HINDU RASHTRA DARSHAN

VEER SAVARKAR was:

- First political leader who lighted a bonfire of foreign clothes (on 7th July, 1905).
- First India citizen to face a trial in International Court of Justice, Hague.
- First scholar whose title of barrister was withheld for refusing to take oath of allegiance.
- First political prisoner to get two life sentences.
- First writer who despite being deprived of pen and paper, created many literary pieces on walls of Andaman prison with spikes, thorns and even his nails and preserved them for posterity by getting them memorised by his fellow inmates.
- First Indian author to face seizure of his books by two governments, even before they were printed and published.

Tributes Paid to Veer Savarkar by Eminent Persons

"Veer Savarkar led a stormy life of a relentless freedom fighter. He lived an extraordinary life of incessant tireless activity in various fields of national uplift."

—M.S. Golwalkar 'Shriguruji'

"Savarkar means glow, Savarkar means sacrifice, Savarkar means perseverance, Savarkar means element, Savarkar means reason, Savarkar means adolescency, Savarkar means arrow, Savarkar means sword, Savarkar means daze, Savarkar means endurance, Savarkar means bitterness—how many shades his personality had! Poetry and revolution together! The creator in Savarkar flew higher and higher. Savarkar had both highs and lows. His contribution is unforgettable. He will continue to inspire us Indians."

—Atal Bihari Vajpayee

"Veer Savarkar was an exemplary freedom fighter and a great son of India who bore brutalities and atrocities at the hand of Britishers but never gave up. His inspiring life will continue to guide generations to come."

—Lal Krishna Advani

"Veer Savarkar's undying love for India made him fight injustice against our Motherland. He inspired many others to join freedom struggle. His emphasis on social reform and his writing and poetry will continue to ignite the spark of patriotism among people."

—Narendra Modi

"Savarkar ji was a strong votary of an undivided India. His mantra was one nation, one cultural value and nationalism... He was a great patriot, unparalleled freedom fighter and social reformer, great writer, pioneering visionary and strong proponent of Hindu culture."

—Amit Shah

"Mr. Savarkar was one of the earliest revolutionaries who had resorted to remarkable ways of escape. A steady and sturdy worker for the independence of our country, his career was for many a youngster, a legendary one."

—Dr. S. Radhakrishnan

"...if the untouchable class is to be an indispensable part of the Hindu society, then the eradication of mere untouchability will not suffice; but the entire four varnasystem should be uprooted. Very few people have agreed upon the necessity of this. And I'm happy to say, that you are one of them."

—Dr. Babasaheb Ambedkar

"Mr. Savarkar was one of the greatest freedom fighters."

—Dr. Ram Manohar Lohia

HINDU RASHTRA DARSHAN

VEER SAVARKAR

Published by
PRABHAT PRAKASHAN PVT. LTD.
4/19 Asaf Ali Road,
New Delhi-110 002 (INDIA)
e-mail: prabhatbooks@gmail.com

ISBN 978-93-5322-765-4
HINDU RASHTRA DARSHAN
by VEER SAVARKAR

Edition
2025

Price
₹ 1200.00 (Rupees Twelve Hundred only)

Printed at
Narula Printers, Delhi

Author's Foreword

In spite of the fact that the past is ever rapidly receding from us further and further, the indefatigable exertions of a band of Maratha scholars, led by Messers Rajwade and others, had thrown such a flood of new light on the history of the Hindu Empire of Maharashtra that the salient features of that great movement have become far more clearly discernible now than they were to those who were constrained for want of better means to view the history through the distorted and dim glasses of foreign scholarship alone. But as the monumental material, comprising state records, documents, original letters and contemporary narratives that the Maratha scholars have discovered and laid under contribution, is to a very great extent confined to the Marathi language and as no attempt, excepting that of Justice Ranade, has been made to rewrite, at least concisely, the history of Maharashtra in the light that these valuable researches throw on it, in a language that would place before the non-Maratha scholars and readers the fruits of their labours, the Indian public, not to speak of that of any other nation, has still very dim, curious and even perverted notions regarding both the heroic principles that animated the Maratha movement as well as the far-reaching effects it had on the course of the larger history of the Indian people. In the absence of such a comprehensive work as would marshal out all the details of this history under a masterly review in this new light thrown on it, we had long intended to write at least a monograph, a small handbook that would pave the way to a large work and acquaint the non-Maratha readers with the great message that the movement came to deliver, the outline of the momentous mission it strove to fulfil. In 1910, we had, just after finishing the work we` wrote on the history of the Sikhs but which was throttled even in the hour of its birth by the ruthless shocks of revolutionary struggle, even commenced such a handbook in the English language on the history of the Marathas.

Just then duties more imminent and exacting involved us in a dreadful combat with forces of darkness and death in the solitary cells of the Andamans and blotted out the very hope of ever surviving to resume our labour of love.

But ultimately it has pleased Providence to grant us liberty and strength enough to take up our pen again, and, thus, we are able today to pay this humble and loving tribute to the mission of those of our illustrious forefathers who, in the 17th and the 18th centuries, fought so gallantly and succeeded so well in vindicating the honour, and winning back the freedom of our Hindu race.

Even an essentially provincial movement, whether it be a Rajput or a Sikh, a Maratha or a Madrasi, achievement is bound to reflect its greatness on the history of Hindudom as a whole. The achievement of a section necessarily reveals the latent possibilities of the whole race. But apart from that reason, the Maratha movement under review transcends the limits of a provincial movement so decisively and so deliberately that it seems pre-eminently entitled to a Pan-Hindu importance and treatment. In fact, we will fail to understand its significance altogether unless it is perceived from a pan-Hindu standpoint. Therefore, our chief aim in writing this critical work, which is primarily addressed to the public outside Maharashtra, has been to ascertain and appraise the value of the Maratha movement in terms of Hindu history. The book is, therefore, meant, not primarily to tell a detailed story of the Hindu Empire of Maharashtra, but to bring out the salient principles and ideals that animated it. Nevertheless, we have devoted the first part to draw a running sketch of the Maratha history, giving in more or less correlated form such events and details as we thought absolutely necessary to substantiate general observations made in the second part. As the public outside Maharashtra is acquainted better with the life of Shivaji and as Mr. Ranade, the gifted author of *The Rise of the Maratha Power*, has unravelled to that public the inner moral grandeur of the mission and of the activities of the Marathas down to Rajaram's death and Shahu's return, we have referred to that period, but in passing and concerned ourselves more with the period that follows it.

The grand message that the story of the rise and fall of our Hindu Empire has to deliver to our Hindu race is writ large on every page of the book. So, we need very little to say and introduce it to our Hindu brethren.

To our Mohammedan readers, however, a word of explanation is needed. The duty of a historian is primarily to depict, as far as possible, the feelings, motives, emotions and actions of the actors themselves whose deeds he aims to relate. This he cannot do faithfully and well, unless he, for the time being, rids himself not only of all prejudices and prepossessions but even of the fears of the consequences the story of the past might be calculated to have on the interest of the present. That latter end he should try to serve by any other means than the falsification or exaggeration or underestimation of the intentions and actions of the past. A writer on the life of Mohammed, for example, would be wanting in his duty, if he tries to smoothen down the fierce attack on 'idolatory' and the dreadful threats held before the unbelievers by that heroic Arab, only to ingratiate himself with the sentiments of those of his fellow-countrymen or readers who do not belong to the Moslem persuasion. He should try to do that by being himself more tolerant, or even by drawing a moral more in consonance with reason and freedom of thought and worship, if he can honestly do so, after he has faithfully recounted the story of that life with all its uncompromising episodes. If he cannot do that, he had better given up the thought of writing the life of Mohammed altogether. Just as this responsibility lies on the shoulder of an honest biographer of Mohammed, there is a corresponding obligation on the part of those of his readers who do not fully or at all contribute to the teaching of Mohammed, which they owe to the writer. They too ought to know that an author, who in the discharge of his duties as a historian of yesterday, of Mohammed or Babur or Aurangzeb, depicts their aspirations and deeds in all their moods, fierce or otherwise, faithfully and even gloriously or appreciatingly, need not necessarily be wanting in the discharge of his duties as a citizen of today, may even be most kindly disposed to his fellow-countrymen or fellowmen of other religious persuasions or racial lineage. In dealing with that period of Hindu history, when the Hindus were engaged in a struggle of life and death with the Mohammedan power, we have never played false to our duty of depicting the great actions and their causes in relation to their environments and expressing the sentiments of the actors almost in their own words, trying thus to discharge the duty of an author as faithfully as we could. Especially our Mohammedan countrymen, against the deeds of whose ancestors the history under review was a giant and mighty protest which we hold justifiable, will try to read it without attributing, solely on that ground, any ill feeling to us towards our Mohammedan countrymen of this generation or towards the community itself as such. It would be as suicidal and as ridiculous to borrow hostilities and combats of the past only to fight them out into the present, as it would be for a Hindu and a Mohammedan to lock each other suddenly in a death-grip while embracing, only because Shivaji and Afzal Khan had done so hundreds of years ago.

We ought to read history, not with a view to find out the best excuse to perpetuate the old strife and stress, bickerings and bloodsheds, whether in the name of our blessed motherland, 'of our Lord God', that divided man from man and race from race, but precisely for the contrary reason of finding out the root causes that contributed to, and the best means to the removal of that stress and strife, of those bickerings and bloodsheds, so that man may be drawn towards man because he is man, the child of our common father God—and nursed at the breast of our common mother—Earth—and wield humanity in a World-Commonwealth.

But, on the other hand, the brilliance of this ultimate hope ought not to dazzle our eyes into blindness towards the solid and imminent fact that men and groups, and races, in the process to consolidating into larger social units, have under the stern law of Nature, got forged into that large existence on the anvil of war through struggle and sacrifice. Those alone who can stand this fierce ordeal will prove their fitness, not only the moral but even the physical, that entitles races and types to survive in this world. Therefore, before you make out a case for unity, you must make out a case for survival as a national or a social human unit. It was this fierce test that the Hindus were called upon to pass in their deadly struggle with the Mohammedan powers. There could not be an honourable unity between a slave and his master. Had the Hindus failed to rise and prove their strength to seek retribution for the wrongs done to them as a nation and a race, even if the Mohammedans stretched out a hand of peace, it would have been an act of condescension and not of friendship, and the Hindus could not have honourably grasped it with that fervour, a sincerity and confidence which a sense of quality alone breeds. But the colossal struggle which the Hindus waged with those who were then their foemen in the name of their *Dev* and *desh*, really paved the way to an honourable unity between the two combating giants. That is why we said, in our work on the history of the National Rising of 1857, that the day that witnessed the forces of *Haribhaktas* of

Hindudom, enter Delhi in triumph and the Moslem throne and crown and standard lay hammered and rolling in dust at the feet of Bhau and Vishvas in 1761, was the day which made an honourable unity between the Hindus and the Moslems more or less feasible. For, that day, the Hindus won their freedom back, proved even their physical fitness to survive on equal and honourable terms in this world. They conquered the conqueror and then could honourably embrace him, if he so wished, as a fellow-countryman and friend. Viewed in this light, the history of the Marathas is so far from standing in the way of any real and honourable unity between our Hindus and our Mohammedan countrymen that, if properly understood, it makes a frank and lasting union far more feasible than it would otherwise have been, and deserves, therefore, to be especially recommended to the attention of all Indian patriots, Moslems as well as Hindus.

It cannot fail to act as a sedative on blustering snobbery on the one hand and as a stimulant to mopping self-diffidence on the other.

For the general reader, too, the story of a movement that presents the imposing spectacle of a nation in arms in defence of their just and human rights, that enlists itself on the side and in the cause of freedom and national independence, and that brings into action generations of warriors and statesmen and builders of kingdoms, and saints and poets—Shivaji and Bajirao, Bhausaheb and Jankoji, Nana and Mahadaji, Ramdas and Moropant—cannot fail to be of an absorbing human interest.

SHIRGAON
15th February, 1925 **—V.D. Savarkar**

Contents

PART—I

Hindu Empire of Maharashtra

PART—II
Hindu Rashtra Darshan

PART—III
Essentials of Hindutva

Part - I

Hindu Empire of Maharashtra

A New Era

स्वधर्मराज्यवृद्धि कारणे। तुम्ही सुपुत्र निर्माण आहां

—Shahaji's letter to Shivaji

It was in the year 1627 that Shivaji was born. That year was destined to be the beginning of an epoch on account of that birth. Before Shivaji was born, hundreds of gallant souls had fought and fallen martyrs in resisting the onslaughts of the Mohammedan foes and in defence of the honour of the Hindu race, fighting as bravely as any of these martyrs and warriors who fell vanquished in the field before him. Shivaji was destined to win and create a wave of triumph which gathered in strength as it proceeded and carried the Hindu banner on its crest from glory to glory, from achievement to achievement, for a period of hundred years or so. The tide of Mohammedan conquest that followed the arms of Mohammed of Ghazni rolled down with irresistible force till all Hindusthan lay submerged under it. Shivaji was the first person to raise his head above it and to command, in his stern Maratha accent: 'Thus far shalt thou go' but no farther.' Till the appearance of Shivaji on the political scene, it could be roughly stated that from the Himalayas to the seas—wherever the Hindu arms met those of the Mohammedans, before 1627, the Hindus were sure to lose, neither because of the sudden disappearance or death of their leader, nor through the treachery of a minister here or a general there—but somehow or the other, every decisive struggle was sure to prove disastrous to the Hindu flag. One has only to recall Dahir's fate, Jayapali's fights, Anangapal's stand, Prithviraj's fall, the black day of Kalingar Sikri, Devagiri or Talikota, to convince one of the melancholy truths of the above statement. But the hand of Shivaji took hold, as if bodily, of this cursed destiny of our people and gave a right about-turn and set her there, facing our opponents as sternly as she did us till then. Never again had the Hindu flag to bend before the Mohammedan crescent.

From the Himalayas to the seas, wherever the Hindu arms met those of the Mohammedans after 1627, the Hindus were sure to win and the Mohammedans sure to lick the dust, whatever be their strength or however tumultuous were their war-cries of 'Allah-ho-Akbar!'—God be victorious! God doubtless proved victorious, but it was the Hindu god. After 1627, one finds god definitely enlisted on the Hindu side—on the side of the image worshipper, and setting his face sternly against the image-breaker; one has only to recall the capture of Sinhgad, the defence of Pavankhind, the careers of Govind Singh, Banda Bahadur, Chhattrasal, Bajirao, Nana, Bhau, Malharrao, Parasharampant, Ranjit Singh and other numerous Maratha, Rajput and Sikh generals who beat the Mohammedans wherever and as often as they met. This turn, so momentous and so triumphant, which the political fortunes of the Hindu took, was doubtless due as well to the great spiritual and national ideal which Shivaji and his spiritual preceptor Shri Ramdas placed before our race, as to the new strategical methods and the new weapons they introduced into the battlefield. Maratha warfare was as truly an addition to the science of war as it was in vogue then among the Hindus, as the Maharashtra Dharma was a new force animating the dying spirit of the national life of the Hindu race.

The ideal which inspired the leaders of that war of Hindu liberation with such faith and gave such vitality was Hindu *Pad-Padashahi*—the establishment of an independent Hindu Empire; and the method of warfare, that made Maratha arms more than a match for the Mohammedan power, and, ultimately, crowned the Hindu brow with laurels of victory, was the surprise or guerilla warfare.

We shall observe how the consciousness of this noble ideal animated their efforts from generation to generation, gave to their distant and widely scattered activities a unity of aim and kinship of interests, made them feel that their cause was the cause of their Dharma and their *desh*—a mission worthy of the efforts of their saints and soldiers alike—carried the Marathas in triumph from step to step to the gates of Delhi, to the banks of the Indus in the north and the seas in the south; and how it raised the story of their deeds to the grandeur of a great national epic that every Hindu mother could proudly sing to her infant, in strains far more triumphant and ennobling than the ballads that tell us how our day was lost, how our banner was torn and how, ultimately, our foes triumphed.

It was in 1627 that Shivaji was born. The ancient chroniclers of his life tell us that, as he grew, the lad began to feel keenly the political subjugation of the Hindu race. He saw with his bleeding heart how the temples of his god were trampled down by alien feet and how the ashes of ancient glory were dishonoured and desecrated. His brave mother, Jijabai, fed his spirit on the glories of our Hindu race, on the memories of Shri Krishna and Shri Rama, of Arjuna and Bhima, of Abhimanyu and Harishchandra; nay, the very atmosphere that he breathed was tense with great expectations and aspirations. All talked of a deliverer to come to rescue the Hindu world—the people whose ancestors talked face to face with gods and angels and whom Shri Krishna had pledged his word never utterly to forsake. The very traditions of the lad's family assured him that his own house was destined to be the cradle of such a national deliverer as that. Was it possible that it all foretold his coming? Could he be the chosen champion of his people, the chosen instrument of god? Whether it was to be so or not, one thing was certain—his duty was clear. He for one would not succumb to the paltry hopes of the easy life of a satisfied slave, a humoured and patted dependent of an alien master who had smashed the throne of his nation and battered down the altar of his gods. He for once would risk all and work and fight and, if need be, die in facing fearful odds for the ashes of his forefathers and the temples of his gods; or, if he be destined to win and survive and remain a victor in the field, then he would lay the foundation of a great and glorious Hindu Empire, even as Vikramaditya or Shalivahana did—an empire that would be a notable realisation of the anxious dreams of generations of his people, of the object of the longing prayers of the saints and sages of his faith.

□

Hindavi Swaraj

—Shivaji's letter

The youth rose in rebellion. He writes in 1645 A.D. to one of his compatriots severely protesting against the allegation of being faithless to the Shah of Vijapur, and appealed to superior morals by reminding him that the only faith they pledged was not to any Shah, but to god alone. Did he not in the company of Dadoji, his guardian, and his comrades solemnly swear in the presence of god on the summits of Sahyadri to fight to a finish and establish 'Hindavi *swaraj*', a Hindu *Pad-Padashahi* in Hindusthan? 'God is on our side and He shall win!'

This word 'Hindavi *swaraj*', coming from the pen of Shivaji himself, reveals, as nothing else could have done, the very soul of the great movement that stirred the life and activities of Maharashtra for a hundred years and more. Even in its inception, the Maratha rising was neither a parochial nor a personal movement altogether. It was essentially a Hindu movement in the defence of Hindu Dharma, for the overthrow of the alien Mohammedan domination and for the establishment of an independent, powerful Hindu Empire.

It was not only the leader of the Maratha who was actuated by this patriotic zeal, but it was more or less shared throughout his camp and his country. The people were as fully conscious of the patriotic spirit that actuated the efforts of Shivaji, as he himself was. He was everywhere hailed as a deliverer of the Hindus.

And even those who still ranged themselves on the Mohammedan side were doing so either through their natural failure to conceive that a rebellion against the great Mohammedan Padshah could ever succeed, or through a natural hesitation to accept the lead of a raw and young enthusiast as Shivaji must have appeared, to the more callous and calculating minds, as well as to those who had vested personal interests in the permanence of the Mohammedan rule.

But to the Hindu people as a whole, not only in Maharashtra, but throughout the Deccan and even in the North, he was the one great champion of their cause, the chosen hero of his race who was destined to win the political independence of his land and his race. History, tradition and literature of that period teem with passages and events that give noble expression to his popular regard and appreciation which the mission and work of Shivaji, Ramdas and their generation won throughout Hindudom, district after district, and town after town, longed and pressed for the coming of the Marathas under Shivaji and rejoiced to see the Mohammedan flag being torn asunder from its flagstaff and the sacred *geruva* of the Marathas rise and wave triumphant in its stead.

To cite only one example to substantiate this statement, let us refer to the letter which the people of Savnoor sent to Shivaji when the Hindus of that district could no longer tolerate the Mohammedan rule: 'We are groaning under the tyrannical sway of the aliens and our Dharma is trampled under foot. Come! Oh, champion of the Hindu faith, come! Oh, destroyer of the wicked and the unbelieving aliens' rule! Here we are at the mercy of the Mohammedan General, Yusuf and his army who, because we sympathise with thee and conspired to invite our Hindu compatriots under thee, have made us prisoners in our own house, placed guards at our gates and are trying to starve us out by interdicting food and water. So, turn thy nights into days and come, oh Deliverer of the Hindu race!'

It is needless to state that Shivaji did not turn a deaf ear to this moving appeal of his co-religionists beyond the borders of Maharashtra. Hambirrao, the famous Maratha captain, hastened to the scene and inflicting crushing defeats on the forces of Bijapur in more than one battlefield, delivered the Hindus from Mohammedan clutches and rid that district of their rule.

Having put in order his little Jahagir, comprising Poona and Supa, and organising the 12 *mavals* (districts) when he was but 14 to 16-year-old, Shivaji with his chosen band, took Torana and other important forts by tactful surprises and daring raids. After gaining one of his moat decisive victories over the forces of Bijapur under Afzal Khan, Shivaji came in open conflict with the Moguls too. Having routed several of their captains and Generals now surrendering, now surprising, but always outwitting them, he struck such a terror in the hearts of his foes that even Aurangzeb thought it prudent to drop opposition for a while and lure him into a trap. But Shivaji proved more than a match even for an Aurangzeb in his intrigues, and frustrating his treacherous designs at Agra, escaped unscathed from captivity and reached Raigad safe. The war with the Moguls was resumed and Sinhgad was recaptured by Shivaji. Several other captains, distinguished themselves by inflicting crushing defeats on the Mohammedans wherever they met, till at last Shivaji thought it prudent and safe to have himself formally crowned as the Hindu Chhattrapati—the champion of Hindu Dharma and Hindu civilisation. Since the fall of Vijayanagar, never had a Hindu prince dared to have himself crowned as an independent ruler, as a Chhattrapati. This coronation broke the spell of Mohammedan superiority in arms. Never again did they prove a match for the Hindus in the battlefield.

The results seemed miraculous even to the actors themselves. Ramdas, himself the high priest and prophet of that war of Hindu liberation, sings in one of his mystic utterances of the vision he had seen and triumphantly asserts that much of what he had seen in his vision had already come to pass. 'In utter darkness I dreamt: behold, the dreams are realised. Hindusthan is up, has come by her own and those that hated her and sinned against god are put down with a strong hand. Verily, it is a holy land and happy. For god has made her cause his own and Aurangzeb is down. The dethroned are enthroned and the enthroned are dethroned! Actions speak better than words. Verily, Hindusthan is a holy land and happy; now that Dharma is backed up by *rajadharma*, Right by Might, the waters of Hind, no longer defiled, can enable us once more to perform our ablutions and austerities.'

It was this consciousness of fighting under the banner of god that made Shivaji, when he succeeded in founding an independent Hindu kingdom, to lay it all at the feet of his spiritual and political guide, Ramdas Swami. It is again this consciousness of a great mission that made Ramdas return it all to his illustrious disciple as a trust to be administered for the good of man and to the glory of god, and declare:

राज्य शिवाजीचें नव्हे - राज्य धर्माचें आहे।

Witness again in what glowing terms, the author of *Chhatra Prakash*, the historical poem that narrates the deeds of Chhatrasal, though a Bundela Hindu by birth, as well as Bhushan, a great national poet who though not himself a Maratha by birth, yet feels as much proud of the victorious march of the Maratha warriors from Shivaji to Bajirao, and going up and down all over Hindusthan roused all Hindusthan into action and achievement in that war of Hindu liberation, sings the deeds of Shivaji and his comrades, in what light they view his achievements. For want of space, we can cite only a line here and there:

कासी हूकी कलाजाती मथुरा मसीत होती सिवाजी न होती तो सुनति होत सबकी॥ राखी हिन्दुवानी हिन्दुवान को तिलक राख्यो अस्मृति पुरान राखे वेद विधि सुनी मैं। राखी रजपुती राजधानी राखी राजन की धरा में धरम राख्यो राख्यो गुन गुनी में॥ भूषन सुकवि जीति हद्द मरहट्टन की देस देस कीरति बखानी तब सुनो मैं। साहि के रजपूत सिवराज, समसेर तेरी दिल्ली दल दाबि कै दिवाल राखी दुनी मैं॥

Thus, the stirring appeal and the battle-song that the Maratha trumpet sounded from the summits of Sahyadri in the name of Hindu Dharma and Hindu *pad-padashahi* touched and roused all Hinduism far beyond the borders of Maharashtra and made them feel that the cause that was being fought out by the Marathas aimed at nothing short of the deliverance of the Hindu people and the Hindu land from the hated alien bondage.

□

A Nation Succeeds Shivaji

'God, we enter our last fight
Thou dost know our cause is right.
Make us march now in thy light
On to Victory!
Let us not thy wrath deserve
In the sacred cause we serve
Let us not from danger swerve.
Teach us how to die!!'

Shivaji died in 1680 and Ramdas in 1681. They had achieved much, but much more had yet to be achieved. The two died, but even their death would not kill the movement they had brought into being. It was not based on the narrow and shifting foundation of an individual life. It had struck its roots deep into the life of the nation. This is one of the most important features of the history of the Marathas, which we wish to emphasise and impress on the mind of our non-Maratha readers. As it is, the life and work of Shivaji and Ramdas being more or less known outside Maharashtra, and the later part of Maratha history being more or less unknown or vaguely and confusedly known, the general readers of Indian or Hindu history feel that Shivaji and Ramdas were the first and the last of Maratha patriots who aimed at the establishment of Hindu *pad-padashahi* and championed the cause of all Hindudom. Not only this, but the general understanding of Maharashtra seems to be that the real history of the Marathas not only began, but also ended with the life of Shivaji; all that follows is confusion worse confounded by selfish and demoralised struggle of stray adventurous bands of freebooters. Both these suppositions are utterly wrong. The fact is that the real greatness of Shivaji and Ramdas lay in the very fact that their movement not only survived them long, but characters as able and patriotic organisers and captains, heroes and martyrs, rose in hundreds and in an unbroken succession and fought for the same cause mightily, pressing towards the same goal of Hindu *pad-padashahi* and achieved such glorious results as would have dazzled the eagle eye of Shivaji himself. When Shivaji was crowned, he had hardly a province under him and yet it was a great achievement. But was it not an achievement, single and great, when his successors under Raghoba Dada entered Lahore and the Maratha horse pranced triumphantly on the banks of the Indus and a continental country lay at their feet? When Shivaji died, Aurangzeb still lived. It was not Shivaji but his Maratha nation that at last succeeded in burying down Aurangzeb and his anti-Hindu ambitions in a common grave at Ahmednagar. The seed that fell at Raigad had become so noteworthy on account of the imposing tree into which our Empire grew. Otherwise, it would have proved barren and been lost into the dust of oblivion like so many other seeds that never grew into fruitful trees. Shivaji ruled at Raigad, but the day was yet to come when his people would rule in Delhi. Nay, had not Dhanaji and Santaji, Balaji and Baji, Nana and Bhau, Malhrrao and Dattaji, Madhavrao and Parshurampant, Nana and Bapu risen, thought, fought and won his cause, the result that Shivaji achieved would have seemed so bald and unimposing as those of the founders of some small principalities, like the Patwardhan or the Bundela states, and could not have claimed such unparalleled and pan-Hindu significance in the history of our Hindu race. Shivaji is great because his nation proved worthy of his greatness, could grasp and press on his mission to ultimate success, could realise what he could merely hope, could accomplish what he could merely desire. The death of Shivaji was the mere beginning of Maratha history. He founded a Hindu principality—it had yet to grow into a Hindu Empire. This was all done after the death of Shivaji. The real epic opens as soon as Shivaji, after calling into being the great forces that had to act it up, disappears from the scene.

□

A Royal Martyr

धर्मासाठीं मरावें ॥

—Ramdas

Aurangzeb was himself mistaken in sounding the death of Mararashtra Dharma and the vitality it had breathed into the movement of Hindu revival in Maharashtra. Like so many other movements, personal or parochial, he thought the Maratha movement too must have received its death-blow at the death of its able leader Shivaji and by the fact of his being succeeded by his brave but incapable son Sambhaji; so Aurangzeb thought his opportunity had come. With the vast resources of an empire at his command in men and money from Kabul to Bengal, he descended into the Deccan with an army estimated at about three lakhs of all arms. Even Shivaji had never to face such overwhelming forces at a stretch. Aurangzeb was not wrong in his calculations, for the whole of the weight of the Mogul Empire thus masterfully concentrated could have crushed a kingdom ten times as large as the new and disorganised Maratha state. To make any attempt to resist the Moguls yet more hopeless, the Marathas had for their leader a man quite incapable of guiding a great nation. In addition to this incapacity to lead, Sambhaji had a bad temper and, at times, indulged in excesses.

But in spite of all these drawbacks and failure to rise equal to the occasion in life, the son of Shivaji proved worthy of his father and of the national movement which he had to represent in rising, not only equal, but even superior to circumstances in the hour of his death. Even when he stood a hopeless prisoner in front of his ferocious foes, he stood erect and refused to barter his religion for his life. He indignantly refused to accept the alternative to death of embracing Islam and, affirming allegiance to the faith of his forefathers, hurled insult for insult against the Muslim persecutors, their logic and their theology. Finding it impossible to tame the Maratha lion into a lap-dog, Aurangzeb ordered to put the *kafir* to death. But the threats failed to overawe the son of Shivaji. His eyes were pierced and pulled out by red-hot iron pincers, his tongue was cut out piecemeal. But still it all failed to overawe the royal martyr. At last, he was beheaded, falling a victim to Muslim fanaticism, but bringing eternal glory to the Hindu race. Sambhaji, by this one act of supreme self-sacrifice, represented the spirit of Maharashtra Dharma—of the great Hindu revival—as nothing else could have done. A leader of freebooters would have acted otherwise. All the material gains of Shivaji were lost beyond hope. His treasury was emptied out, his castles were dismantled and destroyed, his very capital fell into the hands of the alien foes. Sambhaji could not prevent it all. Sambhaji could not preserve the material gains of Shivaji. But Sambhaji, by his great martyrdom, not only preserved, but added immensely to the brilliance and strength of Shivaji's moral and spiritual gains. The war of Hindu liberation gained mightily in grandeur and moral strength, when it could thus feed itself on the blood of its royal martyr to the Hindu faith.

□

The Royal Martyr Avenged

धर्मासाठीं मरावें। मरोनि अवध्यांसि मारावें।
मारितां मारितां ध्यावें। राज्य आपुलें॥

—Ramdas

The whole Maratha nation rose in arms to avenge the death of their king, whose misdeeds and mistakes were readily forgotten and forgiven in this last greatest act of self-abnegation. They resolved, resourceless and penniless, to secure their national independence and assembling together under the presidency of their leader Rajaram, the second son of Shivaji, solemnly swore to fight and die in defence of their Hindu faith and Hindu *rajya*. The teachings of Ramdas:

धर्मासाठीं मरावें। मरोनि अवध्यांसि मारावें॥
मारितां मारितां ध्यावें। राज्य आपुलें॥१॥
मराठा तितुका मेळावावा। आपुला राष्ट्रधर्म वाढवावा।
येविशीं न करितां तकवा। पूर्वज हासती॥2॥

were not forgotten after his death, but, on the contrary, became the living faith of a whole people. Rajaram, Nilo Moreshwar, Prahlad Niraji, Ramchandra Pant, Sankarji Malhar, Parashuram Trimbak, Santaji Ghorpade, Dhanaji Jadhav, Khanderao Dabhade, Nimbalkar, Nemaji Parsoji, Brahmins, Marathas, Prabhus, princes and peasants—it was a nation that rose in arms against the Mohammedan foe.

All Deccan had by this time fallen back into the hands of Aurangzeb. All Maharashtra with all its castles and even the capital of Shivaji was groaning under the military sway of Mohammedan commanders. It seemed as if Shivaji and his generation had fought and died in vain. But what of castles and capitals! The strongest castle that a nation determined to win its independence can have is the castle of its heart; its ideal is its flag and wherever it flies, there lies its capital. 'If all

Maharashtra is lost, let us carry the fight to Madras if Raigad falls, let us plant the banner of Hindu *pad-padashahi* at Jinji; but let us not give up the struggle.' With such undying resistance, the Marathas faced the mighty forces of Aurangzeb for some 20 years or so, and ultimately sent him back broken, discomfited and disillusioned, to die in agony at Ahmednagar in 1707.

The peculiar tactics of war which go by the name of Maratha warfare—*ganimi kava*—stood them in good stead in this long-drawn war. The Maratha forces rallied and dispersed, sallied for them and retired, marched and moved, fought and fled, hurried and held out, with such lightning-like rapidity and matchless generalship and dogged bravery and daring that, the Moguls were harassed and beaten by the Marathas everywhere, but could not fix them anywhere. Every renowned Moslem general was defeated or disgrace, captured or killed. Zulficar Khan, Ali Mardan Khan, Himmat Khan, Kassam, everyone suffered crushing defeat at the hands of Dhanaji, Santaji and other Maratha generals who in great pitched battles at Jinji, Kaveripak, Dudhari and several other places, cut whole Moslem armies to pieces and ultimately destroyed the ambitions of Aurangzeb to re-conquer Maharashtra. The Marathas marched straight against the Imperial camp and literally bearded the lion in his den. The Emperor would have been captured alive, had he not by a stroke of fortune been absent from his Imperial golden tents which the Marathas cut off and carried away in triumph.

To illustrate the patriotic spirit that animated the chief actors in this period, it is enough to refer to the attempt of Khando Ballal to win over the few Maratha nobles who still sided with the Moguls and took part in pressing the siege of Jinji. Secret negotiations were opened with Nagoji Raje to convert him to the Maratha cause. It was explained to him how it was easy to destroy the Mohammedan forces at Jinji, if but he would join Rajaram, and how it was his duty to help the Marathas in their attempt to defend the land and the faith of their forefathers. This appeal did not fail to win over Nagoji Raje who took the first opportunity of deserting the Moslem camp with 5,000 followers and joined the Maratha forces. Thereupon, Khando Ballal decided to persuade even Shirka, who still remained in the Mogul's service. But Shirka grew indignant at the mention of Rajaram's danger and rejoined, 'What do I care, if not only Rajaram, but the whole family of the Bhonslas, are wiped out from this earth? Has not Sambhaji massacred wherever a Shirka was found? Has not the word 'Shirkan' become a synonym for massacre?' Thereupon Khando Ballal persuasively put in, 'Listen friend! What you say is all true. But is it not also true that Sambhaji had three members of my family trampled to death under the feet of elephants? But then the present question is not a family feud. We are fighting here, not for the elevation of the Bhonslas, or of any other individual or family, but for the defence of the comonwealth of the Hindus:

हिंदूंच्या साम्रज्यासाठीं आम्ही झटत आहों।'

Shirka could no longer resist this appeal to his national feeling. He forgave and forgot his private wrongs and family feuds, and promised to help Rajaram to escape from the Moguls and rendered most valuable services, when, at last, Rajaram slipped out of the Mogul hands and re-entered Maharashtra in triumph.

Thus, not only the generation of Shivaji, but the generations after him, were animated by the same noble spirit of patriotism, the consciousness of continuing the same sacred mission of winning back the political independence of the Hindu race and defending the Hindu Dharma from the attacks of an alien and barbarous foe. Here freebooters and plunderers could not have obtained success in such a war against such a foe. It was a great moral and national force that braved and nerved and enabled the patriots of the generations to accomplish the deliverance of their country from a danger which no other race in India had been able to withstand.

□

Maharashtra Mandal

आहें तितुकें जतन करावें। पुढें आणिक मेळवावे ॥
महाराष्ट्र राज्यचि करावें। जिकडे तिकडे ॥

—Ramdas

While Aurangzeb, weighed down with the wreck of all his hopes and anti-Hindu ambitions, sank in a gloomy grave, the Marathas carried the war far and wide into the Mogul territories of Khandesh, Gondvan, Berar and even Gujarat. The release of Shahu, the formal recognition by the Mogul Emperor of the claims of the Marathas to *swaraj* in Maharashtra proper and to *chowth and Sardeshmukhi* over the six *subas* of the Deccan, as well as in the tributary states of Mysore and Travancore, strengthened the hands of the Marathas as never before and gave them breathing time to put their house in order and dress their wounds of fierce party passions and the centripetal tendencies and interests and to constitute the Marathas into an organised whole, with all its inherent and, perhaps, inevitable weakneses, gave so splendid an account of itself that the 'Maharashtra *mandal*' or the Maratha Confederacy actually became the Hindu *pad-padashahi* and ruled, not in name but, in fact, all over Hindusthan.

To these weaknesses and these drawbacks that we have just referred to as being inherent in the Maratha Confederacy because they were the inevitable results of the faults or foibles of the national character and institutions which the Marathas shared in common with all other Hindus, we will return later on. It is enough to state here to avoid all misunderstanding that no one can be more conscious of them than we are. In tracing and illustrating the great national and moral principles that propelled the Marathas as a nation, inspired and sustained them in their Herculean efforts to win the war of Hindu liberation, we do not forget or mean to minimise the fact that, at times and in individual cases, selfish and even vile aims, personal pique, unbridled avarice, got better of their national duty and inclinations. Had it not been so, they would have been a nation of angels and not of men. But here we are concerned, not with what is true in details here and there, but mainly with what is true of the great Hindu movement in general, as a whole; with the outstanding superiority of the great task they had undertaken, the national grandeur of their efforts and their sacrifices and the measure of success they attained—all of which, even when due allowance is made for individual stray aberrations, cannot fail to elicit grateful homage and appreciation from every patriotic Hindu. This, too, we have attempted to do as far as possible in this summary sketch by quoting unimpeachable evidence, by citing at times the very words and illustrating them by the deeds of the chief leaders and actors themselves who led the national movement.

Balaji Vishvanath, having thus put his house in order, found himself in a position so strong as to play an effective part even in the Imperial politics at Delhi. The Marathas no longer stood in danger of any great Moslem offensive against them and the Moslem Emperor himself craved their protection against his own rebellious generals and ministers—so completely had the Maratha war of independence broken the power of the Moslem Empire. In 1718, the Marathas, 50,000 strong, marched forth to Delhi under Balaji Vishvanath and Dabhade to assert the claims of the Sayyad brothers against their Moslem rivals at the court, as the Sayyads had acknowledged the Maratha claims to levy *chowth* and *sardeshmukhi* throughout the Deccan. The Mohammedans at Delhi very naturally resented to see the hated Hindus enter the capital at the head of 50,000 Marathas. So, they conspired to waylay and kill the chief of the Marathas, if ever he succeeded in exacting the Imperial *sanads*, confirming the Maratha claims to *Swaraj* and *chowth*. When this was known in the Maratha camp, Bhanu came forth and offered to risk his life to shield that of his chief and die for him if need be. So, it was arranged that Balaji Peshwa should, after getting the Sanads, leave the Durbar and proceed by an unusual route under cover to the Maratha camp; while Bhanu personated him and, occupying Balaji's palanquin, marched with due ceremony by the usual route. The Mohammedan fanatical mob, watching the palanquin of the Peshwa as usual, suddenly fell on it and with overwhelming numbers, cut the few Marathas to pieces, including Bhanu, whom they took for the real Balaji while Balaji with the state documents under his arm reached the Maratha camp in safety. Such sacrifices of one's life in the interests of one's nation raise the story of that nation to epic grandeur and greatness. Still, in a summary sketch like this, we can but cite a case here and there, feeling sure that even one such case illustrates the national and moral greatness of the movement far more effectively than volumes of detailed and dry criticism can do.

□

The Appearance of Bajirao on the Scene

Independent Maharashtra must lead the War of Hindu liberation.

'Who for Scotland's king and law
Freedom's sword will strongly draw,
Freeman stand or freeman fall
Let him on with me!
By oppression's woes and pains,
By your sons in servile chains,
By your sons in servile chains,
We will drain our dearest veins,
But they shall be free!!
Lay the proud usurpers low,
Tyrants fall in every foe
Liberty's in every blow,
Let us do or die!!!'

After his return from Delhi, Balaji Vishwanath died in 1720 and his son Bajirao became the leader of the Maratha Confederacy, presided over by Shahu. After the birth of Shivaji, the second great personal event that constitutes a landmark in the history of the Marathas is the appearance of Bajirao on the political scene. Great questions of policy were then hanging in the balance. The political independence of Maharashtra was won. The Marathas had grown into a power so strong and so organised as to be able to stand on their feet and defend their land and their faith against all odds; and if they dabbled no more in the imperial politics and confined their aspirations to Maharashtra alone, it was to enjoy peacefully what they had won. Such thoughts very naturally suggested themselves to a few Maratha leaders and they tried to impress these on the mind of Shahu Chhatrapati himself. Even if they had succeeded in convincing the nation and persuaded the people to refrain from carrying the war of Hindu liberation beyond the borders of Maharashtra, it is very doubtful if they could have lived long in peaceful enjoyment of what they had won. But even if they could have held Maharashtra against all comers and lived an isolated political life, unconcerned with whatsoever happened outside Maharashtra, the question was—should they have done so? Why had they fought and bled for the last two or three generations so bitterly and so profusely? Not for mere peace and enjoyment. And could that have been ever an honourable peace and enjoyment which could listen with guilty equanimity to the shrieks of their oppressed Hindu brethren outside of Maharashtra? Shivaji and his comrades aimed at an *'HINDAVI SWARAJ'* and not only at a 'Marathi *rajya.*'

The Hindus of Maharashtra were freed from the foreign yoke, but there remained millions upon millions of their Hindu brethren who were still groaning under it in other parts of India. Ramdas had enjoined 'धर्मासाठी मरावें' and bewailed that 'तीर्थक्षेत्रें भ्रष्ट झालीं'! But how can the Marathas feel themselves acquitted of mission of the fighting and dying in defence of their Dharma when the crescent still waved triumphantly on the Temple of Vishveshwar at Kashi, and how can the mission of Shivaji of *Hindavi swaraj*, of Hindu *pad-padashahi,* be said to have been fulfilled when the alien sat on the Hindu throne of Yudhishthir at Delhi? The Marathas had driven the Mohammedan crescent from Pandharpur and Nasik was no longer open to the insults of Moslem fanatics. But what of Kashi? Of Kurukshetra? Of Hardwar? Of Rameshwar? Of Gangasagar? Were they not as sacred to the Marathas as Pandharpur or Nasik? The ashes of their forefathers had fallen not in the Godavari alone, but in the Ganges as well. The temples of their gods stood scattered from the Himalayas to Rameshwar, from Dwarka to Jagannath. But the waters of the Jumna and the Ganges were still, to quote Ramdas, defiled and unfit for the ablutions of the faithful as they still reflected the triumphant crescent of the Moslem conqueror. Ramdas bitterly complained and charged the Marathas to...

धर्मासाठीं मरावें। मरोनि अवध्यांसि मारावें ॥
मारतां मारतां ध्यावें। राज्य आपुले ॥2 ॥

But did that tyrannical sceptre of the Moslem break, and had all Hindusthan shaken and smashed the chains of political and religious servitude as yet? Hindu Dharma cannot rule triumphant, nor can Hindavi *rajya* flourish, unless and until the Moslem supremacy and strength were smashed, not only in Maharashtra but throughout Hindusthan. As long as there remained an inch of Hindu soil under the Mohammedan sway, so long the mission of Shivaji and Ramdas, and the generations that fought and fell in the war of independence for the past 50 years or so, must remain incomplete and unfulfilled. 'Then ye, who rose proclaiming loud, that ye will not sheath your sword till ye had cut asunder the chains that hold your Hindu land and your Hindu race in abject subjection, till ye made it safe for all Hindus to practise their faith unmolested and till ye have consolidated them into a great and powerful Hindu Empire—how can ye sheath that sword and sink back into an ignoble peace while a mosque is rising on the ruins of the temple of Vishveshwar at Kashi, the alien horse crosses unchecked and unopposed the sacred waters of the Sindhu and the alien sails float triumphant on the waves of the Hindu seas? It is a crucial test—if indeed this great movement was ushered into being for no parochial, no provincial, not to speak of personal ends, but for Hindu Dharma and a Hindavi *swaraj*, Hindu *pad-padashahi*, then pour out, ye Marathas in your hundreds and your thousands, and carry this sacred Gerua banner across the Narmada, across the Chambala, across the Jumna and the Ganges and the Indus and the Brahmaputra, down to the seas. And even as Ramdas has exhorted you to strive, strive.'

देव मस्तकीं धरावा। अवधा हलकल्लोळ करावा॥
मुलुख बडवा बुडवावा। धर्मसंस्थापनेसाठीं॥1॥

Thus argued the great leaders of thought and of action, warriors and statesmen, saints and sages of Maharashtra—Bajirao, Chimaji Appa, Brahmendra Swami, the Dixits, Mathurabai Angre and several other leaders—were animated by these motives and pressed for further expansion of the Maratha activities. It was not only a question of what ought to be done, but even of what must be done. Maharashtra could not, even if it wished, remain in political isolation. The fate of the Hindus of Maharashtra was indissolubly bound with that of their coreligionists and countrymen on the banks of the Indus on the North and the shores of the seas in the South.

The political acuteness of the Maratha statesmen could not fail to see that it was the provincial, parochial spirit of isolation that led in the past, first to the political and, consequently, to the racial and religious ruin of the Hindu race. If possible, they would now strive to make a pan-Hindu stand. That is what Bajirao wrote to the various Hindu princes when Nadir Shah invaded India. Moreover, it was not only the spiritual or the emotional necessity of their national being, but their material and individual interests too demanded that they should neither rest nor retire from the field till they carried their aspirations towards political independence to its logical conclusion, and founded a great and mighty empire that would hold together and consolidate the whole Hindu race. No Hindu could remain long in peace and realise his ideals so long as his race was dominated by alien supremacy and no Hindu could grow to the full height of his being, so long as his race was condemned to servile stuntedness under the over-growth of alien tyranny. For all these reasons, not only these leaders, but even the rank and file in the Maratha camp were fully alive to the fact that they would not be able to rule at Satara unless they ruled at Delhi too. On the memorable occasion, when the leaders of the Maratha Confederacy assembled together under the presidency of Shahu to decide this momentous question of the future policy of the Marathas, Bajirao rose up and gave impression to this, the deepest conviction and aspiration of his people when he, conscious of his own power and enthusiasm and the sublimity of his theme, exclaimed: 'Towards Delhi! Towards Delhi! Will we press and strike straight at the root of this growth of Moslem *swaraj*. Why stand ye hesitating and faltering here? Press on, ye Hindu warriors, ahead; the hour of Hindu *pad-padashahi* has come! Impossible? Oh, no, I have measured my sword against theirs and I know their mettle. I ask for nothing more, neither men nor money, from thee, Chhatrapati. Only sanction this and bless me, oh King, and I shall go straight and strike and bring down this old noxious growth root and branch.'

The most irresistible eloquence in this world is the eloquence of a warrior. Shahu Chhatrapati, thrilled with emotion, felt the blood of Shivaji rise in him and replied, 'Go, hero of my people. Go and lead my armies from victory to victory to whatever direction thou chooseth. What of Delhi! Take thou this, our sacred *geruwa* banner and plant it triumphantly on the summits of the Himalayas and further—even in the 'Kinnar *khand*!' And which was this *geruwa* banner that Shahu referred to? It was decked, not in gold, not in silver, but in the *sanyasin's geruwa*—the colour that is the emblem of renunciation, of devotion to god, of service to man. The Maratha armies followed this *geruwa* banner. This was given to them as a constant reminder of their mission, of the great ideal that should lead them on as defenders of the Hindu faith and liberators of the Hindu race from the alien yoke. Bhawani was their sword, Bhagava was their banner; Ramdas raised it, Shivaji fought under it, and planted it on the summits of Ṣahyadri, and now Shahu and his generation had resolved to carry it aloft to the very confines of Kinnar *khand*.

The Assembly broke up and the history of the Maratha Confederacy became the history of Hindusthan.

□

Forward to Delhi!

अरे बधतां काय। चला जोराने चाल करून।
हिंदुपदपादशाहीस आतां उसीर काय।

—Bajirao

How thoroughly Bajirao and his companions were brought up in the traditions of Shivaji and how closely they had studied the political policy and military strategy of that great leader, could best be seen both in the eloquent appeal Bajirao made to the Maratha leaders in the presence of Shahu, in which he expressly drew a telling comparison between the arduous circumstances under which Shivaji strove to carry the war of Hindu liberation to the South and the relatively more favourable turn the events had taken since then, when his generation, instead of daring more in carrying the war to the North, sat doubting and deliberating as well as in the splendid campaigns against the Nizam, Bangesh and other Mogul generals. The first thing he had to do was to humble the opposition of the Nizam who was the most capable of Mohammedan generals and statesmen of his time.

Bajirao soon proved himself as worthy a student and follower of Shivaji on the field, as he had done in his aspirations and eloquence in the Council Chamber. On the 7th of August, 1727, when it was raining in torrents, Bajirao led his army to the field. Entering Aurangabad, he first levied war contributions on Jalna and the districts around about it, which were held by the Nizam. As soon as the Nizam's forces under Ewaz Khan advanced to meet him, Bajirao, engaging them half-heartedly a while and suddenly, out-marching his opponents, rushed towards Mahur and thence to Aurangabad, giving it out that he would extract a heavy contribution from that city. The Nizam hastened to join Ewaz Khan with a view to protect that wealthy city. But Bajirao, seeing his ruse succeed and the Nizam completely misled, left Khandesh and entering Gujarat informed the Mogul Viceroy there with grim humour that he was invading that province under the Nizam's orders.

The Nizam, hastening towards Aurangabad, learnt to his dismay that the enemy, he wanted to protect that city from, was already in Gujarat. Furious at this, he wanted to beat back Bajirao with his own weapons by imitating the Maratha tactics of surprise marches, to invade Poona and plunder Bajirao's territory as he went. But he was too late in learning his lessons of Maratha strategy. For, Bajirao, anticipating all this, had already left Gujarat and with lightning rapidity entered the Nizam's dominions again.

While the Nizam was advancing towards Poona and fancying he was performing a splendid military feat, he learnt, to his utter discomfiture, that before he could plunder Bajirao's territory, Bajirao had already plundered his. So, abandoning his plan of marching on Poona, he hastened to meet Bajirao along the banks of the Godavari. The Nizam's forces were by now thoroughly tired out and Bajirao wanted to give them a fight even though the Nizam did not wish to do so. Instead of flying away and avoiding them as before, Bajirao by skilful manoeuvres succeeded in tempting the Moguls to occupy a position near Palkhed almost at his bidding. Now Bajirao suddenly took the offensive, as cleverly as uptil now he was avoiding it, and the Nizam, in spite of his big guns and heavy artillery, was completely caught and found to his dismay that it was impossible to shake off the Marathas and that either he should consent to the utter destruction of his forces, or agree to whatever Bajirao dictated. The Nizam chose the latter course and recognised Shahu as the sole King of the Marathas, agreed to the payment of all arrears of *chowth* and *sardeshmukhi* and to the re-instatement of all the Maratha revenue officers in his own dominions.

Reference has been made in detail to this campaign, for, this is a typical example of the Maratha warfare and shows that lessons that Shivaji had taught them were not only not forgotten, but improved upon and successfully employed on the battlefields in a far more extensive and intensive way by the Maratha generals that followed him.

Nor did the Mogul Viceroy of Malva fare better than the Mogul Viceroy of the Deccan did. The Marathas, ever since 1698 when Udaji Pawar raided Malva and camped at Mandwa, were attacking the Mogul forces in that province from several sides. The Hindus of that province were so disgusted with the Moslem tyranny and religious oppression that the wave of Hindu national revival that preceded the War of Hindu Liberation did not fail to find enthusiastic advocates of Hindu *pad-padashahi* in Malva. The Hindu people at large, led by their natural leaders, the landlords, the Thakurs and the priests of Malva, saw, in the growing power of the Marathas and the great ideal of a Hindu Empire that informed and inspired their actions, the only hope of their country's freedom from the foreign yoke.

Fortunately, for the Hindus, the most influential prince in Malva was one of the most enthusiastic advocates of the cause of Hindu independence. He was Sawai Jaisingh, prince of Jaipur. The wisdom of Chhatrasal who, when he found himself unable to defend the freedom of his little kingdom against the alien foe and was faced with the grim alternative of being reduced to vassalage of a Hindu sovereign or to 'prosper' under a Mohammedan and non-Hindu alien, patriotically chose rather to lose his little provincial self and identify himself with the movement of a pan-Hindu Empire, whether that was led by the Marathas or the Rajputs or the Sikhs or any other Hindu section than to live by kneeling at the Mohammedan throne at Delhi. This wisdom of Chhatrasal guided Jaisingh too.

Jaisingh championed the cause of all the oppressed Hindus of Malva—of peasants and landlords groaning under overtaxation, of Thakurs and priests who could no longer tolerate the insolent extortion, humiliation and insult of their faith and their race, which the existence of Moslem rule made inevitable—and advised them all to invite the Marathas to free them and found a Hindu rajya. The noble Rajput was patriotic enough to see that of all the Hindu princes then ruling, the only organised Hindu power that could cope with and crush the Moguls and consolidate the Hindus was the power of the Maratha Confederacy. If he could not take the lead and free the Hindus from the Mogul yoke, the next best thing for him to do was to sacrifice his personal ambitions, suppress all thoughts of mean unpatriotic and parochial jealousy and help those who could and would do it.

Jaisingh was enthusiastically backed up in this plan by the influential Thakur Nandlal Mandavai. They, on behalf of the Hindus of Malva, opened negotiations with the Marathas and invited them to Malva, 'to drive the *Mlechhas* and vindicate the honour of Hinduism'. The Marathas readily responded to this call of their co-religionists in

Malva and soon the province was attacked on all sides by the Maratha captains under Chimaji Appa, the brave brother of *Bajirao*. The Mogul Viceroy mustered all the forces he could, but the Marathas showed no mind to retire and finding a favourable opportunity, they all suddenly attacked the Moslems and in a battle at Dewas, killed their Viceroy.

But the Emperor did not like to part with one of the richest provinces so easily as that. A new Viceroy was sent to give battle to the Marathas there. The Malva Hindus who sympathised with the Marathas joined their ranks. The Mogul Viceroy laid terrible plans and with the help of his huge army, tried to destroy the Marathas in the passes of Mandava Ghat and other places. But the Marathas outwitted him completely with the help of the Malva Hindus and under Malharrao and Pilaji and Chimaji Appa, harassed the Mogul forces as never before and ultimately offered them terrible battle at Tiral where the Mussalmans were completely crushed and their Viceroy killed.

The joy of the Hindus of Malva at the news of this second success knew no bounds. The Marathas were welcome wherever they went, and the sight of a triumphant Hindu banner—witnessed after centuries of defeat and discomfiture—sent a thrill through the hearts of the Hindus, a feeling of patriotic elevation and racial rejoicing.

Jaisingh himself writes in one of his grateful letters thanking all the actors for fighting out the sacred cause and congratulating the Marathas upon the success they achieved. 'A thousand thanks! Splendidly indeed you have won! You have driven the alien out and delivered the Hindus of Malva and vindicated the honour of our Hindu Dharma and Hindu race.'

The Marathas soon restored order, dismissed all Mogul officers and began to administer the province as a regular part of the Maratha Empire.

But the Mogul Emperor at Delhi persisted in hoping against hope and sent a new Viceroy named Muhammad Khan Bangash, a brave Rohilla Pathan, who was so renowned amongst Mohammedan circles for his martial qualifications as to win the title of 'The Lion of War'. From the Imperial court, he was specially charged to crush the rising spirit of the Bundela chief, Chhatrasal first, and then from that vantage point to expel the Marathas from Malva.

Muhammad Khan Bangash attacked the Bundelas who, led by their illustrious chief Chhatrasal, had shaken off the fetters of Moslem rule and had been living a free political life. Chhatrasal was a great admirer of Shivaji, who was the source of his inspiration and whom in his youth he had acknowledged as his master and guide. Since then he, faithfully to the advice of his master to carry the mission of Hindu liberation to Bundelkhand, strove so mightily and successfully to free that province from the foreign rule and defend Hindu Dharma and Hindu *desh* as to earn the title of 'The Shield of Hindudom' from his countrymen.

Now in his old age, he found himself face to face with fierce hordes of the Rohilla Pathans in overwhelming numbers, bent on crushing his little Hindu kingdom. It was but natural for an old Hindu warrior like Chhatrasal, brought up in the pan-Hindu spirit of Shivaji, Ramdas and Prananath Prabhu, to turn instinctively to Bajirao who, as the leader of the Maratha Confederacy, represented not only the strength but even the mission of Shivaji. He wrote a pathetic letter to Bajirao, appealing to those tender traditions of Hindu mythology, which more than anything else rouse the deepest sentiments in every Hindu heart of a common Hindu brotherhood and a pan-Hindu spirit.

'Come, oh Baji! And deliver me from the clutches of this faithless foe, even as Vishnu saved the Gajendra.'

This old friend and disciple of Shivaji, being beset by the Moslems when he turned to the Marathas for help as a Hindu to a Hindu, could not but rouse them to mighty patriotic efforts. With breathless speed, Bajirao, with Malharrao and Pilaji Jadhav and twelve other Maratha generals, marched out at the head of 70,000 men. Meeting the old Hindu hero, Chhatrasal at Dhamorah, he picked up the remnants of the Bundela forces with him and continued his march, though the rainy season had set in.

Muhammad Khan, puffed up with the easy victories he had won over the little Hindu kingdom of Chhatrasal whom he had driven from his capital, thought himself entitled, during the rainy season, to a rest which a victor deserved. While he was thus living in a fool's paradise, the Hindu armies, paying no heed to the torrential rains, dense forests and forbidding mountains, suddenly fell upon Muhammad Khan Bangash and held him fast in their clutches at Jaipur in 1729. Beseiged, beaten and defeated so thoroughly by the Marathas was the Moslem 'Lion of War' that to save his very life he had to ignominiously flee from the battlefield, leaving all Bundelkhand and Malva in the hands of the triumphant Hindus. The old Bundela King re-entered his capital in full state, amidst the welcoming cheers of the citizens and the deafening boom of the victorious Maratha cannons.

So grateful did the old hero feel towards the Marathas that he adopted Bajirao as his third son. On his death, true to this, a third portion of his kingdom was actually handed over to Bajirao. This touching incident in itself is enough to prove how noble had been the underlying principles that formed the spring of their actions and made the Hindus of Bajirao's generation rise above personal or parochial considerations and feel themselves bound together by ties of blood and race and religion, and inspired them to mighty efforts to achieve political independence and found a great Hindu Empire.

The flight of this third Mohammedan Viceroy from Malva and Bundelkhand made the Marathas master of those regions and provided them with a vantage point from which they aimed to carry the war of Hindu liberation into the very heart of the Mogul Empire.

While these campaigns were being fought out in Malva and Bundelkhand, the Maratha arms and statesmanship were achieving results as great and abiding in Gujarat. Pilaji Gaikwad, Kanthaji Bande and, later on, Chimaji Appa himself kept on harassing the Mogul forces in Gujarat so strenuously as to force the Mogul Viceroy to sign a treaty by which he agreed to pay *chowth* and *sardeshmukhi* to the Marathas. But the Mogul Emperor, indignant at this humiliating engagement, sent Abhayasingh and charged him to drive the Marathas out of Gujarat. Abhayasingh, unlike Jaisingh, was out for himself and his self-glorification, and this tendency made him blind to the fact that he was in no way better equipped to take the lead of the Hindus in their struggle for political independence than any other Hindu prince. The Maratha Confederacy was the only Hindu power which had shown itself capable of achieving this noble task. But Abhayasingh's love for personal advancement made him blind to this fact and drove him so far in his opposition to the Marathas in Gujarat as to invite Pilaji Gaikwad, under the pretext of negotiations, to the city of Dakore—a spot sacred to the Hindus and, therefore, safe from suspicions—and in spite of its sanctity and the pledged word of a Rajput, get him assassinated. But he soon realised that he was guilty not only of a crime, but a great blunder.

For the Marathas were not the people who could be cowed down by the murder of a leader here or there. War and battle and death were their playmates from their youth, and for generations, they had grown in the camp.

It should be noted that as in Bundelkhand and Malva, so in Gujarat, the Hindus as often invited and usually sympathised with the Marathas and, at times, actively fought under their banner. For the very Kolis, Bhils, Waghris and other martial Hindu tribes in Gujarat were fiercely enraged at the murder of Pilaji, whom they loved and rose to avenge his blood, against the Mogul forces. The Marathas poured in from all sides, took Baroda by storm in 1732, made it what still it is, the Maratha capital of that province and made it impossible for Abhayasingh to maintain his ground; while Damaji Gaikwad invaded Jodhpur itself and forced Abhayasingh to hasten back to the defence of his hereditary principality. Damaji thereupon whirled round and soon took Ahmedabad itself, and rendered it not only impossible but even unnecessary for the Mogul Viceroy to return to Gujarat again, as that whole province was lost to the Moslem Empire around 1735.

□

To Free the Hindu Seas

आरमार एक स्वतंत्र राज्यांगच आहे, ज्याचे जवळ आरमार त्याचा समुद्र
…जलदुर्गसहित होते त्यास नुतनच जलदूर्ग करून पराभविले।

—Ramchandra Pant Amatya-Rajneeti

While the Marathas were thus carrying the War of Hindu Liberation into the very heart of the Mogul Empire to free the Hindu land, they were no less strenuously striving to free the Hindu seas too, from the domination of the foreigners that threatened them from the West. They had very early realised that the safety of the Hindu Empire was threatened as much by the European mercantile nations that visited their seas, as it was by the Moslems who had already made themselves masters of their lands. How thoroughly Shivaji and his generation were bent on checking and frustrating European ambition and greed on the western coast could best be seen in the clear rules and the line of policy enunciated in the famous treatise on 'State Policy', written by the distinguished Maratha leader and statesman, Ramchandra Pant and issued for general information by the orders of the Maratha cabinet as a state document. Shivaji strove as strenuously to free the coastline of all foreign domination as he could under the circumstances, and laid the foundation of a strong Maratha navy, backing it up by a line of newly built and powerfully equipped sea fortresses, which were destined to defend and guard the freedom of the Hindu seas for a century to come.

In the days of Rajaram, when Aurangzeb overran the Deccan and the Marathas were no longer able to conduct an organised concentrated state, each began to fight against the common foe as best he could and wherever he could, the responsibility of driving the Moguls from the coastline fell on the shoulders of Kanhoji Angre, the Gujars and other distinguished Maratha Admirals. They discharged their duties so well that neither the English, nor the Portuguese, nor the Dutch, nor the

Siddis, nor the Moguls could singly nor, as at times happened, combinedly check or kill the rising naval power of the Marathas. The English had to suffer much as Kanhoji Angre, the Admiral of the Maratha fleet, was in possession of the island of Khanderi, only 16 miles south of the Bombay harbour. They knew that the Maratha Admiral would make short work of them if he was left free from the Moslem power of the Siddi of Janjira and the extensive sway which the Portuguese held over the western coast long before the rise of the Maratha power.

To retain his possessions against all these enemies, Kanhoji Angre was obliged to maintain a large force, and to pay his men, he had to levy the usual *chowth* from the ships trading on the Arabian Sea. The Marathas justly thought themselves masters of the Hindu seas and it was but natural that they should levy their *chowth* on the Hindu waters from the foreigners who sailed their seas with or without permission. But the English and other European nations strongly resisted this claim and Kanhoji had to punish them by taking their ships with all cargoes and men and hold them to ransom. When in 1715, Charles Boone was appointed the Governor of Bombay, he decided to destroy Angre's strongholds. He strove much and bragged more. A powerful naval expedition was fitted out and soon attacked the Maratha sea-port of Vijayadurga. The English breathed fury. The very names of their warships were meant to hurl defiance at the Marathas. One was named 'Hunter', another was 'Hawk', the third was 'Revenge', the fourth was 'Victory'—before the contest began! This formidable fleet was backed up by a division of land forces, comprising thousands of chosen English soldiers who were meant to march against the fort by land. On the 17th of April, 1717, the furious fleet began to bombard the fortress of Vijayadurga, but only to find that the Maratha fortifications were not made of wax. They and the garrison behind them stood bravely the heavy guns of the frigates and the Maratha garrison kept all along jeering at the futile efforts of the English from the secure shelter of the walls. Enraged at this, the English tried to escalae, but the Marathas soon sent them back discomfitted. All hope was lost and the English began to retreat. No sooner did the Marathas see this than they opened such a heavy fire on them as to speed them back far more quickly than they had come on.

Next year Mr. Boone attacked Khanderi, but was badly beaten back. Thereupon the Maratha menace to the English power in India grew daily to such an extent as to force the English King to fit out a special squadron of four men-of-war and entrust it to the command of a highly placed and distinguished officer, Comodore Mathew of the Royal Navy. To render success doubly sure, the Portuguese too were invited and they too readily agreed to march together against the Marathas. The Marathas received the united attack of these two powerful European nations in 1721 and fought so gallantly and skilfully, both by land and sea, as to make it impossible for the European forces to scale the walls of their fortresses. Chafing with impotent rage, Commodore Mathew personally sallied forth in the heat of the action, only to fall a prey to the lance of a Maratha trooper who drove it in his thigh. The Commodore of the English forces was not to be cowed down by one lance wound; he galloped after the trooper and fixed his two pistols instead of one at him only to find that he had forgotten to load them. Nor did the allied forces prove more lucky than their Commodore. For, when they made their last and determined attack, reached the walls and tried to scale them, the Marathas opposed them with such skill and resolution as to send them shrieking back, while another Maratha squadron attacked the Portuguese flank by land. A panic seized the Portuguese, who fled for life and soon the English too followed them, leaving several of their guns and almost all of their ammunition in the hands of the victorious Marathas. When, whatever little spirit of fighting was still left in the allied army, was naturally spent in a war of words in charging each other with the responsibility of the two disgraceful defeats, the Portuguese marched back to Chaul and the English sailed back to Bombay. For a long time, the English Company had to convey their trading ships by armed vessels, lest the Maratha admirals should carry them off for that cursed *chowth*. Soon the English 'Victory' like its Commodore found, after firing that it had forgotten to load its pistol, and the English 'Revenge' not only failed to avenge, but got itself captured by the Marathas and held in ransom. In 1724, the Dutch too had their go. They attacked Vijayadurga with no less than seven warships, two bomb vessels and a body of regular troops, but they too failed to make any impression on the rocks of the Maratha fortitude, and the stout old Maratha admiral sailed the Hindu waters unchallenged—unchallengeable—and all this he and his nation had to achieve in spite of the constant wars with the Moslem Siddi by land in Konkan, the Nizam in the Deccan, the Moguls in Gujarat, Malva and Bundelkhand.

Kanhoji Angre died around 1729. Just then another historical figure entered the political arena in Konkan, and soon began to exercise an influence over the minds of the leaders of the Maratha Confederacy, which, when all is said and sifted, was doubtless a powerful factor in keeping the great mission undimmed by lower passions in the minds of the Maratha people. It was Brahmendra Swami, the guru of Shahu, of Bajirao, of Chimaji, of the Angres and thousands of the rank and file. He was undoubtedly moved by great and noble patriotic emotion and principles and never failed to bring, out of confusion of details, the spiritual and moral aspect and hold the ideal of *swadharma* and *swarajya* before the eyes of his people. The Swami had practised severe austerities in his early life and developed wonderful yogic powers, as of going into *samadhi*—trance for a full month every year and living buried underground during that period. He had travelled far and wide, like Ramdas, all over India and visited every great Indian shrine and had keenly felt the sting of Hindu enslavement and political dependence. A spark was still needed to blow the patriotic fire of his soul into a huge and steady conflagration. The Moslem rulers of Janjira supplied it. The Siddis were the determined foes of the Maratha kingdom and knew that they were soon to lose their ill-gotten possessions in Konkan, if the Maratha power grew daily as it did. Therefore, they always sided with the English, the Dutch and the Portuguese against the Marathas and often raided the Maratha possessions. Not only this, but with the barbarity peculiar to Mohammedan zealots, used to kidnap hundreds of boys and girls, and convert them and others forcibly to Mohammedanism, raze Hindu temples to the ground and commit numerous outrages on the Hindus. The shrine of Parasharam, the beloved and sacred scene of the Swami's austerities and meditation, fell a victim to one of such outbursts of fanaticism. The Siddi pulled the temple down, stone by stone, plundered it of all its treasures and tortured such of the Brahmins as he could lay hands on. This outrage aroused such an inextinguishable pious wrath in the mind of Brahmendra Swami that it cured him of the vacuous and sickly sentimentality to which the Hindu *sadhus* get generally addicted and which makes them equally disposed towards all, good or bad or indifferent. He determined to consecrate all his life to the furtherance of the war of Hindu liberation and the cause of Hindu independence. So great was the influence of the Swami that the Siddi himself could not dare to turn him into an inveterate enemy and prayed that he should still live at Parasharam's shrine as before, without any further molestation. But the Swami retorted: 'You have wrought evil on the gods and the Brahmins; just revenge may they wreak on you.' Even Angre could not appease him and make him stay in Konkan. 'Never will I live nor take a drop of water to drink in a land where the faithless foreigners rule. I will re-enter Konkan again—but as the head of avenging Hindu forces.' Saying so, the Swami went to Satara and, since then, never ceased preaching a crusade against the faithless foes of the Hindus, and especially against the Siddis of Janjira and Portuguese at Goa. His correspondence, which is now available to the general reader, shows how strenuously he kept feeding the sacred fire of Maratha resolution to free Hindudom, to fight in defence of Hindu Dharma and win back the political independence of the Hindus from Kashmere to the Cape.

Shahu and Bajirao, both disciples of the Swami, soon determined to avenge the crimes perpetrated by the Siddi and Maratha agents, were busy plotting against and preparing the ground for a general campaign in Konkan against the Siddi as well as the Portuguese. They had simultaneously to fight against the several powers from Delhi to Arcot, and so they had to watch and wait for a favourable opportunity. Just then a civil feud drove one of the claimants to the throne of the Siddi to the Maratha camp for help. The Maratha Potnis quickly grasped his hand and wrote to Shahu that Maratha diplomacy had done its work. So excited was the king at this longed-for news that he wrote to Bajirao with order: 'Don't read this letter; mount your horse first and then read it.' The campaign opened in 1733 and the Maratha armies descending Sahyadri took the fort of Tala-Ghosala and overran the territories of the Siddi, inflicting defeat after defeat on the Moslem forces. Soon Bajirao attacked and retook Raigad itself. This famous fortress was the seat of Shivaji's throne, the scene of his coronation, which, since the days of the War of Independence, had still been in the Moslem hands. The news of the recovery of the capital of their great King caused universal rejoicing throughout Maharashtra. Nor were the Maratha arms less successful on the sea: Manaji Angre inflicted a severe defeat on the Siddi's fleet near Janjira. The English, too, became alarmed and, first secretly and then openly, helped the Siddi with arms and ammunition and later on sent a substantial force under Captain Haldane to fight against the Marathas. But Khandoji Narhar, Kharde, More, Mohite and even ladies like Mathurabai Angre—that distinguished woman whose correspondence with Brahmendra Swami reveals the depth of her patriotic eagerness to see the Hindu land freed from the hands of the foreigners and the pride with which she watched the Hindu flag rise triumphantly over towns and cities won back from the enemy—all continued the struggle, till at last, in 1733 Chimaji Appa came on the scene and in a battle near Rewas, won a splendid victory over the Abyssinian forces when their leader, the Arab enemy of the Hindus in the Konkan, who had pulled down and levelled to dust the temple of Parasharam, was beheaded and made to pay the price of his crime with his life. With him on that day fell fighting the Moslem Commander of under eleven thousand men on the Mohammedan side.

All Konkan, all Maharashtra showered their grateful blessings on their victorious champion who had so signally wreaked a just vengeance on the enemies of their faith and vindicated the honour of the Hindu race. The King himself was overjoyed and wrote back; 'The Sat-Siddi' was a demon, no less terrible than Ravan. In killing him thou hast uprooted the Siddis. Thy fame spread everywhere.' Summoning the young general to his court, the king showered on him presents and robes of honour while Brahmendra Swami, who had been the prime mover of this campaign and kept the Marathas steady at their post, whenever their efforts flagged through silly bickerings or mutual jealousy, by rousing them to the sense of their duty towards their *desh* and their Dharma and by constantly emphasising the spiritual and moral aspect of the great war of Hindu liberation they were engaged in, could hardly express his gratitude to god, or thank his illustrious disciple in lines adequate to convey the fulness of his feeling. At last, he had succeeded in liberating the holy land of Parasharam, in defending the cause of Hindu Dharma. शामलांचो क्षिति केली कोंकणांत धर्म राखिला।

Thus, the Siddi was subdued and this Moslem principality reduced to insignificance and subordination to the Hindu Empire. But this left the Portuguese to fight single-handedly against the Marathas. Their easy conquests in India and the vast influence they wielded all over the western coasts from Khambayat to Ceylon, had been steadily declining since the rise of the Maratha power. The religious tyranny and the inquisitional outrages they perpetrated in India were no less hideous than those of the Mohammedans and could only be equalled by the Spanish record in Europe. When the Hindus, who had groaned under this religious persecution and political servitude for over a century, saw that their co-religionists and countrymen in Konkan who were under the Siddi had successfully shaken off the fetters and stood free, they naturally looked forth to the coming of the Maratha troops to liberate them too. A wave of great expectation and patriotic fervour passed over the Hindu mind and stiffened their resistance to the mad attempts of the Portuguese inquisition of Goa to crush Hindutva throughout the Portuguese Konkan. The success of Bajirao and the approach of the Maratha arm to their very borders only made the Portuguese madden through fear. With the folly that despair engenders, the Portuguese began to suppress the Hindu movement and crush the new hopes and new spirit of resistance it infused, with an iron hand. The old records state: 'They confiscated extensive estates of Hindu landlords. They surrounded and converted whole villages at the point of the bayonet. They carried away Hindu children, arrested and killed or enslaved those who refused to disown their Hindu faith. The Brahmins were the chosen victims of their wrath. They made them prisoners in their houses. The public performance of all Hindu rites was prohibited and if a Hindu dared to perform any rite, his house was surrounded, the inmates arrested and sent to the Inquisition, either to be forcibly converted to Christianity or sold as slaves or put to death.' But in spite of all this reckless persecution, the Hindu leaders persisted in resisting these monstrous orders of the Portuguese government. Thousands fell victims to Portuguese wrath. At last the leaders of the Hindu populace—the Deshmukhs and Desais of Vasai (Bassein) and other places—opened secret negotiations with Bajirao and Shahu, pressing them to strike for their freedom and vindicate the honour of the Hindu freedom and Dharma and *desh*. Antaji Raghunath, the Sardesai of Malad, brave, popular and a Hindu of Hindus, who had openly flouted the Portuguese order against Hindu rites and encouraged the people on his estate to defy it, fell a prey to the Portuguese persecutions, was arrested, had his land confiscated and was sent to the fatal ordeal of the Inquisition at Goa. But, fortunately, for all Hindus, he effected his escape and managed to reach Poona in safety. He thereupon organised a secret scheme, promised help and local succour and guidance to Bajirao as soon as the Marathas would enter the Portuguese possessions and assured Bajirao that the whole Hindu populace of Portuguese Konkan looked up to him as an *avatar* sent to the earth to punish the faithless foes of Hinduism and longingly looked for his coming as for that of a divine deliverer.

In spite of great issues being fought out in the North and his being hard-pressed by the expenses of the extensive campaigns that the Marathas were carrying on all over India, Bajirao was not a man to turn a deaf ear to such moving appeals of his downtrodden countrymen and co-religionists in the Konkan. With great speed, secrecy and diligence Bajirao collected a large force at Poona under the pretence of a more than usually elaborated festival in honour of Goddess Parwati and ordering out each his task, settled the outline of the coming campaign. Chimaji Appa was appointed generalissimo. Ramchandra Joshi, Antaji and Ramchandra Raghunath and other captains and commanders were sent out to their different posts. In 1737, the Maratha troops attacked the fort of Thana, which the Portuguese defended to the last, and had to in the end surrender. Delighted with the success, the Marathas poured into Salsette. Shankaraji Keshav took the fort of Arnala, Joshi took Dharavi and Parsik. The Viceroy of Goa, deeply concerned at these disasters, sent a gallant warrior named Antonio to continue the struggle. New forces of fresh Portuguese soldiers were specially requisitioned from Europe. Thus reinforced, Antonio took a vigorous offensive and planned nothing less than the re-capture of Thana. Led by the gallant Pedro Mello, four thousand five hundred men marched out to attack and re-take Thana. But, on the Maratha side, in charge of Thana was no less a soldier than the redoubtable Malharrao Holkar. The attack and defence were worthy of heroic fame. But, the Marathas, with the help of their artillery, mowed down the Portuguese so vigorously that their strength grew weaker. 'Seeing this, the brave leader, Pedro Mello, began to rally his men when a well-aimed Maratha cannon-ball struck him down to death. The Portuguese thereupon broke and fled back to their ships. Mahim, too, was regained by the Marathas after a heroic fight, while Venkatrao Ghorpade advanced as far as Rakhol near Goa itself. The power of the Portuguese seemed doomed.

Just then came the news of the invasion of Nadir Shah. This was the greatest danger that India, or rather the only Hindu power represented by the Marathas—that was able to oppose the foreign hordes—had to face. This naturally gave a new lease of life to the Portuguese. Bajirao with an eagle's eye took the whole situation in view and wrote: 'The war with the Portuguese is as naught. There is now only one enemy in Hindusthan. The whole power of all India must get concentrated. I for one will spread our Marathas from the Narmada to the Chambal.

Then let me see how Nadir dares to slip down towards the Deccan.' He directed the Maratha representatives at the courts of Delhi, Jaipore and other northern states to organise, not a Maratha Confederacy alone, but a great Hindu coalition of Rajputs, Bundelas, Marathas and others. The letter of the Maratha statesman of that period, now available in print, refers clearly to a grand Hindu scheme that aimed to dethrone the Mogul emperor altogether and place the Maharana of Udaipore on the throne of entire Hindusthan.

But, although the aspiring mind of the Maratha leader was evolving such vast schemes of Hindu conquests elsewhere, so great were the resources of Bajirao that he could provide both an army to besiege Bassein and fight with the Portuguese and another large enough to drive Nadir Shah from Delhi. So, the Portuguese soon found to their cost that even Nadir Shah could not effectively slacken the Maratha grip that kept clutching at their throat. The Viceroy of Goa learnt of the fall of one after another of the Portuguese strongholds dotted throughout their possessions. Sirigaon, Tarapore, Dahanu were taken by the Marathas by storm and the garrisons put to the sword. Bassein was besieged by the Marathas. The heroic story of the valour of those who stormed and those who defended the fortress is so well-known as to need no description in such a short review as this. The Marathas fought so sternly throughout this war that, to quote the evidence of an eye-witness: 'Even high officers fell fighting where they stood. Unable to bear the reproaches of Bajirao, their beloved leader, they threw away their lives and fell fighting on the battlefield. The Portuguese, too, general after general, fell sword in hand. The Marathas attacked but were repulsed with heavy loss. They attacked again and again and were thrown back with terrible losses to both sides. The explosion of their own mines at times blew and took life of hundreds of their storming parties. But the revengeful and tenacious Marathas gave in not. They delivered no less than eighteen attacks. The Portuguese too repulsed them eighteen times, but each time found themselves left more and more exhausted, and, thus, the siege went on from day to day. Nadir Shah came and went back, but the siege continued and Bassein could not be taken. At last, furious with despair, Chimaji Appa roared out to his warriors: 'Behold, I must enter the fortress of Bassein. If you cannot carry it in my life today, let your guns blow my head over the ramparts tomorrow, that I may enter it at least after death.' Such indomitable valour could not fail to enthuse the stupendous efforts of the men he led. Manaji Angre, Malharrao Holkar, Ranoji Shinde vied with each other in trying to scale the walls of the doomed fort. Just then, another Maratha mine blew off, levelling to the ground an important part of the Portuguese fortifications. The Marathas followed the explosion with indomitable courage and established themselves in the ruins. The Portuguese valour that had lionised itself on both the hemispheres could not shake the Marathas from the position they had taken up. The Portuguese could resist the Marathas no longer, as they kept enfilading and storming the garrison of their foes with such persistence and effect that the long expected end soon came. The Portuguese surrendered and the Maratha banner, triumphant after the tortures of the Hindu faith and the Hindu race, was carried and planted over Bassein, amidst the universal applause of all Maharashtra.

Almost all Konkan was now freed. The Portuguese power never recovered from this shock, though it managed to eke out a miserable existence at Goa, as the Marathas had ever their hands full of other important issues elsewhere. The Portuguese power that once dominated the Asiatic waters from the Cape of Good Hope to the Yellow Sea was broken up by the Marathas by land and by sea, never to raise its hand against the Hindu people.

One can very well understand the relief the Hindus felt, the sense of national elevation and strength and triumphant pride that filled their hearts, at the sight of these great deeds of heroism of their warriors, before whom lay humbled those tyrants and oppressors of their land and faith, who for centuries past seemed as if born to rule over them and they destined to be ruled by them. For centuries, the Hindus in Portuguese Konkan had not seen a Hindu banner aloft, unbent a Hindu sword that struck in defence of a Hindu cause and, instead of getting broken, broke the skull of the alien tyranny and insolence and avenged the wrongs done to their faith and their nation. Well, may the correspondent of Brahmendra Swami write to him when informing him of this brilliant success, 'This valour, this tenacity, this triumph—these deeds seem as if they belong to those times when gods visited our earth. Blessed are they who survive to see these triumphant days, and doubly blessed are they who fell *fighting to render this triumph possible!*'

□

Nadirshah and Bajirao

बघूं नादिरशाहा कसा पुढें येतो तो ।

—Bajirao

But splendid as these successes in the Konkan were, the Maratha arms were prevailing elsewhere as splendidly. Bajirao after the conquest and stallement of Gujarat, Malva and Bundelkhand and, thus, extending the power of the Hindu Empire up to the Chambal, was not likely to cry halt there forever. His aim was a consolidated Hindu Empire that should embrace all Hindusthan in its sweep. His anxiety was to see all the religious shrines of Hindus freed and cleansed from being polluted by the alien and faithless touch of the enemies of Hindu Dharma.

His mission did not, therefore, confine itself to the sacred temple of Parasharam in Konkan alone. Kashi, Gaya and Mathura were still groaning under the sway of the Moslem insolence and fanaticism. So, we find Bajirao and other Maratha Generals again and again trying to strike for the liberation of these holy cities with as restless anxiety as they did in the case of Pandharpur or Nasik. Not daunted by the tremendous odds against which the Marathas were fighting in Konkan by land and by sea, Bajirao threatened the Moslem emperor with nothing less than an attack on Delhi itself if his demands—including the recovery of Kashi, Gaya, Mathura and other religious places thereabout—were not conceded. The Moslem leaders at Delhi, wild with terror, strained their every nerve; not less than 22 Generals marched against the Hindu rebel; and when they could show no real success against the Marathas, they resorted to imaginary ones to tickle their fancy and wrote exaggerated accounts to their Emperor to the effect that Bajirao was utterly crushed in a great battle which was never fought and the Marathas were so completely routed that they could be seen nowhere in the North. The Emperor, thereupon besides himself with glee, insolently dismissed the

Maratha envoy and ordered festivities in honour of this great victory!

When informed of these proceedings at Delhi, Bajirao, with a grim smile on his face, muttered: 'Well, I will take my Maratha forces to the very walls of Delhi and prove our existence in the North to the Moslem Emperor in the dismal light of the flames of his capital.' He kept his word. With Santaji Jadhav, Tukoji Holkar, Shivaji and Yashwantrao Pawar, he was soon knocking at the gates of Delhi. The disillusioned Emperor sent forces after forces of his own Imperial troops, but only to be beaten by the Marathas. Trembling now for his very life, the fool paid for his credulity that fancied the Marathas crushed. This was the first occasion when the tide of the Maratha valour knocked against and shook the gates of Delhi in open opposition. Unable to bear this progress of the Maratha arms in the North, the Nizam hastened with 34,000 soldiers and the best artillery India could then boast of, and marched up to Sironj. The Rajputs too thought it fit to join him against the Marathas. But Bajirao soon came treading on their heels and with splendid generalship and valour speedily made the Nizam realise that he had once more fallen a prey in the hands of the evil Marathas. Their constant and dogged charges forced him to shut himself up behind the walls of Bhopal. He tried to sally forth, to rally round him his exhausted forces again and again, but he was so completely out-generalled and out-marched and his forces, Moslem and Rajput, so thoroughly beaten, besieged and starved that the renowned Moslem General could not but sign a peace almost to Bajirao's dictation.

But, just then, a great Mohammedan plot bore fruit and Nadir Shah crossed the Indus. The Mohammedan hopes of revivifying their dying Emperor rose high. The Nizam and many other Moslem chiefs, who were brought up in the traditions of Aurangzeb, very nearly fraternised with the invader, with the hope that he at least might do what the emasculated Mogul could not and wield a powerful sceptre and strike with might the rising Hindu power of the Maratha Confederacy and raise the Moslem Empire once more to its former pinnacle of glory and might. It all would have been so, but for the dauntless front and resistance that the Hindus led by Bajirao offered to the allied Moslem power led by the fierce foreigner.

Instead of being depressed or daunted, the soaring genius of Bajirao rose to higher altitudes and aspirations at this great national crisis. In the coming of Nadir Shah, he saw an unique opportunity of compressing centuries of Hindu history in years. His able envoys at the different courts in the North watched zealously and led the diplomatic circles as imperiously and effectively as their distinguished Generals led the armies in the fields. Vyankojirao, Vishwasrao, Dadaji, Govind Narayan, Sadashiv Balaji, Baburang Malhar, Mahadeo Bhat Hingne, and several others distinguished themselves and achieved as great diplomatic triumphs as the Pawars, the Shindes, the Gujars, the Angres and other Maratha Generals won military ones.

In fact, it is these Maratha diplomats who preserved the unbroken traditions of the state policy and ideals of the great Hindu movement and prepared with admirable skill the ground for the successful operations of the Maratha Generals. The letters and state dispatches of these distinguished and talented statesmen have now become available in print and their study cannot fail to impress the reader with the grandeur of the schemes and hopes and stupendous efforts which the Maratha diplomats, statesmen, soldiers and sailors conceived and put forth with the single and all-absorbing aim of establishing a consolidated Hindu Empire, which would be the bulwark of the political independence of the Hindu race. It was to defeat this Hindu scheme that Nadir Shah was invited and passively or actively assisted by those Mohammedan leaders who had been trained under Aurangzeb and could ill brook the rising power of the Hindus.

But Nadir Shah soon found that he was brought face to face, in 1739, with a Hindu power far different in nature from that which Muhammad Ghaznavi had to face in 1120-1124. In diplomacy, statesmanship, patriotic fervour and, above all, military strength and organisation—not only readiness to sacrifice but skill in sacrificing in such a way and only when it was found to rebound with tremendous force on their opponents and make the oppressors suffer more than the victim—in all these qualities the Hindus of Maharashtra had proved more than a match for the Mohammedans ever since they rose as a nation in the name of their land and their faith and fought in the belief that they were doing so in the fulfilment of the will of Shri Rama and Shri Krishna. They feared no Nadir Shah; 'Nadir Shah is no god; he cannot destroy the creation; he is bound to come to terms with those who prove strong enough. The talk of friendship can begin only after a trial of strength. Peace can come only after war. So, let the Maratha forces advance. If only the Rajputs and other Hindus, led by Your Excellency (Bajirao), present a bold front, great things would be accomplished; Nadir Shah, aided by the Nizam, is not likely to go back, but will directly march on the Hindu kingdoms. So, all these Hindu Rajas and Maharajas, including Sawai Jaisingh, are anxiously waiting for Your Excellency's (Bajirao's) arrival. If but led by you, our Marathas, the Hindus can march straight on Delhi and dethrone the Moslem, and seat the Maharana of Udaipore on the Imperial throne of Delhi.'

In this strain wrote the Maratha envoys and diplomats to Bajirao. Bassein was still holding on. Maratha armies were conducting great campaigns from the Karnataka to Katak and Allahabad. But Bajirao did not hesitate a moment, or discourage in the least the high hopes his agents had raised in the minds of the Hindus in the North and the vast responsibilities they had undertaken. When some of his colleagues began to express diffidence, he exclaimed: 'Oh, ye heroes: Why ye doubt and deliberate? Advance unitedly and the day of Hindu *pad-padashahi* is at hand. I will spread out my Marathas from the Narmada to the Chambal. Then let me see how Nadir Shah dares to step forward towards the Deccan.'

It is this stubborn attitude of the 'revengeful' Marathas that checked and chilled to death the anti-Hindu ambition of the Persian conqueror. Writing a long and ridiculous letter to Bajirao, whom he addressed as 'a devotee towards the Moslem faith', commanding him to obey the Mogul Emperor at Delhi and threatening how otherwise punishment would be meted out to the rebels. Nadir Shah beat a clever retreat. This scrap of paper that Nadir Shah wrote to the Marathas was relegated to a heap of rubbish and Shahu, the Maharaja of the Marathas, openly proclaimed in the Royal Assembly on 14th June, 1739 that 'Nadir Shah has fled the country through fear of the Marathas'.

Nadir's precipitate retirement left the Nizam in the lurch. The Marathas marched forth towards Delhi to inflict a condign punishment on him for his participation in the anti-Hindu designs of Nadir Shah and hesitation to carry out the terms of the treaty he signed at Bhopal. But just then, Bajirao, the greatest General that ever led them, passed away on 22nd April, 1740.

No man strove more honestly or more successfully for the furtherance of the great cause of Hindu independence. When but a boy, he drew his sword against the enemies of his race and religion and sheathed it not even in the hour of death. He died in the camp in the very act of leading his forces against the enemies of the Hindu race. Throughout his long and arduous campaigns against the Siddis or the Rohillas or the Moguls or the Portuguese, he knew no defeat. His premature death, due to super-human exertions he underwent for the speedy realisation of the great ideal of Hindu *pad-padashahi,* was a greater blow to the Hindu cause than half a dozen invasions of Nadir Shah could ever have been.

□

Nana and Bhau

दशरथ देउनि राज्यश्रीस राम लक्ष्मणाचिया करी,
प्रभाततारा देउनि जाई कांति आपुलि सूर्यकरीं,
तशीच बाजीरावें हिंदु स्वातंत्र्याची ध्वजा दिली,
या नरवीर नानांच्या या भाऊंच्या दुर्दान्त करी॥

—महाराष्ट्र भाट

Bajirao died. But the spirit he had infused in his people could not die. It braced them up to sterner efforts and greater achievements under their new leader Balaji, alias Nana Saheb, the son of Bajirao and Bhau Saheb, the son of Chimaji, the victor of Bassein. Although he was only 19, Balaji had already seen service under his father and proved to be capable of the leadership of a great people. Shahu, ever ready to recognise merit, did not hesitate to appoint the brilliant youth in his father's place as the prime minister of the Maratha Empire. The ceremony of investiture was an imposing one. On the completion of it, a Royal letter of instructions was handed over by the Maharaja to the youthful minister signifying in a few inspiring sentences the very heart of the great idea that had ever been struggling itself to actualise in the mighty movements of Maharashtra. 'Your father Bajirao,' wrote the King, 'had served most faithfully and achieved mighty deeds. He aimed to extend the bounds of Hindu rule to the farthest limits of Hindusthan. You are his son: realise your father's ideal, achieve what he aspired to and lead your horsemen beyond the walls of Attock!'

Faithful to the Royal command, Nana and Bhau strove even unto death to drown with triumph the work which Shivaji had begun. Nor did they require any exhortation to do that. Hindu *pad-padashahi* was the vision of their childhood, the ambition of their youth. To strive and fight and die for it was a labour of love to them. They hated even the cringing sense of fidelity and slavish regard which Shahu at times experienced in spite of himself towards the Mogul court at Delhi, where he had passed his days of captivity, enlivened by occasional royal smiles.

Immediately after the ceremony of investiture was over, Shahu ordered Balaji to go to Poona and sent Raghoji Bhosale on an expedition to the South.

Taking advantage of the civil war that broke out amongst the Marathas after the return of Shahu, the Mohammedans, led by an able General, Sadat Ulla, had brought back the whole of the south-east of the peninsula under the Moslem sovereignty and pressed hard the little Maratha colony at Tanjore. Pratap Singh, the Raja of Tanjore, naturally turned towards Shahu for assistance. Sadat Ulla died in 1732 and his nephew Dost Ali succeeded him as the Nawab of Arcot. He was a powerful chief and a sworn enemy of the Maratha power. Early on 19th May, 1740, the Marathas pressed through a gorge to the south of Dost Ali's position and attacked his front and flank and rear. In a few hours, the Moslem army was totally destroyed and Dost Ali lay dead in the field. The Hindus, long groaning under the Moslem tyranny, rejoiced at the triumph of their coreligionists and made common cause with the Marathas. Raghoji, levying heavy contributions of war as he went from cities and towns, moved against Arcot. Safdar Ali and Chandasaheb, the son and son-in-law of Dost Ali, were holding out at Vellore and Trichinopoly with powerful forces under them. Raghoji thereupon gave it out that as the campaign had been a great pecuniary loss, he meant to abandon it. He actually fell back some 80 miles from Trichinopoly. Even a man of Chandasaheb's activity and tact was so completely taken in by this device that he drafted away some 10,000 men of his forces to attack Madurai, the richest city of Hindu pilgrimage. But the Hindu leader, seeing the Moslem so well caught in his trap, suddenly wheeled round and with forced marches appeared before Trichinopoly. Barasaheb, who had been dispatched to wreak vengeance on Madurai and sack the Hindu sacred city tried to hurry back to reinforce his brother; but Raghoji, detaching a part of his forces to interrupt him, engaged him in a gory fight and knocked him down dead from his elephant. The Mohammedans were totally routed and the dead body of their chief was carried to Raghoji's tent. The Maratha leader had it clad in rich clothes and sent it to Chandasaheb, his brother. The siege of Trichinopoly continued for months. But the Moslem leader, in spite of his brave defence, could not but surrender to the hated Hindu. Raghoji took Chandasaheb a prisoner and sent him to Satara, and appointed Murar Rao Ghorpade to hold Trichinopoly with a garrison of 14,000 soldiers. Safdar Ali too had already surrendered to the Marathas who promised to recognise him as the Nawab of Arcot on the condition that he paid 10 millions of rupees and—be it noted—reinstated all the Hindu princes whom his father had dispossessed since 1736.

But while Raghoji was winning these splendid successes in the South, his government had already come in conflict with Alivardi Khan, the Moslem ruler of Bengal, Bihar and Orissa. Mir Habib, the leader of the party that was opposed to Alivardi Khan, invited the Marathas to assist him. Bhaskarpant Kolhatkar, the Dewan of Raghoji, eager to catch the first opportunity to humble the Moslem power in Bengal and to extend the Hindu sway to the eastern limits of Hindusthan, accepted the invitation and the Maratha horse, some ten thousand strong rushed marching through Bihar, stamping underneath its hoof the prestige of the Mohammedan power there. As soon as Alivardi Khan, who was by no means a despicable leader, came upon them, the Marathas cleverly caught him in a fix, cut off his supplies, crushed his forces and forced him to fall back on Katwa. Mir Habib pressed Bhaskarpant to change his mind and remain in Bengal throughout the rainy season, and live by levying contributions of war on the enemy's territory. The Marathas thereupon attacked Murshidabad, took Hoogly, Midnapur, Rajmahal and almost all the Bengal districts west of the Ganges, except Murshidabad. They intended to celebrate the Kali festival there with unwonted pomp for having favoured the Hindu cause and humbled the pride of non-Hindu bigots in Bengal. Although just then, Alivardi Khan suddenly crossed the Hoogly and took the Marathas by surprise and engaged them to the frontiers of Bengal; yet it was destined, to be merely for a while. For Raghoji soon returned. Baiaji too, at the head of another Maratha army, entered Bihar, ostensibly as an Imperial General but, in fact, to levy revenue there for himself and to settle his own account with Raghoji Bhosale. As soon as the Maratha Generals reached an understanding between themselves, Balaji withdrew and Bhaskarpant demanded a large sum of indemnity and the inevitable Maratha *chowth*. Unable to meet him in the field, Alivardi Khan decided to resort to a treacherous plan and inviting Bhaskarpant to discuss the question of indemnity to his tent as a guest and an envoy, caused assassins to attack and murder him as soon as, at the given signal, the cry of 'kill the *kafirs*' was raised. No less than 20 Maratha officers fell there on that ghastly day. Only Raghoji Gaikwad survived and led the surprised and confused Maratha forces through a hostile country and in the race of the repeated efforts of the exhilarated foe to hem them in and cut them to pieces.

But a murder here or a surprise there was not likely to roll back the tide of the Maratha movement, which the Imperial resources of an Aurangzeb failed to repress. Yet Alivardi Khan was stupid enough to write this ridiculous letter to Raghoji: 'Praised be the Lord! The horses of the faithful feel no dread of encountering the infidels. When the lions of Islam shall so engage the monsters of idolatry....that one part begs for quarters, then alone peace would be possible.' Raghoji retorted that, while he had advanced a thousand miles to meet Alivardi, that lion of Islam dared not move even a hundred to meet him and refusing to carry a war of foolish words any longer, ordered the Maratha light horse to invade and levy revenue throughout Burdwan and Orissa. Year in and year out, the Marathas continued to harass Alivardi Khan, levy regular revenue where they could, impose and collect heavy war contributions where they could not; overran districts, marched in and out, fought or fled as suited them best, till they made it impossible for the Moslem ruler to conduct the government in all the three provinces of Bengal, Bihar and Orissa. Defeat could not deter them, nor disasters depress—they must have their *chowth*.

At last in 1750, Alivardi Khan, that 'lion of Islam' had enough of the 'infidels' and conceived such a 'dread of encountering' them that he begged for quarters and ceded Orissa for the *mundkatai* or the blood-fee for the dastardly murder of Bhaškarpant and engaged to pay 10 lakhs of rupees a year for the *chowth* of Bengal and Bihar. Thus, it was 'the heroes of faith' who at last begged for quarters 'at the hand of the monsters of idolatry', one wonders if they 'praised the Allah' for it on that day.

While Raghoji Bhosale was thus successfully striving to root out the Mohammedan power from Bengal, other Maratha Generals were distinguishing themselves as brilliantly in battering the strongholds of the Moslem power in the North. The fanatical Rohillas and Pathans, who held in their grip all the territory from the Jumna to the borders of Nepal, formed a combination so terrible as to force the Vazir of the Mogul Emperor at Delhi to seek the aid of the Marathas in his attempt to defeat the ambitious intentions of the Pathans to re-establish an Afghan monarch in India on the ruins of the Mogul Empire. The Marathas, who had taken such pains to bring about that ruin, naturally hated any attempt or ambition on the part of any Moslem or non-Hindu people to despoil them of their gain. So, the Marathas gladly responded to the invitation of the Vazir and their leaders, Malharrao Holkar and Jayajirao Shinde, crossed the Jumna and marched against the position the Pathans were holding at Kadarganj. The Pathans held out doggedly, but the Marathas ultimately won a splendid victory and routed their forces. Not only that, but they immediately marched out and hemmed in Ahmed Khan, the great leader of the Pathans, who was hastening to help his comrades at Kadarganj. Ahmed Khan entered Farukkabad and the Marathas invested it. For weeks, the dogged fight continued. But the Pathans could not be crushed, owing to the succour they kept receiving from the other side of the Ganges at the hands of the powerful army of the Rohillas. The Marathas managed to build a bridge of boats, crossed the Ganges in time and while a part of them was pressing the siege of Farukkabad as strenuously as ever, the main part of their forces attacked the combined power of Rohillas and Pathans 30,000 strong, and utterly defeated them in a fierce fight. Ahmed Khan at Farukkabad attempted an escape and tried to engage the diminished forces of the Marathas there, but failed and was hotly pursued. The Marathas routed the Moslems, looted their camp and carried away an enormous booty—elephants and horses, camels and banners and baggage.

The moral result of the campaign, too, was as great as the military glory was brilliant. For the Pathans, just to spite the Marathas and give a religious colouring to their cause, had attacked Kashi and committed outrages on the Hindu temples and priests, swaggering loudly that the *kafirs* could never face the Pathans. For Allah was on their side and, in a way, that came out true. For the Marathas, too, found it very difficult to face them for the simple reason that the Pathans in every pitched fight turned their backs to the Marathas, no sooner had they faced them. The crushing defeats, the hot and persistent pursuit of the Moslems, made the Hindus feel that the wanton insults to their temples and hearts had been amply avenged. The letters of that period are all penned in this triumphant tone. 'The Pathans had insulted Kashi and Prayagji. Well, *Haribhaktas* have triumphed at last....The foes had sown the wind at Kashi; well, god had made them reap the whirlwind at Farukkabad.' Nor were the political results less brilliant. The Moslem Emperor, thoroughly cowed down, conferred on the Marathas the right to levy the *chowth*—which was only the thin end of the wedge—in the remaining parts of the Indian Empire. Thus, Multan (Sind), the Punjab, Rajputana and Rohilkhand were brought under Maratha influence and the *Haribhaktas* could rightly claim to have driven the Maratha lance into the very heart of the Mogul Empire. On receiving news of these momentous events, Balaji, the leader of the Maratha confederacy, wrote back to the armies: "Superb is the courage! Indomitable the bravery! The armies of the Deccan, crossing the Narmada, the Jumna and the Ganges, have challenged and fought and destroyed the armies of such precious foes as the Rohillas and Pathans! Officers and men! You have achieved a triumph that is truly uncommon. You are the pillars of this Hindu Empire. Your name, as the maker of kings, has penetrated to Iran and Turan farther." (1751).

Once again the leaders of the Maratha Confederacy attempted to recover Kashi and Prayag from the Nawab of Oudh and the Vazir of Delhi. As representatives of the great movement of Hindu liberation, they keenly felt the humiliation that the Moslems should still hold the foremost religious places of the Hindus. Again and again, we find the Marathas restless over it all as the correspondence of that period clearly shows. Impatient of arriving at diplomatic results, Malharrao once went so far as to decide to effect a raid and march right towards Kashiji, pull down the mosque that stood over the holy site of Dnyana-wapi and, thus wipe off the standing insult to the Hindu people and their faith. For, the mosque ever reminded the Hindus of those dark days when the Moslem crescent rose insultingly on the ruins of the foremost temples of the Hindu faith. But the Brahmins of Kashi, afraid of the vengeance that the Yavanas, still so dominant round about Kashi, would wreak on themselves and the city, prayed that 'the proposed raid be abandoned till a better chance presented itself.' No wonder that these Brahmins of Kashi expressed in that very letter a pious anxiety as to the sin that would accrue to them for this piece of advice that dissuaded Malharrao from avenging a national insult merely for the safety of their lives and their city (18 June, 1751).

Shahu died in 1749. Since then, Balaji, who had been invested with the supreme power by Shahu himself, became the head of the Maratha Confederacy and the soul of their national ambition and ideals. In spite of civil strifes and petty palace intrigues that, at times, rose to serious dimensions, this able man strove far more consciously and determinedly than several of his predecessors, to rear up a great and independent Hindu Empire, under the leadership of the Marathas, on the ruins of the Mogul Empire and conducted a gigantic struggle with all the foreign rivals in the field, Moslem or Christian, Asiatic or European.

Among these, the French were already accumulating great influence and power in the lower Deccan. Balaji was not unmindful of them. But as he had simultaneously to conduct great campaigns in distant parts in India and face the numerous enemies who from all sides strove to crush the one great Hindu power of Maharashtra, Balaji could not for a long time take the French by themselves and settle accounts with them. But, ultimately, by a series of clever manoeuvres of diplomacy and their irresistible pressure brought to bear on them in the battlefield, Balaji succeeded in baffling the French so completely as to force them and their protege, the Nizam, to sign a treaty at Bhalaki in 1752 by which the Marathas gained all the territories between the Tapi and the Godavari and greatly undermined the French influence in the various courts in the Deccan.

The Peshwa had already undertaken to punish all the rebellious Nawabs in the Karnataka and lower Deccan and now inflicted a serious defeat on the Nawab of Savnur and forced him to hand over an extensive territory to the Marathas and to pay 11 lakhs of rupees as tribute for what he still held. Then the Marathas, 60,000 strong and led by Balaji and Bhau, appeared before Shrirangapattan, exacted 35 lakhs of rupees for accumulated *chowth*, retook Shivre and punished minor Mohammedan chiefs. Then Balvantrao Mehendale marched against the Moslem Nawab of Cuddapah. All the Moslem chiefs in the lower Deccan, who kept trembling at the mention of the Marathas, rallied round the Nawab. Even the English sided with him. But, in spite of the rains, Balvantrao Mehendale attacked the Moslem forces and in a pitched and fierce battle, put to the sword thousands of Pathans and killed the Nawab himself. Annexing half of his dominions to their kingdom, the Marathas proceeded against the Nawab of Arcot, who was strongly backed by the English. But neither he nor his patrons could afford to flout the Maratha demands—had to pay 4 lakhs to pacify them. In 1759, the Marathas besieged Bangalore, took Cheenapattan and forced Haider, who was just then trying to make himself master of Mysore, to pay the stipulated sum of 34 lakhs of rupees. Balaji had a mind to crush him then, but the great campaigns that the Marathas were carrying on elsewhere in India constantly forced him to recall his troops from the lower Deccan and leave the work there half done.

Meanwhile, in 1753, Raghoba took Ahmedabad and extracted 30 lakhs of rupees from the Jats for opposing the influence of the Marathas at Delhi. Just then there arose a civil war amongst the Rajputs about the claim to the Gadi of Jodhpur. Ramsingh courted the assistance of the Marathas against the other claimant, Bijaysingh. The Marathas consented and Dattaji and Jayappa Shinde personally led the expedition. After a bloody fight with the Rajputs, some 50,000 strong, the Marathas inflicted a severe defeat on Bijaysingh, who thereupon fled to Nagore. Jayappa invested it, but soon found that it was an unpleasant work. Rajputs fighting with Marathas, Hindus with Hindus, Balaji again and again pressed Shinde to effect a compromise in Rajputana and proceed to undertake the task so dear to every Maratha heart of liberating the holy cities of Hindusthan—Kashi and Prayag.

But, just then, Bijaysing resorted to a crime which sent such a thrill of horror throughout Maharashtra as to make any effort at compromise impossible. It would be remembered that the uncle of Bijaysingh had formerly got Pilaji Gaikwad assassinated while a guest at his camp. Bijaysingh, too, determined to follow in the footsteps of his uncle, in spite of the knowledge that Pilaji's murder had only sharpened the edge of Maratha revenge and been dearly paid for. Three Rajput assassins started from Bijaysingh's camp, disguised as beggars, kept picking up grams dropped on the floor of the Maratha stable in front of Jayappa's tent and as soon as he came out for bathing and covered his face with a rubbing towel, punched upon him and thrust their daggers in his sides. Jayappa fell mortally wounded. Two assassins were caught and one escaped. Immediately the Rajputs came out, attacked the forces, intending to crush them while leaderless and confused. It would have been so, but for the undaunted spirit of the great warrior who lay there foully done to death. Jayappa, with his dying breath, exhorted his mourning comrades to sally forth and face the fighting foes first and then to weep like women over his wounds. Fired with these words of their dying chief, the Marathas rushed forth and Bijaysingh was once more beaten. Other Maratha Generals too hurried to Shinde's help. Antaji Manekshwar, with 10,000 soldiers, entered Rajputana and inflicted condign punishment on all those Rajput states which supported Bijaysingh. Thus, utterly helpless, Bijaysingh sued for peace, acknowledged the claims of Ramsingh, whom he had dispossessed, to Nagore, Madata and other districts and gave Ajmer and paid all the expenses of the campaign to the Marathas.

Just then the widowed mother of the infant King of Bundi sought Shinde's assistance against her scheming rivals. Dattaji Shinde did the work to the satisfaction of the Rajput queen who thereupon paid 75 lakhs of rupees to him as his reward.

□

On to the Indus

फेडून नवस माहारास गेले लाहोरास जिकित शेंडें ॥
अरे त्यांनी अटकेंत पाव घटकेंत लाविले झेंडे ॥
सरदार पदरचे कसे कुणि सिंह जसे कुणि शार्दुल गेंडें

—Prabhakar

Meanwhile, Raghoba was dominating and shaping great events at Delhi. He helped Gaziuddin to assume the office of the Imperial Vazir. He forced the Emperor to cede Gaya and Kurukshetra to the Marathas. He personally advanced and occupied Mathura, Vrindavan, Gadmukteshwar, Pushpavati, Pushkar and several other religious places of the Hindus: the sacred city of Benares, too, was entered and occupied and held by a strong Maratha detachment. Thus, one of the most cherished dreams of the Hindu people was at last realised and Raghoba could proudly report to the Peshwa of having liberated and recovered almost all the holy sites and cities of Hindudom from the Moslem hands. The Hindu colours waving triumphantly over those sites and cities in north, that were so endearing to every Hindu heart by a thousand holy associations, supplied yet another moral justification to the claim of the Marathas to represent and lead the great movement of Hindu liberation and Hindu *pad-padashahi*. The Emperor too thought that he had enough of the Marathas and should fight. As soon as the new Vazir Gaziuddin became cognizant of the Emperor's secret design against himself and the Marathas who had raised him to the office, he invited Holkar with 50,000 soldiers, who easily routed the Imperial forces so thoroughly that the very ladies of the harem were left unprotected and fell in the hands of the Marathas. They, with Gaziuddin, entered Delhi, forced their way into the palace, dethroned the old Emperor and seated a new one on his throne and, as if to render the vengeance of nemesis poetically complete, named him Alamgir-II.

Alamgir—the conqueror of the world: Alamgir-I and Alamgir-II. Aurangzeb (Alamgir-I) fancied that he could blow out the lamp of Hindu life that burned in the temple just with a breath of his Imperial wrath. He swore by Allah and blew but, to his utter dismay, discovered that the faintly flickering lamp scorching his beard burst suddenly into a wildfire: the hills of Sahyadri caught it and, setting aflame a million hearts and towers and turrets, and hills and valleys, by land and sea, it grew into a great sacrificial conflagration. Alamgir I, despised the Marathas as 'mountain rats'. Since then, the Hindu rats developed such terribly sharp and powerful claws that many a lion of Islam lay torn and bleeding at their feet in the capital of Alamgir-II. Emperor Alamgir-I did not condescend to recognise Shivaji even as a mere Raja: but his descendant, Alamgir-II, could call himself Emperor only because the descendant of Shivaji did not mind it much to allow him the luxury of the name.

The Indian Mohammedan world was thoroughly alarmed and kept chafing with impotent rage at the extension of the Hindu power and influence. Rohillas and Pathans so badly beaten at Farukkabad and elsewhere, the displaced Vazir and Nawabs and the Moulvis and the Maulanas who could ill bear the triumph of the *kafirs* and the sight of the daily diminishing splendour at their ever-weaning crescent, the Emperor himself who could not feel it very comfortable in keeping up his position poised on the point of the Maratha lance, the dispossessed, the hopeless and the ambitious—all Moslem interests vowed vengeance against the Marathas, and began to weave dark schemes of driving and destroying them altogether. Strange to say—and yet not so strange—the extension of the Maratha power in the North gave rise to a deadly antipathy even in the hearts of some of the Hindu princes. Madhavsingh of Jaipur, Bijaysingh of Jodhpur, the Jats and some other minor Hindu chiefs did not hesitate to ally themselves with their natural and national enemies against the Marathas and encouraged the disaffected Moslem elements to hatch up some great plot to get rid of the only Hindu power that could cope with all who aimed at the destruction of the Hindu faith and Hindu independence. The leader of the Moslem world instinctively fell back on the old traditional scheme of inviting their coreligionists from beyond the Indian Frontier against the hated nation of idolaters and *kafirs*, who none of them could face in a fair fight, nor dupe, nor outwit in any Maschiavelian move or Aurangzebian treachery.

This extensive plot found fit leaders in Nazib Khan, who was a Rohilla chief and had everything to gain from the downfall of the Marathas, and in Malakazamani, who had ever been the most intriguing figure in the Imperial harem and could not bear that she had to beg for her bread at the hands of the hated Hindus. They decided to initiate the tactics of their predecessors who, under similar hopes and fears, had invited Nadir Shah. They established secret communication with Ahmedshah Abdalii and sent him pressing requests to invade India and save the Mohmmedan empire from the attacks of the unbelievers. Ahmedshah, too, had his own reason for accepting this invitation. The guilty lust of conquest had ever been his passion. But, above all, the telling fact that the sphere of Maratha influence and power had already touched his frontiers near Multan and daily threatened to widen yet further had already made it incumbent on him to fight the Marathas out.

He had already annexed Multan and the Punjab to his dominions. But in 1750 the Marathas had undertaken to preserve order in and defend the provinces of Thatta, Multan and the Punjab against any internal and foreign aggression and had secured the right of levying their *chowth* in them. Accordingly, they had helped Gaziuddin, the Vazir of their own choice, to recover the Punjab and Multan from the hands of Abdalii in 1754. This was a direct challenge thrown out to Abdalii. Just then the intrigues which Nazib Khan conducted assured Abdalii of the support of a widely spread and powerful Mohammedan section in India. This whetted the ambition of the Pathan conqueror to such an extent that he began to dream of winning the Imperial crown of India for himself and to achieve what Nadir Shah had failed to achieve. Learning that the chief leaders of the Marathas were preoccupied in the Deccan about 1756, he crossed the Indus with 80,000 men, occupied the Punjab, took Delhi almost unopposed and assumed the Imperial titles. True to the traditions of a Pathan conqueror, he even got angry and celebrated this assumption of the Imperial dignity by ordering a ghastly general massacre of the citizens of Delhi for a few hours. In those few hours, not less than 18 thousand persons were put to the sword in cold blood. Thence he started to vindicate his title as the defender of the Moslem faith by devastating the sacred places and the holy cities of the Hindus, which the Marathas had but recently recovered from the Mohammedan grip. Mathura was the first victim to fall. But, it fell as does a martyr. Some 5,000 Jats gave a heroic fight to the overwhelming forces of the enemy, as long as they lived. After wreaking his vengeance on Mathura, if only to spite the

Marathas, the Moslem conqueror came to Gokul Vrindavan, only to find a deathless resistance offered to him by some 4,000 armed Nangas who had assembled there to fight or die in defence of their Gokulnath. Some two thousand *Bairagees* fell on the field, but succeeded in repulsing the foes and saving the temple of (their faith. For Abdalii soon marched towards Agra, took the city and attacked the fort there. Gaziuddin, the Vazir, who led that Moslem section in the North which hated the Pathans and opposed the establishment of a Pathan or Persian dynasty in India as fiercely as the Marathas did, had taken refuge in that fort and was hourly expecting the news of the Marrathas hastening to his rescue.

But what were the Rajputs of Jaipur, Jodhpur and Udaipore and several other Hindu princes and chiefs doing there? They hated the Marathas much and questioned their claim to lead the movement of Hindu *pad-padashahi.* Well then, this was surely the time for them to prove that they were better fitted to lead it than the Marathas were by defending the Hindu interests in the North and by striking either singly or unitedly, in defence of the Hindu faith and the Hindu *pad-padashahi.* But not a man stirred. Ahmedshah Abdalii simply walked down over the plains, teeming with millions of Hindus, to Delhi, to Agra, and would have done so, as he loudly proclaimed to do, right down to the Deccan. The Moslem hordes poured down unresisted and under the very eyes of the Rajputs and Jats and several other Hindu princes and chiefs, loudly calling for vengeance on the *kafirs*, trampled over the Hindu hearts and homes, temples and *tirthas*. But, no one could raise a finger against them till the Marathas came.

The news of Abdalii's invasion did no more damp or depress the Maratha leaders in Poona than the news of Nadir Shah's advance had done. A powerful army led by Raghunath Rao was forthwith dispatched to the North. Abdalii received the news near Agra. He was a clever and experienced General and had seen some reverses in his life. He immediately saw the danger of advancing further in the teeth of such opposition offered by such a foe and like his master Nadir Shah, decided not to risk what was already gained by courting a probable defeat. So, he immediately fell back, reached Delhi, married the daughter of Malkazamani to strengthen his claim to the Mogul crown, left a garrison of 10,000 soldiers to guard Sarhind and, appointing his son Taimur Shah as the Viceroy of Lahore, hurried back to his country as suddenly as he had come down.

The Marathas, in spite of their preoccupation in the Deccan, advanced as rapidly as they could, undoing all that Abdalii had done. Sakharam Bhagwant, Gandadhar Yashwant and other Maratha Generals entered the Doab and put down the Rohillas and Pathans, who had meanwhile revolted against them. The Vazir Gaziuddin was rescued. Vithal Shivdeo marched on Delhi and, after a strenuous fight for a fortnight or so, took the capital and captured alive Nazib Khan, the arch enemy of the Marathas and the chief instigator of the Pathan plot. Thence the Marathas advanced to meet the forces of Abdalii, some 10,000 strong, stationed at Sarhind, under Abdul Samad and routing them, took their general captive. Now they were determined to press on towards Lahore. The rapid successes of the Marathas had so alarmed Taimur Shah, the son and Viceroy of Abdalii, who held the Punjab and Multan for him, that he dared not face them in the field. So, he withdrew. Raghunathrao entered Lahore in triumph. Jahan Khan and Taimur attempted to effect a clever and well-ordered retreat, but the Marathas soon came chasing them so hotly that the retreat soon became a rout. Abandoning all that was less valuable than life, the forces and the son and Viceroy of him, who had come to crush the Marathas and conquer an Indian Empire, could only seek their safety in an ignominious flight before the Marathas. Their camp was looted, an immense booty in money and material was taken, and the *geruwa* banner, that Ramdas handed over to Shivaji, was at last planted on the very northern frontiers of Hindusthan.

The Hindus reached Attock. For the first time since the dismal day when Prithviraj fell, a triumphant Hindu flag waved proudly on the sacred river of the *Vedas*. The Hindu horse of victory drank the waters of the Indus, gazing fearlessly at himself as reflected in its crystal tides.

As the news of these splendid achievements of their forces reached Maharashtra, it simply electrified the nation. Antaji Mankeshwar wrote to Raghunath Rao: 'Lahore is taken; the foe driven out and chased beyond the frontiers: our forces reached the Indus: glad news indeed! It had cowed down all the disaffected elements in the North, Rajas and Raos, Subedars and Nawabs. Only the Marathas could avenge the wrongs done to our nation. They alone have wreaked the vengeance of all Hindusthan on Abdalii. Words fail to convey the fullness of my feelings. Heroic deeds have been done, no less heroic than those of the *avtars*!'

It is no wonder that the Marathas were thus surprised at their own achievements. From Dwarka to Jagannath, from Rameshwar to Multan, their sword had triumphed, their word was law. They openly proclaimed themselves as the defenders and successors of the Indian Empire, and vindicated their claims against all those who came to contest it from Iran, Turan or Afghanistan, from England, France or Portugal. Shivaji's mission of Hindu *pad-padashahi* was almost realised. The teachings of Ramdas had been translated into deeds. They had carried the Hindu colours in triumph to the very banks of the Indus and, as Shahu had commanded Bajirao to do, were likely to carry them yet further.

For the occupation of Attock suddenly widened the sphere of their influence and the horizon of their political activities. It could no longer confine itself within the four walls of Delhi. Agents and emissaries and ambassadors poured in the Maratha camp, from Kashmere, Kandahar and Kabul. A time was when the dispossessed Hindu elements to a *gaddi* invited help from the Moslems of Kabul and Persia. Now the tables were turned. Petitions and prayers were daily received by Raghunath Rao from the disaffected elements of Kabul and Kandahar. Writes the General of Nana Saheb on the 4th May, 1758: 'The forces of Sultan Taimur and Jahan Khan were routed and their very camp, with all their belongings, fell in our hands. Only a few could recross Attock alive. The Shah of Iran has defeated Adbali and has personally written to me, pressing me to advance further on to Kandahar and proposes that, when Abdalii is thus crushed between our allied forces, he would recognise Attock as the frontier of our empire. But I do not know why we should confine ourselves to Attock. The two provinces of Kabul and Kandahar belong to our Hindusthani empire ever since the days of Akbar to Aurangzeb. Why then should we hand them over to the foreigners? I think that the King of Iran would be glad to confine himself to Iran and refrain from contesting our claim to Kabul and Kandahar. But whether he likes it or not, I have decided to treat them as a part of our empire and exercise our sway over them. Already the nephew of Abdaliii, who claims his position has approached us, pressingly requesting help from us against Abdalii. I mean to appoint him as our Governor of that part of our empire that lies beyond the Indus and dispatch some forces to back him up. For the time being, I must hasten back to the Deccan. My successors will see that these extensive designs bear fruit and our regular administration is introduced in the provinces of Kabul and Kandahar.'

□

Hindu *Pad-Padashahi*

'इराणपासुनि फिरगणापर्यंत शत्रुची फळी
सिंधुपासुनी सेतुबंधपर्यंत रणागण भू झाली
तीन खंडिच्यी पुंडांची ती परंतु सेना बुडविली
सिंधुपासुनी सेतुबंधपर्यंत सम्रभू लढवीली'

Soon after penning the letter, Raghunath Rao hastened back with his forces to the Deccan as the rainy season was imminent. It was, however, unfortunate that he had to do so and leave the newly conquered but weakly garrisoned provinces. A yet more fatal factor that was not satisfactorily dealt with was that Nazib Khan, the most intriguing leader of the Pathan plot, was yet spared even after he was captured by the Marathas and in spite of the desire of almost all the Marathas to make him pay with his life for his treacherous dealing with Ahmedshah Abdalii, in instigating him against the Maratha power. But, that wily chief was a consummate actor. He offered numberless apologies, adopted Malharrao as his father and begged him to spare his penitent life as he would that of his son. Malharrao was ever anxious to adopt as his son all those who forfeited their lives as the enemies of the Maratha cause, pleaded so pressingly for Nazib that Raghunath Rao had to give in against his will. It will soon he seen how Nazib spent his penitent life in fomenting most dangerous intrigues against those who had so foolishly spared it.

Upto this time, the Marathas, for diplomatic reasons, were more or less acting in the name of the Emperor of Delhi. That was the line of least resistance and it paid them well. The position they occupied then was analogous to that which the English held in India before the fall of the Marathas in 1818. The same political and diplomatic reasons, which forced the English to pretend to be merely the agents of the Emperor down to 1857, even when they were the de facto Emperor themselves, made the Marathas not hurry the process much, which could only be done by raising a storm of opposition, not only from Indian Moslems but from the English, the French, the Pathans and even the Hindu princes themselves. For each of these had an eye to the dying empire's crown and inheritance, but each one willed that it should linger on its death-bed till rest of the claimants disappeared and it fell an easy prey to him alone.

But, the great successes in the North, coupled with those which the Peshwa had himself won in the South, raised the Maratha power to such a position that, from Balaji and Sadashivrao Bhau to the very man in the street, the whole nation felt itself strong enough to give the finishing stroke to the great work they had undertaken. Grand schemes came up for discussion before the Maratha councils. They felt their strength. They knew they had dealt a death-blow to the Moslem Empire in India. They knew that they had grown into an Asiatic power and that Poona had begun to be the centre, not merely of Indian, but of Asiatic politics. The Mogul Empire lay smashed at their feet. Now they decided to sweep off all that still impeded them in taking the last and crowning step of openly assuming the Imperial crown. Sadashivrao Bhau, more than any other leader in the Maratha camp, felt himself the chosen instrument of this great cause and was determined to render it possible or die fighting for it. They had brought about the downfall of the Moslem Empire; the Hindus had conquered the conqueror; and, fired at the eloquence of Bhau, they decided to strive in such a way as to 'free' all India and bring it directly and openly under the Hindu sway within the next few years.

The great campaigns were laid out with this object in view. Dattaji Shinde was ordered to march towards the Punjab and Multan and introduce order and regular government in the newly conquered provinces. He had thence to come down to Kashi, Prayag, where Raghunath Rao was to meet him at the head of another army. Thence the allied Maratha armies were to march on to Bengal and free the whole province right to the seas by sweeping it clear of the Moslem and of the English, who but recently, had won a battle at Plassey (1757) and aimed to make themselves the masters thereof. While Dattaji, Jankoji and Raghunath Rao were thus charged to reduce all North from Sind and Multan to the seas, the task of liberating all South was undertaken by Balaji himself with Vishwasrao, his son and Sadashivrao Bhau.

Accordingly, Dattaji, with his forces, started towards the North.

Balaji and Bhau first undertook the task of reducing the Nizam to a mere non-entity in the Deccan. They marched against him with a powerful army and up-to-date artillery and after several manoeuvres and fights, won one of the most decisive victories at Udgir in 1760. The Moslem forces were simply crushed, the Nizam so cowed down as to deliver his own Royal seals into the hands of Bhau and humbly express his readiness to sign any conditions the victors dictated. A treaty was signed by which the great forts of Nagar, Barhanpur, Salher, Mulher, Ashirged and Daulatabad, as well as the four districts of Nanded, Fulumbri, Ambed and Vizapur, were handed over to the Marathas. Even Bhau was satisfied with the result. 'The Nizam ceases to be a power. But for the North, all Deccan would have been liberated before this year passed.' At last, the Maratha colours rose above the reduced capitals of Nagar and Vizapur, the kings whereof used to laugh contemptuously at the little rebel when Shivaji took Torna and openly hoisted the flag of a Hindu revolt.

After these great diplomatic and military achievements, the victor of Udgir meant to march on and crush Haider Ali who, besieging Mysore and trying to upset the ancient Hindu dynasty there, had set himself in its stead. The Hindu King and his minister sent pressing and personal appeals to the Marathas to save them from the new Moslem adventurer's ambition. Sadashivrao Bhau, only too eager to seize this opportunity to crush Haider Ali and complete his task of liberating all Deccan, meant immediately to march against Haider Ali, but for the serious news that just then reached the Peshwa from the North. The cup of success Bhau writes was snatched away from his hands even while he was raising it to his lips.

The northern division of the Maratha forces that Dattaji led reached Delhi by the end of 1758. Thence, as ordered, Dattaji proceeded to settle down in the newly conquered province of Lahore and Multan. He appointed Sabaji Shinde and Trimbak Bapuji to govern them up to Attock and garrisoned Sarhind, Lahore and other important places. Then he left the Punjab and came down to undertake the second task allotted to him of crossing the Ganges and marching on Patna and then to settle his account with the English and extend the Hindu sway to the sea.

But here he committed a great mistake in not carrying out the orders of the Peshwa as regards Nazib Khan, who, instead of being severely dealt with by the Shindia, was actually allowed to increase his power and influence in return for the vaguest promises he gave to help Dattaji in his campaign in Bengal and render faithful service. The Peshwa wrote almost angrily: "You write that Nazib promises to pay 30 lakhs of rupees to us if we appoint him as a Bukshee; touch not a farthing. Nazib is half Abdalii; trust him not, nor feed a vile and treacherous reptile." (*Patar-roop itihaas*). But Dattaji was almost hypnotised by that consummate hypocrite and actually depended on his promises to build a bridge of boats to cross the Ganges. Thus, delaying the Maratha campaign in Bengal on the one hand, Nazib got ample opportunity, on the other, to form in secret a second and far more formidable coalition against the Marathas and succeeded in inducing the Moslem Emperor himself to send autographed letters to Abdalii to try again and invade India once more. Fervent appeals were made to rouse Pathan fanaticism in the name of religion and Allah and all that was sacred to Moslems. Would not Abdalii be the defender of the faith, a Gazi and rescue the Mohummedan Empire in India from the death-grip of the unbelieving idolators? Abdalii too was simply smarting under the defeats the Marathas had inflicted on his son. They had snatched away the Imperial Crown of India from him. Nay, they had driven him from the Punjab and Multan and were actually claiming Kabul and Kandahar as a part of their Indian Empire and yet he could do nothing to pay them back.

But, now he saw his chance had come again and under better auspices than ever. Once more he determined to bid for the Imperial Crown of India and crush the ambitious designs of the Marathas to establish a Hindu *pad-padashahi* in India which well nigh been actualised. So Adbali eagerly promised to lead the coalition and with a mighty army crossed the Indus and rapidly reached Lahore and occupied it.

As the news of Abdalili's invasion reached Dehli, Nazib threw off the mask and openly gave himself out as his sworn adherent. Now Dattaji saw the fatal mistake he had committed in not acting on the Peshwa's advice. He saw also how thoroughly he had been duped by Nazib and Suja and how dangerously he was hemmed in by powerful armies of the foe. On one side was Suja, on another Nazib and the Rohillas and Pathans and Abdalii from behind was rapidly advancing with a mighty force. The small Maratha garrisons at Attock and Lahore had necessarily to fall back before the overwhelming forces of Abdali. The only Hindu section that, besides the Marathas, kept opposing the Mohummedan power in the North was the new rising Sikhs. These brave people did all they could to hamper and hit the alien foes. But, they were as yet but getting forged into an organised power and had not been able to liberate even their own province. That day was yet to come. So, Abdalii led his mighty forces rapidly on Sarhind without facing any serious opposition. The majority of the Hindu princes of Rajputana and elsewhere in the North actually sympathised with Abdali, the destroyer of Mathura and the sworn enemy of Hindudom. The only obstacle that stood between Abdalii and the Imperial Crown at Delhi was that one division of the Marathas which Dattaji led. He had written to Holkar to march forthwith to his help. But, that General, the adopted father of Nazib, thought it fit to busy himself in wrangling with petty chiefs here and there. Thus, hemmed in by the overwhelming forces of the foe all round, there was only one way for the Maratha division to save themselves, and that was to leave Delhi and fall back. Every experienced and even brave man pressed Dattaji to withdraw and wait till Holkar joined him. Even Jankoji, the gallant youth, requested his uncle to fall back. But, Dattaji would not listen. The consciousness of having been the cause of involving his section into an overwhelming catastrophe through his credulity weighed heavily on his mind. He was determined not to add cowardice to the credulity that had spared and trusted Nazib, the arch enemy of the Marathas. He returned only one reply to all pressure to withdraw: "Let them withdraw who like, I press none. But I myself must stick to my post; how can I show my face to Nana and Bhau in this life? I will face Abdalii and, god willing, vanquish him in the field, or die fighting in the attempt." (*Bhausahebanchi Bakhar*)

In the meanwhile, Gaziuddin had discovered that the Emperor was a party to the Pathani plot against his life and position. So, he took the Emperor out, put him to death, seated another person on the throne and joined the Maratha forces.

True to his words, Dattaji faced Abdalii at Kurukshetra. His personal valour so enthused the Maratha soldiers that they actually forced Abdalii to fall back and convinced him that he could not hold out long single-handed against the Shindia. So, he attempted to cross and succeeded in crossing the Jumna and joined Nazib Khan's forces at Shukratal. Suja too met him there and Ahmed Khan Bangash and Kutub Shah as well. The Moslem coalition grew more formidable than ever. It was now clear that the single division under Dattaji could not stem the tide. Again his advisers requested Dattaji to fall back: 'Let him go who likes: Dattaji must do the duty of a soldier.' Such words, from the lips of such a General, could not but have their effect. None left him. On 10th January 1760, the Marathas marched out to hold the *ghats* of the Jumna and repel the forces of Abdalii that attempted to cross the river. The fight began. Bayaji, Maloji, leader after leader of the Marathas, fought valiantly and fell facing heavy odds. The opponents mixed and gripped each other. Accidentally, the banner of Maharashtra got surrounded by the crowding Pathan and Rohilla forces. The Marathas rushed to rescue it. The fight thickened, Dattaji and Jankoji, unable to bear the sight of their national banner in danger, both rushed in and engaged in an epic fight. Just then a bullet struck Jankoji and the gallant youth fell wounded from his horse. Dattaji saw it and, instead of fighting back to a safer position, rushed headlong ahead, striking the foes as one possessed and followed by his faithful follower, soon got inextricably mixed with the enemy forces. At last, the inevitable came. Dattaji was hit by a bullet and fell mortally wounded on the ground.

Kutub Shah, the religious preceptor of Nazib Khan and one of the zealots who led the Pathani plot, saw it. He advanced towards the fallen Maratha General and inquired, with ironical bitterness: 'Well Patel; will you fight again and against us?' 'Yes,' replied the dying and undaunted Dattaji. 'If I survive, I will fight again.' These words exasperated the zealot still more and angrily he kicked the fallen hero, drew his sword, cut off and carried Dattaji's head in triumph as that of a *kafir*.

Thus, Dattaji fell. No soldier in the world defended his national colours more faithfully, or died in defending them more valiantly than he.

The news of the fall of Dattaji and the mean dastardly insults heaped upon that dying hero reached Maharashtra and set it aflame. The whole people rose like one man and demanded vengeance.

They had only that week won a splendid battle at Udgir and meant to crush Haider and finish the task of liberating all South. Just then the news of Dattaji's defeat and death reached them. Balaji and Bhau lost not a moment in preparing themselves to meet the momentous issue. In spite of their having that very week fought out a great campaign in the South, they denied themselves and their forces the rest of a single day, ordered their Generals and councillors to assemble at Patdur, discussed the serious question in all its bearing and decided to dispatch a powerful army to face Abdalii and fight him out before he could reach Malva.

The flower of the Maratha nation joined the forces, Samsher Bahadur, Vithal Shivdeo, Manaji Dhaigude, Antaji Mankeshwar, Mane, Nimbalkar and several other veterans and Generals assumed their respective commands. Bhau the victor of Udgir was appointed generallisssimo and the youthful prince, Vishwasrao, the eldest son of Balaji, who had only recently distinguished himself at Udgir and was the rising hope of his nation, accompanied Bhau. Ibrahim Khan Gardi commanded the most efficient artillery of the time. Damaji Gaikwad, Santoji Wagh and other Maratha Generals continued joining, as the army advanced. Letters and messengers were dispatched to the several Rajput courts in the North to win them over to the Hindu cause and persuade them to join hands with the Marathas, at least in their attempt to fight the foe of Hindudom, the destroyer of Mathura and Gokul. Crossing Vindhyadri and the Narmada, the Maratha army reached the Chambal. All North stood awed at the sight of the strength and the splendour it presented. All disaffected elements, Rajas and Raos, Nawabs and Khans, got cowed down and dared not raise a finger against them. Soon Jankoji Shinde, too, came with his division and joined Bhau. The whole Maratha camp received that young prince, as handsome as brave, with enthusiasm and love, and in him honoured the memories of Dattaji, his uncle, who fell in the battle of Badan. Bhau called a general assembly in honour of the valiant prince who, though within his teens, had fought battles, won victories and borne several dangerous wounds in the defence of his people and his faith and publicly showered on him valuable presents and robes of honour. When Vishwasrao, the gallant and noble youth who in the absence of Balaji, was the beloved leader of the Maratha nation, advanced to meet the valiant young Jankoji, every Maratha heart in that vast national concourse was moved. The two splendid youths—both so handsome, so brave and so devoted to the aspirations and ideals of their people—were the rising hope.

Malharrao Holkar, too, came in. He had already paid a heavy price for his suicidal folly in adopting Nazib Khan and in being deliberately negligent in advancing to Dattaji's help before it was too late, had been badly beaten by Abdalii after the fall of Dattaji. Now Bhau meant to cross the Jumna and beat Abdalii before he could advance to face him on this side of the river. He had ordered Govindpant Bundela to attack, whenever possible to do so, the rear of Abdalii's forces and cut off his supplies. But the rivers were in flood and it was difficult to cross them in the face of the powerful enemy moving along the other bank. So Bhau decided to march on to Delhi and recover it from the hands of Abdalii's forces there. Of all Hindu princes in the North, the Jat alone came over to the Marathas. Bhau personally advanced to receive him with great honour and both of them swore by the scared waters of the Jumna to fight out Abdalii, and to fight to a finish.

The eyes of all people now turned towards Delhi. The Hindus and the Moslems both realised the great moral effect that the occupation of Delhi—the historical capital—meant. Bhau sent forth the forces of Shindia, Holkar and Balwantrao Mehendale to attack Delhi. The Pathans who held it fought well. But unable to hold it against the Marathas, they ultimately surrendered the city. The fort too held out bravely, but well directed guns of the powerful Maratha artillery soon rendered it untenable and the Mohammedan forces there gave in. The news of the fall of the capital and the fort caused great rejoicings in the hearts of all lovers of the Hindu cause. The Maratha forces made a triumphant entry into the capital and Bhau planted the Maratha colours on the fort of the capital of the Pandavas. It was for the first time that the Hindu forces, or as they proudly styled themselves, 'The forces of the *Haribhaktas*, the worshippers of Hari', effected a triumphant entry into Delhi under an independent Hindu banner ever since the days of Prathviraj. The Moslem crescent set; the banner of Hindu *pad-padashahi* rose at last over the capital of the Indian Empire in spite of all that the Pathans and the Rohillas, the Moguls, the Sheiks or the Sayeds, could do against it. Abdalii, with all the powerful allied forces of the Moslems, was but on the other bank of the Jumna and yet could do nothing to prevent it.

Sadashivrao Bhau felt that his dream of the Hindu *pad- padashahi* was—be it for a day—but realised before his eyes. To bring about and render the birth of even one such day possible justifies the existence of a nation. Such a day, even in its short span of life, focusses in its rising splendour the activities and achievements, the rejoicings and sufferings, the trials and tribulations, of centuries of national existence. For, that day proved, beyond cavil or criticism, that seven centuries of Moslem persecution and power had failed to crush the Hindu spirit or its vital faculty of rejuvenation. They had not only proved themselves equal to, but had ultimately prevailed over their foes.

Bhau, left to himself, would have got Vishwasrao crowned as the Emperor of all India, and thus ceremoniously ushered in Hindu *pad-*

padashahi. But he rightly doubted the political wisdom of such an immediate step. For, he knew that not only the Mohammedans who still hesitated to take sides through the fear of the Marathas—but alas!—also even the Hindu princes in the North would be totally alienated by such a step as that. Still he determined to test the temper of the people and also not to let pass such a unique occasion without impressing its momentous meaning on the minds of the people of all Hindusthan, friends and foes alike. So, he ordered an Imperial Assembly to be held in honour of the great event and the gallant and valiant Vishwasrao presided over it. All Maharashtra was represented there; nay, the flower of Hindu valour and wealth and statesmanship and learning shone brightly there. Royal rejoicings commenced. Cavalry and artillery, thousands of horses and elephants, tens of thousands of soldiers and warriors that had carried the Hindu colours from the Godavari to the Indus in the North and to the seas in the South, burst forth in victorious salutes through thousands of trumpets and horns and guns and big martial drums. Then Generals after Generals and statesmen and sardars and governors and viceroys, humbly advanced, paid hearty homage to their beloved prince, as they would do to their Emperor, who presided over their nation and tendered him the honours of a victor. All who witnessed that splendid scene knew what it meant. All who took part in it realised that it was but a rehearsal of a great coronation wherein this youthful Hindu prince would—god willing—be crowned as the greatest Hindu Emperor of all Hindusthan.

□

Panipat

'From the field of his fame fresh and glory:
We carved not a line, we raised not a stone,
But we left him alone with his glory.'

—C. Wolfe

The Mohammedans could not fail to realise the momentous meaning of these proceedings at Delhi. The news spread like wild fire that the Marathas had crowned their prince as the Emperor of Hindusthan. Nazib Khan and other Mohammedan leaders pointed at those events as justifying their fears and attempts to rouse the Mohammedans to the gravity of the situation. They loudly declared that the much-dreaded Hindu *pad-padashahi* nay, as Nazib and Mohammedan zealots would deliberately have it—the Brahman *padashahi* had become an accomplished fact. Let every Mohammedan who was true to his Prophet strike against the forces of the *kafirs*!

But in spite of all these emotional ebullitions, self-interest began to weigh more than all Nazib's and Maulvis' exhortations in the name of Mohanmmedanism, with Suja and other Moslems. The eyes of even such bigots as the Rohillas began to open. Impressed by the successes the Marathas had won in the very teeth of Abdalii's opposition, the supineness with which he could not but keep tolerating them, made them doubt Abdalii's power to check the Marathas. Suja actually wrote to Bhau, expressing regret for having joined Abdalii. Bhau, too, thought it prudent to have him on and declared, through his envoys, that the Marathas did not mean to upset the Mogul Emperor and they would gladly appoint Suja himself as the Vazir of Shah Alam whom they acknowledged as Emperor, provided Suja left Abdalii. The Rohillas, too, began to hesitate and talk of deserting Abdalii Seeing how matters were seriously going against his fortune, Abdalii decided to open negotiations with the Marathas and sent his envoys to discuss the terms of peace. But Bhau was the last man to cede the Punjab to Abdalii as he proposed. Nor was he likely to be duped by hollow discussions and, thus, let his opportunity pass of striking the iron while hot. So, even while these negotiations were half-heartedly carried on, he determined to advance towards the North and dislodge Abdalii from one of the most important positions he was holding at Kunjpura. It was guarded by a strong force under Samad Khan. Kutub Shah too was there. As soon as they were informed that the Marathas meant to attack it, they made great preparations to defend the place against all comers. Abdalii, too, from the other bank of the Jumna sent imperative orders to Samad Khan and Kutub Shah to hold out at all costs and assured them that he had dispatched more forces to their help.

Bhau, leaving Delhi, felt it necessary to replenish his treasury. He had expected Govindpant Bundela to cut off Abdalii's supplies and harass his rear and keep raiding and unsettling the provinces of Suja and the Rohillas. Govindpant disastrously failed in accomplishing any of his allotted tasks. Failing to receive any substantial monetary help from Bundela, Bhau looked round for some other source of replenishing his treasury which was to him the real sinews of war. His attention was drawn towards the rich silver ceiling of the Imperial seat worth some dozens of lakhs of rupees. He ordered that it be hammered out and sent to the mint. The slavish and the superstitions croaked hoarsely; it is said that even the Jat got displeased, thinking it was a sacrilege to, thus, insult the Imperial seat of the mighty Moguls whom god had willed to enthrone as the Emperors of India. If so, the Jat ought to have remembered that if every accomplished fact, not excepting even a successful usurpation, betokened the will of Providence and was, therefore, sacred and divine, then surely the throne that Shivaji had raised at Raigad and which rested, not on any aggression or fanatical tyranny, but on the sacred right of self-defence and freedom and national will to lead an independent life, was also an accomplished fact and, therefore, divine. But when Aurangzeb came to the Deccan, carrying fire and sword and all the forces of fanaticism and aggression to crush the national life of the Hindus and throttle, thus, the young Hindu state, did he hesitate to hammer to pieces the throne of Shivaji? Then, why should they now care a two-pence for the Imperial seat of the Moguls which, to them and to all Hindus, including the Jat himself, meant but an emblem and a source of Satanic power—was bathed in the blood of thousands of Hindu martyrs, was built on the ruins of their temples and homes and hearths and whose very existence was their national and political death? Aurangzeb raised his iron hand to hammer the Imperial seat of Hindudom to pieces. Time and nemesis and the guardian angel of Hindusthan snatched the hammer from his hand—and behold! Today his own Imperial seat lay smashed under it.

Paying out the arrears to his soldiers, Bhau advanced towards Kunjpura. Shinde and Holkar and Vithal Shivdeo led the front. The Pathans fought as brave men do. The fort and the town were famous for their natural strength. But, when the Marathas brought their excellent guns to bear on it, backed up by the valiant forces of Shindia and other Maratha Generals, the Moslems could not hold out against them long. As soon as some breaches were effected in Moslem defences, Damaji Gaikwad ordered his division to rush them and at a formidable shout of Har! Har! his soldiers jumped along with their horses headlong through them. A bloody battle ensued. Thousands of Pathans were put to the sword. The fort was taken, the camp of the Moslem was looted and hundreds of their soldiers got captured. Their very General, Samad Khan, fell into the hands of the Marathas. He was captured once before by Raghunath Rao in his last campaign, but was ransomed and spared. He persisted in his deathless opposition to the Marathas and now again fell into their hands.

Bhau, when his battle was well nigh won, was standing, issuing some directions to Holkar and Shindia and admiring the valour of the Hindu forces who finished that work in three days which the enemy expected to cost them as many weeks, if not months. Just then two important prisoners of war were brought, mounted on elephants, into his presence. The first was Samad Khan, the General of the Pathans who commanded Kunjpura; and the second? He was Kutub Shah, the religious preceptor of Nazib, one of the most active leaders of the Pathani plot and the man who had kicked the valiant Dattaji while dying and heaped dastardly insults on him as a *kafir*.

The sight of Kutub Shah inflamed the Maratha blood. The vengeful memory of Dattaji hovered over the scene. 'Are you the man who kicked our dying Dattaji as a *kafir*?' 'Yes,' replied Kutub Shah. 'It is considered pious in our religion to kill an idolater and to treat him contemptuously as a *kafir*.' 'Die then as a dog,' retorted Bhau. The soldiers carried the culprit a little aside and beheaded him. Dattaji had been avenged; Samad Khan, too, shared the same fate.

The family of Nazib Khan, too, with his son-in-law and other members, fell captives in the hands of the Marathas. But, they were not dealt with so severely as Kutub Shah was. In fact, had those, who were caught fighting, been dealt with thus? Abdalii at any rate had no moral right to question the humanity of such a step. For he and his allied Moslem princes were guilty of such barbarous atrocities as to cut the noses of all those Marathas who fell in the battles in the Punjab and at Badan and other places and cutting their heads off, heap up that ghastly pile as a trophy of war in front of his royal tent. Those savage methods could have been imitated by the Marathas too, but all along they refrained from doing so, nor did they distinguish themselves in razing the mosques or burning the *Korans* or committing sacrileges at the sacred places, as Abdaliis and Aurangazebs and Nadirs and Mohammedans did on principle.

The fall of Kunjpura was another tremendous blow to Abdalii's prestige. The Marathas had been inflicting a crushing defeat on his forces, some 1,00,000 strong, and were celebrating the festival of Vijayadashmi, or the day of victory, with great eclat and military pomp almost under his eyes. An able General that he was, he knew that, unless he immediately risked much and distinguished himself by some act of great daring, his cause was lost. Promptly, he decided to try the fort at Bagpat and at any cost cross and Jumna and cut the Maratha forces at Kunjpura from their base at Delhi.

He succeeded in doing it and thrusted his powerful army numbering hundred thousand strong like a wedge between the Marathas and their line of communication with Delhi. He had secured by this one more advantage to himself that proved in the long run more profitable to him than all his martial strength. It was that, while the Marathas were cut off from their base, his line of communication with the Rohillas and Suja's territory remained intact. But even this he owed, not so much to his move, as to the failure of Govindpant to cut off his supplies as directed by Bhau.

Abdalii found the Marathas fully prepared to face him. No sooner had he succeeded in crossing the Jumna at Bagpat than Bhau advanced to meet him on the famous field of Kurukshetra and encamped at Panipat. The Marathas felt confident that they would crush Abdalii on his ground, if but Govindpant and Gopal Ganesh would do their task well and cut off supplies and harass his rear. But, that work Govindpant miserably failed to do. Pressing—Bhau had recourse to all, but Govindpant would not exert himself even as much as he could have done. The Jat had already left the Maratha camp and kept watching the game at a safe distance from his capital at Bharatpur. Still, be it noted to his credit that he, at times, sent some supplies to the Marathas. But the Rajputs would not do even that. None of them dared to oppose the Marathas, but many of them wished that they were utterly crushed. How far this suicidal hope of these Hindu princes was fulfilled, the future history will show. So although both parties were trying hard to cut each other's line of communication and starve out the adversary and then come to blows; yet, as days passed, it was discovered that starvation vexed the Marathas far more than it did Abdalii.

At last on the 22nd of November, Jankoji Shindia marched out of his camp and attacked the Moslem forces. The battle raged furiously all along the line. Unable to hold out longer against the splendid valour of the youthful Maratha General and his veterans, the Moslems fell back by the evening and were beaten and hotly pursued to their camp. Darkness alone saved them that day from a general defeat. The Marathas received their warriors back with victorious salutes. To remove the demoralised effect that this defeat had on the minds of his people, Abdalii, a fortnight later, ordered his chosen divisions to march at dusk and attack the centre of the Maratha position, as soon as night came, under the cover of darkness. But as they advanced, they were surprised to find that Balwant Rao Mehendale had forstalled them and was marching with 20,000 picked troops to meet them in the field. Immediately, the Pathans opened their batteries on the Marathas. As these had not come out with their battery, they began to suffer much. Soon it seemed as if the Marathas would waver. But, lightning like their General galloped forth, exhorting his men not to stain the honour of their flag, rallied them round and, flourishing his sword formidably aloft, ordered a general assault. The Marathas fell on their foes at a gallop, silenced their batteries and came to a death-grip—foremost amongst them being Balwant Rao Mehendale, their valiant General. In the bloody struggle that ensued a bullet struck the General and he fell dead on the field. The Moslems, seeing this, pounced upon him to cut his head off and carry it in triumph, but Nimbalkar threw himself between their swords and the General's corpse and receiving ghastly cuts on him, covered his body till the Marathas rescued it from the foe. By this time, thousands of Pathans were cut down and the Moslems found it difficult to hold on any longer. So, they first wavered and, then badly beaten, turned their backs and made for their camp, leaving thousands of their comrades dead on the field in front of the Maratha centre. The Marathas had won a great battle, but they had lost a great General. They lovingly bore his corpse to their camp and the military honours of a victor were accorded to his memory. Bhau bewailed the loss more than anyone and personally attended the funeral. The wife of the hero, no less heroic than her husband, determined, in spite of all persuasions that Bhau himself could employ, to mount his funeral pile and immolate herself on it. The whole army came out to pay their last loving respects to their heroic dead. Tens of thousands of souls stood reverently round the pile, saluting the distinguished dead and the constancy of the Maratha girl that sat wrapped in flames, fondling the head of her dead lover securely resting on her lap.

Thus, Abdalii gave two battles and in both of them, he was worsted. But, this did not enable the Marathas to solve the question of starvation. Doubtless Govindpant had, by this time, begun to stir himself and cut off the food supplies of Abdalii; but, then, it was too late now. Moreover, that too did not last long. For, Attai Khan, with 10,000 Pathans, attacked Govindpant under false colours. The Marathas, seeing the colours of Holkar, took the advancing Pathans to be friends till they actually began to cut them down. At last, Govindpant, too, was cut down and lost that life, which, had he risked it four months earlier, when Bhau commanded him to do so, would have in all probabilities saved his nation as well as himself from a great catastrophe. The Pathans cut off Govindpant's head and Abdalii was humane enough to send it to Bhau with a number of bragging lines. Still, from a military point of view, there was every chance of crushing Abdalii yet; for, in spite of all his watch and ward, information, as to the fix the Marathas were in, reached the Deccan and Balaji with another powerful army, some 50,000 strong, was marching to the help of his people. If the Marathas could hold out a month longer at Panipat, Abdali would simply get smashed between the two forces. But what to do with starvation? Hundreds of beasts of burden and even horses daily died for want of fodder. The rotting stink grew into a menace to the health of the army, as dangerous as starvation. The only alternative was a premature fight. The spirited soldiers daily crowded Bhau's tent and movingly prayed that they might rather be allowed to face death in the battlefield than keep rotting and starving out. But was there not yet another alternative to starvation, namely, unconditional surrender of the Hindu cause that generations of their forefathers had lived for, worked and died for? Would they do that and acknowledge Abdali as the Emperor of India and surrender their national independence? No, by no means. No Maratha would vote for that; they would rather brave fearful odds, distressed and starved out though they were, and facing the foe fight in such a way that even if they be not able to gain success for themselves, they would yet render the success of their foe utterly futile to him. Amongst men of this temper stood Bhau like a pyramid of strength and unconquerable courage, dauntlessly determined not to give in, not to do anything derogatory to the national honour of his people. But if the worst came to the worst to win—if not a success—yet at least such a defeat as would be a greater source of constant inspiration and pride and national glory to generations of his people yet unborn than many a success could ever be.

A military council of urgency was summoned and it was decided to move fully prepared for a battle and march forth to Delhi and, if opposed, to attack Abdalii, cut his ranks and fight their way out. The 'if' was unnecessary. Abdalii was not the man to let them pass.

Thousands upon thousands of warriors, the forces of the 'worshippers of Hari', gathered round the great *jaripatka*, the golden *geruwa* standard of their nation. Soon Bhau, their Commander-in-chief, rose to announce the decision their leaders had arrived at, as to their future move. As soon as it was told that they had decided to give a decisive battle to the foe, the vast armed concourse burst out in a tremendous shout of approval. The plan of action was explained. Then the great leader made a stirring appeal to his men, pointing to the great national standard under whose folds they stood and which with mute eloquence traced its far-famed history; how Ramdas handed it over to Shivaji as a constant reminder of a great mission of *swadharma rajya* of Hindu *pad-padashahi*; how their fathers, how their immortal dead, carried it from triumph to triumph and brought all Hindusthan from Attock to Arcot and further to all the seas under its fold; how the foes of Hindudom bowed low or fell worsted as it marched forth. Would they now surrender it or bend it low or die fighting in defence of the cause it represented? A hundred thousand warriors burst into '*Har Har* Mahadeva!' and flourishing their swords, swore allegiance to the national colours and to the great cause they represented and to their Commander, who had led them from victory to victory.

As the morning of 14th January rose, it found the Marathas marching out of their camp in full battle array. Bhau and Vishwasrao led the centre. On their right side stood Jankoji and Malharrao Holkar at the head of their forces. Their left was led by Damaji Gaikwad, Yeshwantrao Powar, Antaji Mankeshwar, Vithal Shivdev, and Samsher Bahadur. They had posted their excellent artillery in front of them all, under the command of Ibrahim Khan Gardi, a brave officer who, though a Mohammedan, remained faithful to his masters even unto death. Thus, formidably arrayed, the Marathas left their camp. Hundreds of war drums, trenchant trumpets and battle horns suddenly sounded the march.

As soon as Abdalii learnt that the Marathas were marching forth, he, too, came out to meet them. His centre was led by Shah Nawaj Khan, his Vazir. On the right were the Rohillas and on his left stood Nazib Khan and Suja. He, too, had posted his batteries in front of his line.

Soon they met. The guns began their gory work, the march of those vast armies raised huge columns of dust and the smoke of the batteries blackened the sky. The sun lay covered till long after it rose. When the opponents clearly discerned each other, Yeshwantrao Powar and Vithal Shivdev gave the first attack. The fight thickened. The Marathas, at a gallop, forced the Rohillas to fall back and cut down not less than 8,000 of their men. Under the heavy blow, the right of the foe reeled and fell back. The central position of the Moslems, Bahu and the gallant young Vishwasrao attacked so vigorously that the armies met in a literal death-grip. The Pathans were not enemies to be despised. On the other hand, the Marathas, too, led by a man like Bhau and their young prince Vishwasra were not likely to lose their ground. After a bloody struggle lasting for an hour, Bhau and Vishwasrao broke the iron front of the Pathans led by their Vazir himself. Thousands of them lay slain on the battlefield. The son of the Vazir was cut down and himself unhorsed. The centre of the Moslems fell back. Bhau and Vishwas marched forth, dislodging their foes from position to position. Seeing this, Nazib Khan hastened to the rescue of the Vazir. But following him hotly came the youthful Jankoji, too, at the head of his veteran soldiers to strengthen Bhau's position.

The battle grew fierce as never before. All along the line set, epic duels began. Abdalii saw clearly that his right and left and centre—his whole army—had fallen back and were on the point of getting broken. Soon his men took to flight. But even then he stood undaunted. He ordered his own troops to cut down those who left his ranks and took to flight. The battle had begun at about 8 o'clock in the morning. Since then, the formidable struggle was relentlessly going on. It was now nearly 2 o'clock in the afternoon. But the soldiers knew no rest or respite. Rivers of blood literally swamped the field. The fearful cries and groans of the wounded and the dying rose and mixed with furious sounds of war drums and trumpets and guns and the war-cries of the brave in a bloody harmony.

It was past two in the afternoon. The Maratha valour and dogged resistance told at last seriously on their Moslem foes. Even Abdalii, a veteran General that he was, grew anxious and thought of leaving the field and crossing over to the other side of the Jumna. But, he had most wisely left a reserved force of some 10,000 soldiers at hand. Detecting that this, if ever, was the psychological moment to throw them in the balance, he ordered them to face Bhau himself. This fresh force fell with lightning speed on the Marathas.

Still Bhau and his men, exhausted since the morn, wavered not. Still the Marathas bore the fresh rush and their first impact with undaunted valour. Once more it was clear that the Marathas had well nigh won the battle. Abdalii had played out his last trump.

But, just then a bullet, like death's errand, came whizzing by. It struck the heroic prince of the Marathas, and Vishwasrao fell, wounded in the *howdah*. The gallant youth, so handsome and so brave, the hope of a nation, lay mortally wounded in his *howdah*. The news came to Bhau who was fighting at the head of his soldiers, enthusing, guiding, smiting and sustaining the most heroic struggle the world had ever seen. The news came on him like a bolt from the blue. The Commander hastened towards his beloved nephew and saw him fall mortally wounded, rolling in his blood in his princely *howdah*. The admantine heart of the victor of Udgir broke down for a while, and tears rolled down his cheeks. His voice choked with emotion. 'Vishwas! Vishwas!' he called out sobbing. The dying youth opened his princely eyes and in heroic accent replied: 'Dear uncle, why tarry with me now? The battle may go against us while its Commander is away.' Even death's agony could not make that gallant young prince of Maharashtra forget his duty. His foremost thought was still of the battle, and his anxiety to win it, even if after his death. His words roused the warrior once more and Bhau came to himself. 'What matters now?' He exclaimed; 'I will crush the foe myself.' Saying so, he galloped forth, rallying once more his mighty host. The truest and the bravest were still contesting the field and its fortune was still with the Marathas.

But the news of the death of Vishwasrao spread like wildfire amongst the Maratha forces and told disastrously upon their already over-taxed nerves. Just then another mishap happened. A couple of thousands of Pathans had, a month or two ago, deserted Abdalii and were employed by Bhau in his army. In order to distinguish them in the battle from the enemy, they were made to wear the strip of the Maratha *geruwa* colours on their head. They, mostly out of preconcerted intrigue, suddenly threw away their Maratha colours and spreading a false alarm and the rumour of Vishwasrao's death, rushed to the rear where the camp followers stood and straightaway began to loot and kill. The sight of these Pathans at the rear unsettled the minds of the Marathas and those who fought at the front took it to be a success of a flank attack of the enemy and thinking that the day was lost, broke and fled.

The foe could hardly believe the sight. He had already thought himself well nigh vanquished. The Marathas had won on the right and the left and in the centre as well. While he was busy, taking strictest steps and cutting down his own flying soldiers and, thus, alone sustaining his lines from breaking into a general rout, to his sudden delight, he saw the Maratha rear somehow or other panic—struck and taking to flight. Before they knew why, the forces of Abdalii attacked the panic-stricken line of the Marathas. This was the last straw that broke the back of the Maratha resistance. On their right, the battle ceased and became a rout.

But still the battle raged furious where Bhau and his chosen few stood at bay, defending their national standard unto death. 'Fight! Kill! Slay!' Smiting and shouting out to his men, Bhau grew hoarse. When he could no longer speak out his fury he nodded encouragement and exhortation as he galloped forth into the very jaws of death. Mukund Shinde, seeing him desperate ventured to hold his horse awhile by the rein and humbly pressed: 'Commander, thine had been a superhuman valour. Our men have done all that heroes humanly could do. But now it is wise to retire!' 'What? Retire?' exclaimed Bhau. 'General, seest thou not that Vishwas is dead and the flower of our army fallen on the field? General, after General I called out by name and at my bidding, fell fighting against the foes. How can I now leave the field and survive to show my face to Nanasaheb and my nation? Smite, smite; smite the foes unto death; this is my last command!'

Mukund Shinde saluted his Commander and, in obedience to his last order, jumped down from his horse, raised his sword with a '*Har Har Mahadeva*,' flung himself headlong in the midst of the foes, The youthful Jankoji, Yeshvant Rao Powar, hero of the heroes, did the same; and Bhau? He, too, as if possessed by the spirit of war, rushed headlong, got inextricably lost in the thickest of the battle, true to his words, smiting in defence of the national cause, 'even unto death'.

This was the last news that ever reached the world about the valiant Commander-in-chief of the Hindu forces at Panipat—that he redeemed, by the spiritual grandeur of his valour and dutiful death, the material loss that his nation suffered at Panipat.

□

The Defeat that Vanquished the Victor As Well

'दंतच्छेदोहि नगावाम श्लाध्यो गिरिविदारणे'

The loss was formidable, for, while Bhau along with the bravest that followed him was sustaining an unequal struggle round their national standard, the Marathas were getting completely routed all along the line, hotly pursued by the foes. Thousands fell dead. Thousands were made prisoners whom the next morning their furious victor made to stand in row after row and butchered in cold blood. The booty the Afghans got was also immense.

But, immense also was the price that the Maratha valour had succeeded in exacting from their foes. The Pathans won the victory, but it was pyrrhic. On the last day alone they lost no less than 40,000 Moslem soldiers on the battlefield. Attai Khan, the General who cut off Govindpant's head, Usman and several other leaders of their forces were cut down. Nazib was seriously wounded. Moreover, they knew that they owed their success as much to chance as to their estimable valour and excellent generalship.

The Marathas lost the battle but not without inflicting on their foe such severe wounds as to invalidate him permanently to win the war.

For, what if the battle of Panipat was lost? The Marathas at Panipat were crushed; but then, the Marathas yet lived in Maharashtra. Each home, they say, had to mourn the loss of some-one of their relations, that fell on the ghastly day of Panipat. Yet there was scarcely a home then in Maharashtra that did not vow to redeem their national honour and render the martyrdom of their soldiers and Generals fruitful by winning the cause for which they fell. Already the Peshwa had crossed the Narbada as the head of some 50,000 Maratha forces to check Abdalii's programme. On learning of the catastrophe that befell his people and his family in particular, Nanasaheb decided to press ahead in spite of Panipat and destroy Abdalii's strength before he could utilise the defeat and resulting demoralisation of the Maratha armies in the North. Although his personal sorrow was truly unbearable and his health already seriously broken, yet it only added to his zeal to avenge his people and beat Abdalii back. He wrote letters to all the Hindu princes in the North full of courage, remonstrating with them on the suicidal policy they thought it wise to adopt of standing aside while the foes of their faith and of all Hindudom were putting forth united efforts to crush the cause of Hindu independence altogether. He invited them all to join him in the war of Hindu liberation and assured them that, in spite of the defeat at Panipat, he would render futile the ambition of Abdalii to re-establish a powerful Moslem Empire on the ruins of that of the Moguls. 'What matters it?' he wrote: 'True it is that my young prince Vishwasrao fell fighting his foe even as Abhimanyu did and ascended to Heaven. My brother Bhau and the gallant Jankoji—none knows what has become of them; several other Generals and men have fallen on the field. But then, after all it is war. The question of success or defeat often depends on chance—the will of god. So, it matters not much. We will see to it again in spite of it all.'

Such undying tenacity—this faculty of staying out, that the Marathas displayed under great national disasters made them masters of India. Abdalii was too shrewd to misunderstand the temper of his foes or undervalue their capacity. No sooner was the day of Panipat won than he saw that, unless he rapidly withdrew to his country, he would soon be forced to disgorge what little he had gained. Nanasaheb had rallied round himself all his Sardars and men that survived Panipat. Malharrao Holkar, Vithal Shivdev, Naro Shankar, Janoji Bhosale and several other Generals with their forces were concentrating in Gwalior and along with them, Nanasaheb threatened to march on Delhi. This attitude of the Marathas made Suja and even Nazib Khan, nervous, who got convinced that the winning of the battle of Panipat was not to win the war against the Marathas. So, they independently opened negotiations with and made flattering advances to Nanasaheb who had already come so far as Gwalior. Suja realised the fact that Abdalii could not singly, or allied with them, crush the Hindus, or prop up the tottering edifice of the Moslem Empire. The Mohammedan camp broke up. Each began to seek his safety. Suja left Abdalii. Abdalii came to Delhi and remained there for a few weeks. Nanasaheb, with 50,000 men, was pressing him from behind. The Persians were reported to have invaded his home. This distracted the great conqueror who determined to leave Delhi and the Imperial politics to themselves and in March 1761, hurriedly re-crossed the Indus without being able to realise even one of those ambitious designs which goaded him on to cross it.

This was the last of the series of attempts the Indian Mohammedans made to save their Empire from the attacks of the Hindus by joining hands with their fierce co-religionists across the frontiers. They won the battle of Panipat and in winning it, they lost the last chance of either crushing the great Hindu power of the Maratha Confederacy or rescuing their Moslem Empire from the death grip with which they clutched at its throat.

Never again were the Pathans able to reach Delhi. Soon they were to cease to cross the Indus itself.

For, on the ruins of Panipat, another Hindu power rapidly rose in the Punjab. That power was the rising confederacy of the Sikhs. These brave people had slowly built up their Church which often cemented by the blood of martyrs, promised soon to rise into a powerful state. Under the leadership of their tenth Guru, the lion-like Govind and Banda, the warrior and the martyr—both of whom will ever continue to be worshipped amongst the greatest of national heroes of the Hindu pantheon—the Sikhs fought for the cause of Hindu independence in the Punjab. Under Banda, they succeeded for a while in liberating a part of their land. But the task of dealing a death-blow to the Mohammedan power in the Punjab and bringing the holy land of the five rivers under Hindu sway was reserved for the Marathas. This they accomplished and though they were fighting far off from their homes and had to beard the lion in his own den, they did it and carried the Hindu standard right upto Attock for the first time, since the days of Prithviraj. While the repeated attempts of the Moslems and of their great coalitions under Nadir Shah and Abdalii to revive the Moslem power in India were being brought to naught by the dogged resistance of the Marathas, the Sikhs were getting breathing time to organise themselves into a powerful confederacy. This new Hindu power deprived Abdalii of whatever little satisfaction he might have reaped, in return for the tremendous price he had to pay throughout his

Panipat campaign by annexing the Punjab anew to his dominions. For, although the Punjab, thus, slipped off from the hands of the Hindus of Maharashtra, it could not continue in the hands of the Moslems. For, the Hindus of the Punjab attacked Abdalii's posts as soon as he turned his back and in spite of his twice crossing the Indus again, recovered their native land. Soon the Marathas too re-entered Delhi—once more became the leading sovereign power of all Hindusthan. The Sikhs, too, though they never could extend their sway beyond their frontiers even upto Delhi on the eastern side, yet grew powerful enough to maintain their independence against all comers from across the frontiers. Never again would the fierce fanaticism or the insatiable lust of land of the Pathans or the Turks goad them on to cross the Indus. On the contrary, the Sikhs crossed it and carrying the Hindu standard triumphantly up to the banks of the Kabul, paid back the compliment. So thoroughly had they cowed down the fanatical turbulence of the Moslem tribes of the frontier districts that the name of the Sikhs became a synonym of terror in the Pathan homes.

Thus from the pan-Hindu point of view, the Mohammedans failed to gain their objective. They won the battle of Panipat, but in winning it, they lost the war they had been waging against those who aimed to establish Hindu *pad-padashahi* and in spite of Panipat, had to leave the Hindus, masters of all Hindusthan from Attock to the seas.

But, while the Hindus were fighting out this gigantic national struggle against their Mohammedan foes in the North, yet another combatant managed slyly to creep into the list and kept watching the fierce game. It was he who, more than anyone else, had every reason to chuckle at the fall at Panipat, which, dealing out heavy blows to both the combatants there, forced the Marathas to postpone their intended invasion of Bengal and consequent strangling of the infant English power that was only recently born there on the plains of Plassey. If anyone really won at Panipat, it was neither of the combatants who so furiously fought there; it was that sly intruder who kept watching the game and was clever enough to take advantage of the weakness of both the combatants.

But, although it is true that Panipat gave a new lease of life to the East India Company and forced the Marathas to drop a while their intentions of settling their final accounts with the English, yet it must not, thereof, be supposed that the English secured any very lasting advantage thereby alone. For the Marathas—as we shall see as we proceed—soon recovered from the shock of Panipat and, but for the civil war that broke out amongst them and the untimely death of their able leaders, would have perhaps been able to win even against the English in spite of Panipat. The English owed their success not so much to the defeat of the Marathas at Panipat as to the civil war that later on broke out amongst them.

For, as Major Evans Ball writes: 'Even the battle of Panipat was a triumph and a glory for the Marathas. They fought in the cause of India for the Indians and though they were defeated, the victorious Afghans retired (had to) and never again interfered in the affairs of India.'

As the news of Abdalii's precipitate return and Suja's and Nazib's supplicating overtures reached the Maratha camp, they naturally rejoiced at the favourable turn events had taken. Naro Shanker wrote just within a couple of months after Panipat: 'God be praised, the Marathas—or to quote Hingne—'the forces of the worshippers of Hari' still continue to be the masters of Ind.' The heroic phrase that their great leader had uttered leapt from lip to lip and everyone in Maharashtra was found exclaiming, 'What does it matter? After all it is a war. We will see to it again.'

In the meanwhile the health of Nanasaheb was going from bad to worse. For the last two years or so, he was showing signs of a general breakdown. Just then came the harrowing news of Panipat. He strove as bravely as a man could under the stress to bear it all and suppressing his personal sorrow, enthused and enabled his nation to tide over the demoralisation of a defeat and rise equal to the occasion to present a bold and conquering front to all. But in his heart, the loss of his Vishwas and his Bhau and the bravest of his Generals and men overwhelmed him with the grief that nothing could solace. His already declining health rapidly broke and soon this great leader of Maharashtra who had made her mistress of all Ind passed away on the 23rd of June, 1761. He was only 41 when he died.

It is needless to say anything here as to his capacity and character. His deeds have already spoken louder than words can ever do. His civil administration too was so just and popular that his reign is still gratefully remembered by his people. It was reserved for him to practically realise Shivaji's ambition of establishing Hindu *pad-padashahi*. He, in fact, freed almost all Hindusthan from the hands of Moslems. Under him, the Hindus reached the highest pinnacle of glory they ever attained for the last seven hundred years or so—ever since the fall of Prithviraj. He was undoubtedly one of the greatest personalities—if not the greatest—of his time in the world.

This untimely death of Balaji, alias Nanasaheb, was a loss as great as—if not greater than—the loss the Marathas had to face at Panipat. The two crowded so disastrously together that the nation very naturally took some time to recover from the shock.

□

Madhao Rao, The Virtuous

'भुवमधिपतिर्बालावस्थोप्यल परिरक्षितुम्
न खलु वयसा जात्येवायं स्वकार्यसहोभरः

The enemies of Maharashtra, seeing it left practically leaderless by the death of Nanasaheb and expecting the Maratha Confederacy to collapse under the heavy blow it had to face at Panipat, rose and beset her on all sides. Haider found the opportunity to usurp the Government of Mysore from the hands of his Hindu master and sovereign and to invade the Maratha territories from the South. The Nizam at Hyderabad had made feverish preparations to avenge his defeat at Udgir. The English strove to snatch as much as they could. Not only the Mohammedans in the North, but even the Rajputs and the Jats and several other principalities revolted against the Marathas, each trying to feather their own nest as best as they could. To make the matter yet worse, the treacherous ambition of Raghunath Rao threatened to usher in a civil war and divide the Maratha camp into hostile factions, precisely when their nation was likely to be overwhelmed by their foes and the cause of Hindu independence it represented, fall with its fortunes.

The enormous responsibility of leading the realm under such exceptional difficulties fell on Madhao Rao, the second son of Balaji, who was then but a youth of 17. But, fortunately, for his nation, he was endowed with such extraordinary abilities and personal magnetism and was so devoted to the great mission of Hindu *pad-padashahi* for which his fathers had bled, that under his guidance, his nation tided well over the difficulties and held the position as the leading political power of India against all those who challenged it.

First, the Nizam tried his luck. Fancying the Marathas were dead as a power, he aimed to advance straight towards Poona. To flout their claim as the defenders of the Hindu faith, he even insulted and destroyed the Hindu temples at Tonk. But, he was bitterly disappointed when he found that the Marathas rushed from all quarters to defend their capital and faced him, 80,000 strong. He suffered a defeat at Urali and had to fall back. But as Raghunath Rao was mean-minded enough to begin his intrigues and divided the Maratha people against his own nephew, the young Madhao Rao, the Nizam once more came out with a powerful army to crush the Marathas while they were yet divided. Bhonsle and some other Sardars had actually gone over to his side. But, as often happened in the Maratha history, the denationalised and selfish tendencies, which broke from time to time the political solidarity of their people, were sooner or later counter-balanced and even corrected by the instinctive national impulse that, in spite of all egoistic aberrations, remained long the chief determining factor in their character. The Maratha Sardars who, owing to the bitterness engendered by the civil war, had joined the Nizam against the Peshwa, deserted their unnatural ally and at a very critical moment came over to the Maratha camp. The Nizam was left in the lurch. A great battle was fought at Rakshas Bhuvan in 1763, in which once again the united power of the Marathas won a splendid victory over the Moslems. The Diwan of the Nizam lay slain. Not less than 22 of his Sardars were wounded and captured, his guns and all military stores falling in the hands of the Marathas. Humiliated and humbled, the Nizam, who came out to recover all he had lost at Udgir and had the audacity to claim the right of nominating the Karbhari at Poona, had to hand over to the Marathas, a territory yielding 82 lakhs of rupees for being allowed to go back. This was the first battle in which the young Peshwa fought and distinguished himself so splendidly that his people instinctively recognised in him a leader fit to guide their nation and lead it against all odds.

Having thus convinced the Nizam that the Hindu strength remained unchallengeably superior in spite of Panipat, Madhao Rao proceeded to teach the same lesson to that adventurous soldier who, taking advantage of the Panipat campaign, had founded a new Moslem state at Mysore on the ruins of the old Hindu principality and invaded the Maratha territories up to the Krishna river. In 1764, Madhao Rao marched against Haider. Dharwar was re-occupied by the Marathas and Ghorpade, Vinchurkar, Patwardhan and other Generals pressed Haider and hemmed him in all sides. A clever general and a tough soldier though he was, Haider soon found it impossible to hold out long against his foes after a tenacious fight at Rattihalli. At last he tried to effect a clever retreat, but was forestalled by Madhao Rao on his way to Bednur. A battle was forced upon him with disastrous results to the Moslem forces. Madhao Rao personally led the charge with such a vigour that Haider's army was thoroughly routed. Even the most efficient troops trained by the French that Haider possessed got badly beaten and thousands of horses and camels and field artillery fell in the hands of the victorious Marathas. All further opposition was useless. Haider sued for peace, left the Marathas masters of all they had conquered and paid 22 lakhs of rupees as the arrears of his tribute and the *chowth*.

Madhao Rao, left to himself, would not have allowed Haider to escape even on these terms. But the vile greed of Raghunath Rao proved a greater curse to the Maratha arms than a Haider or a Nazib Khan. He, more than once, rose in open revolt against the young Peshwa, just when he was carrying on victorious campaigns against the foes of the Hindu power. Nothing could quench Raghunath's thirst for power and the power he was most incapable of all men to wield. Left free, he returned to his treacherous designs of allying himself with the non-Hindu states against his own nephew. Whenever defeated and captured and imprisoned he, like so many other sickly sentimentalists, refused to take food and threatened to die of self-imposed starvation. The fate of such a troublesome claimant to a Mogul throne would have been speedily and easily determined by a small drop of poison or a sharp little dagger covered by smiles or even the tears of the ruling chief. But the young Brahmin prince was nobility and piety personified. He even went so far as to write to his uncle on a proposal of partitioning the kingdom being advanced by him in terms of utter surrender. 'Uncle,' wrote Madhao Rao, 'you talk of partitioning this realm. But think who is the master of this mighty kingdom. Is it a private and personal property? Thousands have worked for it to render it so great, so glorious. The power of state must ever remain concentrated in one guiding hand. But how can this kingdom continue to maintain its greatness and strength when it gets divided and parcelled out as personal effects are? No, no; far better for me to efface myself altogether and leave you the sole and uncontested leader of this commonwealth than consent to its division and be a party to its weakness. I will rather resign all my claim to leadership and enlist myself as a common soldier in your ranks, picking up whatever morsels you throw out to me, than hand down my name to further generations as that of one who scarificed the Empire of Maharashtra to his personal greed.' (*Madhavrao Charittar-Sehstrabudhey*)

But, the Marathas as a nation could never have tolerated a man so fickle-minded and so incapable as Raghoba, even if he had assumed the leadership of Maharashtra, while the brave, the just and the most virtuous of the Peshwa yet lived.

□

Panipat Avenged

> 'To their benefactors the Marathas are grateful, to their enemies relentless. If they are insulted, they will risk their lives to avenge themselves.'
>
> **—Hiuen Tsang**

Neither these domestic distractions, nor the treacherous civil wars, nor the rise of such new and dangerous enemies as Haider and Tippu could make the Marathas forget their duty to avenge the day of Panipat and inflict condign punishment on all those who dared to go against them there. For some time, after the death of Nanasaheb, Holkar and Shinde were the two chief Maratha Sardars who kept guarding their national interests in the North as best as they could. When the civil troubles and intrigues of Raghoba could be fairly managed, Madhao Rao in 1769 determined to dispatch a punitive expedition to the North under the command of Binivale. All Maratha Generals in the North were ordered to join the force. Crossing the Narbada with a set purpose of resuming the direction and control of the Hindu Empire and of inflicting a crushing penalty on all those Indian principalities who had dared to pray for the ruin of the Maratha power since 1761, the powerful Maratha army reached Bundelkhand, quelled the petty disturbances their and punishing the recalcitrant princelets and princes on their way, reached the Chambal without much serious opposition. The Jat showed fight and refused to hand over Agra and other forts he had usurped since the day of Panipat. Near Bharatpur, a pitched battle was fought. The Jats contested the field as bravely as heroes do, but were unable to hold long against the Maratha forces. They broke and fled, leaving thousands of their comrades dead on the field and all their camp with elephants and horses and war material fell in the hands of the Marathas. Soon after their leader, Nababsingh, sued for peace and returning all Maratha possessions he held, paid 65 lakhs of rupees to them, as his accumulated tribute. Now the advancing Maratha army marched forth towards the gates of Delhi, expecting their sworn enemy to put up some fight against them. But, the old fox, that wily Nazib Khan, was again all humility and repentance. The very news of the victorious march of the Marathas brought him to the camp as a supplicant for life. He returned all his spoils in the Doab, smoothened the way of the Marathas to Delhi and would do anything for them, if but pardoned and allowed to live that he might conspire once more against them as soon as a favourable opportunity presented itself. But this time nothing seemed likely to shield him from the vengeance of the Marathas had not Death himself intervened and shielded the author of Panipat from the wrath of the countrymen of those who had fallen there.

The Marathas entered Delhi. There was none to contest the capital of Akbar and Aurangzeb. Ahmedshah Abdalii, who contested it last, had at least come to terms and had already opened negotiations with the Peshwa and sent his envoys to Poona. There, after protracted deliberations, the parties reached an understanding by which Ahmedshah Abdalii virtually promised to cease to dabble in the Imperial politics of India and acknowledged the Marathas as the protectors of the Indian Empire. Thus, the victor of Panipat himself confessed the political futility of his victory and of the ambition that led to the battle and acknowledged the Hindus to be the paramount power of Hindusthan. Having thus eliminated the Afghan element from the Imperial politics of India and taken possession of Delhi, the Marathas completely isolated the Pathans and the Rohillas who were only two really powerful Mohammedan centres in India that still would have, if they could, contested the Imperial power at the hands of the Hindus. But their day of reckoning had come. The memory of the outrages and indignities the Rohillas and Pathans had inflicted on the Marathas at Panipat had set on edge the steel of the Maratha vengeance and roused the forces of retribution that could perhaps be crushed, but never coaxed. This the Pathans knew as well as the Rohillas. They, under their old leaders, Hafiz Rahimat and Ahmed Khan Bangash, both of whom had seen Panipat, joined hands and determined to present a bold front to the Maratha hosts as they came.

Halting for a while at Delhi, the Marathas entered the Doab. They found that the forces of their old enemies were growing menacingly great. Some 70,000 Moslems were in arms. But the Marathas did not wait to count them. Field after field was furiously fought. But field after field, the Pathans and Rohillas got mercilessly hewn down. Wresting fort after fort and town after town from the hands of their foes and sweeping the whole Doab clean of Pathan resistance, the advancing army of Maharashtra invaded Rohilkhand and crushed the Rohillas as mercilessly as they had done the Pathans. Death had shielded Nazib Khan from their vengeance, but his son Zabeta Khan still lived to pay for the sins of his father and his own. He had taken shelter behind the walls of the impregnable fortress of Shukratal. The Marathas marched straight against the fort, opened a furious bombardment against it and inflicted such a terrible loss on the contingent inside that Zabeta Khan could no longer hold it against them. One night he fled away and crossing the Ganges entered Bijnoor. Crossing the Ganges quick, the avenging army of the Marathas, too, forthwith marched towards Bijnoor in the very teeth of the fearful fire that the Moslem batteries, kept by Zabeta Khan to guard the gates, opened on them. They carried the batteries, they routed the two powerful armies that contested their way, they put thousands of Rohillas to the sword and entered Bijnoor. The whole district lay trampled under the hoof of their horses. Zabeta Khan fled to Nazibgad. The Marathas pursued him there and took Futtehgarh. Here to their boundless delight the immense booty that Nazib Khan and his Rohillas had carried away from the Maratha camp at Panipat, fell back in the hands of the victorious Marathas. Their triumph was complete. Even the wife and children of Zabeta Khan were captured by them. The cruel and brutal fate that had met the few Maratha women and hundreds of youth at Panipat at the hands of those very fierce Rohillas would have justified the Marathas in dealing out vengeance in terribly equal measures to the family of Nazib and Zabeta now, but true to the tradition of the Hindu triumph, the Maratha vengeance did neither contemplate their forcible conversion, nor their victimisation to the brutal passions of the camp bazaars. The Hindu arms, even without resorting to these barbarous and brutal acts, had struck such terror in the hearts of the Rohillas and Pathans all over the land that the very sight of a Maratha trooper was enough to make a whole village of Rohilla Moslems take to their heels. Those of their leaders who survived, fled away to the interior of the forests of Terai. There too, it was only the setting in of the rainy season alone that shielded them from the steel of the Maratha vengeance. So terribly had they to pay for Panipat.

Having thus carried their colours to the very borders of the forests of Terai and cowed down all their foes, the return march was sounded and the armies of Maharashtra marched back towards Delhi in 1771. There their diplomats had already reaped the fruits of the victories of their Generals and outwitting and frustrating the designs of the English and Suja to secure the person of Shah Alum, the Mogul claimant to the throne and, thus, assume the position of the paramount power in India, had forced Shah Alum to resign to the Marathas all rights and responsibilities of conducting and defending the Indian Empire in return for nominal recognition of him as the Emperor of India. Even this nominal recognition he would not get till he agreed to pay back all accumulated arrears since the day of Panipat and *chowth* to the Marathas and consented to divide equally any new acquisition of territory. Once what was nearly done in 1761 was fully done in 1771. After the crushing defeat of the Rohillas and Pathans there remained no Moslem throughout India who could contest the sovereignty of the Hindus in Hindusthan. That year really marked the end of Mohammedan independence and power and ambition. The Moguls, Turks, Afghans, Pathans, Rohillas and Persians, northern and southern, all sections and sects of the Moslems, strove to contest and seize the Imperial power of India and rescue their Empire from falling into the hands of the avenging forces of Hindudom. But the Marathas made all their endeavours come to naught, held the Imperial power of India as the protectors of Indian Empire for over 50 years against all who came to contest or challenge it. After 1771, we may dismiss the Moslems as a power in the political field of India. The Hindus had finished them and had recovered thus Hindusthan and the independence of their Hindu race from Attock to the seas. The only claimant against whom they had thenceforth to struggle and strive was not the Moslem but one far different in nature and character and calibre from the Mussalman. It was the Englishman.

It would have been strange if the drafting away of these two great armies from the Maratha camp to the North had not induced the redoubtable Haider to try his luck again and challenge the Maratha supremacy in the South. Madhao Rao immediately crossed the Tungabhadra and, at the head of a powerful army, went on capturing fort after fort and giving battle after battle to the foes. A second army was posted to harass Haider when he entered the woods of Anavadi. One night while it was lying encamped near Mattoo, Haider, with a picked force of some 20 thousand men came out of the woods and, supple as a tiger, fell upon the unsuspecting Maratha forces. But, fortunately, the very first boom of Haider's gun roused Gopalrao, the Commander of the Marathas. He instantly sensed the danger, knew that the whole Maratha army would be cut off before it woke if the slightest hesitation or weakness was shown. He jumped on his horse, unfurled his national colours and, taking his position, ordered the war-drums to sound the alarm. At the terrible sound, soldiers after soldiers started up and rushed from his camp-bed to the battlefield. The terrible fire of the foe thickened. Trooper after trooper was hit down, but the Marathas wavered not. The thunder of Haider's guns and the fury of his bombardment threatened to round the Marathas off but Gopalrao stood immovable, intrepid—his colours flying defiance. The war-drums still sounded the alarm. His aide-de-camp was standing by. A cannon ball burst and smashed off his head to pieces. A column of blood spouted up so forcibly that it fell in shower all round and drenched the Maratha Commander in a gory bath. Still Gopalrao stood his ground on his horse. A bullet struck down his horse—he mounted a second. No sooner had he mounted it than that too was hit by a bursting shell; the General was unhorsed again. But again he mounted a third charger and kept his post in the very jaws of death. Unshaken, intrepid, a slight tremour of a nerve, an inch of the ground lost would have meant a panic and the whole army to fall in the hands of an exultant foe. But the Commander's courage grew contagious and the whole army of the Marathas, men and officers, bore the fire, fronting it as an iron wall. Haider, as he came near, stood awed at the sight of this indomitable fortitude and, dismayed, wheeled back suddenly as he had come out. The campaign continued. Pethe, Patwardhan, Panse and other Maratha Generals gave a ceaseless chase and pursued Haider from field to field and at Moti Talao caught him so completely in their clutches that his whole army was cut to pieces and all his camp with arms and ammunition fell in the hands of the victorious Marathas. Now the Marathas meant to remove Haider altogether from the political field, but, just then, a letter reached their camp from Poona, commanding them to end the campaign and return to the capital as the Peshwa was lying seriously ill. Grudgingly, the Maratha Generals drew up a treaty and got it signed, by which Haider had to cede all the territories that comprised Maratha *'swaraj'* and pay 50 lakhs of rupees as his tribute to the Peshwa besides all expenses of war.

Amidst such glorious events, the news of the illness of their leader, under whose capable guidance the Marathas had avenged the wrongs done to them at Panipat and restored their nation to the height of her past greatness, reached the different Maratha camps and capitals from Delhi to Mysore and affected the whole people as a great national calamity. It was not only his martial qualities and achievements that rendered Madhao Rao so popular amongst his people. His civil administration, too, was just and equitable, his concern for the welfare of his subjects, princes and peasants alike, was as deep and sincere, his efforts to see justice done to the high and low alike were so strenuous and watchful that his subjects even to the meanest came to bear a personal love and devotion to him. The powerful feared his probity and strictness. The peasant and the poor confided in him and knew him to be their beloved protector. In spite of domestic troubles and ruinous civil wars caused by the ambitions of his silly uncle he, within ten years of Panipat, made his nation forget it or rather remember it as a battle that was nobly lost, and yet won and struck down with his mighty hand all those who raised their hands against the cause of Hindu independence and Hindu *pad-padashahi*. While he was yet but in the flower of his youth, he was at the height of his popularity and fortune and his nation was expecting at his hands things even more glorious than the achievements of his great father. Madhao Rao fell a prey to consumption when he was only 27 or so. While he lay seriously ill in his palace, he tried to please and placate his incorrigible uncle who even then was conspiring with the Nizam, managed to pay off all his public debts and ordered his royal physician to administer to him such phials as would leave his power of speech unaffected even unto his last moment, so that it might enable him to die with the Lord's praise on his lips. As the news of the serious illness of the Peshwa spread abroad from all sides of his realm, his devoted people poured into Poona to have a last look of their national hero and beloved father. He, thereupon, ordered that the gates of his palace be closed to none and that the meanest of his subjects be not prevented from seeing him. On the 8th of *Kartika* (1772) the noble prince summoned the learned and the pious to his presence. Bowing low to them all and in front of those who kept thronging round his palace as they would round a temple, the prince asked for their leave: 'We depart! said he, 'bound for the last great pilgrimage, we depart; bid ye all a kind farewell unto me.' Then repeating the name of the Lord, the young prince, like a great yogi, yielded his last breath amidst the sighs and sobs of a whole people with the Lord's name Gajanan, Gajanan lingering on his lips. His young, childless and devoted wife Ramabai gave away her jewels and other valuables to the pious and the poor and discarding the persuasions and the pressure of her royal relations, mounted the funeral pyre of her lover. Immolating herself in the leaping flames, she lighted the torch of her soul to illumine the secrets of the deathless love and the divine beauty that could yet be attained by man. Down to this day, Maharashtra offers her loyal and loving tribute of tears at the mention of these, her prince and her princess—Madhao Rao and Ramabai. Down to this day, the national bards bewail: 'Fled is the light of our life and lost the jewel of our heart.'

□

Civil War and Popular Revolution

'इंग्रजाना खडें चारिले नाहीं लागू दिला धारा
भले बुहिहचे सागर नाना ऐसे नाहिं होणार

That a Madhao Rao, the hope of a whole people, should die young, while Raghoba, the curse of whole people, should survive a generation after him, is one of those events that make men doubt at times if god is really omnipotent as it is said to be.

The death of Madhao Rao was a great national calamity, but the survival of Raghoba was a calamity even greater than that. No sooner was the childless Madhao Rao succeeded, in accordance with his wish and the nation's will, by his younger brother Narayan Rao, than did Raghoba begin anew to hatch up bloody conspiracies against the young boy and those who supported him. He took the hired guard of the palace in his confidence and ordered them to surround and arrest the young Peshwa, which plan his demoniacal wife, Anandibai, replaced by inciting them to assassinate him altogether. On 30th August, 1773, the guards suddenly rose in mutiny and confronted Narayan Rao, clamouring insolently for pay. As soon as one of the faithful attendants of the Peshwa remonstrated with them, they drew their swords and killed him there and then. Alarmed, the young Peshwa hastened away from room to room, hotly pursued by the mutineers, till he reached Raghoba's hall and throwing his arms round his waist piteously prayed that his life be spared. 'Save uncle, save me, thy child: I will recognise three as my Peshwa and will ask no more than a few crumbs of bread for my maintenance.' But the assassins were upon him. Raghoba disentangled himself from his clasp and the murderers fell upon the youth. Chaphaji Tilekar threw himself between the swords of the assassins and his master, and covering the body of Narayan Rao, entreated the guards to spare their master. But murder was on them and the guards dealt strokes after strokes with their bloody swords and slew the young Peshwa along with the faithful Chaphaji who lay covering him unto death. Thereupon the mutineers proclaimed Raghoba as the Peshwa of Maharashtra and took possession of the palace.

The news, as it spread through the capital, inflamed the citizens who, gathering in groups, swore not to recognise the murderous Raghoba as their chief. Enough of national spirit was still left in Maharashtra and a horrible palace intrigue was not likely to cow them down into obedience to a chief that they did not tacitly choose. The leaders and the prominent officers of the state formed themselves into a secret revolutionary committee, and Ramshastri, the Chief Justice of the realm, was called upon to carry an investigation into the crime, who soon got convinced of the complicity of Raghoba and Anandibai—his evil genius—in the dastardly murder. Thereupon the dauntless Brahmin repaired to the palace and, entering the hall where Raghoba sat as Peshwa guarded by his partisans, charged him straight to his face as the murderer of his nephew and of the Peshwa of the people. The question of purificatory rites being raised, he exclaimed, 'What purification can there be for such a dastardly crime as this? The only expiatory rite that is prescribed is death by instant execution!' Being warned by someone, he retorted; 'I fear no Raghoba, I have done my duty as the Chief Justice of my people. If he likes, let him add to his crime by murdering me too. I will neither reside nor take food in a city where such a criminal reigns.' Before the awed partisans of Raghoba could fully realise it all, the indomitable Brahmin, burning with pious rage like a flame of fire was off—out of the palace, out of the city, nor touched food nor drink, till he reached the banks of the sacred Krishna river.

Just then, it was ascertained that Gangabai, the young widow of the prince, was pregnant and an issue to Narayan Rao, the deceased Peshwa, was expected. This news strengthened the hands of the revolutionary committee as nothing else could have done. Morobadada, Krishnarao Kale, Haripant Phadak, Trimbakrao Mama, Raste—the chief of the artillery, Patwardhans, Dhygude, Naro Appaji and several other leading citizens and officers of the realm, led by two most prominent statesemen, Nana Fadanavis and Sakharam Bapu, decided first to take Raghoba out on an expedition and then to break out in open revolt against him. They soon succeeded in forcing Raghoba to undertake an expedition in the South. No sooner did he turn his back on Maharashtra than they rose in Poona, took possession of the capital and proclaimed Gangabai as the head of the administration of the realm and the expectant mother of the future Peshwa. The popular revolution soon spread out from the capital to the country. Fort after fort and town after town acknowledged the authority of the new government, which to all practical purposes became a republic and came to be known as 'the Barbhai's administration' or the republican rule. When the startling news of this national outbreak reached Raghoba, his first thought was to march on Poona with the forces under his command, but finding the revolutionary army already coming upon him, he, along with the few who still clung to him, and his hired forces turned towards the North, looting and devastating the people and the country on his march, as though he was passing through an alien land at war. He still hoped that if Gangabai failed to give birth to a son, then a popular reaction would soon set in his favour. At Koregaon, he even gave a battle and defeating the revolutionary forces slew their chief Trimbakrao Mama Pethe. This was a heavy loss to the revolution; for Pethe was one of their staunchest leaders. Still Nana and Bapu held out and backed up by the bulk of the Maratha nation continued the struggle unabated.

Now the eyes of all Maharashtra, nay, all India, centred on Purandar, where the young Maratha princess Gangabai was kept under the strictest and the most solicitous watch and ward. She was fast approaching the critical time. As day followed day, and no news from Purandar came, the popular anxiety grew tense. Crowded congregations sent forth moving prayers from temples and *tirthas* that their young princess at Purandar be blessed with a son and a male heir, so that the wild ambitions of the hated Raghoba be utterly frustrated. From the public squares to the princely halls, all India stood on the tiptoe of expectation and the royal courts at Delhi, Indore, Gwalior, Baroda, Hyderabad, Mysore, Calcutta and several other centres of Indian politics waited for news from Purandar with breathless curiosity. At last, on 18th April, 1774, the longed-for news arrived. Gangabai, the Maratha princess at Purandar, delivered of a male heir. All Maharasthra hailed the birth and recognised him as their national head and the destined first minister of the their realm. Even foreign courts, carried away by the general public enthusiasm, showered congratulations on the infant prince. The relief felt by the revolutionaries all over Maharashtra and the patriotic hopes and aspirations could best be seen in the con temporary correspondence and records. Sabaji Bhonsle writes from his camp: 'As soon as the news reached us, here it conveyed a world of joy; God has heard our prayers; the camp is all aglee; martial music is playing. The guns are booming forth royal salutes. May the Lord bless our beloved Peshwa with long life:' The news caused equally great rejoicing in the revolutionary forces wherever they were. 'Haripant Tatya, our General, immediately ordered great celebrations throughout the army. Martial music and bands and peals of cannon could hardly give vent to the public joy. Sugar was distributed from the *howdahs* on elephants to celebrate the auspicious ceremony. Doubtless, god is on our side. For the welfare and protection of our people and for the propagation of our faith, the Lord has blest our cause. Long live the infant Peshwa! Long live the darling of our people!'

The child was named Madho Rao, which name people fondly devoted to the princely lad, soon replaced by 'Savai Madhao Rao' or Madhao Rao the Greater. His birth changed the political prospect of all India by strengthening the hands of the revolutionists in Poona who now all the more boldly and vigorously declared Raghoba an outlaw and ordered all Maratha Sardars to chase and arrest him wherever found. It enabled the party of those statesmen and patriots who were brought up in the tradition of Hindu *pad-padashai* under Nansaheb and Bhau and who had the vision and the ability to maintain the exalted position Maharashtra had attained, as the great paramount Hindu power in India, to hold the reins of the realm in their hands and keep their nation true to its mission for a longer time than it would otherwise have been, had that man, who could hardly manage his wife, come to manage the Maratha Empire. But, mere news of the birth of a son unto Narayan Rao and the great enthusiasm and wild national rejoicing with which all Maharashtra hailed the birth and lovingly recognised the princely infant as the chosen Prime Minister of their Empire, could not exercise that man of the devilish ambition that had possessed him. For Raghoba, like a frightened bull, ran his wild career all the more madly, the more hotly pursued he was by his ill-luck and the victorious arms of the revolution. At last, defeated and deserted by his own people, he did not hesitate to seek the shelter of the worst enemies of his nation.

Of all the nations and states that were still cherishing an ambition to wield the Imperial power in India at the time under review, there was none who could have challenged the paramount position of the Hindu Empire of Maharashtra while it stood united in itself. All those who tried to do so were either utterly crushed or thrown into the background to keep chafing there with impotent rage, held rightly in subordination. The Mohammedans, whether Pathans or Persians, Moguls or Turks, whether from beyond the Indus or Indian—the Mohammedans were so completely crushed as a power as never again to raise their head against the Hindu Empire. They had ceased to be a factor in the political sphere of India. Of the other combatants, the Portuguese power that once dominated half of Asia reeled and fell, never to recover again under the heavy blows dealt out by the Marathas by land, by sea, in the war they waged for the liberation of Konkan. The French, too, though they never dared to strike against the Marathas face to face, had often attempted to dominate Poona through Hyderabad and Arcot, but were as often frustrated in their aims and partially owing to that and partially as a result of their European conflicts, had so far ceased to be a danger to the Hindu Empire as to render their existence relatively desirable for a while to it as it served no useful purpose of letting it be played as a power to countercheck the ambitious impudence of their English rivals. The English, too, ever since the days of Shivaji, knew well that if they existed on the western coast, it was not so much because they were desired there or their political aims and ambition had escaped the scrutiny of the Maratha statesmen, but simply because the Marathas had to fight far more powerful and pressing foes elsewhere and so tolerated them as a relatively lesser danger that could be more conveniently dealt with later on, or could be more easily crushed if it ever became imminent. The English, too, gifted with an acute political insight knew very well that they held Bombay on the western coast, not so much in the teeth of the Maratha opposition as by virtue of their serious preoccupation elsewhere and their resultant toleration. So, they too, though ever willing to wound, were always afraid to strike. Nanasaheb had utilised them in destroying the power of Angre, but this he did on conditions that were, had his reasonable expectations come out true, far from being harmful to the Maratha power as a whole, whether military or naval. Had not things taken a sudden turn which no one of his generation could have expected as more likely to happen than not, the destruction of Angre's centripetal tendencies would have actually contributed to the strength of the naval power of the Marathas as a state, by concentrating the divided and, therefore, weakened, command of their navy in the hands of the central power. England, in spite of this transaction, derived no very important accessions to their actual possessions so far as the western coast was concerned. These possessions remained confined to the original magnitude ever since the days of Shivaji. But, in Bengal, England found a veritable 'open sesame', and Clive literally awoke to find himself a victor of a field that was fought while he was asleep and master of opportunities that could have, but for the Marathas, carried him straight to Delhi even then. But thereby we do not mean that the successes of the English in Bengal were anyway undeserved. The very fact that people could utilise their success, however accidental or thrust upon them by the cowardice or incapacity of their opponents more than their own prowess, proves that they deserved their luck. The successes the English won against the French in Madras were really due to their pluck. Thus, both their luck and their pluck enabled the English to grow into a power in Bengal and in Madras, without so seriously and directly challenging the supremacy of the Marathas as to provoke their immediate hostilities. But, in spite of this, even this surreptitious growth of the English power in Bengal and Madras had in no way escaped the acute vision of the Maratha leaders. Nanasaheb and Bhau were too seasoned, watchful and foresighted as statesmen to allow any of the opponents of the Hindu Empire, however insignificant their actual power be, to steal a march over them. It was this sudden succession of the English power in Bengal that was one of the causes which made Bhau mark out Bengal in the comprehensive programme of conquest he drafted for 1760-61 as a special objective and direct two powerful Maratha armies to liberate the whole province from the yoke of the non-Hindu powers under which it groaned ever since the days of Laxmansingh, our last Hindu king of Bengal. The northern division of the Maratha forces had actually started on the expedition under Dattaji Shinde in 1760. But, as already described, the invasion of Ahmedshah forced the Marathas to postpone the question of Bengal and face that mighty foe first. Then came Panipat, followed by the death of Nanasaheb. These calamities overtaking the Marathas in rapid succession afforded a new lease of life to the English which they most tactfully and assiduously utilised to strengthen their position in Bengal and Madras and prepare themselves with a set purpose of dominating the Imperial affairs of Delhi, by wresting the leading string of the Indian Empire out of the hands of the Marathas as soon as an opportunity presented itself. But, that opportunity they could not find as yet and Panipat or no Panipat, they dared not contest openly the united strength of the Marathas, which still continued to be the sovereign political power in Hindusthan. The little line of red colour that dotted Calcutta on the map of India swelled and coloured half of Bengal red. The little drop of red that coloured Madras on the map of India suddenly overflowed and submerged half that Presidency. But, the little line of red that marked out Bombay as British in the days of Shivaji remained the little line it had been even to the days of Nana Fadanavis. Not an inch of ground could it bring under its influence on the western coast, even when whole presidencies got tinged in red elsewhere on the map of India. For here on the peaks of Sahyadri, the Maratha sentinel stood on guard balancing his fiercely pointed lance ready to pierce fatally the first alien who dared to step ahead. So, none of the non-Hindu people, whether European or Asiatic, whether Christian or Mohammedan, were in a position to venture to contest or question the supremacy of the Hindu Empire of Maharashtra, as the sovereign political power of India while it stood solid and undivided in itself.

For though it is true that as a nation to a nation, the English were doubtlessly better fitted than the Marathas in those national qualities which make people subordinate and sacrifice their individual ambition and interests to their national aims and instinctively feel a religious repugnance at the thought of betraying their civil and communal interests or of selling their national freedom for a mess of pottage; yet, even then, we must guard ourselves against the fallacious tendency to read the past entirely in the borrowed light of the present. Everyone is wise after the event. But, if we take into consideration only those facts and factors which could be reasonably known or foreseen, then the relative forces, whether civil, military or political, ranged on both sides, it would have required only a prophet to foretell exactly who were destined to win amongst the two rivals. No politician could have precisely foretold it. The scientific or constitutional progress that England recorded then was not so hopelessly in advance of the Maratha activities as to disable them permanently in the political race for the Imperial crown of India. Moreover, there were natural and immense disadvantages on the English side inasmuch as they had to fight on an alien ground, thousands of miles away from their chief base of operation and their mother country. Japan, who began to grid up her loins a century later, could make up the immense distance that separated her from her European rivals in science and constitutional experience within half a century or so. The

Marathas, too, other things equal, could also have done that, especially as in the time under review the English were not so much in advance of the Marathas even in those spheres as to mark them out as pre-eminently destined to oust the Marathas from the paramount position they held as the de facto Imperial power in India in the teeth of the armed and simultaneous opposition of the Moguls and the Afghans and the Persians, of the French and the Portuguese and the English themselves.

The English themselves knew it well and so they never directly challenged the Maratha power while it stood untied and free from serious civil discords. But even when broken into factions and at war with themselves, none but the English possessed that vision and capacity to dare to provoke hostilities and invite opposition with some chance of success. Pampered on the spoil of Bengal and Madras, they had now grown fat enough to venture to kick against the Marathas in Bombay as soon as they found them involved in a serious civil end. Even Raghoba could see that and so when defeated, deserted and driven by his own countrymen, he took it into his head, giddy with the mad ambition of ruling Maharashtra against the will of the people, to seek the shelter of the English and promise to sell the freedom of his nation to its worst foes and let them in through the breach which his fratricidal hands effected in the ramparts of the Maratha Empire. The English eagerly grasped that fratricidal hand and on the condition of receiving a territory yielding 20 to 25 lakhs of rupees of revenue—Salsette and Bassein and Bhadoch, undertook to reinstate Raghoba as Peshwa of the Maratha people. Immediately the English forces with Raghoba opened hostilities against the Marathas and invaded their territory. The news that war had broken out between the English and the Marathas encouraged all the disaffected princes and principalities to rise in revolt against the Marathas all over India. But, Nana Fadnanavis, who had by this time concentrated into his hands the supreme power of the revolutionary government, stood four square against all the adverse winds that blew. In spite of the extremely disorganised state of the newly born government at Poona, Nana gathered whatever forces he could and dispatched them under Haripant Phadke to check and harass the advance of the English forces under Col. Keating. This task Haripant and his men performed well. At Napar and some other places, they inflicted severe losses on the foe, though he kept bravely sustaining them all. Just then, in 1777, there came about a change in the constitution of the English government in India by which the Governor of Calcutta was vested with supreme power over all their possessions in virtue of which he disowned the war with the Marathas undertaken by the Governor of Bombay and sent an envoy to Poona to negotiate a treaty with the Maratha government. Nana, very anxious to get breathing time to quell the risings and revolts that had taken place all over India against the Marathas, signed a treaty by which the English undertook to surrender Raghoba and were to receive Salsette and Bhadoch.

No sooner did the English hostilities end than Nana sent Mahadji Shinde to quell all internal disturbances and ordered Phadke and Patwardhan to chastise Haider for his invasion into the Maratha territory.

But, while those Maratha Generals were away on their several missions, the English refused to surrender Raghoba as agreed by the treaty and once more resumed hostilities with a view to crush Nana before his armies could return to Poona to strengthen his hands. To overawe the Marathas, they undertook, under Col. Egerton, a daring march against Poona itself in 1779. The Marathas, too, having never liked the treaty of Purandar and being now relatively free from internal disturbances which Mahadaji had ably quelled, challenged the English to do their worst and resorting to their traditional tactics of guerrilla warfare, lured the English further and further, taking good care to cut off their communication with Bombay. Bhivrao Panse kept hanging about the skirts of the advancing English forces so persistently, yet so elusively, that the English General could neither thrust a battle on the Marathas nor avoid one when thrust by them on his forces whenever they found him tightly cornered. His parties were constantly cut off; his supplies were interrupted and at last as he came to the top of the passes, his line of communication with Bombay was utterly broken. Still undaunted, he marched on. The determination of the Marathas too grew in intensity and bitterness as the foe approached their capital. They decided to desert and desolate the whole territory from Talegaon to Poona and, if need be, to burn down their beloved capital to ashes than surrender it to the hated foes. This grim national resolve could not fail to impress even the English forces. At Khandala, Col. Cay was mortally wounded by the Marathas. At Kirkee, another important officer, Captain Stewart was hit down to the great grief of the English. At every step, the English losses grew severe. But, admirably disciplined, they still advanced and entered Talegaon, if only to find themselves confronted by a powerful army led by Mahadaji Shinde and Haripant Phadke. The English boldly attacked them, but to their surprise, found that the Maratha army suddenly withdrew, got itself divided and spreading out kept charging the English on all sides and yet from a safe distance. Neither food nor fodder could be had for miles around and reliable rumours reached the English camp assuring them that the further they advanced, the more thoroughly desolate a tract they would have to pass through. Seasoned, brave and haughty, even then the English attempted to march on. But, the wily Marathas had well nigh surrounded them and deliberately informed them of the grim determination of their people to rather burn the capital down than surrender it to their foes. The commander of the English forces had seen enough of the Marathas to cure him of his infatuation and got convinced that the march towards Poona was not a march towards Plassey. There was only one way to get out of the fix—to march back to Bombay. Disgraceful though it was that there was no other go. Even a march back was impossible if openly resumed. So, the English Commander, determined to take the Marathas by surprise, ordered a stealthy march back. But, to take the Marathas by surprise was like teaching grandma to suck. They had known it all and as soon as the English came out, they closed their ranks and at a sign fell on their foe with irresistible might. The English fought with their traditional stubbornness, but the Marathas could not be shaken off. At last, beaten and broken at Vadgaon, the whole army numbering some nine thousand men, surrendered unconditionally to the Marathas. Nana and Bapu and Shinde demanded that Raghoba be immediately handed over to them and all the Maratha districts that the English had squeezed by the treaty of Purandar should forthwith be returned. Moreover, two English officers were taken as hostage to stand security for the carrying out of the terms of the treaty. The English Commander accepted all the terms as a price for being allowed to take back his army to Bombay after remaining captives in the hands of the victorious Marathas for more than a month. The news of the splendid victory sent a thrill of joy throughout the nation. The Union Jack, so stiff, had bowed low to the orange and gold of Maharashtra. In spite of civil feuds and the disorganised state into which their country and people had consequently fallen, their nation had risen equal to the occasion and the people's government had inflicted so indisputable a defeat on such an audacious and stubborn a foe. Even the one remaining adversary, who of all had not yet dared to strike or question the supremacy of the power of Maharashtra in India, had to confess to humiliation as soon as he ventured to do so. 'Our nation,' to quote the contemporary correspondence, 'had taught such a lesson to the English as none else could teach them. Never had they been so thoroughly humiliated.' The people fondly devoted to their infant Peshwa, who had been the centre of the popular cause, lovingly attributed their victories to the luck of that princely lad. 'Even from his very birth, the life of our beloved Bal Peshwa, our dear infant prince, had as miraculous a career as that of the divine child of Gokul. Our enemies stand vanquished and god has blessed the cause of our nation and of our Hindu faith in this holy war.'

□

The English Humbled

'प्रतापमहिमा थोरजळामधिं परि जळचर बुडविला
नधि मोहिम दरसाल देउनी शाह टिपू तुडविला।'

As soon as the news of the capitulation of a great English army reached Calcutta, the English were so wild with rage as to make them utterly unscrupulous and refusing to sanction the treaty their Commander had at Vadgaon signed. After the captured army had been allowed to pass back to Bombay by the Marathas, according to the treaty, they renewed hostilities with added zeal. In the meanwhile, Raghoba, too, who would have in other states, been shot for high treason or betrayal, was so leniently treated as a prince would have been, abused that liberty and once more effected his escape and went over to the English camp. Then the war again grew furious. Goddard descended from Gujarat and marched on Bassein. He was opposed by Ramchandra Ganesh who contested the English advance with admirable pertinacity, fighting action after action against the foe whenever and wherever he could. He led his last assault with such magnificent courage and valour as to win admiration even from his foes. But, unfortunately, this gallant and skilled Maratha General, struck by a bullet, fell in the very thick of the fight and Goddard took Bassein in 1780. Encouraged by this success, the English thought of wiping out the stain that the surrender of their army at Vadgaon had left on their arms, by accomplishing the task of carrying the very capital of the Marathas, which they had formerly so disgracefully failed to do. So, the English advanced against Poona, aiming to browbeat Nana and his associates into surrender. But, the matchless genius of that Maratha statesman had already woven a subtly dangerous net into which he threatened to entangle the English power all over India. He made Haider promise to attack Madras, Bhonsle to invade Bengal and undertook himself to crush the English power at Bombay. Accordingly,

Haider, with the aid of the French government, achieved a signal success at Madras. Parashrambhau with 12 thousand men kept hanging around and harassing the flanks and the rear of the advance of the English forces towards Poona. While Nana, Tukoji Holkar and Haripant Phadke faced the English with 30 thousand Maratha forces, General Goddard found himself as he advanced, in the same predicament as Col. Egerton did. He could not advance further unless he invited the fate of his predecessor and yet he had advanced far enough to render a march back as dangerous as it would be disgraceful. So, standing where he was, he strengthened himself. But, that too could not continue long. The vigorous and most harassing attacks the Marathas delivered against Captain Machay and Col. Brown while striving to carry supplies to Goddard made any further attempt to maintain communication with Bombay extremely risky and ruinous. At last, even General Goddard, to his utter chagrin, had to decide to drop the advance against the capital of the Marathas, and retire. As soon as the crest-fallen English army took a right-about-turn and began a march back, the Marathas led by Bhau and Tukoji Holkar closed upon the prey from all sides and, in spite of the stubborn discipline and bravery of the English, beat them so badly as to make their boastful Commander whose arrogance aspired to crown him with the honours of triumphant entry into the Maratha capital, thank his stars for having somehow been able to reach back Bombay alive, even though at the cost of leaving hundreds of his soldiers slain and strewn, marking the track of his return march with their corpses and almost all ammunition, guns, tents and camp furniture, thousands of cannon shots and stores, thousands of bullocks abandoned and fallen in the hands of the triumphant Marathas. Thus, twice did the English come audaciously forward to fight their way on to Poona; and twice had they to face the utter humiliation of retiring beaten and crest-fallen back to Bombay. Never did a boastful going out end in a more sadly disgraceful return home.

Nor did the English forces fare much better in the North. In spite of some initial success which they, with the help of the Rana of Gohad, who had taken their side against the Marathas and the capture of the fort of Gwalior, the English under Colonel Carac failed to achieve anything so substantial as to enable them to hold long against the most harassing attacks of Mahadji Shindia. Colonel Muir, too, who hastened to succour his comrade out of the fix, failed to improve their position. Thus, foiled in the South by Haider, on the Bombay side by Tukoji Holkar and Patwardhan and in the North by Mahadji Shindia, the English tried to break up the chain of alliances that the genius of Nana Fadanavis had woven round them by making overtures to Mahadaji Shindia and requesting him to influences his government to sign a separate peace with the English. But, Nana would have nothing to do with the separate peace and refused to enter into any negotiations without consulting Haider. The Maratha navy too gave a good account of itself. Anandrao Dhulap, their Admiral, in a daring attack, won a signal victory and captured an English man-of-war named Ranger and carried it away as a prize. But just then, Haider died, even while the negotiations were going on. So, Nana signed the peace in 1783 by which the English had to deliver up Raghoda, who was the chief bone of contention, into the hands of the Marathas, surrender all territories they had taken in the war or received by the treaty of Purander except Salsette, and undertake not to help or encourage any Asiatic nation or state at war or inimically disposed towards the Marathas, who too promised not to have political dealings with any European rivals against the interests of the English. Above all, the English had to pledge not to dabble with the Imperial politics of India at Delhi and acknowledge the right of the Marathas to directly control them as freely as they chose.

Thus ended the first-Anglo-Maratha war. Thus did Maharashtra vindicate their claim and position on the battlefield as the premier and paramount political power of India by discomfiting and defeating, amongst the rest, the only European power that had not till then ventured and challenged the Marathas to challenge to an open combat. They taught England a bitter lesson that in spite of the accession to their strength and possession in Bengal and Madras, the English would only get their head smashed if they dared to defy the Sahyadrian ramparts of the Hindu Empire of Maharashtra with the same insolence that served them so well against and in overawing the effeminate Mohammedan Nawabs of Bengal and Arcot.

Soon after the treaty of Salbai was signed, Raghoba too, had to end his ignominious career of intriguing against his own nation and betraying the interests of his country and selling them to the worst enemy of his race. He had by his foul ambition been the cause of diverting the energies of the Maratha Confederacy into the barren channels and poisonous and fatal bogs of civil war, from the ennobling pursuit of fulfilling the great mission that generations of Maharashtra had worked for and died for. His life was at least as great a national disaster as the battle of Panipat had been. Fortunately, that life did not continue long after the treaty of Salbai. Yet it did neither end without calling into existence another life that was to be even a greater curse to the Maratha people. Even while Raghoba was being utterly foiled in his foul intrigue with England, a son was born to him who, as irony would have it, was named Bajirao the Second, after his illustrious grandfather Bajirao I, and who was destined to fulfil the Satanic mission which his father was forced to abandon and succeed in doing what his parents failed to do and selling the independence of Maharashtra for a mess of pottage and encompass the ruin of the last great Hindu Empire.

But, that was not yet to be, not at any rate till Nana and Mahadji lived.

□

Savai Madhaorao—The Peshwa of the People's Choice

दैन्य दिवस आज सरले सवाई माधवराव प्रतापि कलियुगिं
अवतरले ॥ ध्रु. ॥

सुंदररूप रायाचें कुंगावर नाहिं रागे भरणें ॥
कलगितुरा शिरपेंच पाचुचीं पडत होतिं मुखावर किरणें ॥
महोत्साह घरोघर लागले लोक करायाला ॥
परशाराम प्रत्यक्ष आले जणुं छत्र धरायाला ॥

For Nana and Mahadji, the brain and the sword of Hindudom, meant on their Atalantian shoulders to bear the weight of the mightest of monarchies. Of all the best of statesmen and swordsmen, of Hastings and Wellesley and Cornwallis, that England or France or Holland or Portugal sent out to India to conquer an Empire, none could outwit or oppose these with any great measure of success. Both of them had seen the palmiest days of the Hindu Empire. Both were trained in the principles and aims and traditions of their nation and its mission in the Imperial school of the great Nanasaheb and Sadashivrao Bhau. Both had seen Panipat and survived it, determined to carry on the mission of the heroic generation that lay slain on that gory field. They found their kingdom smitten by the civil war, on the verge of ruin, with a non-entity for its king, a lad for its Prime Minister and an ambitious and powerful European foe for its sworn antagonist. Yet, they faced all odds with dauntless courage and an undimmed vision, quelled revolts and rebellions within the realm and with a mighty hand and unerring eye threw down and forced their foes, whether European or Asiatic, to drink the cup of humiliation.

They had taken upon themselves the risky responsibilities of calling into existence and controlling the uncertain and fitful moods of a popular revolution. Now that the revolution had triumphed over all its enemies and its government, based on the firm foundation of national will, had proved invincible in the field, it was as natural as politically imperative that the achievement be signalised by some imposing celebration. The marriage ceremony of the young Peshwa, Savai Madhao Rao, furnished the fittest occasion for national rejoicings. He was the Peshwa of the people's choice. It was for him that the nation went to war. Now that their beloved young prince had survived not only open wars, but even clandestine, cowardly and criminal efforts of their enemies to poison, assassinate and murder him, the nation could not refrain their imagination from comparing the miraculous vicissitudes of his life with those of the divine child of Gokul and longed to see their princely darling grow to a happy boyhood. People from far and near flocked to Poona to join in the royal celebration. Princes, chiefs, flourishing poets, famous authors, great Generals, veterans that had seen service at Udgir and Attock, diplomats and statesmen, all flocked to Poona to celebrate the marriage and have a look at their beloved and august prince. To impress the world with the solidarity of the confederate constituents of the great Hindu Empire and to disillusion those aliens and enemies who fondly believed the Maratha Mandal was bound to break up and disperse and could never survive the civil war, Nana had intentionally invited and received with Imperial honours the Great Chhatrapati of Maharashtra himself when he reached Poona to grace the occasion of the marriage of his Prime Minister.

There, in the stately Royal Hall, the Chhatrapati sat on his throne, surrounded by brilliant throngs of his Viceroys, and Generals, and Admirals, and statesmen and chiefs, and princes, several of whom had commands over provinces as large as kingdoms in other continents. There were Patwardhans, Rastes and Phadkes. There were represented Holkar and Shindia and Pawar and Gaikwad and Bhonsle. The learning of all India, from Hardwar to Rameshwar, was represented there. The Hindu kings of Jaipur, Jodhpur and Udaipur were cordially invited and represented there through their royal envoys. The Nizam and the Mogul and the European powers in India had sent then their presents and congratulatory gifts through their princes and envoys. Horse and cannon and infantry camped round the capital for miles representing the sword and shield of Maharashtra. Angre and Dhulap represented the Navy, the former being fitly charged with the work of receiving the guests on behalf of the Peshwa. Gathering that mighty concourse under its spacious folds floated those colours, the golden *geruwa*, the orange and the gold—reminding the nation of their great mission or *swadharma rajya*—of Hindu *pad-padashahi*.

At a given signal infantry and cavalry and artillery, all arms burst in a cheering acclamation and saluting, shouted: 'Victory! Victory to our beloved prince!' The Peshwa, so handsome, so young, accompanied by the most impressive pomp and ceremony, by heralds and retinue, slowly advanced and entered the hall of assembly. The assemblage stood up, bent low and bowing in fealty paid the homage of the heart of a nation to the Peshwa in person who, so long had been the theme and the hero of popular songs and myths. But what was the wonder of the assembly when they witnessed the young prince who was the real ruler of all India advance to the Chhatrapati, the King of Satara—who sat enthroned amidst the magnificent assembly—advance with his hands folded and thrice tied and wrapped round with garlands of flowers: for strict decorum required that the Prime Minister must enter the presence and approach the King of Maharashtra with his hands folded and tied in sign of submission! The scene drew tears of joy and national emotion from the eyes of many a sturdy warrior—even the non-chalant and serene face of the minister could not but betray emotion and big tears of joy were observed rolling down his cheeks. The political impression that this majestic celebration and display of unity, solidarity and oneness of aim, which in spite of occasional aberrations still ruled, informed and inspired the constituents of the Maratha Confederacy, produced on the minds of other Indian European princes and powers, did not belie the expectations of Nana and other leaders of Maharashtra. Nor did it contribute little to the strengthening of the ties that bound the confederacy itself by emphasising and accentuating the consciousness belonging to a great and glorious commonwealth, in virtue of which each constituent derived more strength and prestige and splendour than it could have done if left to itself.

As the wounds of the civil war gradually healed, Maharashtra embarked on decades as prosperous and glorious and happy as any recorded in its history. Nana Fadanavis and his able co-adjustors put the administrative and financial and judicial machinery of the state on such a sound footing that, of all people and principalities in India, Maharashtra proper and the vast territories that were held by them under their direct control were the best ruled. The system of assessment and collection of taxes, the efficiency of popular control of justice and the relatively easy opening which all princes and peasants could have to careers, great and glorious, and, above all, the realisation of being the instruments in the fulfilment of a great mission for which their ancestors fought and which their gods and saints sanctified and of belonging to a race that was sustaining on its mighty shoulders an Empire dedicated to the defence and the propagation of the cause of the Hindu faith and Hindu independence, made the people feel literally 'blest for having been born in such days—worked for and witnessed such glorious achievements.' The national atmosphere was charged with a sense of elevation and everyone could not but breathe in it. News of some military triumph or other, of some new national achievement, poured constantly in. Even the lowest felt the times to be extraordinarily gifted and fondly attributed it all to the auspicious star that ruled over the moment of the birth of their fortunate and young beloved prince, Savai Madhao Rao, to whom a nation knelt in homage before he was born. It was the disappointed aspiration of Madhao Rao I, went the popular story, to destroy and avenge the rule of the Mussalmans, the alien and the faithless oppressors, and establish from sea to sea a powerful and godly Hindu Empire that made him take the birth of Madhao Rao II, their beloved prince. That is why, god blessed and fortune ever smiled on their national banner ever since the days the princely lad was born. Such popular and even fantastic beliefs are at times but the dreamy babblings of the sub-conscious longings of a nation's soul and reveal in what light even the rank and file view their national undertakings and achievements.

Soon after the treaty of Salbai, Nana ordered Parasharam Bhau Patwardhan to chastise Tippu who had succeeded Haider and proved as redoubtable an enemy of the Marathas as any. Hostilities opened in 1784 as the Hindu principality of Nargund was grossly oppressed by Tippu and craved assistance from the Marathas. The Marathas under Patwardhan and Holkar, in alliance with the Nizam, forced Tippu to sign a treaty by which he promised to pay his arrears of tribute to the Marathas and cease to trouble Nargund any longer. But, no sooner did the Marathas turn their backs than Tippu, bent upon practising a gross deception, tore off the treaty, took the fort of Nargund, treacherously seized the Hindu chief and his family and in keeping with the best traditions of the faithful, barbarously tortured them to death and carried away the daughter of the Hindu chief to his seraglio; then to lay for himself stores of heavenly merit and to earn the recommendations of the pious Moslem Maulvis and historians who readily raised to the dignity of a defender of the faith and a Gazi an Aurangzeb or a Taimur. Tippu began to break demoniacal vengeance on the Hindu population between the Krishna and the Tungbhadra by committing all the horrors of forcible conversions to Islam that ever accompanied its spread. He, as if to challenge the claim of the Marathas as the protectors of the Hindu faith, subjected many Hindus to forcible circumcision and other acts of indescribable violence. Be it noted to the credit of the unfortunate victims that, though they failed to fulfil the best and foremost duty of men of rising en masse and—as Ramdas had exhorted the Hindus and taught the Marathas to do—to die killing the torturing foes of their faith and put down violence by force, yet they did not fail to do the next best thing of preferring death to dishonour. Not a man here or there, but not less than 2,000 Brahmins alone who were the chief targets of Tippu's ghoulish fury chose to put an end to their lives rather than allow themselves to be subjected to the horrors of forcible conversion and apostate life. They voluntarily martyred themselves to their faith. Before the rise of the Maratha power, such things had been the order of the day. 'Rather get killed than converted' was the best that the Hindu could do. Ramdas rose and standing on the peaks of Sahyadri, exclaimed: 'No, not thus. Better get killed than converted is good enough, but it would be better so to strive as neither to get killed nor violently converted by killing the forces of violence itself. Get killed if that must be, but get killed while killing to conquer—conquer in the cause of righteousness.' With hundreds of his disciples preaching this war-cry through their secret societies from *math* to *math*, from house to house, he taught the Hindus to covet, not only the crown of thorns, but also, and along with it, the laurelled diadem of victory. And yet, in the face of all this, Tippu dared to torture the Hindus into conversion and play the part of an Aurangzeb, while the descendants of Shivaji still ruled at Poona. The piteous cry of thousands of Brahmins and other Karnataka, Andhra and Tamil Hindus who had been the victims of the fanaticism of Tippu reached Poona, loudly calling for deliverance from the Moslem rule. Can the Brahmin kingdom bear this all? Can the Hindu Empire of Maharashtra listen with equanimity to the accounts of the horrible fate that had overtaken their co-religionists across the Krishna? It was a challenge to the Marathas as a Hindu power and they accepted it. Though their armies were busy in the North, as we shall presently see, fighting great battles against their foes, yet Nana determined to hasten to the rescue of his co-religionists and countrymen in Karnataka. He bought off the Nizam by a promise of allotting him one-third of whatever conquests they made in the territories of Tippu and ordered the Maratha forces to open a mighty offensive against the Moslem fanatic. Patwardhan and Behre and other Maratha Generals, now concentrating and then spreading out in divisions, took Badami and other strongholds of the foe, harassed and thrashed him so often and so furiously as to drive him to take shelter in the mountainous districts. There, too, unable to hold out any longer against the Hindu forces, the hero of Islam, who had distinguished himself so much by molesting women and children and by torturing peaceful Hindu priests and violating the chastity of Hindu girls, sued for peace and pardon at the hands of those very Hindus as soon as they proved themselves strong enough to blow his brains out. The humble and unresisting sufferings of thousands of Hindus and Hindu girls did not blunt the edge of his fanatical violence, but it rather sharpened it all the more. But what unresisting martyrdom failed to do, righteous and resisting force did and rendered tyranny impotent to do further harm. Tippu was forced to hand over the state of Nargund and Kittur and Badami to the Marathas besides paying down 30 lakhs of rupees then and there as the arrears of his tribute to the Hindu power and promising to pay 15 lakhs more within a year. Now, had the Marathas meant to be mean like the Moslems, they were in a position to convert the Mohammedan population, those very Maulvis and Maulanas, by forcibly subjecting them to the comparatively harmless Hindu ceremony of keeping the *shika*, who had but so recently exhibited such criminal activities in outraging the Hindu under the orders of Tippu Sultan. But, the Marathas neither pulled down mosques, nor forcibly took Mohammedan girls to their seraglios, nor outraged the faith of other communities by persuading them at the point of the bayonet to embrace the Hindu faith. Such heroic deeds were obviously beyond their reach, as they failed to believe in the Koran as read by Taimurs and Tippus and Allauddins and Aurangzebs. Only the 'faithful' are entitled to commit such acts of vandalism and violence, not so the '*kafirs*'.

Having delivered the Hindus from the fanatical fury of Tippu in the

South, the Maratha armies were now able to concentrate their efforts in subduing a great coalition that their enemies had formed in the North and whom Mahadaji Shindia had single-handedly held in check so long. After the treaty of Salbai, Mahadji had returned to the North. He had been deeply impressed by the efficiency of the disciplined troops under the European Commander and his first care was to carry out the scheme of Sadashivrao Bhau, the hero of Panipat, who was the first great Indian Commander, not only to appreciate, but to attempt on a large scale, the use of a regular army manned and drilled and disciplined after the European model. Mahadaji raised a powerful force under De Boigne, a French General and equipped it so efficiently as to challenge the strength of any European army. Backed up by these, he soon found himself in a position to dictate terms to all those who dared to oppose him in his designs in the North. Although the English had to promise to withdraw from the lists of Imperial politics at Delhi and leave the Marathas free to do as they liked, still they did not cease to foment as much discontent and put as many difficulties as they secretly could in the way of Mahadji by trying to keep the Emperor Shah Alam in their hands and prevent him from going over to the Marathas. But, in spite of all that, Mahadji held the reins of Imperial politics firmly in his hands, brought the Emperor to Delhi and defeated the wretched Mohammedan claimants to the post of Vazirship and to the utter chagrin of his Moslem and European rivals, drove the last nail in the coffin of the Moslem Empire by making the Emperor declare Mahadaji his Vazir, hand over the command of the Imperial forces to him and deliver up the two provinces of Delhi and Agra to his administration. Not only that, but the Mogul Emperor conferred the dignity of Vazir-i-Mutalik on the Peshwa and, thus, virtually empowered him to act in the name of the Emperor and as a '*maharajadhiraj*, the king of Kings, in return for receiving 65,000 rupees for his private expenses and the luxury of being called an Emperor. The situation that this startling constitutional change created, could be best described in the words of a contemporary Maratha correspondent. 'The Empire has become ours. The old Mogul is but a pensioner and a willing pensioner, in our hands. He is still called Emperor: that is all that he wants and we must continue the show for a while.' The English, too, after they had found themselves in a similar situation, could not but keep up that show right down to 1857. Mahadji wished to signalise this event by some great moral appeal to all

Hindudom. So, the Hindu regime was heralded by the issue of orders preventing the killing of bullocks and cows all over the Indian Empire. Nor did Mahadji allow this change in the political status to be merely a verbal one. The Marathas were not likely to be a king long. They immediately began to reduce all recalcitrant elements and fuse them into a great and mighty Hindu Empire, led by the Maharashtra Mandal. The first act of Mahadji was to demand from the English themselves the arrears of Imperial tribute and the Maratha *chowth* and *Sardeshmukhi*. His next step was to levy revenue and reduce those Vicerorys and *zamindars* of those provinces who had for years acted as if they were independent rulers. This step raised a storm all over the North. Nobles and Amirs and Khans, all rose in arms against the Maratha power. Not only that, even the Rajas and Raos joined hands with the Moslems and the English against the only Hindu power that could have established a Hindu Empire in India. It was very natural, but very unfortunate. The two great Rajput states, Jaipur and Jodhpur, formed a coalition against the Marathas, stronger than they had ever formed against the Moslem or the English and in co-operation with the Mohammedan forces all over the North, gave a great battle to Shindia's army at Lalsote. In the thick of the fight, the Imperial Moslem forces under the command of Mahadji, went bodily over the Rajputs at a preconcerted signal and the Marathas, thus suddenly betrayed, suffered a defeat. But, nothing tested the mettle of the Maratha commander as this sudden reverse did. Undaunted, he immediately succeeded in rallying the forces of Maharashtra; Lakhobadada, the Maratha General, who held the fort of Agra which was sorely pressed by the Mohammedans, offered a brave and stubborn resistance and, thus, stayed the swelling tide of Mahadji's foes. Just then Gulam Kadar, the grandson of Nazib Khan whom the Marathas had not either forgotten, or forgiven, appeared on the scene with the Rohillas and Pathans, among to rescue Delhi from the hands of Mahadji. The foolish Emperor encouraged him and he entered Delhi, while Mahadji was busy fighting about Agra against the forces of Mohammedans and Rajputs risen in arms against him on all sides. Mahadji had already acquainted Nana of the unfavourable turn events had taken in the North and represented that it was the disappointed ambition of the English that was at the bottom of all this trouble. They dared not oppose the Marathas face to face. They had tried to do it and failed. Yet they knew that, if the Marathas were allowed to use the name and authority of the Emperor for a little longer, they were sure to tear even the thin veil that kept up the show and openly assume the Imperial dignity themselves, which in fact they had already almost done. So, the English were most eager to possess and hold in their hand the power of the old Mogul, the painted Emperor. 'Let us not forget,' the great Maratha Commander eloquently exhorted his people at home in his letter to Nana, 'that we live and work and will die in the interests of this our great Empire, that we owe allegiance to one common master, the head of our commonwealth. Let us disavow all feelings of jealousy or personal aggrandisement. If any one of you personally entertains any suspicions as to my intentions, I humbly beg of you to banish them all. My services to the commonwealth are enough to silence calumniators who are our real enemies and try to feather their nests by keeping us divided. Let us all rise equal to the occasion, rally round the national standard; and let the cause of our nation, the great mission handed down to us by our forefathers, be upheld in all Hindusthan. Let us prevent our great Empire from being disunited and overthrown.' Nana was not the man to listen to this noble appeal with indifference when the national cause was in danger. As we have already seen, he had been conducting a war against Tippu and as soon as he had sufficiently humbled him, he dispatched. Holkar and Alija Bahadar to strengthen Mahadji's hands. He regretted to find that the Rajputs and the Marathas should have come to blows and, thus, afforded an opportunity to the enemies of Hindudom to raise their heads just when the grand dream of their forefathers was all but accomplished and a great Hindu Empire brought into being, that promised well to unite within its folds all Hindusthan. So, Nana tried to open negotiations with the Rajputs, and especially the King of Jaipur, in the name of the Peshwa and tried to persuade them not to make common cause with the foes of Hindudom and somehow find out a way to reconcile themselves with the Hindu Empire that the Marathas had well-nigh established. Supported by the Maratha armies dispatched from Poona, Mahadji soon humbled his foes. He sent forward Rana Khan. Appa Khanderao and other Maratha Generals, supported by two regular battalions of De Boigne, to oppose Gulam Kadar, the grandson of Nazib Khan, the author of Panipat. The Mohammedans determined to give a battle. Two hotly contested battles were fought. The Mohammedans were broken and beaten as never before. They fled in all directions. Ismail Beg and Gulam Kadar ran towards Delhi, hotly pursued by the

Marathas. The Emperor trembled. Gulam Kadar demanded money. The Emperor could not produce it. Mad with fury, the cruel and barbarous Rohilla chief commenced a systematic train of violence and rapine. He pulled the Emperor down from his throne and threw him on the ground and with his knees planted on his breast, thrust his dagger in the eyes of the old and helpless descendant of Akbar and Aurangzeb and destroyed them in their sockets. Not satisfied with this cruelty, he drove and dragged out his wives and daughters, exposed them rudely and ordered his menials to outrage them before his very eyes. One of the causes of this inhuman fury was that Gulam Kadar was castrated and emasculated in his youth under the orders of this Emperor Shah Alam. Plunder ran riot in the capital. Mohammedans committed such atrocities over Mohammedans as they were wont to commit on others in the name of Mohammedanism. Thus, a tyrant outside, sooner or later turns out a tyrant at home. Thus does tyranny fall a victim to itself. But, who will save now the Mohammedan Emperor, citizens and Mohammedan girls from these barbarous tortures and beastly outrages perpetrated by the followers of Islam? Who else but *kafirs*, the Hindus—the Marathas? It was the occupants of this Mogul and even before that the Mohammedan, throne of Delhi that had razed the temples of the Hindus to the ground, had smitten their images into dust, had carried by force queens and princesses to their harem, had violated the chastity of their girls and the faith of their youths had snatched mother from child and brother from brother and had their hands and hearts red in the Hindu blood that they might invite the honours of a Gazi and a defender of the faith in this world and gather a large harvest of meritorious rewards in the other and now these very Hindus are coming to Delhi not to raze mosques to the ground, not to smite the crescents or the tombs into dust, not to violate—why violate?—not even to touch the princesses or even a peasant girl in the poorest Moslem cottage, not to forcibly convert and snatch away mother from child or son from father, not to indulge recklessly in the wine of ruin or get intoxicated with bloodshed, not to measure the greatness of their success by the height of the ghastly columns of heads cut off from the trunks of their slain foes, or by the flames of their burning capitals. They could have done so. Had they done so, at any rate, the Mohammedans could not have blamed them. The Hindus are fast approaching only to relieve the Moslem occupant of that very throne and that very capital from tortures and outrages, ghastly and ghoulish at the hands of the Moslems themselves! The city prayed for the arrival of the Marathas and the whole populace, Mohammedans and Hindus, burst into the most hearty reception when the armies of the Hindu Empire entered the city gates. Alija Bahadur, Appa Khanderao, Rana Khan and De Boigne took possession of the city, but found that the criminal, Gulam Kadar, had already left it. He was the grandson of Nazib and a hereditary enemy of the Marathas. He was not likely to escape the punishment he deserved. The Marathas did everything which humanity dictated to relieve the descendants of Aurangzeb from the torturing hands of Moslems themselves, in spite of the fact that he had only very recently conspired against the Marathas and joined the very Gulam Kadar in fomenting a coalition similar to that which his grandfather Nazib had formed against the Marathas at Panipat. A large body had already been sent to pursue Gulam Kadar who entered the fort of Meerut and began to offer a vigorous defence. But, it was impossible to hold out long against the Marathas. So, he mounted a horse and fled, but in the confusion of the pursuit he fell from his horse and lay stunned in a field, whence some villagers, recognising him, carried him to the Maratha camp. No one was louder in demanding for an exemplary punishment of that fiend than the Mohammedan public itself. The wretch was produced before Shinde to whom the family of Gulam had for three successive generations borne implacable hatred. Gulam had to pay for all that. He was subjected to fearful mutilations and as he still persisted in abusing, his tongue and eyes too were pulled out and pierced. At last, horribly mutilated, Gulam, the grandson of Nazib Khan, was sent to the Emperor who longed to learn that the human fiend who had subjected him to such fearful tortures was as fearfully punished and killed. Thus, the family of Nazib Khan, who had sworn to destroy the Marathas at Panipat, got himself destroyed at the hands of the Marathas and not a trace of them or their principality was left behind.

By the year 1789, Mahadji, along with other Maratha Generals, had succeeded in subduing their opponents, defeated and destroyed the Mohammedan clique and their Rajput partisans and humbled the English by fronting them with such a display of power as to make them think the better part of valour. The old Emperor was again secured and when he again wished to confer the honour and titles of the highest Imperial office of Vakil-i-Mutalik on Mahadji, the latter waived it once more in deference to his master, the young Peshwa at Poona.

But while the Maratha forces were thus fully occupied in the North, Tippu wanted to try his hand again. In 1798, he assumed a threatening attitude. But, instead of provoking directly the Marathas by attacking their territory, he aimed to extend his possessions—if it was made difficult on the side of Krishna by the presence of the Marathas, then, by attacking the Hindu chief of Travancore, his weaker neighbour. So, Nana, in alliance with the English and the Nizam, declared war on Tippu and Patwardhan invaded his territories. As the Marathas advanced, be it noted, the local inhabitants made common cause with them against the fanatical tyrant of Mysore and helped the Marathas in driving Tippu's officers and men, and aided in collecting the outstanding revenue. Taking Hubli, Ghodvad, Misricot, the Marathas advanced with irresistible might. Dharwad, that had lately fallen in Tippu's hand, was besieged. The Mohammedan General there offered a stubborn resistance. The English, in spite of the advice of the Maratha General, once attempted to take the fort by storm, but disastrously failed. The struggle continued and was doggedly maintained by both the sides. At last, the Marathas with valorous skill lodged charge after charge and took the fort. Panse, Raste and other Maratha Generals crossed the Tungabhadra, took Santi, Badnoor, Maikoda, Hapenoor, Chengiri and other posts under the enemy. The Maratha navy too lay not idle. It guarded the coast and marching along, it drove the Moslem officers from many a place in Karwar and Hansar. Narsinhrao Deoji, Ganpatrao Mehendale and other Maratha officers took Chandavar, Honawar, Girisappa, Dhareshwar, Udgini and then the Maratha armies marched towards Shrirangapattan itself. There, from the other side, was marching the English force led by Cornwallis. But, at that time they were so thoroughly starved and tired out by the tactics of Tippu that they could hardly have a full meal a day. The cavalry, for want of fodder, got automatically converted into infantry as the horses fell in heaps. What was their joy when the English forces in this helpless and starved out condition beheld the columns of the Maratha army advancing towards them, well furnished like a gay bazaar with all the necessaries of life and even its luxuries! Haripant Phadke evinced a human anxiety to relieve the furnished camp of his allies. The confederate armies remained for ten days together and if the Marathas were minded so, they could have surely crushed Tippu's kingdom out of existence. But, Nana's policy did not sanction Tippu's annihilation. He wanted him to continue a little longer as a useful check on ambitious English designs in Madras. So, when, after some further conflict and a sound thrashing at the hands of the English and the Marathas, Tippu abjectly sued for peace, Parasharam Bhau and Haripant Phadke intervened and persuaded the English to grant terms. By these Tippu had to hand over half of his kingdom to Marathas and pay an indemnity of 3 crores of rupees and refrain from molesting the Hindu state of Travancore. Two of his sons were held as hostages by the allies. The gains were divided equally amongst the Marathas, the English and the Nizam, by which the first recovered a vast territory yielding 90 lakhs of rupees a year and a crore of rupees as their share of the indemnity. Thus ended the third great war with Tippu and the Maratha forces reached their capital back in 1792 with honour and military distinction.

But loaded with honours as splendid and military distinction more dazzling than any, the northern commander of the Maratha Empire too, was just then winding his way towards the capital of Maharashtra. The concourse of these mighty forces, Phadke and Raste who had subdued the South and delivered Hindudom there from the fanatical fury of Tippu, and Mahadji who had subdued all North, reduced the Moslem Emperor practically into a pensioner of the Hindu Empire and assumed, in the teeth of the English and French, the Pathans and Rohillas, Imperial powers all but in name—the concourse of these mighty men at Poona threw every foreign court in India and outside into consternation and suspense as to its future fate. What must be the object of this concourse? What would be the next step that the mighty Hindu Confederacy of Maharashtra was likely to take and who could be its next object or victim? All eyes in India turned towards Poona; for Delhi no longer counted for anything. Delhi had been reduced into a mere suburb of Poona. But Maharashtra herself grew uneasy with misgivings of quite a contrary nature. The two giants, Nana and Mahadji, had come face to face. All knew that slowly but surely a suppressed sense of rivalry was growing into mutual fear between these two patriotic men, held up till now in check only by the noble devotion and love which both equally bore towards the great Hindu commonwealth that generations of Maharashtra had built up and in whose defence and for the augmentation of whose power and glory no two men had more whole-heartedly worked than these two themselves. Was that suppressed sense of rivalry now likely to burst out in open hostility? Woe to the Hindu Empire if it ever did! All Maharashtra trembled to think of it and watched with breathless anxiety the giant struggle between the foremost of their warriors and the foremost of their statesmen.

We have already stated how the old Mogul, who was still allowed by the Marathas to style himself as an Emperor, wished to confer on Mahadji the highest honour and title that he could bestow, of Vakil-i-Mutalik and *maharajadhiraj*, and how Mahadji refusing to accept them for himself, secured them for his master, the young Peshwa at Poona. This was no empty show. Although in the hands of a powerless and incapable courtier, these titles would not have been worth the paper on which they were written yet they were not likely to remain the mere hollow-sounding words that they were. They empowered their holder with full power to rule in the name of the Emperor; they meant, in fact, the resignation of the imperial power on the part of the Emperor. The rivalry between the English and other non-Hindu powers and the Marathas for the Imperial Crown of India had made it a point to let the Imperial Crown and titles remain, even if in a name with the old Mogul. To divest him of it was sooner done than said. But, as the English and other Mohammedan powers knew that if once they allowed them to drift in the hands of the Marathas, they would place them almost beyond their reach, they jealously persisted in burning incense to the fetish of the old Mogul, and made a show of recognising him as the Emperor just to spite the Marathas. How this tendency was evident in the public life of India could best be seen by the English anxiety to secure for them the permission of the Emperor Shah Alam to hold the northern sarkars, which they had already been holding through the right of their own might. So, the Marathas too were not a whit behind their rivals in trying to make immense capital out of the shadows of the Imperial dignities that still clung to the name of the old Mogul, long after they had firmly grasped the substance of it in their hands. That is why Mahadji made the Emperor confer the titles and powers of a *maharajadhiraj* and Vakil-i-Mutalik of the Emperor on the head of the Maratha confederacy. And now that he had come all his way to Poona after a long and glorious career in the North, homesick and anxious to see his beloved infant-chief grown into a young god, his first step was to invest him with these titles and Imperial powers with great ceremonial pomp.

But while the Maratha Commander was anxious to formally invest the Peshwa with the honours and insignia of a *maharajadhiraj*—the king of kings—which in fact he already was, Nana, the Brahmin minister, led the party that objected to it as derogatory to the Maratha king of Satara. There could be cited several examples of citizens and even officers of an independent kingdom accepting honours and even services at the hands of and under another state and without forswearing or betraying their own state, nay, at times with the explicit motive and purpose of advancing its interests. Even then, not to wound any national susceptibilities in the least Mahadji applied to and of course secured, the permission of the Maharaja of Satara, the Chhatrapati of the Marathas himself, for the investiture. The constitutional difficulty being thus overcome, the grand ceremony was most imposingly celebrated and the dignity and insignia of Vakil-i-Mutalik was formally conferred on the Peshwa as an inalienable *inam* to descend in his family as a hereditary office. The Peshwa could now act in the name of the Emperor, nay, his Commander Mahadji was bestowed with a power even to choose an heir to the Moslem Emperor from amongst his sons. Now the great *farm* prohibiting the massacre of bullocks and cows throughout the Indian Empire was formally read out. The Shindia and Nana Fadanavis, along with other officers of the Peshwa, made presents of congratulations to him. Now the Marathas had empowered themselves with an effective instrument with which they could stab the jealousy of their rivals, whether European or Asiatic, which pretended to look upon the Emperor as the only source of all legal and constitutional powers in India just to spite the Marathas. Even constitutionally, as in fact, the Marathas claimed to be recognised and meant to act in the place of, pertinent to say, the Emperor of India. They were the Commander-in-Chief of the Imperial forces, the Vazir of the Empire, they could nominate the heir to the throne and above all were Vakil-Mutalik and *maharajadhiraj* inalienably and hereditarily.

But, when once the ceremony was over, the vast concourse of people assembled to witness the procession back to the palace, the shouts of the populace, the salvos of cannon, volleys of musketry had produced all the effect that the projector of this state ceremony could possibly have desired. After the procession arrived at the palace and he was invested with the great honours by the Peshwa, Mahadji, the Commander-in-Chief of the Indian Empire, laid aside all pomp and power, advanced along and, picking up the slippers of the Peshwa, lowly spoke: 'Sire! Maharaj! Princes and Potentates, Rajas and Ranas, Moguls and Turks and Rohillas, the Moslems and the Firangees have been vanquished and reduced to obedience to thee—the head of our Hindu Empire. Thy servant has spent the best part of his life ever since thy birth, sword in hand in distant lands in the service of our commonwealth. But, all the honours and emoluments, all the pomp and power that vanquished kingdoms could yield have failed to appease my thirst for the honour of being allowed to sit at thy feet, and, resuming the duties of my ancestors, take charge of these, thy royal slippers. I long more to be addressed by the cherished epithet of a simple 'Patel' and in Maharashtra, than as the Grand Vazir of the Mogul Empire. So, please do relieve me of these mighty cares in distant lands and let me serve thee. Give me leave to serve, even as my ancestors served, as one of thy favoured personal attendants.'

Mahadji was a master of winning phraseology. Savai Madhao Rao, the noble-minded Peshwa, was a youth, goodnatured and frank and not without a trained insight in politics. Mahadji was doubtless attached and devoted to him and soon succeeded in drawing his young chief towards him. Encouraged by this, Mahadji began to aim at the position of being the chief minister of the realm and handle the power which Nana Fadanavis held. As time went on, he openly intervened in some cases against the decision of the minister and catching a favourable opportunity in one of those occasional excursions which the young Peshwa often loved to enjoy along with Mahadji, the latter openly touched the subject. But he was surprised to find the goodnatured Peshwa seriously rejoin, 'Listen, Nana and Mahadji are two hands of my realm—the first is my right hand, the second the left, each best fitted to do its work. Through their united help, the Empire prospers. They can neither be exchanged nor cut off and cast away without fatally disabling me.'

This conversation, in spite of precautions that Mahadji took could not escape the watchful and masterly scrutiny of the intelligence department organised by Nana. The report alarmed Nana, Haripant Phadke and all the ministerial party in Poona. The grand object of their life of uniting all India under the colours of the Hindu Empire of Maharashtra with the Peshwa at their head and preventing all attempts of the confederates to assert their independence seemed to them in danger. That they could not tolerate so long as they lived. But, if it was only a question of their being removed from the position they occupied, then it was their duty to withdraw, dangerous though, they really dreaded such a withdrawal was bound to be in public interest, rather than risk an open civil war. So, Nana hastened to come to an explanation with the young Peshwa and enumerating the services he had rendered to the state and to the person of the Peshwa over since his birth, he lamented the evil effects that would ensue if he allowed himself to be misled by Shindia's ambitious designs which tended towards reducing the Peshwa to a helpless puppet in his hands as the Mogul Emperor had been. Any sudden attempt to introduce so great an innovation in the constitution of the Maratha Confederacy would bring on a civil war, so terrible as to cause for the ruin of the great Empire they had built and furnish an opportunity to the Moslems who, even then were making great preparations at Hyderabad to overwhelm the Hindu power and the English who, of all, were the most capable of realising the ambition of overthrowing the Hindu Empire of Maharashtra. But, if it was only a question of his personal removal from power—if the young Peshwa was anxious only to get rid of Nana, then, moved to tears, the grand old minister said, 'Here is my resignation. If that could save the realm, avoid a civil war and please thee, sire, then accept this and allow me to proceed to Benares and to retire from the world.' The young Madhao Rao was greatly affected. Touched to the quick by this pathetic prayer of his most revered minister, that builder of an Empire, the Peshwa exclaimed, 'What makes you minded thus? Thou hast been, not only a minister, but a guide and friend and philosopher unto me. This realm rests on thy shoulders and would come down in a crash as soon as thou withdrawest.' Nana, his voice vibrating with emotion, said, 'Sire, ever since thy birth, nay, even before thy birth, I have been incurring the hostility of a host of enemies for having been faithful to thy cause and persisting in my dutiful services towards this realm. But, now the services are forgotten, the enemies alone survive.' The generous-minded youth, thrown at this in a transport of grief, forgetting that he was the chief and the other his minister and overpowered by simple human affection, threw his hands round the neck of Nana and sobbed out, 'Forsake me not, nor grieve: thou hast been not a minister only but a veritable father unto me since my infancy. Forgive me if gone astray, I will not permit thee either to resign or to retire. I will not forsake thee.'

Strengthened by these moving assurances of the Peshwa, Nana, Haripant Phadke and other leaders of the ministerial party took Mahadji, too by an equally effective surprise. Mahadji, whatever his personal ambition be, was as devoted as any of his co-workers as to the magnificent Hindu Empire their nation had built and would have been amongst the first to sacrifice his life to prevent any non-Hindu alien from any attempt to dominate or undermine it. Mahadji was not a Raghoba Dada. In spite of his ambition to hold absolutely in his hands the helm of the Maratha realm, he did not mean to embark on a civil war, and so readily undertook to come to an understanding with the ministerial party and abide by the wishes of the Peshwa. When on being confronted all of a sudden by Haripant Phadke and others, he was informed that, whereas he meant to concentrate all ministerial powers in his own hands and whereas the rivalry between themselves was sure to do the greatest harm to the cause of Hindu Empire they so dearly loved, by strengthening the hands of their foes. Nana had decided to lay down that pen which made and unmade kingdoms and voluntarily resigned his powers rather than involve his nation into a disastrous civil war. Mahadji could not but be deeply touched and promised to withdraw all oppositions to Nana and his party. As it happened on several other occasions, so on this one, too, the patriotic and noble national instincts of the Maratha people got better of their selfish proclivities and the two most powerful men once more met as friends. Sitting at the feet of the Peshwa, they swore to forget all that had passed between them and to continue in their respective capacities to serve their common chief and the great national commonwealth that stood for the holy cause of the defence and the propagation of the Hindu faith and Hindu *pad-padashahi*.

The news of this happy event that the giants had shaken hands, that the misunderstanding between the two most prominent leaders of their Empire had disappeared, gladdened Maharashtra from end to end. How great was the relief felt by every lover of the Hindu cause could best be seen in the eloquent letter dispatched by Govind Rao Kale, one of the most talented and patriotic diplomats of Maharashtra, on learning this happy news. He writes to Nana Fadanavis from the capital of the Nizam where he held the position of Political Resident of the Maratha Empire, 'Your letter thrilled me with joy and made me inexpressibly happy. It spoke volumes and gave rise to a flood of thoughts in my mind.' All the country that lies from River Attock to the Indian ocean, is the land of the Hindus—a Hindusthan, and not a Turkistan, the land of the Turks. There had been our frontiers from the times of the Pandavas down to those of Vikramaditya. They held it against all aliens and ruled over it. But, those who succeeded them as rulers turned out so incapable and impotent to wield the sceptre that the Yavanas, the aliens, conquered us and deprived us of our political independence. The descendants of Babar seized the kingdom of Hastinapur, of Delhi and eventually, during the reign of Aurangzeb, we were reduced to such straits that even our religious liberty was denied to us and the wearer of a sacred thread was required to pay a poll-tax and forced to buy and eat impure food.

At this critical time in our history was born the great Shivaji, the founder of an era, the defender of the Hindu faith. He liberated a corner of our land and that afforded protection to our faith. Then came Nanasaheb and Bhausaheb, heroes of pre-eminent prowess, the grandeur of whose greatness shone amongst men as does that of the Sun. Now everything that was lost had been regained by us under the benign, auspicious reign of His Excellency the Peshwa, owing to the astute skill and invincible sword of our Patel—our Mahadji Shindia. But, the wonder is how could all this happen? Success once surely won makes us blind to its marvellous achievements. Had the Mohammedans won any such triumph, volumes of history would have sung its glory. Amongst the Moslems a trifling deed is immediately extolled to the skies. But amongst us Hindus, however magnificent our exploits be, not even a mention is made of them by us. But, in fact, the marvellous has happened. The inaccessible is won. The Moslems openly lament that the kingdom has passed into the hands of the *kafirs*; the *kafir-shahi* has come.

'And really everyone who dared to raise his head against us in Hindusthan, Mahadji smashed him down. Indeed, we have achieved what seemed beyond human achievement to consolidate and put all in order and to enjoy the blessings of sovereignty and empire even as the mighty emperors of old did. Yet much remains to be done. No one in the meanwhile can tell when or where our merit will fail us, or the evil eye of the wicked cause harm. For our achievement is not limited only to the acquisition of territory, merely material rule, but it also means and includes the preservation of the *Vedas* and the *Shashtras* of Hindu civilisation, the propagation of righteousness, the protection of the cows and the Brahmins, of the humble and the good, the conquest of an empire and national suzerainty, the diffusion of fame and far-reaching triumph. The secret of the alchemy that yielded such miraculous results lies in your hand and that of Mahadji. The slight estrangement between you two strengthens the hands of our foes. But, the news of your mutual concord has now set all my misgivings at rest, encompassed as we are by malevolent foes and secret enemies on all sides. Now let these our forces lie encamped in the plains of Lahore and press on towards the frontiers. Let the enemies get bitterly disappointed who expected them to come in collision amongst themselves. I was so restless about it all, but your letter has cleared the mist. Well done, splendid indeed. Now I feel quite at ease.' This one single letter penned with such ease and grace by one of the actors gives a truer expression to the spirit of our history than many a dull volume had done.

But, amidst this clash of great fears and hopes, Mahadaji, to the intense grief of all Maharashtra, was caught by a violent fever and breathed his last in his camp at Wanavadi, near Poona on 12th February, 1794.

As was very natural, this sudden death of the most powerful of the Maratha chiefs and commanders revived the designs of her enemies against her power and made them eager to attack her before she recovered her strength again after this blow, which they fondly fancied to be a dreadful one. Amongst these enemies, the Nizam of Hyderabad had of late been making great preparations for wreaking a terrible vengeance on that Hindu power which for generations had held him under its thumb and reduced him to be a mere tributary to it. He had increased his force from two regular battalions to 23 regular infantry under the command of a capable French officer. His minister, Mushrulmulk, was an ambitious Moslem who could not tolerate the latest assumption of Imperial prerogative and power by the Marathas under Mahadji's directions. The Moslem population of the state was sedulously whipped into a war fever and kept bragging from bazar to bazar of the day that was soon to come when the standard of the faithful would float over Poona and the *kafirshahi*—the rule of the Hindu—come to an end. The bellicose attitude of the minister of the Nizam grew so daring as to demand, when he was presented with claims for *chowth* by the Political Resident of Maharashtra there, the presence of Nana himself at Hyderabad to explain the claims. 'If,' he continued, 'Nana will not come, I will soon bring him.' As if this insult was not deemed sufficient to excite a war, the Nizam arranged for a royal show to which envoys were deliberately invited and in their presence, made some of his courtiers masquerade the parts of Nana and Savai Madhao Rao—the Peshwa himself—to the great merriment of the Mogul court. Thereupon Govindrao Pingle and Govindrao Kale, the two Maratha envoys at the Nizam's court, got up and entered a strong protest against the insolent treatment meted out to them. 'Listen,' said the spirited Maratha in the end, 'Oh Mushrulmulk! Thou hast more than once assured thyself of thy power to compel Nana, the minister of all Maharashtra, to come to thy court. Thou hast also made thy courtiers exhibit the mask of my master. Here I throw a counter-challenge that I am no Govindrao Kale if thou art not captured, carried away alive by the Marathas and exhibited in person in the streets of the capital of our Hindu Empire.' With these ominous words, the Maratha envoys left the court of the Nizam, retturned to Poona and demanded a war. The English attempt to arrogate to themselves the right of negotiating between the parties was so sternly rebuked that they gave up all thought of dabbling in Maratha affairs, and dared not even to raise a finger in favour of the Nizam in spite of his solicitations. The Nizam had made great preparations for the war. The Moslem element in his state was roused by appeals of their sentiments, till they talked of a holy war against the *kafirs* and secured the sympathies of Moslems from far and near for the undertaking. Poona was to be burnt and looted by the armies of the faithful. These vaunts of the populace were nothing to the vain glorious bombast that Mushrulmulk, their minister, publicly indulged in, when he seriously declared that he was bent on delivering the Moguls once and for all from the tyrannical sway of the Marathas and send their head, the young Brahmin Peshwa, to Benares with but a rag about his loins as a mendicant to beg from door to door.

While the minister at Hyderabad was bragging and boasting to no end, the minister at Poona was coolly calculating his forces and laying down his plans. In spite of the death of the most powerful of their Generals and chiefs, Mahadji Shindia, the Marathas rose equal to the occasion. The genius of Nana never shone so brilliantly, his influence over his people never proved so supreme, as now. His word moved armies from distant capitals of the farflung Maratha Empire. His wisdom rallied the most recalcitrant constituents into a harmonious whole. The great national standard of war was unfurled at Poona and round that hope of Hindu *pad-padashahi* began to muster the armies of Maharashtra from far and near. Daulatrao Shindia, who had succeeded Mahadaji, was summoned there with Jivba Dada Bukshee, the defender of Agra, and others of his Generals and troops that had subdued all North—Pathans, Rohillas, Turks. Tukoji Holkar with his forces was already there. Raghoji Bhosle with a powerful army set out from Nagpur. The Gaikwad led a strong detachment from Baroda to fight in the common cause. Patwardhans and Rastes, Rajebahadur and Vinchurkar, Ghatge and Chavan, Dafle and Pawar, Thorat and Patankar, with several other less conspicuous chiefs and officers and Generals, attended the summons. The Peshwa himself marched out with his armies accompanied by his great minister. This was the first time that the young Peshwa personally accompanied a battle march. This presence of their popular prince inspired the Maratha soldiers most and constituted the chief attraction of this campaign. The Nizam was first in the field. His army was no less than one hundred and ten thousand horses and feet, supported by powerful artillery, brought to an up-to-date efficiency. His forces presented such an imposing display of martial strength and fanatical fervour that the Moguls grew cocksure of the results. The Marathas, in spite of the fact that large bodies of their efficient forces were necessarily held back to guard the frontiers of their Empire, spread out in all parts of India, mustered one hundred and thirty thousand strong. The two grand armies came in touch with each other near the frontiers of the Maratha territory about Paranda. Nana had asked for written opinion from his chief Generals as to the best plan of campaign and chose what he deemed best. He entrusted the post of the generalissimo of all Maratha armies to Parasharam Bhau Patwardhan. As soon as the advanced guards of both the hostile parties came within musket shot, the fight began. In the few first skirmishes, the Pathan force detached parties of the Marathas to fall back and Parsharam Bhau, happening to be in one of these on a reconnoitering expedition, the affair was magnified in the Mogul camp into so big a success as to be celebrated by a public congratulatory Durbar. But, the Nizam soon found out his mistake when the main body of the Maratha forces came to close quarters. Ahmed Ali Khan, with 50,000 picked force met the Marathas and charged them with great vehemence. The Maratha division belonging to Bhosle's forces received them with a terrible discharge of rockets. Soon the batteries of Shindia opened a dreadful side fire. The fight was furious, but caught between the Maratha fires, the Mohammedans, in spite of the exhorting shouts of Allah-o-Akbar, could not hold their ground. They broke and their cavalry was utterly routed. The Marathas advanced and closed them in to complete their discomfiture. The Nizam too got alarmed out of his wits, withdrew from the field and could only find shelter behind the darkness of the approaching night. Irregular fight continued all the night, causing so great a havoc and confusion in the Mogul army that the forces of the faithful, in spite of the stimulating assurance of frothy Maulavis of their being engaged in a holy war, did not desist from plundering their own camp and take to heels as fast as they could. But, the Maratha camp-followers were on their track and soon eased them of all that ill-gotten booty. The morning revealed the Nizam taking up a new position behind the fortifications of a village fort at Kharda and his army, numbering some ten thousand men, posted round in battle array. The Marathas thereupon brought forth their cannon, and from every hill and hillock in the vicinity a dreadful fire opened. Two days the Mogul bore it all. Not only his beard, but even his moral courage got literally scorched by the batteries of Maharashtra. At last, on the third day, parched with thirst, smothered and throttled, the enemy asked for cessation of arms. The Maratha answer was: 'Mushrulmulk first and then the talk of anything else. He must make amends for the gross and cowardly insults he so wantonly flung at the Maratha envoy, nay at the minister of all Maharashtra.' Crestfallen, the Moslem handed over his faithful minister, Mushrulmulk to the Marathas and signified his wish to sign any terms the Marathas dictated. All the territory lying between the Paranda and Tapti was handed over to the Marathas, besides 3 crores of rupees as the arrears of *chowth* and indemnity of war in addition to 29 lakhs to be separately paid out to Bhosle. On these conditions, the Marathas allowed the man to go back alive to his capital as one who came out to burn and loot Poona and send the Peshwa to Benares to beg from door to door.

Mushrulmulk was escorted to the Maratha camp through rows of the victorious *'kafirs'*. As he passed a captive through the camp, the rank and file raised uncontrollable shouts of victory of 'Har! Har Mahadev'. They had caught him, the person who had bragged of capturing Nana. They had kept the promise of their envoy, but after having done this, the noble-minded minister and the amicable Peshwa of Maharashtra treated their fallen foe with distinction and having proved that they could have exhibited him in person from door to door in Poona, spared him any further humiliation. Nana forgave as the Marathas were prone to do after having proved that they possessed the power to punish.

The Peshwa with all his officers entered the capital of Maharashtra in a great triumphal procession. Great multitudes from far and near poured into the capital to offer a national welcome back to their warriors and their beloved young Peshwa. Poona was gaily decorated and accorded the grandest and heartiest reception to her victorious sons.

The ladies lined the balconies and galleries and terraces of the princely mansions of (the richest capital of Hindusthan and showered flowers and the auspicious *'lahyas'* on the warriors, commanders, statesmen and the Peshwa as the procession passed by. Young maidens and damsels stood waiting in front of their doors and loyally waved their little lights about the noble person of their youthful prince. He proceeded towards his palace, receiving Imperial salutes from his devoted people. Many of the most distinguished Commanders and chiefs of the Empire lay encamped with their vast and victorious armies for miles and miles round their national capital and presented to the world such a bold and united and conquering front as to make all recall the palmiest days of the magnificent Hindu Empire when the great Nanasaheb ruled and the heroic Bhau led its forces.

Let us leave them there for a while; the young fortunate and happy prince to enjoy the devoted popularity of his people; the grand mighty minister busy now in distributing the splendid acquisitions of the conquest amongst the constituents of the commonwealth, in settling the different claims and complaints and various questions of policy and in consulting with envoys, Viceroys and Commanders, as to the future activities and undertaking of the Confederacy for the maintenance and extension of the magnificent Hindu Empire they had built; the people of Maharashtra to enjoy the national triumph they had so deservedly earned: the bards and the minstrels to compose and sing to stirring tunes the glories of their sires and the no less glorious and mighty deeds of their sons in accents which even today draw tears of joy and set nerves tingling with heroic emotions whenever listened to: the veteran standing erect amidst admiring groups of villagers and citizens in public places, slowly twisting his mustaches and he listened to the recitals of the fresh ballads telling the story of Kharda to eager crowds at the mention of his personal or regimental exploits; the peasant proprietor singing happy songs over his plough, confident that no harm could come to him or the fruits of his labour as long as Nana ruled at Poona; temples proudly raising their fearless heads to which devotees in their thousands brought their offerings and conducted their worship as freely and as variously as they chose; the pilgrim and the *sannyasin* and the saint and the philosopher from Hardwar to Rameshwar to think or to pray as pleased him best—Carrying and diffusing to broadcast the highest moral precepts as he passed through the land: the savant and the scholar carrying on their studies in flourishing colleges and monasteries relieved from all cares of the necessaries of life through the liberality of the rich chiefs who spent millions in encouraging ancient learning and *Shastras*; the sailor and the soldier each relating his deeds of valour by land and by sea to his young sweetheart or doting mother, displaying his share of booty carried home from the hostile camps or ships in pearls and in gold to substantiate his tale: the capital, the town, the village— Let us leave the whole nation to enjoy the fruits of independence and national greatness which the labour of generations of their sires have so deservedly won. Imagination itself loves to linger on that pinnacle of glory, although it knows that it must be but for a while and although it is prepared to face the abrupt fall, which is soon to be the fate of this great Hindu Empire: let it rejoice over it while it lasts.

In the meanwhile, let us review this sketch which we have so summarily drawn of the modern history of Maharashtra with a view to appraise, correlate and fit it in the long and noble history of Hindusthan, of which it forms an organic and important chapter.

□

A SYNTHETIC REVIEW

'Go, Freedom, whose smiles we shall never resign.
Go, tell the invaders, the Danes,
'Tis sweeter to bleed for an age at thy shrine
Than to sleep but a minute in chains.'

—Thomas Moore

The Ideal:
An All-India Hindu Empire under the Hegemony of Maharashtra

स्वामी हिंदुराज्यकार्यधुरंधरः राज्याभिवृद्धक्तें तुम्हां लोकांचे आंगे-जणीने पावले। संपूर्ण हिंदुस्तान निरुपद्रवी राहे तें, संपूर्ण देशदुर्ग हस्तवश्य करून वाराणशीस जाऊन, श्रीविश्वेश्वरस्थापना करितात॥

—रामचंद्रपंत अमात्य

Our motive in undertaking the review of Maratha history was to bring out prominently from a general confusion of details those events which, when cogently arranged, were most likely to enable us better to appraise and appreciate the value of the modern history of Maharashtra from a pan-Hindu point of view and to correlate and fit it in a comprehensive whole—the history of the Hindu nation itself—of which the first forms but a chapter, however glorious and momentous in itself it be. Therefore, it was necessary to narrate as briefly as possible the story of the Maratha movement and to ascertain the source, the spring, the motive power that propelled a whole people like that to struggle and strive and sacrifice, till they built a mighty Hindu Empire. As the first part of this history is better known outside Maharashtra and even better appreciated than the latter one, which roughly may be taken to open from the rise of Balaji Vishwanath and the formation of the Confederacy and as scholars, like Ranade, had already done justice to the period it covered by presenting the activities of Shivaji's and Rajaram's generations in their true aspect, we have but very cursorily referred to a few events in that period and dealt in our sketch more fully—though not at all exhaustively—with the second part of Maratha history, since it ceased to be Maratha History proper and assumed such magnitude as to cover and get essentially identified with Indian history itself.

In reviewing the story from a pan-Hindu standpoint and in our effort to ascertain the principles that animated it, from generation to generation, we have, so far as necessary, tried to let the actors and thinkers who led that movement to speak for themselves and their motives. Although these mighty generations were so absorbed in solid deeds, breathlessly busy at the hammer and anvil, forging the destiny of a nation, as to be very laconic in words and although their deeds spoke their message more eloquently than mere words could do, yet even their words, few though they be, sounded as mighty and expressive as their deeds. With the help of these together, we tried to prove that the main theme of that great epic, the burden of that mighty song, the great ideal which animated the whole movement and inspired the generations, not only of Shivaji and Ramdas, but essentially even those that followed them to a monumental national achievement, was the liberation of Hindudom from the political and religious shackles of non-Hindu alien domination; and the establishment of a powerful Hindu Empire that should serve as a bulwark and an unassailable tower of strength to the Hindu civilisation and the Hindu faith against the attempts of alien aggression of fanatical fury. From the *swadharma-rajya*, dreamt of by Shivaji, the 'Hindavi *swaraja*' which, at the very outset of this sketch—the great Shivaji assured his comrades to be his devoted goal, down to the Hindu *pad-padashahi* of Bajirao and the triumphant assertion of the talented envoy Govindrao Kale in 1795—'It is a land of the Hindus and not a land of the Turks'—we find this noble conception, this living ideal of a Hindu Empire dedicated to the service of the *deva* and Dharma, of righteousness and god, throbbing and pulsating throughout the mighty movement. The fundamental principle of liberty, spreading out its eagle wings of *swadharma* and *swarajya*, sits hatching and brooding over a century and a mighty people sprang up into existence to act out its will.

People, not a man or two, not even a generation, but a nation, and this is the second and most important fact that our sketch convincingly reveals and which we wish to impress on the minds of our non-Maratha readers. Although this War of Hindu Liberation was initiated by the generation of Shivaji and Ramdas, yet it did not cease with them, but was carried on to its logical and triumphant termination by the generations that followed them. The theme of the great national epic evolves, as we proceed, in heroic magnificence and vastness of effects as great characters—men and women, statesmen and warriors, diplomats and heroes, kings and king-makers, swordsmen and penmen—pass crowding in thousands and tens of thousands and the action thickens on the ever widening stage of centuries, all concentrated round the one Jari Patka, the golden *geruwa*, the standard of Hindudom.

This fact, considered along with the peculiar political organisation into which the Maratha state soon instinctively got itself transformed as a national confederacy, owning a national commonwealth, convinces us that the Maratha movement was not only a non-personal and national movement, but a great advance towards the evolution of political thought and practice in Indian life. For, in the modern history of India, there is no example on such a vast scale as wherein a confederated nation succeeded in rearing up and maintaining so long an Empire which, to all intents and purposes, was a real commonwealth and a national commonwealth in which the principle of personal rule was so little in evidence and the theory and practice of a national commonwealth so effectively inspired the actors with oneness of life and interests and all constituents had duties, responsibilities, rights so well marked as the Maratha Confederacy. People who are trained to confederated national rule can step on to a Republican United States more easily and efficiently than those accustomed to a rule, personal in theory and practice. The second example of a confederated national state, in our modern history, was that of our Sikhs; but it was on a relatively much smaller scale, was more informal and could not last so well and so long. But, as that too was inspired by principles and ideals similarly patriotic and noble, it deserves an honourable mention as another important example of a confederated Hindu power.

But, in emphasising this national and pan-Hindu feature of the Maratha movement, facts as revealed by our sketch would not justify us in assuming that, therefore, all the actors, at all times, were inspired in their actions by public good or pan-Hindu interests alone. Civil feuds and civil wars were constantly going on side by side with the noble activities of the nation in defence and propagation of the Hindu cause. The fact is that, as the Marathas were Hindus first and Marathas afterwards, they, therefore, naturally shared to some extent the essential virtues and vices, the strength and the weakness of the general and particular temperament of the race they belonged to. At the time of the first inroads of the Mohammedans, the fierce unity of faith, that social cohesion and valorous fervour which made them as a body so irresistible, were qualities in which the Hindu proved woefully wanting. This is not a place to discuss relative weakness and strength of the parties as they stood in the days of, say Prithviraj and Muhammad Ghori, but still it must be clearly mentioned that in whatever manner the absolute merits or demerits of a militant church be judged from the point of view of expansion of political and religious conquests, the community that is out for the propagation of their faith and is taught in the fierce doctrines of believing other religions as passports to hell and all efforts to root out these satanic strongholds by force or fraud as highly meritorious is, other things equal, better fitted to fight and vanquish its opponents and rule over them when opposed to a community which belongs not to a militant church at all, condemns the use of force, nay going further, would not like to receive back into its fold even those who were forcibly carried away from its bosom, which prizes individual worship more than a public one and, thus, develops no organ nor organisation for a common defence of their faith as a church and which, lacking thus in the cohesion and the public strength that it engenders, fails to replace it by any other principle like love for the common motherland or, common race, or a common kingdom, or a state powerful enough to wield them all into an organic whole and render them dedicated to its defence and glory with as fierce a fervour as their opponents put forth. The Mohammedans, when they came, found a source of irresistible strength in the principle of theocratic unity, indissolubly wedded to a sense of duty to reduce all the world to a sense of obedience to a theocracy, an Empire under the direct supervision of god. The Hindus wedded to individual liberty and philosophic views of life and the ultimate cause of causes, fallen a prey to the most decentralising and disabling institutions and superstitions, such as the one that prevented them from crossing their frontiers and, thus, threw them always on the defensive and whose political organisations were more personal than patriotic, had naturally, from a national point of view, degenerated into congeries of small states, bound together, but very loosely by a sense of a common civilisation, were more conscious of the differences that divided them provincially, sectionally and religiously, than of the factors that bound them and marked them out as one people. So in spite of some frantic attempts to unite under a Hindu banner, they fell one by one before the first assault of fanatical fury and valorous greed. As an individual to an individual, the Hindu was as valorous and devoted to his faith as a Moslem. But, community to a community, people to a people, the Mohammedans were fiercely united by a theocratic patriotism that invited them to do or die under the banner of their god and invested every effort to spread their political rule over the unbelievers with the sanctity of a holy war. But, as years and even centuries rolled by, the Hindus too learnt the bitter lesson and under the pressure of a common danger, became more conscious of those ties that united them as a people and marked them out as a nation than the factors that divided them. They too began to feel as Hindus first and everything else afterwards and sadly realised the weakness that had crept into their national life by an inherent tendency to isolate thought and action, a general lack community feeling and pride and national sympathy. Slowly, they absorbed much that contributed to the success of the Mohammedans. A pan-Hindu movement was set on foot and struggle for political independence and founding of a great Hindu Empire was carried on. Studying all these movements and the political situation of the Hindu world as it existed then, one cannot help coming to the conclusion that Maharashtra alone was fitted to take the lead in the war of Hindu liberation and carry it to success. That was what Ramdas asserted when, on his return from an all-India tour, he painfully and yet hopefully, declared, 'Throughout this Hindusthan, there was no Hindu left so powerful and so willing as to deliver this land and this nation from the political bondage of the Moslems—only some hope could still be cherished of Maharashtra alone.' With this conviction, he and his school made it a point to first consolidate Maharashtra herself and then lead on their forces in a holy war for winning the independence of all Hindusthan and deliver their *rajya* and *Dharma*, the Hindu temple and Hindu throne, from the foreign yoke by subduing all India to a consolidated and powerful Maratha Empire which, being dedicated to the Hindu cause, would serve as a defender of the Hindu faith and a champion of the Hindu race. But, in this attempt, they could not and would not have eradicated at a stroke the denationalising tendencies of the Hindu race entirely either in Maharashtra or, of course, in Hindusthan. All that they could do was to eradicate them to such an extent as to enable the patriotic impulses of the Hindus of Maharashtra on the whole to hold in check the lower instincts of the people that goaded them on to self-aggrandisement or to sacrifice their national and pan-Hindu interests to their parochial private ends. That is why, we find civil strife breaking every now and then in Maratha history but, on the whole, the nation as such at many a critical point succeeded in enabling their national pan-Hindu and patriotic instincts to have the better of their degrading tendencies and hold them in check if not eradicate them altogether. This pan-Hindu spirit, this longing and capacity to deliver all Hindudom from the bondage of the foreign and unbelieving races, this patriotic fervour that could hold in check the lower selfish and individualistic tendencies of their nature or make them subserve the cause of their nation and their faith which the Marathas rapidly developed and displayed, rendered them decidedly superior in all national qualities to the Mohammedans and pre-eminently fitted them amongst all other Hindu people to rear up and sustain a mighty Hindu Empire which, for the very reasons above indicated, could not but be a Maharashtra Empire.

For the Hindu *pad-padashahi,* which so indubitably inspired the efforts of the Maratha nation, had to be realisable at all under the circumstances, necessarily to be a Maharashtra-*padashahi* too. The Hindus could not have risen to be a great power and able to repulse the formidable attacks of all the haters of the Hindu cause and maintain their independence unless they got themselves consolidated into a strong and enduring Empire, a Hindu *pad-padashahi*. And there was, under the circumstances, no centre, no pivot, no mighty lever that could be used as an instrument in this gigantic task of uplifting the Hindu race from the political servitude into which they had sunk, other than the people of Maharashtra. In spite of the fact that they, too, though far more patriotic and public-spirited than the Mohammedans and far more united and politically willing and capable to fight the War of Hindu Independence than all other sections of their countrymen and co-religionists, still fell far short of ideal patriotism and public virtues, say, relatively to the English who, therefore, beat them in the long run.

In spite of this fact, the Marathas were right in insisting on keeping the strings of the Hindu movement in their own hands and in assuming themselves the insignia and office of a Hindu *pad-padashahi*. They dared first, succeeded so well, sacrificed so much and judging from the circumstances under which they stood, were naturally justified in aiming to consolidate all Hindusthan under their standard, in brining all the scattered rays of Hindu strength into a focus and by subordinating all the Hindu principalities of their sceptre. They took upon themselves the responsibility of championing the Hindu cause. They must be held justified in doing so from a pan-Hindu point, for as our sketch would show, they proved themselves capable of championing it effectively against all hostile attacks. Of course, had any other section of our Hindu people dared first and achieved results so mighty and then called upon Maharashtra to pay homage to it and forced her into subordination to their Hindu Empire, they would have, from a pan-Hindu point, been equally justified. It mattered little whether the Hindu Empire, the Hindu *pad padashahi*, was a Rajput-*padashahi* or a Sikh or a Tamil or a Bengali or even a Kolarian one; it would have been entitled to equal honour and gratitude from us all so long as it championed the cause of Hindudom so well and so effectively by welding all our people into a grand Hindu Empire even though controlled and led by its own province or caste or community.

□

The Best Solution under the Circumstances

—Ramdass

But, could it not have been more patriotic of the Marathas if they had been able to find out a better way to found a Hindu Empire by persuading all other Hindus, rather than coercing them to form a commonwealth, a true commonwealth into which the Marathas, the Bengalis, the Punjabis, the Brahmins and the Mahars, all ceased to be as such and remained only Hindus? Surely, it would have immensely more patriotic. But, had the Hindus been capable of being welded into such a political unity at a stroke, the Mohammedans would not have been able to cross the Indus at all. We must take the facts as they are and judge people in the light of their environment. No nation, any more than an individual, can rise entirely above their environment or can help breathing the general atmosphere of their times. If any claim is made to an ideal excellence and perfection of the Hindu movement as led by the Marathas, this absolute supposition would be perhaps a fit rejoinder. But, it would be a travesty of truth to put forward any such claim. The Marathas were men living amongst men, not angels living amongst angels. Therefore, we have said they shared to some extent the political weaknesses common to all other Hindus and could not find a more patriotic way to compass their ends. Nor could any other Hindu section do it. Nay, none could do it even so well as the Marathas did. Secondly, to persuade others to a better mood depends as much on the skill of the person who persuades, as on the honesty of the purpose or moral sensitiveness of the person to be persuaded. Even had the Marathas taken only to persuasion, would others have allowed themselves to be persuaded to lose voluntarily their individual existences as principalities and kingdoms, in the name of Hindu *pad-padashahi*, in which all equally shared the rights and responsibilities? Where was this patriotic impulse to come from? Amongst those Hindus whose petty thrones were often soaked in the blood of civil feuds before they could ascend them, who freely invited the Moslems and English to decide their civil wars and would rather bow down to the Mogul, who trampled upon their *Vedas* and broke their images than to their brothers? It is foolish to expect a people at this stage of political level and national integrity to rise at a bound to the height of political thought and feeling and practice, which is implied in such absolute supposition as that and to blame only one amongst them for not doing that which none else of his generation could even conceive the probability of doing and especially the performance of which depended at least as much on others as on that one, is not only unjust but even absurd. If the question of the blame of the failure of devising such an ideal and an etymologically precise Hindu Empire is to be discussed at all, then it must be primarily shared by all Hindus alike and secondly, more by those who could not succeed in contributing even so much to the realisation of a Hindu *pad-padashahi* and smashing down the fetters of the foreign and fanatical tyrants as the Marathas did.

And still as it is, efforts to persuade other Hindu brethren to join hands in the great task of building up a Hindu power were not altogether wanting, nor were noble responses wanting from some of the noblest of our Rajputs, Bundelas, Jats and other northern and southern Hindu comrades to such appeals. The sketch teems with such instances and having once collected and related these, all important details bearing out our general remarks in this section, we will not tire out our readers by needlessly quoting them over and over again.

Sufficient time and progress of political thought and training all round amongst the Hindus would have certainly, at least conceivably, brought about an expansion of the Marathas Confederacy into such a pan-Hindu state, or even a Hindu Republic. As their Empire extended, the Maratha Confederacy had shown every sign of being so progressively elastic as to include under its fold several non-Maratha Hindu states, small and great, from the Deccan and the North, and assign to them a definite place in the Imperial organisation with common rights and responsibilities in their Commonwealth; their attempts were often directed to invite the other Hindu states, too, to join hands with them on confederate basis, to form a great Hindu commonwealth. In fact, by the time of the death of Nana Fadanavis in 1800, almost all India was recovered by the Hindus and was held from Nepal to Travancore by Hindu princes more or less held together, controlled and often led by the Maratha Confederacy. Had not a nation, so indisputably superior in national and patriotic virtues and skill and strength even to the Marathas and, of course, to other Indian sections as England was, come on the scene at a very inconvenient time, the Hindu Empire of Maharashtra that had well nigh become the Hindu Empire of Hindusthan would have, with the great assimilative and expansive power they ever displayed, probably altogether ceased to be provincial and evolved into an organic and well-consolidated United Hindu States or Indian Empire. As the Hindus, especially the Marathas and the Sikhs had to the Hindus suffered at the hands of the Mohammedans and succeeded in reforming and recasting their people and their nation so as to render all the peculiar weapons of the Moslems blunt against their armour, even so they would have soon assimilated all that was best in their European antagonists and even as Japan did rehabilitate their Empire in such ways as to beat back all European encroachments. The very fact that the Marathas had already detected one of the most important factors that contributed to the success of the Europeans and had nearly mastered the art of military drill and discipline as introduced by them and proved themselves quite capable of wielding those new weapons and even in manufacturing them as efficiently under such able leaders as Mahadaji Shindia, Bakshi and others, proves that the Maratha Confederacy that had already nearly grown into a Hindu Empire, was quite likely to expand and assimilate all that was best in the Europeans, beat them even as they did the Moslems and evolve into a United States of India, or more likely into a Hindu Empire based on confederated Hindu states, as the German Empire had been on German principalities.

But, as it is, we must leave all this speculation aside and deal with solid facts as revealed by history and try to appraise and apprèciate them by the standards of their time and the possibilities of their environments. Judged from this historical standard, we cannot blame any section of the Hindus, particularly for their failure to have established a Hindu republic at a bound and least of all blame the Marathas any more than we can blame Shivaji for not riding a motor car or Jaisingh for his failure to introduce a state press to carry on a pan-Hindu propaganda. Such a speculative blame must, if at all, be shared by all or by none. Taking into consideration, then, only the relative merits of the case, one realises that the Hindus as such were yet far from developing a pan-Hindu sense so intensely as to render them willing to sacrifice their individual, parochial or provincial existence altogether and entirely to the Hindu cause. Bearing also in mind the fact that the Marathas themselves, in spite of the relatively more consolidated public life and more intense national spirit that they developed as a people and in spite of their being passionately devoted and dedicated to the great and holy cause of delivering the Hindu race and the Hindu faith from the political bondage of alien fanaticism, were naturally far from nationalistic or pan-Hindavi perfection though steadily and even rapidly progressing towards it; and finding, after a careful analysis of the relative strength of the different Hindu states or people of entire Hindusthan, that of all the scattered centres of Hindu life the only nucleus round which the forces of Hindu revival could rally and offer resistance to the mighty foreign foes with some chance of success was to be discovered in Maharashtra alone. We cannot, even from the pan-Hindu point of view, help justifying the tenets and efforts of Ramdas and Shivaji's generation to rally all Maharashtra under the banner of Hindu faith to create first a Maratha kingdom, strong and independent, to serve as a basis, as a powerful lever for the uplift of the Hindu race and then to extend the War of Hindu Liberation beyond the frontiers of Maharashtra, beyond the Narmada to Attock in the North and beyond the Tungabhadra to the seas in the South, and consolidating all the scattered centres of Hindu strength, as they advanced in extending the frontiers of the Maharashtra kingdom, to get it ultimately identified with the Indian Empire itself as the most efficient and practical way of achieving the liberation of all Hindudom and of establishing a Hindu *pad-padashahi*.

Proceeding on this design, the only one that, under these circumstances, had some chance of success and one which now stands vindicated by events and the results achieved, it was inevitable that at times the Marathas had to encounter bitter opposition from some of the Hindu people and states. Of these, some had grown so callous and insensible to the fetters they wore—fetters riveted by Moslem power—that they actually prided themselves on them. They would not mind calling themselves dependents and tributaries, subjects or even slaves of the Moslem, of this Nawab or that, of the Nizam, or the big Padashah at Delhi, but would not tolerate any proposal on the part of the Marathas to pay fealty to the Hindu Empire that stood before their eyes, warring for the rights and honour of the Hindu race. They had to thank but themselves for the chastisement they received at the hands of the Maratha horsemen who naturally looked upon them as allied to the Moslem, and did not cease teasing them, till they were coerced into acknowledging the sovereignty of the Hindu Empire of Maharashtra, or till their Moslem ruler became a tributary to it. Some of those of our brethren who opposed the Marathas were not so dead to appeals of the pan-Hindu movement, but, were as anxious as the Marathas themselves to root out the alien and recover the lost independence of the Hindus. However, they could not understand why the Marathas alone should arrogate to themselves the right of leading this war of Hindu liberation and insist on the submission of all other Hindus to their Empire. Why should not they themselves, some of the non-Maratha Hindu princes and people, urged to try to get themselves acknowledged as the paramount Hindu power in India? The ancestors of a few of them were amongst those who championed the cause of Hindudom in the worst days that ever befell their nation. The decline of the Mogul Empire invited them all equally to carve out a Hindu kingdom, great in proportion to the abilities of each. The Marathas were trying to carve out one for themselves. Why should they not try to do the same? Their claim was just, nor was the claim of the Marathas unjust. From a pan-Hindu point of view every one of them had equal right, nay, owed even a duty to strike the Moslem as best as he could and, failing to found a powerful one and an invincible Hindu Empire, at least try to carve out as many Hindu kingdoms, small or great, as possible. But, when the question of consolidating them all into one Empire arose, they could not, under those peculiar political environments and at that stage of national and pan-Hindu spirit help coming into conflict with each other, doubt each other's abilities and even suspect each other's sincerity of purpose. The Marathas thought they had proved their right to lead the Hindu Empire by their national valour and splendid results. They, as the people, had doubtlessly achieved, by maintaining and by triumphantly maintaining, an uncompromising struggle against the Moslems and Portuguese and the English and the French and all other enemies of the Hindu cause. But, that was no reason, the others thought, why the Marathas should try to swallow the individual independence of other Hindu states by forcing them when unwilling to pay the blessed *chowth* as a token of their subordination. It was but natural; natural also it was for the Marathas, who had achieved so much, to aspire to achieve more and sincerely believe that in consolidating their power and building up a centralised empire alone, the hope of maintaining the independence and the political and the civil existence of the Hindus as a nation and a faith lay in consolidation. And as consolidation necessarily meant reduction, submission and sacrifice, willing or forced, of all constituents to the dictates and interests of the supreme and sovereign constitution, the highest interests of Hindudom demanded the subordination of all Hindus to the Maratha Empire which, of all other Hindu sections, was the only organised state that could, as in fact it well nigh did, establish and maintain a Hindu *pad-padashahi*. This thought of having championed the cause of the Hindu race and the Hindu Dharma so valorously and having inflicted such severe chastisements on the alien foes, they felt it was their right and they possessed the might too, to lead and not to surrender the mastery of the Hindu Empire they had so bravely built. The others naturally questioned their right even though, and even after, they had realised that they lacked the might to dare and do what the Marathas had done in rearing up so great a Hindu power to repulse the worst attacks of alien assailants. Under these circumstances the only way to decide who deserved to lead the Hindu Empire was a trial of strength, and so now and then a conflict between the Marathas and some Hindu states and people who were themselves trying to carve out Hindu kingdoms and so far were, from a pan-Hindu point of view, to be congratulated on their efforts, became inevitable. All movements for national consolidation and great political unions must need to face this regrettable necessity to an extent inversely proportional to the keenness of the desire for such national cohesion and the intensity of the patriotic fervour that counts no individual sacrifice too great in the furtherance of the national cause. Let us take the cause of the Marathas themselves. The petty Hindu *zimindars*, chiefs and princes, that ruled in subordination and vassalage to the Moslem kings in Maharashtra, were naturally tenacious of their relative freedom and some of them were even cherishing an ambition just like the Bhosles to shake off Moslem fetters and establish themselves as independent Hindu princes. Those who did not like to bestir themselves or to be disturbed even by others out of their slavish ease and canine comforts of bondage, as well as those high-spirited souls who aimed to smash down that bondage for themselves, rose in anger against Shivaji and his brave band and opposed their efforts to rally all the Marathas and establish a untied and powerful Hindu kingdom of Marharashtra. They questioned the sincerity of Shivaji very naturally attributing his constant appeals to the necessity of national consolidation and Hindu unity to the secret ambition of the Bhosles for personal aggrandisement under the cloak of liberating the Hindus and winning the independence of Maharashtra. Some of them pointedly asked why Bhosle should expect subordination from them? Why, if Shivaji's intention was really the establishment of a Hindu Empire, should they not acknowledge them as his superiors which in social status they doubtless were, and crown them as Chhatrapati? The mean and the slavish did not scruple to invite or join the forces of other Moselms themselves in meeting the arrogant challenge of the Hindu upstart. Those who were not so degraded, but doubted honestly either the capacity or the justice of Shivaji's claim to arrogate to himself the leadership of the movement, chose the less objectionable course of fighting out their battles against him themselves. Thus rose the necessity of unsheathing his sword at times against the Hindus themselves, and history cannot but acquit Shivaji of any special blame attaching to him, or, for the matter of that, dare to take away the credit of being the foremost champion of the Hindu race, the defender of the Hindu faith and the builder of the nation and the kingdom of the Maratha people. National interests demanded the reduction of all petty chiefs into a united and national state. If the other Hindu chiefs wanted to do that, well they could have risen in rebellion against the common foe, dared as Shivaji did, achieved what he accomplished, and founded a strong and united Maharashtra kingdom before he rose, rendering it superfluous for him to do it, or even in spite of him, thus, proving their superiority to him as nation builders—and Hindu history would have justified them too, as it now does Shivaji and his associates. But, as all other Maratha chief and persons, whether through their fault or not, failed to do that, they ought to have allowed Shivaji to do it for them and in thrusting on him the responsibilities and the risks of the national movement, they ought to have also relinquished in his favour the right of placing himself at its head and even to get himself crowned as the king of all Maharashtra: who else in national interest should be a King but he who could be a 'King', the Koning, the able man!

What acquits Shivaji of any special responsibility or guilt for facing the inevitable, though regrettable, necessity of at times unsheathing his sword against some of his Maratha brethren themselves or Ranjit Singh for reducing the several Sikh misals and coercing them into submission towards him, acquits the Maratha Confederacy, too, for forcing many a recalcitrant Hindu chief to submission to their Empire. It must again be clearly pointed out that a few of those Hindu chiefs, though not all, cannot also be blamed for their opposition to the Maratha claim of sovereignty. For they too were, taking into consideration the general level of political and pan-Hindu thought, as well as their own ambitions to carve out independent Hindu kingdoms for themselves, naturally and rightly tenacious of their individual independence. But, as the very existence of the Hindus as a race, as a civilisation, as a faith, and as a nation, depended on the establishment of a powerful, consolidated and pan-Hindu Empire, whether it be monarchical or confederate, autocratic or plutocratic, Bengali or Rajputi, Tamilian, or Telugu, but a pan-Hindu and centralised and mighty empire, the Marathas who alone of all Hindu people could vanquish the foes of Hindudom and found and maintain that Empire, must be absolved from any special guilt or responsibility for using at times force against the Hindus themselves. The responsibilities, as we said, must be shared either by all Hindus alike or by none, at any rate not by the Marathas alone. Their fitness to lead the war of Hindu liberation and establish a mighty Hindu Empire gave them the right to expect all other Hindus to forego their individual ambitions and interests and submit and if recalcitrant, to be forced to submit to its suzerainty.

□

Viewed in the Light of Ancient and Modern History

'ज्या प्रकारें वानरांकरवीं लंका घेवविली त्या प्रकारें हे गोष्ट झाली, सर्व कृत्यें इश्वरावतारासारखीं आहेत, जे सेवक हे पराक्रम पाहत आहेत त्यांचे जन्म धन्य आहेत। जे कामास आले त्यांनीं तो हा लोक आणि परलोक साधिला। हे ततुद, हे मर्दुमकीए, या समयांत हे हिंमत, ही गोष्ट मनीहि कल्पवत नाहीं।'

—ब्रह्मेंद्रस्वामींचा पत्रव्यवहार

That is the reason why our ancestors not only justified, but, actually sanctified the institution of *chakravartitva*, of the right of a Hindu conqueror of all other states to hold the reins of sovereignty and wear the crown of all Hindusthan. In spite of many and obvious drawbacks and dangers attendant on it, that institution served as one of the effective means which under those environments our forefathers could find to develop slowly a national organisation that could train all Hindudom into political solidarity and oneness of public life. It always brought forward the best man, the best organisation, the best people best fitted to lead the Hindu nation and forced all mediocrities to restrain their blustering ambitions from aiming beyond their worth to the detriment of national interest and entrusted the defence and the leadership of the realm to the strongest and the best-fitted man his times could produce. It rallied the moral forces of the nation to the side of the most capable and demanded as a national duty submission to him from the incapable, but vainly ambitious, recalcitrant element in the society whose claim to the leadership of the realm rested on no other ground than the dubious one of heredity or sheer malice. Accordingly the centre of the political power of the Hindu shifted from province to province, from Hastinapur to Pataliputra, from Pataliputra to Ujjain, from Ujjain to Pratishthan, from

Pratishthan to Kanouj, and so on, as fitness and public and organised capacity to defend the Hindu Empire against all alien attacks dictated from time to time. Whenever national exigency demanded formation of a strong empire, the moral forces of the Hindu people instinctively rallied round the banner of a Hindu world-conqueror and not only condoned his fighting with and vanquishing all other Hindu rivals to that honour, but actually hailed it as the only test practicable under the circumstances to hit upon the best candidate to whom they could safely entrust the preservation and defence of their land and people. Nor did they look down on those also, who challenged him in the field before they acknowledged his right to suzerainty over them. Harsha could not consolidate his empire in the North, nor Pulkeshin in the South, without forcing into submission their mutual rivals, even if they too were Hindus like them, sometimes their castemen or actually their blood relations. We condemn not these latter, for it was but human, nay in the absence of any other higher motive, even manly, that they did not surrender their individuality for the mere asking of it. But for the matter of that, we surely do not hesitate to acknowledge the grand national services that Harsha and Pulkeshin rendered by succeeding in the establishment of two such great and mighty Hindu Empires imparting solidarity of political thought and life to the Indian people. Nay, later on, when Harsha and Pulkeshin both came to measure their swords against each other, we from the pan-Hindu point of view watch the struggle with parental impartiality and tolerate the sight of this internal fight even as a gymnast or a general tolerate, as necessary evil, the combat between his own disciples or tournament parties with a view to train them and find out the best of them who could safely be trusted to face the hostile camp when and if the time comes. If India and our Hindudom have developed any national instinct, any feeling that we, in spite of all divisions, are a people essentially one, sharing a common blood, a common sacred language, a common polity, philosophy, institutions and thought, it is doubtless chiefly due to these great empires that were fostered by that institution of chakravartitva and which, as they shifted their centres from Ksahmere to Kanouj and Patliputra, to Kanchi and Madura and Kalyan, carried with them, to and fro the different currents of our provincial lives and intermingling fused them all into a mighty national stream. It is for this service that we prize all these ancient empires in our history and reckon both those who were valorously vanquished and those who valorously won Harsha and Pulkeshin are the cherished names of our history and we pride ourselves on the achievements of the empires of the Magadhas or of the Andhras or of the Andhra Bhrtiyas, of the Rashtrakutas or of the Bhojas or of the Pandayas, even though none of them could rise into big Hindu states unless they subjugated some lesser Hindu states to their rule and altogether absorbed others, without waiting to hackle them as to why they failed to find out a better and more patriotic way to such political amalgamation, even when we know that their empires had to subjugate and rise at the cost of those very provinces which we today happen to recognise as our provincially separate localities. The Maratha movement, too, for identical reasons, for having succeeded in rearing up a Hindu Empire, larger and stronger than any of those ancient ones and at the cost of far less amount of civil bloodshed in civil feuds and wars, is entitled to the same amount of respect, admiration and honour from us Hindus, irrespective of our province or creed or caste.

Nay, more, for, as the national urgency that propelled the Maratha movement was far more pressing, the moral justification for a pan-Hindu standard for these efforts and wars and conquests must also be far nobler than a Harsha or a Pulkeshin could claim. It was not a mere zeal or a lust of conquest that made them draw their sword. It was not only the glory of being a *chakravartin* that made them subjugate others to their rule. It was the question of the very existence of the Hindus as a nation—as a faith. The northern bard's tribute 'काशीजी की कला जाती मथुरा मशीद होती, शिवाजी न होत, तो सुनत होत सबकी' is no empty eulogy. Recentness sometimes strips an event of grandeur and hallowedness that, if remote, would have invested it with a sanctified halo. Otherwise the services rendered to the Hindu cause by the Maratha Confederacy are no less important in nature and far more superior in magnitude than those rendered by our ancient Hindu warriors, either in the glorious days of Vikram or of Shalivahan or of Chandragupta himself. Though the empire of Chandragupta was undoubtedly the most glorious and mighty than our post-Pandaviya history records, yet the national danger which it had actually to ward off was far less serious and the means it had at its disposal far more effective than in the case of the Maratha movement. Foreign historians talk glibly of Alexandar's India conquest, but, in fact, it means only the conquest of the Punjab. The centre of Hindu strength at Pataliputra remained unhit though supine. The genius of Chanakya and the strength of Chandragupta forced Nanda to abdicate for his failure to drive Mlechhas out, took upon themselves the Imperial burdens and with resources of this Empire at their command ably drove away the Greeks from the Indian soil. But, compared to this, how difficult was the task the Marathas had to undertake, how gigantic the contrast of the dreadful magnitude of the danger and the poverty of the means they had to face! All India lay trampled under the feet of the Moslem, the Portuguese and several other alien and powerful foes for centuries, all virility and even hope squeezed out of it; demoralisation borns of constant defeats fed itself on the vitals of the nation till it grew into a superstition that the Mogul Emperor was born to rule and possessed a divine right to do so; the sword literally broken, the shield literally torn, and, yet, they rose, yet they fought and yet they won in a contest the like of which the Hindus as a nation were never called upon to confront. The Huns and the Sakas, though they had penetrated further in India than the Greeks had done, yet never rose into such formidable foes and never could subdue all India to their rule. Even when a Toraman or a Rudradaman ruled, the national civilisation, the essence of a national life, was not assailed with such perilous and fatal hostility as Moslem or Portuguese fanaticism did. The valour and the patriotic fervour and sacrifice that defended our land and our nation from the attacks of the Huns and the Sakas were glorious indeed and deeply are we indebted to those of our national heroes and warriors and statesmen who not only freed our land from the hated yoke of the foreigners, but contributed so much to our national solidarity and strength by uniting all Hindudom under the Imperial standard of the Magadhas or the Malavas, under the sceptre of a Chandragupta or Vikramaditya or Shalivahan. Every patriotic Hindu, irrespective of his province or caste, in spite of the fact that the empires they built had necessarily to subdue and subjugate the provinces which he happens to own today as his own, in spite of the fact that perhaps they had to shed the blood of his own ancestors in those internecine wars that their *digvijays* then necessarily implied, every patriotic Hindu, knowing fully well that national interest demanded that these necessary evils must be tolerated as the only price that under those circumstances could secure for our nation the inestimable blessing of independence, of glorious peace, of invincible strength, bows down in reverence at the mention of their names and worships the memory of a Chandragupta, of a Pushyamitra, of a Samudragupta or Yeshodharman, or the illustrious 'grandson of Gautami' for having delivered this land from the political bondage of the Huns and the Sakas. Should not a Hindu bow down in reverence and deep gratitude at the mention of Shivaji and Bajirao, a Bhau, a Ramdas, a Nana, a Jankoji and cherish with feelings of love and national pride the memory of that Empire, which saved our Hindudom from a danger which in magnitude and intensity, was so immensely more threatening than what Chandragupta or Vikrama had to face; a danger that almost spelt death, with the means so hopelessly inferior to what those our ancient heroes had at their disposal and achieved results so glorious that, barring a couple of instances, no ancient empire recorded in our history can claim even to equal?

Even in these days of steam and electricity, even a Mazzini or a Garibaldi found impossible to consolidate all Italy by moral propaganda alone. In spite of their high intentions of effacing all provincial distinctions and fuse all their people into one Italian kingdom, they could not dispense with means of relatively doubtful character. Neopolitans and Romans failed to understand why they should sacrifice their individual independence and identity for a vain cry of united Italy. When the King of Piedmont and other leaders like Garibaldi, Crispi, Cavour and others, all Piedmontese, went on deliberately annexing province after province to the Piedmontese Empire, these provincialists naturally questioned the sincerity of their actions and professions. They did not mind the yoke of Austria or France, so immuned they had grown to it, but, as slaves are generally wont to do, could not tolerate the idea of obeying and acknowledging one of their equals as superior to them, as their master. So, even for the sake of Italian unity, Garibaldi, Victor Emmanuel and others had to fight, not only with the foreigners, but with the Italians themselves. But, history absolves them of any guilt of fratricide and all Italy today including the sons of those very Neopolitans and Romans whom they vanquished in war, takes off her hat in utter reverence and kneels down in gratitude and love at the mention of those makers of Italy. As that very King of Piedmont was later on recognised as the King of Italy, so also time and circumstance favouring, the King of the Marathas was almost destined to be formally crowned as the Emperor of India which in fact he virtually had been. Viswasrao was even reported, by friends and foes alike, to have been proclaimed by Bhau as the Emperor of India. The history of the modern German states and their independence and unification affords a nearer parallel to the probable development of Indian politics in the Maratha period, which approached so near fulfilment into a confederated empire of the Hindu princes with the King of the Marathas as their Emperor. As the Italian kingdom of Piedmont, as the German Empire of Prussia, even so the Hindu Empire of Maharashtra constitutes, in spite of civil feuds, a national and pan-Hindu achievement, for which every Hindu patriot must be grateful, feeling proud of the memory of those who worked and fought and died in its cause.

□

The Means: Maratha Warfare

'आपणांस राखुन गनीम ध्यावा. स्थळास गनिमांचा वेढा पडला तो रोज झुंजुन स्थल जतन करावें, निदान येऊन पडलें तरी परिच्छिन्न वार होऊन लोकीं मरावें। पण सल्ला देऊन, स्थळ देऊन, जीव वाचविला असें सर्वथा न घडावें।'

—राजाज्ञा

'ऐसें अवघेंची उठता। परदळाची। काय ती चिंता।
हरिणें पळती उठतां चित्ता। चहूंकडे॥'

—रामदास

We have said at the outset in our sketch that the new era that the birth of Shivaji introduced into the modern history of our Hindu race, so momentous and so triumphant was doubtless due as much to the great spiritual and national ideal which Shivaji and his spiritual preceptor Ramdas placed before our race, as to the new strategic methods the Marathas introduced into the battlefield. We believe the record of events even as cursorily reviewed by us, has convincingly borne out the proposition that the Maratha warfare was as truly an addition to the science of war as it was in vogue amongst the Indians, as the Maharashtra Dharma was a force animating the dying spirit of the Hindu race. It, of course, suited Shivaji's circumstances best and was perhaps a natural outcome of them. But, even the generations that followed Shivaji found it so peculiarly adapted to their genius and so flexible that they used it with singular effect against their foes, even when they marched at the head of armies, instead of a few bands of revolutionists as Shivaji had to do in the first days of his career. The military tactics of their great leaders were gradually adopted and extended to the movement of larger masses by the succeeding Maratha Generals and, as our sketch shows from page to page, used so effectively as to render it hopeless for their foes to face them and to avoid them. The Maratha cavalry dispersed in all directions in the presence of a superior enemy and observed him from the neighbouring hills or woods. Their opponents generally took the movement as a sign of cowardice and hesitation to face them and kept exultingly marching on till they were lured into a difficult position and sometimes occupied the very ground the Marathas had actually chosen for them. Then, suddenly, the Marathas rallied together, closing their ranks as deftly as they dispersed them, and fell like a thunderbolt on their devoted prey and crushed their foes before they could realise it all. Whenever they chose to fight, they fought with such dogged bravery as to strike terror into the hearts of their foes; the battle that Hambir Rao gave, the battle at the Ghat of Badau and several other actions reveal the valorous tenacity of the Maratha warriors who were rendered as dangerous for the Moslem to face the Marathas in a pitched battle when he chose it as to force him to give battle when he chose it not.

The tactics of war and the theory of sacrifice that inspired them were based on the principle of शक्तीनें मिळतीं राज्यें। युक्तीनें यत्न होतसे—रामदास. Righteous war they worshipped, for without war neither independence nor kingdom could be won. Sacrifice, unstinted valour, even Tanaji-like were their pre-eminent qualities that made them masters of Hindusthan. But, still they placed above valour which, without it, was brutal. Sacrifice was adorable only when it was, directly or remotely, but reasonably, felt to be indispensible for success. Sacrifice that leads not to ultimate success is suicidal and had no place in the tactics of Maratha warfare, कातर्य केवला नीति: शौर्यं श्वापदचेष्टितम् was that theme when Ramdas preached शक्तीयुक्ती मिळतीं जयें ठायीं। तेथें श्रीमंत नांदती. They were always eager to devise much ways as to inflict in the long run more losses on the enemy than they themselves incurred. So, calculating, and yet so reckless when the hour came, when recklessness at the moment meant caution in the long run, the Marathas avoided pitched battles, but once they entered into one, deathless was their opposition.

They first kept hanging and whirling round their foes, ready to cut off solitary foremen or surprise small parties in ambush. If pursued they would disperse. When the pursuers gave up the useless chase, in a minute they were upon them. These tactics they employed on such vast scales when they commanded divisions that, instead of interrupting and dispatching few stragglers, they dispatched or captured whole armies of the enemy. The campaigns of Holkar and Patwardhan against the English in the first Anglo-Maratha war show how successfully the

Marathas extended and adopted the military tactics of their illustrious master down to the days of Nana Fadanavis and Mahadji Shinde.

Another important feature of their warfare was the care they generally took to throw the enemy on the defensive as soon as war broke out. Thus, they would generally be the first to invade, taking good care to cover their country and force the hostile territory to undergo the devastations of war. They would march to and fro avoiding battle, cutting off supplies of food and spreading a general panic in the subjects of the enemy which sooner or later was sure to upset the mental vigour of his soldiers and demoralise them. The consequent disorder ended in cessation of all regular government, in scarcity and famine. While on the one hand they hampered and harassed their foe, they levied heavy contributions of war, freely assessed revenue on their own account and thus forced the enemy to maintain not only his army, but also the army of his opponents. The enemy could never avoid them nor face them. He exclaimed in despair: 'To fight with these Marathas is to battle with the wind, is to strike on water.' The best example of these tactics is Raghoji's campaigns in Bengal. We have shown how year in and year out he harassed the realms of the impudent Moslem ruler of Bengal till he was forced to surrender, hand over Orissa and become tributary to the Hindu power.

This campaign would show that it is not correct to say that although those tactics of devastating enemies' land and realm were justifiable in Shivaji's days; they were doing nothing but plundering in the days of the Peshwas as they could have maintained their armies out of their regular revenue. For, first of all, such a warfare was practised as a recognised weapon of war by all nations alike especially in those days. Moslems, fighting against the Moslems or the Hindus, freely resorted to it. The Portuguese, the English and all other nations, whether in Asia or Europe, deemed it necessary to levy contributions of war on those hostile towns and territories which they succeeded in occupying. Secondly, the Marathas who had to fight simultaneously with several foes, the majority of them aliens, oppressors and aggressors, could not have, and even if they could, should not have maintained vast armies simultaneously engaged in campaigns so far from their base at Poona, as, the Punjab on one side and Arcot on the other, should not have abandoned these tactics, for it was a most effective weapon in their hand which hitting the very sinews of war of their foes brought him to his knees sooner than otherwise.

It is this feature of the system of Maratha warfare which their enemies have often dubbed as loot or reckless plunder. As far as this hackneyed, and at times intested, charge is concerned, apart from the military principle that is deemed as sufficient excuse in a Boer war, in a German war, in the annexations of Dalhousie and the campaigns of Neil in 1857, and which, therefore, one should expect to be an excuse in the war of Hindu liberation, too, especially when Aurangzeb, Tippu and Gulam Khader were to be dealt with—apart from that argument that everything is fair in a war, or without citing the just rule that everything is fair in a righteous war—we need waste no words beyond quoting the reply which the great Shivaji himself gave to his opponents once for all: 'Your Emperor,' wrote he, 'had forced me to keep an army for the defence of my people and my country, that army must be paid by his subjects.' Even the English contemporary writers admit that 'on his way as he goes he gives *kaul* (assurance), promising them that neither he nor his soldiers shall in the least do any wrong to any that obeys him which promise he hitherto kept.' And we may add that similar promises given by the Maratha Generals as a rule were as faithfully kept down to the days of last war with the Nizam which ended in the glorious Maratha victory at Kharda in 1795.

It is true that, in such campaigns, often the Hindu subjects of the enemy suffered. We need not reiterate any more reasons that led to these cruel necessities of war, that under such circumstances rendered it impossible to discriminate minutely, nor at times even advisable to discriminate thus. For, as the Moslems or other hostile people had to pay contribution as indemnity, so also the Hindus, too, who ought to have actively sided with the Marathas and yet remained supine, nay, even hostile to them and would not pay for the national struggle and were, therefore, often made to pay it. It was a war-tax informally levied and collected from all Hindus for the maintenance of those armies of the Hindu Empire to whose valour alone they owed the existence of temples, race and civilisation, and but for whose might they would have probably been converted perforce to Mohammedanism and ceased to be Hindus at all.

Of course, we do not mean to condone any particular excess that at times were committed by the Maratha soldiers here or there. But this also must be borne in mind that they were as nothing to those which were held as pardonable, nay even at times advisable by the Moslems,

Portuguese and other nations with whom the Marathas had to fight. They never forced even the very fanatical Maulvis who were guilty of converting Hindus perforce to non-Hindu faith to embrace Hinduism perforce, when they had the power to do so. They razed no mosques or churches to the ground, when they knew that their temples had been mercilessly pulled down to prove the might of Allah or the Lord—although they could have done so to vindicate the might of Shri Rama or Shri Krishna too. And so far as acts of vandalism and moral outrages were concerned, not even their worst enemies could attribute to them any wholesale butchery, or crimes against the honour of womanhood, or reckless and fanatical persecution, burning of the sacred books of hostile faiths and the like. The levying of war contributions and rendering a country barren of all food and fodder as a necessary military step which went by the name of loot was all that even their enemies could allege against them. But how necessary a weapon it was under the circumstances could best be seen by the fact that the Marathas resorted to it even as regards to themselves when a foreign foe invaded their land. The campaign of Aurangzeb in Rajaram's time and the two attempts of the English to march against Poona failed so ignominiously, chiefly because the Marathas hesitated not to desert, devastate and deprive their own territory of all food and fodder and even threatened to burn down their own capital, if ever the English succeeded in approaching it. That clearly shows that it was no sign of reckless hatred or disregard for the interests of their Hindu brethren in other parts of India, that made them take to the tactics of quartering their troops on the enemies' land and upset all peace and order and government in it, thus, to undermine all his supplies and revenues, and even moral prestige and moral courage. This also continued as long as the war lasted or the demands of the Marathas were not aquiesced in. But as soon as the province was regularly annexed or reduced to be a tributary to their Hindu Empire, their inroads ceased. Where the inhabitants had themselves invited the Marathas to free them from Moslem or European bondage, or at least sympathised with them when they came of themselves to wrest that province from the alien hands, it needs no mention that they treated the inhabitants of that province with as much lenity and love as possible.

Occasional excesses must be condemned. But it must be borne in mind that occasional excesses marked even the return of Garibaldi from Rome, marked every great revolutionary movement from the

French Revolution to the Irish Sein Fein, from the American War of Independence to the War of German Liberation and Imperial Unification. As those excesses and civil feuds do not darken the essential grandeur of those brilliant national movements and render their noble and patriotic message doubtful even so in spite of a few excesses here and there—so few compared to those committed on them by their foes—or inevitable civil feuds, the movement that gathered up the standard of the Hindus from the dust of centuries of slavery and impotence raised it in the teeth of mighty opposition of emperors and kings, of Shahis and Badshahis, and planted it on Attock, forcing those very Shahis and Badshahis to kneel and to pay homage to it—that movement and that Hindu Empire which it ushered into existence did not cease to be entitled to the loving and grateful tribute of every patriotic Hindu heart.

□

The Empire Fosters an All-Round Hindu Revival

शास्त्रेण रक्षिसते राष्ट्रे शास्त्रचिंता प्रवर्तते।

Although the Hindu revival that was signalised by the rise of the Marathas had necessarily to assert itself first in the political and military spheres of Hindu life and create a powerful and national state, which must ever remain the *sine qua non* of a nation's progress in all other departments of life, yet it did not fail to manifest itself in these as soon as the categorical imperative of national political independence was achieved under the aegis of the Maratha power. The Hindu Empire of Maharashtra initiated, patronised, financed and promoted several activities and reforms that were inspired by this revivalist movement amongst the Hindus. Assimilating much that was best in their adversaries, they strove to liberate and free all Hindu life from the grip of the killing overgrowth of the foreign influence. The Hindu languages all over India were well nigh dominated to suffocation by the invasion of Persian and Arabian influences. The state records were generally in Persian. But, the Marathas as soon as they created a Hindu state ordered that state records must cease to be in Persian. Then they tried to purify their language, which, but for their timely efforts, must have by this time succumbed to Arabic or Urdu as ignominiously as for example, the current literary language and even the script of the Punjab and Sind did. But, a national state revived the national language. A learned Pandit was commissioned to compose an authoritative dictionary called *Rajavyavahara-kosha,* wherein were collected and enlisted suitable equivalents to all those alien Moslem words that had monopolised the political records and thoughts of that generation. Public opinion, too, was created and encouraged against the use of alien words. The effect of this campaign on the Maratha language was remarkable. The political letters and despatches show much improvement and at times betoken studied attempts to boycott all alien words. While literature, historical or political, poetical or prose, grew slowly chastened, till we come to the *magnum opus* of Moropant's *Mahabharata,* in which monumental work one would hardly detect a dozen foreign words. The *bakhars,* too, are no mean production. Nay, some of them write a Marathi, which throbs with life and seems inimitable in its vigour and impressive simplicity. Political life made history living and the language of a generation whose time was almost wholly claimed by grand and mighty deeds necessarily leaving little to spare for words, naturally developed a laconic eloquence that remains the despair of our age which has to write history without making it to sing of valorous deeds without the daring abilities and opportunities that can actualise them in life.

Not only Marathi, but even Sanskrit, the sacred language of the Hindus, naturally received a great impetus under the Maratha rule. Ancient learning in all its branches, *Vedas, Vedangas, Shastras, Puranas,* poetry, astronomy and medicine, all branches of Hindu literature revived. The dozen and more capitals, great and small, of the Hindu Empire, scattered all over India, became centres of Hindu learning and patronised Hindu scholars and students, started and maintained colleges and schools in all parts of India. Moral education of the people was not neglected. Saints and *sadhus* could go up and down freely under the protection of the Maratha arms from Rameshwar to Hardwar, from Dwarka to Jagannath, preaching and teaching men and women the best principles of Hindu morals, Hindu philosophy and Hindu traditions. To maintain and help those and do what they wished, the great Kings and Viceroys and Governors and Generals of the Empire vied with each other. Great and organised agencies like the one founded by Ramdas had spread out a regular network of *mathas* and convents throughout India, were financed by the Empire and served as so many centres, not only of religious but also of political propaganda. Besides all this, a yearly assembly of learned men, from all over India, met in every *Shrawan* in Poona under the patronage of the Peshwa himself whose regular examinations were held in all branches of Hindu learning and prizes, degrees and endowments were distributed and conferred on the deserving candidates. No less than a hundred thousand rupees were spent yearly on this occasion alone in encouraging and rewarding Hindu learning. These gatherings served to unite and focus all the divergent currents of Hindu thought and moral forces—help to fuse them into a correlated whole, make them feel that they were, in spite of all divergence in creed and caste, Hindus united under one national banner that had vanquished the foes of Hindudom and floated triumphantly over the Hindu Empire, shielding and championing the cause of their faith their country and their civilisation.

Works of public utility, too, received the special attention of the Peshwas and their vassals. If wealth flowed in tribute from Attock and Rameshwar to Poona, it did neither lie miserly hoarded there, nor was wantonly squandered away in dissolute luxuries but eventually flowed back in most useful channels to *tirthas* and *kshetras* all over the land of Hindusthan. There is no sacred river in India that owns not useful and beautiful *ghats*; no important *ghat* that is not adorned by a spacious *dharmashala* or a towering and graceful temple; no famous temple that is not endowed with a rich donation as *inam* or as allowance and stands not a witness to the generous munificence of the Hindu Empire of Maharashtra. In spite of great and pressing military preoccupations, wars and rumours of wars, the people that inhabited the vast territories which were under the direct rule of that Empire from Jinji and Tanjore to Gwalior and Dwarka to Jagannath, were far more lightly taxed and justly governed, enjoyed more peace and plenty than those under any other Indian state. The roads, the postal systems, the jail administration, the medical relief and departments of public utility, we have ample evidence before us to show, were in better state and more regularly conducted than they were in many other contemporary states. That the people on the whole appreciated the blessings of independence and in spite of occasional disorder not only loved their government, but felt themselves intensely proud of their state and thankfully acknowledged their indebtedness to him for being born in those glorious days, could best be seen by a perusal of first-hand evidence of letters, poems, ballads, *bakhars* and other contemporary literature.

Nor were other far-reaching and liberalising movements altogether wanting. Many a custom or superstition that hampered the political or social progress of the people was either rendered less rigid or altogether got rid of. Notable attempts were made to introduce reformed worship, intermarriages amongst castes, to encourage sea-faring habits, revive naval daring and strength, readmit those who crossed the seas and had visited European shores or went beyond Attock, to effect reconversions of those who had been converted to the alien faith either through force or through fraud by the Christian or the Moslem. As regards the last movement, interesting details have come to light that show that the *shuddhi* movement was anticipated by our ancestors ever since the rise of the Maratha power. The Portuguese records tell us of occasional efforts of leading Brahmins to organise reconversions, when they secretly administered purificatory baths to those whom the Portuguese had forcibly converted and readmitted them into the Hindu fold. On one of such occasions the Portuguese, having scented it suddenly, surrounded the secret assembly and dispersed them at the point of the bayonet, when a Gosavi earned the admiration even of these fanatical foes by his refusal to budge an inch till he was cut down. The case of Nimbalkar—a great Maratha Sardar who was forcibly converted by the King of Vijapur and who subsequently gave his daughter in marriage to the convert, but who, in spite of it all, escaped, joined the Maratha camp, was with the permission of the Pandits purified and taken back to the Hindu fold under the patronising directions of Jijabai, the illustrious mother of Shivaji and, to lay at rest all the misgivings of the orthodox element, was allowed to marry his eldest son to the daughter of Shivaji himself—is now well known. Another notable case is that of Netaji Palkar. That brave Maratha Commander who was respected as a second Shivaji, falling in the hands of the Moguls, was taken to the frontiers and forced to live amongst the ferocious tribesmen under the order of Aurangzeb after being converted to Mohammedanism. But, he somehow found an opportunity to return to Maharashtra and implored his people to allow him to re-embrace Hinduism. The Pandits recommended his case to Shivaji and he too was readmitted into the Hindu religion. The Peshwa continued this policy down to the days of Nana Fadanavis and longer. We have original orders and documents, published in the *Diary of the Peshwas,* to show that several cases used to happen wherein a repentant person or persons forced to take to Mohammedanism or Christianity were taken by the Hindus and their castes were consequently asked to resume all intersocial relations with them as before. For example, one Putaji, a soldier in the army serving in Surat district, fell in the hands of the Moslems and was forcibly converted to Islam. But, when Balaji Bajirao was returning from Delhi, Putaji escaped and joined the Peshwa's camp. All his caste people gathering in a meeting declared their willingness to take him back into their caste and intimated their decision to the Peshwa and were by the issue of a special order allowed to do so (pp. 215-6). Tulaji Bhat Joshi, who was converted not by force but by 'allurements' to Mohammedanism repented of his action, repaired to Paithan and standing as a supplicant before the assembly of Brahmins, admitted his guilt and implored for pardon and permission to re-embrace the Hindu faith. Whereupon the assembly of the Brahmins of Paithan—which was looked upon as a stronghold of orthodoxy—decided to readmit him on the sole ground of honest repentance and dined with him. Consequently, orders were issued by the officer of the government to see that the decision of the Pandits was properly respected and Joshi was invested with all the rights and privileges of his caste. Even the disturbed days of Sambhaji proved no exception to this practice. An interesting order, issued by the authorities under the direction of the King and the Chhatrapati Sambhaji Maharaj, shows us not only that a man named Gangadhar Kulkarni, who was, after being forcibly converted to Mohammedanism readmitted into the Hindu fold but also the details of the purification rites he had to undergo and concludes with an emphatic injunction—perfectly consistent with a well-known verse of Manu, that those who would refuse to resume interdining and other acts of social intercourse with him would be guilty—they would be guilty of betraying the cause of *devas* and Brahmins and would themselves be looked down upon as sinners. We may also mention here in passing the case of Princess Indra Kumari of Jodhpur who, long after her marriage with the Mogul Emperor was readmitted into the Hindu fold by the Rajputs after her return from Delhi.

It was but natural that those who took upon themselves the mission of healing the political wounds that our motherland had so grievously sustained should also try their best to heal the social and religious wounds too, which, in a way, were far more deadly than the political. The movement of Hindu liberation and Hindu revival that had inspired great achievements in the political and military fields was not likely to betray a deadly callousness in feeling and striving to retrieve the deplorable losses that our civilisation, policy and faith had to undergo during the stupendous fight we had to face from century to century. But, still while in less than a hundred years, the Mohammedan rule spread their faith throughout the Deccan to such an extent as to claim hundreds of thousands of Hindu converts to their proselytising swords, how regrettable is it that the Hindus, in spite of the Hindu rule that could conquer and crush Moslem thrones and crowns, could not convert or even reclaim a few hundred Moslems back to Hinduism or even when that proselytising Moslem sword was broken to pieces by their valour and when they could have done so, had they willed it—had they been brought in that tradition. The reason is that although fetters of political slavery can at times be shaken off and smashed, yet the fetters of cultural superstition are often found far more difficult to knock off. In addition to this human characteristic, when we take into consideration the second fact that much of the energy of the people of Maharashtra was necessarily consumed in the first and imperative necessity of achieving and maintaining political independence of their nation and the great Hindu Empire, nay, build in the teeth of such deadly opposition from so many enemies sworn to destroy the political supremacy of the Hindus—we cease to wonder much that they could not spare more of it for such secondary movements—though in themselves of utmost importance—of social reform and *shuddhi*. The real wonder is that they could initiate so revolutionary a movement as *shuddhi* at all and succeed in attacking the centre of old superstition so effectively as to actually change the Hindu mentality and public opinion in favour of readmission of apostates into the Hindu fold and—what is far more difficult to bring about—to reinstate them into their old castes and guilds.

□

A Debt of Love and Gratitude

सौख्य स्मरुनि राज्याचें मीनापरि अखंड तळमळती।

—प्रभाकर

And now let the curtain fall—alas so abruptly—on this our last and, so far as the past history of our race is concerned, one of the foremost of our Hindu Empires.

On the black day on which Dahir, our brave Hindu King of Sind, fell on the Indus, with him fell our fortune too. Trilochanpal, the Hindu King of Kabul, Jaipal and Anangpal of the Punjab, Prithviraj of Delhi, Jaichand of Kanoj, Sang of Chittoor, Laxman Sen of Bengal, Ramdeorao and Haripal of Deogiri, Vijayanagar kings and queens, crowns and coronets, one after another rolled in dust from the Indus to the seas; and the intrepid, the insolent, the irresistible foe stood with his knee firmly planted on the gasping breast of our race. Not only Chittoor, but on a vaster scale and in a less glorious manner, all India was reduced to a monumental heap of ash with but a few cinders of martyrdom glowing out now and then in momentary sparks and with that monumental heap of ash, of the hopes of our race lying at his feet sat Aurangzeb, securely seated on his Imperial peacock throne with a hundred thousand swords ready to flourish out death at the slightest stamp of his angry foot.

Just when 'या सकळ भूमंडळाचिये ठायीं, हिंदु ऐसा उरला नाहीं', a band of Hindu youths gathered in a secret conclave in a little corner, *'eka lahanasha konant'* and by their dead kings and queens, by those fallen crowns and coronets, by that monumental heap of the hopes of their race, swore to rise in revolt against their formidable foe to avenge the wrongs inflicted on their nation and their faith and to vindicate the honour of the Hindu arms and the Hindu flag. The band of youth came out with but a few rusty swords to swear by, 'Absurd' naturally exclaimed the world; 'Pooh!' snorted out Aurangzeb; 'suicidal' warned the wise. Nor were they very much in the wrong. For, Shivaji was not the first to rise in revolt. Many a spirited youth had risen before him and failing, paid the dreadful penalty of a revolt. But, the band still persisted, very warily though, believing that if they too happened to fail and had to pay the dreadful penalty of a revolt, such a revolt that would leave its memory like a seed to germinate in apparent oblivion, should still be more covetable than a lifelong servitude.

Some twenty years pass by; the brow of Aurangzeb is perceptibly sad and his speech low. For that little band of Maratha youth have become the nucleus of a Hindu kingdom, 'Never mind,' said the mighty Mogul. 'I will stamp these *kafirs* out of existence while they are still confined to that wretched little corner.' Soon, with those hundred thousand flashing swords of his, the angry Moslem fell upon that devoted little Hindu kingdom and in his formidable wrath, stamped so mightily on the soil, that gave those wretched rebels birth, that the soil cleft under both his feet. The mighty Moslem tottered. He could neither steady himself nor get out of the yawning, ever widening and deepening gulf. The more furiously he stamped and strove, the deeper he sank, never to rise again. It was only over his grave and on that of those of his hundred thousand flashing swords that the soil of that little corner closed again and by the very steps of that Imperial grave rose that little Hindu kingdom to the heights of a Hindu Emprie.

For, soon the brave bands of Maharashtra came out and led by their *geruwa* banner, the sacred symbol of Hindudom spread far and wide the War of Hindu Liberation. Gujarat they entered; Khandesh they entered; Malwa they entered, Bundelkhand they entered; they crossed the Chambal, they crossed the Godavari, they crossed the Krishna, they crossed the Tungabhadra, they camped at Tanjore, they held Jinji, they held Nagpur, they held Orissa. Step by step, stone on stone, they built, till from the Jamuna to the Tungabhadra and from Dwarka to Jagannath, the whole territory was systematically and entirely freed from the Mohammedan yoke and held and consolidated into a continuous, contiguous and powerful Hindu Empire. Then they crossed the Jumna and the Ganges and the Gandaki; held Patna, the capital of the Guptas, worshipped the Kali at Calcutta and the Vishveshwar at Kashi. They—the descendants of that band which in tens and dozens had met in a secret conclave and sworn by a few rusty swords—their descendants marched no longer in tens but in hundreds of thousands, no longer in secret, but with banners unfurled and bands playing—marched on the very capital of the Moslem Empire and knocked mightily at its gate. The blustering Maulanas and Maulvis, who till then had ever been busy in convincing themselves and forcing others to get convinced of the truth of the Koran by citing the political victories of Islamite arms over the forces of the followers of the *Puranas*, saw to their utter dismay that the Hindus, in spite of their caste and creed, their image worship and beardless chin, knocked down the gates of Delhi and advancing in irresistible might, planted the *geruwa* on all the strongholds of Islam. No Zebrial came to contest the triumph of *Puranas* over Koran, as in days of old the Moslems fancied he was wont to do. No longer could it be said that the victory which attended the arms of the Moslem was one of the most convincing proofs of the truth of the Moslem faith that the dust of the temples bore witness to the falsity of the teaching of the Hindu faith. This argument, so spacious, but, in times of racial panic and national defeat and consequent demoralisation so overwhelming, that it could claim more converts from the Hindu fold to the Moslem faith than all over learned discourses and theological persuasions and proofs could do, was knocked so dreadfully on its head that it could have easily been made to tell quite the contrary tale. The temple towered high above the mosque. The crescent waned and gasped for its life and the sun rose, heating the proud and splendid summits of Hindudom in molten gold. Delhi once more was held and ruled by the descendants of Prithviraj and as Bhau would have it, the Hindus conquered back the kingdom of Hastinapur. Aurangzeb had snorted out, 'Rats'; the rats bearded the lion in his own den and pulled out his claws and teeth one by one; the cows killed the butcher; even as our Guru Govind foretold, the hawks were hacked to pieces by the sparrows.

Thence, their forces bathed at Kurukshetra as warriors do, as martyrs do and carried their triumphant Hindu arms to the walls of Lahore. The Afghans intervened and were driven beyond Attock. There the Maratha soldier drew in the reins, lighted down from his horse and rested a little, while his Generals and leaders at the headquarters were busy laying out their plans of a campaign to cross the Indus which would take their Hindu forces to Kabul and the Hindu Kush. Embassies from the Persians, the English, the Portuguese, the French, from Holland and from Austria, visited Poona and requested that they should be allowed to reside there as ambassadors of their nations at the Imperial Court of Maharashtra. The

Moslem Nawab of Bengal, the Moslem Viceroy of Lucknow, the Moslem Nizam of Hyderdabad, the Moslem Sultan of Mysore, not to mention the chiefs and chieflings from Arcot to Rohilkhand, paid them tribute and *chowth* and *sardeshmukhi* and what not, if but permitted to live. The Nizam was reduced to a revenue collector of the province he held, a bit troublesome, but who somehow was made to pour out from time to time all he used to collect into the Imperial treasury of the Marathas. Nor were the Moslems the only foes they had to encounter. As we have seen, the Shah of Iran and the Shah of Kabul, the Turks and the Moguls, the Rohillas and the Pathans, the Portuguese and the French, the English and the Abyssinians, each and all had challenged their supremacy, had maintained and fought field after field, by land, by sea; but, the forces of the Hindus struck in the name of their *deva* and *desh* and smote all the haters of the Hindu cause, of Hindu Independence, wherever they met them by land or by sea. Rangana, Vishalgad and Chakan; Rajapur, Vengurla and Barsinor; Purandar, Sinhgad, Salher, Oombrani, Sabnoor, Sangamner, Phonda, Wai, Phaltan, Jinji, Satara and Dindori; Palkhed and Petlad; Chiplun, Vijayagad, Shrigaon, Thana, Tarapur and Vasai; Sarangpur, Tiral and Jaitpur; Delhi and Durai; Serai and Bhopal; Arcot and Trichinopoly; Kadarganj; Farukkabad, Udgir, Kunjpura and Panipat; Rakshabhuvan, Unavadi, Motitalao and Dharvad; Shukratal and Nasibgad; Vadgoan and Borghat; Badami, Agra and Kharda; breaches mounted, sieges sustained, trophies captured, navies vanquished, battles won. These are but a few of those fields where their armies and navies won such glorious distinction that each of them would have occasioned, in our ancient history and the history of any other nation, the erection of commemorating columns. The *Haribhaktas* from the birth of Shivaji to the death of Nana Fadanavis literally knew no defeat. As they advanced, they dropped secondary capitals, as large as the metropolises of many a sovereign nation in the world, as carelessly and copiously as you drop coppers from your overflowing pockets. Satara, Nagpur, Kolhapur, Tanjore, Sangli, Miraj, Gunti, Baroda, Dhar, Indore, Jhansi, Gwalior, not to mention a host of lesser ones, were the capitals of provinces and districts as large as kingdoms in Europe. They had freed Haridwar and Kurukshetra, Mathura and Dakore, Abu and Avanti, Parasharam and Prabhas, Nasik and Trimbak, Dwarka and Jagannath, Mallikarjun and Madura, Gokul and Gokarn from the iconoclastic fury of the haters of the Hindu faith. Kashi and Prayag and Rameshwar once more raised their towers and turrets, fearlessly high and 'thanked the Lord that a Hindu Empire yet lived' to avenge their woes—a Hindu Empire that comprised nearly all the territories forming the ancient kingdoms of the celebrated Imperial dynasties of old; of the Maukharis, Chalukyas, Pallavas, Pandyas, Cholas, Keralas, Rashtrakutas, Andhras, Kesaries, Bhojas, Malvas, of Harsh and Pulkeshin, of the Rathods, and Chavans. Its Governors and Commanders ruled at times over territories, as in the case, say, of Mahdaji Shindia, so vast as would have entitled a king to perform an *ashwamedha* in ancient days. Barring the glorious Empire of Chandragupta-I and perhaps of the second Guptas in their palmiest days, no Hindu Empire in our history, written and mythological, could match it in extent or in magnitude or in achievement and so far as national services and sacrifices are concerned almost none was called upon to face to such awful difficulties, dangers and disasters and yet none succeeded, if so magnificently, in surmounting them all.

We feel that in our ancient history, a technical distinction seems to have at times been attached to the words *chakravartin* and Vikrama or Vikramaditya. A king who subdued all Hindu kings and proved his title to the assumption of the dignity of a paramount emperor was *chakravartin*. But he, who was not only as great a conqueror as *chakravartin*, but had won that distinction not only by subduing our countrymen, but by subduing some foreign powers, had liberated our nation or civilisation from some alien domination, was honoured by the special distinction of being designated as Vikramditiya. The first Vikrama is reputed to have driven out the Scythians, the second too, liberated our motherland and our race from the fetters of the Western Sakas. The third, yasho dharma Vikrmaditya, drove away the Huns and killed their king in a great battle. If then this our suspicion be true and the high title and designation of Vikramaditya denoted essentially a warrior, who warred in a righteous and holy cause against the alien foes of our land and our nation, a conqueror who went on a *digvijaya*, not only for the sake of military glory, but for a moral and patriotic duty—national necessity—and saved our people from some imminent and great public danger by conquering the forces of aggressive fanaticism and lust, then those who built this last of our Hindu Empires—last, so far as the past history of our race is concerned—performed deeds no less heroic and sublime in motive and far more glorious in magnitude than many a chakravartin and Vikramaditya of old, are, therefore, entitled to the same respect and love and gratitude that we Hindus cherish and bear towards the celebrated and hallowed names in our ancient history. For, they took up the banner of our race from the dropping hands of our Rajput kings, declared a holy war against all those who hated the Hindu cause and avenged the martyrdom of Dahir and Anangpal, Jaipal and Prithviraj and Harpal and Pratap and Pratapadittya and Chittoor and Vijayanagar which, the genius of Madhavacharya and Sayanacharya and the might of Harihar and Bukka, had built as a temple unto our gods.

They won a gigantic war that continued so fiercely for some six centuries and more and by demonstrating what triumphs the Hindu race, even when partially organised and but half awakened, could achieve, indicated its magnificent potentialities, if ever it rouses itself to fulness of corporate life and effort.

Let us acknowledge then our deep debt of love and gratitude that we all Hindus owe to them and pay the fealty and homage of a grateful people at their feet, even while they sit on the pinnacle of power and glory, and have a last lingering look at them and the great Hindu Empire they have so triumphantly built—for the curtain is soon to fall, alas so abruptly and sharply switch out the magnificent past from the weeping eyes of the present.

□

The Curtain Falls

'... ... ... In his eyes
Was mingled with surprise
The stern joy which warriors feel
In foemen worthy of their steel.'

'हिंमत सोडूं नये सर्व पुन्हा येईल उदयाला'

—प्रभाकर

We have brought our review down to the battle of Kharda, 1795. All our remarks passed in the preceding chapters necessarily refer to this period under review. Ours has never been the intention of recounting and examining all the details of the Maratha movement, but only to bring out those which would enable us better to ascertain the leading motive, the underlying principle, that inspired and informed it and ascertain, in that light, its real place in the history of our Hindu people. That task is done. Yet the period from 1795 to 1818, when the Maratha Empire fell, is too tragic to be passed by without a sigh or a tear.

The Marathas, as we have seen, had but just given a finishing stroke that won the long-lasting war of centuries of Hindu liberation and laid low their ancestral Moslem foe. Exhausted, they fetched a sigh of relief and were just resting a while on their muskets. This was precisely the moment when a new and a far more powerful enemy, in spite of his being twice worsted, entered, the lists again and assailed them with irresistible might.

Even then, they could have won, at any rate repulsed him for the third time, but just then, as fate would have it, Nana died and Bajirao II became the undisputed master of his people and the undisputing slave of their foes. These two men, Nana and Bajirao II, embodied the two antagonistic tendencies that we find in conflict throughout the

Maratha movement—one that inclined towards mean selfishness and denationalising self-aggrandisement; the other to patriotic sacrifices and public disinterestedness that made one glory oneself more in the greatness and independence of one's own nation than in crowns and coronets secured for oneself at their cost. The Marathas, although they could not eradicate it altogether, yet succeeded in holding the meaner instinct in check till the days of Nana and his generation—the result was the great Hindu *pad-padashahi* they built. But now Bajirao-II and by naming him we name his entire generation who typified the meaner instinct—had secured the upper hand and the Empire, without a principle of cohesion to hold it together, could not but totter to its fall assuredly; for just then, as we have seen, it was assailed, not by and Indian or Asiatic power, for in that case the Marathas being still on the whole better organised and more patriotic than any of them would have held their own—but by England; the result of the combat was a foregone conclusion.

For, England was then relatively far better equipped in all those essentials that contributed to great conquests. Their nation had long since passed the period of incubation, civil feuds and Wars of the Roses and religious persecution and star chamber tyrannies. Unlike the Marathas, they had long been trained into all those public virtues of how to obey and order and of how to rule and submit, of patriotic loyalty to their country and their King—the national emblem of sovereignty—and above all, racial cohesion and solidarity of aim and aspiration and loving subjection which a strongly consolidated nation, state engenders in a people. Even the Marathas—who of all Indian people were best fitted in all these qualities—were woefully lacking in them relatively to the English.

Still single-handed they stood, they found even frantically, knowing later on fully well that it was a struggle for existence. Some, even like that last great patriot-Maratha, Bapu Gokhale determined not to surrender even when despair and death stared them in the face. 'We may be,' said he to an English officer, 'we may be carrying our shrouds about our heads, but we are determined to die with our swords in our hands.' But with all their capable statesmen, Generals, Mahadaji and Nana, Tukoji and Raghoji and Phadke, removed almost simultaneously by death, with exhaustion in their ranks and worthless men at their front and that Bajirao II at their head—and England for their dreadful antagonist, the result of the combat was a foregone conclusion. The Marathas lost and with them fell the last great Hindu Empire—the last great Indian Empire. Only in the Punjab, the Sikhs yet kept alive a little flickering flame of Hindu independence; but that too was destined and for identical reasons, soon to die out.

We acknowledge that it is not without a keen agony that we write this epitaph on the grave of this our great national Empire. But we grudge not England her victory. Like a good sportsman we admire her skill and might that, stretching her hand over oceans and seas, over continents and countries, snatched an Indian Empire from our struggling hand and on that foundation has raised a magnificent world empire, the like of which history has scarcely recorded.

Here, then in the year 1818, lies the grave of the last and one of the most glorious of our Hindu Empires. Watch it. Hope, with frankincense and offerings even as Mary did, in loving solicitude. For, who knows when the Resurrection comes!!

□

Part - II

Hindu Rashtra Darshan

PRESIDENTIAL ADDRESS

19th Session of the Akhil Bharatiya Hindu Mahasabha held at Karnavati (Ahmedabad)—1937

Ladies and Gentlemen,

I thank you most cordially for the trust you have placed in me in calling upon me to preside on this 19th session of the Hindu Mahasabha. I don't take it so much as an honour bestowed upon me by my nation for service rendered in the past as a command to dedicate whatever strength is still left in me to the sacred cause of defending Hindudom and Hindusthan—our common motherland and our common holyland, and pressing on the fight for our National Freedom. So far as the Hindus are concerned, there can be no distinction nor conflict in the least between our communal and national duties, as the best interests of the Hindudom are simply identified with best interests of Hindusthan as a whole. Hindudom cannot advance or fulfil its life-mission unless and until our motherland is set free and consolidated into an Indian state in which all our countrymen to whatever religion or sect or race they belong to are treated with perfect equality and none allowed to dominate others or is deprived of his just and equal rights of free citizenship as long as everyone discharges the common obligations and duties which one owes to the Indian nation as a whole. The truer a Hindu is to himself as a Hindu, he must inevitably grow a truer nation as well. I shall substantiate this point later on as I proceed.

With this conviction and from this point of view, I shall deal in this my presidential address with some fundamental aspects of the Hindu Sangathan movement as expounded by this Mahasabha or as

I understand them and leave detailed and passing questions to be deliberated upon and decided, to the representatives assembled in this session.

Homage to the independent
Hindu kingdom of Nepal

But, before proceeding further, I feel it my bounden duty to send forth on behalf of all Hindus our loyal and loving greetings to His Majesty the King of Nepal, His Highness Shree Yuddhsamasher Ranajee—the Prime Minister of Nepal and all of our co-religionists and countrymen there, who have even in the darkest hour of our history, been successful in holding out as Hindu power and in keeping a flag of Hindu independence flying unsullied on the summits of the Himalayas. The kingdom of Nepal stands out today as the only Hindu kingdom in the world whose independence is recognised by England, France, Italy and other great powers. Amongst some twenty-five crores of our Hindus in this generation, His Majesty the King of Nepal is the first and foremost and the only Hindu today who can enter in the assemblage of kings, Emperors and presidents of all the independent nations in the world, with head erect and unbent, as an equal amongst equals. In spite of the passing political aspect of the question, Nepal is bound to Hindudom as a whole by the dearest ties of common race and religion and language and culture, inheriting with us this our common motherland and our common holyland. Our life is one. Whatever contributes to the strength of Hindudom as a whole must strengthen Nepal and whatever progress the latter records is bound to elevate the first. Hence all Sangathanist Hindus long to see that the only independent Hindu kingdom is rapidly brought to an up-to-date efficiency, political, social, and above all military and aerial so as to enable her to hold out her own in the national struggle for existence that is going on all around us and march on and fulfil the great and glorious destiny that awaits her ahead.

Message of sympathy to the Hindus in the greater Hindusthan

Nor can this session of the Hindu Mahasabha forget to send forth its message of sympathy and loving remembrances to those of our co-religionists and countrymen abroad who have been building a greater Hindusthan without the noise of drums and trumpets in Africa, America, Mauritius and such other parts of the world and also to those who, as in the island of Bali, are still holding out as remnants of the ancient world Empire of our Hindu race. Their fortunes too are inextricably bound up with the freedom and strength of greatness of Bharatvarsha which is the *pitrabhoo* and *punyabhoo*—the fatherland and the holyland of the Hindudom as a whole.

Hindusthan must ever remain one and indivisible

Nor can the Hindu Mahasabha afford to be forgetful of the Hindus who reside in the so-called 'French India' and 'Portuguese India' in India! The very words sound preposterous and insulting to us. Apart from the artificial and enforced political divisions of today, we are indissolubly bound together by the enduring ties of blood and religion and country. We must declare, as an ideal at any rate, that Hindusthan of tomorrow must be one and indivisible, not only a united but a unitarian nation from Kashmir to Rameshwar, from Sindh to Assam. I hope that not only the Mahasabha, but even the Congress and such other national bodies in Hindusthan will not fight shy of claiming Gomantak, Pondicherry and such other parts of Hindusthan as parts of inalienable and integral parts of our nation as is Maharashtra or Bengal or Punjab.

The definition of the word 'Hindu'

As the whole superstructure of the mission and the function of the Hindu Mahasabha rests on the correct definition of the word 'Hindu', we must first of all make it clear what 'Hindutva' really means. Once the scope and the meaning of the word is defined and understood, a number of misgivings in our own camp are easily removed, a number of misunderstandings and objections raised against us from the camp of our opponents are met and silenced. Fortunately for us, after a lot of wandering in wilderness, a definition of the word Hindu which is not only historically and logically as sound as is possible in the cases of such comprehensive terms, but, is also eminently workable is already hit upon when 'Hindutva' was defined as:

॥ आसिंधुसिंधुपर्यता यस्य भारतभूमिका ॥
॥ पितृभूः पुण्यभूयैश्चैव स वै हिंदुरितिंस्मृतः ॥

'Everyone who regards and claims this Bharatbhoomi from, the Indus to the seas as his fatherland and holyland is a Hindu. Here I must point out that it is rather loose to say that any person professing any religion of Indian origin is a Hindu, because that is only one aspect of Hindutva. The second and equally essential constituent of the concept of Hindutva cannot be ignored if we want to save the definition from getting overlapping and unreal. It is not enough that a person should profess any religion of Indian origin, i.e., recognise Hindusthan as his *punyabhu* his holyland, but he must also recognise it as his *pitrabhu* too, his fatherland as well. As this is no place for going into the whole discussion of the pros and cons of the question; all I can do here is to refer to my book *Hindutva* in which I have set forth all arguments and expounded the proposition at great length. I shall content myself at present by stating that Hindudom is bound and marked out as a people and a nation by themselves not by the only tie of a common holyland in which their religion took birth, but by the ties of a common culture, a common language, a common history and essentially of a common fatherland as well. It is these two constituents taken together that constitute our Hindutva and distinguish us from any other people in the world. That is why, the Japanese and the Chinese, for example, do not and cannot regard themselves as fully identified with the Hindus. Both of them regard our Hindusthan as their holyland, the land which was the cradle of their religion, but they do not and cannot look upon Hindusthan as their fatherland too. They are our co-religionists, but are not and cannot be our countrymen too. We, Hindus, are not only co-religionosts, but even countrymen of each other. The Japanese and the Chinese have a different ancestry, language, culture, history and country of their own and are not so integrally bound up with us as to constitute a common national life. In a religious assembly of the Hindus, in any Hindu Dharma-Mahasabha they can join with us as our brothers-in-faith having a common holyland. But, they will not and cannot take a common part or have a common interest in a Hindu Mahasabha which unites Hindus together and represents their national life. A definition must in the main respond to reality. Just as by the first constituent of Hindutva, the possession of a common holyland—the Indian Mohammedans, Jews, Christians, Parsees, etc. are excluded from claiming themselves as Hindus which in reality also they do not—in spite of their recognising Hindusthan as their fatherland, so also on the other hand, the second constituent of the definition, that of possessing a common fatherland exclude the Japanese, the Chinese and others from the Hindu fold in spite of the fact of their having a holyland in common with us. The above definition had already been adopted by a number of prominent Hindu *sabhas* such as Nagpur, Poona, Ratnagiri Hindu *sabhas* and others. The Hindu Mahasabha also had in view this very definition when the word 'Hindu' was rather loosely explained in its present constitution as 'one who professes any religion of Indian origin'. I submit that the time has come when we should be more accurate and replace that partial description by regular definition and incorporate in the constitution the full verse itself, translating it in the precise terms as rendered above.

Avoid the loose and harmful misuse of the word 'Hindu'

From this correct definition of Hindutva, it necessarily follows that we should take all possible care to restrict the use of the word 'Hindu' to its defined and definite general meaning only and avoid misusing it in any sectarian sense. In common parlance, even our esteemed leaders and writers who on the one hand are very particular in emphasising that our non-Vedic religious schools are also included in the common Hindu brotherhood, commit on the other hand, the serious mistake of using such expressions as 'Hindus and Sikhs', 'Hindus and Jains', denoting, thereby, unconsciously that the Vaidiks or the Sanatanists only are the Hindus and, thus, quite unaware, inculcate the deadly virus of separation in the minds of the different constituents of our religious brotherhood, defeating our own eager desire to consolidate them all into a harmonious and organic whole. Confusion in words leads to confusion in thoughts. If we take good care not to identify the term 'Hindu' with the major Vedic section of our people alone, our non-Vedic brethren such as the Sikhs, the Jains and others will find no just reason to resent the application of the word 'Hindu' in their case also. Those who hold to the opinion that Sikhism, Jainism and such other religions that go from our Hindu brotherhood are neither the branches of nor originated from the *Vedas* but are independent religions by themselves need not cherish any fear or suspicion of losing their independence as a religious school by being called Hindus if that application is rightly used only to denote all those who own India, this Bharatbhoomi, as their holyland and fatherland. Whenever we want to discriminate the constituents of Hindudom as a whole we should designate them as 'Veidiks and Sikhs', 'Veidiks and Jains', etc. But to say 'Hindus and Sikhs', 'Hindus and Jains', is as self-contradictory and misleading as to say 'Hindus and Brahmins' or 'Jains and Digambars' or 'Sikhs and Akalis'. Such a harmful misuse of the word Hindu should be carefully avoided especially in the speeches, resolutions and records of our Hindu Mahasabha

The word 'Hindu' is of Veidic origin

We may mention here in passing that the word 'Hindu' is not a denomination which the foreigners applied to us in contempt otherwise, but is derived from our Vedic appellation of Saptasindhus—a fact which is fully dealt with in my book on *Hindutva* and is borne out by the name of one of our provinces and peoples bordering on the Indus, who are being called down to this day as Sindh and Sindhi.

The Hindu Mahasabha is in the main not a religious, but a national body

From this above discussion, it necessarily follows that the concept of the term 'Hindutva'—Hinduness—is more comprehensive than the word 'Hinduism'. It was to draw a pointed attention to this distinction that I had coined the words 'Hindutva', 'pan-Hindu' and 'Hindudom' when I framed the definition of the word 'Hindu'. Hinduism concerns with the religious systems of the Hindus, their theology and dogma. But, this is precisely a matter, which this Hindu Mahasabha leaves entirely to individual or group conscience and faith. The Mahasabha takes its stand on no dogma, no book or school of philosophy whether pantheist, monotheist or atheist. All that it is concerned with, so far as 'ism' is concerned, is the common characteristic, which a Hindu, by the very fact of professing allegiance to a religion or faith of Indian origin necessarily possesses in regarding India as his holyland, as his *punyabhumi*—the cradle and the temple of his faith.

Thus, while only indirectly concerned with Hinduism, which is only one of the many aspects of 'Hindutva', the Mahasabha is mainly concerned with other aspects of Hindutva resulting from the second constituent of possessing a common fatherland. The Mahasabha is not in the main a Hindu-Dharma *sabha* but it is pre-eminently a Hindu-Rashtra *sabha* and is a pan-Hindu organisation shaping the destiny of the Hindu nation in all its social, political and cultural aspects. Those who commit the serious mistake of taking the Hindu Mahasabha for only a religious body would do well to keep this distinction in mind.

The Hindus are a nation by themselves

Some cavil at the position I have taken that the Hindu Mahasabha as I understand its mission, is pre-eminently a national body and challenge me—'How the Hindus, who differ so much amongst themselves in every detail of life, could at all be called a nation as such?' To them, my reply is that no people on the earth are so homogeneous as to present perfect uniformity in language, culture, race and religion. People are marked out as a nation by themselves not so much by the absence of any heterogeneous differences amongst themselves as by the fact of their differing from other people more markedly than they differ amongst themselves. Even those who deny the fact that the Hindus could be called a nation by themselves do recognise Great Britain, the United States, Russia, Germany and other people as nations. What is the test by which those people are called nations by themselves? Take Great Britain as an example. There are at any rate three different languages there; they have fought amongst themselves dreadfully in the past; there are to be found the traces of different seeds and bloods and races. If you say that in spite of it all, they are a nation because they possess a common country, a common language, a common culture and common holyland, then the Hindus too possess a common country so well marked out as Hindusthan, a common language, Sanskrit, from which all their current languages are derived or are nourished and which forms even today the common language of their scriptures and literature and which is held in esteem as the sacred reservoir of ancient scriptures and the tongue of their forefathers. By *anuloma* and *pratiloma* marriages, their seed and blood continued to get commingled ever since the days of Manu. Their social festivals and cultural forms are not less common than those we find in England. They possess a common holyland. The Vedic *rishis* are their common pride, their *grammarians* Panini and Patanjali, their poets Bhavabhooti and Kalidas, their heroes Shri Ram and Shri Krishna, Shivaji and Pratap, Guru Gobind and Banda are a source of common inspiration. Their Prophets, Buddha and Mahaveer, Kanad and Shankar, are held in common esteem. Like their ancient and sacred language—the Sanskrit—their scripts also are fashioned on the same basis and the Nagari script has been the common vehicle of their sacred writings since centuries in the past. Their ancient and modern history is common. They have friends and enemies in common. They have faced common dangers and won victories in common. One in national glory and one in national disasters, one in national despair and one in national hope and Hindus are welded together during aeons of a common life and a common habitat. Above all, the Hindus are bound together by the dearest, most sacred and most enduring bonds of a common fatherland and a common holyland, and these two being identified with one and the same country, our Bharatbhumi, our India, the national oneness and homogenity of the Hindus have been doubly sure. If the United States with the warring crowds of Negroes, Germans and Anglo-Saxons, with a common past not exceeding four or five centuries put together can be called a nation, then the Hindus must be entitled to be recognised as a nation par excellence. Verily the Hindus as a people differ most markedly from any other people in the world than they differ amongst themselves. All tests whatsoever of a common country, race, religion and language that go to entitle a people to form a nation, entitle the Hindus with greater emphasis to that claim. And whatever differences divide the Hindus amongst themselves are rapidly disappearing owing to their awakening of the national consciousness and the *Sangaṭhan* and the social reform movements of today.

Therefore the Hindu Mahasabha that has, as formulated in its current constitution, set before itself the task of 'the maintenance, protection and promotion of the Hindu race, culture and civilisation for the advancement and glory of Hindu *rashtra* is pre-eminently a national body representing the Hindu nation as a whole.

Is this mission of the Mahasabha narrow, anti-Indian and parochial aim?

Some of our well meaning, but unthinking sections of Indian patriots who look down upon the Mahasabha as a communal, narrow and anti-Indian body only because it represents Hindudom and tries to protect its just rights, forget the fact that communal and parochial are only relative terms and do not by themselves imply a condemnation or curse. Are not they themselves who swear by the name of Indian nationalism in season and out of season liable to the same charge of parochialness? If the Mahasabha represents the Hindu nation only, they claim to represent the Indian nation alone. But, is not the concept of an Indian nation itself a parochial conception in relation to human state? In fact, the Earth is our motherland and humanity our nation. Nay, the Vedantist goes further and claims this universe for his country and all manifestation from the stars to the stone of his own self 'आमचा स्वदेश। भूवनत्रायामध्ये वास॥' says Tukaram! Why then take the Himalayas to cut us off from the rest of mankind, deem ourselves as a separate nation of Indians and fight with every other country and the English in particular, who after all are our brothers-in-humanity? Why not sacrifice Indian interests to those of the British Empire which is a larger political synthesis? The fact is that all patriotism is more or less parochial and communal and is responsible for dreadful wars throughout human history. Thus, the Indian patriots who instead of starting and joining some movement of a universal state, stop short of it, join an Indian movement and yet continue to mock at the Hindu *Sangathan* as narrow and communal and parochial succeed only in mocking at themselves.

But, if it is said justification of Indian patriotism that the people who populate India are more akin to each other bound by ties of a common ancestry, language, culture, history, etc. than they are to any other people outside India and, therefore, we Indians feel it our first duty to protect our nation from our political domination and aggression of other non-Indian nations, then the same reason could be adduced to justify the Hindu *sangathan* movement as well.

When national, communal, or parochial movements are harmful to humanity?

No movement is condemnable simply because it is sectional. So long as it tries to defend the just and fundamental rights of a particular nation or people or community against the unjust and overbearing aggression of other human aggregates and does not infringe on an equal just right and liberties of others, it cannot be condemned or looked down upon simply because the nation or community is a smaller aggregate in itself. But when a nation or community treads upon the rights of sister nations or communities and aggressively stands in the way of forming larger associations and aggregates of mankind, its nationalism or communalism becomes condemnable from a human point of view. This is the acid test of distinguishing a justifiable nationalism or communalism from an unjust and harmful one. The Hindu *Sangathan* movement, call it national, communal or parochial as you like, stands as much justified by this real test as our Indian patriotism can be.

The Hindu Mahasabha is perfectly national in its outlook, for what does the Hindu Mahasabha aim at? As the national representative body of Hindudom, it aims at the all-round regeneration of the Hindu people. But, the absolute political independence of Hindusthan is a *sine qua non* for that all-round regeneration of Hindudom. The fortunes of the Hindus are more inextricably and more closely bound up with India than that of any other non-Hindu section of our countrymen. After all, the Hindus are the bedrock on which an Indian independent state could be built.

Whatever may happen some centuries hence, the solid fact of today cannot be ignored that religion wields mighty influence on the minds of men in Hindusthan and in the case of Mohammedans especially, their religious zeal, more often than not, borders on fanaticism! Their love towards India as their motherland is but an handmaid to their love for their holyland outside India. Their faces are ever turned towards Mecca and Medina. But, to the Hindus, Hindusthan being their fatherland as well as their holyland, the love they bear to Hindusthan is undivided and absolute. They not only form the overwhelming majority of Indian population but have on the whole been the trusted champions of her cause. A Mohammedan is often found to cherish an extra-territorial allegiance, is moved more by events in Palestine than what concerns India as a nation, worries himself more about the well-being of the Arabs than the well-being of his Hindu neighbours and countrymen in India. Thousands of Mohammedans could be found conspiring with the Turkish Khilaphatists and Afghans with an object to bring about a foreign invasion of India if but a Mohammedan rule could thus be established in this land. But, to a Hindu, India is all in all of his national being. That is the reason why the Hindus predominate in the struggle that is going on for the overthrow of the political domination of England over this country. It is the Hindus who went to the gallows, faced transportation to the Andamans by hundreds and got imprisoned by thousands in the fight for the liberation of Hindusthan. Even the Indian National Congress owes its inception to Hindu brain, its growth to Hindu sacrifice, its present position to Hindu labours in the main. *A Hindu patriot worth the name cannot but be an Indian patriot as well.* In this sense, the consolidation and the independence of the Hindu nation is but another name for the independence of the Indian nation as a whole. For, the Hindu Sangathanists know fully well that no regeneration of Hindudom could be brought about and no honour and equal place could be secured for the Hindu nation amongst the nations of the world unless *swarajya* and *swatantrya* are won for Hindusthan, their fatherland and holyland.

But what does this independence of India—
this sawrajya or swatantrya mean?

In common parlance, *sawrajya* is understood as the political Freedom of our country, of our land, the independence of the geographical unit called India. But, the time has come when these expressions must be fully analysed and understood. A country or a geographical unit does not in itself constitute a nation. Our country is endeared to us because it has been the abode of our race, our people, our dearest and nearest relations and as such is only metaphorically referred to, to express our national being. The independence of India means, therefore, the independence of our people, our race, our nation. Therefore, Indian *swarajya* or Indian *swatantrya* means, as far as the Hindu nation is concerned, the political independence of the Hindus, the freedom which would enable them to grow to their full height.

Only geographically speaking India as a land and a state was absolutely independent of any other non-Indian powers when an Allauddin Khilji or an Aurangzeb ruled over her. But, that kind of independence of India proved a veritable death-warrant to the Hindu nation. That is why Sanga and Pratap, Guru Govind Singh and Bir Banda, Shivaji and Bajirao fought and fell and won in the end and established an Hindu Empire under the Marathas, the Rajputs, the Sikhs, the Gurkhas throughout our motherland and saved our Hindudom from the clutches of the non-Hindu aggression. Does it not prove to a hilt that merely the geographical independence or *swarajya* of India does not mean the independence of Hindu nation—nay, may at times prove a positive curse to their race?

India is dear to us because it has been and is the home of our Hindu race, the land which has been the cradle of our prophets and heroes and gods and godmen. Otherwise land for land, there may be many a country as rich in gold and silver on the face of the earth. River for river, the Mississipi is nearly as good as the Ganges and its waters are not altogether bitter. The stones and trees and greens in Hindusthan are just as good or bad stones and trees and greens of the respective species elsewhere. Hindusthan is a fatherland and holyland to us not because it is a land entirely unlike any other land in the world but because it is associated with our History, has been the home of our forefathers, wherein our mothers gave us the first suckle at their breast and our fathers cradled us on their knees from generation to generation.

The cottage wherein our beloved dwell, grows dearer to our eyes than a palace elsewhere. But, let the dear faces disappear from it and go to dwell elsewhere and the cottage shrinks suddenly to the wretched hut that it was. We discard it and follow our beloved to their new abode. So, with the nations also. Look at the Jews or the Parsees! When the Arabians invaded them and only a choice was left to them between their land and their racial and cultural identity, they left the land rather than their religious and racial identity and with their book and culture went away in search of a more congenial abode. They refused to barter away their racial soul for a mere mess of pottage, a mere bit of lifeless earth!

The real meaning of *swarajya* then is not merely the geographical independence of the bit of earth called India. To the Hindus, independence of Hindusthan can only be worth having if that ensures their Hindutva—their religious, racial and cultural identity. We are not out to fight and die for a *swarajya* which could only be had at the cost of our *swatva,* our Hindutva itself!

A united Indian state and the co-operation of the minorities

So far as *swarajya* in this right sense is concerned, the Hindus have ever been in the forefront in the movement and struggle for Indian independence and for founding a united Indian state. It is they who first dreamt of a united Indian state. It is the Hindus again who have by their sacrifices and struggle brought it within the scope of practical politics of today. Taking into account their present strength and weakness, the Hindus have ever been willing to secure the co-operation of all non-Hindu sections of their countrymen in this common struggle with a view to establish a common and united India state. In spite of their overwhelming majority in India, in spite of the consciousness that it is they who have borne the brunt of the fight, struggled single-handedly down to this day while the other non-Hindu sections and especially the Mohammedans, who are nowhere to be found while the national struggle goes on and are everywhere to be found in the forefront at the time of reaping the fruits of that struggle—in spite of all this, the Hindus are willing to form a common united Indian nation and do not advance any special claims, privileges or rights reserved only for themselves over and above the non-Hindu section in Hindusthan.

Let the Indian state be purely Indian. Let it not recognise any invidious distinctions whatsoever as regards the franchise, public services, offices, taxation on the grounds of religion and race. Let no cognisance be taken whatsoever of man's being Hindu or Mohammedan, Christian or Jew. Let all citizens of that Indian state be treated according to their individual worth, irrespective of their religious or racial percentage in the general population. Let that language and script be the national language and script of that Indian state which are understood by the overwhelming majority of the people as happens in every other state in the world, i.e., in England or the United States of America and let no religious bias be allowed to tamper with that language and script with an enforced and perverse hybridism whatsoever. *Let 'one man, one vote' be the general rule, irrespective of caste or creed, race or religion.* If such an Indian state is kept in view the Hindu *Sangathanists* will, in the interest of the Hindu *Sangathan* itself, be the first to offer their wholehearted loyalty to it. I for one and thousands of the Mahasabhaites like me have set this ideal of an Indian state as our political goal ever since the beginning of our political career and shall continue to work for its consummation to the end of our life. Can any attitude towards an Indian state be more national than that?

Justice demands that I must plainly proclaim that the mission and policy of the Hindu Mahasabha with regard to an Indian state have been more national than the present-day policy of the Indian National Congress itself.

The Hindus ask nothing more than what is their due as Indian citizens on the special plea that they are Hindus or that they form the majority of the Indian population, over and above the other non-Hindu sections of their countrymen. Are the Mohammedans ready to join such a truly national Indian state without asking any special privilege, protection or weightage on the fanatical ground that a special merit attaches to them of being Mohammedans and not Hindus?

The anti-national designs of the Mohammedans

Fortunately, for the Hindus, Mr. Jinnah and the Moslem Leaguers have deliberately disclosed their real intentions this year at the Lucknow session of the Moslem League more authoritatively, more frankly and even more blatantly than they used to do before. I thank them for it. An open enemy is safer than a suspicious friend in dealing with him. Their resolutions at Lucknow are, in fact, no news to us. But, up to this time the onus of proving the existence of the Moslem anti-national attitude and their pan-Islamic ambitions more or less lay on the Hindus. But, now we need do no more than point out to the authoritative speeches and resolutions of the League delivered and passed at that Lucknow session to explain the anti-Hindu, anti-Indian and extra-territorial designs of the Moslems. They want the unalloyed Urdu to be raised to the position of the national tongue of the Indian state, although it is not spoken as a mother tongue by more than a couple of crores of Moslems themselves and is not understood by some twenty crores of people in India, Moslems included; in spite of the fact that it can claim no more literary merit than Hindi which is the mother tongue of some seven crores of people and is easily understood by some ten crores more! While the Arabic language itself, on which Urdu is fed is deemed outlandish, be it Kemal and the Turks in the land of the Khaliphas itself, the Moslems expect some twenty-five crores of Hindus to learn it and to adopt it as their national tongue! As to the national script, the Moslems insist on adopting the Urdu script and would have nothing to do, at any rate so far as they are concerned, with the Nagari! Why? Kemal may have discarded the Arabic script itself as unsuited to the present day needs, the Nagari may be more scientific, more amenable to printing, more easy to learn, may already be current amongst or known to twenty crores of people in Hindusthan, yet the Urdu script must be the state-script and the Urdu the state language for the only merit that attaches to them of being recognised by the Mohammedans as their cultural asset and therefore, to make room for it, the cultures of the Hindus and other non-Moslem sections in Hindusthan must go to dogs! The Moslems will not tolerate the *'Vande Mataram'* song. The poor unity-hankers amongst the Hindus hastened to cut it short. But the Moslem would not tolerate even the piece of it cut to order. Drop the whole song and you will find that the Moslems would demand that the very words 'Vande Mataram' are a standing insult to them! Get a new song composed even by an over-generous Ravindra, Moslems would have nothing to do with it because Ravindra being a Hindu could not but commit the heinous offence of using some Sanskrit words as *Jati* instead of *kaum*, 'Bharat' or 'Hindusthan' instead of 'Pakistan'!! They cannot be satisfied unless a national song is composed by an Iqbal or Jinnah himself in unalloyed Urdu, hailing Hindusthan as a Pakistan—the land dedicated to Moslem domination!

When will our unity-hankers understand that the real question at the root of this Moslem displeasure is not a word here or a song there! We would have sacrificed a dozen songs or a hundred words of our own free will if thereby we could really contribute to the unity and solidarity of Hindusthan. But, we know the question is not so simple as that. It is the strife of different cultures and races and nations and these trifles are but the passing and outward symptoms of this malady deep seated in the Moslem mind. They want to brand the forehead of Hindudom and other non-Moslem sections in Hindusthan with the stamp of self-humiliation and Moslem domination and we Hindus are not going to tolerate it any longer not only in the interests of Hindudom alone, but even in the interest of Indian nation as well.

But, if we do not tolerate this, the Hon. Mr. Fuzlul Huq told there and then at Lucknow what would happen to us! From the high altitude of a Prime Minister's *gaddi* he promised to *satana* the Hindus in Bengal (मैं हिंदुओं को सताऊँगा) if other Hindus proved recalcitrant elsewhere to the orders of the Moslem League. Now the *gaddi* of the Prime Minister in Bengal was the outcome of the reforms which were wrested out from the English hands by the martyrdom and sacrifice of the Hindu Patriots in Bengal, The Moslems there as everywhere did not claim a special representation or weightage in those sufferings and sacrifices. But, as soon as the reforms came, who could occupy and deserve the *gaddi* of a Prime Minister but the Hon. Mr. Fuzlul Huq! And now he threatens the very Hindus in Bengal who struggled most and suffered most to whose sufferings alone Mr. Huq owes his *gaddi* that he will *satana*(*satayega*) them, in all shades of the meaning of that word from teasing to oppressing! I should like to assure the Hon. Mr. Fuzlul Huq that the Bengal Hindus, are a hard nut to crack. They have at times forced some of the prancing proconsuls of even the powerful British Empire like Lord Curzon to climb down! But, if he ever does persecute our Bengal Hindus then let him not forget that we Hindus also can in Maharashtra and elsewhere deal out to his comrades the same treatment, measure for measure, full to the brim and well shaken!

I need not refer to the attitude of the Moslems as regards the Communal Award and the federation in which case also they want to humiliate the Hindus and Shylock-like insist on having their pound of flesh! I don't want to tire you out with a plethora of figures which you all know by heart. It is only enough to remind you of the audacious proposal openly debated in the League regarding the Moslem demand to cut up the body politic of our motherland right in two parts—the Mohammedan India and the Hindu India—aiming to from a separate Moslem country—Pakistan—comprising of the provinces of Kashmir, Punjab, Peshawar and Sind!

Hands off, sir, hands off! If you aim thus to reduce the Hindus to the position of helots in their own land, you should do well to remember that a succession of Aurangazebs when they wielded an Imperial power here had failed to perform that feat and in their attempt to carry out that design only succeeded in digging their own graves! Surely, Jinnahs and Huqs cannot accomplish what Aurangazebs failed to achieve!

Real unity can only come when the Mohammedans need it!

Let the Hindus remember that the real cause of this mischief is nothing else but the hankering of the Hindus after the willow-the-wisp of a Hindu-Moslem unity. The day we gave the Mohammedans to understand that *swaraj* could not be won unless and until the Mohammedans obliged the Hindus by making a common cause with them, that day we rendered an honourable unity impossible. When an overwhelming majority in a country goes on its knees before a minority so antagonistic as the Mohammedans, imploring them to lend a helping hand and assures it that otherwise the major community is doomed to death, it would be a wonder if that minor community does not sell their assistance at the higher bidder possible, does not hasten the doom of the major community and aim to establish their own political suzeraignty in the land. The only threat that the Mohammedans always hold before the Hindus is to the effect that they would not join the Hindus in the struggle for Indian freedom unless their anti-national and fanatical demands are granted on the spot. Let the Hindus silence the threat once for all, telling point blank: 'Friends! We wanted and do want only that kind of unity which will go to create an Indian state in which all citizens, irrespective of caste and creed, race and religion are treated all alike on the principle of one man one vote. We, though we form the overwhelming majority in the land, do not want any special privileges for our Hindudom; nay more, we are even willing to guarantee special protection for the language, culture and religion of the Mohammedans as a minority if they also promise not to infringe on the equal liberty of other communities in India to follow their own ways within their own respective houses and not to try to dominate and humiliate the Hindus. But knowing fully well the anti-Indian designs of the pan-Islamic movement, with a link of Moslem nations from Arabia to Afghanisthan bound by their recent offensive and defensive alliances and the ferocious tendencies of the frontier tribes to oppress the Hindus out of religious and racial hatred, we Hindus are not going to trust you any longer with any more blank cheques. We are out to win *swarajya* in which our *svatva* along with the *svatva* of all other constituents will be safe. We are not out to fight with England only to find a change of masters but we Hindus aim to be masters in our own house. A *swarajya* that could only be had at the humiliation and cost of Hindutva itself is for us Hindus as good as suicide. If India is not freed from foreign domination, the Indian Moslems cannot but be slaves themselves. If they feel it to be true, if and when they feel they cannot do without the assistance and the goodwill of the Hindus, let them come then to ask for unity and that also not to oblige the Hindus but to oblige themselves.' A Hindu-Moslem unity which is effected thus is worth having. The Hindus have realised to their cost that in this case seeking unity is losing it. Henceforth the Hindu formula for Hindu-Moslem unity is only this: if you come, with you; *'if you don't, without you; and if you oppose, in spite of you; the Hindus will continue to fight for their national freedom as best as they can!'*

Non-Moslem minorities in India

So far as other minorities in India are concerned, there cannot be much difficulty in arriving at an Indian national consolidation. The Parsees have ever been working shoulder to shoulder with the Hindus against the English domination. They are no fanatics. From the great Dadabhai Naoroji to the renowned revolutionary lady Madam Kama the Parsees have contributed their quota of true Indian patriots, not have they ever displayed any but goodwill towards the Hindu nation which to them had proved a veritable saviour of their race. Culturally, too, they are most closely akin to us. In a lesser degree the same thing could be said about the Indian Christians. Although they have yet done but little to contribute any help to the national struggle, yet they have not acted like a millstone round our neck. They are less fanatical and are more amenable to political reason than the Moslems. The Jews are few in number and not antagonistic to our national aspirations. All these minorities of our countrymen are sure to behave as honest and patriotic citizens in an Indian state.

Those who accuse the Hindus and the Mahasabha of being communal should ponder well on the fact that Hindus have never been found wanting in reciprocating feelings of amicability towards these non-Moslem minorities, nor ever have they grudged to them what is justly due to them—their countrymen.

So far as the Anglo-Indians are concerned, their present arrogance and the lion's share they got in the franchise under the present Reforms Act would vanish in a minute as soon as England goes out. Their sound political instinct will soon bring them in line with other Indian citizens; otherwise they could easily be brought to their senses.

But, with the Mohammedans, the case is quite different. I warn the Hindus that the Mohammedans are likely to prove dangerous to our Hindu nation and the existence of a common Indian state even if and when England goes out. Let us not be stone blind to the fact that they as a community still continue to cherish fanatical designs to establish a Moslem rule in India. Let us work for harmony, let us hope for the best, but let us be on our guard.

Two antagonistic nations living in India side by side

As it is there are two antagonistic nations living side by side in India. Several infantile politicians commit the serious mistake in supposing that India is already welded into a harmonious nation, or that it could be welded thus for the mere wish to do so. These our well-meaning but unthinking friends who take their dreams for realities. That is why, they are impatient of communal tangles and attribute them to communal organisations. But, the solid fact is that the so-called communal questions are but a legacy handed down to us by centuries of cultural, religious and national antagonism between the Hindus and the Moslems. When time is ripe you can solve them; but you cannot suppress them by merely refusing recognition of them. It is safer to diagnose and treat a deep-seated disease than to ignore it. Let us bravely face unpleasant facts as they are. India cannot be assumed today to be a unitarian and homogeneous nation, but on the contrary, there are two nations in the main; the Hindus and the Moslems, in India. And as it has happened in many a country under a similar situation in the world, the utmost that we can do under the circumstances is to form an Indian state in which none is allowed any special weightage or representation and none is paid an extra price to buy his loyalty to the state. Mercenaries are paid and bought off, not sons of the motherland to fight in her defence. The Hindus as a nation are willing to discharge their duty to a common Indian state on equal footing. But, if our Moslem countrymen thrust a communal strife on the Hindus and cherish anti-Indian and extra-territorial designs of establishing Mohammedan rule or supremacy in India then let the Hindus look to themselves and stand on their own legs and fight single-handed as best as they can for the liberation of India from any non-Hindu yoke, be it English or Moslem or otherwise.

Vote only for those who pledge to defend Hindutva and are tried Sangathanists

With this end in view I exhort you all to assert yourselves as Hindus! Down with the apologetic attitude that makes some of us feel shy to proclaim ourselves as Hindus, as if it was something unnational, something like a disgrace to be born of the line of Shri Ram and Shri

Krishna—Shivaji and Pratap and Govind Singh! We, Hindus, must have a country of our own in the solar system and must continue to flourish there as Hindus—descendants of a mighty people Then up with the *shuddhi* which has not a religious meaning alone but a political side as well! Up with *Sangathan* for the consummation of which it is simply imperative for non-Hindus to capture whatever political power has been wrung out by our efforts in the past under the present Reforms Act. The Mohammedans only vote for those who openly and boldly pledge to guard and aggressively secure rights for the Mohammedan people. But, we, Hindus, commit the suicidal blunder of voting for those who openly declare that they are neither Hindus nor Mohammedans and yet are never tired of recognising Mohammedan organisations and dealing with them and of adjusting compromises in the name of the Hindu, ever against Hindus' interests and to unbearable humiliation of the Hindus. You must henceforth vote for those who are not ashamed of themselves of being Hindus, openly stand for the Hindus and pledge themselves not to keep burning incense, always at the cost of the Hindus before the fetish of a dishonourable unity—cult. Let the Varnashram Swarajya Sangha, the Hindu Mahasabha, Shiromani Sikh Sabhas, the Arya Samajists, the political organisations like the Democratic Swarajya Party in Maharashtra that stand for an honourable unity and a truly national Indian state and the great *ashrams*, *sanghas* and *jateeya sabhas*, that take their stand on Hindutva from a united Hindu party in the legislatures and let no Hindu vote for a man who is not a *Sangathanists* and you will find then that your own ministries will be championing the just cause of our Hindu nation as boldly as the Mohammedan ministries are doing theirs. This alone will save not only the Hindu nation of ours but even the Indian state to come. For, truly Hindus are and cannot but be the mainstay of our Indian state! We shall ever guarantee protection to the religion, culture and language of the minorities for themselves, but, we shall no longer tolerate any aggression on their part on the equal liberty of the Hindus to guard their religion, culture and language as well. If the non-Hindu minorities are to be protected then surely the Hindu majority also must be protected, against any aggressive minority in India!

Now in the end I assure you, oh Hindus, that if but you do not lose self-confidence in yourselves and are up and doing in time, all that is lost may yet be regained. There is some such virility and staying power inherent in your race as finds a few parallels in the annals of the world. Let alone the *daityas* and *asuras* you vanquished in your mythological and pre-historical period of your annals—but your very history dates from some two thousand year B.C.! Amidst the terrible struggle for existence which is incessantly going on in creation, survival of the fittest is the rule. The nations of the mighty Incas and Pharaohs and Nebuchadnezars were swept away and no trace left behind. But, you survived those national cataclysms because you were found the fittest to survive. There are ups and downs in the life of every nation. This very England which rules today over an Empire had often fallen an easy prey to the Romans and the Danes, the Dutch and the Normans as well. We too had to face great national disasters. But, each time we rose and tided them over. The Greeks under Alexander the Great came conquering the world but they could not conquer Hindusthan. Chandragupta rose and we drove the Greeks back, inflicting crushing defeats on them, military and cultural. Three centuries after the Huns came on us like an avalanche. All Europe and half Asia lay at their feet; they smashed the Roman Empire to pieces. But, after some two centuries of a life-and-death struggle against them, we vanquished them in the end under our Vikramaditya the great! The Shakas also fared no better. The mighty hands of Shalivahan and Yashodharman beat them to a chip. Where are those of our enemies—the Huns and the Parthians and the Shakas today? The very names are forgotten! Gone, effaced from the face of India and the world as well. The virility and the staying power of our race triumphed over them all.

Then centuries after, the Mohammedans invaded India and carried everything before them. Their kingdoms and empires seemed to reign supreme. But, we rallied again and ever since the day that Shivaji was born, the God of War sided with us. Battle after battle, we beat the Moslems in a hundred fields; their kingdoms and empires, their *nawabs* and *shahas* and *badshahas* were brought to their knees by our warriors till at last Bhausaheb, the Commander-in-chief of the Hindus, as if symbolically raised his hammer and literally smashed the very Imperial throne of the Moguls at Delhi to pieces, Mahadji Shinde held the imbecile Mogul Emperors as prisoners and pensioners in his custody and Hindu supremacy was once more re-established all over the land.

In the meanwhile, before we could recover from the struggle of centuries with Moslems, the English faced us and won on all points. We do not grudge their victory because though we have been vanquished in the field yesterday, yet enough fight is still left in us today. We have not given up the struggle for lost nay, have already returned to the charge.

Who knows that some future and more fortunate president of our Hindu Mahasabha may not be able to rise here; if not in this generation, yet in the generation of our sons and proclaim the triumphant news to that session to come that as happened in the case of the Huns and the Greeks and the Shakas in the past. There is not a trace left behind of the British domination in our land! The banner of Hindudom flies supreme on the summits of the Himalayas, Hindusthan is free again and Hindudom triumphant!!

□

20th Session, Nagpur—1938

Ladies and Gentlemen,

I gratefully acknowledge the confidence you have placed in me in calling upon me to preside over the twentieth session of the All-India Hindu Mahasabha. I promise you in all sincerity that I will try my best to deserve the trust you have thus placed in me, by exerting in full the limited strength which an individual like me can possess. But, you will excuse me if I call upon you in all humility to bear in mind that the only way of justifying yourselves in placing that trust in me can be no other than exerting yourselves in full, in striving and fighting heroically to defend and consolidate Hindudom in such ways as to compel the near future to herald the resurrection of a Hindu nation rising out of the tomb of the Present and grown even greater and mightier, more resplendent than it ever had been in the past in the days of a Chandragupta or a Vikramaditya or the Peshwas at Poona. It is nothing short of a political miracle that we Hindus of this generation are called upon to work out, and no individual howsoever great, can accomplish the task unless and until the whole Hindudom rises like one man to dare and to do and to march on unvanquished through the unavoidable valleys of bitter disappointment and valorous death—through which alone lies the path to the ultimate triumph of such great causes of nations' resurrections. If we quail, we are all lost beyond redemption; if we but dare we are sure to win; for, even today we possess the power, the volcanic fire within us. We only know it not. Rouse it confidently—and it shall burst forth into the column of the sacrificial fire which led the Aryan patriarchs of our Hindu race from victory to victory.

2. When I said that it is out of the tomb of the present that we have to resurrect Hindudom, I said it deliberately so that I may not be guilty of belittling the overwhelming difficulties we have to face today. The

present is indeed a veritable sepulchre into which they have buried our Hindu nation after crucifying it on the charge of committing the crime of claiming to be a nation by itself. It is needless for me to depict to you, brothers and sisters, who have attended this session, to depict the ghastly picture in detail of the dreadful calamities which the Hindus from Peshawar to Rameshwar have to face from day to day. The Session of the Hindu Mahasabha is about the last place today where mere sightseers or job-hunters can find anything attractive enough to attend it here. All avenues to power, pelf, popularity lead but elsewhere. To be a Hindu *Sangathanist* today is not a paying concern. To be a willing delegate to the Hindu Mahasabha session today is to incur the wrath of powers that be, to invite the dagger of a non-Hindu assassin—some 'brother' Abdul Rushid to be slaughtered by some 'brave Moplah patriots' and what is more poignant and unbearable than even the dagger of a non-Hindu assassin—to be hunted and ostracised by millions of one's own Hindu kith and kin for no other fault but of daring to love and defend the Hindu cause and the Hindu people as devotedly and as humanly as the English do the English race, as the Germans do the German cause, or the Japanese love the Japanese self, the Moslems do the Moslem religion and community. To raise aloft the Hindu banner has become today an act of high treason in Hindusthan—in the land of the Hindus themselves, to assert one's self as a Hindu is being dubbed as mean by millions of Hindus themselves. The very fact that under such conditions you all have gathered together here as delegates to this session of the Hindu Mahasabha and dared to rally round this pan-Hindu banner proves it to the hilt that you could not have done so unless impelled by an overwhelming sense of duty, fully conscious of and touched to the quick by the unbearable humiliations to which our Hindu race is subjected to from day to day and fully prepared to defy the intolerable demands of the so-called Indian patriots seeking to smother unto death our very existence as Hindus, as a nation unto ourselves.

3. I shall not, therefore, go into any current and detailed grievances or local questions affecting Hindu interests today but leave them to be dealt with severally in the resolutions and speeches on them to be passed and delivered in the session later on. I shall restrict myself to the two outstanding questions: What is the root cause that has landed the Hindus in this present predicament, striking the life-growth of our Hindu nation

with a sudden atrophy, and the immediate remedy that is sure to rescue the Hindu cause even yet from being lost beyond recovery!

4. Nevertheless inasmuch as this address is meant for those millions of Hindus also who still remain outside the pale of the Hindu Mahasabha and who, in spite of their devoted allegiance to Hindutva in general, are but imperfectly aware of the dangers that beset it today on all sides and wonder, therefore, why the Hindu Sabhaists should make so much ado about nothing or little things here and there. I feel it incumbent upon me just to denote a few points in passing to acquaint them with the real gravity of the situation at least sufficiently enough to set them thinking and in a mood to realise the import of what I have to say later on during the course of the address. Let us just take the constitution in force today. The British have deliberately deprived the Hindus of the political predominance which was their due as the overwhelming majority in India by denying them representation in proportion to their population on the one hand and on the other, loaded the Moslems, Christians, Europeans with weightages, preferences, securities and what not, so as to invest them with political power immeasurably more than what was their due. They broke up the Hindu electorate into watertight compartments with a view to prevent the growth of their political solidarity amongst themselves; why—the very recognition of the Hindus as an electoral unit by themselves is altogether and deliberately denied in the electoral scheme of our country. Spacious apartments, well furnished and honourably named, are reserved for the minorities. The majority, the Hindu, the host is crowded into the lumber-room, the general electorate, unnamed and unrecognised. With a set purpose to starve out the martial qualities in the Hindus, the British Government has been curtailing their recruitment in the army and in the police with the effect that the Moslem minority preponderates in those two vital forces of the nation. In the Punjab and some other provinces, measures like Land Alienation Act seek to crush the Hindus economically while in Bengal an unabashed Act is passed to reserve some 60 per cent of posts for the Moslems in government services. In the Moslem state of Hyderabad, Bhopal and others, the religious and racial persecution of the Hindus is carried on so relentlessly as to remind one of the days of Aurangzeb and Allaudin. In cities and villages all over India, their civil and religious rights are daily trampled under foot to allay the fury of Moslem mobs. The bloody orgies to

which the Hindus were subjected by Moslem fanatics in Malabar and Kohat are enacted on this scale or that even in the Presidency towns all over India every now and then. The Frontier Moslem tribes carry out raids and perpetrate unnameable atrocities on the Hindu people there with a set purpose of exterminating the *kafir* in that region. Only the Hindu merchants are looted, only the Hindus are massacred and only the Hindu women and children are kidnapped and held to ransom or converted perforce to Islam. On top of it all comes in the psuedo-nationalism of the Congressites who practically condone and explain away these Moslem atrocities by inventing such lying excuses; 'There is nothing anti-Hindu in these Moslem raids! It is only economical and sexual starvation of the tribes that goads them on to these crimes. Let us feed those starved souls and they will be good citizens!' But, it is curious that these starved poor raiders leave the rich Moslems in the Frontier towns unlooted, find no young Moslem damsels to kidnap, burn no Moslem houses and go about assuring the Moslem by beat of drums that they shall not hurt a hair of any Moslem provided he shelters not a Hindu *kafir*! Witness only the latest case in the Dadu district Sind. The Moslem raiders attacked an absolutely unoffending archaeological party under Mr. Muzumdar. They asked each one, 'Are you a Hindu?' If he said, 'Aye', he was forthwith shot dead. One Hindu pretended to be a Moslem and he was let go alive and unmolested. This case is only a typical one, illustrating thousands of such dreadful happenings all over India and is the order of the day during all Moslem riots and raids from Malabar to Peshawar, from Sindh to Assam and year in and year out. Add to this the activities of the all-India organisations of the Christian missionaries and the Moslem organisations from the Agakhanis, Hasan Nizamis, Peera Motamiyas to the very village Moslem *goondas*, all seeking and succeeding in converting millions of Hindus to foreign faiths by peaceful or fraudulent or forceful means throughout the length and breadth of India, undermining the religious, racial, cultural and political activities of the Moslem Leaguers and the Moslem States that have already culminated into open resolutions first to divide India into a Moslem federation and a Hindu federation and then to strike down the latter by inviting invasions from outside India by some alien Moslem powers. Such is the present state of the Hindus in Hindusthan, their own land! And yet the worst factor remains to be told. For, even to refer to these calamities to which the Hindus have fallen a prey is damned as a national sin by that new cult which calls itself' 'Indian Nationalists' and leads at present the Indian National Congress. Offering a blank cheque to the Moslems by one hand, they deliver ultimatum to the Hindus, by the other. 'Get looted but don't report, get stabbed, but don't shriek, get repressed as Hindus, but don't organise to resist it as Hindus; or else you will be damned as traitors to the cause of our Indian nationalism!!!'

5. In the face of these facts, who else, but a fool or a foe can accuse the Hindu Mahasabha of making much ado about nothing or fancying grievances where none exists or dealing only with some superstitious and empty contents or religious or racial slogans?

Again, in the face of these facts, what wonder is there that leaving aside those who continue to be counted amongst Hindus, but whose hearts have ceased to respond to their Hinduness or who openly disown any allegiance to Hindudom, we find crores of Hindus all over India, every fibre of whose life vibrates with the racial, religious or cultural consciousness of being Hindus, sorely afflicted to see our Hindu race beset by all these calamities and subjected to such unbearable humiliations. On all sides today the anxious question is asked by crores of Hindus: 'How are we to remedy this evil? How is that we feel? How are we Hindus to rise again as Hindus and recover our position as a nation great amongst the nations in the world?' This recent searching of heart is one of the most encouraging signs to show that the soul of our Hindu race is roused again from the deadly swoon of self-forgetfulness. It is natural that on its return to self-consciousness, it should raise these bewildering questions as to its whereabouts.

Although it is not possible to deal exhaustively with these anxious questions that are daily pouring on us from all sides within the limited compass of an address like this, yet I feel that if but I can succeed in pointing out the root cause which has landed us in this sad plight and the immediate step which we must and fortunately we also can take with a view to come out of it, my address will serve its purpose fairly well.

6. In order to find out the root cause, the first initial error which is leading us into a series of all derivative errors, rendered us Hindus insensible to the very fact that we had a national being at all, we must first have a hurried peep into our racial history.

A peep into our History

It is at least some 5,000 years ago, to the Vedic Age that the beginning of our Hindu nation could be historically and undeniably traced. Our national ancestors lived and flourished then on the banks of the seven Sindhus and were laying foundations of a nation that was destined to grow later on into a mighty Hindu nation. Racially and culturally they were called Aryans; territorially they bore the name of the Saptasindhus or Sindhus. One of our provinces and its people on the banks of the Sindhu river bear the very same name down to this day and are called Sindh and Sindhus respectively. They crossed the Ganges, the vindhyas the Godavari in their vigorous and valorous course of colonisation and conquest till they reached the southern and the eastern and western limits of India. By an admirable process of assimilation, elimination and consolidation, political, racial and cultural, they welded all other non-Aryan peoples whom they came in contact with or conflict with through this process of their expansion in this land from the Indus to the eastern sea and from the Himalayas to the southern sea into a national unit. Politics and religion vied with each other with a conscious policy of ultimately uniting them all into a national being bound together by the ties of a common religion, common language, common culture, a common Fatherland and a common holyland. Witness, for example, the four *dhams*—the religious holy outposts roughly marking the four limits of our holyland—Badrikedar, Dwarka, Rameshwar and Jagannath, identifying them as demarcatingly as it was then possible with the limits of our fatherland as well. Leaving mythological period alone even in the period of our definite history, the mighty centralised empires of Chandragupta Maurya, Chandragupta the Second, Vikramaditya, Yashovardhan, Pulkeshi, Shri Harsha and such other great samrats and chakravartis added to this consolidation of our people and made them vibrate with the stirrings of a common political and national being. Powerful invasions of the Greeks, Shakas, Huns and such other foreign races which threatened our people with a common danger and the mighty conflicts they had to wage to overcome that danger by presenting a common front to it lasting sometimes for centuries vested all the more their consciousness of cultural, political, racial and religious oneness marking them out as a national unit by themselves, in spite of their internal differences in relation to other non-Indian National units. The long period of peace unmolested by external political danger worth the name that intervened between the ultimate triumph of the Hindus over the Huns and the invasion of India by the Moslems was pre-eminently devoted to further consolidation of our people and their religious, cultural, racial and political oneness grew so pronounced, definite and conscious that by the time the Moslems came in they found India fully grown into a homogeneous Hindu people.'

Under the pressure of the Moslem invasions and their consolidation into a powerful Moslem Empire at Delhi, political unity of the Hindus from Kashmir to Rameshwar and Sindh to Bengal intensified still more and the name Hindu derived from the Vedic Sapta sindhus had already become the honoured and beloved common appellation of our race centuries before the days of Prithviraj. Thousands of our martyrs embraced death as 'Hindus' to vindicate the honour of Hindu religion. Thousands upon thousands, princes and peasants alike, revolted and rose as Hindus under Hindu flags and fought and fell, in fighting against their non-Hindu foes. Till at last, Shivaji was born, the hour of Hindu triumph was struck, the day of Moslem supremacy set. Under one common name 'The Hindus', under one common banner, the Hindu banner, under one common Hindu leadership, with one common ideal of the establishment of 'Hindu *pad padashahi*' (The Hindu Empire), with one common aim, the political liberation of 'Hindusthan', the emancipation of their common motherland and Holyland, the Hindus rose from province to province till at last the Maratha confederacy succeeded in beating to a chip the Moslem Nawabs and Nizams, Badashass and padashats in a hundred battlefields. The Marathas advanced victorious East, West, North, and South, dropping their secondary capitals at Tanjor, at Gunti, at Kolhapur, at Baroda, at Dhar, at Gwalior, at Indore, at Jhansi, till they reached the Attuk. They ruled at Delhi and held the Moslem Mogul Emperors as prisoners, pensioners and paupers in their camp. The Sikh Hindus ruled in Punjab, the Gurkha Hindus in Nepal, the Rajput Hindus in Rajputana, the Maratha Hindus from Delhi to Tanjore, Dwarka to Jagnnath. Thus, at last, the Vaidic Sindhus had grown into a mighty Hindu people, a Hindu Nation, a Hindu *pada-padashahi* which is a word used by Bajirao I himself. If your wish to realise fully how the mighty movement was surcharged with the intense consciousness of Hindutva, how our martyrs, heroes, victors from Prithviraj, Pratap, Shivaji, Guru Govind, Banda, down to the days of Nana Fadanavis and Mahadji Shinde owned and gloried in their national and religious oneness as Hindus and were proud of their national appellation as Hindus, you may do well to read, for want of a better book, my historical work named 'Hindu *pad-padashahi.*' Here, owing to limited space, I quote only a stanza out of a letter, by way of illustration written so late as in 1793 to Nana Fadanavis by Govindrao Kale, the Maratha ambassador to the Nizam, so that you may listen to their thoughts in their own words: "From the River Attuk to the Indian ocean extends the land of Hindus, Hindusthan, not Turkestan. These have been our frontiers from the times of Pandavas to Vikramaditya. They preserved them and enjoyed empires. After them came effete rulers and the Moslems conquered our kingdom but now everything has been restored to us and rewon under the Peshwas and by the valorous sword of Mahadji Shinde! The Hindu Empire is established, the fame of our victory goes resounding all round!"

The Hindu nation is an organic growth and no paper made makeshift

7. It will be clear from this hurried peep into our history that ever since the Veidic ages, for some 5,000 years at least, in the past our forefathers had been shaping the formation of our people into a religious, racial, cultural and political unit. As a consequence of it all, growing organically the Sindhus of the Veidic time have grown today into a Hindu nation, extending over India and holding India in common as their fatherland and their holyland. No other Nation in the world, excepting perhaps the Chinese, can claim a continuity of life and growth so unbroken as our Hindu nation does. The Hindu nation is not a mushroom growth. It is not a treaty nation. It is not a paper-made toy. It was not cut to order. It is not an outlandish makeshift. It has grown out of this soil and has its roots struck deep and wide in it. It is not a fiction invented to spite the Moslems or anybody in the world. But, it is a fact as stupendous and solid as the Himalayas that border our North.

It matters not that it had and it has sects and sections, dissimilarities and differences within its fold—what nation is free from them? A nation is not marked out as a separate unit because its people have no subdivisions and diversities amongst themselves but because they, as a whole, present, a more homogeneous unity amongst themselves than they have in common with all other alien national units; because they differ definitely and immensely more from all other peoples in the world than they differ amongst themselves from each other. This is the only test that marks our nation in the world. The Hindus having a common fatherland and a common holyland and both identified with each other have made their nationality doubly sure and stand this test doubly well. As the running outline of our history sketched above unmistakably reveals, for thousands of years our Hindu people had been definitely conscious of their religious and cultural, political and patriotic homogently as a people by themselves, as a nation unto themselves. What is to be specially noted here for the argument in hand is the fact that down to the fall of the Maratha Empire our people, princes, patriots, poets, preachers and statesmen, all and altogether strove consciously and continuously to develop and intensify the conception of Hindu nationality and exerted their might to its best to establish a Hindu *pad-padashahi*, a Hindu Empire in India, which they called Hindusthan, the land of the Hindus.

I shall leave the thread of this argument here to be resumed later on when I shall have to point out its special significance in relation to the problems we have to face today.

The rise of the concept of an Indian Nation

8. We have traced the organic growth and development of our Hindu nation to the fall of the Maratha Empire in 1818 and the consequent advent of the British rule in India. The fall of our Sikh Hindu kingdom also in Punjab enabled the British to establish an unchallenged supremacy throughout our country. The British had found that all the bloody wars they had to fight in the course of their Indian conquest were with Hindu powers. The Moslem as a political factor was nowhere to be faced. The Moslem as a political power was already smashed by the Marathas. The only fight the British had to face single-handed with the Moslems was at Plassey. But, it was such an easy affair that they say, the British Commander won it while he was asleep! Consequently, the first anxiety of the British was to see that the Hindu nation must be undermined, their solidarity as a religious and political unit must be broken. The Moslems came in the picture as a mere handy tool in the hands of the British to compass their design. The British even tried the obvious means of converting the Hindus to Christianity by lending political support of the state to Christian missions in India. But, the Revolutionary Rising of 1857 led mostly by Hindu leaders opened the eyes of the British to the dangers involved in any open attack against the religion of the Hindus and Moslems alike and the British state ceased to lend any open support to the Christian Church. Then they initiated a policy to undermine the very

concept of a Hindu nation amongst the rising generation of the Hindu youth by introducing a de-nationlising scheme of Western education in India. We have the word of Macaulay himself for that. He points out in one of his private letters to his son-in-law that if his scheme of Western education is put into force, Hindu youth would of themselves love to get converted to Christianity, to get Westernised and consequently affiliated and attached to the British people. Unfortunately, for the Hindus, his expectations did not altogether miscarry and the first generation of the Hindu youth who took to Western education with avidity were on the whole cut off from their old moorings of Hinduness of Hindutva. They knew next to nothing of Hindu history, Hindu religion, Hindu culture and all that they knew of Hindutva were only its weak points which were deliberately represented to them as its essence in such ways as to make them ashamed of being Hindus at all. The Moslems on the contrary kept at a hand's distance from this education and consequently it could not undermine their communal solidarity at all.

But, the introduction of the Western education in India did not prove an unmixed evil. Contrary to the expectation of its initiators, it soon brought in new forces into action which were destined to defeat the purpose it was meant to serve and add to the strength of the Hindus in the long run. But, here, we are dealing with its immediate effects only.

And the immediate effect of the Western education was that the two first generations of Hindus who were influenced by it were totally carried off their feet; they fell in love with everything Western. They looked upon the British rule as a Godsend. They prayed for its permanence. Fed on Western literature and history and cut off from any contact with Hindu thoughts and Hindu policy, they naturally came to the easy conclusion that if but they imitated the West and especially England in every detail of individual and collective life, they and their country would be benefitted and saved.

Not that they were not public-spirited or intellectual men. On the contrary, these first batches of English-educated Hindus were allowed to rise very high in the social and official scale by England and were deliberately taken to be the spokesmen of Indian people—of the 'natives'. They got every facility to wield tremendous influence over their own people so that they might impart their admiration about the British people and their loyalty to the British rule to their 'native community'. They, too, with the best of intentions wanted to do good to their people and their nation. But, their idea of doing good and even of what was their nation were entirely outlandish—British—having no relation with the realities obtaining in India.

That was the reason why they naturally thought that their nation meant their country. Like all other ideas and sentiments, their notion of patriotism also was borrowed ready-made from England. They found that the English meant by patriotism love to their country—the geographical unit England, which they inhabited. All those who lived in England were united into a nation, irrespective of religion, race, culture and that was the reason why England had become so consolidated and powerful a nation. The analogy was as simple as attractive. If they too could unite India irrespective of race, religion, culture, caste, creed, their people too might grow into a consolidated and powerful Indian nation. They found that in Europe of their days a national unit meant a territorial unit. All those who inhabited the territorial unit—France were French, Germany were Germans, Spain were Spanish, England were English and each respectively a unitary nation by itself. So, they thought or rather believed, without thinking at all, that the only bond of a territorial unity, the only fact of residing in a common geographical unit was by itself the most efficient, nay, the only efficient factor to mark out a people into a nation by themselves.

'Well, then, all people in India: Hindus, Moslems, Christians, Parsees and others, had been inhabiting the territorial unit called India for centuries together. Therefore, all these people must be a nation by themselves. What if they differed so much in religion, language, culture, race and historical development. Those things had nothing to do with a common nationality. Territorial unity, a common country, was the only foundation required to support and induce a common nationality. Territorial unit must be a national unit. Look at England, France, America.' Thus they argued.

The corollary derived from this assumption was also inevitable. If India, because it was a territorial unit and called a country must be a national unit as well, then all of us must also be Indians only and cease to be Hindus or Moslems, Christians or Parsees. So, they, the leaders of those first generations of English- educated people, being almost all Hindus, tried their best to cease themselves to be Hindus and thought it below their dignity to take any cognizance of the divisions as Hindus and Moslems and became transformed overnight into Indian patriots alone.

It was also very easy for them to cease to be Hindus. The Western education had taught them and they had no other education, that Hindutva meant nothing else, but Hinduism, which to them meant a veritable bundle of superstitions. They had no occasion to stop and think of the other and most fundamental concepts of Hindutva, of Hinduness, in all its racial, cultural and historical bearing.

As they found it so easy for them to renounce their Hinduness and merge themselves at a thought into being Indian and Indians alone, they expected that it would be as easy for the Moslems too to forget that they were Moslems and to merge themselves entirely and totally into the Indian people, the Indian nation, which to those 'Indian' patriots seemed already a fact as tangible as the territorial unit, India.

It must be emphasised here that all these remarks of ours are true in their collective sense only. It is not possible to deal with details and exceptions, either individual or actional, in such a short address as this.

As the Western education went on spreading rapidly amongst Hindus, the idea of an Indian nationality also continued to find a larger and larger following; inversely, the solidarity of the Hindus as Hindus, as a political unit, as a nation by themselves, grew feebler and feebler and at last grew unconscious of itself through sheer starvation.

The British rejoiced at the turn the events had taken. They knew that under those circumstances the only danger to their political supremacy in Hindusthan could come from the revival of the political consciousness of the Hindu nation and the re-emergence of the ideal of a Hindu sovereignty. It is a fact that even after 1857, a Hindu politically proud of his being a Hindu was a suspect. For he brooded over the loss of his Hindu kingdom and was watched as an incipient revolutionist. The armed rising of Ramsing Kooka in the Punjab and Vasudeo Balwant Phadke in Maharashtra even after the defeat of the revolutionary war in 1857, with a view to drive the British out and recover the lost Hindu kingdom, only confirmed the British in their suspicions.

The birth of Indian National Congress

9. It was just after the suppression of the rising of Vasudeo Balwant Phadke of Poona who aspired to revive an independent Hindu kingdom even as Shivaji did, that the birth of the Indian National Congress took place. It is to be noted that the British Government favoured the movement and it was a Viceroy who sponsored it! Many a prominent British civilian, like Mr. Hume, Wedderburn and others led it for a long time. Great

Hindu leaders from the most public-spirited motives nursed it and it became the organised and authoritative spokesman of the new cult of Indian patriotism.

The British, too, while they favoured this Indian movement as an antidote to any possible revival of Hindu nationalism, took good care to see that the Moslem solidarity as Moslems did not suffer in any way by catching the contagion of this new Indian nationalist cult. For, the British knew that if the Moslems also joined that cult as wholeheartedly as the Hindus did, then there would really be a united Indian nation—a contingency likely to prove perhaps more dangerous to British supremacy in India than a Hindu revival could single-handedly prove to be. The British dreaded and hated any real genuine and fruitful rise of Indian nationalism as much—if not more—as they did any revival of Hindu nationalism. So, they, on the one hand, encouraged and helped surreptitiously the fanatical hatred, enmity and distrust, which the Moslems ever bore to the Hindu nation, thus rendering any efficient Indian national unity as delusive as a mirage and on the other hand, encouraged the Hindus, at least in the beginning to pursue that mirage of an Indian nationalism with avidity so that the rise of a homogeneous Hindu nation might be ruled out of practical politics. Of course, it is another matter that the result of this British policy of encouraging Indian nationalism in the beginning did not altogether fulfil their expectations and they had to change it later on. But, that does not belie the fact I have related to above.

The ideal of Indian Nationalism was, in fact, a noble one

10. The Hindus found nothing objectionable in the ideal of uniting all India into a consolidated political unit and very naturally so. For it suited well with the Hindu mentality, with its synthetic trend, always prone to philosophies with a universal urge. It is also true that the ideal of politics itself ought to be a human state, all mankind for its citizens, the earth for its motherland. If all India with one-fifth of the human race could be united, irrespective of the religious, racial and cultural diversities, merging them all into a homogeneous whole, it would be but a gigantic stride taken by mankind towards the realisation of that human political ideal. So far as the ideal language and picture of this conception went it could not but be attractive to people like the Hindus with a religious and cultural ideology, preaching, *sarv khalvid brahma*, all this is but one and indivisible Brahma. But Brahma, even in its political aspect, like its philosophical one, has for its counterpart a *maya*,

the principle of division! And this fact those Hindu Patriots overlooked in their enthusiasm for the ideal—If India was united! Yes, but the 'if, was what mattered most. The new concept of an Indian nationality was founded on the only common bond of territorial unity of India; the Hindus for one found nothing revolting even in that assumption that to their deepest religious or cultural or racial sentiments, because their national being had already been identified with that territorial unit, India, which to them was not only a land of sojourn but a home, their fatherland, their motherland, their holyland and all in one! Indian patriotism to them was but a synonym of Hindu patriotism. Even the territorial unit was as intimately identified with their racial, religious and cultural unit that an Indian nation was but a territorial appellation of the Hindu nation. If Hindusthan was called India, but continued to be a Hindusthan, it made no difference in essentials and for practical purposes might be overlooked.

11. That is the reason why, later on, even those Hindu leaders who in spite of their being highly educated in the Western lore were also deeply imbued with Hinduness, were proud of being Hindus by religion, by race, by culture and joined the Indian national movement for political purposes and worked whole-heartedly with the Congress and even led it so long as it continued to be a purely political body striving assiduously to wrest political power out of the hands of the British Government with a view to establish a real Indian commonwealth, to be held in common with other non-Hindu minorities in India on equitable footing and in honourable company.

12. But, although the Hindus on the whole rallied round the Indian National Congress with unsuspecting enthusiasm and lent their honest devotion to the principle of a territorial nationality that underlay it, that principle seemed to fail miserably in appealing to the Moslems in India. As a community, they held back from the very beginning and by and by began to resent it altogether. The more insistent the Congress demand grew in calling upon all Indians to merge their racial and religious individuality to an Indian nation at any rate for forming themselves into a political unit, the more distrustful and enraged the Moslems grew. For, they instinctively felt that Indian patriotism as defined by the Congress was sure to deal a death blow to the Moslem patriotism which was to be all and end all of their racial, religious and cultural ambitions. The British Government for their own end encouraged them in their

this anti-Congress attitude. The higher the Congress rose in political importance through the strenuous efforts of our Hindu patriots and the more insisting grew its demands and stronger its power to back them up, the more outspoken and determined became the Moslem opposition to it and the more assiduous grew the encouragement and surreptitious assistance to it on the part of the British Government, who came to realise to their dicomfiture that their policy of bringing into being the Indian National Congress movement had in the long run miscarried their expeditions in a large measure.

13. I am the last man to ignore the benefits that even we Hindus reaped from the Indian National Congress movement even from the Hindu point of view. It had though only consequentially and without that special end in view, contributed immensely to the consolidation of Hindudom as a whole by rubbing off their provincial, linguistic and sectional angularities, divisions and diversities and provided them with a common political platform and animated them with the consciousness of a common national being with a definite common goal of a united and central state. Errors that crept in may be rectified but the good that came out need not be disowned. Nor do I decry the introduction of the Western education in India. In spite of the questionable intentions of the British in its inception, we Hindus have succeeded in turning the tables in the long run and are now in a position to give a good and profitable account of our contact with the West.

14. But the point to be specially emphasised here is the fact that just as the benefit we Hindus reaped out of our contact with the West or the receiving of English education through the government universities, was in spite of the evil intentions of the British Government, even so the good that accrued to us Hindus contributing to the further consolidation of our Hindu nation was not in virtue of the new cult of Indian nationality or the proclaimed intentions of the Indian National Congress, but in spite of its efforts, direct or implied, to suppress our racial and religious consciousness as Hindus. The territorial patriots wanted us to cease to be Hindus at least as a national and political unit. Some of them actually gloried in disowning themselves as Hindus at all! They were merely Indians, thinking that they had set a very patriotic example in that which they fancied would persuade the Moslems too to renounce their communal being and also merge themselves in that territorial Indian nation beyond recognition!

15. But the Moslems remained Moslems first, Moslems last and Indians never! They sat on the fence as long as the deluded Hindus kept struggling with the British to wrest political rights for all Indians alike, going to the prisons in lakhs, to the Andamans in thousands, to the gallows in hundreds. And as soon as the unarmed agitation carried on by the Congressite Hindus on the one hand, and the more dreadful and more effective life and death struggle carried on by the armed Hindu revolutionists outside the Congress on the other, brought sufficient pressure on the British Government and compelled them to hand over substantial political power to the Indians, the Moslems jumped down the fence and claimed 'they also were Indians, they must have their pound of flesh!!' Till at last things came to such a pass that the proposal to divide India itself into two parts—the Moslem India and the Hindu India was blatantly put forward and their readiness to ally themselves with non-Indian Moslem nation against the Hindus was avowed by no less a representative Moslem body than the Moslem League. This was the sorry fate of the hopes of these Hindu patriots who from the best of the motives, but with a thoughtless belief and the blindest of the policies persisted in their efforts of consolidating all Indians into one undivided and indivisible Indian nation, irrespective of religions, races and cultures based only on the common bond of territorial unity!

Territorial Unity is not the only constituent of a common Nationality

16. What was then the root cause which brought about this miserable failure in the efforts of the Congress during the last full 50 years to placate the Moslems to allow themselves to be merged into a united Indian nation? To persuade them to be, at any rate, Indians first and Moslems afterwards? Not that the Moslems do not like to form a united Indian nation; but, their conception of unity, national unity of India, is not based on her territorial unity at all. If any Moslem had given out his mind in the most intelligible terms possible, it was Ali Musaliar, the leader of the Moplah rebellion. In justification of his atrocious campaign of forcibly converting thousands of Hindus or putting them to sword—women, men, children—at a stroke, he proclaimed that India must be united into a nation and the only way to bring about a lasting Hindu-Moslem unity could not be other than that all Hindus should become Moslems! Those Hindus who refused to do so were traitors to the cause of Indian unity and deserved death!! Thus, the unsophisticated

Ali Musaliar spoke bluntly in his mother tongue. Polished Moslems, like Mohamed Ali and others speak in elegant Latin and Greek, but the purport is the same. Not territorial unity, but it is the religious, racial and cultural unity that counts most in the formation of a national unit. Congress failed to realise this and this was the root cause of its failure in this matter.

Congress committed the serious mistake at its very start of overlooking this fundamental, social and political principle that in the formation of nations, religious, racial, cultural and historical affinities count immensely more than their territorial unity; the fact of having a common habitat. That also is one of the factors, but, in almost all cases, cannot be the only factor. The example of England and some other European national units which put the Hindu founders of the Indian National Congress on the wrong track, as we have explained above in section eight of this address, was not rightly understood. England has not grown into such a homogeneous national unit only because it is a clear-cut territorial unit. Their territorial patriotism is not the cause but a consequence of their other social and political affinities. England, for example, was as a clear-cut territorial unit in the days gone by, but when their religious susceptibilities were highly irritable, the English Catholics and Protestants felt themselves drawn more to their respective co-religionists outside England than their own countrymen inside it. The English Catholics cared more for the Pope in Rome than their Protestant English sovereigns in England. The English Protestants invited William from Holland to rule over them instead of an English King of Roman Catholic persuasion. Take again the case of Holland. The Hollanders, in spite of their territorial unity, during the religious phase of their history could not be united into a homogenous nation. The Catholic Hollanders joined Spain against their own Protestant Prince William of Orange. Take the case of Austria-Hungary. There was nothing notable to divide them territorially. They were welded together in an Imperial unit and continued to be a political unit under a common state for centuries. But, here there were no racial, cultural, linguistic or historical affinities to draw them towards each other as to be a nation in heart. So, they separated as national and political units as soon as a favourable opportunity arose.

Nor could it be said 'Oh! This your racial and religious bosh is already a thing of the past. The world has grown wiser since. No up-to-date man cares a fig for them today.' To this commonplace exclamation, we rejoin, 'Are the Hindu or Moslem Indians more up-to-date than the Germans or the Irish of today? Are not the latter amongst the most advanced, educated and up-to-date nations of the world? But, do you find that territorial unity counts with the Germans or the Irish more even today than the affinities of a common race, language, culture or history?'

The latest cases of the Sudeten Germans and Ulsterites

The Sudeten Germans and say, the Prussian Germans, knew no common political nationality for a long period. They were not a common people as a state. When the enemies of Germany hit her hard, they cut her into pieces and created a patchwork of a 'nation' and compassed it into a territorial unit called Czechoslovakia, making a mess of the Sudeten Germans, Poles, Hungarians, Czechs, Slovaks, etc. Did they form a nation? Sudeten Germans longed to be one with the Prussian Germans in spite of their being mapped out of it as a territorial unit and revolted against the Czechs who were their next door neighbours in spite of their being mapped together into a territorial and political unit and went over to the Prussians even at the risk of their life. Why? Not because the Sudeten Germans had a more definite territorial affinity with the Prussian Germans than they had with the Czechs, or the Slovaks but because they had linguistic, cultural, racial and historical affinities with the Germans in Germany and gloried in being a part and parcel of the German people. Note, on the other hand, that the German Jews had been not only inhabiting the German land for centuries together with Germans, bound together with the Germans with the common bond of a territorial unit, but had been actually incorporated into a common state, were actually Germans in political parlance, exercised equal rights as citizens of Germany—nay, dominated the German state as members of the national German legislature and executive.

Take again the Irish case. Ireland and England were a political unit and continued to have a common state and common Parliament for centuries together. The English lived in Ireland for generations inter-marrying, inter-dining, speaking the same tongue 'English'. The Ulsterite English and the Irish have the common bond of territorial unity and a distinctly marked out Ireland as a common country. Their religion too is common. Nor is Ireland a very big continental territorial unit. It is hardly as big as a Presidency in India. But did all these common factors, a common and so close a habitat as Ireland, the English and the Irish mould into a common nation? No! The Irish revolted, despised the Imperial advantages they had in common with England, revived their own Irish tongue which was well nigh dead and organised a separate Irish national state. The Ulsterite English on the contrary refused to have any national relation with her next-door Irishmen with whom he has lived for centuries and pines for his union with their English brethren whose face they might have never seen and who resided seas apart from him. Why? Because between the Irish and the English, the want of common racial, cultural and historical affinities repulses each other more than a mere territorial unity can attract.

It is not only a political fact but a human one

17. These few illustrations even of up-to-date nations will show that in almost all cases a common territorial unit, a common habitat, cannot by itself weld people differing in religious, racial, cultural and such other affinities into a national unit. It is not only a political fact but a human one that religious, racial, cultural, linguistic or historical affinities make men feel more akin to each other than the only fact of their residing in a common habitat unless this is an addition to these common ties. This tendency of people having these affinities to form themselves into a group or into a nation and not by the mere fact of being mapped together, has its roots deep down in human or even in animal nature. But, we are not called upon here to go into any psychology of it. Suffice it to say that the efficient factor that constitutes people into an organic nation is their will to be one homogeneous national unit. And this will is induced by such of those affinities as we have indicated above far more eminently and intensely than by the mere fact of their residing in a common country.

Have the Indian Moslems, then, that will to be one with the Hindus

18. That is the question of questions and the Congressite Hindus at the beginning of the Indian National Movement never waited a minute to ponder over it, nor do they even today take it into their head even during the interval when they adjourn the National Congress for hours in deference to the Moslem prayer times. It is useless simply to declare the Moslem League communal. That is no news. The fact is that the whole Moslem community is communal, including the Congressite Moslems. The question that ought to be understood is why are they

so communal? The Congressite Hindus from the very beginning simply dared not study that question. Because they feared that such a study would compel their fad of a territorial nationality of Indian unity in the sense they understand it, to give up the ghost! 'Fanaticism—Folly' you exclaim? But, fanaticism or folly—it is to the Moslems a solid fact. And you cannot get over it by calling it names, but must face it as it stands. To my mind, for reasons alluded to above, it is quite human for the Moslems to bear instinctive apathy to the idea of a territorial nationality, as envisaged by the Congressites who in general are totally ignorant of Moslem history, theology and political trend of mind. This antipathy of the Indian Moslems can be seen through a right perspective if you bear at least the following facts in mind:

(a) The Moslems in general and Indian Moslems in particular have not as yet grown out of the historical stage, of intense religiosity and the theological concept of state.

(b) Their theology and theocratical politics divide the human world into two groups only; the Moslem land and the enemy land. All lands which are either entirely inhabited by the Moslems or are ruled over by the Moslems are Moslem lands. All lands which are mostly inhabited by non-Moslems or are ruled over by a non-Moslem power are enemy lands and no faithful Moslem is allowed to bear any loyalty to them and is called upon to do everything in his power by policy or force or fraud to convert the non-Moslem there to Moslem faith, to bring about its political conquest by a Moslem power. It is no good quoting sentences here or there from Moslem theological books to prove the contrary. Read the whole book to know its trend. And again, it is not with books that we are concerned here but with the followers of the books and how they translate them in practice. You will then see that the whole Moslem history and their daily actions are framed on the design I have outlined above. Consequently, a territorial patriotism is a word unknown to the Moslem—nay, is tabooed, unless in connection with a Moslem territory. Afghans can be patriots, for Afghanistan is a Moslem territory today. But an Indian Moslem if he is a real Moslem—and they are intensely religious as a people—cannot faithfully bear loyalty to India as a country, as a nation, as a state, because it is today 'an enemy land' and doubly lost; for non-Moslems are in a majority here and, to boot it, is not ruled by any Moslem power, Moslem sovereign.

(c) Add to this that of all non-Moslems, the Hindus are looked upon as the most damned by Moslem theologians. For, Christians and Jews are after all *'kitabis'*, having the holy books partially in common. But the Hindus are totally *'kafirs'* as a consequence their land 'Hindusthan' is pre-eminently an 'enemy' and as long as it is not ruled by Moslems or all Hindus do not embrace Islam. This is the religious mentality of the Indian Moslems who still live and move and have their being in religiosity. There are some of them like Mohammed Ali and others who in their individual capacity are not so religious minded but who nevertheless, encourage this mentality in their masses as a very suitable, political, racial and cultural weapon. What wonder then that the Moslem League should openly declare its intention to join hands with non-Indian alien Moslem countries rather than with Indian Hindus in forming a Moslem federation? They could not be accused from their point of view of being traitors to Hindusthan. Their conscience was clear. They never looked upon our today's 'Hindusthan' as their country, nation. It is to them already an alien land and enemy land—'a Dar-ul-Harb' and not a 'Dar-ul-Islam!!'

(d) This is the religious and living mentality of the Moslems. Consequently, their political and cultural mentality also is essentially anti-Hindu and is bound to be so as long as they continue to be Moslems and 'the faithfuls'. They are vividly conscious of the fact that they entered India as conquerors and subjected the Hindus to their rule. They are also gifted with a curious memory that is supremely oblivious of all events which remind them of their defeats and discomfitures. They will never remember that the Hindus beat them like a clip in a hundred battlefields in India and had in the long run freed all India from the Moslem yoke and re-established Hindu *pad-padashahi* as indicated above in section six of this address. They know that they form a powerful minority in India. Their population is growing in every successive Census report. *What is to be especially noted by our Hindu Sangathanist party is the fact that some of our Hindu superstitious and suicidal social customs like untouchability, ban on* shuddhi, *on widow remarriages, etc., offer them a fertile field for Moslem proselytisation and conversion.* So, under the present circumstances, they rightly hope to increase their population and decrease the Hindus with equal rapidity. They know that the British are sure for a long time to come, to offer them every facility and help to strengthen the Moslem position against the Hindus, whose rise and political ambitions the British wholeheartedly dread. They are also sure that the Congressite Hindus in their pursuit of the silly fad of bringing about a Hindu-Moslem unity in India based on the impossible common bond of a territorial unity only, are certain to yield to Moslem demands with an amount of Moslem browbeating as regards weightages, special and larger representation, etc. and especially in suppressing the Hindu *Sangathan* movement that is at present the only thorn in their sides. They realise that in the Indian army and the armed police, the Moslems, in spite of their being in minority, are already the predominant factor holding some 60 per cent jobs. With all these factors in their favour, they are fully confident, wisely or unwisely, that in case the British are overpowered in some big world war, the Moslems with the help of the non-Indian Moslem powers bordering our country may snatch away the political sovereignty of India out of the British hands and re-establish a Moslem Empire here. Then alone they can and will love India as their own country as a 'Moslem land' and sing wholeheartedly by themselves 'Bharat hamara desh hai!!' or 'Hindusthan hamara desh hai.' But, till then, it must remain 'an enemy land' to the Moslem, to the faithful.

I wish the British also take a serious note of the fact indicated at the close of this last paragraph and curtail their policy of encouraging Moslems too much in their anti-Hindu activities. In view of the open declaration of the Moslem League to divide India into two parts, inviting the alien Moslem nations from outside India to form Moslem federation and raise an independent Moslem kingdom in India, the British also should think twice before they trust their 'favoured wife' too much just to spite the Hindus. The harem intrigues in Moslem history are well known and the British may find in the end that in their attempt to encourage their 'favourite wife' just to spite the Hindus they have but succeeded in spiting themselves. Nevertheless, that concerns the British and they can take care of themselves. What concerns us Hindus is the fact that we get determined not to play the part of a handmaid either to the British or to the Moslems, but, are masters in our own house, Hindusthan, the land of the Hindus.

With this end in view what should be our immediate programme

19. Knowing it then for certain that the Indian Moslems, for reasons some of which are referred to above, are about the last people to join the Hindus in forming any common political nation on equal footing in India based on the only common bond of our territorial unity, out of merely

territorial Indian patriotism, let us Hindu *Sangathanists* first correct the original mistake, the original political sin which our Hindu Congressites most unwillingly committed at the beginning of the Indian National Congress movement and are persistently committing still of running after the mirage of a territorial Indian nation and seeking to kill as an impediment in that fruitless pursuit the life-growth of an organic Hindu nation. Let us Hindus resume the thread of our national life where, as I have shown in section seven of this address, our grandfathers left it at the fall of our Maratha and Sikh-Hindu Empires. The life and organic growth of the self-conscious Hindu nation that was suddenly struck with an atrophy of self-forgetfulness must again be revived, resurrected. Let us, therefore, boldly re-proclaim even in the words of Govindrao Kale, who wrote them so early as 1793 in his letter quoted in section six above that the land which extends from the Indus to the Southern seas is Hindusthan—the land of the Hindus and we Hindus are the Nation that owns it. If you call it an Indian nation, it is merely an English synonym for the Hindu nation. To us Hindus, Hindusthan and India mean one and the same thing. We are Indians because we are Hindus and vice versa.

Yes, we Hindus are a nation by ourselves because religious, racial, cultural and historical affinities bind us intimately into a homogeneous nation and added to it we are most pre-eminently gifted with a territorial unity as well. Our racial being is identified with India—our beloved fatherland and our holyland above all and irrespective of it all, we Hindus will to be a nation and, therefore, we are a nation. None has a right to challenge or demand a proof of our common nationality when some thirty crores of us Hindus are with it.

It is absurd to call us a community in India. The Germans are the nation in Germany and the Jews a community. The Turks are the nation in Turkey and Arab or the Armenian minority a community. Even so the Hindus are the nation in India—in Hindusthan, and the Moslem minority a community.

Referring to the Sudeten Germans, the leaders of the Moslem League threatened us the other day at their Karachi session that if their demands in overriding the Hindus are not granted in India, they would play the part of the Sudeten Germans and call in their Moslem co-religionists across the border inside India to their help as the Sudeten Germans called the Germans in Sudeten land. To that threat, I retort that our friends in the Moslem League should not cry till they are out of the woods. They should remember that their illustration cuts both ways. If they grow stronger, they can play the part of the Sudeten Germans alright. But, if we Hindus in India grow stronger, in time these Moslem friends of the League type will have to play the part of German-Jews instead. We, Hindus, have taught the Shakas and the Huns already to play that part pretty well. So, it is no use bandying words till the test comes. The taste of the pudding is in its eating.

Indian Nationalism also is communalism in relation to Humanity

20. If to such an outspoken attitude of being a Hindu Nationalist on your part, an Indian nationalist of the Congress type raises the objection, 'Oh, but do you not see how narrow minded it is to think of Hindus and Moslems, this race or religion and that in sectarian mood? Man to man, we all are one. Let us think of universal brotherhood alone.'

Then inquire of him in return 'Brother, universal brotherhood we Hindus adore even to a fault. But, will you tell us, Oh Indian nationalist, why you think of an Indian nationality in a sectarian sense?' Is it because India is a territorial unit? But, then, there are other territorial units in the world. Why are you an Indian patriot and not an Abyssinian one and go there and fight for their freedom? It is precisely because by company and education you feel yourselves more akin to the Indian people by virtue of racial or religious or cultural affinities than you feel at home with other nationalities—although you may not be aware of this reason. Verily you worship a god you know not. Nor you know that Indian or any patriotism cannot but be communal in relation to humanity, for nationality is as strong a principle of human division as is a racial or religious or cultural community.

Hindu nationalists should not at all be apologetic to being called Hindu Communalists!

21. The fact is that nationalism and communalism are in themselves either equally justifiable and humane or not. Nationalism when it is aggressive is as immoral in human relations as is communalism when it tries to suppress the equitable rights of other communities and tries to usurp all to itself. But when communalism is only defensive, it is as justifiable and human as an equitable nationalism itself. The Hindu nationalists do not aim to usurp what belongs to others. Therefore, even if they be called Hindu communalists, they are justifiably so and are about the only real Indian nationalists. For, a real and justifiable

Indian, nationalism must be equitable to all communities that compose the Indian nation. But, for the same reason, the Moslems alone are communalists in an unjustifiable anti-national and treacherous sense of the term. For, it is they who want to usurp to themselves all that belongs to others. The Indian National Congress only condemns itself as an anti-national body when it calls in the same breath the Hindu Mahasabha and the Moslem League as bodies equally communal in the reprehensible and treacherous sense of that term. Consequently, if, to defend the just and equitable rights of Hindus in their own land is communalism, then we are communalists par excellence and glory in being the most devoted Hindu communalists which to us means being the truest and the most equitable Indian nationalists!

22. Having determined then once for all to revive the concept of an organic Hindu nation and regenerate its life-growth as the first item of our immediate programme, the second and the consequent item must be to review every action and every event in public life from the only standpoint of Hindu interests without mincing matters at all. From the local details of the music and the mosque questions, right up to the question of Indian federation and from the internal Indian political policy to our foreign and international policy and relations, we shall openly and separately take up a stand as Hindus and support, oppose or take every step in the interests of Hindudom alone. Our politics henceforth will be purely Hindu politics fashioned and tested in Hindu terms only, in such ways as will help the consolidation, freedom and life-growth of our Hindu nation.

23. The third item in our immediate programme will be a re-declaration of our attitude to the question of Indian unity even in its territorial aspect. In its own interests, the Hindu nation does not shut the door to any possibility of a united Indian nation provided it is based on an equitable and equal footing. The Hindus will ever be ready to grant equal rights and representation to all minor communities in India in legislatures and services, civil and political life, in proportion to population and merit. The Hindus although they are in overwhelming majority will still waive their right of claiming any preferential treatment, and special prerogatives which, in fact, in every other nation are due to the major community. But, the Hindus will never tolerate the absurd and the unheard of claim of the minorities to have any preferential treatment, weightages or special favours over

and above what the major community obtains. The Hindu nation will go so far as to accept the equitable national principle of 'one man, one vote' irrespective of religion or race or culture in the formation of the common Indian state; but it shall knock on the head any political demand that claims, 'One Moslem, three votes' or 'three Hindus, one vote!' or any cultural demand that antagonises or insults or supresses Hindu culture in its historical, linguistic, religious or racial aspect. The minorities will be free to follow their religion, speak their language, develop their culture among themselves provided they do not infringe on the equal rights of others or is not opposed to public peace and morality. If the Moslems join us on these equitable conditions and bear undivided loyalty to the Indian state and the Indian state alone, well and good. Otherwise our formula holds good, 'if you come, with you, if you don't, without you, but if you oppose in spite of you, we Hindus fight out the good battle of achieving the independence of India and herald the rebirth of a free and mighty Hindu nation in near future!'

24. Our foreign policy also will be guided from an outspoken and unalloyed Hindu point of view. All those nations who are friendly or likely to be helpful to the Hindu nation will be our friends and allies. All those who will oppose the Hindu nation or are likely to endanger the Hindu interests will be opposed by us. All those who do neither, we will observe a policy of neutrality towards them, irrespective of any politicalism they choose to follow for themselves. No academic and empty slogans of democracy or Nazism or fascism can be the guiding principle of our foreign policy. Hindu interests alone will be our test. No more 'Khilafats or Palestine-afats' can dupe us into suicidal sympathies and complications. Our relations with England also will be guided by the same Hindu policy, having the absolute political independence of the Hindu nation in view.

25. Towards the minorities our attitude under the present circumstances must be differential. The Hindus will assure them all that we hate none, neither the Moslems nor the Christians nor the Indian Europeans but henceforth, we shall take good care to see that none of them dares to hate or belittle the Hindus also. Amongst the minorities:

The Parsees are by race, religion, language and culture most akin to us. They have gratefully been loyal to India and have made her their only home. They have produced some of the best Indian patriots and revolutionists like Dadabhai and Madam Cama. They will have to be and therefore, shall be incorporated into the common Indian state with perfectly equal rights and trust.

The Christian minority is civil, has no extra-territorial political designs against India, is not linguistically and culturally averse to the Hindus and therefore, can be politically assimilated with us. Only in religion they differ from us and are proselytising church. So, in that matter alone, the Hindus must be on their guard and give the missionaries no blind latitude to carry on their activities beyond voluntary and legitimate conversion. The Hindus also must continue to reconvert the Christians and carry on the *shuddhi* movement on the same voluntary and legitimate bases. It is only in our Travancore state that the Christians seem to cherish some political design against the Hindu state and it is only there that we shall have to treat them with some political distrust by not allowing them too much latitude in State affairs and offices, till they too cease to be political suspects to the Hindus as the Christians in other parts have ceased to be.

As to the Jews in India, they are too few, have given us no political or cultural troubles and are not in the main a proselytising people, they will to be friendly towards the Hindus who have sheltered them when homeless and can be easily assimilated in a common Indian state. But, this fact must not land us again into the suicidal generosity our forefathers had been guilty of in other cases of inviting colonies of non-Hindus to India. With every sympathy with the Jews outside India, the Hindus must, therefore, oppose the present Congressite proposal of inviting or allowing any new Jewish colony to settle in India. India must be a Hindu land, reserved for the Hindus. While our Hindu overpopulation in some parts of India is hard pressed to find land for extension, how absurd it is to invite non-Hindu colonies to settle in our thinly populated parts! How ridiculous it is to find some Congressites preaching birth control to restrict our own population in order to avoid overcrowding and start straightaway to invite Jewish colonies to settle in India. We must exhort our esteemed Divan of Cochin in particular to take a leaf out of the history of Travancore and set his face sternly against any proposal or outside pressure to allow the alien Jews to colonise the lands in Cochin.

So far as the Moslem minority is concerned, I have already dealt with it at length. In short we must watch it in all its actions with the greatest distrust possible. Granting them, on the one hand every equitable treatment which an Indian citizen can claim on an equality of footing with another, we must sternly refuse them the least preferential treatment in any sphere of life—religious, cultural or political. Not only while we are engaged in our struggle for liberating India but even after India is free, we must look upon them as suspicious friends and take great care to see that the northern frontiers of India are well guarded by staunch and powerful Hindu forces to avoid the possible danger of the Indian Moslems going over to the alien Moşlem nations across the Indus and betraying our Hindusthan to our non-Hindu foes.

But, how to bell the cat?

26. While listening to all this and agreeing with me as to the efficacy of this Hindu policy in future, every Hindu *Sangathanist* here must have been weighed down with one single question. 'But, how are we to bell the cat? How to raise ways and the means to put this policy into practice? How are we to enable ourselves to be in so strong a position as to shape events to our liking in the face of the overwhelming predicaments and powerlessness in which the Hindu *Sangathanist* movement is struck today? I tell you, don't be down-hearted. The most efficient weapon is already lying close at hand; only stretch out your hand in the right direction and you grasp it. Let us just begin at the beginning and...

Capture the political power that obtains in India today

27. If but the Hindu *Sangathanists* capture the seats that are allotted to the Hindus under the present constitution in municipalities, boards and Legislatures, you will find that a sudden lift is given to the Hindu movement so as to raise it to an incredible power in relation to our present all-round helplessness. 'It is a bigger order still.' You may explain, 'How are we to capture even that political power which is allotted to the Hindus today? In a fit of self-forgetfulness it is we Hindus who resigned that power into the hands of the Congressites. It is true that we Hindus made the Congress what it is, but, it has now suddenly turned against us who raised it to a position of power over some seven provinces in India! Now the very concept of a Hindu Nation stinks in its nostrils; it has already declared the Hindu Mahasabha a communal and reprehensible body and ordered millions of Congressite Hindus not to have anything to do with it. It may be that one of those days it may proclaim the Hindu *Sangathan* movement itself as an act of high treason against the Congress fad of an Indian territorial patriotism, But, it is now grown too strong for us to dislodge it from its position and compel it to yield back the political power which as of right was due to us Hindus alone.'

I know that this difficulty stares every Hindu *Sangathanist* in the face all over India. It is true that the Congress looks today like a veritable anti-Hindu tower of strength, but, I assure you it is a painted one! Approach and touch the canvas and you will find it!!

Let the Hindu Sangathanists boycott the Congress and it will come to its senses in no time!!

28. Before we proceed to indicate the easiest remedy to capture the political power and disable the Congress from doing any practical harm to the Hindu *Sangathan* movement, let us declare in unmistakable terms that we are not out to spite the Congress institution itself, nor the leaders and followers thereof. Mr. Jinnah is quite correct in stating that the Congress has been since its inception down to this day a Hindu body manned mostly by the Hindu brains, Hindu money and Hindu sacrifice. Even today, some of them are noble patriots. They are erring, but, cannot be wicked and almost all of them are our own kith and kin. The few Moslems there, although they are allowed to boss the Congress policy at times through the suicidal folly of the Hindu leaders, are but nonentities, are kept there merely as figureheads to run the poor show of a 'united Indian nation'. We are out not to spite the Congress as an institution, but to chastise its anti-Hindu policy, to cure it of the intolerable hypocrispy which is all the more harmful for its strutting about under the mask of truth, Truth absolute and nothing but truth, with its *lathi*-charges and English bayonets going merrily hand in hand with nonviolence, non-violence absolute and nothing but non-violence in thought, word and deed!!

So, under the present circumstances, the Congress has compelled us to disown it and divest it of all power to represent the Hindus in any aspect or capacity whatsoever. They have foolishly challenged the Hindu community and the Hindu Mahasabha and we must take up the challenge.

Just think, Oh Hindu *Sangathanists*, on what meat does this Congress feed that it has grown so great? Only remember that the Congress draws all its supplies—men, money and votes, from the Hindus. Then cut off those supplies and the position which the Congress has taken against the Hindus and which seems to be so impregnable will be untenable in no time.

All the national importance and political power that the Congress has come to wield today, in India and the ministries and majorities it holds in legislatures are but derived from the Hindu electorate. The Congressite Hindu cannot get a single Mohammedan vote, for the constitution itself is communal. The Mohammedans can vote only for a Mohammedan, the Christians for a Christian, and so on. Congressites—and they are mostly Hindus—can but get them elected to the legislature, boards and municipalities, on the strength of the Hindu votes. If the Hindus make it a point not to vote for a Congress ticket, then? Not a single Congressmen can be returned to either a local body or a legislature! They stand on Hindu shoulders as Hindu candidates and as soon as they raise themselves to those high places they kick the Hindus back, disown the Hindus, call Hindu organisations as communal and, therefore, reprehensibly betray Hindu interests at every turn but keep dancing attendance on the Moslem League. But, if you withdraw your that your shoulder, your that support, then? You will find that political power and public importance of the Congress is dead as a door-nail. They call themselves Indian nationalists, but every step they take is communal. They have guaranteed special protection to minorities—Moslems, Christians, Europeans, etc. Is that Indian nationalism? A true Indian nationalist must know nothing of Moslems and Hindus, minorities and majorities. To him all must be Indians only. Why do they then take cognisance of communities, religious or racial, in India? And if they can take congnisance of the communal minorities, then why do they fight shy to take cognisance of the major community, the Hindus, or call those who do so as reprehensible communalists? Nay more; a true Indian nationalist, if honest, will never go abegging for votes from a constituency which is openly tabulated as general, that means non-Moslem, non-Christian, etc. That is an electorate which is not national. A truly Indian national electorate cannot be divided as Moslem one and non-Moslem one or Christian one and non-Christian one, special and general. A truly Indian national electorate must be only an 'Indian' electorate pure and simple without the least mention of the unnational and unreasonable difference of race or religion. If our Congressites are true and conscientious Indian nationalists, they ought to refuse forthwith to stand as candidates to elections under this communal electoral roll and resign their seats forthwith which are tainted with these communal labels. Is there a single Congress minister or member ready to resign and run that ordeal? None, none! Next election when they come to your Hindu doors to beg for votes, tell them in all honesty and humility, 'Sirs, Congressmen, you are Indian nationalists; but I am Hindu and this is a Hindu electorate? Then how can your accept a vote so tainted by communalism? Please go to a truly 'Indian nationalist electorate' to beg for votes wherever you may find it; and if you find it nowhere in the world today, please wait till a pure and simple and truly 'Indian electorate' comes into being!' Do you think you will find a dozen Congress candidates honest enough to do so? None, none!

Then again every candidate under the present constitution has to write his religion and even caste. Then only can he be drafted out to separate electorates, Hindus, Moslems, Christians, etc. These Congress candidates in the election season quietly write down their community as Hindus! They mark down Hindu homes even according to castes—Brahmins, Marathas, Bhangis, etc. and then allot their candidates according to their castes to the caste voters so that he may pool up larger votes. They appeal even to caste pride and caste hatred. In the election season they are communalists of the worst type. But, as soon as the election season is over, the Congress candidate dons on again his Indian national robes and hits back the very Hindu who paid him his vote as a Hindu that it is a shame for a Hindu to call himself a Hindu and to be a member of the Hindu Mahasabha!

But, if you once make it quite clear that you as Hindus are not going to vote for any such seasonal Hindu but only for a Hindu who is born and bred and means to continue to be true to his Hindu race even after the election session is over and if once these gentlemen know for certain that they can never be elected on Hindu votes unless they are members of the Hindu Mahasabha—what do you think will happen? I assure you that 75 per cent of these Indian nationalists will vie with each other to register themselves as members of the Hindu Mahasabha overnight and vow to be Hindus even fanatically throughout their life rather than lose a chance of being members and ministers and somebodies in the government secretariats!

Then the only way which is also unbelievably easy, not only to chastise the Congress nationalist fad, but, even to raise Hindudom to incalculably powerful position in the land at a stroke is under the present circumstances this:

(1) Boycott the Congress; (2) Don't vote for the Congress ticket; and (3) Vote only for a confirmed and merited Hindu nationalist.

29. Let no Hindu *sangathanist* pay a single farthing or lend a single

member or register a single vote for the Congress ticket. We know by experience that even a staunch Hindu has to act against Hindu interests as soon as he is tainted by a Congress ticket under a congress discipline and for the selfish fear that he would otherwise lose his job. When once the Congressites know that the Congress cap or ticket is at a serious discount in the Hindu market, is no royal road to the councils or the local bodies, you will find that the Hindu caps will sell like hot cakes and Hindu Mahasabha tickets will rise in an unsupplyable demand!

30. In a nutshell, the position is this: there is a Moslem electorate to protect the Moslem interests. There is a Hindu electorate in fact, though it is named to spite the Hindus as 'general' which we can use to protect Hindu interests. The Moslems being in majority in some three provinces, they took good care to see that only those Moslems were elected on their votes who pledged openly to save Moslem interests alone. We Hindus are in majority in some seven provinces; we sillily handed over our votes to those who blatantly proclaimed they were not Hindus at all and all of whom promised that they were not going to safeguard the special interests of Hindus, not even the just and equitable interests of Hindus as Hindus. The result is that even in those seven provinces where we are in a majority and of course in those three provinces where Moslems dominate—we Hindus are reduced to be veritable helots throughout our land. In some cases, as in Bengal and the Frontier, our very life and property stand in hourly danger, the honour of womanhood insecure. Thus, we Hindus have thrown away to the winds whatever had not an unsubstantial political power was won by hard struggle carried on and sacrifices undergone by our Hindu patriots and by ourselves amongst them, for the last fifty years and more. While the Moslem ministers are openly members of the Moslem League, they lead it, they avow to be the advocates of Moslem interests, even threaten to *satav* the Hindus, frame themselves and get passed government bills to reserve 60 per cent services for Moslems in Bengal, what do the Congressite ministers and members whom Hindu electorate sent to the councils to represent Hindu interests do? In Bengal, the Congress MLAs practically supported this atrocious Moslem reservation, they have acquiesced all over India in the pro-Moslem communal award and denounce the Hindu Mahasabha also for carrying on an agitation against it!! In every case when Hindu interests are threatened by Moslems, they have leaned towards the Moslems just to parade that they were Indian patriots. Witness the

Congress attitude with regard to the Shahid Ganj affair, Delhi temple struggle, the Nizam and the Bhopal questions. But, is not such an anti-national pro-Moslem attitude also an act of communalism? It is worst on the part of a Congressite, who got himself elected on Hindu votes, it is downright treachery!

Form a solid Hindu Nationalist Front

31. The only way to chastise this anti-Hindu and anti-national policy of the Congress, the best and easiest remedy under the circumstances lies in the fact of forming a Hindu Nationalist Front! Let all our *sadhus*, Sanatanists, Aryasamajists and *Sangathanist* organisations all over India make it a point never to vote for a Congress candidate, but vote for a Hindu nationalist candidate alone. Even today, the strength of all these faithful Hindu parties put together cannot but be counted in millions. We shall and must succeed in forming majorities in almost all provinces where Hindus are in a majority. Even if we fail in some cases through the folly of a number of Hindu renegades, it is still quite possible to begin with, to return a sufficiently strong minority of Hindu nationalists to the councils in provinces and the Centre to make it impossible for any government to function without gaining the support of our Hindu Nationalist Front. If you do this, you will have real Hindu ministries—Hindu national ministries openly avowed to safeguard Hindu interests in seven provinces at a stroke! That will raise the Hindu cause and the Hindu nation immediately to be the greatest political power in the land. You will find as if by a transfer scene that Hindudom has come home, the Hindu Mahasabha suddenly lifted out of its present state of being a persecuted and neglected body and raised to the position of dictatorship in shaping the political destiny of India. Every Hindu will raise his head high and erect, conscious of his importance and assured of government backing. He is sure to get in the defence and assert all his legitimate rights—religious, racial, cultural. If a Hindu girl is molested in any part of the land by a Moslem *goonda*, such a condign punishment will promptly be indicted on him as to render all Moslem *goondas,* tremble to touch any other Hindu girl as in the case of molesting an English girl.

If any riot on the part of the Moslem fanatics seeks to force the Hindus to forego their civil rights, the armed police and the military forces will be so promptly and vigorously made to function against the aggressive party that Moslem riots will be a thing of the past and they will learn to tolerate Hindu music by the public thoroughfare as kindly as they do now the government and English bands and processions. The peasants and the labourers will get what is due to them as the very foundation of national life and industry and commerce. Hindu language will be safe, Hindu script will be safe, Hindu religion will be safe; no illegitimate or forceful conversion of a Hindu to non-Hindu faiths will be tolerated for a minute. No Hindu advances will be made begging on knees before the Moslems for unity. For, confident in our own Hindu strength to achieve Indian independence through our own sacrifice and struggle even as we did in the past, our Hindu nationalists will be prepared to fight any non-Hindu power that stands in the way of our onward march towards the achievement of the independence of Hindusthan and its maintenance against all non-Hindu invasions. The very concept and ideal and right of a powerful Hindu nation will bring out all that is best and bravest in the Hindu spirit to the forefront as nothing else can do. If the Moslems pass an Act, e.g., in Bengal, to reserve 60 per cent services for Moslems, our Hindu national ministries will at once get an Act passed in Hindu majority provinces to reserve 90 per cent services for Hindus even where we are only 80 per cent in population, as a retributory measure without making the least apology for it. When we will be in a position to retaliate thus in this way and do retaliate, the Moslems will come to their senses in a day. We shall not only, save Hindu rights and honour in the Hindu provinces but even in provinces where we Hindus are in a minority. Knowing that every attempt to tyrannise the Hindus is sure to recoil on themselves and react for the worse on Moslem interests in all India, the Moslems will learn to behave as good boys and it is then that they will be anxious to open unity talks and knowing they are in a hopeless minority in India and no more dreams of mass conversions of Hindus by force and fraud and by kidnapping Hindu children in sight—the Moslems will inevitably and soon be in a frame of mind to acquiesce in equitable Hindu-Moslem unity pacts.

We shall, in Punjab and the Frontier, have an allied party with our Sikh-Hindu flank. Our Sikh Hindus, though they have a separate electorate and rightly so under the present circumstances, are strong enough to defend Sikh culture and honour and interests which are but our own culture and honour and interests and we will work hand in hand against all non-Hindu aggressions from outside the Frontier. In the Central Legislature also, the Hindu nationalists will compel the government, if you only return staunch Hindu nationalist members in majority, to take drastic military steps against the Frontier Moslem tribes, beat them like a chip in no time and render our Hindu life and property as safe as that of a handful of Europeans continue to be. In Maharashtra, our Hindu National Party shall ally itself with the Democrats of the present day under that redoubtable champion of equitable and truly national policy—Jamnadas Mehta, the eminent leader of the opposition, Dr. Ambedkar and in all other provinces with every party and everyone who stands for and insofar as the stands for safeguarding the just and national and equitable interest of Hindus in common with all other citizens of India, irrespective of race or religion.

32. Nor need there be any fear of breaking up the so-called united front against the British Imperialist. The present Congress united front is a feigned show, a house of cards. The Hindu national united front will be a realistic, homogeneous living front. We shall not only be able to advance the just interests of the Hindu nation but side by side will be in a position with our equitable and truly Indian national policy as I have outlined in Section 23 of this address,—even to advance the interest of the Indian nation in its territorial sense also far more rapidly and solidly and vigorously than this present Quixotic Congress policy with its proposals of doing away with armed military and guarding the frontiers with girl volunteers with *charkhas* in their hands can never do! Down with all that nonsense forever and up with the matter-of-fact Indian politics and the consequent Hindu Nationalist Front.

Remember, oh Hindus, that in raising the standard of this Hindu Nationalist Front, you are exercising but your legitimate constitutional right and can give unjustifiable affront to none. Every Hindu is required by the constitution to vote for whomsoever he likes. So long as bayonets do not extort your votes against your own will for an anti-Hindu candidate, so long it is the easiest and legitimate thing for you to vote for a Hindu nationalist. If but every Hindu does that easy duty for his race, Hindudom is saved. And if the Hindus do not do even that much and determine to commit a cultural and political and racial suicide by voting for an anti-Hindu and anti-national organisation as the Congress has grown today into one—not even Brahmadeva can save you.

Then begin, at least you Hindu *Sangathanists* who are determined to see that Hindudom asserts itself, begin at once at the beginning, form a united Hindu National front under an unalloyed Hindu national flag and capture the political power that even today obtains by voting only for Hindu nationalists and you will see that the larger part of your present local and detailed grievances dissipate like a mist at the very sight of Hindu nationalist ministries formed in seven provinces in India and at the Centre. When you have this much, more shall be added unto you—-and one of these days you shall have heralded an independent and strong and mighty Hindu nation which is but tantamount with a mighty Indian nation based on perfect equality of citizenship for all loyal and faithful Indian citizens irrespective of race and religion from Indus to the seas. Remember 'those who have more will be added unto them but those who have not even that, will be taken away from them which they have!' This is the inexpungeable law in this matter-of-fact world! Capture and have then first the political power that exists! Raise the standard of a Hindu nation! See to it that India must remain a Hindusthan forever: never a Pakistan! An Anglisthan, never, never!!! And, let all India resound with. HINDU DHARMA KI JAI! HINDU RASHTRA KI JAI!! VANDE MATARAM!!!

□

21st Session, Calcutta—1939

Delegates to and Members of the Hindu Mahasabha

I gratefully acknowledge your appreciation of whatever services I have been able to tender to the Hindu cause during the past two years of my tenure of this presidential office, which has persuaded you in calling upon me to preside over this session also for the third time in an unbroken succession. The keen consciousness of the overwhelming contrast between the stupendous amount of the work which ought to be done if we want to realise our noble aspirations in full and the relatively scanty output of work actually done by us all, weighs so heavily on my mind that you all know how I wished and tried to transfer the task of leading the Hindu movement to some mightier Herculean shoulders and re-enter the rank of soldiers as a fighting unit. But firstly, because the commander also is a soldier in part and must obey the common will and secondly, because the very fact that the actual output of work falls a short of the enormous requirement makes it incumbent upon us all not to cease from doing even that little which we can do standing by our posts against all odds under the most adverse circumstances which our generation has to face and thirdly, on account of the encouraging fact that thousands of eminent brave and devoted new workers have entered the field and assure me that they shall see to it in the spirit of a Pratap that the Hindu cause triumphs before this generation passes away and have actually given just a glimpse in fact of their grim resolve during the Nizam civil resistance struggle—do I yield to your kind and almost compelling pressure to accept the office of the president of the Hindu Mahasabha for the third time in spite of my failing health.

Within the limited space of a Presidential Address like this, it is hardly possible to take even a cursory notice at the thousand and one events and problems which Hindudom had to face during this year locally, provincially and generally from Sindh to Assam. The bloody orgies in which the Moslem mobs indulged only recently in the anti-Hindu riots at Sukkur and other places in Sindh, the continuous campaign of raids committed by the Moslem tribes on the North-West Frontier Province rendering Hindu life and property in daily danger; the looting of towns and villages by Moslem gangs proclaiming all along with drum-beating, 'No Moslem need be disturbed, only Hindus will we loot; hundreds of anti-Hindu riots and outrages committed by the Moslem fanatics at various places in U.P, Bihar and Bengal; this Moslem *goondaism* on the one hand and the polished and parliamentary Moslem League on the other, which, treating Hindu minority with the gentle civilities indicated above in Sindh, Punjab and Bengal complains with righteous indignation that the Moslem minority is the only suffering saint throughout the world; then the Congress-League-government negotiations which threaten to prove damaging to Hindu interests in a far more alarming degree than even the notorious communal decision has proved to be and above all, the war situation which has given a handle to the government to restore autocracy in all its pristine glory, putting the hands of the clock of constitutional progress in India fully 50 years back—all these and several other events require to be dealt with in detail. But I must leave them to be treated thus by the several resolutions which will have to be proposed in special connection with them and to the leading speakers who in cases may deal with them more authoritatively, either owing to their local acquaintance with the details or their expert study of the special questions in hand. So that the little space at my disposal may be better utilised in dealing with those basic principles, policies and programmes which should guide our movements in general and on which we must now concentrate our attention and efforts for at least a couple of years to come. Nevertheless, while dealing with these, I shall of course have occasion to treat with some of those outstanding current events too, but only by way of illustrating their central message and bearing on the Hindus movement in general.

II

The Nizam civil resistance movement.

Of all these events, which took place during the current year, the most outstanding one from the Hindu *Sangathanist* point of view and one which has an abiding message for our future policy and programme is of course, the campaign of civil resistance which we had to carry on against the anti-Hindu policy of the Nizam government for full six months during this year. It was a veritable crusade, as righteous as heroic. Our Arya Samaji brethren had to bear the brunt of the fight: not less than ten thousand Arya joined the fight and fought so bravely as to demonstrate that the sacrificial fire lighted up by Maharishi Dayanand Swamiji, the first and foremost Hindu *Sangathanist* of our age, burns brighter and brighter as days pass by and his mission has not fallen into undeserving hands. Not less than five thousand civil resisters defied the anti-Hindu bans of the Nizam government and kept up the fight with unflinching courage and admirable tact on the Hindu Mahasabha flank. But what is more encouraging to note from the pan-Hindu point of view is the fact that it was not only the Arya Samaj and the Hindu Mahasabha, though these two in the main led the struggle, but it was the whole Hindu brotherhood in general which joined hands and participated in the movement so wholeheartedly and with such fervour under the Hindu flag that without this pan-Hindu co-operation, sympathy and sacrifice throughout India, we could not have carried on the struggle to such a successful termination. This fact, to my mind, constitutes the really abiding achievement we could record, apart from the detailed demands which the Hindu *Sangathanists* had compelled the Nizam government to grant. For, this *dharma yuddha*, this fight for the righteous Hindu cause proved to demonstrate that in spite of caste and creed, sect and section, Hindudom as a whole does still pulsate with a common national being. Behold, the thousands and thousands of Hindus leaving their hearths and homes, their nearest and dearest marching on even at the risk of their lives to the rescue of their co-religionists and compatriots in the Nizam's state whom they had perchance never seen or known personally: the Punjabees and Sindhis, Bengalis, and Biharis, Marathas and Madrassis, Brahmins and Bhangis, Santanists, Arya Samajists, Sikhs, Jains, Lingayats, the rich and poor—everyone who was proud of being a Hindu marched on under a common Hindu banner for the vindication of Hindu honour and faced untold miseries, outrageous riots, bayonets and *lathis* charges, hunger and thirst and even death but kept asserting to his last breath 'Hindu *dharma ki jai,* Hindusthan *Hinduon ka.*'

Take for example the case of Sjt. Reddy or some of those Hindu *Sangathanists* who were ordered to be flogged or *lathied* for raising shouts of '*Vande mataram*' and 'Hindusthan *Hinduon ka*.' For each stripe and *lathi* stroke, they went on repeating '*Vande mataram* and Hindusthan *Hinduon ka*.' Many a brave son died under torture. Amongst them was master Sadashiv Pathak, a Maratha boy under sixteen years of age who had to carry daily heavy stones on his head in spite of his bitter complaints that he suffered keen pangs in his chest, but, he would not apologise and had to lay down his life in consequence. You will read such numerous examples of heroic devotion to the Hindu cause in the authenticated histories of this movement which are going to be published shortly, both by the Arya Samaj and the Hindu Mahasabha. Why, there are present in this very *pandal* here, leaders and gentlemen of unimpeachable integrity who had themselves passed through such ordeals while they were under imprisonment in the Nizam jails as leaders or soldiers fighting out this *dharma yuddha*, this crusade in vindication of Hindu faith, Hindu freedom and Hindu honour.

These crusaders received no pay nor were their families promised pension. Many of them had resigned their services and professions, earning in cases thousands a month. All of them knew they were unarmed, marching against an armed force and from the fate which those who preceded. Them they knew they will be tortured, starved, *lathied* and bayoneted too and yet they marched forth voluntarily, for there was no conscription but moral. You will be surprised to know that after the news of the outrageous *lathi* charge at Aurangabad on the Hindu *Sangathanist* prisoners, volunteers came in larger numbers to our *shibirs* to register their names and some who had then only recently returned after serving their first term in the Nizam jails as civil resisters, insisted on being sent again to defy the anti-Hindu bans in the Nizam state. The fact that such a Hindu force consisting of fourteen to fifteen thousand civil resisters could be raised at the very first blare of the trumpet call by the Hindu *Sangathanist* Party today is a lesson for us and for all those who dare to treat our demands lightly. These fifteen thousand Hindu *Sangathanists* constituted a force superior to those English or German forces who are now fighting in Europe, for their respective nations in moral courage and had it not been only a civil resistance movement and had we been in a position to face our opponents' bayonet for bayonet and rifle for rifle, chances are they would have proved superior to them in an armed resistance too. But, even if we let chances alone, what is also enough is to encourage our Hindu *Sangathanist* Party in India with a self-confidence, with the bracing up consciousness of having won a moral victory and on the other hand, to *warn all anti-Hindu forces that they should henceforth think twice before they treat the resolutions of the Hindu Mahasabha as lightly as they were wont to do.* What we resolved in heroic words at Nagpur or Sholapur last year has been translated into heroic deeds before we re-assembled at Calcutta on the eve of this ensuing year.

One more aspect of this struggle deserves a special emphasis inasmuch as it is sure to exercise a liberating influence on the future of the Hindu movement in general. The Nizam civil resistance campaign has broken the demoralising spell which weighed like an incubus on the Hindu mind for some 20 years in the past that no cause, howsoever righteous it may be in itself from the Hindu point of view, should be deemed righteous unless the Congress was pleased to certify it as 'national', which word in 99 cases out of a hundred proved to be tantamount with the word 'anti-Hindu' and that no movement on an all-India scale should be or could be carried out successfully unless it was sponsored and led on by the Congress flag. Even in the case of the murderous Moslem riots at Kohat or the general massacre of Hindus perpetrated by the Moplahs from village to village in Malabar, the Hindus did not even dare to condemn the Moslem fanaticism on a pan-Hindu scale all over India, because the step was not certified by the Congress as 'national'. The Congress wanted to play the same game even in this case and dictatorially anathematised the Nizam civil resistance movement as 'communal,' as 'anti-National.' But this time the Hindu *Sangathanist* Party had an ideology of its own conception of what is really national or otherwise interpreted in the light of reason that had freed itself from the blind and unquestioning subservience to any inner voices which on their own admission were sure passports to Himalayan errors or new lights which scarcely made darkness visible and subservience to any Papal bulls issued by the Congress Church and marched on to the rescue of their Hindu co-religionists and compatriots in the Nizam state led on by the Hindu flag. The movement rapidly spread throughout the length and breadth of the country, from Peshawar to Madras. On that one single evening, for example, of the 'Nizam Nisheda Day' as well as 'Hindu Nation Day' not less than a core of Hindus were found gathered under the Hindu flag in capital cities and towns throughout India in pursuance of the mandate to the Hindu *Sangathanist* Party to back up the Hindu movement which seemed only to flourish all the more, the more the Congress anathematised and opposed it as communal and anti-national.

Why did the Congress oppose it? The Congress wanted to reform the states: Well, was not Hyderabad the biggest and yet the worst ruled autocratic state in India? It was at least as worthwhile to introduce constitutional reforms and restore civil liberties in the Nizam state as in the tiny *taluka*-like state of Rajkot. Did not Gandhiji want us to believe that the reform movement of that petty Rajkot had assumed the magnitude of an all-India question, that the whole Indian Ocean was set on fire in the tiny tea cup of Mr. Veerawala? And yet, the question of demanding constitutional reforms for nearly a crore of subjects in the Nizam state which the Hindu Mahasabha had undertaken and was fighting for, seemed to him so remote and unconnected with the Indian question that he could not spare even as much sympathy or interest as he would for the Abyssinians in Africa, for the Spanish or the Czechs in Europe. Not only Gandhiji, but no Congressite, neither the backward nor the forward nor the inward block or their heads, stepped out to condemn the Nizam government even after the inhuman *lathi*charges on the Hindu civil resisters at Aurangabad jail or the bloody riots at Hyderabad. Then again, did not the Congress patronise civil liberties? Was it not a fact that under the Nizam government, even the life and property of millions of Hindus was held in daily danger, no freedom either of speech or worship or association worth the name existed? Then why did not the Congress join hands with Hindu *Sangathanists* who were engaged in a life and death struggle to secure these civil liberties in the state or at least pass a resolution to support the justice of their demands? Was it because the Hindu *Sangathanists* went to the field as Hindus instead of as Indians? Well, it may be a sin for a Hindu to do even a good thing as a Hindu—except on the election day when he has to vote for a Congressite who has to state himself as a Hindu, as a unit in the Hindu electorate! But, when the Moslems in Kashmere rose with the help of outside Moslems in an armed revolt against the Hindu King, demanding representation for the Moslems as Moslems, did not Gandhiji write as a born democrat, that if the Hindu King of Kashmere could not satisfy and allay the discontent of the Moslems who formed 85 per cent of his subjects, he had no moral right to rule but should forthwith abdicate and retire to Kashi? Well, more than 85 per cent of the subjects of the Nizam are Hindus; they had only resorted to unarmed civil resistance to the intolerable religious, cultural and political persecutions with the help of their coreligionists outside the state: but did Gandhiji, the born democrat, advise the Nizam too to abdicate and retire to Mecca? No, on the contrary, he wrote in so many words that he was overwhelmingly concerned throughout the civil resistance movement as 'not to embarrass His Exalted Highness, the Nizam.'

I can recount a hundred and one petty mischiefs also which Congressites of the 'national' brand were busy playing to defeat this Hindu *Sangathanist* movement against the anti-Hindu policy of the Nizam government, but that is not what I intend to deal with here. Suffice it to say that the Hindu Mahasabha could secure the sympathy even of some English MPs in England and persuade them to protest against the horrible oppression at the Aurangabad jail and during the Hyderabad riots the Hindus had to undergo, but no Congress ministers in all the seven provinces touched the subject even with a pair of tongs, initiated not even a discussion in the Congress or Indian legislatures, nor uttered a word in defence of the Hindus against the Nizam government; although these very Congress ministers could threaten to resign altogether in the case of the pettiest Rajkot affair.

The moral is plain and must be plainly told. So long as the Congress continues to hug to the 'pseudo-national' ideology as it does today, its policy is bound to be anti-Hindu, is bound to betray Hindu interests, howsoever just and legitimate they may be. Just think; if the Hindu electorate had voted for the Hindu *Sangathanist* representative and thus had Hindu Mahasabha Ministers in Bombay, Madras and other parts, could they have remained so callously indifferent to the oppression the Hindus had to undergo in Hyderabad? What tremendous pressure they could have brought to bear on the Nizam government in staying its hand from out-Heroding Herod!

It was essentially to emphasise this point that whenever the Hindus are oppressed as Hindus and especially at the hands of the Moslems, the Congress simply will not raise a finger in their defence, that the Hindus *Sangathanists* must take up the task of defending themselves on their own shoulders and if they mean to do so, they can do it in spite of the Congress indifference or even opposition, that the Nizam civil resistance movement was launched by the Hindu *Sangathanist* leaders independently of the Congress under a Hindu flag. The struggle was a test case to begin with the prospective pan-Hindu movement and we Hindu *Sangathanists* were not only not Rajkoted at Hyderabad, but on the contrary, came out with flying colours out of this testing ordeal inasmuch as we have recovered and actualised through this struggle our racial and cultural homogenity, our real National self which under a swoon of self-forgetfulness during the last hundred years or so was all but obliterated.

One word about the political reforms announced by the Nizam government and the undertaking it has given to grant Hindu civil, cultural and religious liberties in consideration of which the civil resistance movement was *suspended by the Hindu Mahasabha* in the spirit of responsive co-operation and accommodation for which H.E.H. the Nizam had graciously pleaded in his announcement. The Hindu Mahasabha thanks the Nizam government for the general amnesty of all Hindu civil resisters. It was a step in the right direction, but since then, the Nizam government has not moved as quickly as it ought to have done in introducing the reforms in themselves inadequate and halting in practical operation. The Mahasabha is extremely anxious to open out some way to peaceful constitutional progress and restore lasting amity between the Hindus and Moslems in that state and therefore, it begs to draw the pointed attention of the Nizam to the fact that any unreasonable delay in putting the reforms in actual operation cannot but prove dangerous and give rise to discontent, which is perfectly avoidable if but the Nizam government takes time by his forelock before it is too late. And the second thing that is most urgent is the fact that the Nizam government should hold some of the fanatical local Moslem officials in leash who, counting on an ultimate support from the Central Government, are still harassing the Hindus every now and then.

If the local fanatical Moslem rabble and such officials are strictly dealt with by the government in some cases, the Moslem zealots will soon come to their senses all over the state. I hope these warnings will be taken by the Nizam government in the amicable spirit which prompts me in sounding them.

The Shiva Mandir satyagraha *at Delhi*

The splendid and sustained struggle the Hindus have carried on at Delhi in connection with the Shiva Mandir affair deserves also an all-India homage. It too sounds the same warning that the Congress does not and will not and cannot defend a Hindu cause against any anti-Hindu aggression. But in spite of it all, the overwhelming suffering and sacrifice in men and money in connection with the Shiva Mandir at Delhi shall not go in vain if but only those Hindus, who pledge to safeguard Hindu interests and are not enslaved to the Congress ticket, are sent by the Hindus on a Hindu *Sangathanist* ticket to represent them to the corporation. The pan-Hindu spirit which this struggle has lit up will prove the real Shiva. On the site where stood the tiny mud hut which has been so high-handedly destroyed, I already see rising before my mind's eye a magnificent temple of Shiva and thousands of pilgrims crowding to worship at it before a decade passes away. The successful resistance the Hindus offered in defence of their legitimate rights at Khamgaon, Mahad, Bhagalpur and several other places during this year are also full of significance and testify to the fact that the spirit of self-assertion is consolidating the Hindus under the Hindu Mahasabha's lead. But I must not lose myself in the labyrinths of detailed events any longer and address myself to the chief task I have set before me in this address of outlining the fundamental basis and general policy and programme on which I wish we all concentrate our attention for at least a couple of years to come.

III

Some of the basic principles and tenets of the Hindu movement.

It is encouraging to note that thousands of those who were brought up from their early days under the influence of the pseudo-nationalistic ideology current in the Congress camp and were consequently so thoroughly prejudiced against anything that was connected with Hindutva that they militated against the very word Hindu as something superstitious, out-of-date, unworthy of a progressive patriot to own, should now be evincing a genuine desire to know all about the Hindu Mahasabha, its policy and immediate programme. The case of no less a personality than Mr. Tairsee whose sad demise all Bombay lamented only a couple of months ago can serve as a case in point. He was reputed to be one amongst the first ten citizens of Bombay, a rationalist of rationalists, one of the foremost Congressites. Yet after I had casually explained to him the Hindu *Sangathanist* ideology as expounded in my Nagpur speech, he publicly confessed that the rationalism which made him shun the word Hindu or Hindu *Sangathan* as a crass superstition was itself the crassest of superstitions. He not only joined our party but proudly accepted the presidentship of the Bombay Provincial Hindu Sabha. Throughout my extensive tours I have come across thousands of the intellectual class who simply militated against the Hindu idea at its first mention, when cogently explained rubbed their eyes in a doubting mood at its second mention and half of them pressed for a closer acquaintance with it, while the other half simply capitulated at its third mention. There has grown of late enormous curiosity throughout India to know something of the Hindu Mahasabha, its aims and as to what is its programme and this demand at times comes from foreign countries as well. That is the reason why I wish to devote this address mainly to enumerate categorically the leading principles and tenets on which the Hindu movement is based and to outline its general policy and some outstanding details of its immediate programme. It will serve as a cogent statement of our case and may be utilised as a basis for a manifesto in future to an organised Hindu party in the legislatures as well as a handy guide to our workers and propagandists in the press and platform. It may involve some repetition, but endless repetition of truth as also of a falsehood is about the only means to cast the mentality of a whole people into a required mould. As long as falsehood holds, the propagandistic field truth must speak out to silence it as many times as the former repeats a lie.

The following are some of the basic tenets and aspects of the Hindu movement:

- Every person is a Hindu who regards and owns this Bharat *bhumi,* this land from the Indus to the sea, as his fatherland as well as his holyland, i.e., the land of the origin of the religion, of his religion, the cradle of his faith.

The followers, therefore, of Veidicism, Sanatanism, Jainism, Buddism, Lingaitism, Shikhism, the Arya Samaji, the Brahma Samaji, the Devasamaji, the Prarthana Samaji and such other religions of Indian origin are Hindus and constitute Hindudom, i.e., the Hindu people as a whole.

Consequently, the so-called aboriginal or hill tribes also are Hindus because India is their fatherland as well as their Holyland of whatever form of religion or worship they follow.

This definition, therefore, should be recognised by the government and made the test of Hindutva in enumerating the population of Hindus in the government Census to come. The definition rendered in Sanskrit stands thus:

॥ आसिंधु सिंधुपर्यंता यस्य भारत भूमिका ॥
॥ पितृभू: पुण्यभूश्चैव स वै हिंदुरितिस्मृत: ॥ १ ॥

- *The word 'Hindu' is not of a foreign origin nor it is connected with the advent of the Moslems in India,* as was erroneously suspected for a time under the mischievous influence of some alien scribes. Our land and our people were at times called Sapta Sindhus or Sindhus even by our Veidic *rishis*. The following verse, for example, from the *Rig Veda* itself will conclusively testify to this fact:

॥ आ ऋक्षाद्दहंसोमुचदयो वार्यासत्त सिंधुषु ॥
॥ वधर्दासस्य तु विनृम्ण नीनम: ॥ २ ॥

Thousands of years before Mohammed, the Moslem prophet was born, the ancient Babylonians knew us as 'Sindhus' and the ancient *Zend Avesta* refers to us as Hindus. One of our provinces on this side of the Indus has retained this ancient appellation of our land and people down to this day refer to it as Sindhu *desh* and its people as 'Sindhis' (Sindh). In our modern Prakrit, the Sanskrit 'I' is often transformed into a 'g' just as the word *Kesari* in Sanskrit or *Krishan* has been transformed into Hindu Prakrit as *Kehari* and *Kahna;* even so the word *Sindhu* has been transformed into modern Prakrits as *Hindu*. Those who want to have this point exhaustively and conclusively treated may read my book *Hindutva*.

- *Hinduism, Hindutva and Hindudom:* In expounding the ideology of the Hindu movement, it is absolutely necessary to have a correct grasp of the meaning attached to these three terms. From the word 'Hindu' has been coined the word 'Hinduism' in English. It means the school or system of religions the Hindus follow. The second word 'Hindutva' is far more comprehensive and refers not only to the religious aspect of the Hindu people as the word 'Hinduism' does, but comprehends even their cultural, linguistic, social and political aspects as well. It is more or less akin to Hindu polity and its nearly exact translation would be 'Hinduness'. The third word 'Hindudom' means the Hindu people spoken of collectively. It is a collective name for the Hindu world, just as Islam denotes the Moslem world or

Christiandom denotes the Christian world.

- (*We Hindus are a nation by ourselves.* In my presidential speech at Nagpur, I had, for the first time in the history of our recent politics, pointed out in bold relief that the whole Congress ideology was vitiated *ab initio* by its unwitted assumption that the territorial unity, a common habitat, was the only factor that constituted and ought to and must constitute a nation. This conception of a territorial nationality has since then received a rude shock in Europe itself from which it was imported wholesale to India and the present war has justified my assertion by exploding the myth altogether. All nations carved out to order on the territorial design without any other common bond to mould each of them into a national being have gone to rack and ruin, tumbled down like a house of cards. Poland and Czechoslovakia will ever serve as a stern warning against any such efforts to frame heterogeneous peoples into such hotch-potch nations, based only on the shifting sands of the conception of territorial nationality, not cemented by any cultural, tacial or historical affinities and consequently having no common will to incorporate themselves into a nation. These treaty-nations broke up at the first opportunity they got, the German part of them went over to Germany, the Russian to Russia, Czechs to Czechoslovakia and Poles to Poland. The cultural, linguistic, historical and such other organic affinities proved stronger than the territorial one. Only those nations have persisted in maintaining their national unity and identity during the last three to four centuries in Europe which had developed racial, linguistic, cultural and such other organic affinities in addition to their territorial unity or even at times in spite of it and consequently willed to be homogeneous national units—such as England, France, Germany, Italy, Portugal, etc.

Judged by any and all of these tests which go severally and collectively to form such a homogeneous and organic nation, in India we Hindus are marked out as an abiding nation by ourselves. Not only we own a common fatherland, a territorial unit, but what is scarcely found anywhere else in the world we have a common holyland which is identified with our common fatherland. This Bharat *bhumi*, this Hindusthan, India is both our *pitrubhu* and *punyabhu*. Our patriotism, therefore, is doubly sure. Then we have common affinities, cultural, religious, historical, linguistic and racial which through the process of countless centuries of association and assimilation moulded us into a homogeneous and organic nation and above all, induced a will to lead a corporate and common national Life. The Hindus are no treaty-nation, but an organic national being.

One more pertinent point must be met as it often misleads our Congressite Hindu brethren in particular. The homogeneity that wields a people into a national being does not only imply the total absence of all internal differences, religious, racial or linguistic of sects and sections amongst themselves. It only means that they differ more from other people as a national unit than they differ amongst themselves. Even the most unitarians nations of today, say, the British or the French, cannot be free from any religious, linguistic, cultural, racial or other different sects or sections or even some antipathies existing amongst themselves. National homogeneity connotes oneness of a people in relation to the contrast they present to any other people as a whole.

We Hindus, in spite of thousand and one differences within our fold are bound by such religious, cultural, historical, racial, linguistic and other affinities in common as to stand out as a definitely homogeneous people as soon as we are placed in contrast with any other non-Hindu people, say, the English or Japanese or even the Indian Moslems. That is the reason why today we, the Hindus from Kashmere to Madras and Sindh to Assam, will be a nation by ourselves—while the Indian Moslems are on the whole more inclined to identify themselves and their interests with Moslems outside India than Hindus who live next door, like the Jews in Germany.

Some well-meaning but simple-minded Hindus amuse themselves with the thought and hope against hope that inasmuch as the majority of Indian Moslems also are in fact allied to us by race and language and in cases had gone over to the Moslem fold in living memory of this very generation, they could easily be persuaded to acknowledge this homogeneity and even blood relation with the Hindus and merge themselves into a common national being if, but, we only remind them of these affinities and appeal to them in their name. These innocent souls are really to be pitied. As if the Moslems do not know of it all!! The fact is that the Moslems know of these affinities all but too well: the only difference to be taken into account being that while the Hindus love these affinities which bind the Hindu to a Hindu and to dwell on them with pride—the Moslems hate the very mention of them and are trying to eradicate the very memory of it all. Some of them fabricate histories and genealogies to connect their origin with Arabs or Turks; they are trying to carve out a separate language for themselves and graft it as best as they can on the Arabs stock; they are carrying on a campaign against the Hindu family names, such as 'Tambe' and 'Modak', which in parts like the Konkan convert-Moslems still bear and replace them by Arabs ones and are bent on widening the cleavage deeper and broader by removing every trace which may remind them of having once something in common with the Hindu stock. Their religious and theocratic traditions join hands in impressing upon their mind that Hindusthan is not and cannot be a Dar-ul-Islam, their country which they may love until and unless the Hindus—the *kafirs*—are either converted to a man to Islam or are reduced to helotage paying the *jaizia* to some would be Moslem sovereignty over this land. The very word 'Hindusthan' stinks in their nostrils. I am not referring to these items here in any spirit of either condemnation or justification. I am telling the simple fact which no Moslem can honestly contest that Islam as a whole wants a deliberate design to assert itself in India as a nation altogether heterogeneous with the Hindus and having nothing in common with them. Consequently, it ought to be clear even to these well-meaning Hindu simpletons that this refusal of the Indian Moslems to merge in a common national unit leaves the Hindus, negatively too, as a nation by themselves.

- *Swarajya to the Hindus must mean only that 'rajya' in which their 'swatva' their 'Hindutva' can assert itself without being overloaded by any non-Hindu people, whether they be Indian territorial or extra-territorials.* Some Englishmen are and may continue to be territorially born Indians. Can, therefore, the overlordship of these Anglo-Indians be a *swarajya* to the Hindus? Aurangzeb or Tippu were hereditary Indians, nay, were the sons of converted Hindu mothers. Did that mean that the rule of Aurangzeb or Tippu was a *Swarajya* to the Hindus? No! Although they were territorially Indians, they proved to be the worst enemies of Hindudom and therefore, a Shivaji, a Gobind Singh, a Pratap or the Peshwa had to fight against the Moslem domination and establish a real Hindu *swarajya*.

Consequently, under the present circumstances too all that an Indian national state can mean is that the Moslem minority in India will have the right to be treated as equal citizens, enjoying equal protection and civic rights in proportion to their population. The Hindu majority will not encroach on the legitimate rights of any non-Hindu minority. But, in no case can the Hindu majority resign its right which as a majority it is entitled to exercise under any democratic and legitimate constitution. The Moslem minority in particular has not obliged the Hindus by remaining in minority and, therefore, they must remain satisfied with the status they occupy and with the legitimate share of civic and political rights that is their proportionate due. It would be simply preposterous to endow the Moslem minority with the right of exercising a practical veto on the legitimate rights and privileges of the majority and call it a *swarajya*. The Hindus do not want a change of masters, are not going to struggle and fight and die only to replace an Edward by an Aurangzeb simply because the latter happens to be born within Indian borders, but they want henceforth to be masters themselves in their own house, in their own land.

- *Consequently, the name 'Hindusthan must continue to be the appellation of our country*. Such other names as India, Hind, etc. being derived from the same original word 'Sindhu' may be used but only to signify the same sense—the land of the Hindus—a country which is the abode of the Hindu nation. Aryavarta, Bharat *bhumi* and such other names are of course the ancient and the most cherished epithets of our motherland and will continue to appeal to the cultured elite. In this insistence that the motherland of the Hindus must be called, but Hindusthan, no encroachment or humiliation is implied in connection with any of our non-Hindu countrymen. Our Parsee and Christian countrymen are already too akin to us culturally and are too patriotic and the Anglo-Indians too sensible to refuse to fall in line with us Hindus on so legitimate a ground. So far as our Moslem countrymen are concerned, it is useless to conceal the fact that some of them are already inclined to look upon this molehill also as an insuperable mountain in their way to Hindu-Moslem unity. But, they should remember that the Moslems do not dwell only in India not are the Indian Moslems the only heroic remnants of the faithful in Islam. China has crores of

Moslems, Greece, Palestine and even Hungary and Poland have thousands of Moslems amongst their nationals, but being there a minority, only a community, their existence in these countries has never been advanced as a ground to change the ancient names of these countries which indicate the abodes of those races whose overwhelming majority own the land. The country of the Poles continues to be Poland and of the Greeks as Greece. The Moslems there did not or dared not distort them but are quite content to distinguish themselves as Polish Moslems or Grecian Moslems or Chinese Moslems when the occasion arises. So also our Moslem countrymen may distinguish themselves nationally or territorially whenever they want, as 'Hindusthani-Moslems' without compromising in the least their separateness as a religious or cultural entity. Nay, the Moslems have been calling themselves as 'Hindusthanis' ever since their advent to India of their own accord.

But, in spite of it all, some irrational Moslem sections amongst our countrymen object even to this name of our country and that is no reason why we should play cowards to our own conscience. We Hindus must not betray or break the continuity of our nation from the Sindhus in Rigvedic days to the Hindus of our own generation which is implied in 'Hindusthan' the accepted appellation of our motherland. Just as the land of the Germans is Germany, of the English England, of the Turks Turkishan, of the Afghans Afghanisthan—even so, we must have it indelibly impressed on the map of the earth for all times to come a 'Hindusthan'—the land of Hindus.

- *The pan-Hindu flag: The Kundalini Kripanankiti gerwa* flag shall be the flag of the Hindu nation. With its OM, the *swastik* and the sword, it appeals to sentiments cherished by our race ever since the Veidic days. Those who like to realise the inner spirit and know the *raison d'etre* of its design and the symbols would do well to read the special tract I have written styled 'the Pan-Hindu *dhwaj*.'

It must be emphasised in this connection that all those Hindu flags other than this which are current amongst the Hindus as the colours of the different constituents which go to form our pan-Hindu brotherhood, such as the Sanatanists, the Sikhs, the Jains, the Aryas, etc. will be respected by every Hindu as his own, inasmuch as they are but different manifestations of the common pan-Hindu spirit.

Nor should it be supposed that the Hindu flag implies any inherent antagonism to the several colours of our non-Hindu countrymen. The Moslems are welcome to have their own religious colours to represent their own community. In short, we shall respect any flag which any section of our countrymen adopts, whether religious or political, whether it is the Moslem League flag or the Congress tri-colour or the red one, so long as it continues to respect in return the pan-Hindu flag and does not antagonise it but continues as allied colours. But Hindudom as a whole will be represented by the pan-Hindu Flag alone.

- The Sanskrit shall be our devbhasha, our sacred language and the 'Sanskrit *nishtha*' Hindu; the Hindi which is derived from Sanskrit and draws its nourishment, from the latter, is our *Rashtrabhasha*, our current national language. Besides being the richest and the most cultured of the ancient languages of the world, to us Hindus the Sanskrit is the holiest tongue of tongues. Our scriptures, history, philosophy and culture have their roots so deeply embedded in Sanskrit literature that it forms veritably the brain of our race. Mother of the majority of our mother tongues, she has suckled the rest of them at her breast. All Hindu languages currently today, whether derived from Sanskrit or grafted on to it, can only grow and flourish on the sap of life they imbibe from Sanskrit. The Sanskrit language, therefore, must ever be an indispensable constituent of the classical course for Hindu youth.

In adopting Hindi as the national tongue of Hindudom no humiliation or any invidious distinction is implied as regards other provincial tongues. We are all as attached to our provincial tongues as to Hindi and they will all grow and flourish in their respective spheres. In fact, some of them are today more progressive and richer in literature. But nevertheless, taken all in all, Hindi can serve the purpose of a national pan-Hindu language best. It must also be remembered that Hindi is not made a national language to order. The fact is that long before either English or even the Moslems stepped into India, Hindi in its general form had already come to occupy the position of a national tongue throughout Hindusthan. The Hindu pilgrim, the tradesman, the tourist, the soldier, the pandit travelled up and down from Bengal to Sindh and Kashmere to Rameshwar by making himself understood from locality to locality through Hindi. Just as Sanskrit was the national language of the Hindu intellectual world even so Hindi has been for at least a thousand years in the past the national Indian tongue of the Hindu people. Added to that and as a consequence of that we find even today that it is understood and even spoken as a mother tongue by a far larger number of people than is the case with any other Hindu language. Consequently, it must be made compulsory for every Hindu student through secondary schools at any rate to learn Hindi as his pan-Hindu national language without neglecting in the least his training in his provincial mother tongue.

By Hindi we of course mean the pure 'Sanskrit *nishtha*' Hindi, as we find it for example in the *Satyartha Prakash* written by Maharishi Dayanand Saraswati. How simple and untainted with a single unnecessary foreign word is that Hindi and how expressive withal. It may be mentioned in passing that Swami Dayanandji was about the first Hindu leader who gave conscious and definite expression to the view that Hindi should be the pan-Hindu national language of India. 'This Sanskrit *nishtha*' Hindi has nothing to do with that hybrid, the so-called Hindusthani which is being hatched up by the Wardha scheme. It is nothing short of a linguistic monstrosity and must be ruthlessly suppressed. Not only that, but it is our bounden duty to oust out ruthlessly all unnecessary alien words, whether Arabic or English, from every Hindu tongue—whether provincial or dialectical. We are not against English or any other language; nay, we insist on the study of English as an indispensable necessity and a profitable passport to world literature. But, we must not allow the influx of alien words into our language without checking their past and testing their necessity. Our Hindu brethren in Bengal are especially to be congratulated upon in this connection because the Bengali literature is admirably free from any such unclean admixture of unnecessary alien words which cannot be said regarding our other provincial tongues and literature.

- *The Nagari shall be the national script of Hindudom*. Our Sanskrit alphabetical order is phonetically about the most perfect which the world has yet devised and almost all our current Indian scripts already follow it. The Nagari script too follows this order. Like the Hindi language, the Nagari script too has already been current for centuries all over India amongst the Hindu literary circles for some two thousand years at any rate in the past and was even popularly nick-named as the *shastri lipi*, the script of our Hindu scriptures. With a little touch here and there, it could be reformed so as to render it as suitable to modern mechanical printing as the Roman script. Such a reform movement was set on foot in Maharashtra about some 40 years ago by Mr. Vaidya and others. An organised movement later on under my lead met with an amount of practical success and has already popularised it. I strongly recommend that as an immediate step to popularise Nagari as our national script, all our Hindu papers in different provinces should begin to publish at least a couple of columns of their provincial languages in Nagari script. It is a matter of common knowledge that if Bengali or Gujarati is printed in Nagari, it is more or less understood by readers in several other provinces. To have only one common language throughout Hindusthan at a stroke is impracticable and unwise. But, to have the Nagari script as the only common script throughout Hindudom is much more feasible. Nevertheless, it should be borne in mind that the different Hindu scripts current in our different provinces have a future of their own and may flourish side by side with the Nagari. All that needs to be immediately done as indispensable in the common interest of Hindudom as a whole is that the Nagari script must be made a compulsory subject along with the Hindi language in every school in the case of Hindu students.

It is interesting to remind you here how two prominent Congress presidents proposed to solve this problem of a national tongue and a national script. Pandit Nehru thinks, leaving even Maulana Abul Kalam Azad far behind who only proposes Hindusthani which he assures us is tantamount to Urdu, that the highly Arabic Urdu of the Aligarh School or the Osmania University School is best fitted to be the national language of India including of course, some 28 crores of Hindus, while *desh gaurav* Subhash Babu, improving upon the situation, beat even Panditjis ingenuity hollow by proposing from the presidential chair of the Indian National Congress that Roman script would suit India as the best national script. That is how the Congress ideology approaches things national! Roman script to be the national script of India! How imminently practicable, to say the least! Your *Basumati*, *Ananda Bazar Patrika* and all Bengali papers to appear everyday in Roman script! The *Bande Mataram* song to be printed in this new national style as *Tomari pratima ghadibe mandire mandire* and the *Gita* to begin within this following attractive setting as:

'Dharma kshetre kurukshetre sama-vetah yuyutsavah' and so on and so on. It is true as Subhash Babu says that Kemal Pasha abolished the Arabic script as unsuited to print and took to Roman script, but this fact has a lesson for our Mohammedan zealots who want the Urdu script, that is this very Arabic style, to thrust even on the Hindus as an up-to-date national script and it has no connection with the Hindus. Kemal Pasha took to the Roman script because the Turks had nothing better of their own to fall back upon. The Andamanese pick up *kauris* and make a necklace of them, but is that the reason why Kuber also should do the same? We Hindus should rather call upon Arabia and Europe to adopt the Nagari script and Hindi language; such a proposal should not sound very impracticable to such inveterate optimists at any rate who seriously advance it as a very practical proposal to make Urdu the national language of the Marathas and to expect all our Arya Samaj *gurukuls* to study the *Vedas* in Roman script.

- *The Hindu Mahasabha is a national organisation of Hindudom*. It has come to my notice that a very large section of the English-educated Hindus hold back from joining the Hindu Mahasabha and political circles in India and outside in general feel themselves totally unconcerned about it under the erroneous idea that it is an exclusively religious organisation, something like a Christian Mission. Nothing could be far from the truth. The Hindu Mahasabha is not a Hindu mission. It leaves religious questions regarding theism, monotheism, pantheism or even atheism to be discussed and determined by the different Hindu schools of religious persuasions. It is not a Hindu Dharma Mahasabha, but a Hindu national *mahasabha*, Consequently, by its very constitution it is debarred to associate itself exclusively as a partisan within any particular religious school or sect even with the Hindu fold. As a national Hindu body it will of course propagate and defend the national Hindu church comprising each and all religions of Hindusthani origin against any non-Hindu attack or encroachment. But the sphere of its activity is far more comprehensive than that of an exclusively religious body. The Hindu Mahasabha identifies itself with the national life of Hindudom in all its entirety, in all its social, economical, cultural and above all political aspects and is pledged to protect and promote all that contributes to the freedom, strength and glory of the Hindu nation; and as an indispensable means to that end to attain *purna swarajya*, absolute political independence of Hindusthan by all legitimate and proper means.

- *The Hindu Mahasabha must continue its mission even after Hindusthan is politically free.* Many a superficial critic seems to fancy that the Mahasabha was only contrived to serve as a make-weight, as a reaction checkmating the Moslem League or the anti-Hindu policy of the present leaders of the Congress and will be out of court or cease automatically to function as soon as it is shorn of this spurious excuse to exist. But, if the aims and objects of the Mahasabha mean anything, it is clear that it was not the outcome of any frothy effusion, any fussy agitation, to remove a grievance here or oppose a seasonal party there. The fact is that every organism, whether individual or social which is living and deserves to survive, throws out offensive and defensive organs as soon as it is brought to face adversely changing environments. The Hindu nation too as soon as it recovered and freed itself from the suffocating grip of the pseudo-Nationalistic ideology of the Congress brand developed a new organ to battle in the struggle for existence under the changed conditions of modern age. This was the Hindu Mahasabha. It grew out of a fundamental necessity of national life and not of any ephemeral incident. The constructive side of its aims and objects make it amply clear that its mission is as abiding as the life of the nation itself. But, that apart, even the day-to-day necessity of adapting its policy to the ever-changing political currents makes it incumbent on Hindudom to have an exclusively Hindu organisation independent of any moral or intellectual servility or subservience to any non-Hindu or jointly representative institution, to guard Hindu interests and save them from being jeopardised. It is not so only under the present political subjection of Hindusthan, but it will be all the more necessary to have some such exclusively Hindu organisation, some such Hindu Mahasabha in substance, whether it is identical with this present organisation or otherwise, to serve as a watch-tower at the gates of Hindusthan for at least a couple of centuries to come, even after Hindusthan is partially or wholly free and a national Parliament controls its political destiny.

Because, unless something altogether cataclysmic in nature upsets the whole political order of things in the world which practical polities cannot envisage today, all that can be reasonably expected in the immediate future is that we Hindus may prevail over England and compel her to recognise India as a self-governing unit with the status contemplated in the Westminster Statute. Now a national Parliament in such a self-governing India can only reflect the electorate as it is, with the Hindus and the Moslems as we find them, their relations a bit bettered, perhaps a bit worsened. No realist can be blind to the probability that the extra-territorial designs and the secret urge goading on the Moslems to transform India into a Moslem State may at any time confront the Hindusthani state even under self-government either with a civil war or treacherous overtures to alien invaders by the Moslems. Then again, there is every likelihood that there will ever continue at least for a century to come a danger of fanatical riots, the scramble for services, legislative seats, weightages out of proportion to their population on the part of the Moslem minority and consequently a constant danger threatening internal peace. To checkmate this probability which if we are wise we must always keep in view even after Hindusthan attains the status of a self-governing country, a powerful and exclusive organisation of Hindudom like the Hindu Mahasabha will always prove a sure and devoted source of strength, a reserve force for the Hindus to fall back upon to voice their grievances more effectively than the joint Parliament can do, to scent danger ahead, to warn the Hindus in time against it and to fight out, if need be, any treacherous design to which the joint state itself may unwittingly fall a victim.

The history of Canada, or Palestine, or the movement of the Young Turks will show you that in every state where two or more such conflicting elements as the Hindus and Moslems in India happen to exist as constituents, the wiser of them has to keep its exclusive organisation intact, strong and watchful to defeat any attempt at betrayal or capture of the national state by the opposite party; especially so, if that party has extra-territorial affinities, religious or cultural, with alien bordering states. This tussle between such constituents of such a state must continue till slowly, if ever they all learn to get themselves merged, by developing a spirit of corporate patriotism into a consolidated nation. If the Hindus take this realistic truth to heart, they will try their utmost to consolidate and strengthen the pan-Hindu organisation which is already gathering force and has struck its roots deep in the Hindu soil. The nearer you are to *swarajya* the more indispensable grows the necessity of a strong and consolidated pan-Hindu organisation or rather the stronger grows the pan-Hindu organisation the nearer it takes you to real '*swa*' '*rajya*'.

IV

The practical policy of the Hindu movement

I have so far dealt with some of the basic principles and tenets and set out the national and political ideals of the Hindu *Sangathan* movement as I perceive them. But the very fact that we have still to frame, emphasise and propagate the very ideals and ideology of the Hindu movement added to the fact that they imply an entire re-orientation of the public activities of the Hindu people so as to revolutionise the conception of the Indian state and its formation as we find it today, shows how we have hardly taken a step ahead and how strenuous and sustained a struggle we have yet to undergo before we are able to realise the goal, the creation of an independent Hindusthan as we define it. Once the ideal is fixed, it is this struggle that matters most. And we must, therefore, chalk out as urgently as possible, the lines on which our struggle can be carried on with the greatest effect and if possible, with the least resistance.

It must be noted also that although the ideal remains fixed, the struggle to realise it can scarcely be on a straight line. We have now to confront, now to compromise now to fight on, now to fall back and keep marking time. At times, we shall have to ally ourselves on a given point with one of our opponents and then to oppose the former ally. This very inconsistency in detail resorted to in a long-drawn life and death struggle to reach a goal in consistent enough but if it leads us on the whole irresistibly onward and onward to the great ideal we aim to realise. The policy I am going to outline should also be viewed from this tactical perspective. It is only related to our present circumstances and should not be taken as final. As our movement goes on gathering strength, we may soon arrive at a point when it may march on with irresistible strides of a giant and may grow powerful enough to demand and dictate things with a reckless heroism, which the puny beginnings today can hardly conceive or dare to express.

I should also make it clear that in outlining this practical policy, I am only expressing my personal views. They cannot bind the Hindu Mahasabha unless they are sanctioned by its corporate resolutions.

- Our first and foremost aim in our political activities must always be to guard the integrity of Hindusthan intact. Hindusthan to us does not only mean the so-called British India but comprises even those parts which are under the French and the Portuguese possessions; Gomantak and Pondicherry are as integral parts of our motherland as Maharashtra or Bengal. From the Indus to the Himalayas, from the Himalayas to Tibet, from Tibet to Burma and from Burma to the southern and western seas run the lines of the boundaries of our land. The whole territory including Kashmere and Nepal, Gomantak, Pondicherry and other French possessions constitutes our national and territorial unit and must be consolidated in a free and centralised state. It must ever remain undivided and indivisible. Any attempt to divide this territorial and national unity of Hindusthan so as, for example, to break it up into Hindu and Moslem zones, must be opposed tooth and nail and chastised as an act of treason and treachery.
- Towards our neighbouring States of Burma and Tibet on the eastern and north-eastern frontiers our policy will always be, so far as possible, of wholehearted friendship and if they choose, even of a political alliance. They are our co-religionists and our political interests too are not inherently antagonistic. Nay, we will only find, in general, our mutual political strength augmented if we continue to be political allies.
- But towards those Moslem States and tribes which border our North-West Frontier, our policy cannot but be a guarded one. Their tendency for centuries in the past had been fanatically inimical towards the Hindus and is likely to continue to be so for at least a century to come. The Hindu Sangathanist Party must always see that this Frontier is garrisoned with overwhelming Hindu troops and is never entrusted to Moslem ones. We will always be ready to establish friendly contact with those bordering States and shall give no cause for unnecessary strife but should keep our forces there always in a state of

war and vigilant to resist any sudden aggressive eruption on the part of those Moslem tribes or any threatened invasion through the passes by any anti-Hindu alien army.

- To the independent Hindu kingdom of Nepal, all Hindudom feels itself most loyally attached and would ever strive to strain every nerve in defending its honour and integrity. It is the only part of our motherland which continues down to this day as a Dharma *kshetra* unsullied by the humiliating shadow of an alien non-Hindu flag. The independence of the Hindu Kingdom of Nepal, the home of a heroic Hindu race, constitutes at once the pride and the centre of Hindu hope. Every atom of strength added to Nepal elevates and strengthens the prestige and position of Hindudom all round. On the other hand, anything that weakens or humiliates Hindudom in any other part of Hindusthan must weaken the strength of Nepal in the long run. The danger of the Moslem upheaval on the North-Western Frontier, for example, cannot but be a standing menace to the independence of the Hindu kingdom in Nepal too. If Hindu history has not endowed us even with this much foresight, then it must be said that all the lessons which the invasions of Gaznis and Ghoris were meant by destiny to teach us are lost on us.

Nevertheless, it will be foolish on our part to do anything to drag Nepal into the muddled and slogan-ridden politics which disfigures the British Indian territory. The politics of a subject race can be no guide to the exigencies of an independent kingdom situated as Nepal. I, therefore, feel no hesitation whatsoever in justifying the present policy of the Nepal Government to maintain friendly relations with the British Government and to continue an informal political alliance with the British with a view to guard against any other non-Hindu aggression on India. Consequently, it is also a very wise policy on the part of Nepal to supply as many Nepalese recruits to the Indian forces as it is possible to do in conformity with its own security and strength. The political complications in Europe and the Far East are almost sure to persuade the British Government too to depend more and more on Nepal's friendship and military help to secure Indian defence.

In this connection, it must be emphasised that the British Government should also restore some of those territories on the borders of Nepal which the British had wrested from her in the past, back to the King of Nepal.

Such a step will cement the friendship between the two nations as nothing else can do.

Nepal has doubtlessly a great future before her if she takes time by the forelock and has the prophetic vision which a rising nation must necessarily possess. She must bring up her military strength to an up-to-date European efficiency and must be able to defend herself not only on land, but against any aerial aggression too by equipping herself with a powerful aerial force. Her strength being the strength of an ally, the British Government too is not likely under the present circumstances to hamper her in this attempt with any feeling of uneasiness but would rather wish her to hasten on this project. The influence which Nepal is likely to exercise on Indian politics in the near future will be better pointed out in the words of Mr. Perceval Langdon, the well-known author of the voluminous work on Nepal.

Says Mr. Langdon, 'It invests Nepal with an importance which it would be foolish to overlook. Englishmen should attempt to understand a little more thoroughly the high position which Nepal holds in the general southern Asiatic balance and the great and growing importance that she will possess in future in the solution of the problems which beset the present state of India. Nepal stands today on the threshold of a new light. Her future calls her in one direction and one only. In all the varied theatres of Indian politics, there is nothing which surpasses in interest the ultimate destiny of Nepal. Inevitably, she will become of greater and greater importance if we persist in our present policy of lessening British influence in India. It is not impossible that Nepal may even be called upon to control the destiny of India itself.

- *The National Constitution of Hindusthan: The Hindu Sangathanist Party aims to base the future constitution of Hindusthan on the broad principle that all citizens should have equal rights and obligations, irrespective of caste or creed, race or religion, provided they avow and owe, an exclusive and devoted allegiance to the Hindusthan State. The fundamental rights of liberty of speech, liberty of conscience, of worship, of association etc. will be enjoyed by all citizens alike. Whatever restrictions will be imposed on them in the interest of public peace and order of national emergency will not be based on any religious or racial considerations alone but on common national grounds.*

No attitude can be more national even in the territorial sense than this and it is this attitude in general which is expressed in substance by the curt formula 'one man, one vote'. This will make it clear that the conception of a Hindu nation is in no way inconsistent with the development of a common Indian nation, a united Hindusthani state in which all sects and sections, races and religions, castes and creeds, Hindus, Moslems, Christians, Anglo-Indians, etc. could be harmoniously welded together into a political State on terms of perfect equality.

This attitude which the Hindu Mahasabha takes up with regard to the national Hindusthani constitution is in fact more definitely and expressively national than either the League or even the Congress which calls itself Indian national has as yet dared to take up uncompromisingly and it is the Hindu Mahasabha and the conception of the Hindu nation which is tabooed by the Congress and the League as most dangerously anti-national and uncompromisingly communal! The fact is that the National Congress itself is not only communal in its legitimate sense but perversely communal, inasmuch as it recognises a majority and a minority, the Hindus and the Moslems and on the top of it all forces the majority to forego its just share in the franchise, in the public services, in cultural rights and offers them to a minority based on religion to buy its patriotism and attachment to the common national state. On the other hand, by asking for the Moslems as a religious entity wanton advantages over and above what they are entitled to on a national basis at the cost of the Hindus at the point of a dagger, with a threat to secede and join hands with an alien power, the Moslem League takes up a position which is anti-national to the point of treachery. In demanding three votes for the Moslem, the Moslem League is outrageously communal, while in calling upon the Hindus to yield to this demand and accede to the proposal of one vote for three Hindus, the Congress is cowardly communal! And, yet, it is precisely these two bodies, the pseudo National Congress and the confessedly anti-national League which have the temerity to accuse the Hindu *Sangathanist* Party as communalistic and anti-national simply because they are not ready to betray their birthright for a mess of pottage, to play second fiddle to the Moslems or care for a worthless certificate from the Congressites of being 'nationalistic'!!

- *The rights of non-Hindu minorities:* When once the Hindu Mahasabha not only accepts but maintains the principles of 'one man, one vote' and the public services to go by merit alone added to the fundamental rights and obligations to be shared by all citizens alike, irrespective of any distinction of race or religion, any further mention of minority rights is on principle not only unnecessary but self-contradictory, because it again introduces a consciousness of majority and minority on communal basis. *But, as practical politics require and as the* Hindu Sangathanists *want to relieve our non-Hindu countrymen of even a ghost of suspicion, we are prepared to emphasise that the legitimate rights of minorities with regard to their religion, culture and language will be expressly guaranteed on one condition only that the equal rights of the majority also must not in any case be encroached upon or abrogated. Every minority may have separate schools to train their children in their own tongue, their own religious or cultural institutions and can receive government help also for these, but always in proportion to the taxes they pay into the common exchequer. The same principle must of course hold good in case of the majority too.*

Over and above this, in case the Constitution is not based on joint electorates and on the unalloyed national principle of one man one vote, but is based on communal basis, then those minorities who wish to have separate electorate or reserve seats will be allowed to have them, but always in proportion to their population and provided that it does not deprive the majority also of an equal right in proportion to its population too.

I believe that our Christian, Parsee, Jewish and other minorities, except the Moslems, will be perfectly satisfied with the constitution based on these principles as broadly outlined above. Because the Christians, the Jews and, most eminently, the Parsees are too allied to us in culture and too patriotic, while the Anglo-Indians, too sensible to fail to see that no Constitution if it has to keep the integrity, sovereignty and strength of the national State safe, can go any further and that is all that is really required to safeguard any genuine special interests of the minorities as distinguished from those of the majority. Only that minority will insist to have still more and yet more to the last pound of flesh which, in fact, cherishes secret designs to disintegrate the State, to create a State within a State or altogether to subvert the National State and hold all others under its subjection. Fortunately, no section of our countrymen belonging to the non-Moslem minorities mentioned above harbours this treasonable design. It is only with regard to the Moslem minority that this cannot be asserted with confidence and, therefore, I shall deal separately with it later on.

In this connection, a point of far-reaching importance and one which has a very serious bearing on the political and religious and cultural interest of the Christian, Jew and Parsee countrymen of ours in particular, must be mentioned in bold relief. *The anti-national and aggressive designs on the part of the Moslem minority constitute a danger to all non-Moslem Indians in India and not only to the Hindus alone. It is too clear a point to require any further elucidation here. It is the anti-national attitude of the Moslem minority alone which is giving a handle to the British Government to obstruct further political and constitutional progress in Hindusthan. But, in order to camouflage their own special responsibility for this guilt, the Moslems always try to drag in other minorities also in support of their attitude and want the world to believe that all non-Hindu minorities are as determinedly uncompromising in the anti-national demands advanced by the Moslem League.* The League always wants to pose as the champion of all non-Hindu minorities, but the fact is that the relations of Christians, Jews and above all our Parsee brethren have been for centuries most cordial with us Hindus and these non-Moslem minorities have never advanced any anti-national or unreasonable claims or had ever indulged in political hooliganism or fanatical riots as a silly means to impress their political importance. *My earnest suggestion, therefore, to our Christians, Jews, Parsees and such other non-Moslem minorities would be that they should openly and definitely disown the League designs, protest against being bracketed with the Moslems under the misleading and mischievous common term 'minorities', call upon the Moslem League not to speak in general on their behalf and above all, should definitely declare through their respective political organisations that they are perfectly willing and contented to form a common national front with the Hindus under the conditions referred to above. But, if the Christians, the Jews, the Parsees and all non-Moslem minorities and the Hindus present a common understanding and a common front at any would-be Round Table Conference or Constitutional Assembly, the Moslems will find themselves singularly isolated and will be forced to cease to speak in the name of 'the minority problem' but will have to shoulder by themselves the responsibility of their anti-national and fanatical claims.* These supercilious pretensions of Moslems of being a chosen minority and the bluff claiming political importance and historical traditions investing them with an incomparable superiority to the Indian people in general, constitutes a challenge and an insult to our Christians, Jews, Parsees and other countrymen too.

- *The Hindu Mahasabha and the Congress:* I have no space here nor the inclination to frame a charge-sheet against the Congress, enumerating the grievous errors it has been committing under the dictatorship of Gandhiji and the leaders of his persuasion ever since the Khilafat agitation; setting at naught even the protests of such eminent Hindu patriots as Lokamanya Tilak, Lala Lajpat Rai, Swami Shradhanand and others, which errors have weakened and humiliated Hindudom at every step. I have no inclination to do so or condemn them even in such harsh terms as the gravity of the errors, in fact, demand because I know that some of them have rendered eminent services to our motherland and many of them meant well. Although the Congress as a body has been ungrateful to a degree in failing to appreciate the patriotic sacrifice and service the Hindu Mahasabhaists have rendered equally with and in cases even far more intensely than the Congressites in the fight for the freedom of Hindusthan, yet let every Hindu *Sangathanist* be just and generous in brotherly appreciation of the patriotic motives of those of the Congressites who had been highly selfless and sacrificing. It is not their motive but their judgement and in a couple of cases a monomaniac incompetence which was responsible for the erroneous policy they persisted in which has done incalculable harm to the Hindu cause and which, if not checkmated, is likely to jeopardise not only the legitimate interests of Hindudom far more dangerously than in the past but even the vital interests of the 'Indian nation' too as the Congress itself understands it and loves so well.

It is not, therefore, to rake up fruitlessly the sad memories of the most grievous errors which the Congressites committed in their identification with the Khilafat agitation but to warn against the imminent dangers of a similar type that I must refer to a few facts regarding the attitude of the Gandhist politicians in that ill-fated movement. In spite of the warnings of the great Tilak, Gandhiji committed the Congress to the purely communal, religious and extra-territorial Khilafat agitation to placate the Moslems and himself went to the length of insisting on the point that the question of *swaraj* itself should be subordinated to the

Khilafat issue; nay, he said it was the religious duty of the Hindus to help the kalipha! And, yet, the same Congress leaders forbade the Congress even to touch the Nizam's civil resistance movement as a thing unclean and denounced it as communal because it demanded the religious and cultural rights of Hindus! Not only that, but true to their words, these Congressite Hindu leaders did not subordinate *swaraj* to the Khilafat question only in its figurative aspect, but, were hand in glove with the Moslem leaders who instigated Amir Amanullah Khan to invade India as he actually did. We have the word of Swami Shradhanandji for it. The Swamiji publicly wrote to that effect in protest in his *Liberator* and produced some documentary evidence and a draft telegram in Gandhiji's handwriting to the Amir which Maulana Mohamad Ali had shown to Swamiji. In his own *Young India,* Gandhiji admitted that the Afghans, if successful, were sure to establish their kingdom in India (*see Young India* 1-6-21) and yet these Congressite Hindu leaders did not dissociate themselves from the Moslem leaders in their open and secret activities to egg on the Afghan invasion, but, on the contrary, promised support to this treacherous move. Gandhiji writes in his *Young India* (4-5-21): 'I would in a sense certainly assist the Amir of Afganisthan if he waged war against the British Government, by openly telling my countrymen that it would be a crime to help the government etc'. If you like to see the length these gentlemen had gone in this affair you may read a useful tract recently published by Mr. Karandikar of Poona which is full of original extracts from the speeches and writings of the then Congress leaders and Gandhiji's *Young India*. What is most surprising to note is the fact that these Hindu leaders outbid even the Ali Brothers, the 'national' Maulana Azad and other Moslem leaders in maintaining that if the Amir succeeded in capturing Delhi, we would have won swaraj!—for, they definitely stated that the rule of the Afghans was in itself a *swaraj*, We Hindu Moslems are one, an indivisible nation.' I vividly remember conversations I had with these Hindu leaders of Gandhist persuasion when they used to meet me then in prison. How expectantly they waited for the invading armies of the Amir to capture Lahore! Well, after all the Khilafat was guillotined by the Turks themselves and Amir Amanullah, instead of being Emperor at Delhi, was dethroned by a Bachha Suku in Kabul itself and all that India reaped from the Khilaphat agitation was the intensified pan-Islamic fanaticism roused by that movement amongst the Indian Moslems all over India, aided and abetted by the

Hindus themselves who paid dearly for their folly there and then in Malabar, Kohat, Punjab, Bengal—and will have yet to pay unless they learn to react.

While the Khilafat was on his brain, in a reply he gave to the correspondent of the *Daily Express*, London, Gandhiji disclosed his plan of converting the Afghans from fanatical turbulence into a peaceful citizenship thus, 'I would introduce the spinning wheel amongst the Afghan tribes also and then that will prevent them from attacking Indian territory. I feel the tribesmen are in their own way God-fearing people.'

Yes, 'in their own way'. That is the trouble, for, we can clearly discern their own way of God-fearingness in the ghastly light of Hindu habitations set on fire throughout the frontier line from Sindh to Kashmere. Only Hindus looted, only Hindus killed, only Hindu women and men kidnapped!! Is not a Fakir also a god-fearing man in his own way! And the spinning wheel to persuade them from attacking India! How many centuries after, sir? And what are we Hindus to do in the meanwhile? To garrison the frontiers with hosts of Hindu damsels with the charm of the spinning wheel in their hands, as Gandhiji has suggested quite seriously at one of the sittings of the Round Table Conference?

Well, gentlemen, I am not referring to these few details in any light mood. I want you to realise the mentality and the ideology of these Hindu leaders who still happen to be at the helm of the Congress. Neither Gandhiji nor Pandit Nehru, nay, not even Subhash Babu or Mr. Ray, who, although they do not contribute in any way to some of the above vagaries of the Gandhist school, are still votaries—I call it, victims—of the school of thought which says in so many words, 'Give to the Moslems so much that they would not wish to ask for anything more.' They may sincerely believe that to be the crux of nationalism and wisdom, but do you, who do not wish to see Hindudom humiliated and browbeaten into servility, believe it to be so? If not, are you going to authorise these very gentlemen by electing and returning them as representatives who can speak in the name of the Hindus once again at any Round Table Conference to come, to enter into any new pact with the Moslems on behalf of the Hindus or entrust the destiny of the North-Western Frontiers into the hands of the Khan brothers who are the Congress plenipotentiaries and Gandhiji's certified lieutenants there, as once the Ali brothers were? I call upon those thousands of Hindus also who have not ceased to be Hindus but who still follow the Congress with a blind habitual trait to ponder as seriously as possible on these questions.

After the Khilafat came the blank cheques, then the communal award or decision—'lapses of memory' make the Congress leaders call it sometimes this way, sometimes that, but which always remains definitely unrejected and in fact accepted and worked out by them. Then rushed in the flood of circulars issued by Congress ministers in all provinces. Mr. Pant, for example, assuring the Moslems, amongst other things and I quote his words, 'At Barabanki, the Congress Government stopped Hindus from doing *arti* in their own temples and blowing conch-shells during the whole period of Moharram and at several places during the Holi, the Hindus were prevented from sprinkling coloured water even on Hindus amongst themselves. At Jaunpur, the District Magistrate was attacked by Moslems but the accused were released on the recommendation of the Secretary of the Moslem League. The Congress government, has given representation to the Moslems out of all proportion to their numerical strength which came upto only 14 per cent. But, out of the four Collectors appointed by the Congress government, three were Moslems and out of 13 Deputy Collectors, eight were Moslems. So on and so on. Every Hindu should read this whole circular issued by the U.P. Congress government. It is a masterpiece of self-condemnation. It was secretly circulated only amongst the Moslems, but the Hindu Sabhaists, those cursed 'communalist' traitors, got hold of some copies of this our 'national' confession and broadcasted its reprints. Space forbids me from quoting from other circulars issued by the provincial Congress government in C.P., Madras, etc., all fashioned after the same pattern, pleading in substance before the Tribunal of the Moslem League: 'Sir, we have deprived the Hindus everywhere of what is due to them and given Moslems overwhelmingly more than was due, oppressed the Hindus as best as we could wherever the Moslems were pleased to demand it. So, let the League be pleased, therefore, Sir, to certify that the Congress ministers were truly impartial and perfectly national!!!'

And the Moslem League has certified at last by observing the day of deliverance from the Congress tyranny under which the Moslems groaned for the past two long, long enduring years. In a way, it was a tyranny, for, in all those provinces, where the Moslems were only 7 to 12 per cent in numerical strength, the Congress gave them posts in the stingy proportion of 40 to 75 per cent only in education. Police and other administrative departments where they ought to have got cent per cent in consideration of their 'historical importance', for their being the direct communal descendants of the Moghol Emperors! Has not even Lord Zetland referred to the warlike qualities of the Moslems only this month and reminded the Congressite Hindus that the Moslem Emperors ruled over India for a time, implying, thereby, that the Moslems were, therefore, some superior beings to the Hindus! It was fortunate that His Lordship was never sent in his early youth to any primary Maratha school, otherwise he would have been deprived of the advantage of that argument by a little more knowledge of the fate of that Moslem Empire, how the avenging hosts of Hindus had beaten to a chip the forces of these 'warlike Moslems' in a hundred battlefields, smashed to pieces this self-same Mogul Empire, rearing up an Independent Hindu Empire on the ashes of Moslem pride and power and held the Mogul Emperors as prisoners and pensioners in their hands.

But, it is no use now on the part of our Congress friends to fulminate against this latest move of the Moslem League. The deliverance day of today is but the inevitable logical consequence of the Khilafat Day so gaily observed by the Congress yesterday. It is you who have initiated the Moslems into the belief that the more they demand the more you yield, the more they frown the more you placate, the more they pocket the more you offer, the more thankless they grow, the more afflicted you are with craving for their thanks. Did you not offer them blank cheques? Why then get startled, now that they begin to fill them up with whatever ransom they are pleased to demand? Dr. Munje, Bhai Paramanand and other leaders of the Hindu Mahasabha protested against the Khilafat policy against your blank cheques, against your meaningless 'neither accept nor reject vagaries,' but you then denounced them all as wicked communalists, looked down even upon Shivaji and Pratap as misguided patriots, because they conquered by the sword and you gave yourself out as the new messiahs who have come to conquer by love alone, as world guides in direct communications with the inner voice. And now how pitiable it is to find you so sorely afflicted for want of guidance for yourselves to find out a way to appease and win over by love alone a single individual, the president of the League, that you should stand imploring at the gates of all the British Governors and the Viceroys to lend you a helping hand.

Then again, whenever it happened that some British authorities or leaders referred to the policy of the Hindu Mahasabha on a point here or there with a tinge of appreciation, our Congress nationalists used to exclaim in righteous indignation, 'There! What more proof is required to expose the anti-national guilt of these Hindu Mahasabhaite communalists than the fact that the British people should appreciate their policy on this or that point. And now there is a regular scramble amongst these nationalist Congress leaders to secure and flourish in the face of the world certificates of appreciation from the British Governors and the Viceroys to prove that the Congress ministers were after all not so bad and had served under the British Government to its satisfaction. Moreover, it is also very funny to observe that those very Congress leaders who blamed the Hindu *Sangathanists* whenever they claimed a legitimate protection from the British Government against the Moslem outrages on the Frontier or in Malabar or in Bengal, should now be vying with each other in calling upon Governors and the Viceroy to arbitrate as the best judges and save the Congress prestige by declaring it not guilty in the very serious case framed against them by the Moslem League. Is it not now anti-national to appeal to the British, the third party, the outsiders, to step in to settle our internal differences which we may have with 'our Moslem countrymen'?

It is also instructive and, therefore, necessary to point out here that this theory of the 'third party' also constituted a Congress superstition which was responsible for so many of its errors. They always used to fancy that the Moslems, if left to themselves, would never have indulged in any anti-national, ulterior, anti-Hindu designs. The Moslems—including Messrs, Jinnah, Huq and Hayat Khan—were very simple-minded folk, incapable of any political subterfuges and as devotees of Islamic peace and goodwill, had no aggressive political aims of their own against the Hindus. Nay, even the Frontier tribes, the 'brave brothers Moplahs,' the Moslem populations in Bengal or Sindh who indulge in such horrible outrages against Hindus have no taste for it all, nursed within themselves, but were almost compelled to rise and revolt against the Hindus by 'the third party', the Britishers. When the British did not step in, we Hindus and Moslems lived together in perfect amity and brotherly concord and Hindu-Moslem riots was a thing simply unheard of.

Thousands of Congressite Hindus are observed to have been duped into this silliest of political superstitions. As if Muhammad Qasim, Gazanis, Ghoris, Allauddins, Aurangzebs were all instigated by the

British, by this third party, to invade and lay waste Hindu India with a mad fanatical fury! As if the history of the last 10 centuries of perpetual war between the Hindus and Moslems was an interpolation and a myth! As if the Alis or Mr. Jinnah or Sir Sikandar were mere school children to be spoiled with the offer of sugar pills by the British vagabonds in the class and persuaded to throw stones at the house of their neighbours! They say, 'Before the British came, Hindu-Moslem riots were a thing unheard of.' Yet, but because instead of riots, Hindu-Moslems wars was the order of the day.

But, supposing for a while what the Gandhists maintain that it is this third party, the British, who are solely responsible for hypnotising Moslems into anti-Hindu and anti-national tendencies, how is it that Gandhiji and his Congressite lieutenants are invoking the very 'third party', the British Governors and the Viceroys, to act as arbitrators, to judge whether the Congress was really guilty of the accusations levelled by the Moslem League against it? Is the leading abettor the best person to arbitrate? To request him, whom you accuse as the leading instigator, to investigate into the crime? If the Congress superstition was true, then the British are sure to adjudge the award in a way to intensify the ill-will and distrust between the Congressite and the League so as to undermine yet further any chances of Hindu-Moslem understanding and concord. So, then, either your third party theory was wrong and superstitious or you have obviously bungled in approaching the very mischief-making third party to arbitrate.

The simple fact which the Congressite Hindus would do well to make a note of even now and which would spare them from a series of such inconsistent and bungling steps is that the Moslem religion, theocratic traditions and history, all imbue them with inherent ambition of Islamic political sovereignty. The British policy at times when it suits British interests does, of course, act as a match, but the explosive magazine is genuinely Moslem. It could be held in check, but woe to him who overlooks its existence and dupes himself into the belief that the match itself was the magazine. If not the British-make, any other match may serve the same purpose. Nay, spontaneous combustion is also its peculiar characteristic. Secondly, the Moslems are practical politicians to a fault. So, they, in general, yield to and ally instinctively with the stronger, even if he be their worse opponent, and continue to bully the weaker.

Has not England reduced them to a subject race in India and elsewhere? But, today, England is the stronger of the two. So, they will fawn on England and continue to aggrandise against the Hindus. If tomorrow the Hindus grow stronger, they will be yielding to Hindus too and behave as brothers, as they did in Maharashtra and Punjab in the days of the Peshwas or Ranjit Singh. That is why 'Hindu-Moslem riots were a thing unheard of in days gone by' to quote the Congressite slogan.

The best way to counteract the League's day of deliverance is for the Congress to observe the day of rectification.

In all sincerity, I request my Congressite brothers that instead of fulminating against the move of the League or what is more likely especially in the case of Gandhist group, instead of being yet more browbeaten, the best way would be to take it as an effective eye-opener and arrest their steps once for all on the dangerous path they were treading. They should simply refuse to have any further dealing with the Moslems as Moslems. Let the Indian National Congress rectify that fundamental mistake and be once more the real Indian National Congress as it claims to be. Let it be absolutely consistent with its own ideal of territorial nationalism and begin with a clean slate. *Let it proclaim once for all that it stands by these principles alone: firstly, it recognises no Moslem as a Moslem, or Christian as a Christian, or Hindu as a Hindu, but looks upon them all and deals with them all as Indians only; and, therefore, will have nothing to do with any special, communal, religious or racial interests as apart from the fundamental interests guaranteed to all citizens alike.*

Secondly, it does not acknowledge any other constitutional principle with regard to electorates than the rule 'one man one vote' and public services to go by merit alone. Only one alternative it may condescend to subscribe in view of the peculiar situation in India to the effect that if communal representation is to be resorted to at all, then it must strictly be in relation to the numerical strength of the constituents and in the public services too that relation may be observed, but only insofar as it is consistent with merit.

Thirdly, and above all, so long as such a national and just constitution could not be had, let the Congress resist the temptation of participating in any election whatsoever under a constitution which is deliberately meant to divide the integrity of the Indian people and is not only used on communal divisions, but is most unjustly harmful to the majority community and constitutes a standing instigation to the Moslem minority to act against the nation as a whole as the present constitution aims to do. So long as there are separate electorates for the Moslems and the general, which, in fact, means the Hindus, then let the Moslem League and the Hindu Mahasabha participate in the elections and let the Congress stand supremely aloof as a truly Indian national body which can never condescend to identify itself with any particular communal electorate.

But, if the Congress takes courage in both hands, rectifies its pass anti-Hindu and anti-national attitude and takes up the stand I have suggested above, the prestige of the Congress as a truly national organisation will immediately be enhanced. In that case, it will regain in general the whole-hearted confidence of the Hindu Mahasabha at any rate.

But it can on no account continue to play the double-faced game of getting elected on behalf of the Hindu electorate as Hindus and betray the legitimate interests of the Hindus as nationalists. It can no longer hunt with the hound and run with the hare. Otherwise, the Moslems are bound to continue and rightly so to look upon it as a Hindu body while the Hindus will look upon it and rightly too as a pseudo-nationalistic nuisance, dangerous to the Hindu cause as well as the Indian national one. May I hope that the Congress will open its eyes? If it does even now, it is not yet too late! As my friend Mr. Ketkar proposes in the *Maratha* of Poona, let the Congress observe a Day of Rectification to counteract the League's Day of Deliverance, proclaim the truly national orientation suggested above and write to the League the last word, closing all further correspondence: 'Sirs, if you come, with you, if you do not, without you, and if you oppose, in spite of you', we shall continue the good fight to free our Hindusthan as best as we can.

And in case our Moslem friends want to have a royal commission to define their rights, let the Congress tell them uncompromisingly, 'If you want to have a resort to any independent arbitration, well, then the highest tribunal of that nature can be but the League of Nations, which has already framed a Public Law with regard to the rights of minorities all over the world. The case of Indian minorities also should be referred to the League.' In fact, had the Congress taken up this stand as uncompromisingly as possible and as Dr. Munje had already suggested, then at the Round Table Conference, things could never have drifted in this wild way.

- The Hindu Mahasabha will have to frame a detailed programme of its economic policy in the near future when it issues its electoral manifesto. All that I can do now is to suggest a few broad principles, as space forbids dilation. Firstly, it must be remembered that man is not altogether an economical being. It has been well said by Christ that man does not live by bread alone. As it is spiritually true, it is also true in the racial, cultural, national and several other aspects that go to constitute the human nature. Therefore, the attempt to interpret all human history and human activities in economical terms alone is altogether onesided and amounts to maintaining that man has no other urge in him to live but hunger.

Besides hunger, the problem of bread, man has other appetites as fundamental as that—sensual, intellectual, sentimental, some natural, some acquired, some personal, some social and his being is a complex one; so also is his history. Man has a stomach, but the stomach is not man. Therefore, the solution that is sometimes suggested to the effect that the economical community of interest provides the only and the best solvent of all religious, racial, national and other antipathies that divide mankind in the world is as superficial as simple. The fact that in Europe the very races and nations wherein the prophets of this school arose and preached and where giant efforts were made to revolutionise all human institutions and recast them into this economical mould alone, religious, racial and national differences have been assuming formidable proportions and have been persisting to assert themselves in Germany, Italy, France, Poland, England, Spain, etc. in spite of centuries of the most intense propaganda to insist on economical community of interest, is enough to prove that you cannot altogether eliminate all religious or racial or national factors at the stroke, at a thought. Those who advance the easy argument: 'If but you persuade all to unite on the economical plane and to forget every other superstitious difference as racial, cultural, etc.', forget themselves that the very 'but' in their argument rebuts the practical utility at any rate, apart from its theoretical soundness. Consequently the Hindu *Sangathanists* must in no case delude themselves with the belief that the economical programme alone will ever suffice to solve all cultural, racial and national dangers that threaten them throughout India.

Secondly, they should remember that economical questions too are inextricably bound up under the circumstances obtaining in India with religious and racial complications. There are thousands of examples which the workers in the Hindu *Sangathanist* field know through experience that if a Hindu takes to a particular trade which happens to be the monopoly of the Moslems, he is persecuted. A new Hindu Pinjari or Tangewala is threatened at several places with death. Witness the fact that Moslem dacoits who attack cities and villages on the Frontiers and loot them proclaim at drum-beats: 'We will only loot Hindus; no Moslem shopkeepers or money-lenders will we touch.' Hundreds and hundreds of cases of this type could be cited. Now, how are you to afford immediate relief to these Hindus unless by organising them as Hindus? Moslem police, as Moslems, defend them not. It is clearly a religious, racial and cultural plague and only the patent economical pills can afford no cure. To preach to these millions of fanatics, for example, the rioters in Sukkur district, that their economical interests are one with the Hindus and thus convert them into human brotherhood? Well, let them try who like it, but how many centuries will it take? And what are the Hindus to do in the meanwhile? It is just to match the monomaniac remedy of Gandhiji—the spinning wheel, by which he wants to convert the whole world into *ahimsa* and make it resort to eternal disarmament! Yet, let the wise mouse himself be asked to put into practice his excellent suggestion to bell the cat and let all others in the meanwhile take to other practical contrivances and steps to save themselves!

Consequently, leaving aside the doctrinaire solution of a human economical front or the airy hopes that if but we insist on the economical community of interest of all alike and unite all Indians at any rate on the economical plane alone, all religious, racial, national and cultural animosities will vanish like a mist, we Hindu *Sangathanists* should as practical politicians restrict our immediate economical programme to the economical advance of the Hindu national alone.

Taking into consideration the special circumstances obtaining in India and the stage of social progress, the only school of economics which will suit our requirements in the immediate future is the school of nationalistic economy. To express all the lending factors of our economical policy in a suitable formula I should like to style it as the policy of 'national co-ordination of class interests'. This is the economical flank of the Hindu *Sangathanist* platform.

Our immediate Economical Policy—the National co-ordination of class interests

(a) We shall first of all welcome the machine. This is a Machine Age. The handicrafts will of course have their due place and encouragement, but national production will be on the biggest possible machine scale. (b) The peasantry and the working class form literally the chief source of national wealth, health and strength as well; for, a stalwart army also has for its recruit depot to depend chiefly on these very classes which supply the nation with the first two requisites. Therefore, every effort will be made to reinvigorate them and the villages which are their cradle. Peasants and labourers must be enabled to have their share in the distribution of wealth to such an extent as to enable them not only with a bare margin of existence, but touch the average scale of a comfortable life. Nevertheless it must be remembered that they, too, being a part and parcel of the nation as a whole, must share obligations and responsibilities and therefore, can only receive their share in such a way as is consistent with the general development and security of the national industry, manufacture and wealth in general. (c) As the national capital is under the present circumstances mainly individual and indispensable for the development of national industry and manufacture, it also will receive due encouragement and recompense. (d) But, the interests of both the capital and labour will be subordinated to the requirement of the nation as a whole. (e) If an industry is flourishing, the profits will be shared in a large portion by the labourers. But, on the contrary, if it is a losing concern, not only the capitalist but to a certain extent even the labourer will have to be satisfied with diminishing returns so that the national industry as such may not altogether be undermined by the overbearing attitude of the selfish class interest of either the capitalists or labourers. *In short, the claims of the capital and labour will be so coordinated from time to time as to enable the nation as a whole to develop its national industry and manufacture and make itself self-sufficient.* (f) In some, cases of the key industries or manufactures and such other items may be altogether nationalised if the national government can afford to do so and can conduct them more efficiently than private enterprise can do. (g) The same principle applies to cultivation of land. We should so co-ordinate the interest of the landlord and the peasant that the national agricultural production may on the whole be developed and does not suffer owing to any selfish tussle between the class interests of the landowner or the tenants or the tiller. (h) In some cases, the Government may take over the land and introduce state cultivation if it can serve to train up the peasant class as a whole with the use of big machines and agriculture on a large and scientific scale. (i) All strikes or lockouts which are obviously meant or inevitably tend to undermine and cripple national industry or production in general or are calculated to weaken the economic strength of the nation as a whole must be referred to state arbitration and get settled or in serious cases quelled. (j) *Private property must in general be held inviolate.* (k) *And in no case, there should be on the part of the state any expropriation of such property without reasonable recompense.* (l) *Every step must be taken by the state to protect national industries against foreign competition.*

I have hurriedly lined out the above items to serve as illustrations only. The national economical strength must grow and the nation must be made economically self-sufficient; these two form the pivot of the policy.

A special feature of no less importance of this Hindu Sangathanists *economics must of course be to safeguard the economical interests of the Hindus wherever and whenever they may be threatened by the economical aggression of the non-Hindus as happens today a set policy in the Nizam state, in the Punjab, in Bhopal, in Assam and in several other parts of India. Hindu Sabhas in all localities should make it a point to see that the Hindu peasants, the Hindu traders, the Hindu labourers do not suffer at the hands of non-Hindu aggression while the conflicting class interests amongst the Hindus themselves should be solved in the light of the above general principle.*

Our immediate programme for the next two years.

The European WAR: The two explicit resolutions passed by the Working Committee regarding our policy towards the war in Europe leave nothing more to be said on that subject, as no new event has happened to demand a change. I exhort the British Government once more that a definite and immediate declaration of granting the Dominion Status as contemplated in the Westminster Statute to India, as the end of the war at the latest is the only means to secure whole-hearted sympathy of the Hindu people with England in this present struggle and to ensure the willingness even of an Independent India in future to continue a co-partnership in the Commonwealth on equal terms. Any delay in granting the Dominion Status as an immediate step to enable India to tread on the path of evolutionary progress towards her ultimate political destiny would prove dangerous even to the solidarity of the British Commonwealth. The rise and rapid advance of Japan in the East, of Russia, Italy and Germany in the West are events portentous and a contented and self-governing India cannot but be a mighty factor in strengthening the British position in facing any anti-British combination. But, no amount of political sophistry can disarm Indian discontent and make her tolerate the humiliation of continuing as a British dependency. Do you expect any longer to dupe her into the belief that it is only the want of an understanding between the Indian majority and minority, the Hindus and Moslems, with regard to such details as the percentage in representation, etc. that justifies England in delaying the grant of Dominion Status forthwith? The British statesmen have recently stated that their conscience forbids to thrust an understanding on the minority, the Moslems, in India, against their will and would not move an inch till the Hindus and Moslems have produced a willing compromise and a common demand for a progressive constitution. It was really a news to learn that English statesmen have grown so god-fearing and democratic almost overnight as not to be willing to thrust on any people anything against their own will! But, may it be asked that when you thrust your unmitigated political autocracy on India, was their any plebiscite taken to acertain Indian opinion? Or did you take a plebiscite or receive a united request from the minority and the majority when only a couple of months ago you scrapped up the provincial autonomy at a stroke and invested Governors with powers to conduct the government at their own discretion and in their own judgement? And if you could thrust undiluted autocracy, a vassalage on India and hold her at a dependency, can you not thrust a Dominion Status on her in spite of the will of a minority and especially so when the majority has unanimously demanded it? You can thrust curses; can you not thrust blessings? The sooner the British people cease to have a resort to these transparent political subterfuges and to utilise the Moslem minority to comouflage their own unwillingness to grant Hindusthan her birthright, her *swarajya,* while she is still treading on an evolutionary path of political progress the better for England, the better for India. If the evolutionary path is, thus, altogether closed to the Hindus in particular by empowering the Moslems with a definite veto on all equitable progress, a deadlock may ensue, but only for a while, because Nature hates a vacuum: and if evolutionary progress is denied, the gathering forces of Time Spirit cannot but take the other and more dangerous turn.

Next two years: 'Constructive programme for the Hindu Sabhaists

Unless indeed something unexpected and a far more imminent and urgent duty faces us, in the meanwhile I call upon all Hindu Sabhas, whether local, provincial or central, to concentrate their efforts on the following threefold constructive programme in the main.

We have numberless tasks before us, all useful, all pressing, in their own way, but it is always better to begin with the beginning. Instead of getting lost in details or trying to do all at once and ending in leaving everything undone or ill-done or bungled, carried away by anything and everything that comes in the way, it is always wiser to choose relatively what is most fundamental, most effective and, at the same time, within the reach of our present resources and ability and hit upon a plan to intensify our efforts on those items only in the main.

We should also remember that unless we gather strength, we cannot and should not always be after precipitating struggles only for the sake of demonstration and excitement at the risk of courting an inevitable failure, when it is uncalled for. Navigators abide by the tide. Even lions lie in wait. Great dread-naughts are built in silent and hidden quarters of the ports before they are called out in action and can with their multi-throated roar and fire rout their opponents.

I have not selected the following items at random. All the above factors are taken into consideration in their selection. These three items are the most fundamental, the most urgent and yet quite within the reach of almost every Hindu *Sangathanist* who means to do the really needful at the hour which, though it may not be quite exciting to begin with, is yet quite sure to enable the forces of Hindudom to face a righteous fight in defence of its honour and freedom when the hour is struck. Those who can undertake other items of the *Sangathan* work along with these may of course do so. But, our first and foremost attention must be concentrated on these three items for the next two years to begin with. Whatever we will be able to accomplish in this direction within these two years will put us in a position of vantage to solve other questions far more effectively than it can be done if we take them up now. Therefore, intensify your efforts on conducting a whirlwind campaign at every village and town and city to,

(1) *Remove untouchability.*

(2) *Compel all universities, colleges and schools to make military training compulsory to students and secure entry into the naval, aerial and military forces and institutions for your youth in any and every way.*

(3) *Prepare the Hindu electorate to the utmost measure possible to vote only for those Hindus* Sangathanists *who openly pledge to safeguard Hindu interests; and not to vote for the Congress candidates, who can never serve Hindu interests with full freedom and boldness even if they wish or promise to do so, so long as they are bound by the Congress discipline and tied to the Congress ticket.*

The first of these items will enable you to consolidate at least a couple of crores of your own brethren who are religiously, culturally, nationally and in every other way, as much a part and parcel of Hindudom as any of us can claim to be. Every local Hindu Sabha must see to it in its own locality that these our so-called untouchable brethren are immediately elevated to the level of the so-called touchable by securing to them all fundamental rights which every citizen, even non-Hindus, are entitled to exercise in public life. We should persuade our touchable brothers, in cases wherever untouchable brothers are oppressed in any way on the only ground of untouchability based on birth alone, to fight their cause out if need be by resorting to law courts. Of course, we should on no account molest or disrespect the sentiments of our Sanatani brothers so far as their personal freedom is concerned. But, in public schools, conveyances, posts, services and in every aspect of public life, no Hindu should be permitted to deprive other Hindus of their public rights on ground of caste untouchability alone. Whatever social equality we Hindus allow to Moslems and other non-Hindus must as of right belong to our Hindu brothers of whatever caste they be. To act otherwise is in reality an insult to our common Hinduness. *It must be plainly mentioned here that even those who are at present bracketed as untouchables are themselves guilty of this sin just like those who are bracketed as touchable Hindus. For, every untouchable caste treats some other caste supposed to be inferior to it as untouchable as ruthlessly as it is treated itself by others. The sin is common to all of us and, therefore, let us all join hands together and be determined to remove this sore with a supreme effort.* In the meanwhile, our Sanatani brothers may rest assured that barring the fundamental rights which every citizen is entitled to in public life, the Hindu Mahasabha will always refrain from taking any recourse to law to thrust any religious reform on any sect within the Hindu fold even in the case of untouchability. But, those Hindu *Sangathanists* who are convinced of the incalculable harm untouchability has done and is doing should also be free to act up according to their own conscience in their own dealings. The lines on which I call upon the Hindu *Sangathanists* to carry on an intense campaign of removing untouchability would be made clear from time to time as the work proceeds. I may mention here even at the risk of a personal reference that those who can should make it a point to read the report of the 10 years' work done by the Ratrnagiri Hindu Sabha under my lead in conducting such an intense campaign against untouchability which was attended with notable success. *It will also make it clear that the approach of the Hindu Sabha to the question of the removal of untouchability differs at the root from the approach of the Gandhian attempt to remove it. Therefore, although we may co-operate, yet we should not identify our movement with the Gandhian movement.*

In the next two years' time, we Hindu *sabhaists* must do more in removing untouchability than two hundred years could do in the past.

So far as the second item is concerned, the plans will be outlined in the All-India Committee and the sittings of the Working Committee from time to time.

The third item constitutes, of course, the very keystone of the whole programme. Unless and until the Hindu electorate does not return only the Hindu *Sangathanists* to the legislatures and local bodies but allows the Congress the right to represent the Hindu electorate in the eyes of the government, the Hindus must continue to remain as political orphans in Hindusthan, in their own country. The Hindus may fight and win political rights as they have done to a great extent in the past, but so long as they have not cured themselves of this suicidal folly of resigning those rights in the hands of the Congress at the polls, they can never expect to strengthen the legitimate position of Hindudom in India. But on the contrary, will find themselves as non-entities and the Moslems alone more profited by those very rights which the Hindus have won and consequently in a position to suppress the Hindus with all the greater impact.

Remember also that a new Round Table Conference or a sort of a Constituent Assembly may be called in the near future. So long as the Hindus return as their representatives the Congressites alone, the government is bound and justified to look upon the Congress to represent the Hindu view, even if the Congress protests against it. And they will not recognise the Congress as representing the Moslems or the nation as a whole even if the Congress claims that position because the Moslems refuse to return any Moslem on the Congress ticket as a rule. Even Dr. Kichlu was defeated at the Moslem polls because he stood on the Congress ticket. Under such circumstances, there is a grave and sure danger of further surrender of Hindu rights to Moslem demands which are already claiming equality of status even in the Hindu provinces. There will be no use of any protest from the Hindu *Sangathanists* or of the secret bickerings or fulminations of those Hindus in the Congress camp itself who personally hate this attitude on the part of the Congress as an organisation; for, there will be no party with credentials from the Hindu electorate to represent them, who can advocate at the conference the legitimate Hindu rights as freely and boldly and uncompromisingly as the Moslem League representatives can do their.

But, if the Hindu electorate does ever come to its senses, refuses to return the Congressite candidates and returns only the Hindu *Sangathanists* in majority, the Hindus can have a Hindu *Sangathanists* government in at least seven provinces as the Moslems have in the Punjab, Bengal, etc. and the Hindus can capture enough political power so as to be in a position to remove at least 75 per cent of the grievances under which they are groaning now even in provinces like U.P., where they form the majority and the Congress ruled. The provincial police and the public service will be under the command of Hindu *Sangathanist* governments and will not dare to trample on or neglect Hindu rights. Nay, the Moslems themselves will neither dare to encroach upon Hindu rights nor put forward such intolerable anti-Hindu or anti-national demands. *As we have no grudge against the Moslem minority insofar as their legitimate rights are concerned and as the Hindu* Sangathanists *are ever willing to live in an honourable friendship and amity with their Moslem countrymen in Hindusthan, the Moslem minority, too, will have every protection in the exercise of its legitimate rights.*

Therefore, all our efforts must be intensely concentrated during the next two or three years in persuading the Hindu electorate to vote for the Hindu *Sangathanists* alone and not to vote for the Congressites in any future election. *This will require a daily press devoted to the Hindu* Sangathanist *cause and a central fund.* Above all, we shall have to form a Hindu party—including Sanatanists, Arya Samajists and all such other Hindu bodies, sects and sections, who have not as yet any formal connection with the Hindu Mahasabha as an organisation but are as devoted Hindu *Sangathanists* as the Hindu *sabhaists* themselves. The ways and means of effecting it all is a matter of detail and ought to be attended to by the local, provincial and the central Hindu Mahasabha organisations and above all by all Hindu *Sangathanists,* whether they be formal members of the Hindu Sabha or not.

But, if in spite of our efforts the Hindu electorate persists in its suicidal folly and votes for the Congress and we do not secure a majority at the polls? Never mind, our efforts are sure to succeed in securing a minority, as we already find in Maharashtra and some other places that Hindu *Sangathanist* candidates are not only elected in some hotly contested elections against the Congress but in cases have topped the polls. And even the presence of a minority of devoted Hindu *Sangathanists* in legislatures and local bodies acts as an effective check on the waywardness of the majority, gives a tongue unto Hindu grievances and paves way to further progress in power.

But, if we are completely outvoted at the elections and do not secure a single seat? Never mind still, we shall acknowledge the defeat and share the humiliation in general. But, we can proudly claim for ourselves individually that we did not betray our conscience in spite of overwhelming odds. The responsibility of the electoral defeat and the humiliation will lie on the Hindu electorate in general and not on him who casts his own vote at any rate on the Hindu side. Moreover, the very risk of a contest in elections against the Congress on such a righteous issue is bound to compel the Congress to be more and more afraid of sacrificing Hindu interests on the altar of the fetish of a pseudo-nationalism.

To join the national fight, when and while the forces are winning, is patriotic enough. But, when the fight for a righteous cause is almost lost, to persist still in rallying round its banner and refuse to betray one's conscience to the last, in spite of a general defeat and humiliation, is simply heroic! and all that an honest soldier can individually do! If he cannot share the joy of a general victory, nothing can deprive him of the supreme satisfaction of having done his duty well. This should be the faith with which the Hindu *Sangathanists* should continue their contest under the present circumstances. Let us determine, even if the worst comes to the worst, to be the last of the devoted batch of the Hindu *Sangathanist* than to be the first of the Hindu traitors!

□

22nd Session, Madura—1940

Delegates to and Members of the Hindu Mahasabha,

I really cannot find words adequate enough to express my cordial and grateful appreciation of the trust which you have placed in me in electing me this year also, for the fourth time in an unbroken succession, to the presidentship of the Akhil Bharatiya Hindu Mahasabha. During the last three years, I always felt confident whenever I was called upon by you to preside that I would so acquit myself of the responsibility it involved as to justify your choice to your own satisfaction as well as to the satisfaction of my own conscience. But, this year, I felt so uneasy when I learnt of my election to the presidentship for the fourth time while I continued bedridden owing to a long drawn illness with no speedy recovery in sight that I immediately wrote to our esteemed leader, Dr. P. Varadarajulu Naidu informing him of my intention to resign telegraphically the high office, as I was painfully conscious of my inability to discharge its duties with that untiring activity and zeal with which I tried to do it throughout my tenure as the president of the Hindu Mahasabha. But, Dr. Varadarajulu Naidu wired back to me not to take such a step all of a sudden as that would tell disastrously on the success of the session to come. Several of our esteemed leaders and comrades also wired to me to the same effect and urged upon me the necessity of accepting the presidentship in the best interest of the Hindu cause. In deference to this public will and especially due to my unwillingness to cause any additional worry at the eleventh hour to Dr. Varadarajulu Naidu, the band of Hindu *Sangathanist* workers and the esteemed Chairman and the members of the Reception Committee who had undergone such strenuous efforts to hold this first Hindu Mahasabha session in Tamil Nadu, I yielded to public pressure and agreed to preside over this session at any rate.

Now, if my health improves, I shall of course get to the work you have entrusted to me with unsparing and untiring zeal and effort and try to lead the movement to the best of my ability through thick and thin, through sunshine and shower. But, if my ailing health improves not, instead of playing false to my conscience in sticking to the high post without the required strength to discharge its duties as strenuously as it should be done, I should be allowed to resign from the presidentship and shift its onerous responsibility to some stronger and worthier shoulders. Of course, it goes without saying that even if I cease to be the president of the Mahasabha, I cannot but continue to work and fight as a soldier in your ranks who has dedicated his life once and for all to the sacred Hindu cause.

The Mahasabha movement marches ahead
with long and rapid strides

It is encouraging to note that the Hindu movement has been advancing with long and rapid strides throughout the year under the auspices of the Mahasabha. Even a passing reference to some leading items in the report of the work of the Mahasabha during this year will be sufficient to bear out this fact.

Firstly, we have brought this year another great Presidency within the sphere of influence of our ideological realm. Only a year ago there was hardly even a district Hindu Sabha worth the name throughout this Madras presidency. With the exception of the patriarchal personality of Syt. Vijayaraghavachariar of Salem and a handful of leading men here and there, who realised the urgency and importance of the Hindu *Sangathan* movement, the millions and millions of Hindus in this Presidency knew next to nothing about the Hindu movement or the Hindu Mahasabha which led it. While that political section amongst the Hindus who knew of it, knew it only either to pooh-pooh it or to hate it, but fortunately for the Hindu cause, a veteran leader who was thoroughly well versed in conducting mass movements and held a high position in the political life of this Presidency for decades in the past, came forward at the beginning of this year to espouse the cause of the Hindu Mahasabha and organise the Hindu community under the Hindu flag in this Presidency also. He was Dr. P. Varadarajulu Naidu. Very soon a band of enthusiastic pioneers gathered round him and several men of position offered their co-operation in the sacred mission. The result is that within some 10 months' time the whole Presidency of Madras from Trivandrum to Rajahmundry has not only become alive to the growing prestige and power of the Hindu Mahasabha but millions of Hindus in it have been captivated by the ideology of Hindu *Sangathan*. Consequently, the Mahasabha has already become a force to be counted within the political and social life of this Presidency also.

Nay, further, this Session in the very heart of the Tamil Nadu furnishes a visual proof of the great pan-Hindu awakening that has come over the Hindu mind not only in this Presidency alone, but throughout Hindusthan. It is not only the streams of all Indian rivers, the Sindhu and Saraswati, the Jumna and Ganga, the Krishna and Kaveri that have met in confluence at Madura as they did this morning when waters from all the *teerthas* were taken out in procession, but it is also the All-India streams of Hindu life that have met here today in a pan-Hindu confluence. Every pulse that beats in every Hindu individual here in this vast concourse is pulsating with the oneness of our racial, religious, political and national being and the pan-Hindu flag that is waving on this mandap does but symbolise the flame that has set some 20 crores of Hindus hearts aflame with the glad tidings that a resurrected Hindu nation is soon to rise resplendent out of its grave of a self-forgetful swoon.

Another item which deserves to be noted in reviewing this year's work is the remarkable increase in the well-checked and regularly registered membership of the Hindu Mahasabha throughout India. In this connection the Maharashtra Provincial Hindu Sabha and the Bengal Provincial Hindu Sabha deserve a special mention. Some five years ago, the Mahasabha counted its members in thousands. This year we are in a position to count them in lakhs and if but we all work with unabated and untiring energy for some five years more, we shall doubtless be able to count our membership in millions. In addition to this remarkable increase in membership, the Hindu Mahasabha organisation has also thrown out its branches this year in large numbers in places where they did not exist before. Then again in addition to the Hindu Sabhas which are formally affiliated with the Mahasabha there have grown up Hindu Sabha organisations in the states which are for all purposes identical and allied with the Hindu Mahasabha organisation but which for reasons of policy and convenience are not regularly affiliated with it. As prominent amongst these may be mentioned the Travancore State Hindu Sabha and the Shuddhi Sabha; the Kolhapur State Hindusabha and the Shuddhi Sabha; the Bhopal State Hindu Sabha; the Nizam State

Hindu Mandal; the Gwalior State Hindu Sabha; Cutch-Kathiawar State Hindu Sabha and such others. The majority of these have been started very recently and all of them have recorded commendable progress this year. It is also encouraging to note that the Hindu Sabhas are being organised outside India too, in Affrica, Japan, Trinidad and some other countries. Reports show that the Trinidad Hindu Sabha is making good progress.

Of the state Hindu Sabhas, the Nizam Hindu Mandal deserves special attention on account of the fact that not only its extensive activities but even its very existence testify to the fact *how the Nizam civil resistance movement had morally and materially strengthened the position of the Hindus in that state* and how on the whole, the civil and religious liberties that were denied to them before the civil resistance movement began, can now be exercised at least to such an extent as to enable the Hindus to forge ahead and gather sufficient strength to win further liberties and to get strong enough to defend themselves against the outrages of Moslem fanaticism which even today continue to disfigure the state. The Hindu Mandal has already established its branches in important centres in the state and is rapidly consolidating the Hindus there. The awakening that came over the Hindus in that state during the exciting and inspiring days of the Civil Resistance movement has doubtless come to stay and has already made the Hindus in that state more self-confident and manly enough to defend themselves as has been demonstrated in a number of cases this year in which the Hindus counter-attacked and brought the Moslem *goondas* to their knees when the latter took to rioting or looting as they were wont to do with impunity in days gone by. There have been some organised and outrageous anti-Hindu riots even this year in that state as, for example, at Nanded, wherein the very state police and authorities, mostly Moslems, did not hesitate to molest the Hindus; but then such incidents were relatively few this year when compared to the state of things prevailing a few years ago. We must also remember that even in the so-called British India such fanatical outbursts on the part of the Moslems are not quite unknown. The new factor that is to be noted, so far as the state is concerned, is the increasing resistance and even the spirit of counter-attacking to checkmate aggression which are being displayed by the Hindus in the state in an ever-increasing measure. *If but this spirit continues to grow and the Hindus in Hyderabad state get consolidated into a Hindu front voting for those representatives who are pledged to the Hindu cause,* they would certainly be able before long to bring sufficient pressure on the Nizam Government to yield as many constitutional rights to the Hindus in that state as their population strength demands land as the Moslems in the Kashmere state have already acquired on the same plea of being a major community.

The propagandistic activities of the Mahasabha were also carried on, on a more extensive scale throughout this year than it could be done in the past. Our grateful thanks are specially due in this respect to our veteran leader Dharmaveer Dr. Moonje, who in spite of his advanced age, kept himself constantly on the run from province to province throughout the year. Most influential leaders like Sir M.N. Mookerji, Dr. Syama Prasad Mookerji, Dharamaveer Bhopatkar, as well as hundreds of provincial leaders and organisers kept working night and day with the selfless devotion of religious missionary or a *tapaswi* and toured from place to place to propagate the cause. During this year, there were held not less than a hundred provincial, district and even *taluka* conferences; local meetings were held in thousands; while cart-loads of *Sangathan* literature were being freely distributed from all important centers of the Mahasabha organisation throughout India.

In the electoral field also, we have secured this year some notable successes which proved that at least the intelligent part of the Hindu electorate has unmistakably begun to realise that their best interests as Hindus could only be served by voting for the *Sangathanist* representatives and that it is suicidal for Hindus to vote for a Congress candidate so long as he is bound to the Congress ideology. As a case in point, we may mention the hotly contested election to the Calcutta corporation. The Bengal Hindu Sabha came out with flying colours at several polling stations in spite of the fact that it was the first time when Hindu Mahasabha openly challenged the long and firmly established monopoly of the Congress at the Hindu polls, and the consequence was that the Congress could not form a majority party in the corporation on their own ticket. At some other places, as, for example, in Sindh, Mahad, etc. we inflicted almost a cent per cent defeat on the Congressites and got a clear majority. Of course, it is no wonder that at some places, the Hindusabha suffered reverses also. But we shall have to start in every election for at least five years to come fully prepared to face such electoral reverses. The Hindu electorate cannot so quickly learn to unlearn the lesson that has been branded on their mind that its electoral duty consists in nothing else but to vote for the Congress with eyes closed, tongues tied and brains held in abeyance. Nevertheless, the moral of these reverses also should be carefully noted by us. As an illustration of this, let us take the municipal election at Karnavati (Ahmedabad) which took place this very month where the Hindu Sabha lost all the seats it competed for.

In this case of Karnavati (Ahmedabad) also, this was the first time when the Congress monopoly was challenged by the Hindu Mahasabha at the polls. The Congress, although it calls itself 'national', had set up no candidate in Moslem wards. On the election day, all the Congressites sought only Hindu votes and proclaimed even themselves as Hindus. Their nationalism on that day did not fight shy of insisting upon the fact that they were Hindus, an act which is branded by them as below their dignity as 'nationalists' throughout the period till the day of any election dawns. The opposition of the Hindu Mahasabha was also so tough that it taxed the resources of the congress party to its utmost capacity. The arrest of patriot Vallabhbai Patel was deliberately staged at that city just on the eve of the election and after his arrest, a message was broadcasted as his last word to the citizens that no voter should vote for the Hindu Mahasabha. As if that was the real issue for which patriot Patel courted arrest as if not to vote for the Hindu Mahasabha was such a patriotic virtue that it should constitute the only theme for the Congress *satyagrahi* on which the Hindus required to be instructed if India was to be saved. Nevertheless the election campaign served as the best occasion for the Hindu Sabhaists too to preach their ideology to the public and the more the Congress grew excited, the larger was the audience that attended the Hindu Sabha meetings to know the other side of the question. Some of the meetings addressed by such popular Hindu Mahasabha orators, as Syt. Chandragupta Vedalankar and Prof. Deshpande were more largely attended than any meeting held by the Congress. So at long last, came in the last argument which the Congressites are wont to use during every election campaign, the argument of *goondaism*. Hindu Sabha meetings were disturbed and free fights became the order of the day. At the polls also Hindu Sabha voters were molested to cause panic and as the crowning rite of the *ahimsak*

Dharma, the Congressite *goondas* attacked the Central Hindu Sabha office in the city, on the last day of polling, causing serious bloodshed, injuring a number of Hindu Sabha volunteers so seriously that they had to be removed to the hospital, till at last the police stepped in, took the Hindu Sabha office under their protection and kept patrolling the street for a day or so, even after the elections were over.

I have referred at some length to this incident because for the Hindu Sabhaists it has a moral of its own. The Congress at present is resorting to *satyagraha* in order, as some of them say, to vindicate the right of free speech denied by the British Government or as some other Congressites say to proclaim the regime of absolute non-violence in the whole world. In the light of the above incidents at Karnavati (Ahmedabad) during these very weeks of *satyagraha* we are tempted to ask, does the Congress want to secure the right of free speech from the British for the Congress alone so that they may be left freer to gag the mouth of their own countrymen, kith and kin? And does that regime of absolute non-violence mean the ban on all other *lathis* and weapons but those which are to be freely used against the Hindu Sabha offices and meetings? And in that case does not linguistic honesty at any rate require that this Congress campaign be better styled as *asatyagrah* instead of *Satyagraha*? But whatever reflections we may pass on Congress *goondaism* in electoral compaigns, we must not commit the mistake of attributing the Congress success at the polls to *goondaism* alone. We must remember that a large section of the Hindu electorate itself is likely to persist voluntarily and knowingly for some time to come in the suicidal folly of voting for the Congress merely out of the vicious habit of long standing. Consequently, without being discouraged by reverses as at Karanavati (Ahmedabad) or on the contrary, without getting cocksure by electoral successes as in Sindh or at Calcutta, Delhi, Mahad and such other places, we Hindu Sabhaists must continue to contest the elections not caring much, for the time being, for the results. The results in an election generally depend on the folly or the wisdom of the electorate and you can never correct the electorate unless you continue to contest elections and utilise that opportunity for propagating your principles. Even the most powerful parties of today, the Nazis or the Fascists or the Bolshevists or the Democrats did not sweep the polls at a bound. They too had to face reverses in their initial stages. If but we take cautious steps, study the technique of electoral campaigns at big centres and then enter the contest, we are sure even under the present circumstances to secure an influential minority in representation to the legislatures and local bodies and even the presence of a minority of devoted Hindu *Sangathanists* is sure to act as a check on the Congressite majorities, to give a tongue unto Hindu grievances and pave the way to further political power. Nay, even if we fail to secure a single seat in an election, even then the contest itself will repay the trouble and checkmate the Congressite waywardness. The consciousness that it is not a walkover now in winning seats as it used to be, will force the Congressites to prove to the Hindu electorate that they too do not disregard Hindu interests as the Hindu *Sangathanist* rival candidates in the elections allege and will make the Congressites more and more afraid of sacrificing Hindu interests to the fetish of their pseudo-nationalism. If the Hindu party persists in contesting elections, a day will come when the Congressite Hindus shall have to go to the polls with a conspicuous *gandham* besmeared on their foreheads and the *tulsi* rosary in their hands to prove to the Hindu electorate that it was they, the Congressites, who were Hindus of a purer ray serene than the Hindu *Sangathanist* heretics.

That is why, I take this opportunity of rendering special thanks to the Hindusabha of Karnavati (Ahmedabad) for having contested so toughly in spite of all odds, instead of playing false to their conscience and let go the election uncontested for fear of defeat. They have done their duty well. It is that part of the Hindu electorate which voted for the Congress which is responsible for betraying Hindu interests and will soon pay the bill. Curiously enough, every election week at Karnavati (Ahmedabad) demonstrated the fact how this bill will have to be paid and how Hindus will be made to suffer humiliation at the hands of the Congressites. It is a straw but it shows how the wind blows. In a big educational institution at Karnawati (Ahemadabad), wherein there are some eleven hundred Hindu students and some eighty Moslem students, there was a programme wherein only the first stanza of '*Vande Mataram*' which was certified by the Congress itself as quite harmless even from its timid point of view was to be sung. But the Moslem students objected to that too, to the song itself. The school authorities took out of their file a circular which was issued when the Congress was in power and which laid it down that the '*Vande Mataram*' song or any part of it should not be sung if the Moslems objected and in accordance with it, the song was altogether omitted from the programme to the great resentment of the Hindu students. Thus, the sentiments of 80 Moslem students weighed more than and outvoted the sentiment of eleven hundred Hindu students. This is Congress democracy!

The Hindu Mahasabha has been doing all it can to defend the Hindu cause in Sindh

While we are passing the last year's report of the Hindu movement, under review, of all the Hindu Sabhas, the Sindh provincial Hindusabha and in fact the Sangathanist Party in general, in Sindh, including the Hindu *Panchayats* and Dharma Sabhas there, must be specially congratulated upon the unflinching devotion to their Dharma with which they faced daily martyrdom throughout this year during the latest rising of the murderous Moslem fanatics, in Sindh. You know how keenly we feel our helplessness in extending more efficient help to our Sindh brothers than we could do. But, it may safely be stated that short of armed retaliation, the Hindu Mahasabha or rather the Hindu Sangathanist Party in general has been doing all that could be done under the circumstances to safeguard and defend the Hindu cause in Sindh. Only a couple year ago I had been to Hyderabad, Karachi, Sukkur, Shikarpur, Rohri and studied the situation on the spot and presided over the Hindu Conference at Sukkur held under the auspices of the Sindh Provincial Hindu Sabha. It was at that conference that the Hindus determined definitely to oppose the Moslem aggression on the Manzalgah to formulate their grievances and to form a Hindu front which would oppose tooth and nail any attempt on the part of the Congress to sacrifice the Hindu interests in Sindh by handing over the province entirely to Moslem domination. The Provincial Hindu Sabha organisation was overhauled and the Sanatan Sabhas, the Sikhs, the Arya Samaj and other Hindu *Sangathanist* parties were persuaded to work hand in hand and merge themselves into a common Hindu front. Thereupon, the Sindh Provincial Hindusabha repudiated openly the pretensions of the Congress party to represent the Hindus and began to contest elections on Hindu tickets to legislatures and local bodies. At several places, they succeeded in inflicting defeats on the Congress candidates and today representatives of the Hindu sangathanist party form so influential a minority in the provincial legislatures and some of the local bodies as to be able very often to hold the balance, so as to influence the formation of the Moslem Ministries themselves. In addition to that, there are two to three Hindu ministers in the ministry itself who are pledged to the Hindu ticket. When the Hindus were getting thus more and more consolidated and their opposition to the Manzalgah question grew serious, the Moslems broke out in open riots here and there and Hindu life and property were seriously threatened. Even then the Congressite party did not dare to take up the cause of the Hindu minority in hand and the All India Congress took no notice whatsoever of the violent campaign which the Moslems, who were in overwhelming majority in that province, had set on foot to clear out at any rate some districts of Sindh of Hindu population and render Sindh a veritable Pakistan. When the position in Sindh grew so serious and the Moslem Parties fighting with each other could form no stable government, Dr. Moonje Mahashay paid a visit to that province on the eve of this year and presided over the second Hindu Conference at Sukkur. The Hindus once more declared their firm determination to defend their rights and not to sign voluntarily any humiliating surrender not only in connection with the Manzalgah affair but in case of any question which touched Hindu honour. The Hindu *Sangathanists* discarded the Congressite advice of evacuating Sindh altogether. They were and are determined to defend their ancient hearths and homes and keep the flag of Hindudom flying on the banks of the Indus even though and so long as the Hindus continue to be in the minority of one! Just a couple of days after this conference, the Sukkur riots broke out as the Moslems were driven out of the Manzalgah under Hindu pressure and murderous Moslem rising spread from village to village. The Sindh Provincial Hindu Sabhaists taking their own lives in the hollow of their hands strained every nerve to defend the Hindus as best as they could. Hindu Sabhaists, the leaders and the followers were prosecuted, persecuted, externed, interened, stabbed, threatened and had to work every hour at the imminent risk of their life. Still on the whole they stood bravely by their posts and short of an armed retaliation did everything to oppose and quell the Moslem rising and to succour and relieve the Hindus. The Hindu Sabhas in other provinces also extended every sympathy to their coreligionists in Sindh. There had been hundreds of meetings all over India held by the Hindu Sabhas. Resolutions were passed, funds were raised and sent to relieve the Hindu sufferers. Deputations were sent and representations made to the government. I myself urged upon the Viceroy and the Governor of Sindh that the Moslem ministry and provincial Autonomy should be scrapped, that the Governor himself should take over the administration in his hands to begin with and later on the government re-annex Sindh to the Bombay Presidency. I put it to the Viceroy in writing, 'Had so many Europeans, men and women, been butchered or outraged in Sindh as has been the case with the Hindus, would the government have looked on with folded hands as they are doing now? Would they not have raised to the ground the villages and resorts of murderous Moslem conspirators as an act of just reprisals?' It is amusing to see that some people from time to time should question, why the Hindu Mahasabha does not publish a full report of the Moslem atrocities in Sindh? The fact is that the Sindh Hindusabha, the very men on the spot have held investigations from time to time and published regular reports with names, statements, amount of loss of the Hindu sufferers. A couple of reports had even been proscribed by the government. The Hindu *Sangathanist* press had to furnish security for printing that. Almost all Hindu *Sangathanist* papers in India have printed all those details again and again. In fact it is only due to the Hindu Mahasabha activities and the Hindu Sangathanist press that the grievances and calamities of the Hindus in Sindh could at all be known all over India. Moreover, it is only due to the pressure which the Hindu Mahasabhaists brought to bear on the government that the Governor had at last forced the hands of the Moslem Ministry and took such stringent steps that at least some of the leading mischief-makers were brought to book, some effective protection afforded to the Hindus in the villages, some terror struck in the hearts of the malefactors and consequently there could be at least a temporary lull in the anti-Hindu activities of the Moslem fanatics in Sindh. In view of the above fact, I feel no hesitation in stating again that the Hindu Mahasabha through its provincial and local branches and with the help of the Hindu *Sangathanist* public in general all over India have done whatever it could do under the circumstances to extend relief to the Hindu sufferers in Sindh short of armed reprisals or retaliation. But, the latter means cannot fall within the sphere of our discussion here as here we must concern ourselves only with the legitimate and constitutional means. We wish we could do more than what is done and if the situation in Sindh does not improve soon, more stringent steps shall be taken as circumstances permit.

It is the Congress which is primarily responsible for the calamities which have befallen the Hindus in Sindh

When we find that in spite of all these facts it is precisely the

Congressites who accuse the Hindu Mahasabha for having done nothing for the Hindus in Sindh that the necessity arises of reminding the Congressites that, was it not the Congress which insisted on and brought about the separation of Sindh from Bombay Presidency? And was not that the original sin? The Hindu Mahasabha fought tooth and nail against the separation of Sindh warning the Congressite Hindus that such a step would only lead to untold miseries of the Hindus; that it was a part of the Moslem conspiracy to separate Sindh so as to lay the foundation-stone of their pet Pakistan scheme; that wild, fanatical and murderous gangs of Moslems who always prowled about the borders of Sindh would pounce upon the Hindu minority and even the most polished Moslems throughout India would not raise a finger to save the latter but would wait for the moment when the Hindus were either wiped off or evacuate Sindh en masse, leaving it a pure Dar-ul-Islam a Moslem territory. But in spite of this opposition of the Mahasabha, the Congressite Hindus voted for the separation of Sindh just to please the Moslems! And now it is the Congressites who are demanding from the Hindu Mahasabha the explanation of what it was doing for the Hindus in Sindh!! The incendiary who first set the village on fire is now demanding from the citizens an explanation of the fact why they could not exert themselve more in putting down the fire! The Working Committee of the Congress, which everyday brought harrowing news of anti-Hindu outrages in Sindh, did not utter a single word in condemnation of it. Nor was a single meeting held throughout India by the Congress to protest against it. It was only when Hindu Mahasabha activities brought sufficient pressure upon the government to take stringent measures and pressed the government to scrap up the Moslem autonomy that Maulana Azad was hurriedly dispatched by Gandhiji to Sindh. But, with what leading objectives in view?

But Maulana Azad's mission was not so much to safeguard the Hindus as to stabilise the Moslem Ministry

He did not formulate any scheme to recompense or safeguard the Hindus nor did he issue any condemnation or frame any charge-sheet of the Moslem atrocities. His whole anxiety under Gandhiji's instructions was to exhort the Moslems to form a stable government so as not to give any excuse to the Hindu Mahasabha to force the hands of the government to re-annex Sindh to Bombay or empower the Governor to resume the administration in his own hands. If the Moslems fail to form a stable government in Sindh how were they going to prove to the British Government that they would be able to rule their would-be Pakistan as efficiently as the British? That seemed to be the anxiety which drove Maulana Azad to Sindh. For, one fails to understand how a stable government of those very Moslem parties which have been responsible for the plight of the Hindus upto this time could improve the condition and safeguard the life and property of the Hindu minority there. A stable government of these Moslem parties may as well prove more dangerous to the Hindus than otherwise. The temporary cessation of crime in Sindh is the result of the direct pressure exercised by the Governor and the consequent hunt of the Moslem criminals which had already been initiated before Maulana Azad stepped into Sindh. Not a stable Moslem Ministry or any other measure serving only as an eye-wash can ever be an effective way of protecting the legitimate rights of the Hindu minority in Sindh or ensure peace and order. The annulling of the Moslem autonomy in Sindh and the re-annexation of it to the Presidency of Bombay can alone secure that objective.

The pan-Hindu movement animates the Hindu princes too.

It is encouraging to note another factor, while we are reviewing this year's work, that a lively interest is being evinced by the Hindu princes in the Mahasabha activities. The pan-Hindu ideology was sure to stir up, sooner or later, the latent fire in the blood of our historic forefathers which is flowing in the veins of our Hindu princes and make them realise that their duty required them not only to sympathise with but to lead the Hindu movement. The far-sighted amongst them have begun to realise that their present and future interests as well are, in fact, identified with the pan-Hindu movement now growing stronger from day to day. If, up to this time, the Hindu princes failed to lead the Hindu movement or help it with that fervour, courage and religious devotion with which the Moslem princes in India identify themselves with the Moslem political parties in India and share in the pan-Islamic ambition, the fault does not altogether lie on the side of the Hindu princes alone. The Hindu public, in general, and notably the Congressite Hindus, in particular, never extended any sympathy with the Hindu states or realised their importance; but on the contrary, arrogated to themselves the monopoly of patriotism and looked down on the Hindu states as an impediment in the path of India's progress, which, the sooner it was removed, the better it would be for the nation. But, the Moslem public, on the other hand, with a truer insight into political realities had ever been intensely proud of the few Moslem states in India, looked upon them as organised centres of Moslem strength and even tried to augment the power and presitige of their Nizams and Nawabs. Consequently, the Moslem princes, too, ever felt that not only their present interest but even their future greatness and future glory depended on the progress and strength of the pan-Islamic movement, led by the Moslem politicians in India. If but the Hindu *Sangathanists* possess an insight into political realities they would soon find that the Hindu states are, in fact, nearly the only centres of the organised, military, administrative and political Hindu strength and are bound to play a more active and more decisive part in the near future in moulding the destiny of the Hindu nation than any other factor within our present reach. Even as it is, what party of our chatter-box politicians and slogan-ridden ideologues had succeeded in effecting actually social or industrial or military progress on such an extent as, say, for example, the Hindu states of Baroda, Mysore, Travancore or Gwalior have recorded? For want of space and inclination, I do not deal with this question here at any greater length. All that I would like to emphasise here and want the Hindu *sangathanist* throughout India to note is the fact that they should welcome the response which the pan-Hindu ideology is evoking in the hearts of our Hindu princes and to realise that the stronger the Hindu states grow, the lesser will be the danger of any anti-Hindu aggression in any problematical danger of internal anarchy and anti-Hindu aggression. Of all the factors that are likely, under the present circumstances, to contribute to the resurgence and rejuvenation of a consolidated Hindu nation, the Hindu states constitute the most efficient one.

The Moslems with only two or three important Moslem states to depend upon, are hopeful enough—and in the absence of any countercheck on the part of the Hindus are rightly hopeful of utilising the organised Moslem power in those states as a pivot for their plans of Moslem domination. But, we Hindus have never taken it into our head what powerful resources we have in the existence of some 50 Hindu states with armies, organised police forces, treasuries, governmental machineries all relatively at least as efficient as the Moslem states have and some of them as large as independent countries of Europe. When we hear that the Khaksars and the Frontier Pathans are plotting to rally round the banner of the Nizam and raise him to the pedestal of an independent Moslem King, we are startled, get overawed and are at a loss to know how to meet this impending danger. But, it never occurs to us that while the Moslems are building castles in the air for their independent Nizam to lodge, there is already, in fact, an independent Hindu kingdom of Nepal with a hundred thousand seasoned Hindu soldiers shouldering up-to-date rifles in defence of the Hindu cause!

It is not want of resources, Oh Hindus, which forces you to be so helpless and hopeless, but it is the want of practical insight in political realities to know your resources and the tact to use them. You have lost the political eye altogether. Think of the fact that thousands of Congressite Hindus are openly maintaining that the Nepali Hindus are foreigners to us. Indians, while at the same time, they are simply dying to hug the Moslem Pathans even from beyond the Frontier as Indian nationals and it is only the other day that Gandhiji himself stated that if the Nizam became an independent Emperor of India even with the help of the Pathans from beyond the Frontier, that rule would be cent per cent Home Rule, a cent per cent *swarajya*. So then, even the help of the Moslem Pathans from beyond does not vitiate the Congress nationalism. But the help of the Hindu Gurkhas vitiates it; the Gurkhas who are the direct descendants of Rajputs and went to Nepal only some three centuries ago! It is this political lunacy which has affected the Congressite Hindu mind that constitutes the real cause of our present helplessness and the only cure lies in the pan-Hindu ideololgy which will at once give the correct orientation to all our movements and reveal to us what inexhaustible resources lie even now at our disposal and make you realise that organised power of the Hindu states constitutes the most effective and powerful of them. Hence, it is that I lay so much store by that factor and am glad to note that some of the Hindu princes also have come to realise that not only their duty but even their interests demand that the Hindu movement in general should grow from strength to strength. If Hindudom is uprooted, the Hindu states also must fall down and wither as inevitably as the limbs of a body that ceases to live.

The Hindu Mahasabha captures the political stage

It was but a matter, of course, that the progress which the Hindu Mahasabha had recorded in its activities as detailed out above and the rapid strides with which the Hindu movement forged ahead throughout the last two years should have impressed the Indian as well as the British Government too to some extent or the other. It cannot be denied that the unequivocal recognition by the government this year of the Hindu Mahasabha as the political power which must be consulted on a footing of equality with the Congress and the League in matters affecting all-India politics constitutes the outstanding event in the history of the Hindu Mahasabha movement. Upto this time, the Congress and the League were looked upon by the government as the only two representative bodies, whose opinion was tantamount to Indian opinion. The government seems to have framed an equation and learnt it by heart that the Congress and the League was equal to India as a whole. Of these two, the League was rightly taken to express the Moslem opinion in general, because the League openly avows that it is there to safeguard and promote the Moslem interests. But, the government seems to have taken the Congress to represent the Hindu opinion only because out of the two bodies, the Congress and the League, which to the government thought represented the sum total of Indian opinion, that is, the opinion of Hindus and Moslems, if the League represented the Moslem opinion then the Congress must of necessity be taken to represent the Hindu opinion and interests. Although the Congress itself openly resented the charge that they represented Hindus and proved their contention to the hilt by actually betraying Hindu interests a hundred times over, as, for example, in the question of Sindh separation, the Communal Award the Frontier policy, the Hindusthani language, etc., still the government persisted in believing that the Congress and the League were equivalent as a sum total of Hindu-Moslem representation. Thus, the Hindu view continued to be ascertained by the government through the opinion of that very body which indignantly repudiated the advocacy of the Hindu cause. Consequently, the Hindus as Hindus not only continued to be unrepresented but were positively misrepresented in all governmental constitutional deliberations, All-India Round Table Conferences, etc., etc. But the growing prestige, influence and effective activities of the Hindu Mahasabha did at last impress the government with the fact that it was no longer possible to look upon the Congress as a representative Hindu body or to refuse to recognise the Hindu Mahasabha as the real representative Hindu body and as such the third indispensable political factor which must be taken into consideration in gauging the Indian opinion in its entirety. The Indian Government thus unlearnt the old equation, 'Congress + League—Indian people' and had to learn the new equation, 'The Hindu Mahasabha, the League and the Congress—the sum total of Indian representation.' This new equation does really respond to the present political situation in India and I thank H.E. the Viceroy for having deliberately and decisively recognised the position of the Hindu Mahasabha as, at any rate, the most outstanding representative Hindu body, if not the only one. The Moslem League represents the Moslem interests, the Hindu Mahasabha the Hindu interests, and the Congress,—even if it is in majority today, represents none else but a hotchpotch political party of the Congressite persuasion. But although the Indian Government has grasped this situation quite definitely, yet it seems that the British Government has not yet been able to learn the new equation or realise its full import; that is why, the Secretary of State for India does still repeat the old phrase, the Congress and the League or the League and the Congress to express the sum total of the Indian public and when, of late, he did try to use the corrected version and in his speech in the Parliament last November, did use the new equation 'The Congress, the League and the Hindu Mahasabha', he created an unconscious humour by trying to enlighten his parliamentary audience by acquainting them with what this new stranger Hindu Mahasabha actually meant. The Secretary of State knew it that the League represented the Moslems and the Congress represented the Hindus and so very naturally was at a loss to explain to himself and to others whom this Hindu Mahasabha could represent! So, the nearest explanation, he very naturally found, was to the effect that the Congress represented the reformed Hindus in general and the Hindu Mahasabha must consequently be 'a body of the orthodox Hindus in particular' and he introduced the Hindu Mahasabha for the first time to the British Parliament as 'the orthodox Hindu body.' Mr. Amery will himself feel amused if he learns that the very president of the Hindu Mahasabha for the last three years has been a notorious reformer who, being a born Brahmin, interdines freely with the so-called untouchables in his individual capacity. The second time when Mr. Amery made a reference to the Hindu Mahasabha in a speech this month, advocating the principle 'India first,' he referred to it correctly. It is also our duty, to some extent, to acquaint the British public with the true nature and ideology of the Hindu Mahasabha movement by establishing a well-organised and permanent centre of Hindu propaganda in London. The British public as well as the government must be made to realise that the Hindu Mahasabha is neither orthodox nor heterodox. In fact, it has very little to do with any 'doxy' at all. It is not primarily a Hindu Dharma

Sabha, a religious body. The Hindu Mahasabha is the Hindu Rashtra Sabha, a body aiming to represent the Hindu nation as a whole and includes all sections of Hindudom, whether orthodox or heterodox.

This recognition by the government of the Hindu Mahasabha as the most outstanding representative of the Hindu view and the consequent consultations which the Viceroy held with its president, is an event which is certain to have far-reaching consequences on the Hindu movement in general. Because it implies the recognition by the government of the fact that the Congress does not represent the Hindus as Hindus and that just as to ascertain the Moslem opinion they have to consult the Moslem League or any other such Moslem institution which is independent of the Congress, so also the real Hindu interests, rights and claims could only be ascertained by consulting a representative Hindu body which is independent of and apart from the Congress. Once this principle is admitted as now it is done by the government itself and Hindudom shakes of grip that the Congress has tightened round its neck by virtue of no other right but that of an unchallenged usage, the political, social, religious and cultural interests of the Hindus as Hindus could no longer be betrayed by the Congress or go undefended by default. Henceforth in any conference, whether a Round Table one or all parties one or a constituent one that is called to determine constitutional questions regarding India as a whole, the Hindu Mahasabha is bound to be a party to it on an equal footing with the League and the Congress and unless and until this representative body of the Hindus does not sanction any step taken affecting Hindu interests the consent of the Congress alone can never be taken as the consent of Hindudom and can never be binding on the Hindus. Any Congress-League pact can no longer sell, mortgage or barter away Hindu rights unless and until the Hindu Mahasabha is a willing party to it.

It is to be noted in this connection that we must admit and emphasise in our own interests that the Indian as well as the British governments have not only recognised the right of the Hindu Mahasabha to represent the Hindu view independently of the Congress but has tried to meet the wishes of the Mahasabha, at least on one of the vital points affecting the Hindu interests. It cannot be gainsaid that the important speech which the Secretary of State delivered this month dealing with the question of the political and national integrity of India was chiefly the result of the pressure brought to bear by the Hindu Mahasabha and the Sikh organisations on the government to declare in unambiguous accents that the British Government, at any rate, did not encourage or even contribute tacitly to the mischievous Moslem movement to vivisect the integrity of the Indian nation, country and state as the Pakistan proposal demanded. The Moslem League had, of course, godfathered the Pakistan scheme. The Congressite leaders of note, including all their Rajajis and Pradhanjis, had made it clear that they would not oppose it if the Moslems insisted on it. In fact, the Congressite Hindus had expressed their acquiescence in the Pakistan proposal with such an unabashed haste and obsequiousness as was never evinced by the British people or Government even though they at first did not like to veto it altogether. Even Mr. Amery in his speach only a month ago did not deliberately say anything to discourage the Moslems and had said many things to encourage them tacitly in connection with their proposal to divide India into Hindu and Moslem zones. Whence came then the pressure under which the Secretary of State thought it better to positively lay it down that the integrity of India must be inviolate in the interests of all and formed the first principle on which alone any solution of the Indian constitutional framing can be grafted? It was due to the Hindu Mahasabha, the Sikh organisations, the Sanatani Mandals, etc., in short, to the Hindu Sangathanist Party alone which agitated against the Pakistan scheme and demanded that the government should make a clear declaration washing their hands clean of the Pakistan proposal. The Congress had of course uttered no word in the resolutions either of its sessions of Working Committees against the Pakistan scheme. But, the Hindu Mahasabha had emphatically made it a condition for its participation in the war efforts that the government should declare its intention to stand by the indivisibilty and integrity of the Indian nation and the Indian state. Of course, it must have been in response to this demand of the Hindu Mahasabha and the Hindu Sangathanist Party in general that Mr. Amery had to change his ambiguous and dubious attitude which he had taken in his speech in November when he addressed the Parliament and to make this relatively very clear declaration in his speech this month, preaching almost a religious sermon on ' India first'. *In any case, I have no hesitation in expressing my sincere appreciation of the clear attitude which Mr. Amery has taken on the question of Indian integrity and indivisibility as well as of the firmness with which the Viceroy turned down a number of the anti-Hindu and aggressive demands which the League had advanced during the recent negotiations in connection with the war committee and the extension of the Executive Council.* That also could not but be the result of the negotiations carried on, on behalf of and the most legitimate and reasoned out attitude taken up by the Mahasabha in opposing those aggressive Moslem demands. The Congress had said nothing to denounce them and but for the opposition of the Hindu Mahasabha, in all probabilities the Moslems could have secured a very large portion of the ground which they aggressively claimed to be their own.

The Hindus must get themselves cured of the malady of voting for the Congress in the polls if they want to safeguard their rights

Nevertheless, I must again categorically warn the Hindus that in spite of the fact that the Hindu Mahasabha has succeeded this year in capturing the political stage and stands there today on equal footing with the Congress and the League as the most outstanding representative of the Hindus, it would not be able to safeguard and promote Hindu interests to the fullest extent unless and until the Hindu electorate empowers it beyond cavil or criticism to function as the party in majority in the legislatures returned by the Hindu electorate on a Hindu ticket. So long as the Hindu electorate persists in the habitual act of political lunacy of voting for the Congress tickets, the government cannot but accept the Congress, to a very large extent as representing Hindu opinion. But, the Congress constituted as it is, will never and can never represent even the legitimate Hindu interests so boldly and with such whole-hearted devotion to the Hindu cause as the Hindu representatives, who as definitely pledged to the Hindu ticket, can do. If but the Hindu electorate returns the Hindu Sangathanist candidates in an overwhelming majority at the polls to represent the Hindu cause to the legislatures and the local bodies, the government shall have to recognise the Hindu Mahasabha or any consolidated Hindu Sangathanist Party as the only representative of the Hindus without any further necessity of the endless arguments. The Congress will automatically get deprived of any claim or power to play ducks and drakes with Hindu interests or even to speak in the name of the Hindus as Hindus. In fact, it can hardly have a chance of representing any part of the electorate at all so long as they are communally grouped, which arrangement is inevitably certain to continue for at least a score of years to come. The Moslem will never elect a Moslem who is not pledged to a purely Moslem organisation and in particular are sure to reject a Moslem who stands on a Congress ticket. Their interests, therefore, will never be jeopardised. If the Hindus also elect only those Hindus who are pledged to a Hindu ticket, there will be no electorate left worth the name to vote for the Congress ticket. Even as it is the Congress ministries and majority stand on the shoulder of the Hindu electorate alone.

A large section of the Congressite Hindus is also getting anxious of late to see the Hindu Mahasabha grow into the strongest political organisation in India

Throughout this year, hundreds of Hindu Congressites of note have personally congratulated me as the president of the Hindu Mahasabha on the fact that the Mahasabha should have been able to influence the government in several details some of which are indicated above, and made them think twice before they allowed themselves to play into the hands of the Moslem League and at times to turn down their aggressively anti-Hindu demands. Why these Congressite gentlemen, who are Hindus to the core, denounce in their heart of hearts the constant betrayal by the Congress of Hindu interests and feel thankful that the Hindu Mahasabha should have grown strong enough to checkmate this Congress policy, do nevertheless continue to be under the thumb of the Congress and do not forthwith join the Hindu Mahasabha and add the weight of their influence and efforts to it, is a question which must naturally rise in your mind. I may tell you that the only obstacle which stops them, at present, from leaving the Congress camp and going over to the Hindu Mahasabha fold is a wall, which though it is but an inch in height, proves still most effectively insurmountable to them. This inch-high but to them an insurmountable wall is but the Congress ticket—which affords them the guarantee of being elected at any polls whether to the local bodies or the legislatures or assures them of some post or profit here or there. This again emphasises the fact that if but the Hindu electorate is cured of the suicidal malady, grown into a habit with them, of voting blindly for the Congress ticket at the poll and realises that its interests demand its voting for the Hindu ticket, thousands of these halting and hesitating Hindu brothers, who are now in the Congress, would pick up the courage of joining openly the ranks of the Hindu Mahasabha and leave the Congress—a step which they feel it their duty to take but which their interests forbid them to take at a stroke. Of course, I should appeal to the conscience of thousands of these of our Hindu brothers that they themselves should set the example of placing their duty towards their racial, religious and national being as Hindus far above the wretched consideration of pelf, power or popularity. Whatever be the result of this my appeal, I cannot but thank this large number of our Hindu brothers who have this year come to sympathise with the Hindu Mahasabha and are now willing to extend whatever help they can render to increase its prestige and power in spite of their continuing in the Congress camp. Well begun is half done.

Thus it will be clear from the passing review of some of the leading events during the last year in connection with the Hindu Mahasabha movement and some of the details of its work during the last year, that on the whole the Hindu movement is forging ahead. But, while we should know precisely where our strength lies and the point to which we have been able to progress we should also never lose sight of the defects and deficiencies we have yet to face. But, in spite of this dictum, I have nor deliberately made much of these defects and deficiencies and sad plight in which we Hindus find ourselves enmeshed on all sides for the simple reason that the dark side of the situation has been so patent and so persistently dinned into our ears, even to the point of unbearable exaggeration by friends and foes alike, that the Hindus have already come to suffer from an almost incurable inferiority complex. Therefore, for the time being, our motto should rather be thus that

We should neither underrate our progress and strength,
nor should we exaggerate our weakness

We shall surely face our difficulties, organisational deficiencies, selfishness, want of cohesion and even of capacity of which we are already keenly conscious and staring them full in the face, shall try our best to overcome them. But, the very strength to overcome them can only come from the correct estimation of those factors which are in our favour, of our real assets and resources which also are fortunately inexhaustible though as yet unrealised and untapped. That is why, I have dealt with these latter in particular and placed them in bold relief.

Every Hindu must study at least the following books to
know the real springs of the pan-Hindu movement

Before I proceed to deal with other important points after closing this passing review of the last year's report, I feel it my duty to exhort my Hindu brethren in general and those belonging to the Madras Presidency in particular, to study at least the following books before they form any opinion regarding the pan-*Sangathan* movement. The ideology of Hindu *Sangathan* is now fortunately propagated on a scale wide enough in

Maharashtra, Bengal and some provinces in the North, to enable the Hindus there to understand and appraise correctly much that I have said in the foregoing part of my address. But, the Madras Presidency has only recently come into contact with the *Sangathan* movement. Consequently, a study of the fundamental principles and ideology on which the movement is based is an imperative necessity, especially in the case of all those Hindus belonging to this Presidency who wish to see the Sangathan movement strongly entrenched in the South as well and also in the case of those, too, who though they have not yet enlisted on its side, yet wish to assess it as a powerful current of political thought and activity which is bound to affect the future history of India whether one likes it or not. With that end in view, I recommend to all Hindus, even at the risk of a personal reference, the study of the following books to begin with:

(1) *Hindutva* by V.D. Savarkar. (2) *Hindu Sangathan* (its ideology and immediate programme) published by Syt. N.V. Damle. (3) *History of the Hindu Mahasabha* by Syt. Indraprakash. (4) *Hindu Pad-Padashahi* by V.D. Savarkar. (5) *History of the Bhaganagar Struggle* (Nizam Civil Resistance Movement) by Syt. S.R. Date.

Other important topics will be dealt with in separate resolutions to be passed at this session

Want of space and time compels me now to leave even some pressing questions, such as the grievances of our Hindu brethren in Bengal, the Pakistan scheme, the Census, etc., etc. to be dealt with in the separate resolutions which are to be taken up by this session, especially in view of the fact that they will be better discussed and decided by those leaders who, having made a special study of them, are intimately acquainted with the details in connection with them, and to proceed to deal with the foremost of topical questions of how best we can respond to the war situation under the circumstances we are placed in what should be our immediate policy and programme under the war conditions, so as to enable us to safeguard and even promote Hindu interests?

I want to make it clear before I deal with this question that the views, I shall express in connection with it, should be looked upon as my personal views even though I happen to express them from the presidential chair. The delegates to this session should not take those views as any authoritative announcements or recommendations, much less, as any dictation from their president. Although the president of such an organisation as the Mahasabha is expected to recommend and at times even to dictate the policy or programme to the adopted and in general to lead the assembly he presides over, still the outstanding function of such a president is, unless otherwise provided for, to act as the highest executive officer responsible to carry out the corporate decisions of the delegates and representatives composing the deliberative body of that organisation. With this conception of my duty as the president, I shall ever try my humble best to carry out your corporate decisions, especially on this question even though they may differ widely from the views I personally hold and express and shall never look upon this difference as in any way involving the question of the presidential prestige; and my sincere request to you all is also to the same effect that you should consider the view I express on this question as the views of one of the members rather than the views of the president of the Hindu Mahasabha.

The war situation and what should be our immediate policy and programme in response to it

Before I frame an actual programme, I wish to draw your attention to some of the leading considerations which seem to me as best calculated to clear our vision and help to chalk out our line of action in this respect:

- The first point to be noted is the fact that we are in no way morally bound to help any of the belligerents in this worldwide war, whether it be England or Germany or Japan or Russia or China or any other country involved in the war, from only altruistic point of view as has been demanded from us not only by Great Britain and America, but curiously enough by some of the Congressite leaders themselves and some other sections of the Indian public. The Hindu Mahasabha has already made its position clear on this point in a resolution passed by its Working Committee in September 1939, just within a month after the breaking out of the war, when Gandhiji, the de facto dictator of the Congress, was proclaiming in a flattering mood to the effect that he had not been thinking of Indian independence then, but was chiefly concerned with the safety of England and France and proposed to offer them unconditional help in their crusade to save democracy in the world; when even Pandit Nehru was calling upon India to support these British and French democracies in the holy war they were carrying on against the imperialistic German aggression on Poland and other free nations and while the leader of the Forward Bloc, the Communists, the Royists and other parties too were swearing by the anti-imperialistic innocence free from all political greed on the part of Poland and Russia, the Hindu Mahasabha was about the only organised and outstanding political body in India which was firm and far-sighted enough to give the correct lead to the country and to the Congress itself in ascertaining the real motives and objectives of the belligerents by asserting that none of the belligerent powers in Europe, whether England, Germany, Poland, France or Russia, etc. had been actuated by any moral, democratic or altruistic considerations apart from its own self-interest and self-agrandisement. The Viceroy and the Secretary of State for India have more than once wanted us to believe in their various speeches that the only objective which actuated Britain to continue the war had been 'to resist aggression whether against England or others to defend great democratic ideals and without seeking any material advantage to lay the foundation of a better international system and to secure a real and lasting peace'. No better proof can be adduced to disprove these declarations as to the altruistic objectives of Great Britain in going to the war than the fact that they provided an occasion for Hitler to retort when he was asked by Chamberlain to free Poland that he would do so as soon as Great Britain freed India. Verily does the adage say, 'Thieves alone can trace the footsteps of thieves best.'

- Consequently, the demand of the Congressite leaders, like Pandit Nehru calling upon Great Britain to tell their general objectives in going to the war, seems to me altogather idle. Firstly because Britain has been repeating those general objectives in the above strain *ad nauseam* and secondly, because the declaration of any general pious objectives cannot be worth a brass farthing unless they were immediately translated into actions wherever it was possible to do so, as England could have done it in the case of India by granting her a democratic and free constitution. But, she did nothing of the sort. It is crystal clear that the general objective of everyone of those countries engaged in the war or in fact every nation in the world today cannot be any other than to serve, safeguard and promote its own interests and extend its domination on as large a part of the world as it is able to do. If Hitler or Mussolini is out to win a new Empire because he wants more room on the globe for his people and power to expand Churchill and Stalin and Roosevelt want to secure and maintain their mastery over the Empire they already possess. The labels masking that mastery may be different. They may call it an Empire or a democratic republic or a soviet republic but they all are out to thrust the will and the domination of their nations by force upon other people and their territories against their own will. Is not France a democratic republic? But, it has robbed the freedom of so many countries in the world, including our Pondicherry and Chandra Nagar, as to stand only second to England in the extent of colonial possessions. Russia also is a republic and a Soviet republic to boot but extends its mastery almost over a continent conquered by force and has swallowed Poland and other small nations as greedily as Germany did.

- The same thing could be said about the 'isms' each of them follow. Under whatever label their principles are trotted out, whether as Bolshevism or Nazism or Facism or Republicanism or Parliamentarianism, their armed domination over other peoples they have conquered or wish to conquer does not and cannot savour of anything else but autocratic tyranny. Under such circumstances, it would be but a suicidal folly for India to be taken in by the slogans or by the labels on their principles and policies which all of them use with the only purpose to camouflage their real intentions. We should neither hate nor love Nazists or Bolshevists or Democrats simply on the ground of any theoretical or bookish reasons. There is no reason to suppose that Hitler must be a human monster because he passes off as a Nazi or Churchill is a demi-god because he calls himself a Democrat. Nazism proved undeniably the saviour of Germany under the set of circumstances Germany was placed in, Bolshevism might have suited Russia very well and we know what the English democracy has cost us.

Political science and history, both carry out the fact that no constitution or social system can be beneficial under all circumstances and for all alike. No people are so attached to democracy and to individual liberty as the British so far as their own nation is concerned. But, under war conditions, did they not throw the democratical conception and constitution overboard in a day and vote for almost an undiluted dictatorship? Is not Mr. Churchill today to England what Herr Hitler is to Germany, whose word is nearly the only law of the land? Only the last mail from England brought a leading paper in which a British poet sang the dirge of liberty in the following wailing notes, asking,

'We know the war court is intact
But what of the Habeas Corpus Act
The freedom's isle they could not save
Till it was Magna Carta's grave.'

Consequently, there is no meaning in calling upon Indians that it is their duty to fight Germany simply because they are totalitarians and Nazis or to love the French or the English or the Americans simply because they are Democrats or Republicans. The sanest policy for us which practical politics demand is to befriend those who are likely to serve our country's interests in spite of any 'ism ' they follow for themselves and to befriend only so long as it serves our purpose. The Nazis and the Bolshevists were the most deadly enemies to each other on theoretical grounds but when on the given question of Poland and the general interests in this war arose, they thought an alliance would serve the purpose of their nations better; they joined hands overnight in mutual friendship. Had England herself gone to war, say, with Russia and had Hitler taken the English side, can anyone doubt that England would have landed this very Nazi Germany as enthusiastically as they did the Imperialistic Germany in the days of Bismark when he invaded and crushed these very French people with whom England happened then to be inimical ever since the rise of the Republican Revolution in France to the fall of Napoleon III? Were not these very Americans although her own kith and kin, held up by England before the world as the most faithless and treacherous type of humanity in spite of the fact that they were Republicans when they revolted against England and secured their independence? And yet now that a close alliance with America is almost the last refuge guaranteeing any certainty of saving England from a disastrous defeat, what desperate love has locked Johnl Bull and Uncle Sam into an unseparable embrace!? Nay, is not England already casting a wistful eye to woo the very Bolshevist Russia whom she cursed all along and if but the latter accepts England's hand and breaks off with Germany, can there be any doubt that England would immediately begin to bless the Bolshevist Government as 'our noble ally'?

- Nor should the bogey of the Germans conquering India with which the English try to frighten us out of our wits be taken too seriously into consideration in framing our immediate policy in response to the war situation. As things stand, it is not very likely, nay, it is altogether improbable that in this war, England will be defeated so disastrously as to get compelled to hand over her Indian Empire, lock, stock and barrel into German hands. When Columbus, they say, was on the point of effecting his first landing in America, the natives showed fight. Thereupon, Columbus who knew that an eclipse of the sun was imminent, posed as a deputy sent by god and informed the natives that if they did not welcome him and help him in landing, he would remove the sun from the skies and an eternal darkness would set in. Very soon the unsubmitting natives found to their utter consternation that the sun was really getting removed from the skies and darkness setting in. So, they hurried on with fruits, flowers and gifts to the shore and welcomed and helped him to land. The threat which the English hold before the Indian eyes, 'Help us or Hitler will set in' sounds as unreal, ridiculous and crafty as the ultimatum which Columbus delivered to the natives, 'Help me or eternal darkness will set in.' On the one hand, the English are assuring the whole world that they are sure to crush Hitler in the long run, while in the same breath, tell us, 'Help us or the Germans are sure to conquer India!' *The fact is that if ever the English really came to feel so helpless that without our help they were sure to lose India, they would offer us of themselves not only the Dominion Status but some of their colonies and possessions as they are doing today in the case of America.*

Again, even if we take for granted for the sake of argument that the war takes such a turn as to enable the Germans to invade India, there is no reason why we should only take that probability as certainty that the withdrawal of the British from India must only mean the occupation of her by Germany. In such world-earthquakes, when Empires totter to pieces, history abounds with examples showing that subject nations often find their effective opportunity of achieving independence by playing one mighty enemy against the other to the annihilation of the aggressive might of both of them. Secondly, if the war causes the sudden withdrawal of the British from India, without enabling the Germans or any other great power to occupy India at a stroke and brings us Hindus face to face with only an internal anarchy and a consequent civil war with the Moslems, which argument some people try to use as an alternate threat to frighten us into unconditional submission, there would be every chance that the Hindus will prove victorious in such a civil war and remain the undisputed masters in their own house.

In short, none of these pseudo-moral, hypothetical or problematical reasons trotted out mainly to dupe or frighten us with a view to exact unconditional and willing co-operation with the British war efforts should be allowed to form the only ground on which our war policy and programme can be based. We shall, of course, take these reasons also into consideration but only insofar as they are likely to really affect our own national interests in a matter-of-fact way. In framing our programme, so far as it lies in our power, our only consideration should be *how best can we take advantage of the war situation to promote our own interests, how best can we help ourselves in safeguarding and, if possible'even in promoting the Hindu cause.*

In doing so, we should take great care not to indulge in any idle, useless and even harmful bombast by making light of our overwhelming weakness on the one hand as well as not to underrate, on the other hand, whatever strength we even now possess or are likely to possess as the war situation develops from day to day. Within these limitations let us examine some of the leading courses of action which are either likely to prevent themselves for consideration or are actually suggested or acted upon by the different political parties in India.

An armed tevolt on a national scale: The first and the foremost effective course that would have presented itself to any subjected people as best calculated to assert its independence while its adversary was entangled into serious war with some of its powerful foes, would have naturally been to rise in arms to assert its own freedom. But, firstly, disarmed, disorganised and disunited as we are, an armed revolt against England on a national scale is entirely ruled out under our present circumstances. And, secondly, the question of any armed resistance cannot even form a subject of discussion on an open platform of such institutions as the Hindu Mahasabha or the Congress or any other public and open bodies in India under their present constitution and within the sphere of action they have chalked out for themselves under their present aims and objects. Consequently, not on any moral grounds, but on the grounds of practical politics we are compelled not to concern ourselves on behalf of the Hindu Mahasabha organisation with any programme involving any armed resistance, under the present circumstances.

The Gandhist 'satyagraha' based on absolute non-violence: On the other hand, no programme based on the monomaniacal principle of absolute non-violence is worth a moment's consideration. If the first extreme remedy of an armed rising on a national scale is ruled out on grounds of practical politics, this other extreme of absolute non-violence condemning all armed resistance even to an incorrigible aggression must be ruled out not only on practical grounds alone but even on moral grounds.

Without going into deep waters for want of space and time to ascertain what constitutes the criterion of a moral action, whether morality derives its sanction from intuition or revelation or exigency, the most practical factor and one which ought to be common to all of these schools of moral thought and which alone can practically serve to distinguish a moral act from an immoral one, a virtue from a vice, the good from the bad, is the utilitarian principle that everything that contributes under a given act of circumstances to human good is moral, a virtue and the opposite is immoral, a vice under those given circumstances; that all morality is essentially human. Judged from this most practical and yet fundamental test, the principle of absolute non-violence condemning all armed resistance even to incorrigible aggression cannot but be ruled out as absolutely impracticable, anti-human and therefore, positively immoral. If a serpent finds its way slyly into a pack of children sleeping soundly or a mad dog rushes all of a sudden, foaming with insane exasperation into a crowded fair and you do not kill it there and then even if you can, on principle of absolute non-violence, you abet the murderous violence which the serpent or the mad dog commits by biting innocent human beings to death, you are criminally doubly guilty in refusing to save the life of human beings to spare the life of a serpent or a dog and leave it free to take more human lives at leisure as occasion arises. On the contrary, if you kill the serpent and the dog there and then, you are still guilty of violence from the point of your own principle of absolute non-violence or killing no living being. Even this one illustration is enough to prove that the principle of absolute non-violence is not only absolutely impracticable, but anti-human and therefore, absolutely immoral. What holds good in these individual cases does also hold good in matters affecting nations. It must be noted in this connection that even those religions which put the virtue of non-violence, *ahimsa,* above all virtues had to admit exceptions and did not or could not assert that absolute non-violence condemning all armed resistance whatsoever, even to incorrigible aggression, constituted a virtue.

Relative अहिंसा is a virtue; but absolute अहिंसा a crime!

Of course, relative non-violence on the whole is doubtless a virtue so pre-eminently contributing to human good as to form one of the fundamentals on which human life, whether individual or social, can take its stand and evolve all social amenities. But absolute non-violence, that is, non-violence under all circumstances and even when instead of helping human life, whether individual or national, it causes an incalculable harm to humanity as a whole ought to be condemned as a moral perversity and is on the whole condemned likewise by those very religious and moral schools which lauded relative non-violence as the first and foremost human virtue.

The ahimsa *of the Jains and Buddists is opposed to this Gandhist doctrine of* ahimsa

It should be noted in particular that the *ahimsa* preached by the Buddhist or the Jain religion is directly opposed to the absolute *ahimsa* or absolute non-violence as Gandhiji interprets it, condemning all armed resistance under all circumstances. The very fact that the Jains reared up kingdoms, produced heroes and heroines who fought armed battles and Jain Commanders-in-chief leading Jain armies without being ostracised by the Jain *acharyas* prove this point to the hilt that the *ahimsa* of the Jains cannot be the rabid *ahimsa* of the Gandhist school. Nay, the Jain scriptures openly assert that armed resistance to incorrigible aggression is not only justifiable but imperative. To save a saint from being murdered outright by a violent and armed sinner, *ahimsa* itself requires that the sinner should be killed there and then, if that act alone could save the life of the saint. Such a *himsa* is in itself an act of *ahimsa* and the Jain scriptures defend it, almost in the words used by Manu himself to defend it, that the sin of killing in such a case recoils on the murderer himself whose act was responsible for the reaction, *'मन्युस्तन्मन्युमर्हति!'* Bhagwan Buddha also gave the same ruling when questioned by the leaders of a clan as to whether they should take to armed resistance as soldiers against the armed aggression of another clan. 'Soldiers may fight against armed aggression,' said Bhagwan Buddha, 'without committing a sin if but they fight with arms in defence of a righteous cause.'

The defensive sword was the first saviour of man!

Call it a law of nature or the will of god as you like, the iron fact remains that there is no room for absolute non-violence in nature. Man could not have saved himself from utter extinction nor could have but led the precarious and wretched life of a coward and a worm had he not succeeded in adding the strength of artificial arms to his natural arm. In those geological periods, when he evolved to manhood, he was surrounded by such a ferocious brute and serpentine order that he found himself, individual to individual, the weakest being; physically the most unfit to survive in contest during the struggle for existence that was raging round in the formidable primitive jungles, which was his first home. He had neither poisonous fangs nor tusks nor horns nor blood-thirsty claws. We call the cow as physically and by nature the most harmless and the most incapable of self-defence, but even a cow could have cowed down a man in a naked physical combat and even killed him by piercing her pointed horns in his stomach as none of his natural organs were a match for them. It was only his capacity to invent artificial weapons to add to the strength of his natural limbs, which the beasts and the brutes failed to develop, that man could cope with tigers and lions and wolves and serpents and crocodiles and could snatch the mastery of the earth and water from his wild enemies. Throughout the paleolithic and neolithic periods, the Bronze Age and the Iron Age man could maintain himself, multiply and master this earth chiefly through his armed strength. Verily the defensive sword was the first saviour of man!

The belief in absolute non-violence condemning all armed resistance even to aggression evinces no mahatmaic *saintliness, but a monomaniacal senselessness!*

What held good in man's struggle with the brute world continued to be true throughout his social struggle, the struggle of clan against clan, race against race, nation against nation. The lesson is branded on every page of human history down to the latest page that nations which, other things equal, are superior in military strength are bound to survive, flourish and dominate while those which are militarily weak shall be politically subjected or cease to exist at all. It is idle to say, we shall add a new chapter to history with a new lesson. You may perhaps add something new to history but you cannot add to or take away a syllable from the iron law of Nature itself. Even today if man hands over a blank cheque to the wolf and the tiger to be filled in, with a human pledge of absolute non-violence, no killing of a living being, no armed force to be used, then the wolves and the tigers will lay waste all your *mandirs* and mosques, culture and cultivation. Aramis and *ashrams* finish man, saint and sinner alike, before a dozen years pass by! In face of such an iron law of Nature, can anything be more immoral and sinful than to preach a principle so anti-human as that of absolute non-violence, condemning all armed resistance even to aggression?

And yet it is curious to find that even those who condemn this doctrine of absolute non-violence as impracticable seem still to believe that though impracticable for us worldly men, this doctrine is nevertheless highly moral and evince some mahatmaic excellence, some superhuman sanctity. This apologetic tone must be forthwith changed. It raises these probhets of this eccentric doctrine in their own estimation and makes them feel they had really invented some moral law, raising human politics to some divine level. Seeing that even their opponents on practical grounds attribute to them a superhuman saintliness owing to the very eccentricity of their doctrine, they grow, perhaps unconsciously, all the more eccentric and have the insane temerity to preach in all seriousness to the Indian public that 'even the taking up of *lathi* is sinful. The best means of freeing India from the foreign yoke is the spinning-wheel. Not only that, but even after India becomes independent, there would not be any necessity of maintaining a single armed soldier or a single warship to protect her frontiers. If but India believes and acts in the spirit of such absolute non-violence maintaining no army, no navy or no air force, no nation in the world shall invade her and even if some armed nations did invade her, they could be easily persuaded to fall back as soon as they are confronted by the unarmed army of our *desha sevikas* singing to the tune of the spinning-wheel musical appeals to the conscience of the invading forces'. When things have come to such a pass that such quixotic souls are sent as accredited spokesmen by the credulous crowd to the Round Table Conferences and even in foreign lands such senseless proposals are seriously advanced by them in the name of the Indian nation itself in so many words to the great merriment of the foreign statesmen and the general public in Europe and America—the time has surely come to take this doctrinal plague quite seriously and to counteract it as quickly as possible. We must tell them in no apologetic language but in firm accents that your doctrine of absolute non-violence is not only absolutely impracticable, but absolutely immoral. It is not an outcome of any saintliness but of insanity. It requires no ingenuity on your part to tell us that if but all men observe absolute non-violence, there will be no war in the world and no necessity of any armed forces. Just as it requires no extraordinary insight to maintain that if but men learn to live forever, mankind will be free from death. We denounce your doctrine of absolute non-violence not because we are less saintly, but because we are more sensible than you are. Relative nonviolence is our creed and therefore, we worship the defensive sword as the first saviour of man. It was in this faith that Hindus worship the arms as the symbols of Shakti, the Kali, and Guru Govind Singh sang his hymn to the sword: *सुखसंताकरणाम् दुर्मतिहरणम् खलदलदलनम् जयतेगम्* ॥ and we also join with the great Guru in the refrain and sing with him, 'Hail Thee, sword.'

It is in this spirit that I want Hindus to get themselves re-animated and re-born into a martial race. Manu and Shri Krishna are our law-givers and Shri Rama, the Commander of our forces. Let us re-learn the manly lessons they taught us and our Hindu nation shall prove again as unconquerable and conquering a race as we proved once when they led us:. conquering those who dared to be aggressive against us and refraining our-selves, not out of weakness but out of maganimity, from any unjustifiable designs of aggression against the unoffending. It goes then without saying that the Hindu *Sangathanists* actuated by such a faith can never associate with the Gandhist *satyagraha* which demands freedom to preach this immoral principle of absolute non-violence, condemning all armed resistance even to alien aggression, as it is highly detrimental to our Hindu interests in particular. It is indeed more harmful to Hindu interests than it can ever be to the interest of the government's crafty as the British policy has ever been, they like to some extent that someone should always be preaching to the Hindus that the spinning qualities are more spiritual than the fighting ones and that the highest human virtue consists in getting killed by any invading aggressors than killing them in self-defence. It pays the British to some extent. I shall not be surprised if the government allows the Gandhists to preach the doctrine of absolute non-violence provided they do not say a word against the present war. In fact, some such compromise was suggested by the government and may be accepted by the Gandhists later on just to flourish it in the face of the public as a trophy won by their *satyagraha*. But, even if the government allows the preaching of this doctrine, denouncing all armed strength, then in that case it will be the duty of the Hindu *Sangathanists* themselves to offer all legitimate opposition to this vicious principle in their own interests and on their own account from the *Sangathanist* platform. We must whip up military enthusiasm amongst the Hindus. That is the most crying need of today and must form the chief plank of the Hindu *Sangathanist* platform.

The militarisation and industrialisation of the Hindus must constitute our immediate objective under the war conditions

Thus after taking stock of all other courses and factors for and against us, I feel no hesitation in proposing that the best way of utilising the opportunities which the war has afforded to us cannot be any other than to participate in all war efforts which the government is compelled by circumstances to put forth insofar as they help in bringing about the militarisation and industrialisation of our people. Fortunately for us, facilities are thrown open to us in this direction within a single year in consequence of the war which we could not find during the last 50 years and could not have hoped to secure in ordinary course by empty protests and demands for the next 50 years to come. Owing to the Gandhist lead, the Congress had neglected the question of fostering military strength of our people to such an extent that even the wordy resolutions which the Congress used to pass, while it was under the lead of those who were called Moderates but who in this particular respect were more Extremists and far-sighted than this spineless school of Gandhist non-resister, used to pass demanding the repeal of the Arms Act and Indianisation of the Army, were tabooed for the last 20 years under Gandhiji's pressure on the Congress platform. Even when the Congress was in power, it did not take a single step to promote or even to safeguard the military interests of our people. But, throughout the last 20 years, the Moslems, who cared a fig for any non-violent, non-resisting, non-cooperation nonsense in which the Congress kept indulging under Gandhiji's pressure, almost monopolised recruitment into the army and armed police. It was only a few Hindu Mahasabha leaders, like our revered Dr. Moonje and Bhai Paramanand, who were trying their best to counteract the senseless policy of the Congress owing to which the Hindus alone had to suffer and lose whatever numerical strength they had in the army. Not only that, the sophistical teaching of the so-called satyagraha creed sought to kill the very martial instinct of the Hindu race and had succeeded to an alarming extent in doing so. That was the reason why throughout my tours as the president of the Hindu Mahasabha, I made it my duty to put this point above all others and tried my best to give a fillip to military awakening amongst the Hindus by addressing thousands and thousands of Hindu youth from Punjab to Madras with no negligible success.

But, I was always at a loss to know how we Hindu *Sangathanists* can find immediate ways and means to impart to our young Hindu generation the practical and up-to-date military training. Just then the war broke out and the British Government, to serve their own interests, were compelled to raise new military forces in India on a large scale. Naturally, the Hindu Mahasabha with a true insight into practical politics decided to participate in all war efforts of the British Government insofar as they concerned directly with the question of the Indian defence and raising new military forces in India. I emphatically maintain that the results of that policy even within a year of its trial are positively encouraging.

Results in participating in war efforts satisfactory

In examining these results, we must bear in mind that the British are raising these military forces and encouraging industrial development so far as it helps their war efforts with no altruistic motives of helping the Indians. They are doing whatever they have to do to help themselves. We are also participating in these war efforts or at any rate are not out to oppose them, with no intention of helping the British but of helping ourselves. I have put the situation almost bluntly in the above manner to disarm the political folly into which the Indian public is accustomed to indulge in thinking that because Indian interests are opposed to the British interests in general, any step in which we join hands with the British Government must necessarily be an act of surrender, anti-national, of playing into the British hands and that co-operation with the British Government in any case and under all circumstances is unpatriotic and condemnable. It is all the more amusing to find that this spirit of silly bravado is more rampant amongst those very Congressites who did not hesitate to serve the British Government by conducting their provincial ministries, swearing loyalty and allegiance to the British domination in the oath of allegiance which they had to take; who wept over the fancied destruction of Westminster Abbey, only the other day and had served the British Government as their recruiting officers during the last war and are even now promising full co-operation to the British, if but they get some of their fadist demands satisfied and assure the British that they would do nothing even as it is to embarrass the British. But, the Hindu Sangathanists at any rate must realise the difference between a senseless bravado and real act of bravery. As I have explained above in para (c) how, in practical politics, alliances are to be based on any point of common interests in spite of the fact of the conflict in all other interests between the allied parties. Who can say that Hitler or Stalin can be wanting in bravery or can be silly enough to play into the other's hand and yet both of them did not join in alliance, in spite of their opposing interests on all other points, as soon as they found that their mutual interests coalesced on some points during this war? *One who is always afraid of being duped by others must be a simpleton indeed deserving to be duped all round. The Hindu Sangathanists are so conscious of their political wisdom and so self-confident that they can take good care of themselves against being duped even by the crafty statesmanship of Great Britain and, therefore, feel no hesitation and ought to feel no hesitation in extending a whole-hearted participation in the war efforts of Great Britain if but it serves their own purpose better than any other course.*

Examining from this point of view the results of the Hindu Mahasabhas policy of participating in the war efforts so far as the militarisation of the Hindus is concerned, we note that during the last year one hundred thousand new recruits were enlisted in the Indian Army. While in the old army the proportion of the Moslems had risen in some parts even to 75 per cent, we find amongst these new recruits, there are nearly sixty thousand Hindus and thirty thousand Moslems. The strength of the air force also is trebly increased and is being daily increased. It is very encouraging a fact that the Hindus are evincing a special interest and ability in the aircraft and are getting themselves enlisted in large numbers in the air force and many of them are already serving on the war front and partaking in actual air fights against the seasoned air forces of Germany. In the naval forces, it is regrettable to note that the Hindus counted for nothing upto this time. In the very small number of Indians which was somehow connected with the navy, more than 75 per cent were Moslems. Consequently, strong representations were made by the Hindu Mahasabha during this year against this partiality of the government. The sea-faring and sea-fighting Hindu castes on the

Konkan coast in particular, who distinguished themselves so valourously in the days of the Maratha Empire as to inflict several serious defeats on the English sea-forces, but who have been neglected of late by England perhaps owing to the self-same old grudge the English bear to them, were roused from their lethargy and were made to demand entry into the naval forces. Hundreds of meetings were organised by the Hindu Mahasabha this year in the villages and towns which were attended by very large numbers of these castes: the Agris, the Bhandaris, the Kolis and others; and petitions signed by thousands of them were submitted to the government, demanding entry into the naval forces and the opening of shipyards and naval bases on the Konkan coast. In response to this agitation on the part of the Hindu Mahasabhaists on this point throughout India, the government promised to recruit Hindus in naval service without any distinction and have also admitted the fact that the Hindus are showing more inclination to take to that line than they were doing formerly. In order to meet the large demand for technicians to work in the new factories started on a very large scale to manufacture military equipment, rifles and even tanks, the government has already made arrangements for fifteen thousand Indian candidates to be trained immediately as technicians. All experts to train them who were available in India are called upon to take up the work and in addition to them, technical experts in up-to-date war crafts are requisitioned by the Indian Government from England as well. Besides, this large number of Indian workers and technical hands are to be sent to England to receive the training in up-to-date methods. They will all stay together with the British technical hands and labourers, will receive pay on the same scale and will be treated on an equal footing. The cost of it all will also be borne by the British Government. As the raising, equipping and training of the new army of lakh of Indian soldiers is already substantially complete, the government has only recently announced the expansion of the Indian Army to half a million men of all arms. Thus, nearly two lakhs of Indians would be immediately recruited and the ever increasing necessity under war pressure is sure to compel the government to recruit some five lakhs of Indian soldiers before long, bringing up the total strength of the Indian Army to a million soldiers properly trained, equipped and even mechanised to bring them up to an up-to-date efficiency. Then again we must take into consideration the large increase in the armies of the different Hindu states that have been sanctioned by the government under war pressure. Not less than 40 battalions have already been sent to the different fronts of the war and are taking their lessons in actual fighting on modern lines. The old rusty outlook of the forces of the Hindu states has already been transformed as to present a smart, well-armed and well-equipped front.

The sudden increase in the army from some two lakhs to 10 lakhs of Indian soldiers was bound to create an enormous demand for commissioned officers. So, the old policy of army Indianisation by the introduction of special Indianised units has been scrapped and all units have been opened to Indian officers' recruitment. The Viceroy's commissioned officers too have been reintroduced in the Indianised units and, thus, all units are placed on the same footing. There is consequently an enormous field opened out for Indians to serve as officers in the army in all capacities and on equal footing with the British officers who, upto this time, enjoyed a sort of monopoly in officering the army. Besides this expansion of the rank, file and officers in the regular army to a million men, the Indian territorial forces also are soon to be re-touched, more efficiently equipped and expanded.

So far as the question of compulsory military education to be introduced into high schools and colleges is concerned, the Indian Government is still following obstructive tactics. But, it must be noted that the senates of almost all leading universities in India have demanded during this year that compulsory military training must forthwith be introduced and are already knocking at the gates of the government which as the war pressure goes on increasing are sure to yield and get thrown open.

Only a year ago, the Indian Government used to trot out the excuse that it would take at least 50 years to train up the Indians who had lost all their military instinct to form efficient army officers by their own men on such a large scale as that. But, now they have suddenly discovered that Indians, like other human beings in Europe, could be trained as efficient soldiers and officers in lakhs within a few months and could fight on equal terms with European armies on the European fields. Verily, necessity is the mother of invention and as the necessity grows more pressing under international political complications, England shall have to learn that not only a million Indians but a billion Indians are capable of being trained as soldiers and officers as efficient as the European ones within a couple of years to come.

The manufacture of war materials on an enormous scale is also being introduced in India which has already afforded and is sure to afford as days pass by an opportunity for thousands of our artisans, craftsmen, workers and technicians to get specialised in turning out up-to-date rifles, tanks, ammunition and even machines required in connection with them.

Then, again, whatever be their reluctance, the Indian Government has at last been compelled to permit Sheth Walchand Hirachand, who must be specially congratulated on his untiring efforts and able lead in this respect, to open a shipyard at Bezwada financed by Indian capital, worked by Indian labour under Indian management. Permission for opening a factory to manufacture aeroplanes on a large scale has also been granted to Sheth Walchand Hirachand who has already selected a site at Bangalore and is sure to set it going at full speed with his characteristic promptness and efficiency. The government has already lodged an order for a crore of rupees of planes.

With regard to large industries other than the war industries, it suffices to say that this year has given a fillip to many a chemical industry, the paper industry, etc. Within a couple of years, if but the war pressure is continued, we are sure to record an industrial progress which otherwise even a dozen years would not have enabled us to do as the government stood always in our way to economic self-sufficiency. But now that military exigencies have forced England to raise India to a self-sufficient economical and military unit—a centre commanding the defences of the whole eastern part of their Empire from Egypt to Australia, they are compelled to see that the key industries and even industries in general are started and flourish in this country to such a wide extent that if ever the connection of the eastern part of their Empire is at least temporarily cut off from the western Empire, they may be able to depend for all the sinews of war chiefly on India, which abounds in the resources of men and material.

A serious question

Now I ask you all whether you could have ever been able to bring about such rapid militarisation and industrialisation of the country within a year out of your own sources? Could have the Hindu Mahasabha or the Congress or any such public organisation ever been able to recruit, train and equip half a million of our men and send them to learn real fighting on the field on the strength of its own resources? And even if you had aimed to do so, would the British Government have ever allowed you to do so? We could not have conducted even *lathi* clubs on such a large scale. Even last year were we not as alive to the urgency of militarisation of our Hindu people? But were we not unable even last year even to run half a dozen institutions to impart military education even to a few hundred Hindu youth? And now that the war has opened out an opportunity for us to send hundreds of thousands of Hindus to the army, the navy, the air services and to get them fully trained, equipped and armed as up-to-date soldiers and commanding officers and for building shipyards, aeroplane factories, gun factories, ammunition factories and get thousands of our mechanics trained into war technical experts, shall we turn our back on all these facilities, refuse to join the army or to decline to participate in the manufacture of our materials simply because some fools will call it a co-operation with the government or some booby will curse it as an act of violence? If we do so, we shall but deserve even ourselves to be bracketed with the fool and the booby.

Let us note also that these half-a-million or million of men who are finding employment in the army and the thousands of workers and artisans and technicians and specialists who will get work and secure posts in the war material factories and the Industries made possible by the war will bring food and clothing and necessaries of life, to at least 50 lakhs of persons belonging to the very class who are at present suffering most on account of chronic unemployment? Will it not lessen the unbearable burden that at present falls on our agricultural classes who have to depend on the proceeds of land in spite of its daily diminishing return?

The advent of Japan near our frontiers must compel England to depend on India for military help to an ever-increasing extent

The most important point that I want you to bear in mind in this connection is to the effect that the British Government has not initiated this policy of militarising our nation to do which we all know how deadly opposed they were till only the last year, with the only view of helping themselves in the present war in Europe. So long as only European wars were concerned the British knew that they could not depend much on India, nor did they ever want to do so. Their policy in the European wars had for the last two hundred years or so been simple. They used to get a group of European nations on their side, make it fight with the other group of European nations opposed to them. Even if they wanted to get help from India in men and materials, it would have been impossible and would not have also paid to transfer millions of men and enormous war materials to boot, to Europe. That was the reason why England did not run the risk of militarising India whom she naturally did not like to trust, on such a large permanent scale as she is trying to do now. But, the longish shadow of the dwarfish Japan that has of late fallen on the very Bay of Bengal constitutes a new menace to the English supremacy in India which requires a new military policy, quite opposite in some respects to the one which England followed upto this time as denoted above. The ever-advancing forces of Japan with a declared objective of freeing Asia from European influence has naturally scared England and made her realise in all seriousness that a war with Japan in the near future is in all probability inevitable. The British statesmanship, far-sighted as it usually is, realised this also that if ever war broke out with Japan, India itself must be the centre of gravity of all war preparations, the central depot of war resources in men and ammunitions. If there was an impossibility of transferring large armies from India to England in the case of the European wars, the difficulty now was exactly the opposite to it. Nay, England could not under the present circumstances afford to send any substantial number of British forces or quantity of war material to India while such respectable foes as Hitler, Mussolini or Stalin were waiting to pounce on England herself. If Japan is to be fought out, then the millions of men required for that fight must be raised and all the war material must be manufactured in India itself. This new factor, therefore, is bound to render England more and more dependent on Indian military help and therein lies the guarantee for us also that the militarisation of our nation will continue on a far larger scale as years pass by and Great Britain is sure to extend all possible facilities for developing our military capacity, if but we also extend an enthusiastic participation in her war efforts. Chances are that an army with the strength of a couple of millions shall have to be raised, manned by Indians under Indian officers as rapidly as Japan succeeds in advancing near our frontiers.

Now again, I ask you, shall we lose this golden opportunity to acquire this military strength which our interests also demand and British interests compel Britain to help us in that task simply because some fadists call it an act of violence or some fools condemn it as co-operation with imperialism? Or shall we take the wisest step, of allying ourselves with Britain on this point alone and to the extent to which it serves Hindu interests and flood the new army to be raised with Hindu

Sangathanists and re-animate our race with martial spirit and regain the military strength and status we had lost?

Of all courses open to us at present, I emphatically recommend to you this course that the Hindus can best utilise the war situation by helping on their part the militarisation and industrialisation of India which the British on their side are also eager to effect for their own interests. And again, just think of the fact, that even if you Hindus refuse to join the army or the navy or the air force or the factories of war materials, the only immediate result will be that the Moslems will get into the saddle and instead of weakening the British Government, you will find that you have strengthened a second enemy who is no less bent upon subjecting you to helotage in your own land.

The so-called satyagraha *of the Congress can only serve as a stunt for the elections at best*

Again, what is the alternate programme to one adopted by the Hindu Mahasabha? Shouting some slogans and going into the jail? I appreciate the motive of those patriotic men in the Congress; I sympathise with their sufferings. But, I must plainly state, that they have made a mess of all political movements and the *satyagraha* they have now launched can bring no substantial good to the country. It is to some extent useful and was perhaps meant to serve as a stunt for the next elections. Are the Hindu *sangathanists* going to adopt a counter-stunt? We would have been justified in doing that too. But the Hindu Mahasabha as an organisation cannot do the two things at one and the same time. If it participates in the war efforts with a view to reap the most substantial benefits in militarising the Hindus, and allies itself with the Government to that extent, it cannot as an organisation take to any civil resistance to the government, which act will directly prove detrimental to our first and greater objective. You cannot both eat and have the cake. Of course, the Hindu Mahasabha can resort to civil resistance, if the issue is more profitable than the two great objectives which it seeks to gain, viz., militarisation and industrialisation.

The Hindu sabhaists are full of fight

I have consulted almost all leading workers and branches of the Mahasabha and it was very encouraging to find that the Mahasabhaists and especially the youthful workers were extremely anxious to launch a fighting programme, but only in view of the fact that the Congress has adopted one. Their chief anxiety seems to be to take to civil resistance as a counter-stunt to defeat the purpose of the Congress to win the next elections by the cheap method of courting jail under the A and B classes. But we should consider first, why do we *Hindu sabhaists* want to win the elections? Of course, to serve the Hindu interests best. Now nobody realises the importance of winning the election more than I do. But, if the Hindu interests are likely to suffer more by running after the elections, is it not our duty to discard them rather than sacrifice Hindu interests? If the programme, most beneficial under the present circumstances of participating in the war efforts with the two objectives mentioned above, is likely to suffer by civil resistance on issues which do not serve the Hindu interests in any substantial manner and if the elections could only be won by any such harmful means, *it is our clear duty to lose the elections rather than try to win them by pandering to the follies of the electorate to the detriment of the Hindu cause.* The Nizam's civil resistance movement affords a sufficient and the latest proof to convince any sensible electorate that the Hindu Mahasabhaists are even braver than the Congressites, even if going to jail is to be taken as the only test of bravery and patriotism. The thousands of Hindu Sangathanists who braved '*lathi mars*' in the Nizam jails can surely stand the '*laddu mar*' in the A, B, and even the C class in the British jails, standing shoulder to shoulder with their Congressite co-sufferers. If the Hindu *sangathanists* were only out to win elections with a view to form ministries and gain pelf and power, they could have very easily done it by changing a cap as so many other people have done it. But, we chose deliberately to stand by Hindu interests even at the risk of power, pelf or popularity. As I am convinced that the great facilities which we have secured and are sure to secure on a larger and larger scale for militarisation and industrialisation of Hindudom by participating in the war efforts of the government are overwhelmingly more beneficial to the Hindus than any issue we can win by any slogan-shouting civil resistance, I am quite prepared to lose the next election also. It is more patriotic to lose an election in trying to lead the electorate on a right path than to win it by pandering to their prejudices and follies.

The government has, in fact, met the demands put forward by the Hindu Mahasabha at the outbreak of the war in a substantial measure

I must make it clear here that the demands forwarded by the Hindu Mahasabha were not slighted by the government. We asked them to make a declaration that within one year's time after the cessation of the war, Dominion Status should be granted. Now, the Viceroy and the Secretary of State have both made it clear, so far as words can make it clear, that India shall be raised to the position of a self-governing unit of the *Commonwealth which they call British but I claim, must be called Indo-British,* on equal footing even with Great Britain herself immediately after the war at the shortest interval possible. We wanted a word and they have given us a word. We know that the taste of the pudding is in its eating. But, then the question can arise when is the promise to be translated into action? Secondly, we wanted a declaration from the government that they would not encourage the scheme of breaking up the integrity of the Indian state. As I have shown above under the pressure of the Hindu Mahasabha alone, Mr. Amery has made a clear declaration to that effect in his speach on 'India First'. So far as our military demands were concerned, they are almost all being acted upon in a large measure at least up till now. The military service is thrown open to all castes and creeds alike and other facilities we have got are already dealt with in other parts of my speech. The Hindu Mahasabha is already recognised by the government as the foremost representative body of the Hindus. The only point on which the government is still harping is the fact that they are throwing the responsibility of framing a constitution on the Indians and insisting with their tongue in their cheeks 'unless you all Indian parties, the minority and the majority, produce a compromise unanimously voted for, we cannot thrust any constitution on you of our framing'. But, we shall fight out this specious argument in right time. Nay, there is every likelihood that on this point too, the government will have to yield to the most reasonable demands of the Hindu Mahasabha. In short, I find no detail or issue important enough to compel us to resort to civil resistance at the sacrifice of the important facilities we have gained and the opportunity that has presented itself to us, enabling us to effect the militarisation of the Hindu people to a substantial extent.

Consequently, I, for one, recommend emphatically the following programme on which all Hindu *sangathanists* should concentrate their energy. Of course, I put it forward as my personal view and leave you entirely free to come to any corporate decision you choose, which decision I shall try my best to carry out as your chief executive officer, whether the decision coincides with my programme or not. I need not mention that this programme was already adopted by the Working Committee held on the 21st of November last.

I also make it clear that although I wish that the Hindu Mahasabha as an organisation, should stick to this programme as its immediate line of action, yet if some Hindu *sangathanists* find out a more effective way of fighting on their own account for the Hindu cause, no one shall be gladder than myself. The Hindu Mahasabha also cannot but wish that the younger generation should prove braver than the present one. But, it should prove wiser too.

This programme which I recommend for your adoption in my personal capacity is, of course, meant to be an immediate one. If some new factor arises demanding a new solution, we too shall promptly chalk out a different line of action in response to it.

Immediate programme

This immediate programme could be roughly outlined thus:

- To secure entry for as many Hindu recruits as possible into the army, navy and the air forces
- To utilise all facilities that are being thrown open to get our people trained into military and mechanical manufacture of up-to-date war materials
- To try to make military training compulsory in colleges and high schools
- To intensify the organisation of the Ram Sena
- To join the civic guard movement with a view to enable to defend our own people against foreign invasion or internal anarchy, provided always that the civic guards are not used against any patriotic political movements in India or in any activities detrimental to the legitimate interests of the Hindus
- To start new industries on large scales to capture the market where foreign competition is found eliminated
- To boycott foreign articles to defeat the entry of new foreign competitors
- To set on foot an all-India movement to secure the correct registration, in the coming Census, of the popular strength of the Hindus including tribal Hindus such as Santhals, Gonds, Bhils, etc., and to secure their enlistment as Hindus instead of as animists or hill tribes and by taking every other step necessary to secure the object in view

These few items will suffice to illustrate the lines on which the Hindu *sangathanists* all over India should concentrate their attention in the near future.

□

23rd Session, Bhagalpur—1941

Comrades in the Hindu Cause,

I acknowledge gratefully the honour you have done to me and the trust you have placed in me in offering the presidentship of the All India Hindu Mahasabha this year for the fifth time in an unbroken succession. I had even last year tendered my resignation of this high post twice and requested you all in view of my failing health and in the interest of the Hindu cause to spare me and to entrust the lead of the Hindu Mahasabha in some worthier and stronger hands. But, owing to the most cordial pressure of my comrades all over India and at the behest of the All India Committee of the Hindu Mahasabha, I continued to shoulder the responsibility of the presidential office and tried my individual best to justify and deserve the overwhelming confidence and love which the Hindu *sangathanist* the world all over India continued to cherish towards me. It is a matter of public knowledge that this year also when the time for electing the president for the next year drew near, I had made it clear to almost all provincial leaders and workers that this time at any rate I should be allowed to withdraw from the presidential panel. I was even determined to resign after the election, but just then the government made it clear that they were not prepared to raise the ban on the annual Session of the Hindu Mahasabha at Bhagalpur. This government ban compelled me also to banish altogether from my mind the thought of resigning the presidential office. This ban constituted such an intolerable, uncalled for and unjustifiable humiliation to the Hindu honour as to render it imperative on the part of every Hindu *sangathanist* to try his level best to get it removed by all legitimate means within his or her reach. My duty also as the elected president for the very session at Bhagalpur was clear. It was to stick to my guns. I have, consequently, consented even willingly to shoulder the responsibility of the presidentship and the leadership of the All India Hindu Mahasabha for the fifth time for the ensuing year. May I be able to serve the Hindu cause to the best of my abilities and so unsparingly as to deserve the honour you have all done to me and the confidence you have all placed in me by calling upon me once again to lead the Hindu movement.

The casese of this unjust, humiliating and even illegal government ban

When at Madura the last session of the Hindu Mahasabha decided to hold the session in Bihar and when after surveying different places in Bihar, the Reception Committee decided to hold the session at Bhagalpur, even the government must admit that there could not have been the least intention on the part of the Mahasabha to disturb the communal peace of the particular section of Moslems residing at Bhagalpur during the Bakr-Id festival. The Bakr-Id is observed all over India by the Moslems and there could not be any reason why the Hindu *sabhaists* should have a special spite against the Moslems residing at the comparatively insignificant town of Bhagalpur of all places in India. But nevertheless, after the venue was settled in the ordinary course of things and in view of other considerations and conveniences at Bhagalpur, the government of Bihar came out all of a sudden with a communique banning the session and ordering that it must not be held in a number of districts in Bihar, including the town of Bhagalpur from the 1st of December next to the 10th of January, 1942.

The government of Bihar argued that they would find it very difficult to maintain peace and order at Bhagalpur owing to the paucity of police forces at their disposal in case communal disturbances broke out during the Bakr-Id, if the session and the Bakr-Id coincided.

So far as the question of coincidence was concerned, the Working Committee of the Hindu Mahasabha having no intention whatsoever to give any justifiable excuse even to the aggressive section among the Moslems, decided in an accommodating spirit not to hold the session on the dates during which the Bakr-Id was customarily observed at Bhagalpur and resolved that the session should be held on 24th to 27th December next during the X'mas holidays as had been the usual custom with the Hindu Mahasabha to do for years in the past. This arrangement would have enabled the Mahasabha to end the session a couple of days before the Bakr-Id began and let the Moslems alone to celebrate it in any fashion they chose. But, the Bihar Government still refused to raise the ban on the ground that the holding of the session even before the Bakr-Id and even if it was held on dates not coinciding with Bakr-Id was quite likely to inflame the communal tension and passions at Bhagalpur and prevent the peaceful celebration of the Bakr-Id festival! But, they did not seem to mind it much that there was more likelihood of communal passions being inflamed and of communal riots breaking out if the Bakr-Id was allowed to precede the Mahasabha session and thus endanger again its being held just after the Bakr-Id. As a matter of fact, it cannot be denied that it is the Bakr-Id which more often than not is notoriously associated throughout India with communal disturbances and Moslem fanaticism running riot. The sessions of the Hindu Mahasabha on the contrary are as undeniably noted for their peaceful and orderly celebrations. But, even the latest press communique issued by the government of Bihar which modified the ban to the extent that it allowed the session to be held just after the Bakr-Id after the 3rd of January, 1942, instead of the 10th of January, 1942, did not make it clear whether the government would not renew the ban on the Session even if it was held on the 4th of January, in case some communal disturbances were staged during the Bakr-Id just to spite the Mahasabha session to come. Consequently, whether the session was held before the Bakr-Id or after the Bakr-Id, the necessity of facing the ban like the sword of Damocles was kept hanging on its head.

So far as the second reason which was set forth by the government to justify its attitude as to the paucity of the police forces at the command of the Bihar Government, it is enough to point out that the government has more than once emphasised that in case an attempt to hold the session was made in spite of the ban, the Bihar Government would put it down with all the resources at their command. Now if the government is thus on its own admission so powerful, and it is no doubt so powerful as to command sufficient forces to suppress an all-India session of the Hindu Mahasabha which is likely to be attended by tens of thousands of Hindus along with the most outstanding Hindu leaders from all parts of India, can it ever be said that those very forces would not have enabled the Government to hold in check that aggressive section if Moslems at Bhagalpur, if there be any, which was likely to get inflamed and to threaten criminal disturbances of the Hindus were showed to exercise their legitimate right of free association by holding the session of the Hindu Mahasabha at Bhagalpur?

When the all-India session of the Moslem League was held at Madras this year, the government prevented the Hindus under Section 144 from holding meetings, carrying lethal weapons or assembling in more than five persons so that the session of the League might pass of well in spite of the fact that rabid and anti-Hindu speeches and resolutions were delivered and passed in it. Now at Bhagalpur, when the all-India session of the Hindus Mahasabha is to be held, the government, instead of calling upon the Moslems to keep themselves within the bounds of law and order, have put a ban on the Hindu Mahasabha session itself, making it criminal on the part of the Hindus to exercise their fundamental right of citizenship!

Throughout India the same discriminating, partial and anti-Hindu policy is adhered to and Hindu processions, immersion of images and conferences are held up to placate the fanatical *goondaism* on the part of the aggressive Moslem sections.

The reason trotted out for this anti-Hindu policy is also uniform: that it is the duty of the government to maintain peace and order.

But the peace or order which is to be maintained as a duty on the part of the government is that which enables the law-abiding to exercise their legitimate rights and not that peace or order which could only be maintained by compelling the law-abiding to forgo their rights to placate the aggressive and the criminal.

The underlying idea which makes the government resort to this policy throughout India cannot be any other than the notion that the Hindus, as a people being gentle and law-abiding, are more amenable even to such humiliating and unjust restrictions on their liberty than the chauvinistic Moslem fanatics.

The civic and even the religious festivities of Hindus, Christians and Parsees pass off so peacefully as to provide occasions for general rejoicing to people of all communities alike throughout India. But the Moslem festivals, whether civic or religious, like the Bakr-Id or the Mohurrum, are almost always associated with bloody orgies and fanatical anti-Hindu riots. Not only the Hindus, but all non-Moslem communities in India find them a source of constant and dangerous nuisance to life and property. The responsibility for this situation must be shared not only by the riotous Moslem fanaticism, but by the insane policy of the government too, which almost always seeks to maintain peace and order on these occasions not by chastising Moslem fanaticism running riot but by calling upon the Hindus to forgo the exercise of their legitimate rights of citizenship and, thus, by putting a premium on fanatical *goondaism*.

The ban placed on the Hindu Mahasabha session at Bhagalpur is also justified by the government with unabashed frankness by stating that they had to do so for no other urgent or justifiable reason, but to enable the Bakr-id festivities of a handful of Moslems in a solitary town like Bhagalpur to pass off well. If the session of the All-India Hindu Mahasabha is held before the Bakr-Id, the Government contention is that even this legitimate exercise of the right of association by the Hindus may inflame communal passions of the Moslems! If the government suspected such a contingency, it was its duty to take every precaution to hold in check and chastise this aggressive and intolerant fanaticism that gets inflamed at the sight of the exercise by other communities of their legitimate rights. The Christians, who are to celebrate their X'mas during those very days, never get inflamed at the sight of a number of all-India conferences held by the Hindus and other communities throughout India. But, on the contrary, these Christian holidays like the Hindu holidays provide special facility for such all-India sessions. It is only the insane policy of the government to placate Moslem *goondaism* that has rendered the Moslem fanatics so irascible and intolerant. At Nellore, for example, the very government law courts have openly confessed their inability to compel the executive to abide by and carry out their legal orders in connection with Hindu rights. A government whose executive refuses to carry out the decisions of its own law courts and will not protect the civic rights of the Hindus held valid by the law courts when they are opposed to the fanatical whims of the Moslems for the only reason that otherwise that fanaticism would break out in riotous orgies must be said to have lost all legitimate and moral right to govern at all.

In addition to this unjustifiable nature of the ban, its legality also is seriously questionable. Whatever powers are to be exercised by the provincial governments in order to maintain public safety and order under the defence of India Act are to be exercised, 'For the purpose of securing the Defence of British India,' and in case 'such exercise is called for' for the efficient prosecution of war.' Now, by no stretch of imagination can the government maintain that the session of the All

India Hindu Mahasabha is likely to disturb public order or endanger public safety with a view or in a manner of standing in the way of the efficient prosecution of war or the securing the defence of British India. Add to this fact that of all outstanding all-India organisations, the Hindu Mahasabha alone has been the foremost advocate of extending responsive co-operation to the British Government in this war insofar as the question of Indian defence is concerned. Almost all of its prominent leaders and workers have been touring round throughout the country, calling upon the Hindus to join the military forces of all arms and thousands of its members have already secured entry in the army, navy and the aerial forces with a genuine desire of co-operating with the British Forces in a responsive spirit insomuch as the Hindu interests too under the present circumstances dictate such co-operation. There could not be, therefore, any least chance of suspecting any harm or opposition 'to the cause of Indian defence' or 'the efficient prosecution of war'. Nor has the government itself cited any such reason in their order prohibiting this Session. The case, therefore, cannot be said to be covered by the Defence of India Act and consequently the ban that is placed on this session under this Act is *ab initio* illegal. This legal view taken by some of the foremost lawyers in the land proves that the government of Bihar has not only committed a political blunder, but even a legal one.

The Mahasabha has consequently resolved to hold its session at Bhagalpur itself on the scheduled dates in spite of this unjust, humiliating and illegal government ban, in assertion of the civic rights of citizenship in general and of Hindus in particular. The time has come when the Hindus must correct the erring notion under which the government labours that Hindus can be made to tolerate any aggression on their civic and religious rights and can take all kicking more kindly than the chauvinistic Moslem fanaticism and that this is the cheaper way of maintaining the so-called peace and order. The Hindus must now learn to record practical protest against any such anti-Hindu policy on the part of the government or on the part of anyone else whenever and wherever such cases, humiliating to Hindu honour, crop up, by all legitimate means within their reach even if in this their attempt to exercise their legitimate and fundamental rights of citizenship, the government at times threatens most unjustly and illegitimately to cow down the Hindus by flourishing the police bludgeon in their face.

We go to Bhagalpur not to challenge the government but to assert our legitimate rights

Nevertheless, I must make it clear that the Mahasabhaists are going to Bhagalpur to hold this session—even if the ban is not raised in time, not with any the least desire to throw a challenge to the government or to flout the legitimate authority in any wanton manner. We shall all rally round the pan-Hindu flag raised at Bhagalpur with the only object of asserting our civic right of free association. We shall give no justifiable reason whatsoever to inflame any communal passions or do anything beyond asserting our inalienable civic rights without trespassing on those of other communities in the interest of peace and order which, when interpreted in an impartial and constitutional sense, the Hindu Mahasabhaists are as anxious as the government to maintain. Even if we are banned and opposed by physical force on the part of the government, we are all determined to offer ourselves to get arrested or to face the worst without any show or use of physical resistance to the government authorities on our part, beyond the civil resistance implied by our assertion again and again of our legitimate right to continue the sessional activities.

I earnestly hope that inasmuch as the cause the Hindu Mahasabha is going to fight out at Bhagalpur, it is essentially the cause of civic liberty so far as the question of resisting, with all legitimate means, this ban is concerned—not only all Hindus irrespective of party affiliations but even our Christian, Parsee and Jewish countrymen, in fact, every Indian citizen who values the cause of the fundamental right of citizenship of free association and realises that the government policy of bribing fanatical *goondaism* at the cost of legitimate rights of honest and law-abiding citizens constitutes a common danger to all citizens alike, will extend their sympathy and co-operation and strengthen the hands of the Hindu Mahasabhaists in this their struggle to assert the fundamental rights of citizenship on an issue which is of common interest to all Indian citizens alike.

I have no doubt that if but the Hindu *Sangathanists* muster courage at Bhagalpur from all parts of India and fight out this campaign of civil resistance within the legitimate bounds indicated above with a heroic determination counting no imprisonment, *lathicharges* or any sacrifice whatsoever as too high a price to pay for maintaining the honour of the pan-Hindu flag and without giving any the least illegitimate cause on their part for any breach of honourable peace, genuine civic order or malicious communal tension—this 23rd session of the Hindu Mahasabha is bound to prove the most successful session of all the sessions in the past.

II

As it seems more likely than not, that this speech will not be formally read in a formally assembled session at Bhagalpur and also because there is no time now left to write it at full length, I mean to touch only a few categorical points to serve as finger posts at crossroads to guide the Hindu movement in the near future.

Loyal homage to His Majesty the King of Nepal

I tender on behalf of Hindudom as a whole our most loyal homage to his Majesty the King of Nepal as a defender of the Hindu faith, the sovereign of the only independent Hindu kingdom today, the foremost representative of the glorious Hindu past and the hope of still more glorious Hindu future. Fortunately, for the Hindus, the government of Nepal has today at its helm a personality in whose hands the Hindu interests are bound to be safe. His Highness the Maharaja Yudhasamsher Jang Bahadur, the present Prime Minister of Nepal, realises more than anyone else that the future of the Hindu kingdom of Nepal is indissolubly bound up with the future of Hindudom as a whole. Hindus, in fact, are a national unit and it is given to Nepal today to shape its destiny. The war opens out immense possibilities before us even if it threatens to surround us on all sides with imminent danger. Keeping the ultimate goal of Hindu regeneration full in view, it was no doubt wise under the present circumstances that the Hindu kingdom of Nepal should have chosen to ally herself with the British Government during this war and sent our brave Gurkha armies to protect Indian frontiers and to some other theatres of war to check new alien invasions. The British Government too would do well to recompense for this effective assistance they receive at the hands of His Majesty the King of Nepal by restoring to Nepal at least those districts in Bihar and on the borders of the Punjab which were a part of the kingdom of Nepal only a century ago and were then annexed by the British.

It is encouraging to note that the land forces of Nepal are already so efficient and up-to-date as to match the forces of any nation in the world in warlike qualities and dogged resistance. But, we are anxiously waiting for the day when even the aerial forces of Nepal will be as efficient, up-to-date and powerful enough to protect not only herself but even Hindudom as a whole. Nepal is exposed to aerial attacks as seriously as any of the eastern provinces of India. The war which has already touched the Indian shores constitutes at once a danger and an opportunity and I am confident that the virile and far-sighted Prime Minister of Nepal will take time by the forelock and equip Nepal with a powerful aerial force at no distant date.

The second point to which I want to attract the attention of the government of Nepal may seem comparatively less urgent but is nevertheless far from being negligible. From sources which are more or less reliable, it seems that the Moslems are trying to make their influence felt and numbers increased in Nepal by adopting their usual tactics of stealthy and treacherous advances. Mosques are multiplying rapidly in Nepal and the numbers of unwary Hindu girls and lads are being kidnapped or duped in surrounding tribal districts and ultimately converted to Mohammedanism. There are more ways than one by which a well-planned scheme of increasing the numerical strength of the Moslems in and about the Hindu kingdom is long being worked out. I urge the government of Nepal to be as alert as possible and not to minimise this danger to the strength and stability of Hindus in the kingdom. Mosques are first built as houses of prayer but they soon develop, as we have found in so many cases all over India, into hot-beds of anti-Hindu fanaticism. The campaign of kidnapping and abduction does on the face of it seem a stray outburst of individual crime. But, then, if history has anything to teach us Hindus, it teaches us that it was by these means, howsoever despicable they may seem, that the Moslems continued and are even now continuing to increase their numerical strength and strengthen their hold in India. If a Hindu King allowed mosques to be built, he was first flattered as a magnanimous soul who loved all religions and races alike. But, the time has come that we Hindus should despise this species of magnanimity as nothing short of suicidal madness. It was owing to this malady of magnanimity that our ancient Hindu kings allowed foreigners from all parts of the world into Hindusthan and even treated them as our own kith and kin and granted them protection and status equal with our own Hindu brethren, and now the staggering results stare us in the face. The erstwhile guests are threatening to oust the master of the house himself, out of it. Consequently, the government of Nepal should make it clear to all concerned that no anti-Hindu activity or designs would be tolerated in Nepal and should watch ceaselessly so as not to allow any non-Hindu section and especially the Moslems to grow in numerical strength in Nepal beyond what it recorded a century ago.

The Hindu Mahasabha Movement advancing with strides of a giant

Taking stock of events during the last year it can be incontrovertibly asserted that the Hindu movement led by the Mahasabha has progressed throughout India. The *shuddhi* work, the effective and successful efforts to remove untouchability, the Census campaign it conducted throughout India, the defending of the civic and religious rights of Hindus at hundreds of localities, facing and even foiling the wave of armed aggression on the part of the Moslems in their campaign of the so-called Pakistan riots through a large part of India and proving it to those anti-Hindu forces that even their bloody orgies cost themselves dearer and could never succeed in browbeating the Hindu movement, the successes in scores of electoral contest to the Central Assembly and to the local municipalities or boards which the Mahasabhaists won in Maharashtra, Assam, Bengal and in several other parts of India and even the couple of electoral defeats the Mahasabha had to undergo as the one in Berar, do all of them point out incontrovertibly that the Mahasabha is rapidly growing into a power that could no longer be underrated with impunity and that it has already grown formidable enough to hold in check the anti-Hindu forces that had been let loose on India and ran riot unchallenged during the last 50 years or so. But, the crowning achievement of the Mahasabha movement has been, more than these direct and detailed events, the indirect influence which its ideology and propaganda exercised on the Hindu mind to such an amazing extent as could only be fitly described as a mental revolution. The unparalleled enthusiasm displayed by crores of Hindus, classes and masses together with which they welcomed the president of the Hindu Mahasabha and several of its veteran leaders in all quarters of the country and which enthusiasm found its fittest expression, rending the air day in and day out, in that million-million throated *'Hindu Dharma ki Jai; Hindusthan Hinduon ka!!'* proved to demonstrate that the Hindus as a people have shed that inferiority complex which had been their greatest curse inflicted by themselves upon themselves and that they have returned to their national self-consciousness as Hindus. This mental revolution could not have found a better expression to voice forth its significance than that *'Hindusthan Hinduon ka!!'*

This awakening of the Hindu spirit which the Mahasabha movement brought about has already been able to effect breeches even in Congress citadel from within and thousands of those Congressite Hindus who had altogether forgotten that they were Hindus under the baneful influence of the pseudo-nationalistic opiates of the Gandhist school of thought are already searching their hearts and are blessing the Mahasabha in their innermost hearts for fighting for the Hindu cause and are sooner or later destined to fall as willing captives into our hands. This indirect effect of the Mahasabhaist propaganda has already compelled those very Congressites who blamed the Hindusabhaists for calling upon the Hindu electorates to vote for those who pledged to safeguard Hindu interests and for thus rendering the elections tainted with communalism—to assure the Hindu electorates that although they stood on Congress ticket, yet they were nevertheless Hindus of Hindus and would not yield to the Hindu Mahasabhaist candidate in safeguarding Hindu interests!! No compliment to the efficacy of the Hindu movement can be more convincing than these appeals by Congress candidates to the Hindu electorate, even if they be for the time being meant only to capture Hindu votes.

The time is fast approaching when the Congress will either be but a plank of the Hindu Mahasabha or get compelled to shut its shop altogether which deals in wholesale representation, by foregoing the right to represent the Hindus directly or indirectly.

The Moslems must get satisfied with representation in proportion to their population only

The third outstanding achievement of the Hindu Mahasabha has been that it has already proved to be a formidable opponent to the inordinate ambitions of the Moslems in general and the Moslem League in particular.

Whether it be the question of the extension of the Executive Council or the formation of the National Defence Council or the Defence Advisory Committee, the Moslem Leaguers have themselves admitted that they have been discomfited and their swollen headed claims left unheeded. Mr. Jinnah resents that Mr. Amery should have betrayed him in not keeping up the government 'promise' of not turning down the full-fledged Pakistan scheme and should have even gone to the length of delivering sermons on 'India first.' In Bengal, Mr. Huq, who only last year kept roaring like a 'tiger' that he would *sataenga* the Hindus is already so cowed and chastened as to talk sense and prefer to join hands with Hindu Mahasabha even at the risk of getting a divorce from the Moslem League. Nor did Sir Sadullah Khan fare better in Assam and was compelled to resign his premiership overnight. The so-called League governments in these provinces having tumbled down like a house of cards, it was but natural that the Moslem League should have found itself left in the lurch and its bloated ambition fallen flat to the ground.

It cannot be denied that it was largely due to the formidable opposition of the Hindusabhaists that the League thus finds itself today discomfited and foiled on all sides. Nor does the future hold out any more hopeful prospect before it in view of the fact that the Hindus are every day getting influenced more and more by the ideology of the Hindu Mahasabha and are consequently bound to get more and more consolidated and powerful to present a united Hindu front to all anti-Hindu aggression.

The war also has belied the hopes of the Indian pan-Islamite. Only in last April when the Moslem League held its session at Madras, Mr. Jinnah warned the government and the Hindus that if they did not do what he wanted them to do, 'others would come to India and do it and break up Hindusthan into a conglomeration of Pakistans'. Other notable Moslem leaders too asserted in continuation of the threat that their great Moslem nations across the border of India were there and, thus, would not hesitate to join hands with them as the Indian Moslems looked upon them as their destined deliverers from the yoke of the Hindus in India. But unfortunately out of these 'others' or these 'our great Moslem Nations beyond the borders of India', none now can be found at the station. During the last war the Ex-Amir Amanullakhan was to play the part of the destined deliverer of Islam in India and with the treacherous connivance of Gandhi, the two great 'nationalists' leaders, the Ali brothers, conspired to bring him to Delhi as the would be annointed Emperor of India. But unfortunately a Baccha-i-Saku, a son of water carrier, finished the Ex-Amir and the would-be Emperor of India. If this time our Moslem leaders at Madras meant by the 'others' Raza Shah of Iran, who was then hand-in-glove with the Nazis and expected him to play the part of the next best deliverer of our Indian Moslems from the majority tyranny of the Hindus, then now his address also is not quite known and instead of booking for India he seems to have taken a wrong train to Mauritius. Instead of playing the part of the deliverer of Islam in India, poor Persia is desperately searching now for a deliverer for her own sake. The Turks are but literally sandwiched between the German and British forces and they themselves do not know what would be their fate tomorrow and have only a Hobson's choice before them—to surrender to one of these advancing forces. Still if of those 'others' who were to do for the Moslems what the Hindus refused to do and cut up India to order after the Pakistan fashion, any Moslem deliverer is yet willing and able to do the task—we shall be glad to be enlightened by the League as regards his present destination and address. Can it be that His Exalted Highness the Nizam of Hyderabad is the next aspirant to that high office? If so, then all that we can do is to exclaim, 'If these be thy gods, Oh Israel!!'

On the whole, the time has come when our Moslem countrymen should realise that even in their own interests they should accept the inevitable and should cease amusing themselves with airy nothings. They must count with realities, they must know that they are in a minority and that there is not the slightest chance now left for them to reduce the present majority of the Hindus in any appreciable measure. The *shuddhi* movement and the virile awakening that has come over the Hindus have disarmed forcible or fraudulent conversion to Islam in India once and for all. Even if an Allauddin or an Aurangzeb comes down again, he would not be able to convert permanently and from generation to generation a dozen Hindu by force or fraud. Take the latest case of such forcible conversions in Bengal during the Dacca riots this year. In a number of villages, hundreds of Hindu families were forcibly 'converted' to Islam and the Moslem rioters fancied that those villages were then permanently annexed to Pakistan as used to be the case in reality some two centuries ago. But, then, no sooner were the riots put down than did the Moslems find to their utter dismay that all the 'converted' Hindus were *shuddified* in no time and went back to their Hindu fold more intensely Hinduised and more bitterly opposed to Islamite persuasion and practices. If but this factor is once clearly and definitely realised, it follows inevitably that the Moslems in India cannot but continue as a minority and must frame their political programme accordingly. They cannot expect a single seat more either in the legislature or in government cabinets than what their population strength today entitles them to have and so far as their claim of cutting off the Punjab and other provinces from India to form them into Pakistan is concerned, well, they should take it as feasible or otherwise as the claim of the Hindus to annex Afganistan to Hindusthan once again so as to extend the boundaries of Hindudom right up to the Hindukush!!!

III

Our immediate programme

Without touching the day-to-day activities in hundred and one directions which the Hindu Mahasabha branches have to carry on all over the country in connection with *shuddhi*, removal of untouchability, meeting the local needs and suppression of the local grievances of the Hindus in every town and village, the routine of propagandistic work, the conference, meetings, tours, and such all other organisational and *sangathanist* activities, I want to emphasise here categorically the only two most outstanding and urgent items on which for the next few years all Hindu *sangathanists* must concentrate their attention and their energy. The first of these items constitutes the electoral plank of the Hindusabha platform and the second, the militarising one.

The Hindu electorate must vote for those Hindus who stand openly on a Hindu Mahasabha ticket under the Hindu flag and pledge to guard Hindu interests. Thereby alone they will invest the Hindu Mahasabha with an undeniable status as the first and the foremost representative body of the Hindus and the Hindus would be able to capture whatever political power there exists today and is bound to be secured in future in the legislatures. Unless and until the Congress is not deprived of the right of representing the Hindus in the legislatures it is dead certain that the special interests of the Hindus and the Hindus must go to the wall in the long run.

There is pan-Hindu issue involved in every electoral contest

So long as the electorates are based on communal distinctions the Hindus can never have their special interests and aspirations represented in the legislatures unless and until they elect only those candidates who stand on a clear-cut Hindu Mahasabha ticket, who owe no allegiance to any organisation which is not pledged wholly and solely to safeguard and promote the special interests of the Hindudom as a whole. To the Hindus all over India, there can be no distinction between the so-called national interest and the Hindu interest. Because what is after all the ideology the Hindu Mahasabha represents?

Independence of India, indivisibility of India, representation in proportion to the population strength, public services to go by merit alone and the fundamental rights of freedom of worship, language, script, etc. guaranteed to all citizens alike are some of the basic principles on which the Hindu Mahasabha takes its stand. It realises that the best interests of the Hindus themselves demand under the present circumstances that the Indian nation and the Indian state should be based on these fundamental foundations.

The conception of any genuine nationality also, that takes no account of any communal or creedal super-arrogation into consideration, can go no further. That is why, the Hindu Mahasabha claims that there can be no conflict or clash between Hindu interests and interests of the Indian nation as a whole.

The Hindu Mahasabha seeks not an inch more than what is legitimately due to it or than what it is willing to concede to all non-Hindu minorities in India in strict proportion of their population strength. But, it follows from this very just and legitimate conception of true nationalism that the Hindu Mahasabha should not yield an inch of what is legitimately due to the Hindus on ground of national equity to the Moslems or anyone else simply because they do not happen to be Hindus. But, the Congress, the Forward Bloc and all such organisations in India have sinned against this conception of real nationality under the false notion of geographical nationality. They have a set ideology and policy which raise betrayal of Hindu rights to the pedestal of patriotic virtue! To prove that they are above communal level the Hindu leaders and followers belonging to these organisations hesitate even to claim themselves as representative of Hindus!

But, perversely enough they do not hesitate to seek elections at the hands of communal electorates! They thereby betray both their national labels as well as the interests of the Hindu electorates who elect them to represent and guard the special rights of Hindus.

If the Congress or the Forward Bloc do not want to call themselves as representative bodies of the Hindus alone and claim to represent the Indian nation as a whole, the only logical and honest policy for them would be not to seek election on behalf of the Hindu electorate alone as they invariably do at present. So long as the electorates are divided communally, these bodies who call themselves national should refuse to stand for election on behalf of any of those communal electorates. They should wait till a real national electorate is ushered into being.

But, this double dealing and misguided policy on the part of the Congress or the Forward Bloc or any of these so-called national bodies have done an incalculable harm both to the Hindu interests and the national interests as well. The result of this pseudo-nationalistic error on the part of the Hindu Congressites with all its blocs and their heads left the Hindus entirely unrepresented as Hindus all round.

On the other hand, the Moslem representatives in the assembly, in the board, at the Round Table Conferences and at all such vital centres get represented by the Moslem Leaguers or by those Moslems who are pledged to Moslem electorates openly and whole-heartedly to safeguard and promote Moslem interests even to an overwhelmingly aggressive degree.

And, on the other hand, the Congressites and the Forward Blocists and all such bodies duped by the pseudo-nationalistic mentality get themselves elected on behalf of the Hindu electorate as its representatives but when in the legislature or in a Round Table Conferences or even in the day-to-day politics, etc., whenever questions of Hindu interests arise, they refuse to advocate the Hindu cause and even feel themselves insulted if the government takes them as the representatives of the Hindu electorate. In the case of the partition of Sindh, the Communal Award, down to the question of Census this year when Mr. Kripalani declared that the Census being a communal question, the Congress had to do nothing with it, the Hindu interests were actually betrayed in hundreds and hundreds of cases by these pseudo-nationalistic organisations in spite of the fact that they got themselves elected on behalf of the Hindu electorates. I know it personally that some of the foremost leaders of the Forward Bloc were eager only last year to placate the Muslim League at a larger sacrifice of the Hindu interests than even the official section of the Congress did, so that anyhow they must represent to the government a Hindu-Muslim pact. The motives of the leaders of these pseudo-nationalistic organisations were above any personal interests and were even patriotic, but, patriots can also be befooled and betrayed into a suicidal policy. But, whether their policy or their ideology be the cause, the results are what matters most to the Hindus who have been victimised and will continue to get victimised so long as the Hindu electorate persists in the suicidal folly of electing the candidates who have pledged to the ideology and discipline of these pseudo-nationalistic bodies.

It is not enough that some individual candidate on the Congress or Forward Bloc ticket, promises to safeguard Hindu interests, if he is elected by the Hindu electorate for the simple reason that he can never be in a position to do that in spite of himself so long as he is bound to the wheel of the pseudo-nationalistic ideology and policy and discipline of his party, whether it be the Congress or the Forward Bloc.

I affirm that under these circumstances the most effective and the easiest way for those Hindus who feel that Hindudom has a right to be free, flourishing and powerful in their own fatherland and holyland must elect only those representatives on behalf of the Hindu electorate who stand on the Hindu Mahasabha ticket and are consequently pledged and bound uncompromisingly to safeguard and promote Hindu interests under the lead of the Hindu Mahasabha.

As shown above, the ideology and policy of the Hindu Mahasabha is genuinely national. Consequently, in electing the candidate on Hindu Mahasabha ticket, the Hindu electorate can serve and safeguard both their national interests in general as well as their special interests as Hindus in particular. In fact for a Hindu owning the Hindu Mahasabha ideology, there can be no distinction whatsoever between his Hindu interest and his national interest.

But, in electing a candidate who is bound to the ticket of any of the pseudo-nationalistic bodies like the Congress or the Forward Bloc, the Hindu electorate is sure to run the risk of having the special interests of the Hindus knowingly or unknowingly betrayed and even the genuinely Indian national interest hazarded.

I, therefore, call upon all Hindus to follow determinedly the only policy that can save them as effectively as possible under the present circumstances—the policy of electing as their representatives only those candidates who stand on the Hindu Mahasabha tickets or are backed by it. Thereby alone the government will be compelled to recognise the Hindu Mahasabha as the only representative body of Hindudom as a whole and the Congress will be deprived of any legal or legitimate right to speak on behalf of the Hindus.

The government maintains that the Congress cannot represent the Moslems on the unchallengeable ground that the Moslem electorate never votes for a Congress candidate, but votes unfailingly for a

Moslem who is pledged openly to guard Moslem interest and owes no allegiance to any pseudo-nationalistic body. Consequently, if the Hindu electorate which makes it a point never to vote for any candidate who stands on the Congress ticket or the Forward Bloc ticket or the ticket of any pesudo-nationalistic body, the claim of the Hindu Mahasabha to represent Hindu interests will be legally and legitimately established. These elections are a challenge thrown by the government to the Hindu electorate to prove that Hindu Mahasabha represents them and the Congress can no longer sign any pacts like the Communal Award or the Pakistan that is threatening to come into being to the detriment of the Hindu. Conferences to frame the future constitution of India will soon be summoned. If the Hindu Mahasabha can pass the acid test at her polls all over India and has its candidates returned by the Hindus as their accredited representatives, the government will be compelled to recognise the position of the Hindu Mahasabha on par with the Moslem League in these conferences. Then no blank cheques, no Communal Awards, no Pakistan scheme, no weightages can be binding on the Hindus simply because the Congress signs them. The religious, the political and the economical interests, the culture, the language, the script, the honour and the whole future of the Hindu race and the Hindu nation will be safe in the hands of the Hindu Mahasabha and no constitution or law or understanding can be binding on the Hindus unless and until it is signed by the Hindu Mahasabha.

If but the Hindu electorate returns only the Hindu Mahasabha representatives to the legislatures, there will be in almost all provinces Hindu *Sangathanists* ministries formed, pledged to safeguard and promote Hindu interests openly and uncompromisingly and even in the Hindu minority provinces powerful Hindu *Sangathanists* opposition parties in the legislatures will be in a position to exercise an effective check on the Moslem ministries to defeat their anti-Hindu aggressions. Consequently, I call upon the Hindus all over India to realise the significance of this pan-Hindu aspect in all future electoral campaigns.

The second most important and urgent item on which the Hindu *sangathanists* all over India must bend all their energies and activities is the programme for the militarisation of the Hindus. The war which has now reached our shores directly constitutes at once a danger and an opportunity which both render it imperative that the militarisation movement must be intensified and every branch of the Hindu Mahasabha in every town and village must actively engage itself in rousing the Hindu people to join the army, navy, the aerial forces and the different war-craft manufactories.

Japan's entry into the war against Britain and the United States need not cause any change in the attitude taken by the Hindu Mahasabha towards war efforts calculated to contribute to Indian defence. The Hindu Mahasabha holds fast to the belief that, just as Britain, Germany, Italy, America or even Russia have gone to war with no altruistic aim but only in pursuance of their own national interests, Japan too proves no exception so far as the motive which drove her to the war is concerned.

When every nation in the world is following the policy of self-interest and self-aggrandisement, India too must adopt a policy dictated solely by the interest of promoting her own interest, present and future. From this point of view, situated as we Hindus are at present, our best national interest demands that so far as India's defence is concerned, Hindudom must ally unhesitatingly in a spirit of responsive co-operation with the war effort of the Indian Government insofar as it is consistent with Hindu interests, by joining the army, navy and the aerial forces in as large a number as possible and by securing an entry into all ordnance, ammunition and war-craft factories.

Militarisation and industrialisation of our Hindu nation ought to be the first two immediate objectives which we must pursue and secure to the best of our power, if we want to utilise the war situation in the world as effectively as possible to defend the Hindu interest.

Again it must be noted that Japan's entry into the war has exposed us directly and immediately to the attack by Britain's enemies. Consequently, whether we like it or not, we shall have to defend our own hearth and home against the ravages of the war and this can only be done by intensifying the government's war effort to defend India. Hindu Mahasabha must, therefore, rouse Hindus especially in the provinces of Bengal and Assam as effectively as possible to enter the military forces of all arms without losing a single minute.

IV

If but you act according to these instructions, I guarantee, Oh Hindus, that the future of our Hindu race, our religion and of our nation cannot fail to be even more glorious than our ancient past had been. These two steps which I have emphasised above: namely, by voting at the polls for the Hindu ticket alone and by not casting a single Hindu vote for the Congress to capture the political power and the governmental machinery in the land that exists today and secondly, to flood the army, the navy and the aerial forces with millions of Hindu warriors with Hindu *sangathanist* hearts—these two steps are but the first two steps and yet they shall give you such an immediate and high lift that at the end of the next five years, you will find the political situation in India inevitably dominated by the Hindu thought, led by the Hindu hand, and more or less dictated by the Hindu will.

The great war today has dwarfed all other issues and no one can say with certainty who will emerge successful out of this world chaos. But one thing can still be said as the most probable to happen that if but the Hindus stick to this immediate programme and take advantage to the fullest extent possible of the war situation with the Hindu *sangathanist* ideal full in view, pressing on the movement for the militarisation of the Hindu race, then our Hindu nation is bound to emerge far more powerful, consolidated and situated in an incomparably more advantageous position to face issues after the war, whether it be an internal anti-Hindu civil war or a constitutional crisis or an armed revolution.

Whatever, again, be the position and the fate of nations after the war, today under the present circumstances, taking all things together, the only feasible and relatively beneficial attitude which the Hindu *sangathanists* can take up is doubtless to ally ourselves actively with the British Government on the point of Indian defence, provided always that we can do so without being compelled to betray the Hindu cause.

If ever the saying was true that the darkest hour of the night is nearer the golden rise of the morn, it holds good today. The war that has approached our shores from the East and may threaten us in due course even from the West is a danger which may prove unparalleled in its magnitude, ravages and results. But, it is also bound to break into a new day for the world and there are no signs wanting to show us that not only a newer but a better order may ensue out of this world chaos. Those who have lost all may gain much in the end. Let us also bide our time and pray and act for the best.

□

24th Session, Cawnpore—1942

Delegates to and Members of the Hindu Mahasabha,

You have really overwhelmed me with kindness in appreciating my services, quite limited though they are, so highly as to elect me in an unbroken succession for the sixth time to the presidentship of the All-India Hindu Mahasabha, the highest office of honour and duty which lies at the disposal of Hindudom today. If I too on my part do not shirk to accept this responsibility for the present, in spite of the most willing resignations tendered by me from time to time requesting you to relieve me of this post in view of my ailing health, it is only due to the fact that forces from outside the camp of the Hindu Mahasabha have actually been conspiring first to waylay the Mahasabha and then capture it by some crafty *coup d'etat*. Some of them try to browbeat it into submission, others are scheming to kill it with kindness and all of them want it to betray the Hindu ideology and those fundamental principles of independence and integrity of Hindusthan, the holyland and fatherland of us Hindus, which alone form both the charter and the vindication of its existence apart from and independent of the Congress, as the foremost representative organisation of Hindudom as a whole. It is consequently the imperative duty of each and all of us Hindu *sangathanists*, on whom has fallen in this generation the duty to protect Hindudom and this Mahasabha, this holy shrine of our Hindu nation, to stand on guard at each of its gates and serve the post allotted to each with unswerving fidelity. It is this special emergency that has made me take up this post which you have all summoned me again to hold.

2. Before I proceed, I must first take a rapid review of some leading events which happened during this year in connection with the Hindu Mahasabha so as to enable us to realise more precisely where we stand today and what should be our immediate programme.

This year opened just when we were in the very thick of the Bhagalpur civil resistance campaign. The most important aspect of the struggle which constitutes an abiding source of strength and self-confidence to our people is the fact that we Hindus could present a united Hindu front and demonstrated beyond cavil or criticism that in spite of castes or creeds, sects and sections, Hindudom as a whole does still pulsate with a common national being. That pan-Hindu consciousness, which the Hindu Mahasabha has so long been striving to create, has at last become a living reality, forceful and organised enough to resist and at times even to cow down the anti-Hindu forces, which held their sway unchallenged for such a long time in the past. From our esteemed leader, Dr. Syama Prasad Mookerji down to those heroic souls, who laid their lives unknown to fame by name, thousands and thousands of Hindu Sangathanists—Rajas and *Raises*, millionaires and millhands, ex-ministers and M.L.A.s, Sanatanists, Sikhs, Jains and Aryans—all rushed to Bhagalpur from every corner of India animated by the common urge to defend the honour of the pan-Hindu flag. The struggle was not restricted to Bhagalpur alone, but ultimately spread all over the six districts of Bihar which came under the ban and its shocks were felt throughout India. They faced *lathicharges* which were the order of the day. The armed mounted forces of the government charged the processionists and civil resisters at various places, trampling men, women and children under the hoofs of their horses. Organised firing was resorted to in cities and towns and even villages. The Hindu civil resisters faced it all with unabated zeal in defending the honour of the Hindu colours and in winning the goal which was the objective at issue. There can be no exaggeration in proclaiming that the 23rd session of the Hindu Mahasabha held at Bhagalpur despite the government ban proved to be the most momentous and the most successful one of all the annual sessions held till then by any all-India organisation, including the Congress in the modern history of India.

I shall be failing in my duty, if I, as the president, do not express on behalf of this session our deepest gratitude to all those who took part in the Bhagalpur *dharma yuddha* as soldiers in the spirit of crusaders, although the Hindu Mahasabha has nothing else to offer to mark its appreciation of their services but the crown of thorns of martyrdom to those heroes, who laid down their lives in the struggle and their very wounds to those thousands of soldiers who were wounded as the 'iron crosses' they won.

The second aspect of the struggle which must be noted here is the fact that it was fought in defence of Hindu rights as Hindu rights and under the unalloyed Hindu colours. The Nizam's civil resistance movement and this Bhagalpur campaign wherein millions of Hindus rose in protest against the humiliation of the Hindu flag drove the last nail in the coffin of that pseudo-Nationalism which kept dominating the Hindu mind for the last 30 years or so, had penalised an agitation to uphold any special rights of the Hindus as a 'national' sin, throttled the Hindu voice, suppressed the Hindu spirit, reduced the Hindus to political orphans in this land.

These struggles did also prove to all concerned that the Hindu Mahasabha was not only powerful enough to raise a mass movement of legitimate resistance on an all-India scale in defence of Hindu rights, but had a better tactical sense of timing and conducting them strategically to an assured success.

3. Within a couple of months of the cessation of the Bhagalpur struggle, the all-India committee of the Mahasabha was held in February in Lucknow and passed off successfully in spite of the riotous opposition staged by the Moslems there.

4. Then came the Cripps Mission at the end of March The British Government had been for years feigning to believe that the Congress represented the Hindus, the Moslem League represented the Moslems and consequently the political equation followed inevitably that the Congress and the League together represented all India. But in the meanwhile, the Hindu Mahasabha had established itself so firmly as a new political power in the land, challenging both the Congress and the League, whenever Hindu interest demanded it, that the British Government had to recognise the Mahasabha, by the time Cripps Mission came, as one of the three outstanding All-India organisations and as the foremost accredited representative body of Hindudom as a whole. To the Congress and many other parties and leaders, the Cripps scheme seemed at first sight sufficiently alluring to undertake a hopeful survey to discover confidently some oases in that political Sahara. It was the Hindu Mahasabha alone which publicly declared just at the first glance of the scheme that Sir Strafford wanted really to play to the American gallery and carried on those endless negotiations with the

Indian politicians just to make them play the tune he called Not only that, but the Mahasabha unerringly and immediately discerned and pointed out the cloven foot concealed under a heap of roses on which the scheme really stood. It was the clause laying down the condition that the declaration of freedom of India could be made by Great Britain only if the Hindus admitted the principle that provinces should be allowed to have the right of self-determination by their own majority to secede from the Central Indian Government and even to set themselves up as states independent of it. This clause constituted a veritable dagger aimed at the heart of the integrity of Hindusthan as an indivisible nation and a centralised state. The Hindu Mahasabha rejected it unceremoniously and in rejecting the clause, it had to reject the scheme in toto. While all other parties, including the Congress had tacitly accepted the clause and swallowing that camel, kept straining at the gnats of portfolios here and there, this total rejection of the scheme by the Hindu Mahasabha initialised at a stroke the attention of the whole nation in general and the Hindus in particular on the real point that nullified most—while the independence of India was still floating in the hazy clouds of promises alone, the integrity of India was in imminent danger of being stabbed in the back. The lead that the Mahasabha gave by rejecting the scheme at a stroke on this issue was followed after some fuss of negotiations by almost all parties in the land under this or that excuse.

The Working Committee which was immediately held regarding the Cripps scheme reasserted in its resolution that in view of the rapid development in the political situation in the world, nothing short of an immediate and unconditional declaration of India's independence could animate and enthuse the whole country to mobilise its full and willing fighting strength, both in men and the materials to fight out the war which then would have been our own concern as truly as it was in the case of the British people.

5. It was necessary to demonstrate that the Hindu Sanghatanist world was solidly behind the Hindu Mahasabha on these two fundamental points which compelled the Mahasabha to reject the Cripps scheme. It was, therefore, decided that an anti-Pakistan day should be observed throughout India by the Hindus under the pan-Hindu colours on the 10th of May 1942, which being the anniversary of the national rising of 1857, had been annually celebrated by the Hindu Mahasabha as the Independence Day. Accordingly, this day was observed throughout India

under the auspices of Hindu Mahasabha with intense enthusiasm on an unprecedented scale. Jammu, Peshawar, Poona, Amritsar, Lahore, Delhi, Lucknow, Patna, Calcutta, Bombay, Nagpur down to Madras—almost all capital cities and hundreds of towns and villages held innumerable meetings which were altogether attended on that evening by millions and millions of Hindus who took up a public pledge to support the Hindu Mahasabha and to stand by the two fundamental principles on which it has taken its stand—the independence and the integrity of Hindusthan. Although the Moslems were conducting without let or hindrance a pro-Pakistan campaign and men like Mr. Rajagopalachari were allowed to preach vivisection of Hindusthan as freely as they liked, an illegitimate and one-sided ban was placed on the anti-Pakistan demonstrations at places like Patna, Arrah and others on this all-India anti-Pakistan day. But, the Hindu Mahasabha defied those unjust bans, took out their processions and held meetings even though hundreds of them got arrested for the only fault of asserting their basic civic rights. The determination with which Hindudom as a whole expressed on this day its uncompromising opposition to any scheme which involved the granting to the provinces the right of secession, proved once more the strength of the hold the Hindu Mahasabha had come to exercise on Hindu mind and how it had, thus, established its right to represent genuine Hindu feeling far more correctly and effectively than the self-styled Indian National Congress could ever do.

6. The Congress, in the meanwhile, was rapidly on the other hand, yielding to the pressure of the Moslems and had already got itself committed to the promise that it would not oppose the grant to provinces to secede if the Moslems insisted on it. As if the Moslems had not already insisted on it uncompromisingly enough to brow-beat the Congress itself into submission—Mr. Rajagopalachari in particular got simply possessed of the Pakistani spirit. He actually planned a triumphal tour to convert the benighted Hindu all over India to his new faith. He left Madras and selected his own presidency at the outset to infect with the Pakistani epidemic, but the Mahasabhaists were after everywhere and gave him a hot chase throughout his tour from Madras to Bombay. Dharmaveer Dr. Moonje and Prof. Deshpande, the indomitable champion of the Hindu cause who has only recently been arrested under the Defence of India Act, were deputed to tour the Madras Presidency and there, along with the veteran Hindu Mahasabha

leader Dr. Varadrajalu Naidu, they dislodged Rajaji so completely from every platform that like the proverbial hare 'whom hounds and horns pursue', even the redoubtable Rajaji, in spite of the obliging blessing and public sympathies of Gandhiji himself, had to return discomfited 'back to the place from whence at first he flew'. Since then, he seems to have left the forum and taken to his table to busy himself with the more congenial task of issuing statements after statements to convince the benighted Hindus that the Moslem demands were just, that Pakistan was the key to *swaraj*; two and two do not make four but five!

Just then the Congress almost made it clear that it meant to start some kind of civil resistance movement, under the usual non-violent dictatorship of Gandhiji. The Hindu *sabhaists* from all parts of India grew naturally anxious to know what attitude they should adopt towards this Congressite movement which was meant to order Great Britain straightway to 'Quit India' forthwith. Now, it was the duty of every Indian patriot and especially of a Hindu patriot to join a movement which had for its goal the absolute political independence of Hindusthan. But, the question of timing and the ways and means were also of outstanding importance. Even leaving it all aside, the goal to be achieved by any movement was the question of questions which must be decided to begin with. You must know before you go to fight the objective for which you have to fight. The Congress had made it crystal clear by that time that it was ready to agree even to vivisect India as an organic and centralised state in order to placate the Moslems and to persuade them to join the movement. Then again, 'Quit India' was not the only demand which they advanced; but inconsistently enough, they added to it a rider which demanded of Great Britain that though the British should leave India yet they must retain their British forces and even the American forces behind to protect India against the Axis Powers invading her. In short, the war-cry of the Congress movement came to *'Quit India but keep the British Army here and the Americans to boot!.'* And the price of the movement for Indian independence was the vivisection of Indian integrity!! Under such circumstances, it became quite necessary to clear up the issue before the Hindu Mahasabha got committed to any such movement even though it was primarily meant for freedom of India, which was the proclaimed demand of the Hindu Mahasabha itself on its own initiative. Consequently, I laid down the following conditions in my speech at a mammoth meeting in Poona on the Bajirao Maidan on the 2nd of August, the report of which was broadcast and published not only in the Indian press but by the foreign press also, before the A.I.C.C. met in Bombay.

The leading conditions were as follows: (a) The Congress should guarantee the integrity of Hindusthan from the Indus to the seas as an organic nation and an internal centralised state, (b) The Congress should, therefore, openly repudiate the granting of any right to the provinces to secede, (c) Representation in the legislatures, etc. should be in proportion to the population of the majority and the minorities, (d) Public services should go by merit alone, (e) That the Hindu Mahasabha should be recognised as the representative body of Hindudom and consequently no step should be taken affecting Hindu rights without its consultation and sanction, (f) All minorities should be given effective safeguards to protect their language, religion, culture, etc., but none of them should be allowed to create 'a state within a state' as the League of Nations put it, or to encroach upon the legitimate rights of the majority as defined above, (g) The residuary powers should be vested in the Central Government.

Had the Congress agreed to these conditions, the Hindu Mahasabha could have considered whether to co-operate with it on any reasonable lines of action. These conditions were so indisputably national that the Indian National Congress, in fact, ought to have been the first instead of the Hindu Mahasabha, to proclaim them, if it was genuinely and justly representing the Indian nation as a whole. But, the Congress refused stubbornly to have anything to do with these conditions. Nay, in their resolution at Bombay, the A.I.C.C. actually declared that the residuary powers shall be vested in the provincial governments instead of the Central, in addition to the concession the Congress had already made to the Pakistanis of the principle of provincial self-determination to secede. The climax came when Gandhiji, after being proclaimed as the de fecto dictator of the Congress wrote an authoritative letter to reassure Mr. Jinnah of his readiness to hand over the whole Government of India including the Indian states to the Moslem League. I quote the relevant passage from the letter itself:

> 'In all sincerity, let me explain it again that if the Moslem League co-operated with the Congress for immediate independence, subject, of course, to the provision that independent India will permit the operation of the allied armies in order to check Axis aggression and

thus to help China and Russia, the Congress will have no objection to the British Government transfering all the powers it today exercises to the Moslem League on behalf of the whole of India, including the so-called Indian India. The Congress will not only not obstruct any government which the Moslem League may form on behalf of the people, but will even join the government. This is meant in all seriousness and sincerity.'

—M. K. Gandhi

Comments are superfluous. The betrayal of Hindu rights or genuine nationality could have gone no further. Such a letter would have been burnt in protest from thousand platforms throughout India by the enraged Hindu Sangathanist world, had not restraining counsel prevailed in view of the patriotic objective at issue and had we not been passing through abnormal times. Were the Hindu Mahasabhaists asked deliberately to join a fight whose price and inevitable consequences was the vivisection of their own motherland and holyland? Then again there were the tactical questions which were also of no less importance regarding the timing, the ways and the means and above all, the effectiveness which we could depend upon on under sane calculations. This was the crucial and fundamental issue which made the Mahasabhaists in general feel duty-bound not to identify themselves entirely with the Congress movement as it was then vaguely contemplated.

Since then, of course, the Congressites themselves have been disowning avowedly their connection with the present wave of violent disturbances passing over the country. Consequently we need not take upon ourselves the responsibility of labelling it all as a Congress movement and the question of joining it or otherwise does not arise at all so far as the point under discussion is concerned.

7. Then all of a sudden, several hundreds of patriotic Congress leaders, including Mahatma Gandhiji were arrested and later on a violent wave of popular discontent and governmental repression of it threw the whole country into turmoil. Today thousands of our Hindu brethren, Congressites and non-Congressites have already suffered or are suffering untold calamities from detention to death. They are all our kith and kin and our deepest sympathies cannot but go out to them in grateful appreciation of the fact that they have faced these sufferings from a patriotic motive or as the result of the patriotic struggle. Unscrupulous *goondaism* which is inevitably let loose in such great commotions cannot

of course deserve any sympathy. But, even the British Government or the British public could not but admit that the struggle was essentially the struggle of the people for the freedom of their country. If that be a guilt, then we have all been participating in it and are proud to be guilty of it.

8. But, patriotism itself demands that it is a national duty of all of us Hindus to see to it that sympathy with patriotic sufferings must not be allowed to get the better of our judgement and drive us headlong and blindfolded on a path which we conscientiously believe to be detrimental to the best interest of our Hindu nation. To make a common cause on a wrong issue or a line of action which is bound to lead to national 'disaster,' simply to present a 'united front' is not the essence of patriotism, but amounts to a betrayal of national duty. It will be well of those who criticise the Hindu Mahasabha either through indiscretion or impudence for not following the Congress rightly or wrongly for the sake of unity and because the Congress was actuated by patriotic motive, would do well to remember that patriots also are no exception to the general rule that it is human to err. Those who sincerely think that a particular line of action is detrimental to the nation and therefore reject it and choose to serve it in the way and with the means they are convinced to be more effective under the given circumstances to realise a common ideal, cannot be deemed on that ground only as less patriotic than those who acted otherwise. It is regrettable, however, that forgetting this fact, the Congressite press day in and day out have been trying to bring the Hindu Mahasabha into disrepute. Their criticism when reasonable and decent could be met by reasons given above. But, the larger part of the Congressite press and propaganda has thrown decency of criticism to the winds and is growing malicious and mad. In righteous defence of the Hindu Mahasabha such criticism must be challenged and checked. Some of these critics seem to be irritated at the thought that the leaders of the Hindu Mahasabha did not jump over the walls of the jail the very day Gandhiji and others were arrested for raising such a momentous cry as 'Quit India but keep your army here'. So far as the 'Quit India' is concerned, it is enough to point out that some of the outstanding Mahasabha leaders and followers today had been amongst those handful of revolutionists, who publicly raised the standard of Indian independence for the first time in current History and rose in an armed revolt when Gandhiji and some of the present

leaders of the Congress were singing Hallelujahs to the British Empire, extolling its blessings and thinking it their duty as loyal citizens and subjects of that Empire to take its side against Zulus and the Boer who were fighting for their freedom. When further on as a consequence of their revolutionary activities, these Hindu *Sabhaists* of today had some of them to stand under the shadow of the gallows and others were undergoing the sentences of transportation for life, rotting in Andamanese dungeons for decades on decades, if we reason as you do now, were not the present outstanding Congress leaders including Gandhiji 'guilty' for not making a common cause with the revolutionists merely for the sake of 'united front' and for not seeking the gallows or getting themselves locked in the cellular jails in the Andamans? Coming nearer, what have you to say regarding the Congress when it not only kept itself at a respectable distance from imprisonment, but actually joined hands with the Nizam and took up a pledge 'not to embarrass His Exalted Highness' while thousands of Hindu Sangathanists were carrying on a deadly struggle with the Nizam for the most legitimate rights of the Hindus and were facing *lathicharges*, imprisonment and tortures at the hands of the Nizam's government? Far from sharing these sufferings with the Hindu *Sangathanists*, were not the leaders and followers of the Congress strutting about as ministers of provinces under the British Crown, some drawing fat pays, others rolling in the lap of luxury? And what about Bhagalpur? When for the defence of fundamental civil liberties of freedom of speech and freedom of association not less than one hundred thousand Hindu *Sangathanists* carried on an active struggle with the government of Bihar throughout the six districts which came under the ban, against all the forces which the Bihar Government could draw upon—firings, bayonetting, cavalry charges, not to speak of whippings, imprisonments, etc.—did not the Congressites stand totally unconcerned and aloof without uttering a word of sympathy with the struggle for civic liberty which the Hindu *Sangathanists* were carrying on against the foreign government or of condemnation of that government?

If they try to explain and justify this conduct on the part of the Congressites as not due to want of public spirit or to a lack of courage, but due to an honest difference of opinion on patriotic grounds as to the line of action and principles which the Congress had with the Hindu Mahasabhaists and consequently attempt to justify the Congress on not presenting a 'united front' at the cost of national good as Congressites interpreted it by joining the Hindu Mahasabha, then they should have sense enough to perceive that very justification holds good in the case of the Hindu Mahasabha too because they too did not like to be dragged as moral slaves by whatever the Congress resolution decreed or movement demanded.

Similarly, another argument which forms the stock-in-trade of the libellous criticism and propaganda of the Congressites with regard to the policy of the Hindu Mahasabha of occupying centres of political power, howsoever limited it be, springs back upon themselves and unlike the boomerang, hits only themselves hard. The Hindu Mahasabha through its elected or supported representatives has now come to occupy responsible positions in political council, committees, ministries, legislatures, municipalities and such other centres of political power and it is this fact which has pre-eminently contributed to the outstanding political importance which the Mahasabha and, through it Hindudom as a whole, has come to attain throughout India as never before. It is human that some of the unemployed Congressites should get irritated to find that so many of the 'Jobs' should have fallen into other hands and should make them accuse the Hindu *Sangathanists* as mere 'job-hunters'. We pity them for their irritation. But we cannot excuse them for making a virtue of necessity and go about posing as so many suffering saints who never cared a fig for these very worldly and servile 'jobs'.

For, was it not only the other day that the Congress from one end of India to the other went on such 'job-hunting? They agreed to act as ministers—not as kings, but servilely enough as ministers—to the Governors, who, in their turn, were servants of the British Crown. They, who now accuse the Hindu *sabhaists* as helping imperialism took oaths of allegiance to the British Imperial Crown, accepted salaries, invited whole troops of their followers and hangers-on to get the loaves and fishes of the offices, posts and positions distributed only among themselves. They could do only those things which the Governors permitted at their pleasure in the last resort. They laboured under the constitution which they had pretended to despise. Whenever they failed to satisfy this or that section of public, they either pointed out to the limitations under which they held office or they sallied out, firing and delivering *lathi* charges on those of their countrymen who disobeyed them or picketted them. If anybody fasted at their doors in protest of their actions, they told him bluntly, 'You may lie there comfortably till you die, I must attend my office and do my duty as I choose.' Did not Rajagopalachari himself, the foremost of those ministers, who 'followed the Mahatma', tell the world in blunt accents in general justification of the actions of the Congress government that the first duty of the government was to govern!

Do you condemn the Congress for this 'job-hunting' and rough-riding? Or do you justify all this as patriotic? Do the Congressites explain it all away on the ground that larger public interest demanded that even under limitations, the constitution should be worked out to squeeze whatever public good you can get out of it? If you say 'yes' to the latter, then in justifying yourselves, you justify the Hindu Mahasabha too in its policy of capturing centres of political power, limited though it be to begin with and standing on that point of vantage, try to leap over and occupy more effective centres of power.

The Hindu Mahasabha holds that the leading principle of all practical politics is the policy of responsive co-operation. And in virtue of it, it believes that all those Hindu Sangathanists who are working as councillors, ministers, legislators, ministers and conducting Municipal or any public bodies with a view to utilise those centres of governmental power to safeguard and even promote the legitimate interests of the Hindus without, of course, encroaching on the legitimate interests of others, are rendering a highly patriotic service to our Nation. Knowing the limitations under which they work, the Mahasabha only expects them to do whatever good they can under the circumstances and if they do not fail to do that much, it would thank them for having acquitted themselves well. *The limitations are bound to get themselves limited step by step till they get altogether eliminated. The policy of responsive co-operation which covers the whole gamut of patriotic activities from unconditional co-operation right up to active and even armed resistance, will also keep adapting itself to the exigencies of the time, resources at our disposal and dictates of our national interests.*

It must be remembered in this connection that if there be any 'job-hunters', it is precisely these penny-a-liners who betray such a low taste in their criticism of the Mahasabha and happen to conduct the majority of Congressite second rate sheets and owing to that very fact are within easy reach of the masses. The majority of them, we all know, have not suffered a scratch throughout their life in any patriotic movement and would write for any other party if but they are more sumptuously paid. Many of them are actually known to have done so. It becomes inevitable, therefore, in defence of the Hindu cause that from time to time they too must be shown their proper place.

But, I shall do injustice to myself if I fail to make it clear that my criticism against this type of a Congressite does not and cannot mean that all Congressites are equally blind to reason or are deliberately bent on harming Hindu interest or on humiliating Hindu honour which Hindus as they themselves are, cannot but be their own interest and honour.

Nay, I know that many of these patriotic Congressites do actually appreciate the merits of the Hindu Mahasabha as well. Their racial pride as Hindu gets wounded whenever the Congress goes wrong and sacrifices the most legitimate Hindu interests and makes the Hindu undergo most cowardly surrenders. The very fact that thousands of devoted workers and several all-India leaders, who have now rallied devotedly round the pan-Hindu standard had once been actively and prominently working in the Congress camp, is enough to bear out this truth that there are and must be thousands of Hindus in the Congress camp who cannot bear to see the Hindu cause anathematised by the Congress but who nevertheless have not yet got rid of the habitual reluctance to get out of the Congress rut and come openly out of it.

But, this past experience makes me feel more or less confident that thousands of these of my Hindu brethren who are proud of their race, religion and their motherland of the *rishis* and the *avatars*, will have to leave the Congress before long through the very urge of their conscience and can find them but one path to go ahead in defence of Hindutva—the path that leads to that Hindu Mahasabha shrine.

9. As soon as the Congress was removed from the political field as an open organisation under the governmental ban, the Hindu Mahasabha alone was left to take up the task of conducting whatever Indian national activities lay within its scope. For, to call upon the Moslem League to lead any Indian national movement would have rightly enough been taken as an insult by it just as to call the Congress a Hindu body was perversely enough used to be taken by it as an insult. For, India to the Moslem League was but a sub-continent, no nation at all. But, the Hindu Mahasabha believes in an integral Indian nation

even more intensely than the Indian National Congress itself. The first national point that required immediate attention at that time was to expose the hollowness of the British propaganda which wanted the world to believe that the Cripps scheme failed not so much owing to the unwillingness of the British to part with power as to the internecine conflicts of the Indian people. The Cripps scheme was held dazzling before the world as a veritable Magna Carta, conferring on India all that could be offered to liberate a people from political slavery and pointing out to it, the British press and propaganda called upon the world to witness how higher constitutions bestowed upon peoples not politically developed enough to deserve them serve only to worsen their condition. The glorious Magna Carta which wanted to invest India with full freedom proved only an apple of discord. As soon as political power was offered to the Indians, instead of receiving it as a united nation, they sprang at each other's throat, community against community and their ancient civil feuds, instead of being healed, grew only fiercer. There was no united demand and had we not withdrawn that glorious Magna Carta in time, there would have broken up an immediate and bloody civil war. Thus, the British interpreted the episode to India and the world.

That there was and continues to be communal disunity in India need not be denied. Every country had to pass through such phases, including England and America. But the fact that it was the real cause of the withdrawal of the Cripps scheme was a lie and it had to be nailed to the counter, because the British had almost succeeded in duping America and China and even a section in India. The American public and the press which were sympathetic to some extent before the Cripps Mission changed their tone and admitted that England had done all she could and in all sincerity in granting full political freedom to the Indians and that it was really the internal discord amongst the Indians themselves that was responsible for the failure of the scheme.

Above all, in India itself, the Congress and the majority of the Hindus in particular laboured under this supposition that if but we could produce as national demand a united scheme, then it will be simply impossible for England to refuse to grant it. That is why the Congress often went on its knees before the League. That is why so many all-party and non-party conferences had been held. It was necessary, therefore, even to cure the Indians themselves from this self-deception that some strenuous efforts on an all-India scale had to be made.

It was also advisable to find out how far the various parties in India did really differ and whether, on the two or three questions which concerned all alike, some national demand could be framed. It was with this objective in view that the Hindu Mahasabha decided to enter into negotiations with all important political parties and personalities on the three outstanding demands which the Mahasabha had already framed. The immediate declaration of Indian independence; a national government with full powers during the war with the exception of the military portfolio so far as the operative part was concerned and the holding of constitution-framing assembly as soon as the war ceased—formed the leading clauses in this demand.

A special committee was appointed to conduct these negotiations consisting of the president, Dr. Syama Prasad Mookerji, Dr. Moonje, Barrister, N.C. Chatterji, Raja Maheshwar Dayal Seth, Raj Bahadur Meherchand Khanna and Prof. Deshpande. The response that the committee received from different parties and eminent persons was encouraging and spontaneous. Under the able lead of Dr. Syama Prasad Mookerji on whom fell the real burden of carrying the negotiations, the committee succeeded in creating such a wave of enthusiasm all over India that the public attention was centred on this topic only. Representatives of the English, the American, and the Chinese press also took keen interest in the developments and gave prominent publicity in their countries to these efforts of the Mahasabha.

The result also was not quite incommensurate with the troubles taken by the distinguished members of the Hindu Mahasabha Committee and of those Indian organisations and leaders who co-operated with them. Firstly, it was full of significance from the constructive point of view. For, the committee succeeded in producing a national demand on the most crucial issues referred to above, which could not but convince everyone but those who found it inconvenient to get convinced that India as a nation demanded with a united will and voice the declaration on the part of the British Parliament that she should be recognised here and now as an independent nation. When the Hindu Mahasabha—the second great all-India Hindu organisation to quote Lord Devonshire, the present Under Secretary of State for India, with the foremost leaders of our Sikh brotherhood, the president of the Momin Conference and other Moslem organisations, the president of the Christian Federation, the Nationalist League, the Liberal Federation, along with the then provincial ministers of Sind and Bengal and scores of other eminent politicians who had been legislators and administrators and held most responsible positions in the government,—have signed or supported the demand it had every right to claim for itself and to be recognised as being nothing short of a national demand. When you add to it the fact that the Congress resolution too had more or less emphasised the very items, its national character becomes unassailed. It is even pretended that such a demand also falls short of a national demand only because the League or some such section chose to remain aloof, then no demand ever made by any nation could deserve to be called a national one.

It must be remembered that even the national plebiscites on the strength of whose demand the Canadian or the African or the American Federations were formed were not and could not be considered national or univocal on the sole ground that there was not a single citizen or single party opposed to them. Nay, the fact is that in all such national demands or plebiscites, those who voted against them could also count their strength in thousands. *A national demand must always mean the demand of overwhelming majority of citizens or parties forming those nations, irrespective of the dissentient minorities.*

When the Mahasabha succeeded in producing a definite demand signed by such an overwhelming majority, it served to explode the British pretext and had a very salutary effect not only on that large section of Indians themselves, but even on the Chinese, the American and the pro-British foreign press in general which had first acquitted the British for withholding freedom from India and believed that the chaotic disunity in India itself was really responsible for the withdrawal of the Cripps scheme. Many of them changed their opinion, saw through the game and came to the correct judgement that it was really the unwillingness on the part of Great Britain to let go of her hold on India.

As the president of the Hindu Mahasabha, I forwarded this national demand by a cable to the British Prime Minister, the Rt. Hon'ble Mr. Winston Churchill. I received an acknowledgement from him in which the Prime Minister wrote that he noted with appreciation the endeavours of the Hindu Mahasabha to promote unity among the several elements in India's life, but observed that they had not so far resulted in any specific and constructive proposals enjoying the support of all the major parties.

Comments need not be made on this reply as the question is already exhaustively dealt with above. Only one point needs to be touched. The only party in India worth mentioning as a major party that did not support the demand was the Moslem League—not Moslems because we had large Moslem organisations signing the demand. If then, the failure of the League to see eye to eye with all other parties in the land is to disqualify a demand from being national, then it only amounts to invest a fraction of a minority, with a power to veto the will of the overwhelming majority of the nation! Of course, even the League must be knowing that the Prime Minister must have been talking with his tongue in his cheek when he referred to the League with such an awful indispensability! If ever the League asks anything or supports anything which goes against the British interest, even the League cannot be doubting that the Prime Minister will question its right to speak for the Moslems themselves.

The negotiations were also useful to prove the falsity of the dishonest criticisms of the opponents of the Hindu Mahasabha, including the Congressites that it being a communal organisation could have no national programme or policy or could take no national lead. It was made clear that the Hindu Mahasabha was more national in its programme and yet less liable to fall a victim to weak-kneed vagaries, like the Congress or to perverse communalism like the League. In practical politics also, the Mahasabha knows that we must advance through reasonable compromises. Witness the fact that only recently in Sind, the Sind-Hindu *Sabha* on invitation had taken the responsibility of joining hands with the League itself in running the coalition government. The case of Bengal is well known. Wild leaguers whom even the Congress with all its submissiveness could not placate grew quite reasonably compromising and sociable as soon as they came in contact with the Hindu Mahasabha and the coalition government, under the premiership of Mr. Fazlul Huq and the able lead of our esteemed Mahasabha leader Dr. Syama Prasad Mookerji, functioned successfully for a year or so to the benefit of both the communities. Moreover, further events also proved demonstratively that the Hindu Mahasabhaists endeavoured to capture the centres of political power only in public interest and not for the loaves and fishes of the office. Witness the bold and eloquent statement issued by Dr. Mookerji when he threw away the portfolio the moment he saw that the Governor had made it impossible for him to serve the public and continue in the ministry with any degree of self-respect.

10. Even though we do not contribute in the least to the forlorn hope that Americans, Russians or any other foreign nation will risk its own interest and take up cudgels to free India on account of political justice or a high sense of humanity alone, still we cannot altogether dispense with the utility of foreign propaganda, for the very practical reasons, to acquaint the independent nations with the political situation in our country and combat any propaganda set on foot by anti-Hindu parties to mislead their judgement or to secure their sympathies. The very self-interest of each of the nations in the world is so intertwined and got mixed up with the self-interests of others that each of them requires to know and let know the real political situation to the other. Coalitions and counter-coalitions, even though they be based on national self-interest of each nation, could be advantageously formed if each nation knows the correct political situation in all other countries in the world. Ever since the war began, England launched a world-wide propaganda that she was fighting for freedom and democracy all over the world, but the Hindu Mahasabha believed not a word of it and openly said so in its resolutions. England, therefore, had to prove to Americans and others that if she could not free India here and now, it was due to India's own fault. American interest on this and several other grounds required that if India is satisfied it will be an inexhaustible source of men and materials for them to win the war. So, they grew more anxious to study the Indian situation. Before the war broke out, America had some hazy notion that there was a National Congress and the Moslem League. The first was a Hindu body in the main and the League represented the Moslems. Consequently, they thought that the Congress and the League meant the united opinion of the Hindus and the Moslems. They heard now and then something about the Hindu Mahasabha, but they did not know how to squeeze it in between the two. They had not the slightest notion that the Mahasabha had come to occupy an outstanding position as an all-India body.

But, since my cablegram to President Roosevelt, which was featured prominently throughout the American press and through it the world press, the attention of the American public and the press was drawn more pointedly to the Mahasabha and a curiosity grew in foreign countries to know more closely its ideology, position and policy. Several press representatives and public men, who came to study Indian position in general in the year, from America, England and China interviewed the Hindu Mahasabha leaders also. Some of them wrote back to their respective presses, acquainting their public with the ideology and the outstanding position of the Hindu Mahasabha as the representative all-India body of the Hindus, just as the Moslem League was the representative of Moslem interest. A number of cables sent from the presidential office and other Mahasabha centrers on several occasions got good publicity as the American press representatives assured me. Even American film-men got the presidential office and the routine work photoed personally for a movie and I am told that the newsreels are shown on the American screens. At the time of the negotiations also, the foreign press-agents took keen interest and did considerable propaganda to make the voice of the Mahasabha heard outside India. The contact we have thus succeeded in establishing with American, Chinese and even British public men who interviewed personally the President and several other leaders and with the public press overseas, has already grown intimate enough in knowing them realise that any pact signed by the Congress alone will not bind the Hindus, unless and until it is agreed to and sanctioned by the Hindu Mahasabha, the foremost representative body of the Hindus nor can any agreement between the Congress and the League alone be taken as an Indian national agreement if the Hindu Mahasabha is not a party to it. This fact will stand us in good stead at the end of the war when the powers sit together to reshape the map of the world, and if the political constitution of India does form an item on their agenda at all.

11. It was imperative for reasons indicated above that we should send a delegation on behalf of the Hindu Mahasabha to America, England and China at any rate, to defeat the British propaganda which was carried on a governmental scale and also to acquaint the American public with the ideology and the policy of the Hindu Mahasabha. That section at any rate which took interest in India affairs and knew something of the Congress and the League in these foreign countries must be kept well informed of the Hindu Mahasabha activities also. Consequently, a delegation under the lead of Dr. Moonje and Babarao Khaparde was to be sent to America. Another delegation was to go under the lead of Dr. Vardrajalu Naidu to England to counteract any mischief likely to be done by the move on Rajagopalachari's part, who also wanted to go to England. But, as Rajaji was not allowed or did not ask for any facilities, there was no particular point in pressing on for a passport

to Dr. Naidu as they were quits. Other outstanding leaders also from Bengal, Punjab and United Provinces were consulted in this connection and facilities being denied to Babarao Khaparde and others, at the very outset, the question was left further unpursued. The reasons advanced by the government were various. But, the most amusing part of the public criticism in non-Mahasabhaists camp was that they condemned along with the government the very idea of taking out delegations to foreign lands as that would reduce the prestige of our public life and support the British plea that there were dissension's in India. It is bad indeed to wash one's dirty linen in a public square. But, the point is who did it first? Did not the British press propaganda go round the globe at the failure of the Cripps scheme that there were incurable communal dissensions in India with a thousand-tongued voice? Then again do you think that the thousands of Americans and Chinese at present in India have left their eyes and ears in America? And the Germans, and the Japanese? The whole world knows that there are communal dissensions but the whole world must also know and does know that no nation in some of the other phases of its history was without its own communal dissensions, wars of secessions or wars of Roses. The point is that just as in spite of the dissensions England has bestowed the curse of slavery on India in spite of her will, so also England can and, therefore, ought to bestow a blessing of freedom in spite of her dissensions. Just as she is guarding slavery with bayonets, she should guard the freedom too. Or she should openly say that she does not want to free India because of the British imperialistic designs and not owing to our dissensions. If the Hindus Mahasabhaists were allowed to go to America our dissensions could not have been a news to the Americans but by acquainting them why these dissensions arose and what is the solution of the Hindu Mahasabha for them, the delegation would have enabled the foreign public to judge better between the black sheep and the grey wolf.

But, nevertheless the government had done well in inviting Rai Bahadur Meherchand Khanna, president, N.W. Frontier Hindu Sabha to join the delegation to the Pacific Relations Committee. The delegation has already reached its destination. Rai Bahadur Khannaji is bound to have ringing publicity to his thesis ' Pakistan and the Hindu View' to enable you to judge how rapidly, though not sufficiently rapidly, the Hindu Mahasabha has asserted its position in England and the other countries. I give below a couple of extracts from the brochure published by the Oxford University Press recently and written by R. Coupland, who had many occasions to observe the Indian affairs at close quarters when he was touring India, as well as when attached to the Mission of Sir Stafford Cripps, for what they are worth:

(1) 'Still more vociferous was the 'Mahasabha the militant Hindu organisation, which has always maintained that all India is Hindusthan and belongs to the Hindus. For some time past, its leaders have denounced as a vice that very non-communalism which Congress boasts as a virtue. Congress, they say, is an unfaithful servant of Hinduism, and it is one more proof of the existing communal tension that the Mahasabha, which not very long ago had little weight in Indian politics, has been growing fast in membership and influence. Its policy is quite frankly communal. 'Our Moslem countrymen should realise,' says its fiery president, Mr. Savarkar, 'that even in their own affairs they should accept the inevitable', etc. page 16.

(2) 'Militant Hinduism, true to form, was more outspoken'. 'The basic principle of the Hindu Mahasabha,' said its Working Committee, 'is that India is one and indivisible, and it cannot be true to itself or to the best interests of Hindusthan if it is a party to any proposal which involves the political partition of India in any shape or form.'—Page 37.

Lord Devonshire, the Under Secretary of State for India, referred to the Mahasabha as 'the second great all-India Hindu organisation'. If the Congressites were anxious to secure credentials from the Governor, there is no impropriety if we refer incidentally to some references just to know in what light others view our activities.

12. Till a couple of years ago, it were only the Moslems, who were fighting for Pakistan and all our arguments, we had to address to them; but since the Cripps Mission and the Congressites yielding to the Pakistani demand in its worst form as I have shown in paragraph 7 of this speech, a preposterous position has arisen. There has sprung up, politically speaking, a hybrid of pro-Pakistani Hindus and they have been infecting the Hindu mind as rapidly as a contagious and loathsome disease would do. Some of these Congressites are good Hindus, but they have been duped into believing that it is in the interest of the Hindus also to allow the Moslem provinces to secede and bring about a final and eve- lasting unity. Then there are very statesmanly Hindu personalities who recognise no affiliation to any party or body as it behaves statesmanship, but whose commitments, views and votes are nevertheless bound to be counted as Hindu ones. It is regrettable that

many of these esteemed persons should have been ready to admit the principle of provincial secession and thus 'statesmanly' enough betray not only the Hindu cause, but what they worship like a fetish, the nationalism as well. How these pro-Pakistani Hindus are working to persuade the Hindus and even to persuade the government to compel the Hindus to get persuaded can best be illustrated by the untiring effort of Mr. Rajagopalachari. This *acharya* has really been exerting himself with more sincerity and perverse fanaticism than any mad-Mullah known to history. Consequently, the real danger to the integrity of India rises now more eminently from the mentality of the Pakistani Hindus than from the efforts of the Pakistani Moslems. I deliberately choose some of these points to argue, which I know from personal knowledge to weigh heavily on the minds, especially on that section of our Hindu brethren, who still belong to the Congress persuasion but who nevertheless have a Hindu heart.

(a) It must be noted first of all very carefully, that there is a fundamental difference between a provincial re-distribution and provincial self-determination to secede. The latter forms the essence of Pakistan, whatever its other aspects or extents may be. There is no fundamental objection from the Hindu point of view to any re-distribution of provinces, whether on linguistic, military, financial or any other reasonable ground, provided it does not weaken the national strength or cohesion and does not involve any underlying anti-national and anti-Hindu designs. But, the question of provincial secession from the Central state must be altogether ruled out inasmuch as it means nothing short of breaking up Hindusthan into pieces before a century passes away.

(b) Again, the granting of the right to provinces to secede from the Central Government at their own sweet will and allow them to set up as separate states, entirely independent of the Central Indian Government is far more dangerous than the demand for Pakistan, meaning thereby freedom to cut off definite number of provinces, because they contain Moslem majority. The latter case, of a Pakistan demand intolerable as it is and which also we must oppose with all our might, does still come to the loss of a definite number of provinces. But, the principle of self-determination cannot but form a veritable sword of Damocles kept hanging on the head of the Central State. It will be practically an invitation and instigation to any province to secede and blow up at a stroke the whole ground on which the Indian State has to stand. The majority of the Moslems is the only ground in Pakistani demand for secession; but, in admitting the principle of provincial secession, we shall have to face the demand on the part of any province at any time on any economical and any other conceivable ground to secede from the Central Government. Remember that the political centralisation in India is still passing through a phase of formation. The Indian Central State and the political integrity and cohesion are still standing on a fissury rock. We cannot be cocksure against the change that sometime or other even some of those provinces, where there is not a Moslem majority, may be caught up by disintegrating forces and rise against the Central Government and get carried away by the provincial or even sub-provincial egoistic fever, may demand secession and set themselves into separate states. America, Russia and several other nations can serve as danger signals to us in this connection. In fact, even those nations, which today are strongly unitary, had to pass through this phase and it was only a powerful centrifugal force which kept the centripetal tendencies on the part of their components, effectively suppressed, till they got slowly eliminated altogether.

(c) Those who think it matters not much to allow the Moslems to form their independent federation on the North-West Frontier Province, in which there is already an overwhelming majority of the Moslems, should take into consideration the military aspect which makes such a surrender simply suicidal on our part. Can you ever find such a nation on the surface of the earth which would willingly hand over their strongest possible frontiers into the hands of those very people, who seceded from them and had been cherishing a hereditary desire to dominate over it? Then again, remember that on the heels of Pakistan, there comes treading the demand for Pathanisthan. Those Frontier Provinces, if they get entirely free from the control of the Central Government, are sure within measurable time to join hands with the tribal and form a contiguous Pathani State from Hindukush to the very banks of Jhelum. There can be no real unity unless and until their design which for the very existence of 'Hindusthan' we can never willingly allow to fructify, is not cowardly allowed by letting go of our hold on those mountain ranges, which form our national frontiers and frontier guards at once, throughout historical time. But, why should we do it at all? To avoid rupture with our Moslem friends? But what guarantee have you to believe that this rupture instead of getting lessened by our handing over our frontier to them as a free gift will not only get intensified? For, is it not more likely that those, who are now relatively weak and yet are talking of civil war, once they get an independent footing as a state, sufficient time and liberty to organise themselves and entrenched on the powerful frontier ranges, grown stronger precisely in the proportion your position grows weaker by the withdrawal of your frontier? Unity, when it lays our nation exposed to a more dangerous position, is worse than open hostility.

(d) Some of our learned Hindu leaders after most complicated calculations maintain that there is no harm in allowing the Moslems to secede and form Pakistani independent states in the north-western parts and even in Bengal because they are bound to be so crippled financially and economically that they will soon themselves be compelled to repent for secession and go down on their knees. But, this financial weakness need not lead to repentance alone, as our learned Hindu economists expect. So long as we continue to be so cowardly as to yield to any preposterous demand on the part of the Moslems to keep up the show of unity and so terribly afraid of Moslem discontent as to allow even the integrity of our motherland to get broken up into pieces—is it not more likely that this very financial and economical starvation of these would-be Moslem states may goad them on to encroach once more on our Hindu provinces and instigated by the religious fanaticism, which is so inflammable in the frontier tribes even now and urged on by the ideal of a Pathanistan under the lead of the organised forces of the Ameer, may threaten to invade you if you do not hand over to them the remaining parts of the Punjab right up to Delhi to make them financially and economically self-supporting? The example of the tribes is before your eyes already. They carry out incursions almost every year into the Indian provinces and loot, kidnap, murder, hold to ransom only the Hindus in particular as a rule. Although they are goaded on by Moslem fanaticism in the main, yet several Congressite Hindus were not found wanting in disgracefully condoning these nefarious activities of the tribal Pathans on the ground of 'financial and even sexual starvation' from which those 'poor souls' (!) had to undergo inordinate sufferings. I am referring to facts howsoever disgraceful they may be and not fictious. What guarantee there could ever be that given this cowardly and ever-yielding inferiority complex on the part of the Hindus and this monomania for

Hindu-Moslem unity 'at all cost'—that in case these financially starved Pakistani provinces invade the Hindu provinces on their borders with far greater strength than they can now—ever command—a troop of Hindus of such mentality would not similarly condone their encroachments, sympathise with their demands and vote for handing over even Delhi to those invading Moslems before a shot is fired in order just to make a show before the world of a genuine Hindu-Moslem unity or alliance? The 'poor' Moslems in eastern Bengal are even now making their poverty a sufficient excuse and their fanaticism a merit, to loot and harass the Hindus wherever they find an opportunity to do so. When once you allow them to get organised into governmental strength as a separate Moslem Raj, do you think that this very financial starvation which you admit will cripple their would-be state, would provide them with a compelling cause to invade or harass the Hindus in western Bengal and unless you are cured of this unity mania, would you not be faced again with the same bogey—an alternative of handing over some rich slices of Bengal to save the Moslem state from perpetual starvation or be prepared to resist their perpetually growing demand?

(e) But, some of my Pakistani Hindu friends whisper in my ear, 'We know all these things, but our yielding for the time being is the craftiest stroke of policy. When we once get rid of these troublesome Moslem provinces and are left free to organise unhindered by them the unalloyed part of Hindusthan, then we shall consolidate our Hindus and raise them into such a mighty military power so rapidly that the Pakistani provinces of the Moslems would be simply brow-beaten into submission.' The only question that should be put to them by themselves, 'Have you not counted without the host—the British?' Have you got any definite guarantee from the British that as soon as you yield to the Pakistani demand, they would clear out and leave you to organise your Hindusthan as you choose?'

Secondly, even if that is done, where is the magic wand that shall raise the Hindus into such a military power, while Congress mentality continues to dominate a thousand of them? We thank you for your inner intention of raising the Hindus into an independent and strong power and for feeling as a Hindu of Hindus, but do you not think that the Moslems too would utilise that interval with a vengeance to strengthen their position and amalgamating themselves with their kith and kin across the frontier grow quick into a powerful Pathanisthan here or a

Pakistan there? Mind you, they have not a single Congressite among them and, on the other hand, the Moslem minority in every province of yours would-be Hindusthan would be dominating even Congressite Hindus here as they are doing today, creating the same troubles over again and demanding that you must come to terms with the Pakistani states by sacrificing some more Hindu provinces on the altar of the fetish of Hindu-Moslem unity as our 'patriotic', 'Azad' and 'Alli' have been purposively doing today. And if you, as a staunch Hindu, realise that, in that case, somewhere or the other, we shall have to resist the Moslems, then would it not be better to resist them today by flatly refusing even to listen to their insulting and intolerable demand, when they are relatively weaker and when we can prove relatively stronger by simply changing our yielding mentality and replacing it by the Hindu *Sangathanist* ideology, pointing out to the aggressive tendency of the Moslems their right place and command them 'thus far and no further'.

(f) Some of our wise men also are labouring under the misconception that the question of Pakistan is just like the Ulster phase in Ireland. But the fact is that they are committing a grievous error in comparing the two and suggesting that just as the Irish accepted an Ulster, we Hindus should accept the Pakistan. In Ireland there was a question of only a small corner to be set aside as Ulster, but the Pakistani demand seeks to break up India into a number of separate Moslem states and insist that there should be no Central Government of India at all; worst than that the principle of provincial secession at the sweet will of provinces was never raised in the Irish negotiations. Had this principle not been accepted or tolerated by the Irish, there would have been no integral Ireland today. This principle of provincial secession if accepted by the Hindus would sound the death-knell of our national cohesion, integrity and unity.

(g) The chain of reasoning which has succeeded over these Pakistani Hindus comes to this: We want *swaraj*. England is not going to bestow *swaraj* unless and until there is a United demand and univocal constitution framed by Hindus and Moslems together. Moslems have made it clear that they will not join the Hindus in producing a united demand unless and until they are not allowed to break up integrity of India and the Pakistani states are allowed to be set up with no connection with any Central Government. Therefore, we must satisfy the Moslems, yield to their Pakistani demands and get *swaraj*.

Now almost every word in this chain of reasoning is fallacious and the whole chain of reasoning is based on a foolish hope. Although we want *swaraj,* yet that *swaraj* must mean the Hindusthani *swaraj* in which Hindu, Moslem and all other citizens have equal responsibilities, equal duties and equal rights. Such a *swaraj* would not even tolerate a particular community on religious grounds to get itself cut off from the Central Government, demand portions of our country which is the inalienable basis on which this our national *swaraj* stands and any such aggressive claim on the part of a community would be immediately put down as an act of treachery by the united strength of the Central Government. Secondly, it is silly to believe that England is only waiting for a united demand and would walk out of India as that rag, signed by the Hindus and Moslems, is handed over to them. I emphatically assert that even if the Congress, Hindu Mahasabha and the League produce a united demand signed by all the crores of Indian citizens and ask univocally for independence, Britain will never give it for the mere asking. The superstition that if but the Congress and the League demanded with one voice anything in the world the demand would immediately prove irresistible, is responsible for making the real assets of the League inflated beyond all proportions. As soon as the League does join the Congress and even the whole of India goes to England with a common demand, England will say, 'Well boys, you have behaved wonderfully. Hindus, Moslems, all united in a common demand for independence. But, as, all of you united, are still unitedly helpless, disarmed and unable to protect yourself, Great Britain must continue to rule over you even for the moral obligation to save you from foreign aggression and your own internal anarchy.' So, on the whole, all that you do in this bargain is to pay the price knowing perfectly or rather foregoing with open eyes that the substantial thing for which you paid the price can never be delivered over to you. And after all, what is the price? Vivisection of your motherland and of your holyland—the liquidating altogether of the spiritual, racial and above all, the political unity and of the certain chances of its rapid consolidation.

And, above all, if we grant for the sake of argument that paying such a tremendous price for your racial honour and future you are handed over a *swaraj* by the British on conditions laid down by the Moslems, what kind of *swaraj* and whose *swaraj* it can possibly be? It can in no way be a *swaraj* in which the *swatva* of the Hindus is safeguarded for reasons which I have already shown above at some length. Any independence which is achieved at price of admission of and the brittle basis of the principle of the provincial secession is bound to be like a house raised on the crater of a living volcano.

(h) I appreciate in this connection the emphasis the Vicroy has laid at least on the geographical unity of India and the fervent appeal His Excellency has made in his recent Calcutta speech, to maintain the integrity of our country on the grounds of practical politics also. Reasonable safeguards to the minorities must be given and the League of Nations has already shown us the way in one of the world-famous documents formulating what reasonable safeguards to minorities really mean. But, the Viceroy, perhaps inadvertently, used the term 'fully satisfactory to the minorities instead of qualifying the safeguards as 'reasonable.' Fortunately, our countrymen belonging to the Parsee, Jew and Christian communities have extended their readiness to abide by the safeguards laid down as reasonable for the minorities, which the Hindu Mahasabha also is ever willing to guarantee. The fact is that it is not a question of minorities, but, of one minority, the Moslem minority alone. To say that the safeguards must be fully satisfactory to the Moslem minority is to stultify the whole statement because the only safeguard which can be satisfactory to the Moslem minority is, as definitely told by them, to lay an axe at the root of Indian integrity. Thus, we are caught in a vicious circle. The self-destructive solution that, to save the integrity of India as a nation, let us kill it outright in order to satisfy the Moslems, is like that of some clans who, to save their daughters from dishonour when they grew, used to kill them as soon as they were born.

(i) Consequently, taking all these above reasons into consideration, it will be crystal clear to the Hindus who have still kept an open mind on this question that even yielding the principle of provincial secession or Pakistan in certain provinces could never bring about the Hindu-Moslem unity, but such a move will throw Hindus alone into a hopeless predicament. There is no chance whatsoever for the cowardly hope even though they feel that it is a crafty one, to be realised that this or that concession to the Moslems is bound to prove final and usher in a permanent and amicable alliance between the two people, so long as it is you who yield, so long as the Moslems who would be fools to give up the aggrandisation on Hindusthan and the Mohammedans are certainly no fools insofar as this ambition is concerned. Invasions against the *Kafirstans* is in their grain. They are fed on real or boosted up stories of their past conquests and the only way to hold them in check is to make them realise that any such mad dreams would cost them much more than it would, to their opponents. That is why Mr. Jinnah, who speaks in the accents of an Alexander the Great, the conqueror of the world when he addresses some local meetings of his admirers, brandishing a presented sword here or there, threatening the Hindus alone, has never displayed the courage of threatening an armed revolt against the English who in fact are comfortably seated on the very *gaddi* of the Moguls and left no trace of the Moslem Empire throughout India for he knows that the consequences would be immediately terrible.

(j) The only organised body that had the courage to tell the Moslems that the consequences of their efforts to destroy Indian integrity would be in the long run as terrible had been the Hindu Mahasabha alone. Oh! Hindu *sabhaists* and Hindu *Sangathanists,* you form the last citadel in which the Hindu hope and Hindu Future have come to seek refuge and take its last stand for the sake of honour, if not for immediate success and among the faithless crowd of Hindus themselves, you form the last faithful army which has rallied round to defend and hold up the pan-Hindu colours as our ancestors did under such trying circumstances at Chittor! If you, at any rate, oh! Hindu *Sangathanists,* do not betray yourselves and that tradition of Chittor, then rest assured you will in near future be able to sally out or by your falling in the struggle as indomitable and uncompromising warriors enable your race to sally out of the Chittor of martyrdom—to the Raigad of victory! Come out then to assert boldly and uncompromisingly on behalf of Hindudom—that...

> Just as in America, Germany, China and every other country not excluding Russia, so also in Hindusthan, the Hindus by the fact that they form an overwhelming majority are the nation and Moslems are but a community because like all other communities they are unchallengeably in a minority. Therefore, they must remain satisfied with whatever reasonable safeguards other minorities in India get and accept as reasonable in the light of the world formula framed by the League of Nations. We may adapt it to Indian circumstances by concessions more or less on minor questions, but no minority in India shall be allowed to demand to break up the very integrity of Hindusthan from Indus to the seas as a condition

of their participation in the Central Government or provincial ones. No province whatsoever, by the fact that it is a province, shall be allowed to claim to secede from the Central State of Hindusthan at its own sweet will. Hindusthan as a nation can have a right of self determination but a province or a district or a *taluka* can have no right to run counter by the strength of their own majority to the law and the will of the Central Government of Hindusthan. All we can in fairness promise is to grant a representation to all Indian citizens on the general principle of 'one man one vote' or if that is not found to the taste of the Moslems, we may go a step further and base all representation strictly on population proportion. We know for certain that those minorities like Parsees, Christians and others who have expressed unmistakably their loyalty to united, undivided and indivisible Indian nation and the Indian State with reasonable safeguards are with the Hindus and willing to work shoulder to shoulder for Indian independence. It will be well for the Moslems even in their own interest to bear faithful allegiance to the Indian nation on the same conditions offered to other minorities. But, if the Moslems, mistaking the pseudo-national yielding attitude of Congress for the attitude of Hindudom as such persist in their outrageous and treacherous demand for Pakistan or the principle of provincial self-determination then it is time, you Oh! Hindu *Sangathanists*, that you must proclaim your formula from the very tops of the Himalayas, 'We don't want Hindu-Moslem unity at all on such conditions.' If you come, with you, if you don't, without you, and if you oppose, in spite of you, we shall fight as best as we can to secure independence and defend the integrity of Hindusthan! Hindusthan shall and must remain an integral and powerful nation and a Central State from the Indus to the seas, treating any movement on the part of any one to vivisect it, as treacherous and strongly suppress it just as any movement of Negrostan would be promptly punished by the American nation!!

13. All laws are but generalisations primarily based on detailed observations. The detailed observation of the history of Hindus through centuries on centuries points incontrovertibly to the fact that the Hindu nation is imbued inherently with such an amazing capacity of resurrection, of renaissance, of rejuvenation that the moment, which

finds them completely overwhelmed by anti-Hindu forces is precisely the moment which ushers in the day of deliverance—to quote the Puranic style—of the birth of an *avatar*. It was in the darkest hour of the night that Shri Krishna was born. It is this indomitable spirit of the inherent vitality that enabled our national being to prove almost immortal in relation to other races or nations—ancient or modern—and invested it with the strength which ultimately demolished and swept away all anti-Hindu forces, which raised their head from time to time against us. This is no mere rhodomontade I am indulging in. Leaving aside even the Puranic period, and the Huns, Shakas or even taking into consideration the Moslems who came as conquerors, this is the gist of well-authenticated Hindu history.

The Moslems came as conquerors, but stayed too long to be conquered by the Hindus and beaten to a chip in thousand and one battlefields till at last the mighty Moslem Empire which rose like a rocket, fell like a stick, till eventually the Hindu horse of victory rode off unchallenged from Attock to Rameshwar, from Dwarka to Jagannath.

To validate this historical fact, only look at these two following pictures: Just take up the map of India about A.D. 1600 The Moslems ruled all over Hindusthan unchallengeably. It was veritable Pakistan realised not only in this province or that, but all over India; Hindusthan as such was simply wiped out.

Then open out the map of India about A.D. 1700 to 1798 and what do you see? The Hindu forces are marching triumphantly throughout India. The very Mogul throne at Delhi is smashed to pieces literally with a hammer by Sadashivrao Bhau, the Generalissimo of the Maratha! Our Hindu-Sikh brotherhood does ultimately deliver Punjab from the Moslem yoke and rule supremely from the borders of Tibet to the banks of Kabul river; the Gurkha-Hindus rule in Nepal, while the Marathas from Delhi to Rameshwar have planted the triumphant Hindu flag from capital to capital, from temple to temple. The Pakistan actually realised by the Moslems was entombed and out of it rose up once more Hindusthan—resurrected and triumphant. The conquering Moslem had to eat the humble pie in the long end and got completely crushed and weaned of his dominating dreams that even today in his heart of hearts he shudders to think of his fate as soon as he sees the probability of the consolidated strength of the overwhelming Hindu majority in the land.

It should be good to the Moslems themselves if they once realise the import of this historical truth. The fate which overtook them even when they had succeeded in translating whole of Hindusthan into an actual living and mighty Pakistan, ought to warn them of the miserable future they would have in store if they persisted in dreaming wildly of a Pakistan, which is today but an airy nothing, a forlorn hope!

14. The Hindu Mahasabhaists should remember that, as is very probable, they will be called upon to fight out any attempt on the part of the Moslems to thrust Pakistan on us, whether by resorting to the 'revolt', whatever the Leaguers may mean thereby, then the entire burden, responsibility and consequently the merit also will be yours in facing the struggle single-handedly. The Congress-minded Hindus, the worshippers of pseudo-nationality would not only be of no use to you, but would actually try to combat you and put you into a false position by their willing surrender to the Moslem demands as Hindus. You should, therefore, try to mobilise your forces and reserve whatever strength you can command for defence of the integrity of India, which no one else but you alone may defend. You are the salt of Hindudom; but if the salt loses its flavour, with what shall it be salted? Independence of Hindusthan has no meaning at the cost of its fundamental integrity as a state and a nation. It may be thrusted on us even as the British rule is thrust on us but just as that does not deprive us of the right of struggling for our freedom with England, even so, if we but do not betray our own conscience and sign willingly any or all schemes, proposing percentages, plebiscites, which are growing in abundance like mushrooms, either out of panic or pusillanimity, you will find yourself soon in a position to press on both the demands regarding independence and integrity and together get them realised through your own strength.

So far as the most determining factor of all secondary movements the World War is concerned, neither parties of either the Axis or the Allies has as yet secured any result so decisive as to invest it with an unquestionable superiority. Consequently, the best policy for all nations situated as we Hindus are, is to continue to sit on the fence and watch the results, keeping ourselves all the while as well-organised, as well-informed and as tactfully ready to take as much advantage of the last results, when the war ends.

15. In view of this indecisive aspect of the war and the necessity for the Hindu Sangathanists to keep mobilised their forces for the resistance which they are very likely to be called upon to offer and

continue fighting the anti-Pakistani struggle single-handedly and owing to our inability howsoever regrettable but which must be recognised as an actuality, to enter the world combat on our own account to, win back our independence, the most far-sighted and practicable programme which, if carried on faithfully and handicapped though we are, while the war continues without arriving at any decisions, is as follows:

(a) To continue a hundred times more intensely the Hindu Militarisation movement and try to get recruited and enlisted as many Hindus as possible in the army, navy, the air forces, ammunition factories, war technicians, etc. The results of this movement are already so encouraging as to make it quite superfluous now on my part to marshal out all the arguments I had been doing so often. When the war began, the percentage of the Moslems had so dangerously gone high in the Army as 62 per cent. This was the result of the Gandhist policy denouncing the soldier as sinner and the spinner as the greatest spiritual warrior, who alone was the real liberator of the land and was sure with the music of his spinning wheel to win over the hearts of all Hitlers, Stalins, Churchills and Tojios. But, ever since the Hindu Mahasabha found that the war had made it incumbent on the government to throw the doors of the army, navy and the air force open to the Hindus, it whipped up military enthusiasm amongst the Hindus and conducted an organised campaign to send thousands and thousands of Hindus to all branches of the military forces of the land. The result, as has recently been declared, is that the percentage of the Moslems in the army has gone from 62 per cent to 32 per cent. This must also be reduced to some 25 in just accordance with the population proportion of Hindus and Moslems. The Hindu Mahasabha branches all over India must start Militarisation boards to send to the forces of the land the best and the bravest of the Hindus. If any province or a district wants to study an organisation board which has proved most competent in this respect, it should do well to study personally the working and the results achieved by the militarisation *mandal* at Poona under the able lead of our esteemed Hindu *sabhaists* leader, St. L.B. Bhopatkar. Hundreds of promising Hindu youth have already secured King's Commissions, Viceroy's Commissions and are leading the forces with efficiency and merit and getting up-to-date knowledge and practice of warfare in different battlefields. The same can be said of the air force. Believe me that nothing can stand the Hindus in better stead even after the war, as this Hindu militarisation will do. I assure every Hindu soldier and officer, who are now serving in the Indian Army, navy or the air force, etc. that they are doing as patriotic a service to their nation as those who went to jail at Bhagalpur, if not more. The immediate defence of our hearths and homes does also make it incumbent to make a common cause with the British forces, till they are in the field.

(b) Continue to capture all centres of political power from the Central Executive Council, legislatures, defence committees and councils, municipalities, ministries in the civil part of the Government just as on the military side. The men who come to occupy these centres of power must be either elected by the Hindus Mahasabha or supported by it as independent Hindu Sangathanists. But, in no case should a Hindu be trusted with any such centre of power, who by persuation, belongs to the pseudo-nationalistic Congress School and glorifies more in betraying Hindu rights to the Moslems than in defending them against Moslem encroachment.

(c) Do not fritter away your energies or keep your Sangathanist forces shackled down in any untimely and tactless movement which pursuing high-sounding slogans loses more than gains in the long run. Remember it is not the slogan but the strength that counts. Under the war fever, only arms speak and can dictate not slogans howsoever high sounding.

(d) But, you must, because you can, give fight on detailed questions, in defence of the civic rights of the Hindus when they are locally attached or humiliation deliberately offered to the Hindu honour or any just grievance or to face any anti-Hindu riots, as we have already been doing year in and year out. Only those issues which are beyond our power to tackle and are to be fought out on an all-India scale against armed forces overwhelmingly more powerful than those we can rally, disorganised and disarmed as we relatively are, should not be taken up just now. Time and strategy demand that we should leave them till we are in a better position.

(e) In the meanwhile, in order to mobilise our forces and keep them prepared for any emergency, such as the Pakistan struggle, we should continue the constructive activities to make our Hindu Mahasabha organisation as strong as possible. The general and suicidal error which makes us under-value a constructive programme, which we could easily carry out even during the war time, must be immediately corrected.

Even the war-time must be utilised all the more intensely by enlisting as many members, starting branches at as many places down to *talukas* and villages and keeping them well organised and working, is a duty which the Hindu Mahasabha must continue to do and can do even now with hundredfold speed and activity.

(f) Remember also that the removal of untouchability is a task as easy to be tackled as it is bound to strengthen Hindu consolidation. It will be nothing short of a victory won in the battlefield if we, within five years' time, can sweep out untouchability from the face of our country by killing the very idea of not touching our co-religionist on ground of birth in a particular caste alone, and removing automatically the special disability, some economical and some social, from which those of our religious brothers are suffering most unjustly at this hour. It is only a change of mentality and nothing more than that to achieve this seemingly insuperable task. If every one of the Hindu Sangathanists simply says and begins to act on it—'I would not look upon anyone of my co-religionists as untouchable simply on account of birth in a particular caste'—the question will be solved without a farthing's cost or the least measure of suffering and we shall have a veritable army of some three crores of our co-religionists fighting shoulder to shoulder with us under pan-Hindu flag on behalf of Hindudom.

So long as the war continues without reaching any decision, this is the most profitable and the most tactical programme which the Hindu Mahasabhaists and the Hindu *Sangathanists* can work out and must work out before the war introduces any revolutionary factor, concerning our own country so as to demand our first attention that compels us to adapt ourselves to it forthwith.

16. All our present programmes, it need not be mentioned, are based on the assumption that Britain comes out at any rate so successful of this World War, as to continue to be a sovereign power in India. Nothing has happened so far, so cataclysmic as to undermine the probability of this assumption. But, then the forces of Japan are hanging on so persistently on our eastern borders, undislodged to any appreciable measure and on the other hand, the Axis powers have been surrounded at any rate for the moment by a veritable hornet of irritated nations, that no one even among the most optimistic statesmen or commanders or dictators is in a position to predict with any certainty or definiteness the results of the war. Till that along with those nations who cannot but helplessly

watch their destinies tied up with the fortunes either of the powerful combatants on both sides, India too disarmed as it is must bide her time and tide.

The dice of destiny is loaded already and recklessly thrown on a world battlefield! All nations are thrown in the crucible! The very seas are on flames and the skies are garrisoned with showering thunderbolts day and night. No nation after this World War can emerge just as it was. Many of those who were at the pinnacle of their power will be reduced to dust. Many who were trampled down in the dust may all of a sudden find themselves in a position to rise and come to their own. The face of the earth is bound to get revolutionised in any case and in that revolutionary upheaval, which at present lies in the lap of the war gods, one thing only could be said with some certainty so far as India is concerned that she also cannot but be one of the factors whose future is bound to get revolutionised, though we cannot and may not point out definitely the course and the aspects of it. One thing you may rest assured that all possible courses and aspects are already viewed as carefully as human ingenuity can and neither the continuation nor the termination of the war can find the Hindu Mahasabha unprepared to take full advantage of every revolutionary phase the war passes through, near or far off, so as to press on the Hindu cause. As has happened so many times in the Hindu history that it was precisely in the darkest hour that the *avatar* destined to deliver us was born, it is not quite unlikely, nay, it is more likely than not, that the spirit of renaissance of the Hindu race may find an opportunity to assert itself and as if by a miracle similar to those our Puranas sing, Hindudom emerges triumphant over all the forces of evil which are attacking it today. About possibilities and even about probabilities, wise men should not assert anything more definitely in such cases than pious hopes. All that they should do is to conserve the forces of their nation in the meanwhile, and wait for the probable time and tide so that they may not be found wanting, if the probability does arise all of a sudden.

Hindu *sabhaists* and Hindu *Sangathanists*! Only see to it that on the eve of such a probable, miraculous development in near future, do not play coward to your conscience under the weight of the present or get stampeded by the pseudo-nationalistic forces into any unbecoming pacts and do not sell your birthrights for the mess of potages, and play coward to your own conscience! Hold fast to the programme chalked out above for the present, plain though it may seem and get not yourselves trapped into any untimely outburst, which instead of bringing you near success may only serve to find you entirely disabled, to catch the tide of fortune which in all probability is likely to reach your shores under the pressure of the war!

In any case, hold fast to the crux of the Hindu Sangathanist ideology which shall serve you in any event, the future may unfold, namely:

'Hinduise all politics and militarise Hindudom'! Hindu Dharma ki Jai! Hindu rashtra ki jai! Vande Mataram.

□

Statement on Resignation

I

The following statement was issued by Veer Savarkar on 31-7-1943 from his presidential office, Savarkar Sadan, Bombay:

Inasmuch as even the sixth year of my presidentship of the Hindu Mahasabha is rapidly drawing to its close, I feel that the time has come for announcing my decision to resign the presidentship and request the Mahasabha electorate, without in any way impudently trespassing on its right of liberty of choice, to relieve me of this high office, by not including my name even in the first panel of the election of the president for the next year.

The heavy work involved in discharging my duties as the president continuously for six years has visibly affected my health and secondly, I have also felt time and again, as will be shown in my statements issued on the occasions of my former resignations, that I should myself come forward to help the electorate to select someone of our able colleagues to act as a president of the Hindu Mahasabha for the next year.

In this connection, it should be noted that this is not the first time I am tendering my resignation although it must definitely be the last one now. When I fell seriously ill in August 1940 and when in spite of it, I was elected to preside over the Madura Session, I tendered my resignation for the first time. But, owing to the most cordial pressure of Hindu *Sangathanist* public all over India and the Reception Committee in particular which wrote to me that the session itself would not be held with any amount of success if I did not withdraw my resignation, I accepted the presidentship for the fourth time and could only be taken on a stretcher to attend the session. Next year in 1941, I again resigned for the second time, but was elected almost unanimously for the fifth time. Just then, the Bhagalpur question came to a head and to defend Hindu honour, I thought my duty required me to stick to my guns. Consequently, I accepted even the dictatorship of the civil resistance campaign and faced imprisonment at the head of thousands and thousands of our Hindu Sangathanist co-workers who fought out the struggle to an undeniable success. That task over, I tendered my resignation for the third time in July 1942. But the Working Committee refused to accept it and would not proceed to work till I withdrew it.

Just then the Congress movement of 'Quit India, But Keep Your Army Here' was launched and later on it came to my notice that some of the leading Congressites who were outside the jail had actually conspired to capture the Hindu Mahasabha itself because it refused to serve the Congress as a handmaid. They wanted to use it to take the Congress-nuts out of fire and make the Mahasabha accept Pakistan at least in principle. What I then foresaw has been proved to demonstration by later events. In order to ward off this danger in time and to expose and frustrate this conspiracy, I resolved not only not to resign but contest the election. This was the only time when I actually contested it. Backed up by the wisdom and the overwhelming confidence of the Hindu Mahasabhaists electorate, I was again almost unanimously elected for the sixth time in continuous succession to the presidentship. The session at Cawnpore passed an uncompromising and emphatic resolution not only against the Pakistan scheme, but even against the vicious principle of provincial self-determination to secede from the central Indian State. The Hindu militarisation movement received a fillip and all attempts to Congressify the Hindu Mahasabha were brought to naught to the great chagrin of the Congress stalwarts as Mr. Rajagopalachari who publicly bewailed 'Even those few leaders of the Hindu Mahasabha who more or less sympathised with my formula regarding Hindu-Moslem unity fell a prey to crowd psychology at Cawnpore.'

This short recapitulation of events will show that I have time and again tried to lay down the reigns of the presidentship for the very reasons indicated above in para two for which I have now definitely made up my mind to resign. This clarification is meant to forestall any misinformed or mischievous attempt to attribute my resignation to any other reason than those indicated above. It is precisely because I feel that the Hindu Mahasabha is by far the stronger and more consolidated organisation today than ever before that I have chosen this particular time to resign. Even an adversely inclined critic like Prof. Coupland, a member of the 'Cripps Mission' has remarked in his recent booklet, the

Hindu Mahasabha is a militant organisation of Hindus which has been growing fast in membership and influence.'

I rejoice, while tendering this resignation, to see that I have been able to do so while I am in possession of the fullest confidence and affectionate regard of the Hindu *sangathanist* world as a whole throughout India. Millions of my countrymen and co-religionists who participated in the celebrations of my Diamond Jubilee only last month have—through the resolutions passed at thousand and one meetings in almost all capital cities, towns and villages, through the addresses given to me by local bodies, associations and literary and religious institutions, through messages I received from hundreds of most prominent Hindu leaders including those who did not formally belong to the Hindu Mahasabha organisation, through the special numbers of leading periodicals and editorials in papers in the country—given most touching expressions to their grateful appreciation's of the humble services I rendered to the Hindu cause and have assured me of their fullest confidence and trust in me and the Hindu ideology I advocate.

In all humility, I thank the Hindu *sangathanist* public and all my comrades and colleagues in particular for their over-whelming kindness, confidence and even forbearance they showed for whatever shortcomings they might have noticed in me.

It is needless to add that, in spite of this resignation of its presidentship, I shall ever continue as a soldier in its rank and file and serve the Hindu Mahasabha in furtherance of the Hindu cause.

□

Long Live the Hindu Mahasabha!
'Long Live Hindudom!!'

II

The following statement was issued by Veer Savarkar on 17-12-1943 from his presidential office, Bombay:

'I gratefully acknowledge the kindness, confidence and appreciation of the work done, expressed by the Hindu Mahasabha electorate in entrusting me with the presidentship of the Mahasabha for the seventh time in an unbroken succession, in spite of my resignation pending before the Working Committee. But, as I have been fearing long since, my health has steadily declined and I have been confined to bed for the last fortnight by an acute attack of bronchitis. My medical advisers are definitely against my undertaking any long journey, especially to a part where severe cold prevails. I must, therefore, request the Hindu *sangathanist* public to excuse my inability to attend the next Silver Jubilee session of the Hindu Mahasabha at Amritsar.

I have already referred this matter to the Reception Committee and to Dharmaveer Dr. Moonje, the General Secretary of the Hindu Mahasabha, intimating the latter to call the Working Committee as it is laid down in our constitution, to consider this question and select someone of our foremost leaders to officiate in my stead as the president. My personal view in this matter is that Dr. Syama Prasad Mookerjee should be unanimously elected to officiate in my stead as the president, especially in view of the fact that it will be very long for me to recoup my health and energy to work with full efficiency.

Nevertheless, the decision of the Working Committee must be held final.

I exhort every Hindu *sangathanist* who can attend the session at Amritsar. The Reception Committee at Amritsar has left no stone unturned to render this Silver Jubilee of the Mahasabha as grand a success as possible. From my sick-bed, I cannot express at length the special significance why Hindudom should rally round the pan-Hindu flag on the occasion of this Silver Jubilee session so as to demonstrate the mighty mental revolution that has already come to sway the racial soul of the Hindu nation.

All I can say in this short statement is this that if Hindudom does not betray itself and does rise equal to the occasion as it has done a hundred times centuries gone by, then the day of birth of the Hindu Mahasabha is bound to be marked red in the Hindu history before long as the day of the birth of an *avatar*: 'the Saviour of the Hindu Nation'—as the day of the birth of a New *yug*—the Hindu *yug*.

III

The following telegraphic message dated 1-8-1944 was sent by Veer Savarkar to Dharamaveer Bhopatkar, Chairman of the Reception Committee, to welcome Dr. Syama Prasad on the occasion of his visit to Poona:

'I join you in welcoming Dr. Mookerjee. Hindudom is indebted to him so much for his monumental services and his recent condemnation of provincial self-determination to secede from the Central Government and his determination to oppose Indian vivisection that I for one wish that the crown of thorns of the presidentship of the Hindu Mahasabha, the highest honour that Hindudom can offer, be bestowed on him next year.'

□

Part - III

Essentials of Hindutva

Essentials of Hindutva

What is in a name?

We hope that the fair maid of Verona, who made the impassioned appeal to her lover to change 'a name' that was 'nor hand, nor foot, nor arm, nor face, nor any other part belonging to a man' would forgive us for this our idolatrous attachment to it when we make bold to assert that, 'Hindus we are and love to remain so!' We too would, had we been in the position of that good Friar, have advised her youthful lover to yield to the pleasing pressure of the logic which so fondly urged 'What's in a name? That which we call a rose would smell as sweet by any other name!' For, things do matter more than their names, especially when you have to choose one only of the two, or when the association between them is either new or simple. The very fact that a thing is indicated by a dozen names in a dozen human tongues disarms the suspicion that there is an invariable connection or natural concomitance between sound and the meaning it conveys. Yet, as the association of the word with the thing it signifies grows stronger and lasts long, so does the channel, which connects the two states of consciousness tend to allow an easy flow of thoughts from one to another, till at last it seems almost impossible to separate them. And when in addition to this a number of secondary thoughts or feelings that are generally roused by the thing get mystically entwined with the word that signifies it, the name seems to matter as much as the thing itself. Would the fair Apostle of the creed that so movingly questioned, 'What's in a name?' have liked it herself to nickname the god of her idolatory as 'Paris' instead of 'Romeo'? Or would he have been ready to swear by the moon that tipped with silver all the fruit tree tops, that it would serve as sweet and musical to his heart to call his 'Juliet' by 'any other name', such as, for example 'Rosaline?' Nay more; there are words which imply an idea in itself extremely complex or an ideal or a vast and abstract generalisation which seem to take, as it were, a being unto themselves or live and grow as an organism would do. Such names though they be 'nor hand, nor foot, nor any other part belonging to a man', are not all that, precisely because they are the very soul of man. They become the idea itself and live longer than generations of man do. Jesus died but Christ has survived the 'Roman' Emperors and that Empire. Inscribe at the foot of one of those beautiful paintings of 'Madonna' the name of 'Fatima' and a Spaniard would keep gazing at it as curiously as at any other piece of art; but just restore the name of 'Madonna' instead, and behold his knees would lose their stiffness and bend his eyes their inquisitiveness and turn inwards in adoring recognition, and his whole being get suffused with a consciousness of the presence of divine motherhood and love! What is in a name? Ah! Call Ayodhya—Honolulu, or nickname her Immortal Prince—a Pooh bal, or ask the Americans to change Washington into a Chengiz Khan, or persuade a Mohammedan to call himself a Jew, and you would soon find that the 'open sesame' was not the only word of its type!

Hindutva is different from Hinduism

To this category of names which have been to mankind a subtle source of life and inspiration belongs the word Hindutva, the essential nature and significance of which we mean to investigate into. The ideas and ideals, the systems and societies, the thoughts and sentiments which have centred round this name are so varied and rich, so powerful and so subtle, so elusive and yet so vivid, that the term Hindutva defies all attempts at analysis. Forty centuries, if not more, had been at work to mould it as it is. Prophets and poets, lawyers and law-givers, heroes and historians, have thought, lived, fought and died just to have it spell thus! For, indeed, is it not the resultant of countless actions—now conflicting, now co-mingling, now co-operating—of our whole race? Hindutva is not a word but a history. Not only the spiritual or religious history of our people as at times it is mistaken to be by being confounded with the other cognate term, Hinduism, but a history in full. Hinduism is only a derivative, a fraction, a part of Hindutva. Unless it is made clear what is meant by the latter, the first remains unintelligible and vague. Failure to distinguish between these two terms has given rise to much misunderstanding and mutual suspicion between some of those sister communities that have inherited this inestimable and common treasure of our Hindu civilisation. What is the fundamental difference in the meaning of these two words would be clear as our argument proceeds. Here it is enough to point out that Hindutva is not identical with what is vaguely indicated by the term Hinduism. By an 'ism' is generally meant a theory or a code more or less based on spiritual or religious dogma or system. But when we attempt to investigate into the essential significance of Hindutva we do not primarily—and certainly not mainly—concern ourselves with any particular theocratic or religious dogma or creed. Had not linguistic usage stood in our way then 'Hinduness' would have certainly been a better word than Hinduism as a near parallel to Hindutva. Hindutva embraces all the departments of thought and activity of the whole being of our Hindu race. Therefore, to understand the significance of this term 'Hindutva', we must first understand the essential meaning of the word Hindu itself and realise how it came to exercise such an imperial sway over the hearts of millions over millions of mankind and won a loving allegiance from the bravest and best of them. But, before we can do that, it is imperative to point out that we are by no means attempting a definition or even a description of the more limited, less satisfactory and essentially sectarian term 'Hinduism'. How far we can succeed or are justified in doing that would appear as we proceed.

What is Hindu?

Although it would be hazardous at the present stage of oriental research to state definitely the period when the foremost band of the intrepid Aryans made it their home and lighted their first sacrificial fire on the banks of the Sindhu, the Indus, yet certain it is that long before the ancient Egyptians and Babylonians had built their magnificent civilisation, the holy waters of the Indus were daily witnessing the lucid and curling columns of the scented sacrificial smokes and the valleys resounding the chants of Vedic hymns—the spiritual ferver that animated their souls. The adventurous valour that propelled their intrepid enterprises, the sublime heights to which their thoughts rose—all these had marked them out as a people destined to lay the foundation of a great and enduring civilisation. By the time they had definitely cut themselves aloof from their cognate and neighbouring people, especially the Persians, the Aryans had spread out to the farthest of the seven rivers—Saptasindhus—and not only had they developed a sense of nationality but had already succeeded in giving it 'a local habitation and a name'! Out of their gratitude to the genial and perennial network of waterways that ran through the land like a system of nerve-threads and wove them into a being, they very naturally took to themselves the name of Saptasindhus, an epithet that was applied to the whole of Vedic India in the oldest records of the world—the *Rigveda* itself. Aryans or the cultivators as they essentially were, we can well understand the divine love and homage they bore to these seven rivers presided over by 'the river'—'the Sindhu' which to them were but visible symbols of the common nationality and culture इमा आप: शिवतमा इमा राष्ट्रस्य भेषजी: । इमा राष्ट्रस्य वर्धनीरिमा राष्ट्रभृतोपमा: The Indians in their forward march had to meet many a river as genial and as fertilising as these but never could they forget the attachment they felt and the homage they paid to the Saptasindhus which had welded them into a nation and furnished the name which enabled their forefathers to voice forth their sense of national and cultural unity. Down to this day, a Sindhu—a Hindu—wherever he may happen to be, will gratefully remember and symbolically invoke the presence of these rivers that they may refresh and purify his soul.

इमं मे गंगे यमुने सरस्वति शतद्रु सतोमं सचता परूष्ण्या।
असिक्न्यामरूद्वृधे वितस्याजींकीये श्रुणुह्या सुषोमया॥
गंगे च यमुने चैव गोदावरि सरस्वति।
नर्मदे सिन्धु कावेरि जलेऽस्मिन् सन्निधिं कुरू॥

Not only had these people been known to themselves as 'Sindhus', but we have definite records to show that they were known to their surrounding nations—at any rate to one of them—by that very name Saptasindhu. The syllable स (s) in Sanskrit is at times changed into ह (h) in some of the Prakrit languages, both Indian and non-Indian. For example, the word *sapta* has become Hapat not only in Indian Prakrits but also in the European languages too; we have *Hapta,* i.e., week in India and 'heptarchy' in Europe, *kesri* in Sanskrit becomes *kehri* in old Hindi, Saraswati becomes Harahwati in Persian and *asur* becomes *ahur*. And then we actually find that the Vedic name of our nation Saptasindhu had been mentioned as Haptahindu in the *Avesta* by the ancient Persian people. Thus in the very dawn of history we find ourselves belonging to the nation of the Sindhus or Hindus and this fact was well known to our learned men even in the Pauranic period. In expounding the doctrine that many of the मलेंच्छ tongues had been but the mere offshoots of the Sanskrit language, the *Bhawishpurana* clearly cites this fact and says:

संस्कृतस्यैव वाणी तु भारतं वषैमुह्यताम्।
अन्ये खंडे गता सैव मलेंच्छा ह्यानंदिनोऽभवन्॥

पितृपैतरभ्राता च बादरः पतिरेव च।
सेति सा यावनी भाष ह्यश्वश्चस्यस्तथा पुनः ॥
जानुस्थाने जैनश्बदः सप्तसिन्धुस्तथैव च
हप्तहिन्दुर्यावनी च पुनर्ज्ञेया गुरूण्डिका ॥ (प्रतिसर्गनर्व अ.5)

Thus knowing for certain that the Persians used to designate the Vedic Aryans as Hindus and knowing also the fact that we generally call a foreign and unknown people by the term by which they are known to those through whom we come to know them, we can safely conclude that most of the remoter nations that flourished then must have applied the same epithet 'Hindu' to our land and people as the ancient Persians did. Not only that, but even in the very region of the Saptasindhus, the thinly scattered native tribes too, must have been knowing the Aryans as Hindus in the local dialects in accordance with the same linguistic law. Further on, as the Vedic Sanskrit began to give birth to the Indian Prakrits which became the spoken tongues of the majority of the decendants of these very Sindhus as well as the assimilated and the crossborn castes, these too might have called themselves as Hindus without any influence from the foreign people. For, the Sanskrit स changes into ह as often in Indian Prakrits as in the non-Indian ones. Therefore, so far as definite records are concerned, it is indisputably clear that the first and almost the cradle name chosen by the patriarches of our race to designate our nation and our people, is Saptasindhu or Haptasindhu and that almost all nations of the then known world seemed to have known us by this very epithet—Sindhus or Hindus.

Name older still

So far we have been treading on solid ground of recorded facts but now we cannot refrain ourselves from making an occasional excursion into the borderland of conjecture. So far we have not pinned our faith to any theory about the original home of the Aryans, but if the most widely accepted theory of their entrance into India be relied on, then a natural curiosity arises as to the origin of the names by which they called the new scenes of their adopted home. Did they coin all those names from their own tongue? Could they have done so? Is it not generally true that when we meet a new scene or enter a new country, we call them by the very names—may be in a slightly changed form so as to suit our vocal ability or taste—by which they are known to the native people there? Of course, at times we love to call new scenes by names redolent with the memory of the clear old ones—especially when new colonies are being established in a virgin and but thinly populated continent. But, this explanation could only be satisfactory when it is proved that the name given to the new place already existed in the old country and even then, it could not be denied that the other process of calling new scenes by the names which they already bear is more universally followed. Now we know it for certain that the region of the Saptasindhus was, though very thinly, populated by scattered tribes. Some of them seem to have been friendly towards the newcomers and it is almost certain that many an individual had served the Aryans as guides and introduced them to the names and nature of the new scenes to which the Aryans could not be but local strangers. The विद्याधराप्सरोयक्षोगंधर्वकिन्नरा: were not all or altogether enemical to the Aryans as, at times, they are mentioned as being benevolent and good natured folks. Thus it is probable that many names given to these great rivers by the original inhabitants of the soil may have been Sanskritised and adopted by the Aryans. We have numerous proofs of this nature in their assimilative expansion of those people and their tongues; witness the words *Shalkantkata, Malya, Milind, Alsada* (Alexandria), *Suluv (Selucus),* etc. If this be true then it is quite probable that the great Indus was known as Hindu to the original inhabitants of our land and owing to vocal peculiarity of the Aryans, it got changed into Sindhu when they adopted it by the operation of the same rule that स is the Sanskritised equivalent of ह. Thus, Hindu would be the name that this land and the people that inhabited it bore from time so immemorial that even the Vedic name Sindhu is but a later and secondary form of it. If the epithet Sindhu dates its antiquity in the glimmering twilight of history, then the word Hindu dates its antiquity from a period so remoter than the first that even mythology fails to penetrate to—trace it to—its source.

Hindus, a nation

The activities of so intrepid a people as the Sindhus or Hindus could no longer be kept cooped or cabined within the narrow compass of Panchnad or the Punjab. The vast and fertile plains further stood out, inviting the efforts to some strong and vigorous race. Tribe after tribe of the Hindus issued forth from the land of their nursery and led by the consciousness of a great mission and their sacrificial fire that was symbol thereof, they soon reclaimed the vast, wasted and but very thinly populated lands. Forests were felled, agriculture flourished, cities rose, kingdoms thrived—the touch of human hand changed the whole face of the wild and unkempt nature. But, while these great deeds were being achieved, the Aryans had developed to suit their individualistic tendencies and the demands of their new environments a policy that was but loosely centralised. As time passed on, the distances of their new colonies increased and different peoples of their highly developed types began to be incorporated into their culture, the different settlements began to lead life politically very much centred in themselves. The new attachments formed, though they could not efface the old ones, yet grew more and more pronounced and powerful until the ancient generalisations and names gave way to the new. Some called themselves *Kurus*, others *Kashis* or *Videhs* or *Magadhs,* while the old generic name of the Sindhus or Hindus was first overshadowed and then almost forgotten. Not that the conception of a national and cultural unity vanished, but it assumed other names and other forms, the politically most important of them being the institution of a *chakarvartan*. At last, the great mission which the Sindhus had undertaken of founding a nation and a country, found and reached its geographical limit when the valorous Prince of Ayodhya made a triumphant entry in Ceylon and actually brought the whole land from the Himalayas to the seas under one sovereign sway. The day when the horse of victory returned to Ayodhya unchallenged and unchallengeable, the great white umbrella of sovereignty was unfurled over the Imperial throne of Ramchandra the brave, Ramchandra the good, and a loving allegiance to him was sworn, not only by the princes of Aryan blood but Hanuman—Sugriva—Bibhishana from the South—that day was the real birthday of our Hindu people. It was truly our national day for Aryans and Anaryans knitting themselves into a people were born as a nation. It summed up and politically crowned the efforts of all the generations that preceded it and it handed down a new and common mission, a common banner, a common cause which all the generations after it had consciously or unconsciously fought and died to defend.

Other names

A synthetic conception gains in strength if it finds a term

comprehensive enough to give it an eloquent expression. Those terms, Aryavrat or Brahmavart, were not so suitable as to express the vast synthesis that embraced the whole continent from the Indus to the sea and aimed to weld it into a nation. Aryavrat as defined by the ancient writers was the land that lay between the Himalaya and the Vindhya आर्यावर्तः पुण्यभूमिर्मध्यं विन्ध्यहिमालयोः and although it was best suited to the circumstances which gave it birth, yet and, therefore, it could not serve as a common name to a people that had welded Aryans and non-Aryans into a common race and had carried their culture—Empire—far beyond the bending summits of Vindhyadri. This necessity of finding a suitable term to express the expansive thought of an Indian nation was more or less effectively met when the house of Bharat came to exercise its sway over the entire world. Without entering into speculations as to who this Bharat was—the Vedic Bharat or the Jain one—or what was the exact period at which he ruled, it is here enough for us to know that his name had been not only accepted but the cherished epithet by which the people of Aryavrat and Dakshnapath delighted to call their common motherland and their common cultural empire. Thus as the horizon opened out to the South, we find that the centre of gravity had very naturally shifted from the Saptasindhus to the Gangetic delta and the name Saptasindhu or Aryavrat or Dakshnapath gave way to the politically grander expression, Bharatkhand which included in its sweep all that lay between the Himalayas and the seas. This is most clearly indicated by the definition of our nation attempted at a period when the vast conception must have been dawning over the minds of our great thinkers. We have met with no better attempt to define our position as a people than the terse little couplet in the विष्णुपुराण-उत्तरयत्समुद्रस्य हिमादेश्चैव दक्षिणम् । वर्ष तद्भारतं नाम भारती यत्र संततिः ॥

How names are given

But this new word Bharatvarsh could not altogether suppress our cradle name Sindhus or Hindus nor could it make us forget the love we bore to that river of rivers—the Sindhu, at whose breast our patriarchs and people had drunk the milk of life. Our frontier provinces which bordered the course of Indus still clung to their ancient name Sindhurashtar and throughout the Sanskrit literature we find Sindhusauvirs recognised as an integral and an important part of our body politic. In the great Mahabharat war, the King of Sindhusauvir figures prominently and is said to have been closely related to the Bharats. Although the limits of the Sindhurashtar shifted from time to time, yet the language that the people speak—did then and does even now mark them out as a people by themselves—from Multan to the sea, and the name 'Sindhi' which it bears, is an emphatic reminder that all those who speak it are Sindhus and are entitled to be recognised as a geographical and political unit in the commonwealth of our Indian people. Although the epithet Bharatkhand succeeded in almost overshadowing the cradle name of our nation in India, yet the foreign nations seem to have cared little for it and as our frontier provinces continued to be known by their ancient name, so even our immediate neighbours—the Avestic Persians, the Jews, the Greeks and others clung to our ancient name Sindhus or Hindus. They did not merely indicate the borderland of Indus by this term as in days gone by, but the whole nation into which the ancient Sindhus by expansion and assimilation had grown. The Avestic Persians know us as Hindus, the Greeks dropping the harsh accent as Indos and through the Greeks almost all Europe and later on America as Hindus or Indians. Even Hiuen-Tsang who lived so long with us persists in calling us Shintus or Hintus. Barring a few examples as that of Afghanistan being called Shavetbharat by the Parthians, very rarely indeed had the foreigners forgotten our cradle name or preferred the new one, Bharat to it. Down to this day, the whole world knows us as 'Hindus' and our land as 'Hindusthan' as if in fulfilment to the wishes of our Vedic fathers who were first to make that choice.

But, a name by its nature is determined not so much by what one likes to call oneself but generally by what others like to do. In fact a name is called into existence for this very purpose. Self is known to itself immutably and without a name or even without a form. But, when it comes in contact or conflict with a non-self then alone it stands in need of a name if it wants to communicate with others or if others persist in communicating with it. It is a game that requires two to play at. If the world insists that a teacher or a wit must be handed down as an *'ashatvakra'* or a *'mulla dopiyaja'*, well, then he, in spite of his liking, is very likely to be remembered as such. If the name chosen by the world for us is not directly against our liking, then it is yet more likely to shadow all other names. We might bear witness 'Paage', 'Mujumdar', 'Peshve', but if the world hits upon the word by which they would know us as one redolent of our glory or our early love, then that word is certain not only to shadow but to survive every other name we may have. This fact added to the circumstances which brought us first into close contact and then into a fierce conflict with the world at large, soon enabled the epithet Hindu to assert itself once more and so vigorously as to push into the background even the well beloved name of Bharatkhand itself.

International life

Although Indians were by no means cut off from the outside world before the rise of Buddhism and although their world activities had already assumed such dimensions as to give a just occasion to our patriotic poet law-givers to claim,

एतद्देशप्रसूतसय सकाशादग्रजन्मन:
स्वं स्वं चरित्रं शिक्षेरन् पृथिव्यां सर्वमानवा: ॥ (मनु)

yet as far as the present argument is concerned, the international life of India, after the rise of Buddhism, requires chiefly to be considered. Because it was about this time when political enterprise having exposed or exhausted all possibilities of expansion in our own land naturally began to overflow its limits to an extent unevidenced before and the communications with the outsiders began to knock at our doors more impudently and even imperatively than they ever had done. In addition to these political developments, the great and divine mission that set in motion 'the wheel of the law of righteousness' made India the very heart—the very soul—of almost all the then known world. To countless millions of human souls from Misar to Mexico, the land of the Sindhus came to be the land of their gods and Godmen. Thousands of pilgrims from distant shores poured into this country and thousands of scholars, preachers, sages and saints went from this land to all the then known world. But, as the outside world persisted in recognising us by our ancient name 'Sindhu' or 'Hindu', both these in-coming and out-going processes helped mightily to render that epithet to be the most prominent of our national names. The necessity of political and diplomatic correspondence with various states, who knew us as Hindus or Indus, must also have, by making it incumbent on our people to respond to it, revived the use of this epithet first side by side with and then at times even instead of the name Bharatkhand.

But, if the rise of Buddhism has thus enabled this epithet to grow in prominence throughout the world and made us more and more conscious of ourselves as Hindus, then strange to say the fall of Buddhism only carried this process further than ever.

Fall of Buddhism

We fear that the one telling factor that contributed to the fall of Buddhism more than any other has escaped that detailed attention of scholars which it deserves. But, as the subject in hand does but remotely involve its treatment here, we cannot treat it here in full. All that we can do here is to make a few general remarks and leave them to be expounded and detailed out to a more favourable occasion if the work be not done by others better fitted to do it. Can it be that philosophical differences alone could have made our nation turn against Buddhism? Not wholly; for these differences had been there all along and even flourished side by side with each other. Can it be the general inanition and demoralisation of the Buddhistic church itself? Not wholly; for, if some of the *viharas;* sheltered a loose, lazy and promiscuous crowd of men and women who lived on others and spent what was not theirs on disreputable pursuits of life, yet, on the other hand, the line of those spiritual giants of Arhat and Bhikkuz had not altogether ended; nor had such scenes been peculiar to the Buddhistic *viharas* alone! All these and many other shortcomings would not have attracted such fierce attention and proved fatal to Buddhist power in India had not the political consequences of the Buddhism expansion been so disastrous to the national virility and even the national existence of our race. No prelude to a vast tragedy could be more dramatic in its effect in foreshadowing the culminating catastrophe than that incident in the life of the Shakya Sinha, when the news of the gate of the little tribal republic of the Shakyas was carried to their former Prince when he was just laying the foundation stone of the Buddhist Church. He had already enrolled the flower of his clan in his Bhikkusangha and the little Shakya Republic thus deprived of its bravest and best, fell an easy victim to the strong and warlike in the best, very lifetime of the Shakya Sinha. The news when carried to him is said to have left the Enlightened unconcerned. Centuries rolled on—the Prince of the Shakyas had grown into the Prince of Princes—the Lokjit, the great conqueror of worlds. The confines of his little Shakya state expanded and embraced the confines of India; and as if to give a touch of poetical precision and poetical justice, the woeful fate that had overtaken the tribal republic of Kapil-avastu befell the whole of Bharatvarsha itself and it fell an easy prey to the strong and warlike—not like Shakyas of their own kith and kin but—the Lichis and Huns! Of course, the Enlightened would perhaps remain as unaffected as ever, even if this news could ever reach him like the first. But, the rest of Hindus then could not drink with equanimity this cup of bitterness and political servitude at the hands of those whose barbarous violence could ill be soothed by the mealy-mouthed formulas of *ahimsa* and spiritual brotherhood, and whose steel could ill be blunted by the soft palm leaves and rhymed charms. We do not mean to underrate—much less accuse—the services of the great brotherhood and its divine mission. We have only to point out the concomitance that is too glaring to escape the attention of any student of history. We know that it could easily be pressed against this statement that the greatest and even the most powerful Indian kings and emperors known belong to the Buddhist period. Yes, but known to whom?—To Europeans and those of us who have unconsciously imbibed not only their thoughts but even their prejudices. There was a time when every school history in India opened from the Mohammedan invasion because the average English writers of that time knew next to nothing of our earlier life. Lately, the general knowledge of Europe has extended backwards to the rise of Buddhism and we too are apt to look upon it as the first and even the most glorious epoch of our history. The fact is, it is neither. We yield to none in our love and admiration and respect the Buddha—the Dharma—the Sangha, they are all ours. Their glories are ours and ours their failures. Great was Ashoka the Devapriya, and greater were the achievements of Buddhis Bhikkus. But, achievements as great, if not greater, and things as holy and more politic and statesmanly had gone before them and indeed enabled them to be what they were. So, we do not think that the political virility or the manly nobility of our race began and ended with the Mauryas alone—or was a consequence of their embracing Buddhism. Buddhism has conquests to claim but they belong to a world far removed from this our matter-of-fact world,where feet of clay do not stand long, and steel could be easily sharpened, and *trishna*-thirst—is too powerful and real to be quenched by painted streams that flow perennially in heavens. These must have been the considerations that must have driven themselves home to the hearts of our patriots and thinkers when the Huns and Shakas poured like volcanic torrents and burnt all that thrived. The Indians saw that the cherished ideals of their race—their thrones and their families and the very gods they worshipped—trampled under foot, the holy land of their love devastated and sacked by hordes of barbarians, so inferior to them in language, religion, philosophy, mercy and all the soft and human attributes of man and god, but superior to them in strength alone; strength that summed up its creed, in two words—fire and sword! The inference was clear; clear also was the fact that Buddhist logic had no argument that could efficiently meet this new and terrible dualism—this *Duwait*, this strange bible of fire and steel. So, the leaders of thought and action of our race had to rekindle their sacrificial fire to oppose the sacrilegious one to re-open the mines of Vedic fields for steel to get it sharpened on the altar of Kali,' the Terrible so that Mahakaal, the 'Spirit of the Times' be appeased. Nor were their anticipations belied. The success of the renovated Hindu arms was undisputed and indisputable. Vikramaditya, who drove the foreigners from the Indian soil and Lalitaditya who caught and chastised them in their very dens from Tartary to Mongolia—were but complements of each other. Valour had accomplished what formulas had failed to do. Once more the people rose to the heights of greatness that shed its lustre on all departments of life. Poetry and philosophy, art and architecture, agriculture and commerce, thought and action felt the quickening impulse which consciousness of independence and strength and victory alone can radiate. The reaction as usual was complete even to a fault. 'Up with the Vedic Dharma!' 'Back to the *Vedas*!' The national cry grew louder and louder, more and more imperative, because this was essentially a political necessity.

Buddhism—a universal religion

Buddhism had made first and yet the greatest attempt to propagate a universal religion. 'Go, ye Bhikkus, to all the ten directions of the world and preach the law of righteousness!' Truly, it was a law of righteousness—it had no ulterior end in view, no lust for land or lucre quickening its steps; and grand though its achievements were, it could not eradicate the seeds of animal passions nor of political ambitions nor of individual aggrandisement in the minds of all men to such an extent as to make it safe for India to change her sword for a rosary. Even then, to set an example, did India declare her will to 'take more pleasure in the conquest of peace and righteousness than in the conquests of arms.' Nobly she tried, Ah! so nobly as to make herself ridiculous in the eyes of lust and lucre: had she not issued royal edicts to the effect that the very water be strained before it was poured out for horses and elephants to drink, so as to enable the tiny lives in the waters to escape immediate death? And had she not opened cornthrowing centres in the midst of the seas that fish be fed in her oceans of the world, nor had the very fish ceased to feed on each other! Nobly did she try to kill killing by getting killed—and at last found out that palm leaves at times are too fragile for steel! As long as the whole world was red in tooth and claw and the national and racial distinction so strong as to make men brutal, so long if India had to live at all a life, whether spiritual or political according to the right of her soul, she must not lose the strength born of national and racial cohesion. So, the leaders of thought and action grew sick of repeating the mumbos and jumbos of Universal brotherhood and bitterly complained:

ये त्वया देव निहता असुराश्चैव विष्णुना।
ते जाता मलेंच्छरूपेण पुनरद्य महीतले॥
व्यापादयन्ति ते विप्रान् ध्नन्ति यज्ञादिका: क्रिया:।
हरन्ति मुनिकन्याश्चपापा: कि कि न कुवंते॥
म्लेचछाक्रान्ते च भुलोके निर्वषट्कारमंगले।
यज्ञयागादि विच्छेदाद्देवलोकोवऽसीदति॥ (गुणाढ्य)

and when the barbarian hordes of the Shakas and the Huns—who had ravaged their fair land that had in utter confidence clad herself in a Bhikku's dress, changed her sword for rosary and had taken to the vows of *ahimsa* and nonviolence—were expelled beyond the Indus and further, and a strong national state was firmly established, then it was but natural that the leaders of our race should have realised what an immense amount of strength could be derived if but the new national state was backed up by a Church as intensely national.

Moreover everything that is common in us with our enemies weakens our power of opposing them. The foe that has nothing in common with us is the foe likely to be most bitterly resisted by us just as a friend that has almost everything in him which we admire and prize in ourselves is likely to be the friend we love most. The necessity of creating a bitter sense of wrong and invoking a power of undying resistance especially in India that had under the opiates of universalism and non-violence lost the faculty even of resisting sin and crime and aggression, could best be accomplished by cutting off even the semblance of a common worship—a common Church which required her to clasp the hand of those as her co-religionists whose had been the very hand that had strangled her as a nation. What was the use of a universal faith that instead of smoothening the ferociousness and brutal egoism of other nations only excited their lust by leaving India defenceless and unsuspecting? No, the only safe guards in future were valour and strength that could only be borne of a national self-consciousness. She had poured her life's blood for sophistry that tried to prove otherwise.

Then came the reaction!

The reaction against the universal tendencies of Buddhism only grew more insistent and powerful as the attempt to re-establish the Buddhist power in India began to assume a more threatening attitude. Nationalist tendencies refused to barter with our nation's independence and accept a foreign conqueror as our overlord. But, if that foreign invader happened to be favourably inclined towards Buddhism, then he was sure to find some secret sympathiser in the Indian Buddhists all over India, even as Catholic Spain could always find some important section in England to sympathise with their efforts to restore a Catholic dynasty in England. Not only this, but dark hints abound in our ancient records to show that at times some foreign Buddhist powers had actually invaded India with an express national and religious aim in view. We cannot treat the history of this period exhaustively here, but can only point to the half-symbolic and half-actual description given in one of our *Puranas* of the war waged on the *Aryadeshja* by *Nyanpati* (the king of the Huns) and his Buddhist allies. The record tells us in a mythological strain how a big battle was fought on the banks of River *Hahha*, how the Buddhist forces made China the basis of operation (चीनदेशमुपागम्य युद्धभूमिरकात् ।), how they were reinforced by contingents from many Buddhist nations:

श्यामदेशोद्भवा लक्षास्तथा लक्षाश्र्च जापकाः ।
दशलक्षाश्र्चीनदेश्या युद्धाय समु पस्थितः ॥

and how after a tough fight the Buddhists lost it and paid heavily for their defeat. They had formally to renounce all ulterior national aims against India and give a pledge that they would never again enter India with any political end in view. The Buddhists as individuals had nothing to fear from India—the land of toleration—but they should give up all dreams of endangering the national life of India and her independence:

सर्वेश्र्च बोद्धवृन्दैश्र्च तत्रैव शपथं कृतन् ।
आर्यदेशं न यास्यामः कदाचिद्राष्ट्रहेतवे ॥ (भविष्यपुराण, प्रतिसर्गपर्व)

Institutions in favour of Nationality

And, thus, we find that institutions that were the peculiar marks of our nation were revived: Varanashramviastha, which could not be wiped away even under the Buddistic sway, grew in popularity to such an extent that kings and emperors felt it a distinction to be called 'वर्णव्यवस्थापनपर:' (सोनापत ताम्रलेख)—'वर्णारश्रमवयवस्थापन प्रवृतचक्र' (मधवत ताम्रपट). Reaction in favour of this institution grew so strong that our nationality was almost getting identified with it. Witness the definition that tries to draw a line of demarcation between us and foreigners:

'चातुर्वर्ण्यवस्थनं यस्मिन्देशे न विद्यते।
तं मलेच्छदेशं जानोयादार्यार्यावर्तस्ततः परम्॥'

From this, it was but a natural step to prohibit our people from visiting shores which were uncongenial—in some cases, fiercely hostile—to such peculiar institutions as these and where our people could not be expected to receive the protection that would enable to keep up the spirit and letter of our faith. Reckless as the reaction was, perfectly intelligible when viewed at politically, for do we not frequently meet with patriotic thinkers even now in our land who would stand for laws prohibiting our men from emigrating to nations where they are sure to be subjected to national disabilities and dishonours?

Commingling of Races

Thus it was political and national necessity that was at once the cause and the effect of the decline of Buddhism in India. Buddhism had its geographical centre of gravity nowhere. So it was an imperative need to restore at least the national centre of gravity that India had lost in attempting to get identified with Buddhism. When the nation grew intensely self-conscious as an organism would do and was in direct conflict with the non-self, it instinctively turned to draw the line of division and mark well the position it occupied, so as to make it clear to themselves where they exactly stood and to the world how they were unmistakably a people by themselves—not only racial and national, but even a geographical and political unit. On the southern side of our country, the natural and strategic limits were already reached, sanctioned and sanctified. The framework of the deep and boundless seas in which our southern peninsula is set is almost poetical in its grace and perfection. The *smudararshna* had pleased the eyes of generations of our poets and patriots. But on the north-western sides of our nation the commingling of races was growing rather too unceremonious to be healthy and our frontiers too shifty to be safe. Therefore it would have been a matter of surprise if the intense spirit of self-assertion that had found so benign an asylum under the patronage of the Mahakaal of Ujjain had not made our patriots turn to this pressing necessity of drawing a frontier line for us that would be as vivid as effective. And what could that line be but the vivacious yet powerful stream—the river of rivers—the Sindhu? The day on which the patriarchs of our race had crossed that stream they ceased to belong to the people they had definitely left behind and laid the foundation of a new nation—were reborn into a new people that, under the quieting star of new hope and new mission, were destined by assimilation and by expansion to grow into a race and a new polity that could only be most fittingly and feelingly described as Sindhu or Hindu.

Back to the Vedas

Nor was this attempt to identify our frontier line with River Indus an innovation. In fact it was but the natural consequence of the great war-cry of the national revivalists 'Back to the *Vedas*'. The Vedic state based on and backed up by the Vedic Church must be designated by the Vedic name and—so far as it was then possible—identified with the Vedic lines. And this process of events which the very general trend of history should have enabled us to anticipate seems to have actually gone through. For, one of patriotic *Puranas* assures us that Shalivahan, the grandson of the great Vikramaditya, after having defeated the second attempt of foreigners to rush in, expelled them beyond the Indus, and issued a royal decree to the effect that thenceforth the Indus should constitute the line of demarcation between India and other non-Indian nations.

एतस्मिन्ननतरे तत्र शालिवाहनभूपतिः ।
विक्रमादित्य पोत्रश्च पितृराज्यं प्रपेदिरे ।
जित्वा शकान् दुराधर्षान् चीनतैत्तिरिदेशजान् ॥
बाल्हिकान् कामरूपांश्च श्वरोमजान् खुरजान् शठान् ॥
तेषां कोशान् गृहीत्वा च दंडयोग्यानकारयत् ॥
स्थापिता तेन मर्यादा मलेच्छार्याणां पृथक्पृथक् ॥
सिंधुस्थानमिति ज्ञेयं राष्ट्मार्यस्य चोत्तमम् ॥
म्लेचछस्थानं परं सिधोः कृतं तेन महात्मना ॥

(भष्यिपुराण प्रतिसर्गपर्व अ. 2)

Sindhustan

The most ancient of the names of our country of which we have a record is Saptasindhu or Sindhu. Even Bharatvarsh is and must necessarily be a latter designation besides being personal in its appeal. The glories of a person however magnificent, lose their glamour as time passes on. The name that recommends itself by appealing to such personal glories and achievements, can never be so effective and permanent a source of ever-rising consciousness of gratitude and pride as a name that, besides being reminiscent of such national achievements and beloved personal touches, is in addition to it associated with some great beneficent and perennial natural phenomena. Emperor Bharat is gone and gone also many an emperor as great, but the Sindhu goes on forever; forever inspiring and fertilising our sense of gratitude, vivifying our sense of pride, renovating the ancient memories of our race—a sentinel keeping watch over the destinies of our people. It is the vital spinal cord that connects the remotest past to the remotest future. The name that associates and identifies our nation with a river like that, enlists nature on our side and bases our national life on a foundation, that is, so far as human calculations are concerned, as lasting as eternity. All these considerations must have fired the imagination of the then leaders of thought and action and made them restore the ancient Vedic name of our land and nation, Sindhustan—the राष्ट्रमार्यस्य चोत्तमम् ।

The epithet Sindhustan besides being Vedic had also a curious advantage which could only be called lucky and yet is too substantial to be ignored. The word Sindhu in Sanskrit does not only mean the Indus but also the sea—'समुद्ररशाना' which girdles southern peninsula—so that this one word, Sindhu, points out almost all the frontiers of our land at a single stroke. Even if we do not accept the tradition that River Brahmaputra is only a branch of the Sindhu which falls into flowing streams on the eastern and western slopes of the Himalayas and thus constitutes both our eastern as well as western frontiers, still it is indisputably true that it circumscribes our northern and western extremities in its sweep and so the epithet Sidhustan calls up the image of our whole motherland: the land that lies between Sindhu and Sindhu—from the Indus to the seas.

What is Arya?

But, it must not be supposed that the epithet Sindhu recommended itself to our patriots only because it was geographically best fitted. For, we find it emphatically stated that the concept expressed by this word was national and not merely geographical. Sindhustan was not merely a piece of land, but it was a राष्ट्र, a nation, which was ideally if not always actually a state (*ragyarashtram*). It also clearly followed that the culture that flourished in Sindhustan and the citizens thereof were Sindhus even as they had been in the Vedic days. Sindhustan was the *'rashtrmaryasya chottmumm'* as distinguished from *malechhsthan,* the land of the foreigners. However, it must be clearly pointed out that the definition is not based on any theological hair-splitting or religious fanaticism. The word 'Arya' is expressly stated in the very verses to mean all those who had been incorporated as parts integral in the nation and people that flourished on this side of the Indus, whether Vedic or Avedic, Brahmin or Chandal, and owned and claimed to have inherited a common culture, common blood, common country and common polity; while *malechha* also by the very fact of its being put in opposition to Sindhustan meant foreigners nationally and racially and not necessarily religiously.

Hindu & Hindusthan

This royal decree was as all royal decrees in Sindhustan had generally been—the mere executive outcome of a strong and popular movement. For, the custom of looking upon Attak as the veritable Indian land's end as the very word 'Attak' signifies could not have been originated and observed so universally and so long, had it not been inspired by and appealing to our national imagination. This custom that is so tenaciously and reverently observed by millions of people, premiers and peasants alike, is a good proof that strongly corroborates the fact that some such royal edict sanctioning the identification of our frontiers with the ancient Sindhu and associating the name of our land and nation with it as Sindhustan had actually been issued; and that the highest religious sanctification consecrating this royal sanction and popular will must have enabled this attempt to restore the Vedic name of our country to triumph in the end. Of course, centuries had yet to pass and momentous events to happen to shape and mould the destinies of the words, Sindhu and Sindhustan, till they came to be as powerfully influential as to colour the thought of our whole nation and be the cherished possession of our race. But after all, they have done it and today we find that while thousands would not know what Aryavart or Bharatvarsh exactly means, yet the very man in the street will understand and recognise the names Hindu and Hindusthan as his very own.*

---

* The verses from *Bhavishpurana* quoted above seem to be quite trustworthy so far as their general purport is concerned: Firstly because they record a general tradition that, unlike dates or individual successions, can easily be remembered longer. Secondly, independently of that, the general trend of our history as shown points to some such state of affairs. Thirdly, it is not necessary here for our arguments to be very precise either about the date of this decree or even the king by whom it was issued. And, fourthly, the author does not seem to have been writing about things only haphazardly or to which he is entirely a stranger. For, the family table that he gives of the House of Vikramaditya is again given on other parts of the work and the two agree closely with each other. The writer who knows of details about the House is likely to know the *salient* facts of the most distinguished king that belonged to it.

After all, the main resources of our history had been and must ever be our national traditions remembered or recorded in our ancient *puranas*, epics and literature. Their details may be challenged, their dates determined and rejected, but on account of discrepancies here or miraculous colouring there which are, in fact, common to all ancient records of mankind, we cannot dismiss them altogether, especially where the acts recorded have not an impossible or unnatural element in them or when they do not contradict events otherwise proved to be indisputably true. The habit of doubting everything in the *puranas* till it has been corroborated by some foreign evidence is absurd. The sounder process would be to depend on our works especially where general traditions and events are concerned till they are found to be unreliable in the light of any more weighty and less ambiguous evidence and not simply on account of the airy imaginings of someone to whom it does not seem probable! Take the case of this *Bhavishyapuran* itself; because it contains some inaccuracies and even absurdities—and is Plutarch free from them? Are we to reject the personality of Alexander himself because of the supernatural touches given to the story of his birth? Would it be reasonable to doubt, say the following verse:

चंद्रगुप्तस्य सुतः पौरस्याधिपतेः सुताम्।
सुलवस्य तथोद्वहय पावनीं बौद्धतत्पर॥

In fact, we owe a debt of gratitude to these *Puranas* and epics for having preserved all ancient and venerable records of our people through revolutions which had effaced the very traces of whole nations and whole civilisations elsewhere in the world. For after all, these records of our ancient and patriotic *Puranas* and *Itihaas* as are at any rate more faithful, more accurate and more reliable than the modern up-to-date western *Puranas* that have such convincing discoveries to their credit as the one which assures us that *Ramayan* sings of (the foundation of Vijayanagar or the other which asserts that Gautam the Buddha was merely the sun or the dawn personified!

Reverence to Buddha

But before we proceed to state what further developments the history of this epithet had to undergo we feel it incumbent to render an apology to ourselves. We have, while writing this section, wounded our own feelings. So, we hasten to add that the few harsh words we had to say in explaining the political necessity that led to the rejection of Buddhism in India should not be understood to mean that we have not a very high opinion of that Church as a whole! No, no! I am as humble an admirer and an adorer of that great and holy Sangh—the holiest the world has ever seen—as any of its initiated worshipper. We are not initiated not because the Sangh is not worthy of us, but because we are not worthy of stepping on the footsteps of the temple that has lasted longer because it rested on ideas than many a great palace that rested on rocks. The consciousness that the first great and the most successful attempt to wean man of the brute inherent in him was conceived, launched and carried on from century to century by a galaxy of great teachers, Arhats and Bhikkus who were born in India, who were bred in India and who owned India as the land of their worship—fills us with feelings too deep for words. And if these be our feelings for the Sangh, then what shall we say about its great founder—the Buddha the Enlightened? I, the humblest of the humble of mankind can dare to approach thee, Oh *Tathagat!* With no other offering, but my utter humility and my utter emptiness! Although I feel that I fail to catch the purport of thy words yet I know that it must be so. Because while thy words are gathered from the lips of gods, mine ears and my understandings are trained to the accents and the din of this matter-of-fact world. Perhaps it was too soon for thee to sound thy match and unfurl thy banner while the world was too young and the day but just risen! It fails to keep pace with thee and its sight gets dazzled and dimmed to keep the radiance of the banner in full view. As long as the law of evolution that lays down the iron command:

चलानामचला भक्ष्या दंष्ट्रिणामप्यदंष्ट्रिण।
अहस्तानां सहस्ताश्च्व शूराणां चैव भीरवः ॥ (मनु

is too persistent and dangerously imminent to be categorically denied by the law of righteousness whose mottos shine brilliantly and beautifully—but as the stars in the heavens do—so long the banner of nationality will refuse to be replaced by that of universality and, yet, that very national banner hallowed as it is by the worship of gods and goddesses of our race, would have been poorer if it could not have counted the Shakyasing under its fold. But, as it is, thou art our as truly as Shri Rama or Shri Krishna or Shri Mahavir had been and as the words were but the echoes of yearnings of our national soul, thy visions, the dreams of our race, even so, if ever the law of righteousness rules triumphant on our human plane, then thou will find that the land that cradled thee, and the people that nursed thee, will have contributed most to bring about that consummation *if indeed, the fact of having contributed thee has not proved that much already!!*

Hindus: All one and a nation

So far, we have depended upon Sanskrit records in tracing the growth of the word 'Sindhu' and we have left the thread of our inquiry at the point where the growing concept of an Indian nation was found to be better expressed by the word Sindhustan than by any other existing words. It was precisely to refute any parochial and narrow-minded significance which might, as in the case of Aryavrat be attached to this word that the definition of the word Sindhustan was rid of any association with a particular institution or party-coloured suggestion. For example, Aryavrat was according to an authority:

चातुर्वण्यंवयंवस्थानं यस्मिन्देशे न विद्यते।
तं मलेच्छदेशं जानीयादार्यावतंस्ततः परम्॥

This solution, though legitimate could not be lasting. An institution is meant for the society, not the society or its ideal for an institution. The *chaturvarnyavyavsthan* may disappear when it had served its end or ceases to serve it, but will that make our land a *malechhdesha* land of foreigners? The *sannyasis*, the *Arya Samajis*, the Sikhs and many others do not recognise the *Chaturvarnyaviyavasatha* and yet, are they foreigners? God forbid? They are ours by blood, by race, by country, by god.

'तं वर्ष भारतं नाम भारती यत्र संतति' is a definition ten times better because truer than that, we, Hindus, are all one and a nation, because chiefly of our common blood भारती संतति:

Hindusthani language

At this period of our history, the rise as well as the fall of Buddhism were accompanied by a remarkable spread and growth of the vernaculars of India and Sanskrit was fast being shut up in the impenetrable fortresses of classical conventionality to such an extent that new ideas and new names had to be Sanskritised before they could be incorporated in any acceptable work. Naturally, the very day life and the ever-changing phases of national and social activities gradually sought expression through the spoken Prakrit which thus grew better fitted to convey the living and throbbing thoughts of the people in all their freshness and vigour and precision. Consequently, although the words 'Sindhu' and 'Sindhustan' are, at times found in Sanskrit works, yet the Sanskrit writers generally preferred the word 'Bharat' as being more in consonance with the established cannons of elegance. While on the other hand the vernaculars stuck almost exclusively to the more popular and living name of our land Hindusthan (Sindhustan), instead of the ancient and well-beloved names, Bharat or Aryavrat. We need not repeat here how स in Sanskrit gets at times changed into ह in India as well as non-Indian Prakrits. So we find the living vernacular literature of India full of reference to Hindusthan or Hindus. Although the Sanskrit language must ever remain the cherished and sacred possession of our race, contributing most powerfully to the fundamental unity of our people and enriching our life, ennobling our aspiration and purifying the fountains of our being, yet, the honour of being the living spoken national tongue of our people is already won by that Prakrit, which being one of the eldest daughters of Sanskrit, is most fittingly called Hindi or Hindusthani—the language of the national and cultural descendants of the ancient Sindhus or Hindus. Hindusthani is par-excellence the language of Hindusthan or Sindhustan. The attempt to raise Hindi to the pedestal of our national tongue is neither new nor forced. Centuries before the advent of British rule in India, we find it recorded in our annals that this was the medium of expression throughout India. A *sadhu* or merchant starting from Rameshwaram and proceeding to Hardwar, could make himself understood in all parts of India through this tongue. Sanskrit might have introduced him to the circles of *pandits* and princes, but Hindistani was a safe and sure passport to the *Rajya Sabhas* as well as to the bazars. A Nanak, a Chaitanya, a Ramdas could and did travel up and down the country as freely as they would have done in their own provinces, teaching and preaching in this tongue. As the growth and development of our genuine national tongue was parallel to and almost simultaneous with the revival and popularisation of the ancient names,

Sindhustan or Sindhus or Hindusthan or Hindus, it was but a matter, of course that language being the common possession of the whole nation should be called Hindusthani or Hindi.

After expulsion of the Huns and the Shakas, the valour of her arms left Sindustan in an undisturbed possession of independence for centuries on centuries to come and enabled her once more to be the land where peace and plenty reigned. The blessings of freedom and independence were shared by the princes and peasants alike. The patriotic authors go in rapture over the greatness and the happiness that marked this long chapter of our history extending over nearly a thousand years or so:

ग्रामे ग्रामे स्थितो देव: देशे देशे स्थितो मख: ।
गेहे गेहे स्थित द्रवयं धमंश्च्वेव जने जने ॥ (भविष्यपुराण, प्रतिसर्गपर्व)

From Sinhal (Ceylon) to Kashmir, the Rajputs—a single family of princes—ruled often connected closely by marriages and more closely by the tradition of chivalry and culture handed down by a common law. The whole life of the nation was being brought into a harmony as rich as divine, and the growth of the national language was but an outward expression of this inward unity of our national life.

Foreign invaders

But, as it often happens in history, this very undisturbed enjoyment of peace and plenty lulled our Sindhustan, in a sense of false security and bred a habit of living in the land of dreams. At last, she was rudely awakened on the day when Mohmmed of Ghazni crossed the Indus, the frontier line of Sindhaustan and invaded her. That day the conflict of life and death began. Nothing makes self-conscious of itself so much as the conflict with the non-self. Nothing can weld peoples into a nation and nations into a state as the pressure of a common foe. Hatred separates as well as unites. Never had Sindhustan a better chance and a more powerful stimulus to be herself forged into an indivisible whole as on that dire day, when the great iconoclast crossed the Indus. The Mohammedans had crossed that stream even under Kasim, but it was a wound only skin-deep, for the heart of our people was not hurt and was not even aimed at. The contest began in grim earnestness with Mohammed and ended—shall we say with Abdalii? From year to year, decade to decade, century to century, the contest continued. Arabia ceased to be what Arabia was; Iran, annihilated, Egypt, Syria, Afghanistan, Baluchistan, Tartary—from Granada to Gazani—nations and civilisations fell in heaps before the sword of Islam of Peace!! But here for the first time the sword succeeded in striking but not in killing. It grew blunter each time it struck, each time it cut deep but as it was lifted out to strike again, the wound stood healed. Vitality of the victim proved stronger than the vitality of the victor. The contrast was not only grim but it was monstrously unequal. It was not a race, a nation or a people India had to struggle with; it was nearly all Asia, quickly to be followed by nearly all Europe. The Arabs had entered Sindh and single-handedly they could do little else. They soon failed to defend their own independence in their homeland and as a people we hear nothing further about them. But, here India alone had to face Arabs, Persians, Pathans, Baluchis, Tartars, Turks, Moguls—a veritable human Sahara whirling and columning up bodily in furious world storm! Religion is a mighty motive force.

So is rapine. But, where religion is goaded on by Rapine and rapine serves as a hand-maid to religion, the propelling force that is generated by these together is only equalled by profoundity of human misery and devastation they leave behind them in their march. Heaven and hell making a common cause—such were the forces. Overwhelmingly furious that took India by surprise the day that Mohmmed crossed the Indus and invaded her. Day after day, decade after decade, centuries after centuries, the ghastly conflict continued and India single-handedly kept the fight morally and militarily. The moral victory was won when Akbar came to the throne and Dara Shukoh was born. The frantic efforts of Aurangzeb to retrive their fortunes lost in the moral field only hastened the loss of the military fortunes in the battlefield as well. At last, Bhau, as if symbolically hammered the ceiling of the Imperial seat of the Moghuls to pieces, the day of Panipat rose, the Hindus lost the battle, and won the war. Never again had an Afghan dared to penetrate to Delhi, while the triumphant Hindu banner that our Marathas had carried to the Attak was taken up by our Sikhs and carried across the Indus to the banks of Kabul.

Hindutva at work

In this prolonged furious conflict, our people became intensely conscious of ourselves as Hindus and were welded into a nation to an extent unknown in our history. It must not be forgotten that we have all along referred to the progress of the Hindu movement as a whole and not to that of any particular creed or religious section thereof—of Hindutva and not Hinduism only. Sanatanists, Satnamis, Sikhs, Aryas,

Anaryas, Marathas and Madrasis, Brahmins and Panchmas—all suffered as Hindus and triumphed as Hindus. Both friends and foes contributed equally to enable the words Hindu and Hindusthan to supercede all other designations of our land and our people. Aryavrat and Dakshnapath, Jambudeep and Bharatvarsh, none could give so eloquent an expression to the main political and cultural point at issue as the word Hindusthan could do. All those on this side of Indus who claimed the land from Sindhu to Sindhu, from Indus to the seas, as the land of their birth, felt that they were directly mentioned by that one single expression, Hindusthan. The enemies hated us as Hindus and the whole family of peoples and races, of sects and creeds that flourished from Attak to Katak was suddenly individualised into a single being. We cannot help dropping the remark that no one has up to this time taken the whole field of Hindu activities from A.D. 1300 to 1800 into survey from this point of view, mastering the details of the various now parallel, now correlated, movements from Kashmere to Ceylon and from Sindh to Bengal, and yet rising higher above them all to visualise the whole scene in its proportion as an integral whole. For, it was the one great issue to defend the honour and independence of Hindusthan and maintain the cultural unity and civic life of Hindutva and not Hinduism alone, but Hindutva, i.e., Hindu Dharma—that was being fought out on the hundred fields of battle as well as on the floor of the chambers of diplomacy. This one word 'Hindutva' ran like a vital spinal cord through our whole body politic and made the Nairs of Malabar weep over the sufferings of the Brahmins of Kashmere. Our bards bewailed the fall of Hindus, our seers roused the feelings of Hindus, our heroes fought the battles of Hindus, our saints blessed the efforts of Hindus, our statesmen moulded the fate of Hindus, our mothers wept over the wounds and gloried over the triumphs of Hindus.

It would require a volume if we were to substantiate these remarks by quoting all the words and writings of our forefathers that bear on the point. But the argument in hand does not allow us to be drawn aside even by so alluring a task as that. Consequently we must content ourselves with quoting a few eloquent lines either from the lips or the pen of some of the foremost representatives of our Hindu race.

Of all the works written in the Hindu language, old and new, the great epic, *Pirthviraj Raso* by Chand Bardai is, so far as present researches go, admittedly the most ancient and authoritative one. There is only one solitary verse which claims to be an earlier composition. But luckily and strangely enough, this very first composition in our northern vernacular literature refers to the words Hindusthan in terms full of pride and patriotic fervour. The poet Ven, father of Chand Bardai addresses the Raja of Ajmer, the father of Prithviraj:

अटल ठाट महिपाट, अटल तारागढथानं
अटल नग्र अजमेर, अटल हिंदव अस्थानं
अटल तेज प्रताप, अटल लंकागढ़ डंडिय
अटल आप चहुवान, अटल भूमिजस मंडिय
संभरी भूप सोमेस नृप, अटल छत्र ओपै सुसर
कविराव वेन आसीस दे अटल जागां रजेसकर

Chand Bardai, who may justly be called Adkavi of Hindi literature, uses the words Hindi, Hindvan, Hind so often and so naturally as to leave no doubt of their being quite common and accepted terms as far back as the eleventh century, when the Mohammedans had not secured any permanent footing even in Punjab and, therefore, could not have influenced the independent and proud Rajputs to adopt a degrading nickname invented by their foes and make it their national and proud appellation. Describing how Shahabuddin taken prisoner by the Hindus, was let go by the noble Prithviraj on the condition that he would not again attack the 'Hindus', Chand says:

राखि पंचदिन राहि अदब आदर बहु किन्नी
सूज हुसेन गाजी सुपूत हथ्थै ग्रहि दिन्नी
किया सलाम तिनवार जाहु आपन्ने सुथानह
मति हिंदुपर साहि सज्जि आओ स्वस्थानह।

(पृथ्वीराज रासो स. 6)

But, Shahabuddin was not a man to be won over by Hindu chivalry. Again and again he sallies forth and fierce fight ensues to the boundless joy of that divine cynic Narad:

जब हिंदुदल जोर हुआ छुट्टि मीरघर भ्रम
समय अरबस्तान चला करन उदूसाक्रम

And again:

जुरे हिंदु भोरं बहे खगग तारं
मुखे मारमारं बहे सुरसारं

Till at last:

हिंदु मलेच्छ अधाइ घाईन।
नींच नारद युद्ध चायन॥

But, in spite of his efforts to crush the Hindus, Shahabuddin lost the day and the triumphant news sent Delhi mad with joy that Pajjunaray had once more taken Shahabuddin a prisoner. The populace greeted their King Prithviraj:

आज भाग चहुआन घर।
आज भाग हिंदवान॥
इन जीवित दिल्लीश्र्वर।
गंज न सक्कै आन॥

Further pledges solemnly entered by the man who had broken his form, insolent challenge is set by Shahabuddin, the Rawals and Samants are aflame, when Chamundrai tells the Mohammedan messenger to remind Shah of the dust he had licked and add:

निर्लज्ज मलेच्छ लजै नही। हम हिंदु लजवान्॥

The fatal day drew near and both the sides knew it was a desperate game. Chand Bardai almost on the eve of the defection of Hammir, approaches the Goddess Durga and opens his prayer so pathetic and so patriotic thus:

दुगगे हिंदुराजान बंदीन आयं
जपै जाप जालघर तू सहाय
नमस्ते नमस्ते इ जालंधरानी
सुर आसुरं नाजपुजा प्रभानी।

After having narrated the fateful results of the battle and consequent plot that enabled Shahabuddin to strike Prithviraj dead, the poem ends with paying a last touching tribute to the fallen Hindu Emperor:

धनि हिंदु प्रथिराज, जिन रजवट्ट उजारिय
धनि हिंदु प्रथिराज, बोल कलिमझझ उगारिय
धनि हिंदु प्रथिराज, जेन सुविहानह संध्यो
बारबारह ग्रहिमुक्कि, अंतकाल सर बंध्यो।

It is remarkable that although the word 'Bharat' appears often in the *Raso* in the sense of *Mahabharata*, yet it seldom, if ever, is used in the sense of Bharatvarsh. What we find is this earliest of our northern vernacular composition holds good in the later development of our vernacular literature down to the day of the great Hindu revival and the war of Hindu liberation. Ramdas, the high priest and prophet of that movement, in one of his mystical and prophetic utterances sings of the vision he had seen and triumphantly but thankfully asserts that much of what he had seen in his vision has already come to be true:

स्वप्री जें देखि लें रात्रीं, तें तें तैसेंचि होतसें
हिंडतां फिरतां गेलों, आनंद वन भूवनीं ॥ 1 ॥
उडाले सर्वही पापी, हिंदुस्थान बलवालें
अभक्तांचा क्षयो झाला, आनंद वन भूवनीं ॥ 2 ॥
कलचांत मांडिला मोठा, मलेच्छदैत्य बुडावया
कैपक्ष घेतला देवी, आनंद वन भूवनीं ॥ 3 ॥
येथून वाढला धर्म, राजधर्मासमागमें,
संतोष मांडिला मोठा, आनंद वन भूवनीं ॥ 4 ॥
बुडाला औरंगया पापी, मलेच्छ संहार जाहला,
मोडिलीं मांडिलीं छत्रें, आनंद वन भूवनीं ॥ 5 ॥
बोलणें वाउगे होतें, चालणे पाहिजे वरें,
पुढें घडेल तें खरें, आनंद वन भूवनीं ॥ 6 ॥
उदंड जाहलें पाणी, स्नान संधया करावया,
जपतप अनुष्ठानें, आनंद वन भूवनीं ॥ 7 ॥
रमरलें लिहिलें आहे, बोलता चालता हरी,
राम कर्ता, ताम भोक्ता, आनंद वन भूवनीं ॥ 8 ॥

(In utter darkness, I dreamt: Behold, dreams are realised. Hindusthan is up, has come by her own, and those that hated her and sinned against God are put down with a strong hand! Verily it is a holy land and happy! For, god has made her cause his own and Aurangzeb is down! The dethroned are enthroned and the enthroned is dethroned. Actions speak better than words! Verily Hindusthan is a holy land and happy: Now that Dharma is backed up by *rajdharma*, right by might, the waters of Hind, no longer defiled, can enable us once more to perform our ablutions and austerities. Let come what may: Rama has made this land holy and happy!)

Bhushan, the Hindu poet who was one of the most prominent of our national bards that went up and down the country and roused 'Hindwan' to action and achievement in those days of the war of Hindu liberation, challenged Aurangzeb:

लाज धरो शिवजी से लरो सब सैयद सेख पठान नठायके।
भूषण ह्यां गढकोटन हारे उहां तुग क्यों मठ तोरे रिसायके ॥
हिंदुन के पति सों न विसात सतावत हिंदु गरीबन पायके।
लीजै कलंक न दिल्ली के बालम आलम आलमगीर कहायके ॥

(Thou art so busy in winning easy victories over the poor Hindu friars and beggars there, why dust thou fight so shy to face the Hindpati himself?

Thou hast lost fort after fort in the fair field here; that is perhaps why thou art distinguishing thyself by pulling down unoffending convents, churches and chapels there! Art thou not ashamed to call thyself Alamgir, conqueror of the world, when thyself standest vanquished by the Hindu Emperor Shivaji?)

Again at another place, Bhushan says:

जगत मैं जीते महाबीर महाराजन ते
महाराजन बावन हूँ पानसाह लेवाने।
पातसाह बावनौ दिल्ली के पातसाह दिल्लीपति
पातसाह जीसो हिंदुपति सेवाने
दाढी के रखैयन की दाडीसी रहति छाति
वाढी जस मर्याद हद्द हिंदुवाने की
कढि गयि रयित के मन की कसक मिट गयी
ठसक तमाम तुरकानेकी
भूषण भनत दिल्लीपति दिल धकधका सुनिसुनि
धाक सिवराज मरदानेकी
मोठी भयि चंडी बिन चोटीके चबाय सीस
खोटी भयि संपति चक ताके धराने की॥

Speaking of things that Shivaji achieved, Bhushan says:

राखी हिंदुवानी, हिंदुवान के तिलक राखयो,
स्मृति और पुराण राखयो वेद विधि सुनि में
राखी रजपुती राजधानी राखी राजनकी
घरांमें धरम राख्यो राख्यो गुण गुणीमें
भूषण सुकविजीनि हद्द मरहट्टनकी, देसदेस
कीरति बखानी तब सुनि मैं
साहिके सुपूत सिवराज समसेर तेरी, दिल्लीदल
दाबिके दिवाल रखि दुनिमै॥

It was in this light that achievements of Shivaji and his compatriots were viewed by his race throughout Hindusthan. Bhushan, though not a Maratha, felt as much proud of the victorious march of the Maratha warriors from Shivaji to Bajirao (vide *Bhushan Granthawali*) as they themselves did. He was, Hindu of Hindus and till the last day of his life, he kept on singing his stirring songs, emphasising the national and pan-Hindu aspect of the movement and impressing it on the minds of its great leaders. Amongst these, Chhattarsal, the brave Bundela king, was his second favourite:

हवर हरट्ट साजि गैवर गरट्ट समपैदर थट्ट
फोज तुरकान की
भूषण भनत रायचंपनिको छत्रसाल रोपयो रनख्याल
वहैके ढाल हिंदवाने की।

Nor was this tribute paid to Chhattarsal undeserved. Chhattarsal was truly like Shivaji, Raj Singh, Guru Gobind Singh, the *dhal Hindvane ki*. He looked upon himself as the champion of Hindutva. Says Chhattarsal:

हिंदु तुरक दीन द्वै गाये। तिनसो वैर सदा चलि आये।
लेख्यो सुर असुरन को जैसो। केहरि करिन बखाने तैसो॥
जबते शाहा जखतपर बेठे। तब ते हिंदुन सो उर ऐठे॥
सहगै कर तीरथनि लगाये। वेद देवाले मिंदर डहावे॥
सब रजपूत सीर नित नावै॥ ऐड करे नित पैदल धावे॥
ऐड एक शिवराज निवाही। करै आपके चितकी चाही॥
आठ पातसाही झुक झोरै। सूबनि बांधि डांड लै छोरै।

After his historical visit paid by Chhattarsal to Shivaji, the great Bundela leader, greatly encouraged by the latter:

तुम छत्री सरताज। जीत आपनी भूमिकी करो देशको राज॥

met Sujan Singh, who was a powerful Rajput chief in Bundelkhand. In the conversation that followed, Sujan Singh draws a moving picture of the political situation in the country:

पातसाह लागे करन, हिंदुधर्म कौनासु
सुधि करि चंपतराय को लइ बुंदेला सासु
जब ते चंपति करयो प्यानो, तबतै परयो हीन हिंदवाने,
लगयो होग तुरकजको जोरा, को राखे हिंदुन को तोरा
अब जो तुम कटि कसौ कृपानी, तौ फिर चढे हिंदुमुख पानी॥

Sujan Singh, the old Raja, saying thus offered his sword and heart to Chhattarsal and blessed him and his mission:

यह कहि प्रीति हिये उमगाई। दिये पान किदवान वधाइ
दोऊ हाथ माथपर राखे। पूरन करौ काज अभलाखे
हिंदुधरम जग जाइ चलावौ। दौरि दिलीदल हलनि हलयो॥

(छत्रप्रकाश)

(*Chattarparkash*, the historical work that describes the events of Chhattarsal's reign, was composed under his direct order by Lalkavi.)

Tegh Bahadur, the great Guru, who not only championed the cause of this war of Hindu liberation in Punjab, but laid down his life for it, is reported to have advised the Brahmins of Kashmere, who oppressed and threatened with 'Islam or death', solicited his help:

तुम सनो दिजेसु ढिंग तुकेसु अवैसु इमगावो
इक पीर हमारा हिंदु भारा भाईचारा लख पावो
है तेगबहादूर जगत उजागर ता आगर तुर्क करो
तिस पाछे तब ही हम फिर सबही बन है तुरक भरो ॥

(पथप्रकाश)

(Oh Brahmins! Listen, you go and tell the Turks (Mohammedans) without fear 'there is a great Hindu leader of ours with lakhs of followers. His name is Tegh Bahadur, uplifter and awakener of mankind, first make him embrace Islam and then we will all do the same.')

And when he was challenged by the foes of the race and religion he boldly answered:

तिन ते सुन श्री तेगबहादूर। धर्म निहाहन विषे बहादूर ॥
उततर भनयों धर्म हम हिंदु। अति प्रियको किमकरे निकदु ॥

(सूर्यप्रकाश)

('Hearing them, Guru Tegh Bahadur, the hero, the champion of Dharma, replied: 'How can I disgrace the Hindu Dharma, so dear to my heart.')

His illustrious son, Guru Gobind Singh at once the poet, the prophet and the warrior of our Hindu race and our Hindu culture, exclaims in a moment of inspiration:

सकल जगत में लालसा पथ गाजे
जगे धर्म हिंदु सकल भंड भाजे ॥

(विचित्र नाटक गुरू गोविंदसिंह)

(May this Khalsa Panth flourish everywhere (so that) long may Hindu Dharma live and all falsehood vanish!!)

The chronicler of Shivaji in the old work शिवछत्रपतोचें चरित्र, says,

शिवाजीचे मनांत आलें जे आपण हिंदु, सर्व दक्षिण देश यवनांनीं पादा-क्रांत केला. क्षत्रास पीडा केली हिंदुधर्म वुडविला, प्राणही देऊन धर्म रक्षू. आपले पराक्रमें नवीन दोलत संपादू तें अन्न भक्षु.

(Shivaji thought to himself, we are Hindus. The Mohammedans have subjugated the entire Deccan. They have defiled our sacred places! In fact, they have desecrated our religion. We will, therefore, protect our religion and for that we would even lose our lives. We will acquire a new kingdom by our powers and that bread we will eat.')

But the shrewd and trusted Dadaji advised:

आपण म्हणतां तें कार्य चांगले खरें, पण याचा शेवट लागणें दुष्कर. यास मातवर स्थलें असावीं. हिंदु राजे व हिंदु फोजां जागजागीं साह्यकर्त्या असावया. ईश्वराचें आनुकूल्य व सिद्ध पुरुषांचा आर्शीर्वाद असतां आशा गोष्टी घडतील.

(चिटणीस-बखर)

(Your plans are certainly very good, but it would be exceedingly difficult to carry them to a finish. In the first place you are to establish powerful centres. Hindu kings and Hindu armies must afford assistance from place to place. Again God Almighty must be on our side and we must be blessed with the benedictions of consummate saints. And then these things are possible.)

And yet Dadaji was the guiding hand of the whole movement. The youthful Shivaji writes in A.D. 1646 to one of his young compatriots:

'शहास' तुम्ही आपली बेमानीगिरी करीत नाहीं, आदि कुलदेव स्वयंभू, त्यानीं यश दिलें व पुढें तो मनोरथ हिंदवी स्वराज्य करून पुरविणार आहे, हें राज्य व्हावें हें श्रींचे मनात फार आहे.'

(You would not be faithless to the emperor. Our primordial family god is self-existing (and, therefore, all-powerful). He has given success to our efforts so long and in future also will fulfil the object of my life by bringing about the establishment of Hindavi *swarajya* (Hindu independence). Indeed it is the cherished wish of god that such a kingdom should be established.)

Mr. Rajvade has the original copy of this letter which reveals, as it were, the soul of the great Hindu movement in the seventeenth and eighteenth centuries. It was no parochial movement; it was Hindavi *swarajya* the Hindu Empire, that was the great ideal which had fired the imagination and goaded the actions of Shivaji while he was but within his teens. We have his own word for it.

But, when Jaisingh—a Rajput prince—came to subdue Shivaji and his movement, the edge of Shivaji's power of resistance became very naturally blunted. It was disheartening in the extreme to find the Rajputs—the ancient shield of Hindutva—shedding their blood and the blood of their coreligionists and brother Hindus that the Mohammedans may win! Says Shivaji to Jaisingh—

'तुम्हांस जे किल्ले पाहिजेत ते मी देतो. निशाण चढवितो पण मुसलमानांस यश न देणें. मी हिंदु, आपण रजपूत तेव्हा हिंदूच. राज्य मुळचें हिंदूचें हिंदुधर्मरक्षकापुढें मी डोकें शतदा नमवीन. पण हिंदुधर्माची मानहानि होईल असें कधींही घडणार नाहीं'!!

(I am ready to hand over to you all fortresses you might ask for. I myself will plant your flag on them. But let not those Mohammedans triumph. I am a Hindu; you are Rajput and, therefore, a Hindu. The kingdom has originally been of the Hindus. I will humble my head a hundred times before one who protects the Hindu religion. But, I will never agree to do anything that is calculated to impair the honour of the Hindu religion.)

Jaisingh was doubtless touched and replied–' 'औरंगजेब बादशाह पृथ्वीपति. त्याशी तुम्ही सख्य करावें. शत्रुत्वाने राहून या कालों परिणाम लागणार नाही. आम्ही हिंदु जयपूरचे राजे. तुम्ही हिंदुच. तुम्ही हिंदुधर्म स्थापन करतां यास्तव आम्ही तुम्हांस अनुकूल आहों.' (Emperor Aurangzeb is a very powerful sovereign. You should, therefore, agree to make terms with him. You will not be able to live in peace by maintaining hostile relations with him. We, princes of Jaipur, are Hindus; you are also a Hindu. We are in accord with you since you are out to rehabilitate Hindu religion.')

The rise of Hindu power under Shivaji had electrified the Hindu mind all over India. The oppressed looked upon him as an *avatar* and a saviour. Thus, we find that the people of the Savnoor District groaning under the Mohammedan yoke appeal to him:

'हा युसुफ फार खस्त आहे, बायकापोरांस उपद्रव देणे, जूलम, गोवधादि निंद्य कर्मे आम्ही त्याचे हाताखाली वागण्यास कंटाळलो. तुम्ही हिंदुधर्मचे संस्थापक. म्लेच्छाचे नाशक, म्हणून तुम्हाकडे आम्हीं आलों म्हणून आमचे द्वारा चौकी वसली आहे. अन्नपाण्यवाचून जीव घेणयास उद्युक्तझाले आहेत. तरी रात्रीचा दिवस करून येणें.'

(This Yusuf is a very wicked fellow. He oppresses the women and the children, commits atrocities and even resorts to such reprehensible misdeeds as the massacre of cows! We are so disgusted that we can no longer live under him. You are the restorer of the Hindu religion and the destroyer of the Malechhas (foreigners). It is, therefore, that we have come to you for refuge. And since we have so approached you, guards have been stationed at our gates. In fact, they are intent on starving us here without food and water. So, do come with all haste (lit by turning nights into days).

Again after Shivaji had restored the Jahagir to his brother Vayankoji at Tanjore on the condition that he should cease to recognise the sovereignty of the Mohammedan sway. Shivaji writers:

'दुष्ट हिंदु विद्वेषी यांस आपले राज्यांत ठेबू नये.'

(Those who are bitter haters of Hindu should have no footing in your territory.)

Rajaram, in order to express his sense of appreciation of the national services of Santaji and his brothers in the war of independence, conferred on Bahirji the high and proud appellation 'Hindrav'. When the siege at Jinji was pressing, the Maratha forces to try their best to break through it, an attempt was made to win over the Marathas in the services of the Mogul commander:

'Secret negotiations were opened with Nagoji Raje to the effect that if he joins with the Marathas, they would break the enemy's forces and preserve the Hindu religion. He should therefore, come over to them.' Thereupon Nagoji Raje gave up service under the Mohammedans and withdrawing the attack, entered the city with his battalion numbering five thousand...when Shirke entered the service of the Moguls (as Sambhaji had beheaded the Shirke family). Khandoji Ballal said, 'Shirke had been beheaded: but, similarly, three of my ancestors were killed by being trampled under the foot of an elephant. But we are striving for the establishment of the kingdom of the Hindus and you must be our parteners.' Then, Shirke also entered the plot and helped the Marathas, with the result that Rajaram broke through the siege and escaped.

Shah had once entered into a controversy with Jaisingh (Swai) on the point: हिंदुधर्माचे रक्षणासाठी मी काय व तू काय केलेंस।'

(सरदेसाई – मध्यविभाग)

The same spirit animated the generations of Bajirao and Nanasaheb. Says the historian:

'पुष्कळानी बाजीरावाच्याच उद्योगचें अनुकरण व परिपोष केलेला दिसतो. ब्रह्मेंद्र स्वामी, गोविंद दीक्षित वगरे देशभर यात्रा करून अनुभव घेतलेल्या साधु-पुरुषांच्या ठिकाणीं वरील 'हिंदुपदपादशाहीचीं' भावना स्फुरण पावत होती व ते आपल्या सर्व शिष्यवर्गास याच भावनेनें उपदेशित होते' (सरदेसाई) बाजीराव स्वत: म्हणतात, – 'अरे वघतां काय? चला जोरानें चाल करून. हिंदुपदपादशाहीस आताँ उशीर काय?' (बाजीराव)

(It appears that others also followed or supplemented Bajirao in the great work undertaken by him. The above idea of Hindu *pad-padashahi* (Hindu sovereignty) was animating the hearts of such saints as Brahmendra Swami, Govind Dixit and others who had been going over the country of pilgrimages and acquiring experience. They were imparting instructions to their disciples with the same idea. Bajirao himself says, 'Why do you tarry? Rush vigorously and attack, and Hindu *pad-padashahi* (Hindu kingdom) is at hand!'

(Sardesai)

Brahmendra Swami was the central figure of the intellectuals of the period 'परंतु हिंदुधर्मचा उच्छेद ज्या राज्यांत होतो त्यास भेटणें स्वामीस योग्य वाटलें नाहीं... हिंदुच्या साम्राज्यांत देवब्राह्मणांचा छळ होणें ही गोष्ट किती लज्जास्पद आहे ही गोष्ट त्यानें शाहूच्या मनांत भरवून दिली.' – (सरदेसाई)

(But the Swami did not think it proper to meet one in whose territory Hindu religion was being defiled! He impressed upon Shahu's mind how disgraceful it was that deities and Brahmins should be subjected to atrocities in the territory of Hindus!'

Sardesai)

Mathurabai writes to this Swami:

'शंकराजी मोहिते, गणोजी शिंदे, खंडोजी नालकर रामाजी खराडें, कृष्णाजी मोड इत्यादि मातबर सरदारांनीं राज्यरक्षण करून शामलांचा मोड केला व कोकणांत हिंदुधर्म राखला।'

(Shankaraji Mohite, Ganoji Shinde, Khandoji Nalkar, Ramaji Kharade, Krishanaji Mod and other powerful Sardars have preserved the kingdom, exterminated the Mohammedans and protected the Hindu religion in Konkan.)

The letters sent by this brave lady, Mathurabai Angre, are all so full with patriotic fervour and force that they deserve a perusal from all those who want to catch the real spirit of the great Hindu revival.

The Protuguese fanaticism at Goa was an Indian edition of the Inquisition in Europe. Once they prohibited the open observation of all Hindu religious rites and rituals. Then the public-spirited Antaji Raghunath defied the order and encouraged other Hindus to do the same. But, he knew perfectly well that impotent passive resistance is impotent suffering. To be successful under such conditions as then prevailed, it must be backed up by the sword of a Bajirao or a Chimnaji. It was Antaji Raghunath who brought about the revolution in the Portuguese territories in India, enlisted the sympathies of all Hindu leaders on the side of Bajirao and, in fact, was the prime mover who brought about the Maratha invasion which ended in the liberation of almost all the Hindu territories after the triumphant campaign of Chimnaji Appa.

But, in the meanwhile, and before the fall of Vasai, Nadir Shah invaded India and Delhi had fallen in his hands. The Maratha agents of Bajirao write to him:

"Tahmaspkulikhan (Nadir Shah) is not a divine being so as to be able to destroy the whole creation. He is bound to come to terms with those that prove strong. Therefore Your Excellency (Bajirao) should come with a strong force. Peace can come only after a war. We can expect a decisive result if Your Excellency and the entire Rajput chiefs combine now. We must join together all the Hindus including Bundele and such others and we must present a more than brilliant front. Nadir Shah does not intend to go back. He will directly march on the Hindu kingdom. Savai Jaisingh wants that Ranaji (of Udaipur) should be installed on the Imperial throne. The Hindu kings including Savai are looking for the arrival of Your Excellency. In fact as soon as Your Excellency can give a strong backing, Shivaji will send forces against Delhi and will also himself march'.

(Dhondo Govind's letters to Bajirao)

But, as Vasai was still holding out, Bajirao could not go in time. He was chafing under his inabilities. He writes:

"The Hindus are placed in a critical situation. We have not yet captured Bassein. Under the circumstances, all the Maratha armies should combine and cross the River Chambal. The plan is that he (Nadir) should not be allowed to proceed further."

(Bajirao to Brahmendra Swami)

But, his indomitable spirit rose triumphant over all obstacles. He writes again:

"We must lay aside our internal differences (such as punishment of Raghoji and others). The whole of Hindusthan has now one common enemy to encounter. As for myself, I have decided to cross the Narbada and spread the Maratha armies as far as Chambal and we shall see how Nadir Shah proceeds southward."

(Bajirao's letter)

Savai Jaisingh was as intensely proud of his Hindutva as anyone else of the great leaders of the Hindu movement. It was he who directed the people—the oppressed Hindus—in Malva to request Bajirao to extend the war of Hindu liberation to Malva and thus to take a further important step towards the realisation of the mission of generations of the followers of the Shivaji cult all over India—the mission of Hindu *pad-padashahi.* In one of his letters, the enlightened and patriotic Rajput prince writes:

"May you get success and wealth!.... respectful greeting to Nandlalji Pradhan and Bhaiji Thakur, Sansthan Indore, from Maharajadhiraj Jai Singh, camp Amargad. You are informed that the Emperor has started operations, but you need not be anxious. God Almighty will bring the matters to a successful issue. We have secured from Bajirao Peshwa solemn promises concerning you.

Oh splendid! Really creditable. It is right and proper that you and the other chiefs of the Malva unite and bring about the prosperity and growth of the Hindu religion. It was with this object that the Mussalmans were discouraged from Malva and the Hindu religion was preserved intact."

(Jaisingh's letters A.D. 26.10.1721)

Nanasaheb, the son of Bajirao, was, in fact, the greatest leader of men that the great movement of Hindu liberation and Hindu *pad-padashahi* brought to the front. His correspondence is a study by itself. Wherever we find him, we find him the champion of Hindutva. To Tarabai he writes:

"The Moghul (Nizam) is an inveterate enemy of the Hindu power, and yet, while you are yourself carrying on negotiations with them, you accuse (me) your humble servant of crooked ways!"

(Nanasaheb's letters)

Though much was lost on the field of Panipat, yet all was not lost. For, two men survived the battle and saved the cause. Nana Fadnavis and Mahadaji Shinde—the brain, the sword, the shield of the Hindu power—thought and worked and fought for 40 years or so—in spite of the disastrous defeat of Panipat or rather in virtue of it for that defeat was the greatest blow that the victors had ever received—and succeeded in making the Hindus the de facto rulers of Hindusthan. How conscious the national mind had grown of the triumphant turn events had taken and how intensely proud had they been of Hindutva and the Hindu Empire all but established, can best be seen in the letters of the most talented diplomatic writers of the period. Govindrao Kale writes to Nana Fadanavis from the capital of the Nizam on learning the news that gladdened the Marathas from end to end of Maharashtra that the misunderstanding growing between the two men, Nana and Mahadaji, had disappeared:

"When I read your letter, I was simply thrilled with joy. Indeed I felt mightily happy. I cannot express all that fully in a letter. Literally my mind was flooded with thoughts. All the territory from the River Atak to the Indian Ocean is the land of Hindus and not of the Turks. These have been our frontiers from the times of Pandavas down to those of Vikramaditya. They preserved it and enjoyed. After them, the rulers turned out to be quite effete and the *Yavanas* (Mohammedans) rose in power. The Moghuls seized the kingdom of Hastinapur. And eventually during the regime of Alamgir we were reduced to such straits that the wearer of every *yadnyopavita* (the sacred thread) was required to pay a jizya tax of ₹ 3-8 and to buy cooked food.

"As such a juncture was born Shivaji Maharaj, the founder of the era and the protector of the religion. However, his mission was confined to a limited area. Then came Nanasaheb and Bhausaheb of respected memory. Heroes of such pre-eminent prowess that the like of them has not been born. And now everything has been restored to us under the benign and illustrious auspices of Shrimant (Peshwa) owing to the astuteness and valour of Patil Boa. But how was all this achieved! Because we had won, we thought it had been an easy matter. If it had been the case of Mohammedans, volumes of histories would have been written about it. Amongst the Mohammedans even the smallest matter is extolled by them to the skies. While amongst us Hindus, we are inclined not even to refer to our exploits, however, magnificent they may be. Indeed results difficult to achieve have been achieved. The Mohammedans think and say that the accursed Hindus have established their supremacy!

"And really Patil Boa has broken the heads of those who tried to raise them. In fact the unachievable has been achieved. To establish order and reap its benefit like the great kings is still ahead. I am afraid where our merits will fail and the work will be spoiled. The achievements are not limited to the acquisition of territory and regaining of our kingdom, but include the preservation of *Vedas* and *Shastras*, rehabilitation of religion, protection of cows and Brahmins, establishment of suzerainty and the diffusion of our fame and victory. To keep all this intact depends on you and Patil Boa. If there is difference amongst you, the enemy is bound to grow strong. Now my misgivings are a guess. It was really splendid! Very excellent! The enemies are besetting us on all sides. I was very uneasy. Your letter has been a relief to me (A.D. 1793).

This one single letter penned with such ease and grace gives a truer expression to the spirit of our history than many a dull volumes had done. How spontaneously it hits on the right derivation of the epithets, Hindu and Hindusthan and how completely our ancestors down to the last generation loved and revered and identified themselves with these epithets is so eloquently illustrated in this letter as to render it superfluous to cite any more.

Stupid notions must go

Having thus tried to trace the successive chapters of the history of the words, Hindu and Hindusthan, from the earliest Vedic period to the fall of the last of our Hindu empire in A.D. 1818, we are now in a position to address ourselves to the main task of determining the essentials of Hindutva. The first result of our enquiry is to explode the baseless suspicion which has crept into the minds of some of our well-meaning, but hasty countrymen that the origin of the words, Hindu and Hindusthan, is to be traced to the malice of the Mohammedans! After all, that has been said in the previous paragraphs about the history of these words, this suspicion seems to be singularly stupid that to mention it is to refute it. Long before Mohammed was born, nay, long before the Arabians were heard of as a people, this ancient nation was known to ourselves as well as to the foreign world by the proud epithet Sindhu or Hindu and Arabians could not have invented this term any more than they could have invented the Indus itself. They simply learnt it from the ancient Iranians, Jews and other peoples. But apart from all serious historical refutation, is it now clear that had it been really contemptuous expression of our foes, as it is said to be, could it have ever recommended itself to the bravest and best of our race? Surely our people were not quite such strangers either to the Arabic or Persian tongues! The Mohammedans were apt to refer to us as *kafir* also but had our people adopted that name and stuck it up as a distinguishing mark? Why did they submit voluntarily to the national insult only in the case of the other epithets, Hindusthan or Hindu? Simply because they knew more of our national traditions and were less cut off from our national life than some of us had been. That is why some of us kept constantly harping on the fact that this word Hindu is not found in Sanskrit. What of this word alone? The Sanskrit literature makes no mention of Kishna-Banaras-Maratha-Sikh-Gujrat-Patna-Siya-Jamna and thousands of other words that we use daily. But are they to be traced to some foreign source? The word 'Banaras' though not found in Sanskrit is still ours because it is the Prakrit form of Varanasi which is found in Sanskrit. In fact, it is ridiculous to expect a Prakrit word in classical Sanskrit. Nay more; although Hindu being a Prakrit form of a Sanskrit word, should not be expected to be found in Sanskrit, yet as it is it cannot be but a weighty proof of its importance even in its Prakrit form that, that form should be, at times met with in Sanskrit literature: for example, the *Bherupattra* use this word Hindu. Great Sanskrit lexicographers, like Apte in Maharashtra and Taranath Tarakvachispati in Bengal, have also mentioned it. While the line *Shivshiv-n-Hinduran Yavan* is too well known to be quoted.

It may be that in the modern Mohammedanised Persian some contemptuous meaning has come to be associated with the term Hindu but how does that show that the original significance of Hindu was contemptuous and meant 'black'? The words Hindi or Hind are used in Persian but they do not mean black and yet we know that they along with Hindu are originated from the same Sanskrit word, Sindhu or Sindh. If the word Hindu is applied to us because it means 'black', then is that Hind and Hindi are also applied to us though they do not mean 'a black man'? The fact is that the word Hindu dates its origin not from the Mohammedanised Persian but from the ancient language of Iran, the Zend, and then the Saptasindhu meant Saptasindhus alone. It *could not* have been applied to us because we were black *literally*, for the simple reason that the ancient Saptasindhus, i.e., Hindus in Avestic period, were as fair as the Iranians and lived practically side by side and even at times together with them. Even so, as late as the dawn of the Christian era, the Parthians used to call our frontier province as Shavet Bharat or white India. Thus, originally, Hindu simply could not have literally meant a black man.

In fact, after it has been made so amply clear in the foregoing sections that the epithets Hindu and Hindusthan had been the proud and patriotic designations signifying our land and our nation long before the Mohammedans or Mohammedanised Persians were heard of, it becomes almost immaterial so far as the greatness of epithet Hindu and its claim to our love are concerned, what meaning, complimentary or contemptuous, is attached to it by some swollen-headed fanatic here and there. There was a time when the term 'England' had fallen so low in England itself in the estimation of her Norman conquerors that it became a formula of swearing against each other! 'May I become an Englishman!' was the strongest form of self-denunciation and calling a Norman 'an Englishman', an unpardonable insult. But, did the English care to change the name of their land or their nation and call it Normandy instead of England? Or would their disowning their name as the 'the English' have made them great? No; on the contrary, precisely because they did not disown their ancient blood or name, today we find that while the word Norman has become an historical fossil and Normandy has no place on the map of the world, the contemptuous English and their English language have come to own the largest empire the world has as yet seen! And yet great as the glories of the English world are, what on the whole, has it to show to match the glories of the Hindu world?

In times of conflict, nations do lose their balance of mind and if the Persians or others once understood by the word Hindu a thief or a black man alone, then let them remember that the word Mohammedan' too was not always mentioned to denote any very enviable type of mankind by the Hindus either. To call a man Mussalman or better still a 'Musanda' was worse than calling him a brute. Such bitter fulminations and mutual recriminations though they might have the excuse of inevitability in times of life and death struggles while the fume and flame of the angry brutal passions last, should be forgotten as soon as men recover from their fits and claim to be recognised as gentlemen. Nor should we forget that the ancient Jews used the term Hindu to denote strength or vigour. For, these were the qualities associated with our land and nation. In an Arab epic, named *So Hab Mo Alaku,* it is said that the oppressions of kith and kin are bitterer or more fatal than the stroke of a Hindu sword, while 'returning a Hindu answer' is a proverbial way with the Persian themselves, by which they are said to mean, 'to strike bravely and deeply with an Indian sword.' The ancient Babylonians had been in the habit of denoting the finest quality of cloth as Sindhu because it generally came from the Saptasindhus—a custom which also shows that they also knew our country by its ancient name Sindhu; nor have we as yet heard of any other meaning being attributed to this word in the ancient Babylonian language than its national one.

No Hindu can help feeling proud of himself at the curious interpretation put upon the epithet by the illustrious traveller Hiuen Tsang, himself belonging to our highly civilised and ancient neighbours, the Chinese, when he identifies our national name 'Hindu' with the Sanskrit 'Indu' and says in justification that the world had rightly called this nation 'Indus' for they and their civilisation had like the moon ever been a constant source of delight and refreshment to the languid and weary soul of man. Does not all this clearly show that the way of inspiring respect for our name in the minds of men is not either to change or deny it but to compel recognition of, and homage to it by the valour of our arms, purity of our aims and the sublimity of our souls? Even if we allow some of our brethren to ride their hobby horse in all glee and get themselves recognised and registered in the Census reports as 'Aryans' instead of as

Hindus, yet they could only succeed in dragging down the word Aryan to their own level and adding one more synonym to the vocabulary of the words for a 'helot' and a 'coolie'—as long as our nation does not attain to the heights of greatness and of strength as in the days of yore.

But, apart from any serious argument against the absurd proposal of denying the epithets Hindu or Hinduism, and granting for a while, the stupid theory that their origin is to be traced to the malice of foreigners, we simply ask is it possible to deny them and coin a new word for our national designation? As it stands at present, the word 'Hindu' has come to be the very banner of our race and the one great feature that above all others contributes to strengthen and uphold our racial unity from Cape to Kashmere, from Attak to Kattak. Do you think you can change it as easily as a cap? Once it happened that a gentleman, well-meaning and patriotic, intended to get himself registered in the Census records as an Aryan instead of a Hindu, as he had been a victim to the widespread lie that we were first called Hindus by the Persian Mohammdans out of their contempt—that the word meant a thief or a black man. Yet, I could not enter into any detailed discussion about the origin of the word for want of time and so simply questioned him as to what his own name was? He told it was Takat Singh. 'My good friend.' I continued, 'unlike the word Hindu whose origin is at the worst disputable, your name is indisputably a hybrid word and should therefore be first replaced in the register by some ancient and purely Aryan word—say *Maudglayan* or *Sinhasan Singh.* Having evaded the point for a while, he tried to point out how difficult it was to do so and how it would completely upset his economical position and after all how could he get the world to call him by the new-fangled name or what could be gained at all by this risky experiment of calling himself 'Sinhasan Singh' while all others persisted in calling him 'Takat Singh'? 'But,' I rejoined, 'if to change your individual names which is indisputably foreign, seems to you so difficult, nay harmful, then my friend how much more difficult would it be to change the name of a whole race which is so far from being a foreign invention that it is ours as much as *Vedas* are ours, and how much more futile?' Of the futility of any such attempt to change a deep-rooted name, a far more convincing example than this personal one is furnished by our Sikh brotherhood in the Punjab. The band of the best and the bravest of the Hindu race whom our great Guru had chosen, triumphantly exclaiming, नीलवस्त्रके कपडे फाडे तुरक पठाणी अंमल गया for the expressed purpose of धर्म चलावन सन्त उबारण, दुष्ट दैत्यके मूल उपाटण, यहि काज धरा मैं जनम्। समझ लेहु साधुसम मननम्। (परित्राणाय साधुनाँ विनाशाय च दुष्कृ ताम। धर्म संस्थापनार्थाय सम्भवामि युगे युगे) that band of warriors was named 'Khalsa'! The saintly who bewailed, क्षत्रियांहि धर्म छोडिया म्लेच्छ भाषा गहि। सृष्टि सब इकवर्ण हुई की गति रहि is daily greeted with a वाह गुरु जी का खालसा। The words *Darbar, Diwan Bahadur* have crept like thieves to the very heart of our *Harimandir*. They are the scars of our old wounds. The wounds are healed but the scars persist and seem to be incorporated with our form. As long as any attempt to scratch them out threatens to harm us more than profit, so long all that we can do is to tolerate them; for, after all, they are the scars of the wounds received in a conflict that we have won in a gory field in which we remained as the victors of the day.

And yet, if any words, however closely they might have been associated with things sacred, are to be disowned and changed, they are these for they all are indisputably foreign and reminiscent of alien domination. Does it not seem almost insincere that we who cannot only tolerate but love these names, should clamour to disown the epithet Hindu or Hindusthan which is the very cradle name of our race and of our land chosen by our patriarchs, recorded in the most ancient and revered annals of the world—the *Vedas*? An epithet which had proudly been borne by millions of our countrymen on both sides of the Sindhu for the last 40 centuries if not more; which expanded to and embraced the whole of our country from Kashmere to the Cape and from Attak to Kattak- which sums up in a word the whole geographical position of our race and our land Sindhu or Hindu; which had been recognised as the sign of distinction to mark out the *rashtramaryasya chottamam,* an epithet for which our foes hated us and for which our warriors from Shalivahan to Shivaji went forth in their thousands to keep up their fight from century to century. It was this word, 'Hindu', that was found impressed on the ashes of Padmini and Chittor. It was this word, 'Hindu', that was owned by Tulsidass, Tukaram, Ramkrishan and Ramdass. Hindu *pad-padashahi* was the dream of Ramdas, the mission of Shivaji, the polar star of the ambitions of Bajirao and Banda Bahadur, of Chhattrasal and Nanasaheb, of Pratap and Pratapaditya. It was inscribed on the banner defending which a hundred thousand Hindu heroes fell, inflicting fatal wounds on the foes on the battlefield of Panipat—and Bhau at the head of them all and sword in hand within one single day! It was for the Hindu *pad-padashahi* that in spite of all that martyrdom and inviture of it, Nana and Mahadji steered the nation clear of all rocks and shoals and brought it almost within sight of the coveted shores. It is this epithet Hindu or Hindusthan that even to this day, owns a loving allegiance of millions of our people—from the throne of Nepal to the begging bowl in the street. To disown these words is like to cut off and cast away the very heart of our people. You would be dead before you do that. It is not only fatal, but futile. To oust the words 'Hindu' or 'Hindusthan' from the position they hold is to try to oust the Himalayas from theirs! Nothing but an earthquake with all its terrible wrenches and appalling uncertainties can accomplish that!

The objection that is levelled against the appellation Hindu and 'Hindusthan' on account of the mistaken notion which attributed their origin to foreign sources could, if left to itself, be easily laid low by advancing undesirable historical facts. But, as it is, this objection is, in some cases, backed up by a secret fear that if the epithet be honoured and owned, then all those who do so would be looked upon as believers in the dogmas and religious practices that go by the name 'Hinduism'. This fear, though it is not often admitted openly, that a Hindu is, necessarily and by the very fact that he is a Hindu, a believer in so-called Hinduism, makes many a man determined not to get convinced that the epithets are not an alien invention. Nor is this fear totally unjustified. But, it would be more candid if those who entertain this fear should openly advance it as the ground of their objection to being recognised as Hindus and not try to hide it under a false and untenable issue. The superficial similarity between these two terms, Hindutva, and Hinduism is responsible for this regrettable estrangement that, at times, alienates well-meaning gentlemen in our Hindu brotherhood. The distinction between these two terms would be presently made clear. Here it is enough to point out that if there be really any word of alien growth, it is this word 'Hinduism' and so we should not allow our thoughts to get confused by this new-fangled term. That a man can be as truly a Hindu as any without believing even in the *Vedas* as an independent religious authority is quite clear from the fact that thousands of our Jain brethren, not to mention others, are for generations calling themselves Hindus and would even to this day feel hurt if they be called otherwise. We refer to this simply as an actual fact apart from any detailed justification and examination of it which would presently follow. Till then, we hope our readers would not allow prejudicial fear regarding the conclusion of our argument as to its intrinsic merit and bear in mind that we have throughout the foregoing pages been dealing—not with any 'ism' whatever but—with Hindutva alone in its national and cultural aspects.

Now we are fairly in a position to try to analyse the contents of one of the rnost comprehensive and bewilderingly synthetic concept known to human tongue. Hindutva is the derivative word from Hindu. We have seen that the earliest and the most sacred records of our race show that the appellation Saptasindhu or Haptahindu was applied to a region in which the Vedic nation flourished. The geographical sense being the primary one has been, now contracting, now expanding, but ever persistently been associated with the words Hindu and Hindusthan till after a lapse of nearly 5,000 years, if not more. Hindusthan has come to mean the whole continental country from the Sindhu to Sindhu, from the Indus to the seas. The most important factor that contributes to the cohesion, strength and the sense of unity of a people is that they should possess an internally well-connected and externally well demarcated 'local habitation', and a 'name' that could, by its very mention, rouse up the cherished image of their motherland as well as the loved memories of their past. We are happily blessed with both these important requisites for a strong and united nation. Our land is so vast and yet so well-knit, so well demarcated from others and yet so strongly entrenched, that no country in the world is more closely marked out by the fingers of Nature as a geographical unit beyond cavil or criticism. So also is the name 'Hindusthan' or 'Hindu' that it has come to bear. The first image that it rouses in the mind is unmistakably of our motherland and by an express appeal to its geographical and physical features it verifies it into a living being. Hindusthan meaning the land of Hindus, the first essential of Hindutva, must necessarily be this geographical one. A Hindu is primarily a citizen either in himself or through his forefathers of 'Hindusthan' and claims the land as his motherland. In America as well as France, the word Hindu is generally understood, thus, exactly in the sense of an Indian without any religious or cultural implication. And had the word 'Hindu' been left to convey this primary significance only, which it had in common with all the words derived from the Sindhu, then it would really have meant an Indian, a citizen of Hindusthan as the word Hindi does.

Essential implications of Hindutva

But, throughout our inquiry, we have been concerning ourselves more with what would have been or what should be. Not that to paint what should be is not a legitimate pursuit; nay, it is as necessary and at times more stimulating, but even that could be better done by first getting a firm hold of what actually is. We must try, therefore, to be on our guard so that in our attempt to determine the essentials of Hindutva, we be guided entirely by the actual contents of the word as it stands at present. So, although the root-meaning of the word 'Hindu', like the sister epithet 'Hindi', may mean only an Indian, yet as it is, we would be straining the usage of words too much—we fear, to the point of breaking—if we call a Mohammedan a Hindu because of his being a resident of India. It may be that at some future time, the word 'Hindu' may come to indicate a citizen of Hindusthan and nothing else; that day can only rise when all cultural and religious bigotry has disbanded its forces pledged to aggressive egoism, and religions cease to be 'isms' and become merely the common fund of eternal principles that lie at the root of all, that are a common foundation on which the human state majestically and firmly rests. But, as even the first streaks of this consummation, so devoutly to be wished for, are scarcely discernible on the horizon, it would be folly for us to ignore stern realities. As long as every other 'ism' has not disowned its special dogmas, whichever tend into dangerous war cries, so long no cultural or national unit can afford to loosen the bonds, especially those of a common name and a common banner, that are the mighty sources of organic cohesion and strength. An American may become a citizen of India. He would certainly be entitled, if *bona fide*, to be treated as our Bhartiya or Hindu, a countryman and a fellow-citizen of ours. But, as long as in addition to our country, he has not adopted our culture and our history, inherited our blood and has come to look upon our land not only as the land of his love but even of his worship, he cannot get himself incorporated into the Hindu-fold. For although the first requisite of Hindutva is that he be a citizen of Hindusthan either by himself or through his forefathers, yet it is not the only requisite qualification for it, as the term 'Hindu' has come to mean much more than its geographical significance.

Bond of common blood

The reason that explains why the term 'Hindu' cannot be synonymous with Bhartiya or Hindu and mean an Indian only, naturally introduces us to the second essential implication of that term. The Hindus are not merely the citizens of the Indian state because they are united not only by the bounds of the love they bear to a common motherland, but also by the bounds of a common blood. They are not only a *rashtar* but also a *jaati*. The word *jaati*, derived from the root *jan* to produce, means a brotherhood, a race determined by a common origin—possessing a common blood. All Hindus claim to have in their veins the blood of the mighty race incorporated with and descended from the Vedic fathers, the Sindhus. We are well aware of the not unoften interested objection that carpingly questions, 'But are you really a race? Can you be said to possess a common blood?' We can only answer by questioning in return, 'Are the English a race? Is there anything as English blood, the French blood, the German blood or the Chinese blood in this world? Do they, who have been freely infusing foreign blood into their race by contracting marriages with other races and people, possess a common blood and claim to be a race by themselves? If they do, Hindus also can emphatically do so. For the very castes, which you, owing to your colossal failure to understand and view them in the right perspective, assert to have barred the common flow of blood into our race, have done so more truly and more effectively as regards the foreign blood than our own. Nay, is not the very presence of the these present castes a standing testimony to a common flow of blood from a Brahmin to a Chandal? Even a cursory glance at any of our *Smritis* would conclusively prove that the *Anulom* and *Pratilom* marriage institutions were the order of the day and have given birth to a majority of the castes that obtain amongst us. If a Kshatriya has a son from a Shudra woman, he gives birth to the Ugar caste: again, if the Kshatriya raises an issue on an Ugar, he founds a Shabpach class, while a Brahmin mother and a Shudra father beget the caste Chandal. From the Vedic story of Satyakam Jabali to Mahadji Shinde every page of our history shows that the ancient Ganges of our blood has come down from the altitudes of the sublime Vedic heights to the plains of our modern history, fertilising much, incorporating many a noble stream and purifying many a lost soul, increasing in volume and depth and richness, defying the danger of being lost in bogs and sands and flows to-day, refreshed and reinvigorated more than ever. All that caste system has done is to regulate its noble flood on lines believed and on the whole rightly believed—by our saintly and patriotic law-givers and kings to contribute most to fertilise and enrich all that was barren and poor, without famishing and debasing all that was flourishing and nobly endowed.

This is true not only in the case of those castes that are the outcome of intermarriages between the chief four castes and the cross-born but also in the case of those tribes or races who somewhere in the dimness of the hoary past were leading a separate and self-centred life. Witness the customs prevalent in Malabar or Nepal where a Hindu of the highest caste is allowed to marry a woman of those who are supposed to be the originally alien tribes but who, even if the suggestion be true, have by their brave and loving defence of the Hindu culture have been incorporated with and bound to us by the dearest of ties—the ties of a common blood. Is the Nagavansh a Dravidian family? Well then, who is who now, when the youths of Agnivansh have taken to them the daughters of the Nagas and the Chandervansh and the Suryavansh have bestowed their damsels on the youth of both the families? Down to the day of Harsh—not to mention the partial breakdown of the caste system itself in the centuries of Buddhistic sway—intermarriages were the order of the day. Take for example the case of a single family of the Pandvas. The sage Prashar was a Brahmin, who fell in love with the fair maid of a fisherman who gave birth to the world-renowned Vyas, who in his turn, raised two sons on the Kshatriya princeses, Amba and Ambalika; one of these two sons, Pandu, allowed his wives to raise issue by resorting to the Niyog system and they having solicited the love of men of unknown castes, giving birth to the heroes of our great epic. Without mentioning equally distinguished characters of the same period—Karan, Brabhuvahan, Ghatotkach, Vidur and others, we beg to point out to the relatively modern cases of Chandragupta said to have married a Brahmin girl who gave birth to the father of Ashok; Ashok, who has as a prince, married a Vaishya maid; Harsh who being a Vaishya, gave his daughter in marriage to a Kshatriya prince; Viyadhkarma, who is said to be a son of Viyadh with whom his mother, a Brahmin girl, had fallen in love and who grew to be the Yagyacharya of Vikramaditya, Surdas, Krishanbhatt who being a Brahmin fell, so desperately in love with a Chandal girl as to lead an open married life with her and subsequently became the founder of the religious sect 'Matangi Panth', who nevertheless call themselves and are perfectly entitled to be recognised as Hindus. This is not all. An individual at times by his or her iron actions may loose his or her first caste and be relegated to another—शूद्रो ब्राह्मणतामेति ब्राह्मणश्चेति शूद्रताम्।

The injunction:

न कुलं कुलमित्याहुराचार कुलमूच्यते।
आचारकुशलो राजन् इह चामुत्र नंदते॥
उपासते येन पूर्वा द्विजा संध्यां न पश्र्चिमाम्।
सर्वास्तान् धार्मिको राजा शूद्रकर्माणि याजयेत्॥

was not always an empty threat. Many a Kshatriya have by taking to agriculture and other occupations of life lost the respect due to a Kshatriya and were classed with some of the other castes; while many a brave man, in cases whole tribes, raised themselves to the position, the rights and titles of the Kshatriya and were recognised as such. Being outcasted from a caste, which is an event of daily occurrence, is only getting incorporated with some other.

Not only is this true so far as those Hindus only who believe in the caste system based on the Vedic tenets are concerned, but even in the case of Avedic sects of the Hindu people. As it was true in the Buddhistic period that a Buddhist father, a Vedic mother, a Jain son, could be found in a single joint family, so even today, Jains and Vaishnavs intermarry in Gujrat; Sikhs and Sanatanis in Punjab and Sind. Moreover, today's Manbhav or Lingayat or Sikh or Sanatani is yesterday's Hindu and today's Hindu may be tomorrow's Lingayat or Brahmo or Sikh.

And no word can give a full expression to this racial unity of our people as the epithet Hindu does. Some of us were Aryans and some Anaryans; but Ayars and Nairs—we were all Hindus and own a common blood. Some of us are Brahmins and some Namshudras or Panchams; but Brahmins or Chandals—we are all Hindus and own a common blood. Some of us are Dakshanatyas and some Gouds; but Gouds or Saraswats—we are all Hindus and own a common blood. Some of us were *rakshas* and some *yakshas*; but *rakshas* or *yakshas*—we are all Hindus and own a common blood. Some of us were *vanars* and some *kinners*; but *vanars* or *nars*—we are all Hindus and own a common blood. Some of us are Jains and some Jangams; but Jains or Jangams—we are all Hindus and own a common blood. Some of us are monosts some pantheists; some theist and some arthiests. But monotheists or arthiests, we are all Hindus and own a common blood. We are not only a *rashtra* but a *jaati*, a born brotherhood. Nothing else counts; it is after all a question of the heart. We *feel* that the same ancient blood that coursed through the veins of Rama and Krishna, Buddha and Mahavir, Nanak and Chaitanya, Basav and Madhav, of Rohaidass and Tiruvellavar, courses throughout the Hindudom from vein to vein, pulsates from heart to heart. We *feel* we are a *jaati*, a race bound together by the dearest ties of blood—and, therefore, it must be so.

After all, there is throughout this world so far as man is concerned but a single race—the human race, kept alive by one common blood—the human blood. All other talk is at best provisional, a makeshift and only relatively true. Nature is constantly trying to overthrow the artificial barriers you raise between race and race. To try to prevent the commingling of blood is to build on sands. Sexual attraction has proved more powerful than all the commands of all the prophets put together. Even as it is not even the aborigines of the Andamans are without some sprinkling of the so-called Aryan blood in their veins and *vice versa*. Truly speaking, all that any one of us can claim, all that history entitles one to claim, is that one has the blood of all mankind in one's veins. The fundamental unity of man from pole to pole is true—all else, only relatively so.

And speaking relatively alone, no people in the world can more justly claim to get recognised as a racial unit than the Hindus and perhaps the Jews. A Hindu marrying a Hindu may lose his caste but not his Hindutva. A Hindu believing in any theoretical or philosophical or social system, orthodox or heterodox, provided it is unquestionably indigenous and founded by a Hindu may lose his sect but not his Hindutva—his Hinduness—because the most important essential which determines it is the inheritance of the Hindu blood. Therefore, all those who love the land that stretches from Sindhu to Sindhu from Indus to seas as their fatherland, consequently claim to inherit the blood of the race that has evolved, by incorporation and adaption, from the ancient Saptasindhus can be said to possess two of the most essential requisites of Hindutva.

Common culture

But only two; because a moment's consideration would show that these two qualifications of *ek rashtra* and *ek jaati*—of a common fatherland and therefore of a common blood—cannot exhaust all the requisites of Hindutva. The majority of the Indian Mohammedans may, if free from the prejudices born of ignorance, come to love our land as their fatherland, as the patriotic and noble minded amongst them have always been doing. The story of their conversions, forcible in millions of cases, is too recent to make them forget, even if they like to do so, that they inherit Hindu blood in their veins. But, can we, who here are concerned with investigating into facts as they are and not as they should be, recognise these Mohammedans as Hindus? Many a Mohammedan community in Kashmere and other parts of India as well as the Christians in South India observe our caste rules to such an extent as to marry generally within the pale of their castes alone; yet, it is clear that though their original Hindu blood is thus almost unaffected by an alien adulteration, yet they cannot be called Hindus in the sense in which that term is actually understood. Because, we Hindus are bound together not only by the tie of the love we bear to a common fatherland and by the common blood that courses through our veins and keeps our hearts throbbing and our affections warm, but also by the tie of a common homage we pay to our great civilisation—our Hindu culture, which cold not be better rendered than by the word *sanskriti,* suggestive as it is of that language, the Sanskrit, which has been the chosen means of expression and preservation of that culture, of all that was best and worth preserving in the history of our race. We are one because we are a *rashtar*, a *jaati* and own a common *sanskriti*.

What is civilisation?

But, what is civilisation? Civilisation is the expression of the mind of man. Civilisation is the account of what man had made of matter. If matter is the creation of the Lord, then civilisation is the miniature secondary creation of man. At its best, it is the perfect triumph of the soul of man over matter and man alike. Wherever and to the extent to which man has succeeded in moulding matter to the delight of his soul, civilisation begins. And, it triumphs when he has tapped all the sources of supreme delight, satisfying the spiritual aspirations of his being towards strength and beauty and love, realising life in all its fulness and richness.

The story of the civilisation of a nation is the story of its thoughts, its action and its achievement. Literature and art tell us of its thoughts; history and social institutions of its actions and achievements. In none of these can man remain isolated. The primitive *dungi* (Canoe) of the Andamanese can truly claim to have influenced the up-to-date dreadnoughts of America. The latest adventure of fashion amongst the fair sex in Paris is but the lineal descendant of the bunch of leaves stuck in the girdle-string which constitutes the perfection of a toilet of a *Patuya* girl.

And, yet a dungi remains a dungi and a dreadnought, a dreadnought; they are too much more unlike each other than like to be identified as one and the same. Even so, although the Hindus have lent much and borrowed much like any other people, yet their civilisation is too characteristic to be mistaken for any other cultural unit. And, secondly, however striking their mutual differences be, they are too much more like each other than unlike, to be denied the right of being recognised as a cultural unit amongst other such units in the world, owning a common history, a common literature and a common civilisation.

Paradoxical as it may sound to those who have fallen victims to the interested or ignorant cry that has secured the ear of the present world that the Hindus have no history, it neverthe-less remains true that Hindus are about the only people who have succeeded in preserving their history—riding through earthquakes, bridging over deluges! It begins with their *Vedas* which are the first extant chapter of the story of our race. The first cradle songs that every Hindu girl listens to sings of Sita, the good. Some of us worship Rama as an incarnation, some admire him as a hero and a warrior, all love him as the most illustrious representative monarch of our race. Maruti and Bheemsen are the never-failing source of strength and physical perfection to the Hindu youth; Savitri and Damayanti, the never failing ideals of constancy and chastity of the Hindu maid. The love that Radha made to the divine cowherd in Gokul finds its echo wherever a Hindu lover kisses his beloved. The giant struggle of the Kurus, the set duels of Arjun and Kama, of Bheem and Dusshasana that took place on the field of Kurukshetra thousands of years ago, are rehearsed in all their thrill from cottage to cottage and from palace to palace. Abhimanyu could not have been dearer to Arjun than he is to us. From Ceylon to Kashmere—Hindutan daily sheds tears as lovingly and as bitterly as his father did at the mention of the fall of that lotus-eyed youth. What more shall we say? The story of *Ramayana* and *Mahabharata* alone would bring us together and weld into a race even if we be scattered to all the four winds like a handful of sand. I read the life of a Mazzini and I exclaim 'How patriotic they are', I read the life of a Madhavacharya and exclaim 'How patriotic we are!' The fall of Prithviraj is bewailed in Bengal; the martyred sons of Govindsingh, in Maharashtra. An Arya

Samajist historian in the extreme North feels that Harihar and Bukka of the extreme South fought for him, and a Sanatanist historian in the extreme South feels that Guru Teg Bahadur died for him. We had kings in common. We had kingdoms in common. We had stability in common. We had triumphs in common and disasters in common. The names of Mokavassya and Pisall, a Jaichand and Kalapaharh make us all feel as sinners do. The names of Ashok, Bhaskaracharya, Panini and Kapil leave us all electrified with a sense of personal elevation.

But what about the internecine wars amongst Hindus? We answer, what about the Wars of Roses amongst the English? What of internecine struggle of states against states, sects against sects, class against class, each invoking foreign help against his own countrymen, in Italy, in Germany, in France, in America? Are they still people, a nation and do they possess a common history? If they do, the Hindus do. If the Hindus do not possess a common history, then none in the world does.

As our history tells the story of action of our race, so does our literature taken in its fullest sense tells the story of the thought of our race. Thought, they say, is inseparable from our common tongue, the Sanskrit. Verily it is our mother tongue—the tongue in which the mothers of our race spoke and which has given birth to all our present tongues. Our gods spoke in Sanskrit, our sages thought in Sanskrit, our poets wrote in Sanskrit. All that is best in us—the best thought, the best idea, the best line—seek instinctively to clothe itself in Sanskrit. To millions, it is still the language of their gods; to others it is the language of their ancestors; to all it is the language *par excellence*; a common inheritance, a common treasure, that enriches all the family of our sister languages. Gujarati and Gurmukhi, Sindhi and Hindi, Tamil and Telugu, Marathi and Malyalam, Bengali and Singhali constitute the vital nerve-thread that runs through us all, vivifying and toning our feelings and aspirations into a harmonious whole. It is not a language alone; to many Hindus, it is a *mantra;* to all, it is a music. The *Vedas* do not constitute an authority for all Jains but the *Vedas* as the most ancient work and the history of their race belong to Jains as much as to any of us. Adipuran was not written by a Sanatani yet the *Adipuran* is the common inheritance of the Sanatanis and Jains. The *Vasavpuran* is the bible of the Lingayat; but it belongs to Lingayats and non-Lingayat Hindus alike, as one of the foremost and historical Kanaree work extant. *Vachittarnatak* of Guru Gobind Singh is as truly the property of a Hindu in Bengal as the *Chaitanya Charittaramrit* is of a Sikh. Kalidas and Bhavbhuti, Charak and Sushrut, Aryabhatt and Varahmihir, Bhas and Ashavghosh, Jaidev and Jagannath wrote for us all, appeal to us all, are the cherished possession of us all. Let the work of Kamb, the Tamil poet and say, a copy of Hafiz be kept before a Hindu in Bengal and if he be asked, 'What belongs to you of these?' He would instinctively say, 'Kamb is mine!' let a copy of the work of Ravindranath and that of Shakespeare be kept before a Hindu in Maharashtra, he would claim, 'Ravindra! Ravindra is mine.'

The works of art and architecture are also a common inheritance of our race, whether they be representative of Vedic or Avedic school of thought. For, all the labourers who wrought them, the masters who guided them, the tax-payers who financed them and the kings who organised them, whether Vedic or Avedic belonged to the great race that inhabits and owns this land from to Sindhu to Sindhu—the Hindu race. Those who are Sanatanis today have contributed and laboured for the Buddhist monuments of art and architecture, then while those who were Buddhists they have contributed to and laboured for the monuments of the Sanatani art and architecture now.

Common laws and rites

Common institutions and a common law that sanctions and sanctifies them however they may differ in details are nevertheless both the cause and the effect of the basic unity of our race. The Hindu law with the underlying principles of Hindu jurisprudence, whatever the superficial difference be and, howsoever contradictory a detail here on an injunction there may seem to be, is too organic a growth to lose its individuality by the manifold changes wrought by times and climes. In spite of the feverish speed with which the law machines in the different states of America and British Commonwealth keep manufacturing and modelling laws we still acknowledge the principles of jurisprudence and the lines of growth that underlie their code to constitute a single whole. The English law, or the Roman jurisprudence or the American law could not be designated as such if eternal identity or a dead level similarity is expected. The Mohammedan law retains its individuality in spite of such damaging exceptions to it as the Khojas or the Bohras who, like some other Mohammedan communities, observe the Hindu law in regulating some departments of their life, notably in matters of inheritance. Some of the Hindu customs in Maharashtra or Punjab may differ from some in Bengal or Sind, but the similarity in all other details is so great that the law of Maharashtra as a whole seems to be an echo of the law book, ruling our brothers in Bengal or Sind and vice versa. When all the rules, customs and laws observed by any given community are collected together, it can immediately be found to be nothing but a fitting chapter of the Hindu law while no amount of ingenuity or torture can fit in say, the English or Mohammedan or the Japanese law books.

We have feast and festivals in common. We have rites and rituals in common. The Dussehra and Diwali, the Rakhibandhan and Holi, are welcomed wherever a Hindu breathes, Sikhs and Jains, Brahmins and Panchams alike. You would find the whole Hindu kingdom enfete on the Diwali day. Not only Hindusthan, but the greater Hindusthan that is fast growing in all the continents of the world. Not even a cottage in the Terai forests could be found on that night that has not shown its little light! While the Rakhi day would reveal to you every Hindu soul from the delighted damsels of Punjab to the austere Brahmins of Madras tying the silken tie that, 'heart to heart and mind to mind, in body and in soul, can bind', yet we have deliberately refrained ourselves from referring, any religious beliefs that we as a race may hold in common. Nor had we referred to any institution or event or custom in its religious aspect or significance. Because we wanted to deal with the essentials of Hindutva not in the light of any 'ism' but from a racial point of view and yet even from a national and racial point of view do the different places of pilgrimage constitute a common inheritance of our Hindu race. The Rath Yatra festival at Jagannath, the Vaishakhi at Amritsar, the Kumbh and the Ardhakumbh, all these great gatherings had been the real and living congress of our people that kept the current of life and the thought coursing throughout our body politic. The quaint customs and ceremonies and sacraments they involve, observed by some as a religious duty, by others as social amenities, impress upon each individual that he can live best only through the common and corporate life of the Hindu race.

These then in short—and the subject in hand does not permit us to be exhaustive on this point—constitute the essence of our civilisation and mark us out a cultural unit. We Hindus are not only a *rashtra*, a *Jaati*, but as a consequence of being both, own a common *sanskriti* expressed, preserved chiefly and originally through Sanskrit, the real mother tongue of our race. Everyone who is a Hindu inherits this *sanskriti* and owes his spiritual being to it as truly as he owes his physical one to the land and the blood of his forefathers.

A Hindu then is he who feels attachment to the land that extends from Sindhu to Sindhu as the land of his forefathers—as his fatherland; who inherits the blood of the great race whose first and discernible source could be traced by the Himalayan altitudes of the Vedic Saptasindhus and which assimilating all that was incorporated and ennobling all that was assimilated has grown into and come to be known as the Hindu people; and who, as a consequence of the foregoing attributes, has inherited and claims as his own the Hindu *sanskriti*, the Hindu civilisation, as represented in a common history, common heroes, a common literature, a common art, a common law and a common jurisprudence, common fairs and festivals, rites and rituals, ceremonies and sacraments. Not that, every Hindu has all these details of the Hindu *sanskriti* down to each syllable common with other Hindus; but that, he has more of it common with his Hindu brothers than with, say, an Arab or an Englishman. Not that a non-Hindu does not hold any of these details in common with a Hindu but that, he differs more from a Hindu than he agrees with. That is why Christian and Mohammedan communities, who were but, very recently, Hindus and in majority of cases had been at least in their first generation most unwilling denizens of their new fold, claim though they might have a common fatherland, and an almost pure Hindu blood and parentage with us, cannot be recognised as Hindus; as, since their adoption of the new cult they had ceased to own Hindu sanskriti as a whole. They belong, or feel that they belong, to a cultural unit altogether different from the Hindu one. Their heroes and their hero-worship, their fairs and their festivals, their ideals and their outlook of life, have now ceased to be common with ours. Thus, the presence of this third essential of Hindutva which requires of every Hindu uncommon and loving attachment to his racial *Sanskriti* enables us most perfectly to determine the nature of Hindutva without any danger of using overlapping or exclusive attributes.

But, take the case of a patriotic Bohra or a Khoja countryman of ours. He loves our land of Hindusthan as his fatherland which indisputably, is the land of his forefathers. He possesses—in certain cases they do—pure Hindu blood; especially if he is the first convert to Mohammedanism he must be allowed to claim to inherit the blood of Hindu parents. He is an intelligent and reasonable man, loves our history and our heroes;

in fact the Bohras and the Khojas as a community, worship as heroes our great ten *avatars* only adding Mohammed as the eleventh. He is actually, along with his community subject to the Hindu law—the law of his forefathers. He is, so far as the three essentials of *rashtra*, *jaati* and *sanskriti* are concerned, a Hindu. He may differ as regards a few festivals or may add a few more heroes to the pantheon of his supermen or demigods. But, we have repeatedly said that difference in details here or emphasis there, do not throw us outside the pale of Hindu *sanskriti*. The sub-communities amongst the Hindus observe many a custom, not only contradictory, but even conflicting, with customs of other Hindu communities. Yet both of them are Hindus. So, also in the above case of patriotic Bohra or a Christian or a Khoja, who could satisfy the required qualifications of Hindutva to such a degree as that, why should he not be recognised as a Hindu?

He would certainly have been recognised as such but for his attitude towards a single detail—which, though is covered by the words *Sanskriti* or culture, is yet too important to be lost in the multitude of other attributes, and, therefore, deserves a special treatment and analysis; which again brings us face to face with the question which, involving as it does the religious aspect of Hindutva, had often been avoided by us, not because we fight shy of it, but on account of our wish to fight it out all the more thoroughly and effectively. For, we are now better equipped to determine the significance and attempt an analysis of the two terms, 'Hinduism' and 'Hindutva'.

□

Who is a Hindu?

The words 'Hindutva' and Hinduism being both of them derived from the word 'Hindu' must necessarily be understood to refer to the whole of the Hindu people. Any definition of Hinduism that leaves out any important section of our people and forces them either to play false to their convictions or to go outside the pale of Hindutva stands self-condemned. Hinduism means the system of religious beliefs found common amongst the Hindu people. And the only way to find out what those religious beliefs of the Hindus are, i.e., what constitutes Hinduism, you must first define a Hindu. But, forgetting this chief implication of the word Hinduism, which clearly presupposes an independent conception of a Hindu, many a people go about to determine the essentials of Hinduism, and finding none so satisfactory as to include, without overlapping all our Hindu communities, come to the desperate conclusion—which does not satisfy them either—that therefore those communities are not Hindus at all! Because, not that the definition they had framed is open to the fault of exclusion but, because those communities do not subject themselves to the required tenets which these gentlemen have thought it fit to label as 'Hinduism'. This way of answering the question, 'Who is a Hindu?' is really preposterous and has given rise to so much of bitterness amongst some of our brethren of Avedic school of thought, the Sikhs, the Jains, the Dev Samajis and even our patriotic and progressive Arya Samajis.

'Who is a Hindu?' He who is subject to the tenets of Hinduism. Very well. What is Hinduism? Those tenets to which the Hindus are subjected! This is very nearly arguing in a circle and can never lead to a satisfactory solution. Many of our friends who have been on this wrong track have come back to tell us, 'There is no such people as Hindus at all!' If some Indian, as gifted as that Englishman who first coined the word Hinduism, coins a parallel word 'Englishism' proceeds to find out the underlying unity of beliefs amongst the English people, gets disgusted with thousands of sects and societies from Jews to the Jacobins, from Trinity to Utility, and comes out to announce that 'There are no such people as the English at all', he would not make himself more ridiculous than those who declare in cold print, 'There is nothing as a Hindu people.' Anyone who wants to see what a confusion of thought prevails on the point and how the failure to analyse separately the two terms, Hindutva, and Hinduism renders that confusion worst confounded may do well to go through the booklet *Essentials of Hinduism* published by the enterprising Natesan and Co.

Hinduism means the 'ism' of the Hindu; and as the word Hindu has been derived from the word Sindhu, the Indus, meaning primarily all the people who reside on the land that extends from Sindhu to Sindhu, Hinduism must necessarily mean the religion or the religions that are peculiar and native to this land and this people. If we are unable to reduce the different tenets and beliefs to a single system of religion, then the only way would be to cease to maintain that Hinduism is a system and to say that it is a set of systems consistent with, or if you like, contradictory or even conflicting with, each other. But, in no case can you advance this your failure to determine the meaning of Hinduism as a ground to doubt the existence of a Hindu nation itself, or worse still, to commit sacrilege in hurting the feelings of our Avedic Hindu brethren and Vedic Hindu brethren alike, by relegating any of them to the non-Hindu pale.

The limits of this essay do not permit us to determine the nature or the essentials of Hinduism or to try to discuss it at any great length. As we have shown above, the enquiry into what is Hinduism can only begin after the question 'Who is a Hindu' is rightly answered, determining the essentials of Hindutva; and as it is only with these essentials of Hindutva, which enable us to know who is a Hindu, that this, our present enquiry is concerned and the discussion of Hinduism falls necessarily outside of our scope. We have to take cognizance of it only so far as it trespasses in the field of our special charge. Hinduism is a word that properly speaking should be applied to all the religious beliefs that the different communities of the Hindu people hold, but it is generally applied to that system of religion which the majority of the Hindu people follow. It is natural that a religion or a country or community should derive its name from the characteristic feature which is common to an overwhelming majority that constitutes or contributes to it. It is also convenient for easy reference or parlance. But, a convenient term that is not only delusive but harmful and positively misleading should not any longer be allowed to blind our judgement. The majority of the Hindus contribute to that system of religion which could fitly be described by the attribute that constitutes its special feature, as श्रुतिस्मृतिपुराणोक्त Dharma or Sanatan Dharma. They would not object if it even be called Vedic Dharma. But besides these there are other Hindus who reject either partly or wholly, the authority—some of the Puranas, some of the Simritis and some of the Shruties, themselves. But, if you identify the religion of the Hindus with the religion of the majority only and call it orthodox Hinduism, then the different heterodox communities, being Hindus themselves rightly resent this usurpation, of Hindutva by the majority as well as their unjustifiable exclusion. The religion of the minorities also requires a name. But, if you call the so-called orthodox religion alone as Hinduism then naturally it follows that the religion of the so-called heterodox is not Hinduism! The next most fatal step being that, therefore, those sections are not Hindus at all!! But, this inference seems as staggering even to those who had unwillingly given whole-hearted support to the premises which have made it logically inevitable that while hating to own it they hardly know how to avoid arriving at it. And, thus, we find that while millions of our Sikhs, Jains, Lingayats, several Samajis and others would deeply resent to be told that they—whose fathers' fathers up to the tenth generations had the blood of Hindus in their veins—had suddenly ceased to be Hindu!—Yet a section amongst them takes it most emphatically for granted that they had been faced with a choice that either they should consent to be a party to those customs and beliefs which they had in their puritanic or progressive zeal rejected as superstitions, or they should cease to belong to that race to which their forefathers belonged.

All this bitterness is mostly due to the wrong use of the word Hinduism to denote the religion of the majority only. Either the word should be restored to its proper significance to denote the religions of all Hindus or if you fail to do that it should be dropped altogether. The religion of the majority of the Hindus could be best denoted by the ancient accepted appellation, the Sanatan Dharma or the श्रुतिस्मृतिपुराणोक्त Dharma or the Vedic Dharma; while the religions of the remaining Hindus would continue to be denoted by their respective and accepted names Sikh Dharma or Arya Dharma or Jain Dharma or Budh Dharma. Whenever the necessity of denoting these Dharmas as a whole arises then alone we may be justified in denoting them by the generic term Hindu Dharma or Hinduism. Thus, there would be no loss either in clearness, or in conciseness but on the other hand a gain both in precision and unambiguity which by removing the cause of suspicion in our minor communities and resentment in the major ones would once more unite us all Hindus under our ancient banner representing a common race and a common civilisation.

The earliest records that we have got of the religious beliefs of any Indian community-not to speak of mankind itself—are the Vedas. The Vedic nation of the Sapatsindhus was sub-divided into many a tribe and class. But, although the majority then held a faith that we for simplicity call Vedic religion, yet it was not contributed to by an important minority of the Sindhus themselves. The Panis, the Dass, the Vratyas and many others from time to time seem to have either seceded from or never belonged to the orthodox church and yet racially and nationally they were conscious of being a people by themselves. There was such a thing as Vedic religion, but it could not be even identified with Sindhu-Dharma; for the latter term, had it been coined would have naturally meant the set of religions prevailing in Sapatsindhus, orthodox as well as heterodox. By a process of elimination and assimilation, the race of the Sidhus at last grew into the race of Hindus-and the land of the Sindhus i.e., Sindhustan, into the land of the Hindu i.e., Hindusthan. While their orthodox and the heterodox schools of religions have,—having tested much, dared much and known much,—having subjected to the most searching examination possible till then, all that lay between the grandest and tiniest, from the atom to the Atman—from the Parmanu to the Parbrahma,—having sounded the deepest secrets of thoughts and having soared to the highest altitudes of Ecstasy,—given birth to a synthesis that sympathises with all aspirants towards truth from the Monist to the Atheist. Truth its goal, Realisation its method. It is neither Vedic nor non-Vedic, it is both. It is the veritable science of religion applied. This is Hindu Dharma—the conclusion of the conclusions arrived at by harmonising the detailed experience of all the schools of religious thought—Vedic, Sanatani, Jain, Buddh, Sikh or Devsamaji. Each one and everyone of those systems or sects which are the direct descendants and developments of the religious beliefs, Vedic and Avedic, that obtained in the land of the Saptasindhus or in the other unrecorded communities in other parts of India in the Vedic period, belongs to and is a part integral to Hindhu Dharma.

Therefore, the Vedic or the Sanatan Dharma itself is merely a sect of Hinduism or Hindu Dharma—however overwhelming be the majority that contributes to its tenets. It was a definition of this Sanatan Dharma which the late Lokmanya Tilak framed in the famous verses:

प्रामाण्यबुद्धिर्वेदेषु साधनानामनेकता।
उपास्यानामनियम एतद्धर्मस्य लक्षणम॥

In a learned article that he had contributed to the *Chittarmayjagat,* which bears the mark of his deep erudition and insight, Lokmanya in an attempt to develop this more or less negative definition into a positive one, had clearly suggested that he had an eye not on Hindutva as such but, only on what was popularly called Hindu Dharma and had also admitted that it could hardly include in its sweep the Arya Samajis and other sects which nevertheless are racially and nationally Hindus of Hindus. That definition, excellent so far as it goes, is in fact not a definition of Hindu Dharma, much less of Hindutva but of Sanatan Dharma—the श्रुतिस्मृतिपुणोक्त sect, which being the most popular of all sects of Hindu Dharma was naturally, but loosely mistaken for Hindu Dharma itself.

The Hindu Dharma being etymologically as well as actually and in its religious aspects only (for Dharma is not merely religion) the religion of the Hindus, it necessarily partakes of all the essentials that characterise a Hindu. We have found that the first important essential qualification of a Hindu is—that, to him the land that extends from Sindhu to Sindhu is the *pitrabhu*, the *matrabhu,* the land of his patriarchs and forefathers. The system of set of religions which we call Hindu Dharma—Vedic and Avedic—are as truly the children of this soil as the men whose thought they are or who 'saw' the truth revealed in them. To Hindu Dharma with all its sects and systems this land, Sindhustan is the land of its revelation—the land of its birth on this human plane. As the Ganges, though flowing out of the lotus feet of Vishnu himself is even to the most orthodox devotee and mystic so far as human plane is concerned, the daughter of the Himalayas, even so, this land is the birthplace, the *matrabhu* and the *pitrabhu*—of that *tatvagiyan* which in its religious aspect is signified as Hindu Dharma. The second most important essential of Hindutva is that a Hindu is a descendant of Hindu parents, claims to have the blood of the ancient Sindhus and the race that sprang from them in his veins. This also is true of the different schools of religion of the Hindus. For, they too being either founded by or revealed to the Hindu sages and seers are the moral and cultural and spiritual descendants and development of the thought of Saptasindhus, through the process of assimilation and elimination, as we are of their seed. Not only is Hindu Dharma the growth of the natural environments and of the thought of the Hindus, but also of the *sanskriti* or culture of the Hindus. The environmental frames in which its scences, whether of the Vedic period or of Buddh, Jain or any extremely modern ones of Chaitanya, Chakradhar, Basav, Nanak, Dayanand or Raja Rammohun, are set, the technical terms and the language that furnished expression to its highest revelation and ecstacies, its mythology and its philosophy, the conception it contraverted and the conceptions it adopted, have indelible stamp of Hindu culture, of Hindu *sanskriti*, impressed upon them. Hindu Dharma of all shades and schools, lives and grows and has its being in the atmosphere of Hindu culture, and the Dharma of a Hindu being so completely identified with the land of the Hindus, this land to him is not only a *pitrabhu,* but a *punyabhu*, not only a fatherland, but a holy land.

Yes, this Bharatbhumi, this Sindhustan, this land of ours that stretches from Sindhu to Sindhu is our *punyabhumi*, for it was in this land that the founders of our faith and the seers to whom 'Ved', the Knowledge was revealed, from Vedic seers to Dayanand, from Jin to Mahabir, from Budh to Nagsen, from Nanak to Gobind, from Banda to Basav, from Chakardhar to Chaitanya, from Ramdas to Rammohun, our gurus and godmen were born and bred. The very dust of its paths echoes the footfalls of our prophets and gurus. Sacred are its rivers, hallowed its groves, for it was either on their moonlit *ghats* or under their eventide long shadows, that the deepest problems of life, of man, soul and god, of *Brahma* and *maya* were debated and discussed by a Buddh or a Shankar. Ah! Every hill and dele instinct with memories of a Kapil or a Vyas, Shankar or Ramdas. Here Bhagirath rules, there Kurukeshetra lies. Here Ramchandra made his first halt of an exile, there Janaki saw the golden deer and fondly pressed her lover to kill it. Here the divine cowherd played on his flute that made every heart in Gokul dance in harmony as if in a hypnotised sleep. Here is Bodhibriksh, here the deer park. Here Mahavir entered *nirvana*. Here stood crowds of worshippers amongst whom Nanak sat and sang the *aarti*, *'Gagan thaal ravichand deepak bane*!'. Here Gopichand, the King, took on vows of Gopichand the *jogi* and with a bowl in his hand knocked at his sister's door for handful of alms! Here the son of Banda Bahadur was hacked to pieces before the eyes of his father and the young bleeding heart of the son thrust in the father's mouth for the fault of dying as a Hindu! Every stone here has a story of martyrdom to tell! Every inch of thy soil, Oh mother! has been a sacrificial ground! Not only 'where the Krishansaar is found' but from Kammeer to Sinhal it is *yagyabhumi* sanctified with a *giyanyag* or an *Atmayag*. So, to every Hindu, from the Santal to the Sadhu, this Bharatbhumi, this Sindhustan is at once a *pitrabhu* and a *punyabhu*.

That is why in the case of some of our Mohammedan or Christian countrymen who had originally been forcibly converted to non-Hindu religions and who consequently have inherited along with Hindus, a common fatherland and greater part of the wealth of common culture—language, law, customs, folklore and history—are not and cannot be recognised as Hindus. For, though Hindusthan to them is *pitrabhu* as to any other Hindu, yet it is not to them a *punyabhu* too. Their holyland is far off in Arabia or Palestine. Their mythology and godmen, ideas and heroes are not the children of this soil. Consequently their names and their outlook smack of foreign origin. Their love is divided. Nay, if some of them be really believing what they profess to do, then there can be no choice—they must, be a man, set their holy-land—above their fatherland in their love and allegiance. That is but natural. We are not condemning nor are we lamenting. We are simply telling facts as they stand. We have tried to determine the essentials of Hindutva and in doing so, we have discovered that the Bohras and such other Mohammedan or Christian communities possess all the essential qualifications of Hindutva, but one, and that is that they do not look upon India as their holyland.

It is not a question of embracing any doctrine propounding any new theory of the interpretation of god, soul and man. For, we honestly believe that the Hindu thought—we are not speaking of any religion which is dogma—has exhausted the very possibilities of human speculation as to the nature of the unknown—if not the unknowable, or the nature of the relation between *that* and *thou*. Are you a monist—-a monotheist—a pantheist—an atheist—an agnostic? Here is ample room, oh soul! Whatever thou art, to love and grow to thy fullest height and satisfaction in this temple of temples, that stands on no personal foundation but one the broad and deep and strong foundation of truth. Why goest then to fill thy little pitcher to wells far off, when thou standest on the banks of the crystal-streamed Ganges herself? Does not the blood in your veins, oh brother, of our common forefathers cry aloud with the recollections of the dear old scenes and ties from which they were so cruelly snatched away at the point of sword? Then come ye back to the fold of our brothers and sisters, who with arms extended are standing at the open gate to welcome you—their long-lost kith and kin. Where can you find more freedom of worship that in this land where a Charvak could preach atheism from the steps of the temple of Mahakaal; more freedom of social organisation than in the Hindu society wherefrom, the *pandas* of Orissa to the *pandits* of Benares, from the Santhals to the *sadhus*, each can develop a distinct social type of polity or organise a new one. Verily यदिहास्ति न सर्वत्र यन्नेहास्ति न कुत्रचित्। Whatever could be found in the world is found here too. And, if anything is not found here it could be found nowhere. Ye, who by race, by blood, by culture, by nationality possess almost all the essentials of Hindutva and had been forcibly snatched out of our ancestral home by the hand of violence—ye, have only to render wholehearted love to our common mother and recognise her not only as *pitrabhu* but even as a *punyabhu* and ye would be most welcome to the Hindu-fold.

This is a choice which our countrymen and our old kith and kin, the Bohras, Khojas, Mamons and other Mohammedan and Christian communities are free to make—a choice again which must be a choice of love. But, as long as they are not minded thus, so long they cannot be recognised as Hindus. We are, it must be remembered, trying to analyse and determine the essentials of Hindutva as that word is actually understood to signify and would not be justified to strain it in its application to suit any preconceived notions or party convenience.

A Hindu, therefore, to sum up the conclusions arrived at, is he who looks upon the land that extends from Sindhu to Sindhu, from the Indus to the seas, as the land of his forefathers—his *pitrabhu*, who inherits the blood of that race whose first discernible source could be traced to the Vedic Saptasindhus and which, on its onward march, assimilating much that was incorporated and ennobling much that was assimilated, has come to be known as the Hindu people, who has inherited and claims as his own the culture of that race, as expressed chiefly in their common classic language—the Sanskrit and represented by a common history, a common literature, art and architecture, law and jurisprudence, rites and rituals, ceremonies and sacraments, fairs and festivals, and who above all addresses this land, this Sindhustan, as his *punyabhu*, as his holyland, the land of his prophets and seers, of his godmen and gurus, the land of piety and pilgrimage. These are the essentials of Hindutva—a common *rashtra*, a common *jaati*, and a common *sanskriti*. All these essentials could best be summed up by stating in brief that he is a Hindu to whom Sindhustan is not only a *pitrabhu* but also a *punyabhu*. For the first two essentials of Hindutva—*rashtra* and *jaati*—are clearly denoted and connoted by the word *pitrabhu*; while the third essential of *sanskriti* is pre-eminently implied by the word *punyabhu*, as it is precisely *sanskriti* including *sanskaars*, i.e., rites and rituals, ceremonies and sacraments, that makes a land a Holyland. To make the definition more handy, we may be allowed to compress it in a couplet:

आसिंधुसिंधुपर्यन्ता यस्य भारतभूमिका।
पितृभूः पुण्यंभुश्चैव स वै हिंदुरिति स्मृतः॥

Hindus in Sindh

The rough analysis to which the conception of Hindutva was subjected in the foregoing pages has enabled us to frame a working definition embodying or rather indicating the salient essentials of it. It now remains to see how far this general definition can stand a detailed examination that could best be conducted by testing a few typical and some of the most different cases which have in fact made the necessity of a definition so badly felt. While developing it, we have tried at each step to free it, so far as it is possible to do so in the case of so comprehensive and elusive a generalisation as that, from the defect of being overlapping. If we find in testing a few typical cases in the light of this definition that they all fit in well, then we may be sure that it is free from the opposite defect of exclusiveness too. We have seen that it is not open to *ativiyapati*; it remains to be seen whether it is not open to *aviyapati* also.

The geographical divisions that obtain amongst the Hindus would, at a glance, be seen to harmonise well with the spirit of our definition. The fundamental basis of it is the land Asindhu-Sindhu-*paryanta*, and although many of our brethren, and especially those who had been the most undoubted descendants of the ancient Sindhus and who besides are the very people that to this day have never changed the ancient name either of their land or of their race, and are called today as five thousand years ago, Sindhi, the children of Sindhudesh, inhabit on other bank of the Indus yet, as in the mention of a river, the mention of both its banks is implied as a matter of course so that part of Sindh which constitutes the western bank of Indus is a natural part of Sindhustan and is covered by our definition. Secondly, accessories to the mainland are always known by the name of the latter. And, thirdly, our Hindu people on that side of the Sindhu had throughout history looked upon this land of Bharatvarsh as their real *pitrabhu* as well as *punyabhu*. They had never been guilty of matricide in attempting to set up the patch they inhabit as their only *pitrabhu* or only *punyabhu*. On the other hand, their Banaras and Kailash and Gangotri are our Banaras and Kailash and Gangotri. From the Vedic time, they are a part integral of Bharatvarsh. Sindhushivisauvirs are mentioned in *Ramayana* and *Mahabharata* as the rightful constituents of the great Hindu confederacy and commonwealth. They belong to our *rashtra*, to our *jaati* and to our *sanskriti*. Therefore, they are Hindus and their case is well covered by our definition.

But, even if one rejects the contention that the ownership of a river does employ, unless otherwise stated, the ownership of both its banks, yet the definition remains as sound as ever and applies to our Sindhi brethren on other grounds. For, apart from the special case of our Sindhi brethren that inhabit on the other side of the Indus, there are hundreds of thousands of Hindus who have settled in all parts of the world. A time may come when these Hindu colonists, who even today are the dominating factor in trade, numbers, capacity and intellect in their respective lands, may come to own a whole country and form a separate state. But, will this simple fact of residence in lands other than Hindusthan render one a non-Hindu? Certainly not; for the first essential of Hindutva is not that a man must not reside in lands outside India, but that wherever he or his descendants may happen to be, he must recognise Sindhustan as the land of his forefathers. Nay more; it is not a question of recognition either. If his ancestors came from India as Hindus, he cannot help recognising India as his *pitrabhu*. So, this definition of Hindutva is compatible with any conceivable expansion of our Hindu people. Let our colonists continue unabated their labours of founding a Greater India, a Mahabharata to the best of their capacities and contribute all that is best in our civilisation to the upbuilding of humanity. Let them enrich the people that inhabit the earth from Pole to Pole with their virtues and let them in return enrich their own country and race by imbibing all that is healthy and true wherever found. Hindutva does not clip the wings of the Himalayan eagles but only adds to their urge. So long as ye, Oh Hindus! Look upon Hindusthan as the land of your forefathers and as the land of your prophets, and cherish the priceless heritage of their culture and their blood, so long nothing can stand in the way of your desire to expand. The only geographical limits of Hindutva are the limits of our earth!

So far as the racial aspect of our definition is concerned, we cannot think of any exception that can seriously challenge its validity. Just as in England, we find Iberians, Kelts, Angles, Saxons, Danes, Normans now fused in spite of the racial restrictions on intermarriages into one nation, so the ancient racial distinctions of Aryans, Kolarians, Dravidians and others even if they had ever been keen, can no longer be recognised. We have dealt with the point as exhaustively as necessary in the foregoing pages and pointed out that the *Anolom* and *Pratilom* systems recognised in our law books bear indisputable testimony to the fact that a fusion sufficient to keep the flow of common blood through our body politic vigorous and fresh was even then an accomplished fact. Nature again broke the barriers where custom refused to pull them down in time. Bhimsen was neither the first nor the last of Aryans to make love with a Hidimba, nor the Brahmin lady the mother of Viyadhkarma, to whom we have referred already, was the only Aryan girl that took a fancy to a Viyadh youth. Out of a dozen Bhils or Kolis or even Santhals, a youth or a girl may at times be picked up and dropped in a city school without any fear of being recognised as such, either by a physical or by a moral test. The race that is born of the fusion, which on the whole is a healthy one, because gradually, of the Aryans, Kolarians, Dravidians and all those of our ancestors, whose blood we as a race inherit, is rightly called neither an Aryan, nor Kolarian, nor Dravidian, but the Hindu race; that is, that people who live as children of a common motherland, adoring a common holy land—the land that lies between the Sindhus. Therefore, the Santhals, Kollis, Bhils, Panchams, Naamshudras and all other such tribes and classes are Hindus. This Sindhustan is as emphatically, if not more emphatically, the land of their forefathers as of those of the so-called Aryans, who inherit the Hindu blood and the Hindu culture, and even those of them who have not as yet come fully under the influence of any orthodox Hindu sect, do still worship deities and saints and follow a religion however primitive, are still purely attached to this land, which, therefore, to them is not only a fatherland, but a holyland.

There would have been no serious objection raised against the cultural aspect of Hindutva too, but for the unfortunate misunderstanding that owes its origin to the confusing similarity between the two terms 'Hindutva' and 'Hinduism'. We have tried already to draw clear line of demarcation between the two conceptions and protested against the wrong use of the word Hinduism to denote the Sanatan Dharam alone. Hindutva is not identical with Hindu Dharma; nor is Hindu Dharma identical with Hinduism. This twofold mistake that identifies Hindutva with Hindu Dharma and both with Sanatani sects is justly resented by our non-Sanatani sects or religious systems and goads a small section of people amongst them—not to explode this mistaken notion, but unfortunately to commit another grave and suicidal mistake in the opposite direction and disown their Hindutva itself. We hope that our definition will leave no ground for any such bitterness of feelings on either side and based on truth as it is, would be acknowledged by all the fair-minded people throughout our Hindu society. But, as in the general treatment of this question, we could not take any notice of any special case we shall do so now. Let us first take the case of our Sikh brotherhood. No one could be so silly as to contest the statement that *Sindhustan,* 'आसिंधु सिंधुपर्यंता यस्य भारतभूमिका', is their fatherland—the land that ever since the first extant records of the Vedic period has been the land where their forefathers lived and loved and worshipped and prayed. Secondly, they most undoubtedly inherit the Hindu blood in their veins as much as anyone in Madras or Bengal does. Nay more, while we Hindus in Maharashtra or Bengal inherit the blood of the Aryans as well as of those other ancient people who inhabited this land, the Sikhs are the almost direct descendants of those ancient Sindhus and can claim to have drunk their being at the very fountain of this Ganges of our Hindu life before she had descended down to the planes. Thirdly, they have contributed and, therefore, are the rightful co-partners in our Hindu culture. For, Saraswati was a river in the Punjab before she became the deified image of learning and art. To this day, do millions of Hindus throughout Hindusthan join in the enchanted chorus with which the Sindhus, your forefathers, oh Sikhs, paid the tribute of a grateful people to and extolled the glories of the river on whose banks the first seeds of our culture and civilisation were sown and catching their Rig Vedic accents, sing 'अंवितमे नदीतमे। देवीतमे सरस्वती!' The *Vedas* are theirs as they are ours, if not as a revelation, yet as revered work that sings of the first giant struggles of man to tap the sources of Nature; the first giant struggle of light against the forces of darkness and ignorance, that had stolen and kept imprisoned the spirited waters and refused to allow the rays of illumination touch man and rouse the soul in him.

The story of the Sikhs, like any one of us must begin with the *Vedas*, pass on through the palaces of Ayodhya, witness the battlefield of Lanka, help Lahu to lay the foundation of Lahore and watch Prince Siddharth leave the confines of Kapilavastu and enter the caves to find some way out to lighten the sorrows of man. The Sikhs along with us bewail the fall of Prithviraj, share the fate of a conquered people and suffer together as Hindus. Millions of Sikh—Udasis, Nirmals, the Gehangambhirs and the Sindhi Sikhs adore the Sanskrit language not only as the language of their ancestors but as the sacred language of their land. While the rest cannot but own it as the tongue of their forefathers and as the mother of Gurmukhi and Punjabi, which, yet in its infancy is still sucking the milk of life at its breast. Lastly, the land Asindhu-Sindhu-*paryanta* is not only the *pitrabhu* but also the *punyabhu* to the Sikhs. Guru Nanak and Guru Gobind, Shri Banda and Ramsingh were born and bred in Hindhustan; the lakes of Hindusthan are the lakes of nectar and of the freedom—Amritsar and Muktsar; the land of Hindusthan is the land of prophets and prayers—*Gurudwara* and *Gurughar*. Really, if any community in India is Hindu beyond cavil or criticism it is our Sikh brotherhood in the Punjab, being almost the autochthonous dwellers of the Saptasindhu land and the direct descendants of the Sindhu or Hindu people. The Sikh of today is the Hindu of yesterday and the Hindu of today may be the Sikh of tomorrow. The change of a dress, or a custom, or a detail of daily life cannot change the blood or the seed, nor can efface and blot out history itself.

To the millions of our Sikh brethren, their Hindutva is self- evident. The Sehajdhari, Udasi, Nirmal, Gehangambhir and the Sindhi Sikhs are proud of being Hindus by race and by nationality. As their *gurus* themselves had been the children of Hindus, they would fail to understand if not resent any such attempt to class them as non-Hindus. The *Guru Granth* is read by the Sanatanis as well as by the Sikhs as a sacred work; both of them have fairs and festivals in common. The Sikhs of the Tatkhalsa sect also so far as a bulk of their population is concerned, are equally attached to their racial appellation and live amongst Hindus as Hindu. It cannot be but shocking to them to be told that they had suddenly ceased to be Hindus. Our racial unity is so unchallenged and complete that intermarriages are quite common amongst the Sikhs and Sanatanis.

The fact is that the protest that is at times raised by some leaders of our Sikh brotherhood against their being classed as Hindus would never have been heard if the term Hinduism was not allowed to get identical with Sanatanism. This confusion of ideas and the vagueness of expression resulting therefrom, are at the root of this fatal tendency that mars at times the cordial relations existing between our sister Hindu communities. We have tried to make it clear that Hindutva is not to be determined by any theological tests. Yet, we must repeat it once more that the Sikhs are free to reject any or all things they dislike as superstitions in Sanatan Dharma, even the binding authority of the *Vedas* as a revelation. They, thereby, may cease to be Sanatanis, but cannot cease to be Hindus. Sikhs are Hindus in the sense of our definition of Hindutva and not in any religious sense whatever. Religiously they are Sikhs as Jains are Jains, Lingayats are Lingayats, Vaishnavas are Vaishnavas; but all of us, racially and nationally and culturally, are a polity and a people, one and indivisible, most fitly and from times immemorial called Hindus. No other word can express our racial oneness—not even Bhartiya can do that for reasons dealt with in the foregoing pages. Bhartiya indicates an Indian and expresses a larger generalisation but cannot express racial unity of us Hindus. We are Sikhs, and Hindus and Bharatiyas. We are all three put together and none exclusively.

Another reason besides this fear of being identified with the followers of Sanatan Panth which added to zeal of some of our Sikh brothers and made them insist on getting classed separately as non-Hindus, was political one. This is not a place of entering into merits or demerits of a special representation. The Sikhs were naturally anxious to guard the special interests of their community and if the Mohammedans could enjoy the privilege of a special and communal representation, we do not understand why any other important minority in India should not claim a similar concession. But, we feel that the claim should not have been backed up by our Sikh brothers by an untenable and suicidal plea of being non-Hindus. Sikhs, to guard their own interests, could have pressed for and succeeded in securing special and communal representation on the ground of being an important minority as our non-Brahmins and other communities have done without renouncing their birthright of Hindutva. Our Sikh brotherhood is certainly not a less important community than the Mohammedans; in fact to us Hindus they are more important than any non-Hindu community in India. The harm that a special and communal representation does is never so great as the harm done by the attitude of racial aloofness. Let the Sikhs, the Jains, the Lingayats, the non-Brahmins and even, for the matter of that, Brahmins press and fight for the right of special and communal representation, if they honestly look upon it as indispensable for their communal growth. For their growth is the growth of the whole Hindu society. Even in ancient times our four main castes enjoyed a kind of special representation on communal basis in our councils of state as well as in local bodies. They could do that without refusing to get fused into the larger whole and incorporated into the wider generalisation of Hindutva. Let the Sikhs be classed as Sikhs religiously; but as Hindus, racially, nationally and culturally.

The brave people who placed their heads by hundreds under the executioner's axe rather than disown their *guru*—धर्महेत शाका जिन किया। शिर दिया शिरह न दिया।—will they disown their seed, or swear their fathers and sell their birthright for a mess of pottage! God forbid! Let our minorities remember that if union lies in strength, then in Hindutva lies the firmest and yet the dearest bond that can effect a real, lasting and powerful union of our people. You may fancy that it pays you to remain aloof for the passing hour, but it would do incalculable harm to our ancient race and civilisation as a whole, and especially to yourselves. Your interests are indissolubly bound with the interests of your other Hindu brethren. Whenever in the future as in the past a foreigner raises a sword against the Hindu civilisation it is sure to strike you as deadly as any other Hindu community. Whenever in future as in the past the Hindus as a people come to their own and under a Shivaji or a Ranjit, a Ramchandra or a Dharma, an Ashoka or an Amoghwarsha, feeling the quickening touch of life and activity mount the pinnacles of glory and greatness, that day would shed its lustre on you as well as on any other member of our Hindu commonwealth. So, brothers, be not dismayed by the immediate gains, paltry or otherwise, nor be duped by misreadings and misinterpretations of history. I was once told by one who, posing as a Granthi, was nevertheless convicted for committing a dacoity in the house of a Brahmin to whom he owed money and whom be consequently murdered—that the Sikhs were not Hindus and that they could incur no guilt by killing a Brahmin as the sons of Govind Singh were betrayed by a Brahmin cook! Fortunately, there was another Sikh gentleman and a real Granthi and was recognised as such by all learned Sikhs who immediately contradicted and cornered him by several examples of Matidas and others, who had sheltered the *Guru* and proved true to the Sikhs even unto martyrdom. Was not Shivaji betrayed by his kith and kin and his grandson again by a Pisall, who too was a Hindu? But, did Shivaji or his nation disown their race and cease to be Hindus? Many of the Sikhs have acted treacherously first at the time of desertion of the heroic Banda, then again at the time of the last war of the Khalsa forces with the English. Guru Govind Singh himself was deserted by a number of Sikhs in the very thick of a fight and it was this act of treacherous cowardice of these Sikhs which by forcing our lionhearted *guru* to try a desperate sortie, gave occasion to that cursed Brahmin wretch to betray his two sons. If, therefore, for the crime of the latter we cease to be Hindus, then for the crime of the former, we ought to cease to be Sikhs too!

The minority of the Hindus as well as the major communities of them did not fall from the skies as separate creations. They are an organic growth that has its roots embedded deep in a common land and in a common culture. You cannot pick up a lamb and by trying a *kachha* and *kirpan* on it, make a lion of it! If the guru succeeded in forming a band of martyrs and warriors, he could do so because the race that produced him as well as that band, was capable of being moulded thus. The lion's seed alone can breed lions. The flower cannot say, 'I bloom and smell: surely I came out of the stalk alone; I have nothing to do with the roots!' No more can we deny our seed or our blood. As soon as you point a Sikh who was true to his *guru,* you have automatically pointed out a Hindu who was true to the *guru* for before being a Sikh he was, and yet continues to be a Hindu. So long as our Sikh brethren are true to Sikhism, they must of necessity continue to be Hindus for so long must this land, this भारत भूमिका आसिंधु सिंधुपर्यन्ता remains their *pitrabhu* and their *punyabhu*. It is by ceasing to be Sikhs alone that they may, perhaps, cease to be Hindus.

We have dealt at some length with this special case of our Sikh brotherhood as all those arguments and remarks would automatically test all similar cases of our other Avedic sects and religions in the light of our definition. The Dev samajis, for example, are agnostics but Hindutva has little to do with agnosticism, or for the matter of that atheism. The Dev samajis look on this land as the land of their forefathers, their *pitrabhu* as well as their *punyabhu* and are therefore Hindus. Of course, it is superfluous, after all this to refer to our Arya samaj—all the essentials of Hindutva hold good in their case so eminently that they are Hindus of Hindus. We, in fact, are unable to hit upon any case that can lay our definition open to the charge of exclusiveness.

In one case alone, it seems to offer some real difficulty. Is, for example, Sister Nivedita a Hindu? If even an exception proves the rule it does so here. Our patriotic and noble-minded sister had adopted our land Asindu-Sindhu *paryanta* as her *pitrabhu*. She truly loved it as such and had our nation been free, we would have been the first to bestow the right of citizenship on such loving souls. So, the first essential may, to some extent, be said to hold good in her case. The second essential of common blood of Hindu parentage must, nevertheless and necessarily, be absent in such cases as these. The sacrament of marriage with a Hindu which really fuses and is universally admitted to do so, two beings into one may be said to remove this disqualification. But although this second essential failed, either way, to hold good in her case. The third important qualification of Hindutva did entitle her to be recognised as a Hindu. For, she had adopted our culture and came to adore our land as her *punyabhu*. She *felt* she was a Hindu and that is, apart from all technicalities, the real and the most important test. But, we must not forget that we have to determine the essentials of Hindutva in the sense in which the word is actually used by an overwhelming majority of people. And therefore, we must say that any convert of non-Hindu parentage to Hindutva can be a Hindu, if *bona fide*, he or she adopts our land as his or her country and marries a Hindu, thus coming to love our land as a real *pitrabhu*; and adopts our culture and thus adores our land as the *punyabhu*. The children of such a union as that would, other things being equal, be most emphatically Hindus. We are not authorised to go further.

But by coming to believe into the tenets of any sect of the Hindus, a foreign convert may be recognised as a Sanatani, or a Sikh, or a Jain; and as these religions being founded by or revealed to Hindus, go by the name of Hindu Dharma the convert too, may be religiously called a Hindu. But, it must be understood that a religious or cultural convert possesses only one of the three essentials of Hindutva and, it is owing to this disqualification that people generally do not recognise as a Hindu anyone and everyone who contributes to the religious beliefs of our race. So deep our feeling of gratitude is towards Sister Nivedita or Annie Besant for the services they rendered to the cause of our motherland and our culture, so soft hearted and sensitive to the touch of love as a race we Hindus are, that Sister Nivedita or a person like her who so completely identifies his or her being with the being of our people, is almost unconsciously received in the Hindufold. But, it should be done as an exception to the rule. The rule itself must neither be too rigid nor too elastic. The several tests to which we have subjected our definition of Hindutva have, we believe, proved it that it satisfies both these requirements and involves neither अव्याप्ति nor अतिवयाप्ति

Unique natural blessing to Hindusthan

So far, we have not allowed any considerations of utility to prejudice our inquiry. But having come to its end, it will not be out of place to see how far the attributes, which we found to be the essentials of Hindutva, contribute towards strength, cohesion and progress of our people. Do these essentials constitute a foundation so broad, so deep, so strong that basing upon it, the Hindu people can build a future which can face and repel the attacks of all the adverse winds that blow; or does the Hindu race stand on feet of clay?

Some of the ancient nations raised huge walls so as to convert a whole country into a fortified castle. Today their walls are trodden to dust or are but scarcely discernible by a few scattered mounds here and there, while the people they were meant to protect are not discernible at all! Our ancient neighbours, the Chinese, laboured from generation to generation and raised a rampart, embracing the limits of an empire—so wide, so high, so strong—a wonder of human world. That too, as all human wonders must, sank under its own weight. But behold the ramparts of Nature! Have they not, these Himalayas, been standing there as one whose desires are satisfied—so they seemed to the Vedic bard—so they seem to us today. These are *our* ramparts that have converted this vast continent into a cosy castle.

You take up buckets and fill your trenches with water and call it moat. Behold, Varuna himself, with his one hand pushing continents aside, fills the gap by pouring seas on seas with the other! This Indian Ocean with its bays and gulfs, is *our* moat.

These are our frontier lines bringing within our reach the advantages of an inland as well as an insular country.

She is the richly endowed daughter of god—this our motherland. Her rivers are deep and perennial. Her land is yielding to the plough and her fields loaded with golden harvests. Her necessaries of life are few and a genial nature yields them all almost for the asking. Rich in her fauna, rich in her flora, she knows she owes it all to the immediate source of light and heat—the sun. She covets not the icy lands; blessed be they and their frozen latitudes. If heat is at times enervating here, cold is at times benumbing there. If cold induces manual labour, heat removes much of its very necessity. She takes more delight in quenched thirst than in the parched throat. Those who have not, let them delight in exerting to have. But those who have—may be allowed to derive pleasure from the very fact of having. Father Thames is free to work at feverish speed, wrapped in his icy sheets. She loves to visit her *ghats* and watch her boats gliding down the Ganges on her moonlit waters. With the plough, the peacocks, the lotus, the elephant and the *Gita*, she is willing to forego, if that must be, whatever advantage the colder latitudes enjoy. She knows she cannot have all her own way. Her gardens are green and shady, her granaries well stocked, her waters crystal, her flowers scented, her fruits juicy and her herbs healing. Her brush is dipped in the colours of dawn and her flute resonant with the music of Gokul. Verily Hind is the richly endowed daughter of *God*.

Neither the English nor the French—with the exception of Chinese and perhaps the Americans, no people are gifted with a land that can equal in natural strength and richness the land of Sindhustan. A country, a common home is the first important essential of a stable and strong nationality; and as of all countries in the world our country can hardly be surpassed by any in its capacity to afford a soil so specially fitted for the growth of a great nation; we Hindus whose very first article of faith is the love we bear to the common fatherland, have in that love the strongest talismanic tie that can bind us close and keep a nation firm and enthused and enable it to accomplish things greater than ever.

The second essential of Hindutva puts the estimate of our latent powers of national cohesion and greatness yet higher. No country in the world with the exception of China again, is peopled by a race so homogeneous, yet so ancient and yet so strong both numerically and vitally. The Americans too, whom we found equally fortunate with us so far as the gift of an excellent geographical basis of nationality is concerned, are decidedly left behind. Mohammedans are no race nor are the Christians. They are a religious unit, yet neither a racial nor a national one. But, we Hindus, if possible, are all the three put together and live under our ancient and common roof. The numerical strength of our race is an asset that cannot be too highly prized.

And culture? The English and the Americans feel they are kith and kin because they possess a Shakespeare in common. But, not only a Kalidas or a Bhas, but, Oh Hindus! Ye possess a *Ramayana* and *Mahabharata* in common—and the *Vedas*! One of the national songs the American children are taught to sing attempts to rouse their sense of eternal self-importance by pointing out to the hundred years twice told that stand behind their history. The Hindu counts his years not by centuries but by cycles—the *yug* and the *kalap*—and amazed, asks:

रघुपतेः क्व गतोत्तरकोशला ;
यदुपतेः क्व गता मथुरापुरी ॥

He does not attempt to rouse the sense of self-importance so much as the sense of proportion, which is truth. And that has perhaps made him last longer than Ramses and Nebuchadnezzar. If a people that had no past has no future, then a people that had produced an unending galaxy of heroes and hero-worshippers and who are conscious of having fought with and vanquished the forces whose might struck Greece and Rome, the Pharaohs and the Incas, dead, have in their history a guarantee of their future greatness more assuring than any other people on earth yet possess.

But, besides culture, the tie of common holyland has at times proved stronger than the chains of a motherland. Look at the Mohammedans. Mecca to them is a sterner reality than Delhi or Agra. Some of them do not make any secret of being bound to sacrifice all India if that be to the glory of Islam or could save the city of their Prophet. Look at the Jews: neither centuries of prosperity nor sense of gratitude for the shelter they found, can make them more attached or even equally attached to the several countries they inhabit. Their love is, and must necessarily be divided between the land of their birth and the land of their Prophets. If the Zionists' dreams are ever realised—if Palestine becomes a Jewish state and it will gladden us almost as much as our Jewish friends—they, like the Mohammedans would naturally set the interests of their holyland above those of their motherlands in America and Europe and in case of war, between their adopted country and the Jewish State, would naturally sympathise with the latter, if indeed they do not bodily go over to it. History is too full of examples of such desertions to cite particulars. The Crusades again attest to the wonderful influence that a common holyland exercises over peoples widely separated in race, nationality and language, to bind and hold them together.

The ideal conditions, therefore, under which a nation can attain perfect solidarity and cohesion would, other things being equal, be found in the case of those people who inhabit the land they adore, the land of whose forefathers is also the land of their gods and angels, of seers and prophets, the scenes of whose history are also the scenes of their mythology.

The Hindus are about the only people who are blessed with these ideal conditions that are at the same time an incentive to national solidarity, cohesion and greatness. Not even the Chinese are blessed thus. Only Arabia and Palestine—if ever the Jews can succeed in founding their state there—can be said to possess this unique advantage. But, Arabia is incomparably poorer in the natural, cultural, historical and numerical essentials of a great people; and even if the dreams of the Zionists are ever realised into a Palestine state, still they too must be equally lacking in these.

England, France, Germany, Italy, Turkey proper, Persia, Japan, Afghanistan, Egypt of today (for the old descendants of 'Punto' and their Egypt is dead long since)—and other African states, Mexico, Peru, Chile (not to mention states and nations lesser than all these)—though racially more or less homogeneous are yet less advantageously situated than we are in geographical, cultural, historical and numerical essentials, besides lacking the unique gift of a sanctified motherland. Of the remaining nations, Russia in Europe and United States in America, though geographically equally well-gifted with us, are yet poorer, in almost every other requisite of nationality. China alone of the present comity of nations is almost as richly gifted with the geographical, racial, cultural and numerical essentials as the Hindus are only in the possession of a common, a sacred and a perfect language, the Sanskrit, and a sanctified motherland, we are so far as the essentials that contribute to national solidarity are concerned more fortunate.

Thus, the actual essentials of Hindutva are, as this running sketch reveals, also the ideal essentials of nationality. If we would we can build on this foundation of Hindutva a future greater than what any other people on earth can dream of—greater even than our own past; provided we are able to utilise our opportunities! For, let our people remember that great combinations are the order of the day. The Leagues of Nations, the alliances of powers, pan-Islamism, pan-Slavism, pan-Ethiopianism—all little beings are seeking to get themselves incorporated into greater wholes, so as to be better fitted for the struggle for existence and power. Those who are not naturally and historically blessed with numerical or geographical or racial advantages are seeking to share them with others.

Woe to those who have them already as their birthright and know them not, or worse, despise them! The nations of the world are desperately trying to find a place in this or that combination for aggression—can any one of you, Oh Hindus! Whether Jain or Samaji or Sanatani or Sikh or any other subsection afford to cut yourselves off or fall out and destroy the ancient, the natural and the organic combination that already exists—a combination that is bound not by any scraps of paper nor by the ties of exigencies alone, but by the ties of blood and birth and culture? Strengthen them if you can: pull down the barriers that have survived their utility, of castes and customs, of sects and sections: What of interdining?—But intermarriages between provinces and provinces, castes and castes, be encouraged where they do not exist. But where they already exist as between the Sikhs and Sanatanists, Jains and Vaishnavas, Lingayats and non-Lingayats—suicidal be the hand that tries to cut the nuptial tie. Let the minorities remember they would be cutting the very branch on which they stand. Strengthen every tie that binds you to the main organism, whether of blood or language or common festivals and feasts or culture and love you bear to the common motherland. Let this ancient and noble stream of Hindu blood flow from vein to vein, from Attak to Kattak, till at last the Hindu people get fused and welded into an indivisible whole, till our race gets consolidated and strong and sharp as steel.

Just cast a glance at the past, then at the present: pan-Islamism in Asia, the Political Leagues in Europe, the pan-Ethiopian movement in Africa and America—and then see, Oh Hindus, if your future is not entirely bound up with the future of India and the future of India is bound up, in the last resort, with Hindu strength. We are trying our best, as we ought to do, to develop the consciousness of and a sense of attachment to the greater whole, whereby Hindus, Mohammedans,

Parsees, Christians and Jews would feel as Indians first and every other thing afterwards. But whatever progress India may have made to that goal, one thing remains almost axiomatically true—not only in India, but everywhere in the world—that a nation requires a foundation to stand upon and the essence of the life of a nation is the life of that portion of its citizens whose interests and history and aspirations are most closely bound up with the land and who thus provide the real foundation to the structure of their national state. Take the case of Turkey. The young Turks after the revolution had to open their parliament and military institutions to Armenians and Christians on a non-religious and secular basis. But, when the war with Serbia came, the Christians and Armenians first wavered and then many a regiment consisting of them went bodily over to the Serbians, who politically and racially and religiously were more closely bound up with them. Take the case of America; when the German war broke out, she suddenly had to face the anger of desertions of the German citizens; while the Negro citizens there sympathise more with their brethren in Africa than with their white countrymen. American state, in the last resort, must stand or fall with the fortunes of its Anglo-Saxon constituents. So, with the Hindus, they being the people, whose past, present and future are most closely bound with the soil of Hindusthan as *pitrabhu*, as *punyabhu*, they constitute the foundation, the bedrock, the reserved forces of the Indian state. Therefore even from the point of Indian nationality, must, ye, Oh Hindus, consolidate and strengthen Hindu nationality; not to give wanton offence to any of our non-Hindu compatriots, in fact, to anyone in the world, but in just and urgent self-defence of our race and land, to render it impossible for others to betray her or to subject her to unprovoked attacks by any of those 'pan-isms' that are struggling forth from continent to continent. As long as other communities in India or in the world are not respectively planning India first or mankind first, but all are busy in organising offensive and defensive alliances and combinations on entirely narrow racial or religious or national basis, so long, at least so long, Oh Hindus, strengthen, if you can, those subtle bonds that like nerve-threads bind you in one organic social being. Those of you who, in a suicidal fit, try to cut off the most vital of those ties and dare to disown the name Hindu will find to their cost that in doing so they have cut themselves off from the very source of our racial life and strength.

The presence of only a few of these essentials of nationality, which we have found to constitute Hindutva enabled little nations like Spain or Portugal to get themselves lionised in the world. But, when all of those ideal conditions obtain here, what is there in the human world that the Hindus cannot accomplish?

Thirty crores of people, with India for their basis of operation, for their fatherland and for their holyland, with such a history behind them, bound together by ties of a common blood and common culture can dictate their terms to the whole world. A day will come when mankind will have to face the force.

Equally certain it is that whenever the Hindus come to hold such a position, whence they could dictate terms to the whole world—those terms cannot be very different from the terms which *Gita* dictates or the Buddha lays down. A Hindu is most intensely so, when he ceases to be a Hindu; and with a Shankar claims the whole earth of a Benares 'Varanasi *medini*!' or with a Tukaram exclaims,

आमुचा स्वदेश। भुवनत्रयामधयें वास।

my country? Oh brothers, 'The limits of the universe—there the frontiers of my country lie.'

□□□